Life Insurance

Products and Finance

CHARTING A CLEAR COURSE

by
David B. Atkinson, F.S.A.
James W. Dallas, F.S.A.

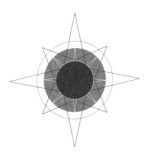

Published by the Society of Actuaries
2000

ISBN 0-938959-67-0

First Edition
Second Printing

Printed in the United States of America
05 04 03   5 4 3 2

Edited by David Anderson
Society of Actuaries Liaisons:
   Sandy Rosen, Practice Area Administrator
   John F. Carey, Scientific Publications Manager
Cover and interior design by Arc Group Ltd., Chicago, Ill.
Typeset at Pro-Image Corporation, York, Pa.
Printed by Mack Printing Group, Ephrata, Pa.

Contents

Preface

Each of us learns in different ways, and often the hard way. In the back seat of an Audi Fox, I learned quite a bit about life insurance products and product development, by listening to my carpool driver and mentor, Claude Thau. I supplemented this by puzzling through a Fortran pricing program, a pricing assumption manual, some articles, some actuarial study notes, and various other disconnected sources. Within a short time, I thought I knew it all—such is the confidence of youth. In fact, I knew enough to be dangerous and at times I was.

In retrospect, I could have benefited from a single, complete source on life insurance products and finance that explained not just how, but why, and what to watch out for. By not having such a source, though, I was able to learn from experience, which is a great and memorable teacher. As a result, I have vivid memories of a great number of mistakes and blunders, most of which are covered in this book.

David B. Atkinson

As David says above, each of us learns in different and (I know personally) sometimes hard ways. My contribution to this book is rooted in the memory of the many hours I spent poring over the study materials on the actuarial exams. The study materials for the actuarial exams were always written by someone quite knowledgeable and comfortable with the concepts and materials. However, I found that, more often than not, the author did not keep in mind that the concepts can be difficult for the first-time reader to absorb. Therefore, David and I have done our best to present concepts and materials with enough detail so that the reader will be able to understand and quickly absorb the material. This may be one reason this book is as lengthy as it is. To the extent that we have failed in some parts, we apologize. To the extent that we have accomplished that goal, we can be proud that we have made, in some small way, a worthy contribution to our noble profession.

James W. Dallas

Intended Audience

Over the years, we have been frustrated by the time required to teach someone the basics of life insurance products, product development, pricing, modeling, and finance. This book is designed to accelerate that process. With the help and guidance of an experienced professional, this book should enable someone new to life insurance or product development to begin making meaningful contributions in a matter of weeks.

Many people with years of experience in life insurance or related fields know a great deal about their business, but find the work done by actuaries to be very mysterious. This book requires no actuarial background and lays bare some of the greatest mysteries of life insurance. No stone is left unturned! Every secret is revealed! Whether you help run an insurance company, manage its assets, report its financial results, underwrite its risks, automate its processes, help set company policy or strategy, or so on, this book can help you complete your mastery of life insurance.

Many institutions of higher learning do a fine job of building the student's understanding of financial and insurance theory. This book may be a logical first step from theory to practice, especially if the student has an opportunity to apply this practical knowledge, such as through summer employment or a work/study program. A student familiar with the material presented in this book could make an immediate contribution to an employer.

Scope

This book is focused primarily on individual life insurance, but also includes some discussion of annuity and investment products.

A valiant effort has been made to make this book international in scope. By ignoring the mind-numbing complexities of country-specific regulations, we were left with the basics that apply to life insurance around the world. We looked for similarities in the practice of life insurance and described the most common patterns. This allowed us to focus on practices that are less likely to change. In contrast, detailed regulations are always under revision in one country or another. In spite of our best intentions and contributions from friends around the world, this book has a clear North American bias.

There are a number of good books that explore the theories of life insurance probabilities, pricing, finance, and the like. This book is not one of them. Instead, the focus is on simplicity (not counting Chapter 15) and ease of application to real-world problems.

Organization of the Book

This book is organized into three major parts:

Part I:	Chapters 1–3	Product Development Fundamentals
Part II:	Chapters 4–13	Product Pricing
Part III:	Chapters 14–16	Modeling and Finance

At the beginning of each part, there is a short overview, which we encourage you to read now.

Toward the end of each chapter, you will find a number of exercises that will test your knowledge and expand your understanding of the chapter. We strongly encourage you to work through these exercises. You will find the answers at the end of each chapter, immediately following the exercises, rather than at the end of the book.

Following Chapter 16, you will find an extensive glossary of life insurance terms. We encourage you to skim through this glossary now, so you will know what is generally included. After reading the book, the glossary can be used to test your knowledge and prepare for examinations. If you find we have missed some terms that would be helpful for future readers, please let the publisher know so we can consider them for the next edition.

Examinations Based on This Book

This book may be used in connection with examinations. If you must take such examinations, please accept our sympathies and condolences.

If you are charged with designing questions for such examinations, please read on. The authors strongly suggest and sincerely hope that this book will be used according to the following principles:

- The memorization of lists, data, variables, and formulas is a waste of time. Such knowledge is quickly forgotten, and rightly so. It can always be looked up.

- It is important to understand life insurance fundamentals, principles, concepts, issues, relationships, risks, opportunities, limitations, and the like.

- It is important to be able to explain and apply the material, to discover problems and develop solutions, and to derive formulas from basic principles to fit a given situation.

These principles are best applied by using an open-book examination format.

Important warning to those taking examinations based on this book: The above principles may not apply. Please check with the organization administering your examinations.

We wish you smooth sailing through the material in this book and hope this helps you chart a clear course through the many opportunities you will encounter.

Acknowledgments

This book is dedicated to our wives, Andrea Maddox-Dallas and Brooke Shoemaker Atkinson, in recognition of their unflagging support and understanding. They kept us going and made it possible for us to find the time to write this book. Our children, Andrew and Greg Dallas and Blaine and Julie Atkinson, and many other family members and friends received much less of our time and attention than we would have liked over the last 18 months. We look forward to catching up with them all.

Our employer, Reinsurance Group of America, and our bosses, Paul Schuster and Greig Woodring, were very generous with their support of this project, freely providing resources and expertise. Our international colleagues provided invaluable and irreplaceable knowledge and insight into their home markets and other markets: David Boettcher, Daniel Cossette, Jean-Francois Lemay, Ross Morton, Dave Pelletier, and Paul Nitsou in Canada; Hamish Galloway and Perry Thomas in the U.K.; Richard Krajewski and David Morris in Australia; and Colin Dutkiewicz in South Africa. In St. Louis, many of our actuarial colleagues gave us their input, help, and advice: Roberto Baron, Mark Buehrer, Greg Goodfliesh, Mike Stein, Lisa Renetzky, and Susan Willeat. Clay Stallard designed and built the eye-catching mortality and interest rate graphs in Chapter 3. Lisa Davis, Kathy Schubert, and Terie Pieper tracked down information, got permissions from other authors, and kept the communication flowing. Special thanks are due to Kathy for her help with the glossary. Finally, Dave Groff, Felisa Marshall, Evan Nichols, Scott Rushing, and Kari Sims "test drove" the first few chapters and gave us their ideas on how to make the book more readable. We thank you all!

At the Society of Actuaries, we want to thank David Banasiak, John Carey, and Sandy Rosen. They were a pleasure to work with and did a remarkable job of managing the project and keeping our editors and us on a tight schedule. We especially want to thank Jill Carpenter,

Linda Delgadillo, Marta Holmberg, and Rich Lambert for their role in getting this project off the ground.

Many Society members freely volunteered their time to review one or more chapters. Their contributions significantly improved the clarity, focus, and accuracy of the book. We warmly thank Kathy Anderson, Jeff Beckley, Graham Bancroft, Boris Brizeli, Ching-Meei Lee Chang, Shiela Companie, John David Currier, Jr., Keith Dall, Michael DuBois, Marv Fineman, Brent Fritz, Tom Kalmbach, Ronnie Klein, Mary Jane Kulig, Rich Lambert, Richard E. Ostuw, Kenton Scheiwe, Pam Schiz, Larry Stern, and Melinda Willson for their guidance and support. In addition, we would like to thank Stewart Citroen, Glen Keller, Herb Pettersen, and Ed Robbins for helping us with ideas, stories, and facts.

David Anderson did a marvelous job as technical editor. After going through many versions of multiple drafts, we would turn a chapter over to David for final markup. In spite of our best efforts, David invariably found hundreds or thousands (or was it hundreds of thousands?) of items in every chapter that needed change. To the extent that the book is clear, consistent, and grammatically correct, we all have David to thank for it.

Finally, we would like to thank the individuals and organizations who kindly allowed us to adapt and include their work in this book: Jim Ericson of Northwestern Mutual Life; Thomas Nagle of Strategic Pricing Group Inc.; Ron McIntosh, Len Savage, Jon Joseph, and Dan Farrell of Fox-Pitt, Kelton Inc.; Doug Doll of Tillinghast-Towers Perin; and Stephanie Philippo of the Life Office Management Association. Their contributions added immeasurably to the book.

St. Louis, Missouri, U.S.
May 2000

Part I
Product Development Fundamentals

Part I introduces the reader to most of the information needed to understand and develop products. The remaining product development topic, product pricing, is presented in Part II.

- Chapter 1, "Life Insurance Overview," introduces life insurance and explains the many purposes it serves. The major types of individual life insurance products are examined, as well as how life insurance is taxed and distributed.

- In Chapter 2, "Product Development," the product strategy is tied to a company's overall plans and goals. Pricing strategies are presented. The product development organization and process are examined in detail.

- Chapter 3, "Pricing Assumptions," explores the key assumptions of mortality, lapse rates, interest rates, and expenses in considerable depth. Average size, sales distribution, and sales volume are also addressed.

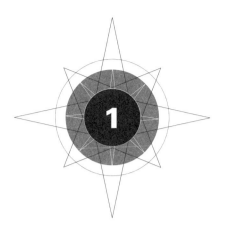

Life Insurance Overview

1.1 Introduction

In this chapter, we will define life insurance and explore how life insurance is used. We will briefly describe the major types of individual life insurance products and examine the effect of taxation on the products sold. Finally, we will discuss the many ways in which life insurance products are distributed.

1.2 Life Insurance Basics

Life insurance starts with a simple proposition: A life insurance company collects premiums in return for a *death benefit* it will pay if the *insured* dies while the policy is in force. The initial death benefit is often referred to as the *face amount*. The definition of *in force* varies by type of product. In general, though, a policy is in force if its scheduled premiums have been paid on time or if it has sufficient value to cover any charges due.

The person who pays the premiums is called the *policyowner*, policyholder, or payor. This person is often the insured, but could also be a company, a partnership, a spouse, or some other person or entity with an interest in the insured.

The person who receives the death benefit is called the *beneficiary*. The beneficiary is most often a relative of the insured. The beneficiary could also be the insured's estate, a trust, company, partnership, or any person with an insurable interest in the insured. *Insurable interest* can be thought of as being in the position of wanting the insured to live rather than die, in spite of the death benefit. A beneficiary with an insurable interest will typically suffer an emotional or financial loss if the insured dies. When the policyowner is not the insured, it is quite common for the policyowner to be the beneficiary.

The insurance company and policyowner enter into a contract that is called a life insurance *policy*. When all requirements have been met, including payment of the initial premium, the insurance company *issues* the policy. In many instances, all or partial coverage begins when both the application for insurance has been submitted and a premium has been paid.

If the policyowner decides to stop paying premiums and cancels the policy before the insured dies, many policies will pay the policyowner a *cash value* for surrendering the policy. This cash value is usually very small or zero in the early years of the policy. The cash value usually grows as the policy ages.

Most policies with cash values allow the policyowner to take out a *policy loan* when cash is needed, as an alternative to surrendering the policy for its cash value. This allows the policyowner to continue the policy while receiving cash from the policy. The policy loan is backed by the cash value and is not allowed to exceed the cash value.

Life insurance policies are often sold with riders. *Riders* are additional benefits and options that enhance the benefits provided by the policy. Riders can be added by the policyowner to customize the insurance program to better meet the policyowner's needs. Some forms of riders limit the policy's benefits.

1.3   Purpose of Life Insurance

The death of one person can adversely affect the lives of many people who depend on that person in one way or another. While life insurance cannot offset the emotional impact of a person's death, it can offset the financial impact, as in the following situations:

Maintain family income: If the insured provides significant income to help support the family, death benefits can make up for the income lost due to death.

Mortgage or other loan protection: If an insured's income is needed to help make ongoing mortgage payments or other loan payments, then life insurance can be used to pay off the loan in the event of death. This protects both the lender and those who no longer have to worry about paying off a loan if the insured dies.

Funeral or final expense coverage: For families with little savings and low incomes, life insurance can be used to cover the costs of a funeral or other final expenses.

Key man (or key person) insurance: In many small- and medium-sized businesses, the loss of one key person can threaten the survival of the business. A death benefit can be used to help the company through the hard financial times that may follow the death of a key person, as well as defray the expenses of finding a replacement.

Buy/sell agreement: Some partnerships specify that, when one partner dies, the other partners must buy out the interests of the deceased partner. For a partnership with just a few partners, it can be very expensive to buy a deceased partner's share. By owning life insurance on the life of each partner in the firm, the partnership can ensure it has the money it needs to buy out any partner who dies.

Estate protection: In some countries, when a wealthy person dies, significant estate taxes must be paid. For large estates, these taxes may equal a significant percentage of the value of the person's estate at the time of death. Because much of the estate's value may be tied up in property and business ownership, estate taxes may force the heirs to sell the family property, the family business, or other assets. Life insurance death benefits can be used to pay estate taxes and avoid such a forced sale.

Life insurance can be a convenient and tax-efficient means of saving for future needs other than death, such as in the following cases:

- By buying a policy with regular premium payments, the policyowner can establish a habit of saving. This can be particularly effective if the premium payments are automatically deducted from the policyowner's paycheck or checking account.

- In a few countries, premiums up to a certain amount per year per worker are tax deductible, to encourage savings through life insurance.

- In most countries, the buildup of a policy's cash value is not taxable unless the policy is surrendered, in which case the excess of cash value over premiums paid may be taxed.

- In almost all countries, the death benefits received by beneficiaries are tax-free.

The money saved through life insurance is often used to fund higher education for children, for retirement income, or to fund a major purchase such as a home or a car.

1.4 Life Insurance Products

A life insurance product is defined by the rules and relationships that govern its premiums, death benefits, and cash values. Through the years, the life insurance industry has developed quite a number of different products, which we will divide into four basic categories:

1. Pre-scheduled products

2. Dynamic products

3. Multiple-life products

4. Riders, additional benefits, and options.

1.4.1   Pre-Scheduled Products

Some products have premiums, death benefits, and cash values that are fixed or known well in advance. So long as the policyowner pays the scheduled premiums, the pre-scheduled cash values and death benefits will be available. We will refer to these as *pre-scheduled products*. They are also called traditional products. They fall into two main categories: term insurance and permanent insurance.

1.4.1.1   Term Insurance

The simplest traditional product is term insurance, which can be identified by its relatively low premiums and low or zero cash values. Term insurance is meant to provide death benefits for a limited period of time (the "term" of the policy). Term insurance often lasts for 10, 20, or 30 years or until a specified age, such as age 65 or 70. Term insurance achieves its low cost by minimizing the cash values. Term insurance comes in many varieties. Not all varieties of term insurance are offered in all jurisdictions. The products offered may be a function of competitive or regulatory constraints.

Level term offers level premiums and level death benefits. *Twenty-year level term* and *Level term to 65* are common level term products. Five-year level term products commonly offer one or more additional level term periods. Some level term products switch to annually increasing premiums after an initial period of level premiums. In such cases there is often a steep premium increase after the level term period, which mainly unhealthy insureds would tend to pay.

Increasing premium term offers annually increasing premiums and level death benefits. It is perhaps better known as annually renewable term (ART) or yearly renewable term (YRT), but these names are misleading. The policy is not truly "annually renewable" because it automatically continues from one year to the next with no action required other than payment of the increased premium.

Decreasing term offers level premiums and decreasing death benefits. The most popular form of decreasing term follows the pattern of a declining mortgage balance, that is, the amount needed to pay off a mortgage. This kind of decreasing term benefit is commonly referred to as *mortgage protection*. Figure 1.4.1 shows the outstanding principle or mortgage balance for a 30-year mortgage loan for 100,000 with an 8% interest rate.

Mortgage protection term products present two special challenges:

1. Customers have mortgages with many different interest rates and number of years remaining. Some companies offer several mortgage protection products with patterns based on different interest rates and years remaining. A few companies have products that can exactly match the customer's actual mortgage pattern, with the premium also custom-calculated.

2. As the death benefits approach zero toward the end of the policy, the benefits are often worth much less than the level premium. To correct this, some companies have the decreasing term policy become paid-up a few years before it expires. Another approach is to establish a minimum or floor for the death benefit, such as 20% of the original death benefit.

Term to 100 offers level premiums and a level death benefit, both of which last until age 100. This product stretches the definition of term

Figure 1.4.1 Mortgage Protection Death Benefit Pattern

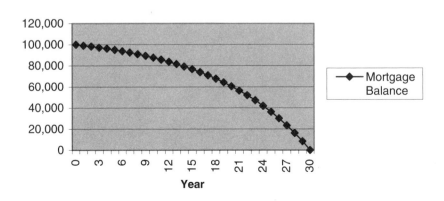

Mortgage Balance
$100,000 Initial Amount
8% Interest

insurance to the point where it is almost permanent insurance. However, Term to 100 premiums and cash values are much lower than those for permanent insurance.

Term insurance products often include one or more of the following features:

Convertible: The term insurance product can be converted to a permanent product, subject to conditions such as converting within a certain number of years or before a certain age.

Renewable: As mentioned previously, "renewable" is misleading. Renewable usually means the policyowner has the right to continue the insurance simply by paying a higher premium. For example, *ten-year renewable term* typically has premiums that increase every ten years.

Reentry: Some products offer lower premiums to those who have recently been determined through additional underwriting to be good risks. A reentry provision allows an insured to be reunderwritten from time to time, often at company expense, with the chance to qualify for lower premiums.

Indeterminate premiums: Some or all of the premiums are not guaranteed. For example, a 20-year level term product might guarantee the level premiums for only the first ten years. The insurance company has the right to redetermine premiums after the guaranteed period. New premiums are based on the insured's original health and risk class, such as nonsmoker, preferred, or substandard. Indeterminate premiums serve two purposes:

1. To minimize reserves that the company must hold (see Chapter 6).

2. To allow the company to adjust for differences between actual and expected experience, both positive and negative. For example, if mortality turns out to be much higher or lower than expected, future premiums can be adjusted accordingly.

Products with indeterminate premiums have two sets of premiums: current premiums and guaranteed maximum premiums. Current premiums may be guaranteed for only a few years or for many years, after which premiums are indeterminate or nonguaranteed. The company has the right to raise or lower current premiums on a class basis (that is, individual insureds cannot be singled out), as long as the new premiums do not exceed the maximum premiums guaranteed in the policy.

Some jurisdictions require that any change in premiums be based solely on the company's expectations of the future. Past gains and losses cannot be taken into account, unlike participating insurance. To ensure compliance, certain jurisdictions require that the assumptions upon which the gross premiums are based be filed before the product will be approved. When the company desires to change the premiums, revised assumptions must be filed. Assumptions are explored in detail in Chapter 3.

Guaranteed upgrade: In Australia, it is common to guarantee that a term policy will be automatically upgraded to match any better terms offered on newer term policies. For example, if a company's existing term policies have guaranteed upgrades, a decrease in term premium rates for new business will force the company to lower its term premium rates for existing term policies. This can be a powerful disincentive to lowering term premiums.

1.4.1.2 Permanent Pre-Scheduled Insurance

The other form of pre-scheduled products is referred to as permanent insurance. There are two major forms of permanent pre-scheduled insurance: whole life and endowment.

When compared to term products, the distinguishing feature of permanent products is that they develop significant cash values. Premiums for permanent products are usually level. In the early policy years, the premiums are much more than adequate to cover the cost of mortality. (In contrast, term insurance premiums more closely match mortality costs.)

Cash values can be thought of as accumulated premiums less mortality costs and expenses. (Mortality costs reflect the death benefits the company expects to pay, which are based on the probability of death.) High expenses in the first year hold down the first-year cash value. After the first year or two, cash values usually increase rapidly, because premiums are much higher than expected mortality costs and expenses, at least for several years. The cash value accumulates with interest. As the cash value grows, interest has a bigger and bigger effect. In fact, interest usually allows the cash value to continue to grow in the later years, even after mortality costs exceed the premium. Figure 1.4.2 gives hypothetical cash values that might result from the premiums, expenses, interest, and mortality costs shown. Premiums and interest add to the cash value, while expenses and mortality costs work to reduce the cash value.

Whole life insurance products provide death benefits over a person's entire lifetime or "whole life," or to some high age, such as age 95 or 100, as long as the required premiums are paid. Whole life products typically provide a level death benefit. They are mainly distinguished by how long premiums are paid:

Figure 1.4.2 Development of Cash Values

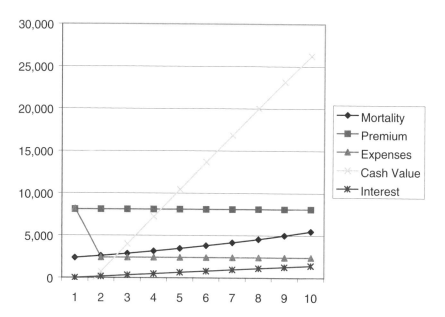

Development of Cash Values
First 10 Policy Years
100,000 Face Amount Policy

- *Single premium whole life* has one premium, paid at the inception of the policy.

- *Limited-pay whole life* has premiums that are most often payable for a specified period of ten years, 20 years, or to age 65. Insurance coverage continues past the point that premiums cease to be paid. For example,
  20-pay life has premiums payable for 20 years, and *Life paid-up at 65* has premiums payable to age 65. Both plans would provide coverage for life or to some ultimate age, such as 95 or 100.

- *Full-pay whole life* has premiums payable for the whole life or to some high age.

Whole life plans typically pay an endowment benefit if the insured lives to the end of the coverage period, such as to age 95 or 100. As a result, they are not truly "whole life."

Endowment insurance products pay a level death benefit for a limited period of time, such as ten years, 20 years, or to age 65. An endowment benefit, equal to the amount of the death benefit, is paid at the end of that period if the insured is still alive. Endowment products generally have the highest premiums and highest cash values. An endowment is used when the policyowner wishes to maximize the savings component of the insurance policy. As with whole life insurance, endowment insurance premiums can be single pay, limited pay, or payable for the duration of the policy.

Participating products pay dividends and are referred to as *par* products. Products that do not pay dividends are referred to as *nonparticipating* or *nonpar*. Historically, par products have been associated mainly with mutual life insurance companies, which are owned by their policyowners. Par policyowners are said to "participate" in the results of the company. Most par products are permanent, but some companies also offer par term products.

The goal of participating insurance sold by mutual companies is to provide insurance at cost with some permanent contribution to the company's capital or surplus. Par products have higher premiums than similar nonpar products. The payment of the premium assures the policyowner of a certain level of guaranteed cash values and guaranteed death benefits. The results of favorable mortality, interest, lapse, expense, and tax experience are shared with the policyowner through dividends. The policyowner dividend is the mechanism through which the company is able to provide value to the policyowner beyond the minimum layer of guaranteed values. The policyowner thereby "participates" in the results of the company. Dividends give the company a means to adjust the net cost of the policy, as experience emerges that differs from that initially anticipated (see Figure 1.4.3).

Years ago, par premiums were typically based on the net premiums calculated for reserve purposes plus a margin for expenses. This meant premiums were based on the same conservative mortality and interest rates used for reserves. Dividends made up for the difference between actual mortality, interest, and expenses and those built into the premiums.

Today, par premiums and dividend scales are more likely to be developed using pricing models. Pessimistic assumptions might be used to establish premiums that will be adequate under adverse conditions. The level and slope of the dividend scale are often part of the product design. In other words, dividends have become more than just a mechanism for returning excess earnings and ensuring equity among

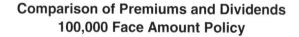

Figure 1.4.3 Participating Premiums and Dividends

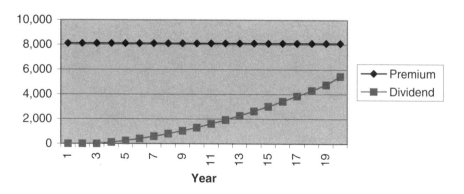

**Comparison of Premiums and Dividends
100,000 Face Amount Policy**

policyowners. The pattern of dividends may be crucial in achieving a goal, such as "vanishing" the premium (by using accumulated dividends or paid-up additions together with future dividends to pay all future premiums). Therefore, the desired level and slope of dividends must be supportable under realistic assumptions. In some cases, regulations may prohibit the illustration of vanishing premiums. Even so, policyowners are free to use accumulated policy values to pay premiums, thereby causing premiums to effectively vanish, at least for a time.

The setting of premiums and dividend scales is a circular process. One affects the other. Both are important in competition. Premiums that are too high or dividends that are too low will have a negative effect on sales. The relative level of premiums and dividends is determined more by competition, company tradition, and intuition than it is by complex formulas. Dividend scales are usually structured to achieve equity among policyowners while leaving a fair profit for the company.

Dividends are usually projected and illustrated at the inception of the contract. As time passes and actual results emerge, dividend scales can be modified. If experience has been better than originally assumed, dividends can be increased, enhancing the benefits available to the policyowners.

Dividend scales should not create unrealistic expectations on the part of agents or policyowners. If experience is worse than originally assumed, dividends can be decreased to bring the profitability of the product in line with original expectations. However, dividend reductions should not be taken lightly, since many products are sold with certain goals in mind. Reducing the dividend scale may cause the originally illustrated goals to not be met. Also, a dividend scale reduction can cause policyowners and agents to lose confidence in the company. If the dividend scale reduction is made because of understandable changes in economic conditions, then there may be less policyowner discontent. Dividend scale reductions should be thought through carefully.

Generally, premiums and cash values are based on conservative estimates of mortality, lapses, interest, expenses, and taxes. More

favorable results in these five areas are shared with the policyowner through the payment of a dividend. Dividends are generally very small or zero in the early policy years and grow as the policy ages.

The par policyowner is usually given a number of *dividend options* that can be changed from time to time:

1. Dividends can be taken in *cash.*

2. Dividends can be left with the company to *accumulate with interest.* The policyowner can later withdraw these funds. Otherwise, they will be disbursed when the policy is surrendered or when the insured dies.

3. Dividends can be used to *reduce premiums,* with any excess dividend applied to another dividend option.

4. Dividends can be used to purchase amounts of paid-up life insurance, which are commonly called *paid-up additions* (PUAs). These additions are neither a policy nor a rider, but rather a supplement to the policy. PUAs have their own cash values and dividends. PUAs can be surrendered. If they are not surrendered, their cash value will be paid when the policy is surrendered, or their death benefit will be paid when the insured dies.

5. Dividends can be used to purchase amounts of *one-year term* (OYT) insurance. This option functions like a term insurance rider, with no cash values and usually no dividends. Each year's dividend is divided by the OYT premium rate for the current age to determine the OYT death benefit for the coming year. OYT premium rates are essentially mortality costs, which typically increase from 8% and 10% per year for most ages over 30. In the early years, dividends increase much faster than do OYT rates, so the OYT death benefit increases. In the later policy years, dividends increase more slowly than do OYT rates, so the OYT death benefit decreases. The resulting pattern of OYT death benefits may be far from ideal.

Some companies offer one or two dividend options beyond those listed above. Combinations of options are also possible. For example, dividends could be accumulated for a number of years and then used to vanish the premiums, by using a combination of accumulated and future dividends to pay all future premiums. As another example, dividends could be split each year between paid-up additions and one-year term to provide a level additional amount of insurance. Because there is always a risk that dividends may be reduced, the company must make it clear that vanishing premiums or level additional amounts of insurance are not guaranteed.

Special riders for participating products: Some par products offer various riders that, when combined with the product in different ways, enable the product to compete with a wide variety of other products. Consider the following example: A company offers a high-commission, high-cost participating whole life policy with two riders:

1. A low-commission, low-cost term insurance rider that has lower premium rates than any term insurance policy on the market. However, this rider cannot be purchased by itself; it must be attached to the high-cost par whole life policy. When a policy is issued with such a rider, restrictions are usually placed on the use of the policy dividends. There is often no explicit additional premium associated with the term rider. Instead, the dividends in the policy must first be used to pay the term rider premiums. Any unused dividends would usually be applied to purchase paid-up coverage or left to accumulate with interest.

2. A low-commission, low-death-benefit, high-cash-value rider that accumulates almost 100% of premiums paid as cash values.

Together, these two riders can match the benefits provided by the par whole life policy, but at a much lower cost. By combining these riders with the policy in various proportions, the agent can select from a broad range of average commission rates and competitiveness.

With-profits: Participating is a North American term. In the U.K., Australia, and South Africa, par products are referred to as *with-profits*. Dividends are referred to as *bonuses*. Besides the terms used, there are several other important differences between North American and U.K. par products:

• In North America, these products are backed primarily by bonds and mortgages. In the U.K., stocks and real estate account for the majority of the assets backing with-profit products.

- For the same age, sex, risk class, and premium, UK with-profit products typically provide lower guaranteed death benefits and cash values than their North American counterparts.

- Cash value guarantees tend to be lower in the U.K. There are no regulations that require companies to offer cash values. The competitive emphasis is on actual cash values, not guaranteed cash values. With lower guaranteed cash values, companies can invest in riskier, higher-yielding investments that, on average, result in higher actual cash values.

- With-profit products have two common forms of bonuses. The annual bonus increases the death benefit and cash value, much like the paid-up additions dividend option in North America. There is also a terminal bonus payable on death or maturity. The insurance company can vary terminal bonuses at any time. This can be done to reflect changes in the market value of the more volatile assets often used to back with-profit products.

- Some with-profit products guarantee a minimum death benefit that functions much like a nonparticipating decreasing term rider: A supplementary death benefit decreases as the with-profit death benefit increases with annual bonuses, thereby providing a level total death benefit. This feature is similar to the low-cost term insurance riders offered on participating products as described in Section 1.4.1.2.

Nonparticipating permanent insurance: Participating policies have historically been associated with mutual companies, which are owned by their policyowners. In contrast, nonparticipating products have been associated mainly with stock companies, which are owned by public or private stockholders. Stock companies have offered participating products, but now more commonly offer dynamic products. Regulatory constraints on par products sometimes make it difficult to earn returns that are acceptable to stockholders.

Nonparticipating permanent products have premiums, cash values, and death benefits that are fixed. Nothing is subject to change after the policy is issued. No dividends are payable. This means nonpar products have no means to adjust for significant changes in mortality, lapses, interest, expenses, or taxes. As a result, the nonpar premium must contain a substantial margin to cover the risk of excess mortality, excess lapses, excess expenses, and, in particular, falling interest rates.

While par premiums are higher than nonpar premiums for otherwise similar products, the net cost of par products (premiums less dividends) usually makes them much more attractive than nonpar products over the long term. This is because par products can adjust dividends to handle the various risks while nonpar products must charge a fixed margin to handle these risks.

Nonpar permanent products may be more competitive in times of low interest rates: A lower perceived risk of interest rates falling may result in a smaller margin to cover the interest risk. Indeterminate premiums can also be used to make nonpar permanent products more competitive and more responsive to changes in conditions. Switching from nonpar to par would seem to be a simpler, more effective alternative to indeterminate premiums.

Nonpar permanent products are most useful in situations where simplicity is more important than competitiveness or value. This is often the case with small-sized policies.

1.4.2 Dynamic Products

Dynamic products differ from pre-scheduled products in that cash values are not determined up front. Instead, a particular policy's cash values are determined on an ongoing basis by first accumulating an *account value* for the policy. The account value is calculated by accumulating premiums with interest or investment results and by deducting charges for mortality and expenses. The mortality charges are also referred to as *cost of insurance* (COI) charges. Premium payments and investment income are added to the account value. Expense and mortality charges are subtracted from the account value. This process is usually performed once a month.

A dynamic product's cash value is usually equal to an *account value* less a *surrender charge*. The surrender charge gradually declines and eventually disappears after a number of years.

With a dynamic product, continuation of a policy is tied to having enough funds available in the account value to cover the monthly deductions for expenses and mortality. This contrasts with pre-scheduled policies, where continuation is tied to the payment of a pre-scheduled premium.

Premiums are often flexible, allowing the policyowner to skip payments or pay more or less than originally planned. Death benefits sometimes vary with the cash value. Some dynamic policies allow for *partial withdrawals* from the cash value, as an alternative to policy loans.

The premium flexibility of some dynamic products allows an appropriate insurance program to be tailored for a particular insured. A flexible premium dynamic product can be designed to provide insurance for a short period of time, like a term product, or for a long period of time, like a permanent product.

After a certain number of years, a *persistency bonus* is sometimes added to the account value. This bonus is usually a refund of a portion of past mortality or expense charges or represents the retroactive crediting of higher interest rates. The bonus may be guaranteed or at the company's discretion. Either way, its all-or-nothing nature can create an accounting and reserving dilemma. For example, a substantial bonus may be payable at the twentieth policy anniversary, but if the policy lapses after 19 years, no bonus may be payable. Should the cost of the bonus be allocated solely to the twentieth policy year, or should the cost be spread over the first 20 policy years in some fashion?

Mortality and expense charges are usually subject to guaranteed maximums. However, actual mortality charges are often less than the guaranteed maximum charges. Actual expense charges usually equal the guaranteed maximum expense charges.

There are two main categories of dynamic products: universal life and variable universal life.

1.4.2.1 Universal Life

Universal life (UL) products credit interest to the account value, usually subject to a guaranteed minimum rate of interest. The insurance company usually decides on the interest rate to be credited to the account value, although the credited interest rate could also be based on a financial index. The policyowner does *not* have a choice of investment funds. The interest rates credited are based on interest rates earned on assets in the company's general asset portfolio, or general account.

There are three main variations of universal life:

- *Single premium* universal life speaks for itself.
- *Fixed premium* universal life requires that a fixed premium be paid for some period of time, just like a whole life product.
- *Flexible premium* universal life allows the policyowner to vary or even stop premium payments, subject to either a minimum cumulative premium being paid or the account value being greater than zero.

The interest rate credited to a UL policy often depends on when premiums were received. For example, premiums received during a period of high interest rates would often be credited a higher interest rate than premiums received during a period of low interest rates. A single UL policy's account value can be composed of many different funds, each earning a different interest rate. To simplify administration, many companies try to minimize the number of time periods that result in different interest rates. However, even two interest rate periods dramatically increase the complexity of administration: Every addition to and deduction from the policy's account value must be allocated in some fashion to one fund or the other or both. For example, should mortality charges be allocated to the oldest fund, the newest fund, or pro-rated among all funds?

A few UL products link the credited interest rate to a bond index. For example, the credited interest rate could equal the rates earned on five-year government bonds minus 0.25% (25 basis points). Another approach would be to link the credited interest rate to an equity index. For example, the credited interest rate could be 70% of the increase in the S&P 500 stock index. When linking credited interest rates to an index, assets must be carefully managed to match the company's obligations. In any case, the credited interest rate would be no less than the guaranteed minimum interest rate.

Each of a company's assets usually has two values. The *book value* is the value shown on the company's books, which is often related to what the company paid for the asset. The *market value* is the estimated amount the asset could be sold for. Book values tend to be stable and predictable. Market values depend on many factors, especially interest rates. When interest rates rise, financial markets calculate present values using higher interest rates. When the future cash flows of an asset are discounted using a higher interest rate, the result is a lower present value. This is why most asset market values fall when interest rates rise. As a result, interest rate changes can be dangerous for life insurance companies.

To reduce this danger, some UL products feature a *market value adjustment* (MVA) that reflects the current market value of the assets backing the cash value. In most cases, this is accomplished through a formula that approximates the effect of interest rate changes on market values. For example, if an increase in interest rates caused the market value of assets to drop to 90% of book value, cash values would be multiplied by an MVA of roughly 90% before being paid out. On the other hand, if a decrease in interest rates caused the market value of assets to rise to 120% of book value, cash values would be multiplied by an MVA of roughly 120% before being paid out.

Fixed premium universal life products usually have level premiums. These products are also referred to as interest-sensitive whole life or excess-interest whole life. Scheduled premium payments are required. Except as mentioned below, if premium payments cease, coverage will be discontinued.

Premiums for fixed premium UL products are usually calculated to be sufficient to mature the policy (that is, to accumulate a cash value that eventually equals the death benefit). The premium is often based on current COI charges and credited interest rates at the time the policy is issued. Some products base the premium on more conservative factors, so the policy will mature even if interest rates decline somewhat or if COI charges increase a little.

As actual experience emerges, the premiums may not be sufficient to keep the policy in force. A drop in interest rates or an increase in mortality charges may eventually force an adjustment to the policy. Policy provisions usually give the policyowner a choice from time to time, such as every five years, as to what to do if premiums are insufficient. The choices offered might include some of the following:

1. Leave the premium and death benefit as is. If conditions do not sufficiently improve, the policy will run out of cash value and expire before its scheduled maturity date.

2. Increase the premium in order to continue the current death benefit to the maturity date, based on current interest rates and COI charges.

3. Decrease the death benefit in order to continue the current premium to the maturity date, based on current interest rates and COI charges.

On the other hand, higher than expected interest rates could cause the cash value to become excessive in relation to the death benefit. To counter this, policy provisions would usually increase the death benefit automatically, in order to maintain a reasonable relationship to the cash value. Alternatively, death benefits could be left as is, and premiums could be adjusted downward, to reflect the better experience.

Sometimes a vanishing premium option is available. This allows the policyowner to stop paying premiums when the account value is deemed sufficient to provide a level (but nonguaranteed) death benefit to maturity. If interest rates drop or mortality charges increase, the policyowner will eventually have to resume paying premiums. This option can be difficult to explain to agents and customers. There is a good chance that most will incorrectly believe that premiums are guaranteed to vanish.

Flexible premium universal life: There is more than just a difference in premiums between flexible premium and fixed premium universal life. Flexible premium universal life usually offers two death benefit options:

1. A level death benefit. This is often called *Option A* or *Type A*.

2. A level amount at risk: The death benefit equals a level amount plus the cash value or account value. This is often called *Option B* or *Type B*. It is also referred as the increasing death benefit option.

Figure 1.4.4 illustrates death benefit patterns for the level death benefit option and the level amount at risk option.

Flexible premium universal life introduces some new variables:

- Large initial premiums are common. The initial premium might come from the cash value of a policy being replaced.

- Premiums may cease without the policy being lapsed or surrendered.

- Premiums may increase, decrease, stop, or resume.

- Death benefits may decrease or, with evidence of insurability, increase. In addition, the level amount at risk option produces varying death benefits.

Increases in death benefit (other than those that naturally occur under the level amount at risk design) will usually involve additional underwriting costs and a high commission rate on any increase in premium. Because of the flexibility of premium payments, lapse measurement is much more difficult. Rather than tracking only policies lapsed or death benefit lapsed, you might also track actual versus expected premium income and actual versus expected cash withdrawals.

Most flexible premium UL products (and VUL products discussed below) pay a high commission on first-year premium up to the amount of a target premium. Premiums in excess of the target premium receive

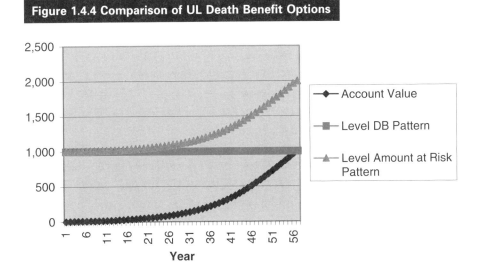

Figure 1.4.4 Comparison of UL Death Benefit Options

a low commission, as do first-year lump-sum (nonrecurring) premiums and renewal premiums. There are often two exceptions to this:

1. If the second-year premium is less than the first-year premium, the excess first-year premium is retroactively assumed to be a lump-sum premium and retroactively receives only a low commission rate.

2. If the agent sells a significant increase in death benefit to the policyowner after the first year, the agent will receive a commission similar to what would have been earned by selling a second UL policy. This removes the incentive to sell a second policy rather than increase the first policy.

While both of these exceptions make sense, they can be very difficult to administer.

1.4.2.2 Variable Universal Life

Variable universal life (VUL) products usually allow the policyowner to allocate the account value among several investment funds, including the company's general account. For example, the policyowner might choose to put half of the premiums into a growth-oriented stock fund and the other half into a long-term bond fund. The investment results of the chosen funds are credited to the account value. Unlike UL, VUL investment results are not subject to a guaranteed minimum interest rate, except for amounts allocated to the general account. For funds that are not allocated to the company's general account, the policyowner bears all of the investment risk while the company bears none. For funds that are allocated to the general account, the company bears the investment risk. This includes disintermediation risk. This is the risk of having to sell assets to fund cash outflows at a time when market values are depressed.

Consumers often choose VUL products in order to participate in the stock market. VUL is most popular when recent increases in stock prices make stocks look more attractive than other investments. Conversely, VUL is least popular after a period in which stock prices have significantly declined or when current interest rates are high.

Variable universal life has three main variations, just like universal life: single premium, fixed premium, and flexible premium. VUL products share many of the characteristics of UL. The major difference is that UL credits interest rates based on rates set by the company while VUL tracks the performance of investment funds. There is an exception: Funds allocated to the general account earn interest rates declared by the company.

Each business day, the total market value, number of units outstanding, and unit value for each investment fund is determined. The unit value is equal to the total market value divided by the number of units. All transactions that affect an investment fund are converted to a number of units by dividing the cash involved by the unit value for the day.

For example, suppose a premium of 1,000 is paid for Policy 1 and allocated 100% to Investment Fund A, with the following additional information before the premium is paid:

Policy 1 Account Value
    Investment Fund A: 100 units
    Investment Fund B: 200 units
Investment Fund A
    Total market value: 10,000,000
    Units outstanding: 500,000
    Unit value: 20.00000

The premium of 1,000 would purchase 50 units of Investment Fund A (1,000 divided by the unit value of 20.00000). This would increase the Policy 1 Account Value for Investment Fund A from 100 units to 150 units. Investment Fund A's market value would increase to 10,001,000. Units outstanding would increase to 500,050. Unit value would remain unchanged at 20.00000.

If the market value of Investment Fund A increased by 10% overnight, the Policy 1 Account Value for Investment Fund A would increase in value from 3,000 (150 times 20.00000) to 3,300 (150 times 22.00000) overnight.

While this explanation focuses on daily unit values, in some countries it is possible to have a VUL product with monthly values. In such a case, all transactions are accumulated and processed at the end of the month. This raises questions as to whether short-term interest should be credited to premiums received early in the month and whether cash payable on withdrawals or surrenders can be disbursed before the end of the month.

Unit-linked: In the U.K. and some other countries, VUL is referred to as unit-linked. In most respects, VUL and unit-linked are the same, but there are some differences:

- VUL and newer unit-linked products tend to offset *acquisition costs* (that is, the costs of acquiring a policy, including commissions, underwriting costs, and administrative costs) with surrender charges that gradually decline to zero over a period of five to 20 years. Older unit-linked products are more likely to use front-end loads (large expense charges in the first policy year or two) to cover acquisition costs. These front-end loads sometimes exceed 100% of first-year premium.

- Older unit-linked products make use of a bid/offer spread as an additional, somewhat hidden expense charge. For example, if the bid/offer spread is 5%, premiums may buy units at a bid price of 102.5% of the unit price, and withdrawals may sell units at an offer price of 97.5% of the unit price. In effect, the company is charging a 2.5% expense charge on premiums paid and a 2.5% surrender charge on amounts withdrawn. Such hidden charges are less common with newer products.

- In Australia, unit-linked products are pure investment products and offer no death benefit beyond the cash value. To compete with other investment choices, commissions and expense loads tend to be low. Surrender charges are more common than front-end loads.

Unitised-with-profits: The U.K. offers a product that is a hybrid between unit-linked and with-profits (that is, participating) products. This product is called *unitised-with-profits.* In most respects, the hybrid product behaves just like a unit-linked product. The main exception is the crediting of investment returns. Unitised-with-profits passes only some of the investment risk to the policyowner, while unit-linked passes all of the investment risk. Unitised-with-profits smoothes the returns credited to the policy. Compared to traditional with-profits products, unitised-with-profits reduces the company's capital requirements. This is because some of the investment risk is passed to the policyowner.

Unlike unit-linked or VUL products, unit values do not track the market value of an investment fund. Instead, the insurance company manages the investments backing the product and controls the unit values. The company usually has a goal of smoothing the returns, to avoid reflecting the ups and downs in the stock and real estate markets. Dividends (bonuses) serve to increase the unit value when they are credited.

Unit values are guaranteed not to decrease. To manage this guarantee, the company may wish to maintain a safety buffer and hold back on the excess investment returns (that is, dividends or bonus rates) credited to the unit value. This safety buffer will help stabilize the company during times when stock and real estate market values are falling. To minimize inequities created by holding back on dividends, the company can pay terminal dividends (or terminal bonuses) to those terminating their policies. The terminal dividends would roughly equal the dividends that have been held back and not yet credited to the unit value.

1.4.3 Multiple-Life Products

Multiple-life products insure two or more lives in the same policy. Multiple-life products can come in just as many forms as single life products, such as term, permanent, universal life, and variable universal life. Outside of group insurance, policies that insure more than two lives are rare. Therefore, we will limit our discussion to the insurance of two lives in the same policy. There are two types of products that cover two lives:

1. *Joint first-to-die* products pay the death benefit when the first death occurs.

2. *Joint last-survivor* or *Joint last-to-die* products pay the death benefit when the second death occurs.

Joint first-to-die products sometimes include a survivor insurance rider. This rider allows the surviving insured to purchase a new single-life policy at regular rates when the first insured dies, regardless of the survivor's insurability.

There are two varieties of joint last-to-die products that behave quite differently when the first insured dies:

1. One variety features a big increase in premium and cash value when the first insured dies. The resulting premium and cash value might be those for an otherwise similar single-life policy on the surviving insured. A less common variation results in a paid-up single-life policy on the surviving insured.

2. The other variety totally ignores the first death, with no change in premium or cash value when the first insured dies.

There are three basic approaches to handling the different ages, genders, and risk classes of the two insureds:

1. An *equivalent single age* approach allows a company to use a single life product to insure two lives. For example, two people age 65 might be issued a policy with premiums and cash values that are the same as those for a single insured age 55. The difference is that the death benefit is not payable until both insureds have died. Reducing the issue age from 65 to 55 offsets the value of delaying the death benefit until the second death. Company rules specify how two ages, two genders, and two risk classes are combined to determine an equivalent single age, gender, and risk class.

2. A *joint equal age* approach allows a company to develop a joint life product that assumes that every joint policy is issued to two people of the same age and same risk class. The joint equal age is adjusted to reflect the actual ages, genders, and risk classes of the two insureds, based on company rules.

3. An *exact age* approach reflects the age, gender, and risk class of each insured. This is most practical for a dynamic product, which can calculate mortality charges for the particular combination of ages, genders, and risk classes for each policy as needed. This calculation is explained in Chapter 4. Given the many combinations of two ages, two genders, and two risk classes, it is impractical though possible to precalculate all the possible premiums and cash values that would be needed for a pre-scheduled product.

Joint products sometimes include a *split rider,* which allows the joint policy to be split into two single-life policies under certain conditions, such as a divorce or change in the law governing estate taxes.

1.4.4   Riders, Additional Benefits, and Options

Life insurance policies are usually offered with a choice of many different riders, additional benefits, and options that enhance the benefits provided by the policy. These can be broken down into three major categories:

1. Modifications to the basic policy
2. Minor benefits that are added to the basic policy
3. Significant benefits that could be sold as separate policies.

1.4.4.1   Modifications to the Basic Policy

Some products offer an *accelerated death benefit option*, often for no extra charge. This benefit comes into play when the insured has a terminal illness that is reasonably certain to result in death within a short period of time, such as six months or a year. In such a case, an accelerated death benefit option allows a discounted death benefit to be paid prior to death. For example, if the insured has six months to live, the company might pay the death benefit six months early, reduced for six months of lost interest and six months of lost premium payments.

When inflation is significant, some products offer a *cost-of-living adjustment* (COLA) that periodically increases the death benefit to keep pace with inflation. There are two main approaches to determining the periodic increases:

1. The increases are tied to an outside index, such as a consumer-price index.
2. The increases follow a fixed schedule specified in the policy, such as an annual increase amount or an annual percentage increase.

The increases are often limited to a certain number of years, such as ten or twenty, or to a certain cumulative percentage of the original death benefit.

COLAs are most commonly used in connection with increasing premium term and dynamic products, because these products can directly charge for the increased death benefit. Typically, if one COLA increase is declined, then the policy becomes ineligible for future increases. Increases can usually be resumed if the insured is reunderwritten and found to be in suitable health.

Another approach to battling the effect of inflation is found in Chile. All financial products in Chile must be denominated in an inflation-adjusted financial unit. For example, you might buy a policy with a death benefit of 300 financial units at a time when one financial unit is worth 700 pesos. After many years of inflation, the policy will still have a death benefit of 300 financial units, but one financial unit may be worth, say, 1,500 pesos at that time.

1.4.4.2 Minor Benefits Added to the Basic Policy

The most common minor benefits added to life insurance policies are waiver of premium, accidental death benefits, family insurance riders, and guaranteed insurability riders. None of these riders typically offer cash values.

Waiver of premium (WP) is one of the most common riders attached to life insurance policies, probably because of its simplicity, usefulness, and low additional cost. The waiver of premium benefit allows the policyowner to stop paying premiums if the person insured by the WP rider becomes disabled. The WP rider usually insures the person paying the premiums.

The definition of disability is usually fairly restrictive and includes a waiting period, such as six months, during which the insured must remain disabled in order to qualify for WP benefits. WP benefits cease if and when the insured recovers from the disability. WP riders typically have two levels of benefits:

1. If disability occurs before a certain age (such as 55), premiums will be waived for the remainder of the policy.

2. If disability occurs after the first age (such as 55) and before a second age (such as 65), then premiums will be waived until the second age (such as 65).

The WP rider typically terminates at the age after which no benefits are payable (such as age 65).

For pre-scheduled and fixed premium products that are issued with a WP rider, the premiums are waived (that is, paid by the company) while the insured is disabled. Also, premiums for the WP rider and other riders are waived while WP benefits are being paid. The premium for the WP rider is typically increased when premiums for other riders are part of the WP benefit.

For flexible premium products, several different WP benefits are possible. The most common are the following:

- The average recurring premium, excluding any lump-sum deposits, is waived. In this case, the premium for the WP benefit would typically be a percentage of recurring premiums paid.
- A flat amount, specified when the policy is issued, is waived.
- Mortality charges and other monthly deductions are waived. Waiving the mortality charges and other monthly deductions ensures the policy will remain in force while the insured is disabled.

In any case, the charges for the WP rider are waived while WP benefits are being paid.

Accidental death benefits (ADB) pay a benefit if the insured dies from an accident. *Accidental death and dismemberment* (AD&D) benefits additionally pay a full or partial benefit in the event of accidental dismemberment, depending on the extent of dismemberment. Sometimes an accidental death benefit is included as part of the basic policy, with the result that the death benefit is increased when death occurs by accident. Some companies issue ADB and AD&D as stand-alone policies.

The justification for these benefits is that death by accident is more unexpected and traumatic to the insured's beneficiaries than death by natural causes. However, a counterargument is that, because of the lower cost of final medical care, accidental deaths require less insurance. Death by natural causes can generate far greater medical costs, such as for the treatment of cancer or coronary bypass surgery. In spite of this, accidental death benefits are often attractive because of their low cost.

Family insurance riders usually provide modest amounts of term insurance on the lives of the insured's spouse and children. This rider is meant to cover funeral and other final expenses plus something more if the spouse dies. The spouse's death benefit often decreases with age while the children's death benefit is typically a level amount until age 18 or 21 and zero thereafter. The premium for the family rider is usually level and independent of the number of children covered.

A *guaranteed insurability rider* (GIR) allows the insured to buy additional policies at the attainment of certain ages or when certain events happen, such as marriage of the insured or the birth or adoption of a child of the insured, with no proof of insurability required. This means the policyowner can increase the amount of insurance on the insured with no underwriting and at guaranteed premium rates. However, the increases are generally limited to fairly small amounts. The rider may include a provision that terminates the rider if the policyowner fails to elect an eligible increase.

Other names for GIR are *guaranteed purchase option* (GPO), *guaranteed increase option* (GIO), and *future insurability option* (FIO). When attached to a dynamic product, these riders would be exercised by increasing the death benefit of the policy rather than issuing a new policy for the amount of the increase.

Beneficiary insurability option: Before joint second-to-die products were developed, other methods were used to provide death benefits on the second death. One of these methods involved using a beneficiary insurability option (BIO) attached to a single-life policy. When the beneficiary died first, the single-life policy would provide a benefit on the second death. When the person insured by the single-life policy died first, the BIO would provide the beneficiary with the right to purchase a new policy at guaranteed rates. The new policy would then provide a benefit on the second death. Either way, a single-life policy with a BIO would provide a benefit on the second death. Another name for BIO was *survivor insurability rider* (SIR).

1.4.4.3   Significant Benefits That Could Be Separate Policies

Many companies offer significant benefits that can be added as a rider to a life insurance policy. Some companies offer the same benefit as a stand-alone policy. Some companies offer the buyer a choice for a particular benefit: It can be added as a rider or purchased as a stand-alone policy. Often, the company gives the buyer an economic incentive to purchase the benefits as riders, either through a discount or avoidance of an additional policy fee.

In this section, we will discuss term insurance riders, critical illness benefits, long-term care benefits, total and permanent disability benefits, disability income benefits, and medical expense riders.

Term insurance riders: Many companies offer term insurance as a rider. Many times the term rider is virtually identical to a separate term policy except that the policyowner pays only one policy fee instead of the two policy fees that would be incurred if two policies were purchased. The term rider may insure the same person insured by the basic policy, the insured's spouse, or some other person. The earlier discussion of term insurance also applies to term riders.

Critical illness (CI) benefits, also known as dread disease (DD) benefits, pay a lump-sum benefit when one of a certain list of illnesses occurs. The list would typically include such illnesses as heart attack, stroke, and cancer. The list could be as short as five illnesses or as long as 50 or more.

When attached to a life insurance policy, the CI benefit is often integrated with the policy's death benefit: Any amount paid out as a CI benefit reduces the policy's death benefit. Some companies offer a *buy-back option* that automatically increases the policy's death benefit back to its original level over, for example, a three-year period following the CI benefit payment.

Another approach is to offer a CI benefit that is totally independent of the policy's death benefit. In this case, any CI benefit paid has no effect on the policy's death benefit. Clearly, this second approach costs more.

Anti-selection is a major problem with CI benefits. For example, someone who suspects they have cancer may purchase a CI benefit before they see a doctor. This kind of behavior results in many early claims. One possible remedy is to have a waiting period after the policy is issued during which certain types of claims (such as certain forms of cancer) are not covered. However, this can result in many misunderstandings and poor customer relations.

Long-term care (LTC) insurance comes in many varieties. It typically pays a monthly benefit while the insured requires daily care. What constitutes a need for daily care varies widely and is carefully defined in the policy. LTC benefits are usually limited to a cumulative maximum amount or a maximum number of monthly payments. The amount of each monthly benefit payment may be a flat amount or tied to the cost of caring for the insured, subject to a maximum.

When attached to a life insurance policy, the LTC benefit is often integrated with the policy's death benefit and cash value: Any amount paid out as a LTC benefit reduces the policy's death benefit. The policy's cash value may be reduced by the LTC benefit paid or by the percentage by which death benefits are reduced.

Another approach is to offer a LTC benefit that is totally independent of the policy's benefits. In this case, any LTC benefit paid has no effect on the policy's death benefit or cash value. Clearly, this second approach costs more.

LTC insurance tends to be very expensive because it is usually purchased late in life when the need for long-term care becomes more likely and not so far in the future. For example, suppose LTC insurance is purchased at age 70, with a benefit that will pay for up to ten years of nursing home costs at current price levels. The annual premium for this coverage will probably be a significant percentage of the annual nursing home cost.

Total and permanent disability (TPD) insurance pays the insured a lump sum when the insured is certified as being totally and permanently disabled. In South Africa, TPD is known as *capital disability*. The definition of disability for this benefit is usually limited to forms of disability that are obvious, clear, and unarguable. For example, disabilities that are difficult to prove or disprove (such as those related to mental conditions or chronic pain) would normally not be covered by TPD insurance.

When attached to a life insurance policy, the TPD benefit is often integrated with the policy's death benefit: Any amount paid out as a TPD benefit reduces the policy's death benefit. Another approach is to offer a TPD benefit that is totally independent of the policy's death benefit. In this case, any TPD benefit paid has no effect on the policy's death benefit. Clearly, this second approach costs more.

Disability income (DI) insurance typically pays a fixed monthly benefit once the insured qualifies as disabled. Some variations of DI pay a monthly benefit that reimburses lost income rather than pay a fixed monthly benefit.

DI benefits may be payable for a certain number of years, to a certain age, or for life. To qualify as disabled, the insured has to remain disabled for a waiting period, which is usually measured in months. Companies that offer DI typically offer a range of choices in benefit periods and waiting periods. Because DI premiums vary by benefit period, waiting period, occupation, age, gender, and perhaps other underwriting factors, the sheer number and complexity of DI premiums can be overwhelming.

There is a wide range in the definition of disability. A liberal definition would be the inability of the insured to perform his or her usual occupation. At the other extreme, disability could be defined very restrictively, along the lines used for TPD benefits.

From the company's point of view, there is a major risk that, when the economy slows down and unemployment rises, many insureds with DI insurance will find a way to be disabled rather than unemployed. Because of this, it is not uncommon for insurance companies to earn profits on their DI insurance block when the economy is strong and then suffer losses when unemployment rises.

Medical expense riders: There are many forms of medical expense riders, but a typical rider would reimburse the insured for hospital expenses up to a certain amount per day in the hospital. While this benefit is unrelated to life insurance, it often satisfies a perceived need at a price that can be attractive to consumers.

1.5 Taxation of Life Insurance Products

The taxation of policyowners, beneficiaries, and life insurance companies has a great influence on the products that are most commonly sold. Taxation varies tremendously from country to country and it accounts for many of the differences between countries in the products offered. Taxes can be a powerful motivation to purchase life insurance. Tax rules can make or break a particular type of product. The tax treatment that applies to life insurance products can be broken into the following categories.

1.5.1 Deductibility of Premiums Paid

A few countries grant a tax deduction for up to a certain amount of life insurance premiums per year, to encourage savings through life insurance. This causes many individuals, especially those subject to high tax rates, to choose life insurance as their preferred method of saving money. The result is that insurance policies tend to sell themselves in great numbers.

The most popular products when premiums are deductible are usually short-term endowments with limited underwriting. Other than investment products, endowments offer the highest savings element and the lowest cost of protection.

1.5.2 Taxation of Death Benefits Paid to Beneficiaries

Most countries do not tax death benefits received by beneficiaries. This is the most common tax break enjoyed by life insurance. When premiums are not tax deductible, it is usually seen as fair that death benefits are not taxable. However, to receive this tax break, you have to die. As a result, this tax break is not usually a major motivating factor when buying life insurance.

However, corporations sometimes will buy life insurance policies on their employees' lives. This is called corporate-owned life insurance (COLI). COLI is often used to fund some of the corporation's future employee obligations in a tax-efficient way. By paying premiums until each employee dies, the corporation receives nothing but tax-free death benefits, thereby earning a more attractive rate of return on its money. There are many variations on the COLI theme: bank-owned life insurance (BOLI), hotel-owned life insurance (HOLI), and motel-owned life insurance (MOLI).

1.5.3   Taxation of Cash Value Buildup

Permanent products can build up substantial cash values. These cash values come from the accumulation of premiums and investment income, net of expenses and mortality costs. The cash values are backed by invested assets that usually earn interest or appreciate in value. In most countries, the policyowner is not taxed on this investment income as long as the funds are left with the insurance company. With more sophisticated, tax-conscious buyers, this tax deferral can be one of the reasons for buying life insurance. This can help greatly with the sale of large permanent policies.

Some countries, such as Canada, tax the annual increase in cash value, adjusted for premiums and distributions. This makes permanent products much less attractive to more sophisticated, tax-conscious buyers.

1.5.4   Taxation of Gain on Distribution

When policyowners receive dividends, cash values, endowment benefits, withdrawals, or other distributions, they may be taxed. A common approach is to tax policyowners on any gain they receive. Cumulative gain is usually calculated as the excess of cumulative distributions over cumulative premiums. For example, a policyowner receiving 12,000 after paying ten years of 1,000 annual premiums would be taxed on 2,000. Some countries deduct a cost for mortality in calculating the gain. In this way, an attempt to tax only the investment gain is made. In the above example, if the cost of mortality were calculated as 3,000, the policyowner would be taxed on 5,000 of gain (12,000 of cash value minus 10,000 of premiums plus 3,000 of imputed mortality cost).

Some countries have tax rules that forgive the tax on the gain if the policy meets certain conditions. For example, Australia forgives the tax on the gain once the life insurance policy has been in force for ten years.

1.5.5 Taxation of Policy Loans

Often, policy loans are not counted as taxable distributions. In this case, policy loan repayments would also be ignored for tax purposes. However, in some countries, policy loan interest is tax deductible. When coupled with no tax on the cash value buildup, this can make a fully loaned life insurance policy an extremely tax-efficient investment choice.

The ultimate product design to exploit the tax deductibility of policy loan interest might have the following features: The product would have a single premium and a cash value that could be fully loaned at issue. The policyowner would only have to pay cash equal to the difference between the single premium and the initial policy loan. For a relatively small net outlay, the policyowner would receive big annual tax deductions on policy loan interest payments while watching cash values build up with no tax currently payable. In effect, the policy loan interest payments would be equivalent to tax-deductible premiums. This situation once existed in the U.S., but was gradually eliminated by tax law changes through the years.

1.5.6 Qualification as Life Insurance

In some countries, in order to enjoy the tax advantages of life insurance, products have to meet certain requirements. For example, the death benefit may have to significantly exceed the cash value for the product to be taxed as life insurance. The U.S. has enormously complex rules that define whether a policy qualifies as life insurance.

In a number of countries, any product sold by a life insurance company is taxed as life insurance. For example, a pure investment product (that is, with no death benefit and no investment guarantees) sold by a life insurance company may be taxed as life insurance. In the U.K., the tax authorities compensate by taxing the life insurance company on the portion of its investment income backing such tax-favored products.

1.6   Life Insurance Distribution

As an old life insurance adage says, "Life insurance is sold, not bought." Many people avoid the subject of their own death and need to be convinced to purchase life insurance. As a result, in most countries individual life insurance has been sold primarily through life insurance agents. Over the last two decades, agent distribution has been declining in a number of markets, while other distribution channels have been growing. In this section, we will discuss the channels for distributing life insurance products.

1.6.1   Captive Agents

A captive field force is the oldest form of insurance distribution. Agents are said to be *tied*, *dedicated*, or *captive* if they sell primarily one company's products. Often, the agent has a contract with the company that limits or forbids sales with other companies. Some companies refer to their captive agents as *career* agents.

Many companies recruit inexperienced agents and subsidize them during a training period. In return for the training and subsidies, the agent is expected to sell only the company's products.

Agents may be organized into *general agencies*, headed by *general agents*. The general agent (GA) would typically provide training, marketing support, and office space for the agents. In return, the GA would receive part of the commission on every policy sold through the agency, referred to as a *commission override*. The GA might also receive a subsidy from the company to defray start-up expenses or ongoing office expenses. Most general agents continue to personally sell insurance. Often, commissions from their personal sales efforts contribute a major portion of their income.

In some cases, GAs have no agents reporting to them. These GAs are called *personal-producing general agents* (PPGAs). In practice, a PPGA is simply an agent who receives a higher commission, because it includes the GA's commission override. Some companies use PPGAs for a major portion of their distribution. Many PPGAs and agents work out of their homes.

Agents may also be organized into *branch offices*. A branch office is an office fully paid for by the company and headed by a company employee called the *branch manager*. The company saves the expense of paying commission overrides but usually pays the branch manager a salary plus a production-related bonus to encourage sales. Some companies support both general agencies and branch offices.

1.6.2 Independent Agents

From the agent's perspective, the captive agency system can be a difficult way to make a living. The products of any one company will not always stand up to the competition, making it difficult for an agent to sell for just one company. From the company's standpoint, maintaining a captive agency force can be difficult. In exchange for being captive, the agents may expect a high level of service. It may be difficult for the company to provide both high levels of service and competitive products.

An alternative is independent agents, also known as *brokers*. The word "broker" often refers to someone who represents the buyer. Therefore, we will not use that term, since an insurance agent is legally an agent of the insurance company, not the buyer. However, business sold through independent agents is usually referred to as *brokerage business*. In the U.K., an independent agent is referred to as an independent financial advisor (IFA).

Independent agents are free to choose the companies they represent. They often represent three or more companies. They can present potential buyers with the most competitive product or the highest-rated company. Also, independent agents are free to sell from an assortment of products that will provide adequate compensation to meet their needs.

Sometimes an independent agent's start-up expenses will be borne by one particular company, as that company strives to gain the agent's business. The independent agent may be more inclined to place business with that company, not only until the start-up costs are repaid, but also thereafter.

Independent agents will expect a certain level of service from the insurance company in return for placing business with that company. On the other hand, the company wants agents who produce sufficient business of reasonable quality. A company will often have a minimum production requirement that the agent must meet in order to continue representing the company. Many companies monitor each agent's persistency and mortality experience. If either falls too far short of the company's standards, the agent will be terminated.

Increasingly, independent agents are organizing themselves into large groups, often called *producer groups*. Some of these groups have developed considerable clout and bargaining power with life insurance companies, often due to a reputation for quality and huge capacity to produce new business. Some insurance companies are willing to cater to a producer group that, in return, will restrict the number of companies it represents. For example, some producer groups have had products designed exclusively for them. Often, these groups perform many of the marketing and new business services typically provided by insurance companies. As a result, producer groups usually receive extra commissions. Some groups own a life insurance subsidiary that receives, through reinsurance, a portion of every policy written by the group.

1.6.3 Banks

In most countries, banks are not allowed to engage in the insurance business by issuing insurance policies and taking insurance risks. Similarly, life insurance companies are not allowed to engage in the banking business by taking deposits. However, many countries allow banks and insurance companies to own one another or be owned by a common parent company. Also, banks are often allowed to sell insurance, acting as an agent for an insurance company.

Some countries maintain a strict separation between banking and insurance activities. Historically, there has been a fear that allowing banks and insurance companies to mix ownership could lead to financial instability. For example, a bank in financial trouble could cause the collapse of an affiliated insurance company. In addition, there has been a fear that a bank in the insurance business would require a borrower to buy insurance at a high price in order to receive a loan from the bank. In spite of these fears, the worldwide trend is toward breaking down the separation between banking and insurance.

Depending on local regulations, there are a number of ways in which banks can sell insurance:

- Banks can sell insurance to customers who visit bank branches. This activity can range from responding to inquiries and requests for insurance to more aggressive selling to customers not seeking insurance. Advertising can be used to stimulate customer inquiries.

- Banks can review customer data and target those customers most likely to need or buy life insurance. Bank employees, often offered incentives like commissions or bonuses, contact the targeted customers and try to sell them insurance.

- Instead of using bank employees to sell insurance, a bank can contract with a life insurance company to do the selling. In exchange for help from the bank with customer leads, the insurance company would pay the bank a commission on all sales.

Banks have experience selling savings-oriented products. As a result, life insurance products that provide tax-advantaged savings are often sold through banks. Term insurance is commonly sold through banks, most often in connection with a loan from the bank. Because other financial products offered by banks can usually be explained and sold in minutes, only the simplest life insurance products tend to be sold by banks. The underwriting and issue process is typically streamlined and simplified for such life insurance products. In some cases, banks are able to issue a policy to a customer during the visit to the bank branch, with the entire process taking less than 30 minutes. This is quite different from the usual time frame for issuing a policy, which can run from weeks to months.

1.6.4   Direct Marketing

We will define *direct marketing* as the insurance company selling directly to consumers without the use of agents. Without agents to explain the choices, direct marketing usually requires simple products. Also, the underwriting process is usually very basic, because there is no agent to push the customer to complete the underwriting requirements and close the deal. As a result of these factors, direct marketing is able to serve only a fraction of the life insurance market. The most common approaches used for direct marketing are the following.

Direct mail: The insurance company can mail material to targeted consumers with the hope that some will read it and decide to buy insurance. The mailings may go to tens of thousands of consumers at once, with success often achieved when the response rate reaches 0.5% to 1.0%. The savings achieved by paying no agent commissions are often offset by the significant costs of printing and mailing.

Telemarketing: The insurance company hires a telemarketing firm to call thousands of targeted consumers and try to sell them insurance. The economics are very similar to direct mail: A low response rate is normal, and commission savings are largely offset by the costs of telemarketing.

Direct response: The insurance company advertises through radio, television, newspaper, or other media. Interested buyers call a toll-free phone number that connects them to a call center. The call center is manned by insurance company or service company employees who obtain all the needed information from the interested buyer. In some cases, an insurance policy can be issued on the spot or within a few days, depending on how quickly the buyer and the buyer's information can be authenticated. In other cases medical exams, blood tests, or other underwriting requirements must be arranged. This can delay the issue of the policy for weeks or months, drastically lowering the chance of closing the sale.

Internet: As a result of advertising, recommendations, price shopping, or an Internet search, an interested buyer visits a web site and completes an application for life insurance. The process is similar to direct response, except the interested buyer keys in the information, has no one available to answer questions, and receives no encouragement to finish completing the application. For some people, the Internet may be the preferred method of buying.

A few companies have had success with direct response beyond simplified products with simplified underwriting. For example, one highly respected company in the U.S. targets the military market. Its reputation for value and service is the envy of many companies, as is its high persistency and low mortality. The company's reputation is responsible for most of its sales, with the help of periodic reminders and new product announcements that are regularly mailed to its customers.

Customers who want to buy insurance call in and talk to highly trained, knowledgeable employees who advise them and collect information. Other employees arrange for medical evidence as needed and follow up to ensure all requirements are satisfied so the policy can be issued. In other words, salaried employees perform most of the functions of an insurance agent, with one major exception: The customer does not have to be sold; customers usually sell themselves before they call the company.

The result of this marketing approach is that the company is able to offer a full range of products (both simple and complex) at highly competitive prices. The company's excellent reputation and low-cost distribution make it possible to offer very attractive products. These products further enhance the company's reputation. Not surprisingly, the company has expanded its scope over the years to include a wide range of financial products and services, all building on and contributing to the same reputation.

1.6.5   Fee-for-Service

People with high income or high net worth have often turned to attorneys, accountants, and other financial advisors for expert advice in structuring their financial arrangements. This advice might include help with wills, trusts, estate planning, investments, taxes, financing, and insurance. These experts are often paid an hourly rate or a consulting fee for a particular assignment. They would not usually require a commission on life insurance purchased as a result of their advice.

Some insurance companies have developed products with low or no expense charges that are aimed at financial advisors who do not require commissions. A product with no commission should be a more competitive product. If it is one of the best buys available, it should be recommended by financial advisors.

In practice, it has been difficult for insurance companies to develop relationships with the multitude of financial advisors who spend a minority of their time on insurance issues. Also, the advisor needs to be independent and give the client the best advice. This means it is often necessary for the advisor to shop around for the best insurance policy for each client, rather than rely on a relationship with one or two insurance companies.

An increasing number of service organizations rank the competitiveness of products or the security of insurance companies. Perhaps the best an insurance company can do is maintain an image of quality and security and keep its products competitive, hoping to rank high enough in both measures to be picked by financial advisors.

1.6.6 Debit Agents

Debit agents sell to the low-income market, also known as *home service* and *industrial insurance*. They typically sell high-cost permanent insurance in small amounts. The death benefit is normally sufficient to cover the cost of a funeral. Premium payments are made weekly or monthly. Many of the customers do not have checking accounts, so debit agents spend a large part of their time collecting premium payments in cash, visiting their customers soon after they are paid. Premiums tend to be small, so a significant percentage of the premium is needed to cover the expenses of collection.

Industrial insurance is a variation of debit insurance. Instead of collecting premiums at the customers' homes, the agent may collect premiums at work, usually at companies where the workers are paid in cash. This tends to be more efficient, as the agent can often collect premiums from multiple workers at the same site.

1.6.7 Employer-Sponsored Sales

A number of insurance companies work with employers to sell individual life insurance to their employees. Insurance sold in this manner is referred to as employer-sponsored sales or worksite marketing. With the employer's support, an insurance company can sell its products to a significant percentage of the employees. However, gaining the employer's support can be very difficult. It helps if the insurance company can demonstrate that its products offer a price or convenience for the employees that they cannot obtain elsewhere. In that case, the employer may see the products as additional employee benefits and be more inclined to lend its support.

The insurance company may send representatives, agents, or enrollment specialists to enroll employees in its life insurance programs. The employer usually recommends the company and its products. The recommendation may be made through group meetings or written communications, such as memos, brochures, or paycheck stuffers. The employer also assists by allowing the company to conduct the enrollment process at the work site and solicit its employees during work hours.

A company will often develop special products or underwriting programs for its employer-sponsored business. To keep costs down, products typically have little flexibility with regard to the options that can be chosen. Death benefits are usually restricted to a choice between several multiples of the employee's salary. Simplified or reduced underwriting programs are often offered. These programs save time for all involved, allow a greater percentage of the employees to be covered, and minimize the underwriting costs incurred by the company.

Most employers will allow the premiums for the insurance to be paid by payroll deduction. The employer's payroll system will need to be able to communicate smoothly with the insurance company's billing system.

1.6.8 Stockbrokers

Stockbrokers focus on buying and selling mutual funds, stocks, bonds, and other investment products for their customers. In some countries, stockbrokerage firms have become important distributors of investment-oriented insurance and annuity products, especially variable products. To win business from stockbrokers, insurance companies have streamlined the application process to come closer to the time and effort required to place orders for stocks and bonds. The commissions earned by stockbrokers typically compensate for the extra time and effort required to sell and place a life insurance policy or annuity contract.

1.7 Alignment

In this chapter, we have discussed many insurance needs, insurance products, tax considerations, and distribution methods. All of these should be considered when a company decides how best to serve a target market. To serve a target market, the company must decide which needs it will fill, which products best serve those needs, whether taxes play an important role, and which distribution systems will be most effective. For example, to serve a target market of middle-income families, a company might decide to protect families from the death of an income earner by selling level term insurance through employer-sponsored sales.

Companies often have more than one target market. However, those that do not have clear target markets run the risk of trying to be all things to all people, a strategy that always fails. A company that is focused on serving a few target markets can build its competencies, tailor its products, hone its distribution methods, and bring all of them into alignment with its target markets. This allows the company to get the most out of its limited resources and serve its target markets more effectively than many larger companies. Alignment of markets, products, and distribution can be a significant competitive advantage. On the other hand, a company with no clear target markets may end up with an unwieldy portfolio of products and multiple distribution systems that point the company in a myriad of conflicting directions.

1.8 Exercises

Exercise 1.1

Explain why cash values develop on permanent, whole life products, and why they are the same rate per thousand of insurance for each buyer of the product with a given risk class, gender, issue age, and policy year.

Exercise 1.2

For a participating whole life product, how can two policies with the same initial death benefit, risk class, gender, and issue age develop different values over the life of each policy?

Exercise 1.3

Explain how cash values develop on dynamic products. Why would two dynamic policies with the same death benefit, risk class, gender, and issue age develop different values?

Exercise 1.4

For dynamic products, if the cash value accumulates to exceed the original death benefit, what amount is paid upon death?

Exercise 1.5

Describe at least three ways to receive cash from a life insurance policy while keeping the policy in force. Consider all the different types of products and product features.

Exercise 1.6

A company designs a life insurance policy with the following pre-scheduled premium pattern: annually increasing premiums designed to cover only mortality, expenses, and profit for the first 20 years, followed by level premiums for the remainder of the insured's life. The death benefit remains level from the issue date to the maturity of the policy. Describe the likely cash value pattern.

Exercise 1.7

Calculate the following UL policy's account value on May 31, given the following information:

Annual interest crediting rate = 6.00%
On April 30: Account value = 5,500
On May 10: Cost of insurance charge = 25.00.

Exercise 1.8

Calculate the following VUL policy's account value on May 31, given the following information:

On April 30: Account value = 5,500 and unit value = 55.0000
On May 10: Cost of insurance charge = 25.00 and unit value =
50.0000
On May 31: Unit value = 55.2729

Repeat this exercise assuming the unit value on May 10 is 55.0879.

Exercise 1.9

Describe the ideal tax treatment of life insurance if the goal is to
encourage the public to use life insurance as a savings and protection
vehicle.

Exercise 1.10

Which distribution channels are best suited to the following types of
sales?

a. A sophisticated use of life insurance to solve estate-planning needs.

b. Burial insurance for someone without a checking account but with
   an employer willing to withhold funds from paychecks to pay life
   insurance premiums.

c. The lowest-cost ten-year term insurance.

d. A UL policy crediting the highest interest rate.

1.9 Answers

Answer 1.1

Cash values develop because premiums in the early policy years are
much higher than mortality costs and expenses incurred. Except for
minor differences due to policy fees (which are constant amounts added
to the premium independent of the size of the policy), each policy of a
given risk class, gender, issue age, and policy year has the same
premiums, cash values, and death benefits per thousand. This is the
nature of the product: Given the characteristics of the insured, all policy
values are pre-scheduled.

Answer 1.2

Participating policies have dividends. The policyowner has flexibility with regard to how dividends are applied. For example, one policyowner could decide to take all dividends in cash, while the other may choose to have all dividends purchase paid-up insurance additions. The underlying guaranteed cash values may be the same for each policy, but since each policyowner uses dividends in different ways, different values will accumulate.

Answer 1.3

In general, premium payments in the early years exceed the amounts deducted for cost of insurance charges and expense charges. The excess amounts accumulate with interest, thereby building cash values. As more premiums continue to be paid in excess of COI charges and expense charges, more cash value builds and earns even more interest.

Two policies with the same death benefit, risk class, gender, and issue age can develop different cash values for several reasons. Different values will accumulate if different premiums are paid, since premiums are often flexible. Even if the exact same premiums are paid, the policies may develop different values. Interest on premiums is usually calculated daily, although added to the cash values only once a month. So, if one of the policies consistently pays premiums later than the other, different values will accumulate because less interest will be credited to the policy that pays premiums later.

Answer 1.4

It is possible, if enough premiums are paid or enough interest is credited, for a policy's cash value to exceed the original death benefit. Many dynamic products define a *corridor* amount or percentage that automatically increases the death benefit when the cash value approaches the death benefit. Often, the corridor is a percentage based on the insured's attained age. Some taxing authorities specify minimum corridor percentages to make sure the tax-free accumulation of the cash value does not offer too great of a tax advantage when compared to non-insurance products.

Answer 1.5

1. For participating products, surrender any accumulated paid-up insurance additions or dividend accumulations.

2. Take a policy loan.

3. Make a partial withdrawal of cash under a dynamic policy.

4. Receive benefits paid under a critical illness rider

5. Receive benefits paid under a long-term care rider

Answer 1.6

Since the first 20 years' premiums cover primarily death benefit payments, no cash values will emerge during the first 20 years. After year 20, since premiums are level for the remainder of life, premiums must be in excess of that needed to pay for the cost of mortality for some number of years. Therefore, cash values will develop, most likely increasing until the cash value equals the face amount of the policy. The probable pattern of premiums and cash values is illustrated below. The premiums and cash values starting in the twenty-first year will be similar to those for a newly issued whole life policy at that age.

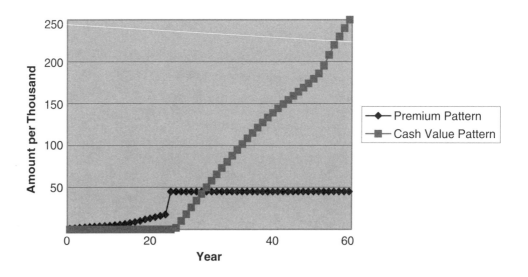

Answer 1.7

On April 30: Account value = 5,500.

On May 10, credit interest for ten days:

$$5,500 \ (1.06)^{10/365} = 5,508.79.$$

Next, deduct the COI charge of 25.00 to get 5,483.79.

On May 31, credit interest for the 21 days since the deduction of the COI charge:

$$5,483.79 \ (1.06)^{21/365} = 5,502.21.$$

Answer 1.8

On April 30, the policy has 100.0000 units (5,500/55.0000).

On May 10, 0.5000 units are deducted for the COI charge (25.00/50.0000), leaving 99.5000 units.

On May 31, the account value equals 99.5000 units × 55.2729 unit value = 5,499.65.

If the May 10 unit value is 55.0879, then:

On May 10, 0.4538 units are deducted for the COI charge (25.00/55.0879), leaving 99.5462 units in the policy.

On May 31, the account value equals 99.5462 units × 55.2729 unit value = 5,502.21.

Answer 1.9

Ideal tax treatment of life insurance would include full tax deductibility of life insurance premiums paid, no taxation of any cash value buildup or any distributions from a life insurance policy, and minimal requirements for a policy to qualify as life insurance.

Answer 1.10

a. Agent or fee-for-service distribution is most likely to have the expertise needed for a sophisticated use of life insurance to solve estate-planning needs.

b. Employer-sponsored distribution would provide the best life insurance value for someone without a checking account but with an employer willing to withhold funds from paychecks to pay life insurance premiums. Debit agent distribution would provide a more expensive alternative.

c. A variety of distribution methods can be used to deliver the lowest-cost ten-year term insurance. Because underwriting is important to obtaining the lowest cost, the distribution system must have some insurance know-how. Some forms of direct response and employer-sponsored sales may offer the best combination of low-cost distribution and the ability to capture underwriting information.

d. Advice is very important when looking for the best UL policy. The policy with the highest credited interest rate is not necessarily the best buy; there may be many hidden costs. Agent distribution or fee-for-service can best provide the needed advice.

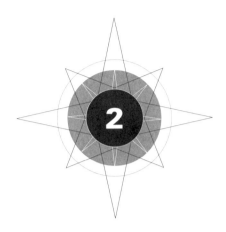

Product Development

Companies are largely defined by the markets they serve and the products they offer. In financial services, companies are further defined by how they develop, distribute, and service their products.

By and large, successful companies target specific markets and develop products that enable them to best serve those markets. Unsuccessful companies, although they may be unsuccessful for other reasons as well, often do not clearly define whom they are trying to serve, nor do they develop products that are tied to a cohesive marketing strategy.

This chapter will explore the following topics:

- *Product strategy:* The most important product development decisions relate to which products to develop. These decisions should be tied to the company's purpose, vision of the future, and other strategies.
- *Product development organization:* How the company organizes its product development efforts relates directly to the success of the products developed, as well as the time and expense of product

development. Possible structures for organizing the product development function are presented.

- *Pricing strategy:* With financial products, product development and pricing are intimately related. To set prices intelligently, one should understand the different types of competitive environments, product life cycles, and pricing strategies that may apply.

- *Product development process:* Each of the major stages of the product development process is discussed: market research, preliminary design, final design, implementation, and product management.

2.2 Product Strategy

Before a company can articulate a product strategy, it needs to clearly understand its purpose and possess a vision of what the company will be in the future. These are often referred to as having a mission and a vision of the future. The company should be focused on serving identified needs of target markets. These market needs will help define which products the company should offer. The company's strategy will guide how it will evolve to better serve its target markets.

In the end, there needs to be alignment between the company's mission, vision, strategy, culture, core competencies, target markets, and products. The greater the alignment, the more successful the company tends to be. Significant misalignment is a formula for failure. A comparison of two hypothetical companies will help illustrate these points:

Company A	Company B
Operations: Individual life insurance	Operations: Individual life, group life, health, and annuities
Policyowner Focus: Upper-income customers	Policyowner Focus: Mainly upper-income customers, but considers a wide range of opportunities
Vision: Dominate target market, growing business even as others struggle to grow	Vision: Become a large, all-purpose insurance organization
Strategy: Focus on individual life insurance sold through captive agents while maintaining reputation of providing the best long-term value for customers	Strategy: Offer a variety of products sold through a variety of distribution channels and operating units, aimed at many different target markets
Tactics: Increase recruitment and retention of agents; offer a small number of high-value products; further lower unit costs through automation and economies of scale; pursue a number of initiatives to enhance persistency, mortality, and investment results	Tactics: Win agents' business through competitive, innovative products and excellent supporting services

Company A would seem to be the company with the better likelihood of success. By being better focused, Company A is likely to (1) maintain a high level of employee and agent loyalty to the company, (2) have a commitment throughout the organization to improve customer value, and (3) maintain competitive advantages in the areas that affect long-term customer value, such as mortality, persistency, and expenses.

Company B has a vision statement that is not as narrowly focused. By trying to provide a variety of products through a variety of distribution channels, Company B will probably have a more difficult time achieving success. Supporting a variety of target markets and products means that company resources will be stretched thin and expenses will be increased. Computer systems for marketing, administration, and agency support will be more complex. It will be difficult to achieve economies of scale with numerous markets and products. This may make it difficult to maintain innovative product development and competitive pricing.

At the close of the twentieth century, one of the most respected life insurance companies in the U.S. was Northwestern Mutual Life, headed by James D. Ericson, CEO and Chairman. Northwestern Mutual's focus has contributed to its success, as explained by Mr. Ericson:

For more than a century, our mission at Northwestern Mutual has been to deliver the greatest possible value to our policyowners. This is still our mission today. We operate as a true mutual company, run for the benefit of *all* policyowners.

This mission helps us stay focused on what we do best. We have long emphasized the importance of life insurance fundamentals. Our industry leadership has been built on performance—low mortality, tight expense control, high persistency, and consistently strong investment results. As a result, in 1999, we paid more life insurance dividends than any other company. Consistent with this focus on quality, we continue to distribute our products exclusively through a career agency force of more than 7,500 Northwestern Mutual agents.

Even though we have not changed our historical emphasis on quality, we have experienced tremendous growth in recent years. We sold about $74 billion of individual life insurance in 1999, or about 50 percent more than four years earlier. We now have more individual life insurance in force than any other U.S. company, with well over $500 billion in force.

2.2.1 Target Markets

It is often helpful for a company to define one or more target markets that it wishes to serve. With a particular market in mind, the company can much more effectively organize its efforts to understand and serve that market. There is no hard and fast definition of what is and what is not a target market. However, for a target market to be a useful tool, it helps if it has these attributes:

- Precise definition or characterization of the target market
- Clear method of reaching those in the target market
- Members of the target market have a number of buying habits, insurance needs, or other useful characteristics in common
- Sufficiently large to make it worth targeting.

Here are some examples of possible target markets:

- Middle-income, single parents with children under the age of 18
- Upper-income people who need life insurance and seek tax-deferred savings
- Married professionals between the ages of 30 and 50
- Middle- or upper-income couples over age 50, with at least one spouse who is still employed.

Once you have identified a target market, you need to learn everything you can about its buying habits, preferences, insurance needs, and attitudes. This will help you develop products that fit the needs and desires of the target market. The alternative is to guess at the need and how to serve it, which some actuaries do. The result can be a product that is unwittingly designed for a very small target market—actuaries!

With a good understanding of the target market, the company should be able to identify in advance a product with only limited potential. This will help the company avoid the costs of developing products that will fail, because of lack of demand or interest. However, in some cases the company may consciously develop a product that it knows will not sell much. This may be done to bolster the company's image by showing that it has a complete line of products.

A company should avoid developing a product that is out of synch with the needs or desires of the target market. Often, a strong advocate in management or the distribution system will sponsor a new product that is not appropriate for the target market. A company with the discipline to stick to serving its target markets will reject such a product. Exercising such discipline is much easier said than done.

2.2.2 Core Competencies

A product should not only fit the target market, but also build on the company's strengths and core competencies, which might include some of the following:

Low cost of capital (able to leverage results using debt or reinsurance; see Chapter 16)

Financial strength (high ratings, high capital ratios, strong earnings)

Operational efficiency (low acquisition and maintenance costs)

Underwriting expertise and discipline (excellent mortality results)

High persistency (high customer value, quality sales and service efforts)

Investment management (superior returns, low investment expenses)

Speed, flexibility, adaptability (ability to pounce on opportunities)

Quality of distribution (high-quality sales and service)

Control of distribution (ability to shift focus, products, and prices)

Low-cost distribution (efficient, no frills, or agents not used)

Sophisticated distribution (able to sell complex products)

Sophisticated home office staff (able to develop and support complex products).

For example, a product to be sold to corporations might require the following competencies:

- Financial strength, with the highest ratings from outside rating agencies
- Sophisticated home office support for illustrations and insurance plan design (sometimes referred to as *advanced underwriting*)
- Experience and comfort with simplified or guaranteed issue underwriting, which will be explained in Chapter 3.

A product to be sold through employer sponsorship may require the company to have the following:

- Trained enrollment teams that can visit employers' worksites to market and efficiently enroll a large number of people in a short period
- Administration and billing systems that can electronically communicate with employers' payroll systems to automatically handle premium payments made through payroll deduction
- Home office support and easy access for policyowner inquiries.

It is rare that a company possesses strength in every area for a given product. When that happens, the company should be able to dominate its target market for that product. Often, a company will make do with what skills and strengths it has. Increasingly, companies are looking outside the organization for ways to bolster their strengths, in order to compete more effectively and profitably. For example,

- The company might outsource its administration or investment management to lower costs or improve service and performance. By using outside resources, a company hopes to immediately tap into expertise instead of developing that expertise on its own.

- The company might reinsure the business to use the reinsurer's expertise and capital, or to "outsource" the mortality cost to the reinsurer, as described in Chapter 7.

- The company might use consultants to help design and price products, providing expertise or resources that are needed. Consultants may also be used to improve operational efficiency or underwriting discipline.

2.2.3   Risk Profile

Deciding which markets to serve and which products to offer are key decisions that have an enormous effect on the company. Adding a new market or a new product should be viewed as a major decision with significant long-term commitments required. The new market or new product should be consistent with the company's mission, vision, and strategy, rather than a diversion.

The product's risk profile—the size and type of risks inherent in the product—should fit the company's goals for stability of financial results. While Berkshire Hathaway's Warren Buffett may be willing to risk a billion dollars on a single catastrophic risk, most companies try to limit their risk exposure to a few million dollars or less. Care should be taken with certain products that produce a large concentration of risk. For example, a product that guarantees current interest rates well beyond the duration of available assets is dangerous, unless sales are held to a modest level. Companies have become insolvent when interest rates fell after they sold too much of these kinds of products. Variable products that guarantee return of principal pose a similar risk. Many risks (not just mortality risk) can be managed using reinsurance, as explained in Chapter 7.

2.2.4 New Markets

Successful companies tend to be those who build on their strengths and stick to what they know best. However, in the end, all markets and products change or disappear. A company that does not change will certainly disappear. Some experimentation outside of the company's mission, vision, and strategy can create new markets for the future, making the company more apt to be a survivor. On the other hand, too much experimentation can be a major distraction.

Some new products may not fit the company's current strategy. If the investment in such new products can be kept to a minimum, the company may learn some inexpensive lessons that could eventually lead it to important new markets or new products.

Experimentation on too grand a scale can lead to financial disaster. For example, over the last two decades, a number of major life insurance companies have rapidly built or acquired some very large new businesses that were outside of their historical expertise (such as health insurance, general insurance, or securities). When large losses emerged after a few years, many of these new businesses were sold. Had the new businesses been launched on a smaller scale, the same lessons could have been learned much less expensively.

It takes strong discipline for a company to design and maintain a rational product portfolio that plays to its strengths, fits its target markets, and aligns with its mission, vision, strategy, and goals. Experimentation can be exciting. It is human nature to want to try new ideas and ventures. However, experimentation can go too far, resulting in a company trying to be all things to all people.

2.3 Product Development Organization

Developing a new product can require support from almost all areas of a life insurance company. The support required for a particular product is a function of what is new about the product. For example, the underwriting area would be involved if there were any new risk classes or underwriting standards. The investment area would be involved if credited interest rates are key or if any new investment strategies or types of investments are needed. The policyowner service area would be involved if the product offers new features or services.

Many, if not most, new products contain nothing that is new to the company. The underwriting, investments, features, and services for a new product may all be the same as existing products. In that case, the main support required from various areas of the company is that they gain an understanding of the new product in order to support it.

Three important skill sets are needed for product development: marketing, actuarial, and implementation. When these skill sets are integrated into one cohesive team, the results can be outstanding. By cooperating fully, the team can develop products that best serve the market and contribute to company goals, while making product implementation as easy as possible.

On the other hand, when marketing, actuarial, and implementation responsibilities are spread out among several areas, cooperation can evaporate. For example, marketing personnel may push for the most competitive product and the highest agent compensation, with little regard for profitability. The actuaries may push for full profitability or high consumer value without regard for either the competitiveness of the product or adequate agent compensation. Both marketing and actuarial personnel may be unaware of or unconcerned with the effect of their decisions on implementation of the new product.

2.3.1 Product Development Team

Unfortunately, the kinds of problems listed above are all too common. A team approach can help overcome many of these problems:

- The team should be comprised of highly competent and knowledgeable people who collectively possess all the needed skills and knowledge.

- The members of the team should develop a close working relationship, learn from each other, and make decisions that reflect their collective wisdom, rather than the wisdom of the strongest personality.
- The team should be led by someone who moves the team along quickly, overcomes obstacles with other areas of the company, and does not dominate the decision-making process.
- The team should have the authority, responsibility and accountability to make product-related decisions within broadly defined parameters. If the team is no more than a committee that makes suggestions to senior management, there is a danger that the team will be ineffective. The team may try to anticipate senior management's biases rather than develop the best product.

A team might include people with marketing, actuarial, implementation, and legal abilities. A lack of strength in any of the four areas could worsen the results. In addition, each member of the team should have more than a rudimentary knowledge of the tasks and skill sets of the other team members. For example,

- The actuary should understand systems constraints and processes.
- The marketing person should understand pricing and how different pricing assumptions might affect the results.
- The implementation person on the team should understand the marketing department's needs.
- The legal person should understand and be able to communicate any limitations with regards to regulatory constraints on pricing, marketing, and issuing the product.

2.3.2 Senior Management Input

Senior management's primary role should be to give guidance by clarifying how the company's mission, vision, strategy, and goals relate to the product being developed. Ideally, senior management should intervene only when the team has deviated from guiding principles and should not second-guess the team's decisions. This can be very difficult for senior management with prior product experience or marketing insights.

It is key that senior management has the confidence to let the team lead the way. The product development team should seek senior management input early in the product development process. Ideally, such input will be used as valuable background information rather than as a mandate for what must be done. This will give the team the freedom to design the best product for the company.

2.3.3 Product Development Staff

Product development can be highly seasonal work. While some companies introduce new products many times a year, many companies do so only once every year or two. Many companies have full-time staff devoted to product development year-round, even when they introduce new products only once a year. Some companies form teams on an as needed or ad hoc basis, while others make use of outside expertise.

The use of full-time staff, ad hoc teams, or outside expertise will vary widely from company to company, and even within a company. Different approaches may be taken by different lines of business within the same company. The approach taken may be independent of the size of the company.

2.3.3.1 Full-Time Product Development Staff

A full-time product development staff can create two problems:

1. With staff devoted to product development, the tendency over time is to develop too many products. The company's product portfolio may become bloated and hard to comprehend. There may be no rhyme or reason to the many product offerings.

2. Work expands to fill available time. If few new products are developed, the time frame needed for product development may stretch out to six months, 12 months, or even longer. The product development staff will find ways to stay busy, often by doing a number of tasks that add little value.

2.3.3.2   Ad Hoc Product Development Efforts

As mentioned, some companies do not have a full-time product development staff. They form teams as needed to develop a new product. While this may overcome the disadvantages of a full-time product development staff, ad hoc efforts have their own disadvantages:

- There may be no continuity in product development, since the people involved tend to change from product to product.

- The company might not build product development experts, especially ones with insights into several key areas of knowledge such as marketing, actuarial, and implementation.

- Without full-time focus, the product development process tends to be reinvented for each new product. There is little process improvement. The same mistakes tend to be repeated.

- There is a strong tendency toward interdepartmental conflict, as noted earlier in this section.

2.3.3.3   Outside Expertise

When developing a product that is new to the company in some fundamental way (such as new underwriting, new investment strategy, or new features), it is often helpful to bring in outside talent with relevant experience. Actuarial consultants are often used to provide pricing support and expertise.

For certain products, especially large-amount term insurance, reinsurers may possess relevant experience. In some cases, reinsurers have designed products in return for reinsurance of a significant share of the mortality risk, allowing the company to lock in a major share of its profit. In essence, the reinsurer advises the company and then guarantees its advice by taking a big share of the mortality risk.

2.3.3.4   Sample Structure

One possible structure might be as follows: A small, full-time product development staff would consist of three to six people from various disciplines. The smaller the staff, the faster products would be developed—necessity *is* the mother of invention. This staff would be formed and supported by senior management, which would also define the parameters for operation of the unit. To minimize time wasted due to the involvement of multiple layers of management and conflicts between various departments, the product development staff would make all product-related decisions, but only after working closely with other departments to gain their input, understanding, and support.

During slow periods, the staff would shift their efforts to market research, process improvement, and reviews and updates of existing products. During busy periods the staff would borrow people from other areas or use outside expertise as needed.

Continuity of staff and cross-training of staff would be essential. The goal would be to give all staff a deep understanding of marketing, actuarial, and implementation aspects. To be successful in such a role would require gaining cooperation from many departments and acquiring a well-rounded knowledge of the business. This kind of success would create good candidates for leadership roles in other areas of the company.

2.4 Pricing Strategy

Many of the pricing strategies that apply to nonfinancial products can be adapted to life insurance. However, there are two important differences between life insurance and most nonfinancial products that result in fundamentally different buyer behavior:

1. Life insurance is not well understood by most consumers. Except for term insurance, most products are very difficult to compare, even for insurance professionals. Permanent life insurance policies have so many elements that can differ (such as premiums, cash values, dividends, and death benefits) that it is impossible to rank them.

2. Life insurance is often sold, not bought. In other words, many buyers of insurance are convinced to buy life insurance by an agent calling on them. Without the agent forcing the issue, the person would not purchase life insurance. In this situation, the buyer usually does not

seek information from other sources on prices and features. The person either buys from the agent or does not buy at all.

Because of these two differences, most life insurance purchase decisions are based on trust. The buyer trusts the agent to select the product that will best meet the buyer's needs. From this, you might conclude that life insurance companies are not subject to competition. This is far from true.

2.4.1 Competition among Life Insurers

Life insurance companies track each other's products. Most adjust their prices (usually downward) when they find they are significantly out of line with the competition. Many companies make these kinds of price adjustments even when the new prices have no measurable effect on sales. This is because most insurance company employees and agents like to feel that their company's products are priced fairly in relation to the competition. In contrast, most other industries would pay closer attention to the effect of price changes on sales levels and try to maximize total profit.

The small percentage of buyers who do shop around and compare products from different companies exert influence well beyond their numbers. The occasional case an agent loses to competition is vividly remembered and frequently shared with company management. Agents hate to lose sales because their company's products are not competitive. The company often hears about such losses loudly and clearly. This keeps pressure on even the most competitive companies to further lower their prices.

Insurance companies generally compete on two different kinds of prices: the price to the consumer and the commission to the agent. When the company sells directly to the consumer, there is only one kind of price competition. In situations where the agent has no competition (such as insurance sold through a loan officer to insure the amount of the loan), the insurance company may compete by charging high premiums and paying high commissions.

In the rest of this section, we will define pricing strategies at two levels: (1) buyer-oriented pricing strategies, which ignore competition, and (2) competitor-oriented pricing strategies. We will then apply these pricing strategies to the product life cycle.

2.4.2   Buyer-Oriented Pricing Strategies

Four main pricing strategies describe how most companies use prices with buyers or consumers:

Penetration pricing involves setting prices low enough to generate a much higher level of sales. An example of this is the pricing of CD players in 1990 at a price equal to that of record players. Because of the higher quality sound of CD players, sales of CD players skyrocketed while sales of record players essentially stopped.

Even though the profit margin may be reduced with penetration pricing, the increased volume of sales may produce a greater total profit. This strategy can help build economies of scale. For insurance products, penetration pricing works best with commodity-like products, like term insurance, where premium outlay is the major factor.

For companies that sell through independent agents, commissions can also be used as part of a penetration pricing strategy. By paying relatively high commissions on a product that is otherwise the same as a competitor's products, the company may induce independent agents to sell much more of its product.

Neutral pricing involves setting prices at a level that most buyers would consider reasonable. In other words, the price would be set at a level that would neither attract nor discourage many buyers. This would normally mean setting prices and commissions at levels not too far from the industry average. Neutral pricing is very common in life insurance.

Segmented pricing involves setting different price levels for different kinds of buyers with different behaviors. For example, in the airline industry, it is common to charge low fares for personal travel booked weeks in advance with a Saturday night stay-over. This helps fill airplanes with consumers who would not travel as much without the low fares. At the same time, the airlines will hold back a number of seats in order to charge high fares to business travelers who book flights at the last minute. Business travelers often have no choice as to whether to travel and must pay the higher fares.

In life insurance, prices routinely vary by age, gender, and risk class. These price differences are mainly intended to balance premiums with expected benefits, rather than to exploit different buyer behaviors. Price discounts are often available on larger policies. These discounts may reflect both expense savings on larger policies (per thousand of insurance purchased) and the increased sophistication and cost-consciousness of large policy buyers. Some products are specially designed for the corporate market. Pricing of these products often reflects lower commissions and a more favorable cost-benefit relationship for the buyer.

Skim pricing involves setting a high price that maximizes a company's profit margins. A good example of this is the initial pricing of large, flat-screen televisions at levels five to ten times the price of similarly sized, traditional cathode ray tube (CRT) televisions. Skim pricing is usually done with products that are in short supply and high demand, which is very rare in life insurance.

2.4.3 Competitor-Oriented Pricing Strategies

Independent pricing is done by a company with no real competitors in its target market. The company sets a price that is independent of prices charged by any other companies. This is most common with specialized market niches dominated by one company. For example, a company might have a custom participating whole life product sold to city employees through cooperative savings associations. Independent pricing is rarely found in larger market segments, which typically attract more competition.

Cooperative pricing is common when a few companies dominate a market segment. From experience, the companies may have learned that each of the other companies will match any price change they make. The companies may not charge the same price, but changes in price will be made in parallel. The companies may settle into a pattern of stable prices, stable commissions, and stable profits.

Cooperative pricing is most likely to occur in the insurance arena where there is a large or expensive barrier to entry, relative to the profits to be made. For example, a barrier to entry might be the high cost of building the infrastructure needed to support a particularly complex product in a market that demands high levels of automation and service. For potential new players, the investment required may not make economic sense in terms of the expected profits. However, if the existing players raise the profit margins high enough, they will attract new competitors.

Adaptive pricing is probably the most common form of competitive pricing behavior. Companies review the prices of other companies and then determine where to set their price. They tend to set their prices higher than the price leaders, reasoning that the extra profit margin gained by charging a higher price outweighs any loss in sales. Their theory is that, as long as their prices and commissions are reasonable in relation to the price leaders, they will not lose many sales. Instead of competing mainly on price, companies using adaptive pricing try to compete based on image, quality, and service.

Adaptive pricing is often the only strategy open to companies that are not strong competitors. While such companies may profess that they are competing on image, quality, or service, the truth may be that they possess no advantage in any of those three areas. They may be forced to charge a higher price merely because they are inefficient. As Jacques DuBois, CEO of Swiss Re in the U.S., likes to say, "Service is the refuge of the inefficient." Over the long haul, many such companies can be expected to gradually lose market share and become even more inefficient. Eventually, most companies in this category will exit the business or be acquired.

Opportunistic pricing uses price as a competitive weapon. The most efficient companies can be expected to use this strategy. By driving prices down to a level where only the most efficient can survive, they can gain market share or force less efficient competitors that match their prices to earn poor returns and eventually exit the business. This is natural selection, or survival of the fittest. Long term, this strategy can only be supported by an unwavering focus on improving productivity, efficiency, and results in the areas of mortality, persistency, and investment returns.

This is the pricing strategy used by Wal-Mart to achieve domination in its business. Some of the largest writers of term insurance use this strategy. When more than a few companies are using opportunistic pricing for the same product and market, prices will change more rapidly and profit margins will be thinner.

Predatory pricing involves charging a price that is below the cost of the product. A company can use such prices to drive competitors out of business, often at a financial loss to the predator. With the competition gone, the company can raise prices and recoup its losses. This was one of several unsavory practices employed by Standard Oil to achieve domination of the U.S. oil industry early in the twentieth century.

In many countries, predatory pricing is illegal. Companies are not allowed to charge less than their costs to gain long-term competitive advantage. In the financial services industry, predatory pricing can mean financial suicide, as the company is literally giving money away.

The insurance industry tends to be highly regulated. Regulators will usually not allow predatory pricing to take place, since it reduces a company's financial strength. Even if a company were successful in driving its competitors out of business, there are few barriers to keep out new players. If one company is perceived as earning high profit margins in a sizable market, competition will return.

2.4.4 Product Life Cycle

Most products go through predictable stages, with a life cycle that runs from birth to death. These stages have a huge effect on competitive conditions. A product's life cycle stage should be carefully considered when setting pricing strategy. Figure 2.4.1 illustrates the four stages of a typical product's life cycle.

2.4.4.1 Development Stage

A product starts its life in the development stage. The product is new and unfamiliar to customers and agents. A substantial effort is required to teach the market about the advantages and features of the product. Because most people learn about new products from the experiences of others, it can take years for a new product to become widely accepted.

Initially, the lack of familiarity with the product will be the biggest obstacle to sales. Price will be a secondary consideration. Therefore, it may make sense to introduce the product with a higher price than the company expects to ultimately charge. Because sales will be low, the company might as well make an extra margin. However, care should be taken not to set the prices so high or the commissions so low that the product's growth is stunted. In addition, sufficiently high prices may encourage competitors to introduce their own versions of the product more quickly.

Another approach is to introduce the product with the prices the company expects to charge long term. While this approach may help the product grow faster, it may also discourage some competition because of the lower profit margins available.

Figure 2.4.1

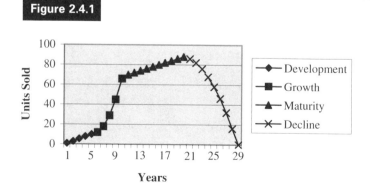

2.4.4.2 Growth Stage

In the growth stage, the product experiences its most rapid growth. Agents and consumers become much more aware of the product. As the product grows, new competitors fuel the growth by entering the market and offering their own version of the product, often with new, improved features or lower prices. The companies that developed the product face increasing competition and need to adapt or exit the business.

The growth stage is usually the most crucial time for competitors to establish their positions in the market. This is the time when large market shares can be built, quality images can be honed, and low-cost, efficient production can be created. Once these competitive advantages have been established, they can be very difficult for competitors to overcome. IBM is a great example of this. They did not develop the first computers. However, by investing $5 billion to create and introduce the System/360 in 1960, they exponentially expanded the market for computers, built a commanding market share, and created an image of quality, reliability, and service that no competitor could touch for decades.

2.4.4.3 Maturity Stage

The maturity stage is a time when sales become more or less static. Companies can grow significantly only by taking market share from competitors. Since sales are static, the strain of writing new business is more than offset by profits being earned on sales from prior years. The product leaders are typically harvesting significant profits while the marginal players are earning enough to get by. In most developed countries, the insurance industry is in the maturity stage, although particular products or markets may be in other stages.

In the maturity stage, companies try to make the best of the competitive advantages they may possess. A company with a well-known brand name may try to increase sales while holding the line on prices. A low-cost provider may pursue a penetration pricing strategy in an effort to grow market share. In any case, there will be a tendency for prices to decline, as companies become more efficient and write off the costs of developing the product and its supporting systems.

To maintain profitability in the face of declining prices, all companies need to find ways to improve their pricing effectiveness. The solutions for life insurance companies may include streamlining and automating operations, altering the product line to more effectively target customers, eliminating unappreciated features and services, revamping distribution, and adding more efficient forms of distribution.

2.4.4.4   Decline Stage

Products and industries eventually decline and disappear or change so fundamentally that they have little in common with their former selves. Nothing lasts forever. When a product enters the decline stage, most companies will experience a decrease in sales, although a few may continue to increase their market share and grow. As sales decrease at a life insurance company, the company's fixed or overhead costs become increasingly significant. For example, if sales drop by 50%, it is unlikely that a company can reduce all of its costs by 50%. As the market shrinks, many companies will reach a point where their fixed costs force them to sell their business to a larger, more efficient company. Compounding this expense problem, some companies in the decline stage try to stimulate sales growth by cutting prices. This is only a temporary help to sales, as competitors react and cut their own prices to rebalance the competitive field. However, declining sales do tend to drive prices down throughout the decline stage.

There are two basic strategies for survival in the decline stage:

1. *Retrenchment* involves pulling out of market segments where the company is weak in order to focus all efforts on market segments where the company is strong. In other words, the company shifts its attention to its most profitable and defensible market niches.

2. *Consolidation* involves buying other players in order to gain a stronger position. This is only viable for a company in a strong financial position. By buying less efficient competitors and streamlining their operations, a consolidator can create value and earnings, allowing it to continue acquiring other companies.

An alternative to survival is an exit strategy called *harvesting*. This involves the company recognizing that it will not be a long-term survivor and deciding to make the best of the situation. Harvesting starts with a retrenchment to focus on the most profitable segments of the business. This is followed by phased withdrawal from each segment as it becomes unattractive. The pricing strategy attempts to maximize the company's profits, not defend its market share. Compared with the results of a failed survival strategy, a harvesting strategy may create more value for the company's owners, especially if the company is acquired.

2.4.5 Distribution System Life Cycle

In life insurance, product variations and features come and go, but truly new products are rare. The product life cycle may be more applicable to product variations and features, but these typically have only a minor effect on a company's success.

Distribution methods also have life cycles. Understanding these distribution life cycles may be very important to a company's future. For example, in certain life insurance markets today, some would say that distribution methods are generally in the following life cycle stages:

Development stage: Internet, direct response, fee-for-service

Growth stage: bank, employer-sponsored, telemarketing

Maturity: direct mail

Decline: captive agents, independent agents, debit agents.

The same pricing strategies that apply to product life cycles can be applied to distribution life cycles. For example, Internet distribution may be a much lower cost alternative to agent distribution. However, during the development stage, companies may share only a small portion of the cost savings with the consumer. Once companies develop more experience with selling through the Internet and competition increases, you can expect prices to drop, sales to climb, and market leaders to emerge during the growth stage.

At some point, sales growth will drop to modest levels as Internet distribution approaches its maximum penetration and enters the maturity stage. With low barriers to entry and the ability to quickly copy the success of others, you can expect most companies to sell through the Internet. However, a few brand names that consumers remember and trust may dominate sales. Finally, at some time in the future, you can expect new developments to force Internet distribution into the decline stage. Those with well-known brand names, large market shares, and efficient operations will survive the longest as other companies gradually close down or sell off their Internet distribution arm.

Sections 2.5 through 2.9 discuss each of the major stages of product development: market research, preliminary product design, final product design, product implementation, and product management. All these steps must have seemed like too much bother to a certain company. As Ross Morton, a life insurance executive from Toronto, tells it:

In the mid-1980s in Canada, Transamerica Life had just introduced a new, trend-setting term product that was taking the market by storm. The product offered very low, competitive premium rates for seven years, after which premiums increased steeply. It quickly became the fastest-selling term product in the Canadian market.

A company that will go unnamed (and that, in fact, no longer exists) decided to copy this product, literally. They went as far as to send Transamerica Life's sales brochures to their printer, substituting their name for Transamerica's and reducing all the rates by 0.01 per thousand. While the plagiarism would have been obvious to most of the industry anyway, they made the embarrassing mistake of leaving Transamerica's name, address and phone number on the back of the brochure!

While shortcuts can be taken, we recommend a more original and thorough approach.

2.5 Market Research

Market research can indicate the need for a new product. It can also identify when an existing product's competitiveness has slipped. When this happens, the product's competitiveness can sometimes be restored without having to resort to redeveloping or repricing the product.

Market research is the first step in developing a new product or adjusting an existing product. A company may conduct market research for a number of reasons:

- To better understand the needs of the company's target markets, with the hope of identifying unfulfilled needs that can be satisfied by new products or modifications to existing products

- To track the movements of competitors operating in the company's target markets, so that the company can react quickly to changes in products, practices, prices, and services

- To investigate other potential target markets, with the hope of identifying markets that are currently underserved and consistent with the company's mission, vision, strategy, and culture.

Timely market research can help a company identify

- Market pressure to change prices such as premium rates, cost of insurance rates, credited interest rates, or dividend rates.

- Competitors who have changed their underwriting requirements. In some cases, existing products can support the changed underwriting requirements with no other change needed.

- Competitors who have introduced new or improved sales tools. The company may be able to improve its own sales tools with no change to its products.

2.5.1 Understanding Customers

The best way to develop an understanding of the company's target markets is to talk to current customers, potential customers, and lost customers. By interviewing current customers, you can find out what they like and dislike about the company and its products. By conducting interviews with potential customers from the company's target markets, you can find out more about their preferences, decision making, and unmet needs. By talking to lost customers, you can find out why they canceled their insurance and what the company could have done to hold on to their business.

A special category of lost customers are those who were approved for insurance but who opted not to buy from the company. By interviewing them, you can find out if there were any problems in the buying process. In addition, for those who ended up purchasing insurance from a competitor, you can find out who the competitor was and what they offered that made the difference to the buyer.

A company could also study the demographics of these three groups to gain a better understanding of each. How do current, potential, and lost customers differ in terms of income level, age group, risk class, and other characteristics? What can be learned from such differences to better position the company and its products?

2.5.2 Tracking Competitors

Tracking the movements of competitors can be a daunting task. To narrow the scope of market research, the company should focus on only the major
competitors in its target markets. Major competitors can be determined in a number of ways:

- By interviewing customers and asking them which other companies they seriously considered for life insurance.

- By tracking other companies that are involved with similar target markets and distribution systems. Find out which of these competitors are most successful in garnering sales from the company's agents.

- By talking to agents and employees from other companies. Many companies are very open about their target markets.

Major competitors can be tracked continuously or sporadically, depending on how often the information is used. For example, if the company insists on updating its products only every two years, it may not make sense to track competitors continuously.

Competitor information can be gathered in many ways. Company employees may build information-trading relationships with employees at other companies. Many companies are happy to give information as long as they receive as much information in return. Industry trade groups, industry meetings, industry databases, and industry publications are often good sources of information. Agents and others involved in distribution are always a good source of what is new and appealing to them. In fact, they often volunteer such information.

The company will want to organize competitor information into some form of database or spreadsheet. Several categories of information should be collected:

- Prices, including premium rates and commission rates. For some products, items such as cash values, credited interest rates, cost of insurance rates, expense charges, or dividends should also be collected and compared. Rather than collect every possible rate, the company will probably want to focus on a few selected issue ages, one gender, one or two risk classes, and one or two size categories.

- Underwriting requirements, such as issue age and amount limits for medical exams, blood tests, and urine samples.

- Product features, such as partial withdrawal provisions, policy loan interest rates, and the guarantee period for premiums or benefits.

- Sales tools, such as illustrations, brochures, and advertisements.

Data should be collected only for similarly designed products sold to similar markets. For example, a company that sells primarily whole life products with low average sizes and large first-year commissions should not collect information on a product designed for the corporate-owned marketplace, since corporate-owned products are often sold in large amounts and are often designed with low, levelized commissions.

2.6 Preliminary Product Design

Once market research has identified the need for a new product or a revision to an existing product, the next step is preliminary product design. Preliminary product design has four stages, all of which reduce the amount of wasted time and effort spent on product development:

1. Develop consensus on as many aspects of the product as possible
2. Determine the feasibility of the product
3. Perform preliminary pricing and develop estimates of sales and profits

4. Perform a cost/benefit analysis and decide whether to proceed to final product design.

For a minor product revision, it may be possible to skip this step and proceed directly to final product design. However, it may be worth spending some time on preliminary product design to ensure that there is consensus on the details of the product revision.

2.6.1 Develop Consensus

Before trying to determine feasibility, it is helpful to pin down how the product will look to consumers. You should try to develop consensus on the customer needs that will be satisfied by the product, how the product will be marketed and sold, what variations or features will be included, and what risk classes will be used. Market research should provide guidance to help answer many of the following questions.

Customer needs: To what kind of customer is this product meant to appeal? What customer needs will this product satisfy? How well does the initial design satisfy these needs?

Distribution needs: What forms of distribution will be used? Does the product fit the needs of these distributors? Will it pay adequate compensation? Are there any special education or training needs for distributors?

Marketing and selling strategies: How will the product be marketed? Is the product designed to reach a new or a current target market? How will that target market be reached? How will the product be sold? In other words, why will consumers buy it? Is having the lowest or close-to-the-lowest price important? Or will a fair price or average price be sufficient? Will special features help sell the product? If so, which features will make a significant difference to the consumer? Is the company's reputation or image a major factor? Are certain measures of financial strength needed for success with this product? At what level should commissions be set to encourage (or not discourage) sales of the product?

Product features and riders: Many common product features and riders were discussed in Chapter 1. Preliminary consensus building should include product features and riders. What standard features will the product include? What optional features will the consumer be able to add to the product? How will these features differ from similar features previously offered by the company or by competitors? How important is each of these features, in case some features have to be eliminated to improve the cost of the product? Which are the most important and least important features? What patterns or formulas will apply to premiums, death benefits, cash values, dividends, or other important product parameters? How will these compare to values contained in current products and competitors' products that are comparable to this product? For products with a significant investment component, such as whole life, endowments, and universal life, it may be necessary to map out an investment strategy. An investment strategy can be designed that will enable the product to credit competitive interest rates while managing the company's investment risk.

Risk classes: How will insureds be classified for premium rate or mortality risk purposes? Will rates vary by issue age and policy year, by attained (current) age, or simply by issue age? Will there be separate rates for males and females? Will female ages be converted to equivalent male ages using an age setback? (For example, a five-year age setback would convert an age 45 female to an age 40 male, for rate purposes.) Will rates vary between smokers and nonsmokers? Will one or more preferred categories be offered?

2.6.2 Determine Feasibility

In order to determine whether a product is feasible, it is necessary to examine a number of areas. Here are some of the questions that usually need to be answered:

- Does the product fit the company?
- Are there any regulatory barriers?
- Are there any implementation barriers?
- What effect will this product have on sales of the company's other products?

2.6.2.1   Product and Company Fit

The product should first be reviewed to see how it fits with the company's mission, vision, goals, strategy, culture, target markets, core competencies, and distribution systems. In some ways, this is one of the simplest steps. However, it is easy to be carried away with enthusiasm for developing a new, appealing product that does not fit the company. It is much more difficult to maintain a rational, disciplined approach and cancel the development of a product that does not fit.

2.6.2.2   Regulatory Barriers

How difficult or expensive will it be to gain regulatory approval for this product? Is it uncertain whether the product will be approved? Will new or different accounting or reserving requirements apply to the product? If the product will be offered in more than one jurisdiction, how many versions of the product will be needed for different jurisdictions? (For example, it is rare that the same product can be used in all 50 U.S. states. Some modifications are usually required to conform to nonstandard regulations in several states.) Are there any special licensing requirements for this kind of product, for either the company or its agents? Are there any special ongoing reporting requirements for this product? Are there any special tax implications or requirements?

2.6.2.3 Implementation Barriers

When a company develops a product unlike any it has offered before, it is normal to encounter some implementation difficulties. These difficulties can range in severity from annoyances to insurmountable obstacles. A truly new product will require new administrative processes and procedures to be developed and implemented, to support the product's features. New or enhanced software will often be required. Training for company staff and agents will usually be required.

For example, suppose a company's existing products are all of the pre-scheduled variety, with premiums, commissions, death benefits, cash values, and dividends known well in advance. To implement universal life, the company will need software that will support flexible premiums and dynamically calculate commissions, death benefits, and cash values for each policy. Modifying the company's existing software to support universal life may be too expensive and possibly disruptive to the company's existing business. On the other hand, buying new software for universal life can also be expensive. Not only does the software have to be paid for and installed, but it also has to be integrated with the company's other software and maintained for many years into the future.

Besides tracking flexible premiums and calculating dynamic values, software changes can be required for other product features, sales illustrations, and policy issuance, and to satisfy regulatory, accounting, and tax requirements. In some companies, something as simple as a rate change may require software changes or other computer-related support.

There are a number of factors to consider related to software changes:

- Does the company have the expertise and resources available to develop the needed software? If not, can software be purchased or can outside resources be hired?

- Whether software is developed or purchased, how long will it take to be ready?
- What will the software cost, including initial expenses (both internal and external) and long-term maintenance expenses? These costs should be considered in the final stage of determining feasibility.

While the major implementation obstacles may be software-related, you should not overlook other potentially important costs, such as

- The costs of instituting new administrative procedures and processes
- The costs of training company staff and agents, and
- The costs of introducing the product to the distribution system, including presentations to explain the product, new sales and marketing materials, and any advertising required for the product.

2.6.2.4   Effect on the Company's Existing Products

Every new product has an effect on the company's existing products. A new product may replace an existing product, reduce sales of other products, trigger upgrades to existing policies, or encourage customers and agents to trade in old policies for the new product.

In many cases, a new product is developed to replace an older product. Sometimes, however, the older product continues to be sold long after the new product is introduced, perhaps as a concession to certain agents. The company's intentions should be clear regarding what is to happen to the older product being replaced. While the costs of continuing one older product may seem small, it is hard to hold exceptions to one product. Over the years, the company may find that many products that were supposedly replaced by new products continue to be sold. The cost of continuing many older products is not small, and they add complexity and take away from the company's sense of direction.

Occasionally, a company is surprised when a new product hurts sales of some older products that it was *not* intended to replace. For example, a new term product could hurt sales of existing permanent products. In such a case, the company may find that customers switching from high-premium, high-profit products to low-premium, low-profit products have unexpectedly cut its overall profits.

If the new product is a better value than the product it is replacing, consideration should be given to upgrading the buyers of the old product. Some companies have a policy of always improving the terms of existing policies to match the improved terms of any new product. Other companies upgrade only recent buyers of the old product.

If the new product is better because the company's results have improved (because of lower mortality, better persistency, or lower expenses), then the cost of upgrading old policies may be insignificant. However, if the company is lowering its rates to be more competitive and is accepting lower profit margins, upgrading old policies could be very expensive.

The effect of an upgrade on recoverability of the old product's acquisition costs should be considered. At the same time, upgrades send a powerful message about the company's belief in treating customers fairly. This can contribute greatly to customer and agent loyalty. In the end, the goodwill generated by fair treatment may benefit the company through increased sales and superior persistency.

A company that does not upgrade old policies will face persistency problems. The company's agents will want to serve their customers and earn another commission by selling them a new, improved product. If the company does not allow this, the agent may take the business to another company. Alternatively, the policyowner may take the initiative to buy a newer, better product.

2.6.3 Preliminary Pricing

Perhaps the most difficult aspect of product development is predicting the future sales and profit margins of the product. Much of the rest of this book is focused on pricing techniques that help predict future profit margins. However, predicting future sales is just as important, since sales times profit margins equals profits.

2.6.3.1 Expected Profit Margins

We will use *profit margin* to mean a measure of the additional profit resulting from an additional unit of sales. The profit margin will take into account only the costs that vary with sales levels. In other words, it will not include the expenses of developing the product or the company's fixed costs. It will reflect all future profits resulting from a unit sold. For example, the profit margin may be the present value of all future profits, expressed as a percentage of the present value of all premiums.

For preliminary pricing, it is necessary to develop pricing assumptions and perform profit margin calculations for a small number of pricing cells. These pricing cells might consist of a few representative issue ages for the gender, risk class, and size of policy with the highest expected sales.

By focusing on a few pricing cells, you can more quickly test the effect of changes in premiums, commissions, cash values, underwriting criteria, investment strategies, product features, and other design factors. By varying one factor at a time, you can measure the effect on profit margins. In addition, you could calculate the premium change or other change necessary to offset the effect on profit margins. Often, varying one factor at a time provides enough information for the company to decide on each design factor independently. Sometimes, however, two or more factors must be considered at once, as in the following example.

Example 2.6.1 Varying Two Factors at Once

The company has asked its Agents Council for help in deciding whether to maintain their liberal underwriting criteria and high first-year commission structure or change to stricter underwriting criteria or a level commission structure. The following table shows the twentieth-year cash values per unit needed to maintain the same premiums and profit margins for two sets of underwriting criteria combined with two sets of commission structures.

Twentieth-Year Cash Value Per Unit

(needed to maintain premiums and profit margins)

	High First-Year Commission Structure	*Level Commission Structure*
Strict Underwriting Criteria	200.00	225.00
Liberal Underwriting Criteria	180.00	195.00

Clearly, either change would help the company be more competitive, which could help the agents sell more business. However, the agents may prefer the status quo, which may result in higher total commissions.

The speed of the preliminary pricing process is often determined by how the company makes decisions regarding the many design factors. If decisions are made by a small, cohesive group that is focused on product development, the process may be very fast. If decisions are made by a large group that often disagrees and rarely meets, the process may be very slow. Companies often involve representatives from a number of areas of the company, such as sales and marketing, the distribution system, finance, and product development.

For some design factors, a number of iterations may be necessary before agreement can be reached. For example, to obtain sufficiently competitive premium rates, the company might vary the underwriting criteria, commission rates, and cash values per unit, looking for the most acceptable combination.

Sometimes a competitive problem has its roots in overly conservative assumptions. This can be explored by solving for the value of a key assumption needed to make the product competitive. For example, you could solve for the mortality assumption needed to make a term product competitive. The required mortality assumption could be compared to recent mortality experience and trends, to see if the company can be more competitive.

Once most of the design factors have been agreed upon, profit margins should be estimated for the range of price levels that the company is considering. The company may have a good idea from its market research as to what price level it would like to offer. Profit margin estimates could be calculated for the desired price level and for prices 5% higher and 5% lower.

2.6.3.2 Price Sensitivity

Most life insurance products are at least a little price sensitive. In other words, the lower the price, the higher the resulting sales. However, the degree of price sensitivity can vary widely by type of product, target market, and even price level. For example, term products may be more price-sensitive than permanent products. Large-amount buyers may be more price-sensitive than buyers of small amounts.

By studying company experience and the sales results of competitors, you may be able to develop some relationships between sales levels and price levels. This information about price sensitivity is extremely important. It is perhaps the least available and yet the most useful information to have when setting price levels for a product. If you can predict the effect on sales of, say, a 1% increase in price, you can then determine the effect on profits, since profits equal profit margin times sales. This allows you to hone in on the price level that will maximize profits.

Even when a product is very price-sensitive, you may find that sales are fairly insensitive to changes in price at the noncompetitive end of the price range. At the same time, sales may skyrocket as the price drops toward the most competitive price offered. Figure 2.6.1 below illustrates a hypothetical relationship between sales and price level.

Figure 2.6.1 Price Sensitivity Varies with Price Level

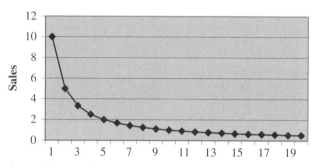

Price as a Percentage above the Lowest Price Offered

Looking at the figure, there is a natural temptation to try to match or beat the lowest price offered, in order to maximize sales. There are two problems with this strategy:

1. The lower the price, the lower the profit margin. At some point, the company cannot afford to lower the price further without earning inadequate returns, in spite of increased sales.

2. You can expect competitors to react and lower their prices to maintain their competitive positions and their sales levels. Your increased sales will only be temporary. You will have to lower prices repeatedly to hold on to an increased level of sales. This squeezes profit margins for all the companies who wish to be price leaders. In the end, few companies, if any, will earn an adequate return on sales of the product. A low price strategy works best for the lowest cost producer.

2.6.3.3 Expected Sales

Sales of a new product come from three sources:

1. *Taking sales from another product:* The company's distribution system sells the new product instead of one of the company's older products.

2. *Taking sales from competitors:* The company's distribution system sells the new product instead of competitors' products.

3. *Creating new sales:* The product may create new sales by attracting customers (or distribution) that would not otherwise have purchased (or sold) life insurance.

Taking sales from another product is predictable. Sales levels of the product being replaced can be used to estimate sales of the new product.

Taking sales from competitors is where most companies pin their hopes of increased sales. Sometimes their hopes are exceeded. More often, emotions and sales goals get in the way of objective estimation of sales from this source, so the resulting sales levels are disappointing. *Taking sales from competitors* may become *giving sales to competitors,* if competitors have improved their products more than the company has. Few companies forecast decreases in sales, but decreases are common.

Creating new sales is usually not a significant factor. However, if the product pushes prices to a level that creates substantial value in the eyes of customers, people may purchase much more life insurance. Occasionally, new product features or streamlined buying or selling procedures can generate increased sales. For example, bank employees may be more apt to sell life insurance if the sales process is simple and short.

2.6.3.4 Combining Expected Sales and Profit Margins

Expected sales should be estimated for the same range of price levels for which profitability was estimated. Expected sales and expected profit margins can then be combined to determine profits for a range of price levels, as in the following example.

Example 2.6.1 Combining Expected Sales and Profit Margins

Price Level	*0.95*	*1.00*	*1.05*	*1.10*
Sales (in thousands)	150	100	70	50
Profit Margin (per thousand)	0.50	1.00	1.50	2.00
Expected Profit	75	100	105	100

If the company's overriding goal were to maximize profits, it would choose a price level close to 1.05. However, if the company valued growth in addition to profits, it might choose a price level of 1.00. Compared to a price level of 1.05, this would involve sacrificing 5% of profits for an additional 42% of sales.

The foregoing discussion assumed price levels could be reduced to a single factor. In reality, price levels are often a combination of many factors such as premium rates, interest rates, cash values, and product features. In addition, commission levels can be considered one of the factors, because of their large effect on sales, profit margins, and profits. As a result, it may be necessary to develop a multidimensional grid of the many factors that make up the price levels. This would result in a corresponding multidimensional grid of expected sales, expected profit margins, and expected profits.

When a number of factors are being considered at the same time, this kind of analysis becomes difficult and the results are questionable. Expected sales are hard to estimate when just one factor is varied. With multiple factors varying, expected sales become pure guesswork, as does this kind of analysis.

2.6.4 Cost/Benefit Analysis

Once all the preliminary design work has been done, you must make a decision as to whether to go forward with development of the product. It is helpful to take an objective look at all the costs and benefits of developing the product. Here is a list of some of the costs and benefits that may apply.

2.6.4.1 Costs

The costs of product development include all the costs listed under *Implementation Barriers* in Section 2.6.2:

- Purchase or development of software
- Maintenance of software
- New administrative procedures and processes
- Training company staff and agents
- Introduction of the product to the distribution system.

In addition, there is the cost to finish developing the product, the cost to manage the product over its lifetime, and the cost of developing this product instead of devoting resources to another opportunity. Finally, you should consider the lost sales and lost profits on the older products that will be replaced by this product, particularly if the older products have higher profit margins than the new product.

2.6.4.2 Benefits

The benefits of the new product may include increased profits (from expected sales times expected profit margin) and increased sales. Increases in profits or sales may be only temporary, as competitors react and introduce improved products of their own. This is especially true if the company sells through independent agents. However, the effect of the new product will be longer lasting if the company has captive agents.

The new product may give the company the ability to develop and sell similar products in the future. If the costs of developing and implementing this product are high, they could be spread over a number of future products of similar design. For example, once a company has implemented its first variable universal life product, subsequent VUL products may incur much smaller implementation costs.

The new product may enhance the company's image as an innovative or leading edge company, making it easier to recruit and retain agents, employees, and customers. The product may be part of a broader company strategy or a key contributor to the company's vision of the future.

2.6.4.3 Analysis

Many of the costs and benefits can be reduced to numbers and compared. However, some of the costs and benefits are intangible and must be weighed using human judgment. Insights from a number of people with different backgrounds and perceptions can help in weighing the intangible costs and benefits.

If the decision is made to cancel the product, it is useful to document the reason behind such a decision, so that all involved understand and learn from the experience. For example, a company's high expenses, high cost of capital, or high profit goal may make it noncompetitive for certain types of products. As another example, the company may decide not to pursue the development of a product if its initial work found that the market was underpricing the product.

2.7 Final Product Design

Depending on the decisions made during preliminary design, final product design can be relatively straightforward or enormously complicated. At one extreme, all of the important decisions may have already been made. In that case, final product design may be no more than extending the decisions already made for selected pricing cells to the rest of the product, with some further refinement and more elaborate profit testing.

At the other extreme, preliminary design may have asked more questions than it answered. For example, price levels, commissions, product features, and risk classes may all be undecided. Final design would then include a search for the best possible combination of all the undecided variables. There may be an infinite number of combinations to test, with no clear way to judge whether one combination is better than another. In this case, preliminary product design continues into the final product design stage. At a minimum, final product design would normally include the following steps:

- A careful review of the preliminary design, looking for and correcting any inconsistencies, errors, and omissions.

- An attempt to reach agreement on as many unanswered questions and design factors as possible before pricing begins, to reduce the combinations of factors to be tested.

- Development of pricing assumptions for all issue ages, genders, risk classes, policy sizes, and product variations. Usually, only a fraction of the pricing assumptions is developed during preliminary design. Final pricing assumptions are more detailed and complete and reflect the latest information available.

- Profit testing (that is, calculation of profit margins) for the selected pricing cells used in preliminary design, to see whether there have been any significant changes to profit margins due to new or more refined assumptions. If so, it may be necessary to redo some of the preliminary design.

- Profit testing for every fifth or tenth issue age for every combination of gender, risk class, policy size group, and product variation that will have different premiums, death benefits, cash values, or other product factors.

- Profit testing for selected pricing cells to measure the sensitivity of profit margins to changes in key assumptions. If profit margins are found to be very sensitive in certain areas, product design or product management may be fine-tuned to minimize the effect of variations in future experience.

2.7.1 Pricing Pitfalls

Over the years pricing mistakes have been made by virtually everyone who has ever priced a product. Some mistakes are more serious than others. To help you avoid them, here are some of the more common and serious mistakes that are made.

2.7.1.1 Inappropriate Pricing Assumptions

All pricing assumptions are estimates, and all are wrong to some extent. Here are some areas where pricing assumptions can be so far off that expected profits become expected losses:

- Developing a product using no more than educated guesses for key assumptions that will make or break the product. For example, because of major changes in underwriting criteria, it may be necessary to estimate the mortality assumption for a new term insurance product.

- Not accounting for the effect on pricing assumptions of a new target market, a new distribution system, or changes in economic conditions. For example, if a company has historically focused on the upper-income market and has decided to expand into the middle-income market, it must be careful to adjust its mortality assumptions upward and persistency assumptions downward, as will be explained in Chapter 3.

- Not accounting for rational buyer or seller behavior. For example, if a term product has very high percentage increases in premium each year, you should expect very low persistency.

- Offering a product with first-year commissions and first-year cash values that together exceed first-year premiums. In this situation, watch out for agents buying large policies for themselves or their families and lapsing them after one year. A disreputable agent can also sell large amounts of insurance by sharing part of the commission with the policyowner or by paying all of part of the first-year premium for the policyowner, allowing the policies to lapse after one year.

- Offering a product with a very low level premium and little or no cash values, where profits depend on policyowners lapsing their policies. When this is the case, as it often is for Term to 100, you can expect that policyowners will persist in droves.

- Pricing a product so that most cells subsidize certain high-profile cells. Although it may appear that the overall product is meeting profit objectives based on an assumed distribution of sales, there may be a "distribution of sales" risk. When sales are more concentrated in the cells that are being subsidized, profitability may be far lower than originally assumed.

- Not clearly understanding the cost of options that certain product features give the policyowner. Policyowners may exercise these options in ways that are harmful to the company. Every guarantee in a policy has an expected cost, unless there is no chance that the guarantee will make a difference. For example, guaranteed cash surrender values can be costly when interest rates rapidly rise.

2.7.1.2   Not Understanding Your Environment

Laws, regulations, and guidelines change. It is important to understand where things stand and where they are heading when the product is developed. Pricing should reflect the environment that the company will be subject to in the years ahead. Here are some common mistakes:

- Not accurately reflecting the effect of accounting guidelines, reserve standards, capital requirements, and tax regulations. For example, accounting guidelines and reserve standards can have a major effect on the timing of profits. Capital requirements can have a huge bearing on the product's rate of return. Complex tax regulations can result in larger and earlier taxes than expected.

- Pricing using terminal reserves that ignore the conservatism in mean reserves; see Chapter 6, Section 6.5.2.

- Not accurately reflecting the timing of cash flows. For example, death benefits and taxes may be paid, on the average, at the middle of the policy year rather than at the end of the policy year.

- Assuming tax advantages for the policyowner are never taken away. If tax advantages *are* taken away, you can hope for "grandfathering," where policies receive the tax treatment originally planned. If there is no grandfathering, policies may lapse en masse.

2.7.1.3 Technical Mistakes

Pricing is a complex process. It is easy to get a little confused and calculate or interpret results incorrectly. Here are some of the more common mistakes:

- Calculating investment income on prior year profits and counting it as part of current year profits. Once profits have been earned and counted, they should be removed. Interest on past profits should *not* be included as part of current profits.

- Discounting using an inappropriate rate. In the financial world, discount rates are tied to the riskiness of the investment. When a company discounts future profits using the interest rate earned on high-quality investments, it is saying that an investment in its insurance business is no more risky than a high-quality investment. In actual practice, the owners of most insurance companies demand a rate of return quite a bit higher than that earned on a high-quality investment.

- Discounting future losses using a high discount rate; see the discussion of generalized ROI in Chapter 11, Section 11.6.2. For example, if future losses are discounted using a 15% discount rate, the company is actually *paying* 15% interest to the policyowner for a period of time.

2.7.2 Pricing Software

Certain pricing software packages are great pricing aids. They accelerate the pricing process by calculating policy values and performing profit testing. These packages typically have preprogrammed calculations that reproduce the effect of accounting guidelines, reserve standards, capital requirements, and tax regulations. In addition, these packages usually have calculations with enough flexibility to allow a company to calculate cash values and other policy values for all the common products in a variety of ways.

Some companies create and maintain their own pricing software. This enables a company to support features or methods that are unique to the company. A number of companies have developed pricing software or related tools built on spreadsheets, at least for some of their more unusual products. In addition, many companies create software to interpolate rates for every age (from the rates for every fifth or tenth age developed in pricing) and to load the resulting rates into their administrative system.

2.7.3 The Pricing Process

Pricing is a process that attempts to find the best combination of many variables. The minimum goal is to develop a product that will generate at least adequate sales and adequate profits. Other companies may wish to maximize sales while producing adequate profits. Some other companies wish to maximize profits while producing adequate sales. Still other companies try to strike more of a balance between sales and profits.

When many variables are to be solved for, a plan of attack is needed:

- Can some variables be determined first, without knowing all of the other variables? For example, is there an absolute profit goal that must be met?

- Are there some good starting points that can be used for certain variables, such as values from a similar product? For example, UL expense charges could be set close to the industry average.

- What relationships should exist between variables? For example, surrender charges could be designed to match the product's cumulative loss, so the company does not lose money on surrenders.

Example 2.7.1 Sample Plan of Attack

Suppose a product has premiums, commissions, and profit margins that are variables that must be solved for. Here is an example of a possible plan of attack:

1. Set premium rates at a level that will beat 75% of competitors' premium rates, set commissions at the greater of the company's normal commission level and the average level of competitors' commissions, and then solve for profit margin.

2. If the resulting profit margin is unacceptable, raise premium rates until profit margin is acceptable, but not beyond a level that will beat less than 45% of competitors' premium rates.

3. If the resulting profit margin is unacceptable, lower commissions until profit margin is acceptable, but not below the lower of the company's normal commission level and the average level of competitors' commissions.

4. If the resulting profit margin is still unacceptable, devise a new plan of attack.

Even when a reasonable plan of attack has been devised, the results of pricing may not produce an acceptable product. It may be necessary to devise and try a number of different plans of attack before the product is finalized. While this can be frustrating for the person doing the pricing, this is the nature of research and development. Success is not guaranteed.

Pricing software is essential to the pricing process. Pricing software should allow you to load all of your pricing assumptions in advance, to efficiently enter or generate your variables, and to automatically solve for variables such as premiums, commissions, interest margins, and cost of insurance rates. The software should be able to handle a number of pricing cells at once and solve for variables based on a weighted average of many pricing cells.

The pricing process differs dramatically between pre-scheduled and dynamic products. However, a few variables apply to all products:

- Most products have *death benefit patterns* that are an integral part of the product. The product defines the death benefit. For example, decreasing term products have a pre-scheduled decreasing pattern of death benefits. Level term products have a level death benefit. Pre-scheduled permanent products usually have a level death benefit, as do certain forms of UL and VUL.

- Most products have *commission rates* that are either agreed to in advance of pricing or determined during the pricing process. Commission rates are usually high in the first policy year and low thereafter, although some companies use level commission rates. For some companies, commission rates must be split between general agents and agents. Companies may have vesting schedules that govern whether the agent receives future commissions after leaving the company. Agent bonuses, pensions, and other agent-related expenses might be tied to commissions. Commission rates can have a big effect on sales. High commission rates may help a product sell better, depending on the level of consumer scrutiny. Low commission rates can effectively kill a product. Then again, a high commission rate adds significantly to the price of the product and can make the product less competitive.

- If the product has preferred or other *underwriting criteria* that are not governed by industry standards, then the details of the underwriting criteria can become a variable for pricing purposes. By tightening underwriting standards, the company can lower its expected mortality and thereby lower the product's price. By loosening underwriting standards, the product may appeal to a wider audience, although its price will usually have to be increased.

2.7.3.1 Pricing Pre-Scheduled Products

We will consider just two categories of pre-scheduled products for pricing discussions: term insurance and permanent participating insurance. Permanent nonpar insurance can be priced as par insurance with no dividends. With-profits products can be priced much like par insurance, although additional testing may be necessary if assets and liabilities are mismatched. Mismatched assets and liabilities are addressed in Chapters 14 and 15.

For *term insurance,* the major variables solved for are premiums, commissions, and profit margins. However, a number of other product features could also be pricing variables, such as

- Cash values: While most term products do not offer cash values, they are required by some countries in some situations.
- Number of years for which premiums will be guaranteed.
- Guaranteed maximum premiums, if different from the current level of premiums.
- Benefit period: For how many years or to what age will premiums and benefits be payable?
- Specifics of any conversion option: Will conversion credits be offered? For how many years or until what age will conversion be allowed?
- If premium rates will be lower for insureds more recently underwritten (that is, select and ultimate premium rates), will the insured have a right to be reunderwritten in order to requalify for lower premium rates? If so, how often may the insured be reunderwritten and who will pay the expenses of underwriting? What premium rates will be charged for those who do not requalify for lower premium rates, since these insureds are likely to be worse-than-average risks?

Premiums can have a number of different aspects. Rarely do term products have only one premium for the lifetime of the term policy. Instead, premium rates may vary by policy year. Annually renewable term has annual increases in premium rates. Ten-year term products often have premium increases after ten years. When premiums vary by policy year, the slope of the premium is very important. The steeper the premium increase, the more policyowners will cancel their insurance, with healthy insureds more apt to cancel their policies than unhealthy insureds. With steep premium increases, the company may experience higher mortality than expected, as the average persisting insured becomes increasingly unhealthy.

The premium pattern usually has a major effect on the reserves built into the pricing; see Chapter 6. This can complicate the pricing process, forcing you to recalculate reserves every time you change the premium pattern.

For *participating permanent insurance,* the major variables solved for are premiums, commissions, cash values, dividends, and profit margins. Solving for all of these variables at once is not possible. It is essential to decide on some of these variables in advance, such as commission rates and profit margins.

At the very least, commission rates should be narrowed to a few choices. Mutual companies sometimes set the profit margin in advance and try to maximize policyowner value. Stock companies would be more apt to aim for a certain competitive position while trying to maximize profit margin, but subject to a minimum profit margin.

Cash values and dividends are usually determined by complex formulas. Cash values may be a function of premiums, interest rates, and mortality rates, such as those used for reserves or guaranteed by the product. Dividends are often based on the difference between assumptions used for reserves and the assumptions used for pricing. For example, the interest rate for reserves might be 3% while the interest rate used for pricing might be 7%. Dividends would pay the policyowner most of the difference between 7% and 3% interest.

If cash values and dividends are not formula-driven or if the formulas are not automatically handled in the pricing software, the pricing process can become extremely labor intensive, with reams of numbers having to be manually input for each iteration. This will likely force a quick decision on cash values and dividends.

Term insurance price comparisons are straightforward, usually involving a simple comparison of premiums. Permanent products are much harder to compare. When pricing to achieve a certain competitive position, it may be difficult to determine which competitive measure to use. Here are some of the more common choices:

1. Net cost, equal to premiums less dividends less cash values after 10 or 20 years

2. Same as (1), but adjusted for the time value of money

3. Same as (2), but adjusted for the cost of expected death benefits.

Consumers and agents will want to know about the aggressiveness of the assumptions on which dividends are based, so that they can assess the likelihood of projected dividends being paid. When comparing your product to other companies' products, you should consider the same question. One company may seem to have a more competitive product only because they have projected the future more aggressively. This makes competitive comparisons of par products very difficult.

2.7.3.2 Pricing Dynamic Products

Development of a dynamic product is part art, part science. The art is finding the best combination of several key components: cost of insurance charges, expense charges, surrender charges, and investment spread. Together, the components must provide both acceptable profitability and a product that will sell. Competitive pressures may drive the choice of a particular component, but proper pricing should emphasize the combined performance of all the components, not the profit margin for each individual component.

We will consider three categories of dynamic products for pricing discussions: fixed premium UL, flexible premium UL, and VUL.

The design of *fixed premium UL* products can be similar to the design of participating permanent products. The premium is important, but projected cash values, in relation to the premium, determine the overall competitiveness of the product. The premium is set by balancing several considerations:

1. The lower the premium, the more competitive the product.

2. The company may want to set the premium to target a certain market or need. For example, the premium might be set to minimize or maximize the cash values, or to match a competitor's product.

3. The higher the premium, the greater the likelihood the policy will mature if interest rates decline or COI charges increase.

UL cash values are calculated as premiums plus credited interest less expense charges, cost of insurance charges (to cover the cost of death benefits), surrender charges (charged only upon surrender), and withdrawals.

Pricing should determine each of the above components of cash values. Competition usually has a major effect on the credited interest rate, which is perhaps the most visible and best understood feature of a UL policy. The product should have a credited interest rate that seems reasonable to both the agent and the customer.

Expense charges often have several components and are harder for the customer to understand and compare. For example, a single product may have expense charges that are a percentage of premium, a flat amount per month, a flat amount per thousand of death benefit, and a percentage of account value. Agents are likely to discern expense charges that are higher than the competition. If the difference is significant, you can expect pressure from agents to bring the expense charges more in line with the competition.

Cost of insurance charges are usually based on a mortality table. They are very hard for people to understand and compare. However, both the agent and customer can compare the cash values that result from all of the components, including COI charges. If the resulting cash values are not competitive, there will be pressure to improve one or more components of cash value.

You will want to test a number of possible future patterns of credited interest rates and COI charges, to ensure the product performs adequately in terms of consumer value and profitably for the company. This is especially important when premiums have been set relatively low, such that there is a fair chance that the policy will not mature if interest rates decline or COI charges increase. In this case, some scenarios may result in the product terminating prematurely, making it difficult for the company to recoup its acquisitions costs. This problem can be overcome by giving the company the right to change the premium from time to time to offset the effect of decreases in credited interest rates or increases in COI charges. However, you can expect that an unplanned increase in premium will result in poorer persistency and some customer dissatisfaction.

Flexible premium universal life: Flexible premiums add an extra layer of complexity. Assumptions are needed for the pattern of premiums and the effect of various premium patterns on persistency. A number of different premium patterns should be tested to ensure that certain patterns do not result in unacceptably low or high profit margins. Profit margins that are too high for certain premium patterns may mean the product is not competitive. Premium patterns with profit margins that are too low are apt to be discovered and exploited by customers or agents.

For example, you may develop what seems to be an adequately priced product, using some general assumptions as to the overall premium pattern. However, the premium pattern that maximizes commissions as a percentage of premiums may be the most popular and unprofitable pattern.

One of the first steps in pricing flexible premium UL is to determine target premiums. Most flexible premium UL products pay a high commission on first-year premium up to the amount of a target premium. Target premiums have a big effect on the overall price of the product. They are often set to reinforce a desirable premium level or to match the competition.

Testing should be done to set minimum and maximum premiums. Minimum premiums are needed to ensure the policy persists long enough to recoup acquisitions costs. Recall that a dynamic product's cash value is usually equal to an account value less a surrender charge. UL products with large surrender charges may have positive account values but negative cash values in the early policy years. However, as long as a minimum premium is paid, the company will usually allow the policy to continue. Failure to pay the minimum premium will cause the policy to terminate if its cash value is less than zero. Without a minimum premium requirement, coverage could continue for a number of years until the account value is exhausted, thereby circumventing the surrender charge.

In some UL products a very large premium can trigger an automatic increase in the death benefit well in excess of the additional premium. In other words, if the insured were dying, the policyowner could increase the death benefit by "dumping in" the maximum premium possible. To minimize such behavior, some UL products have limits as to how much premium can be paid without additional underwriting being required. In addition, if one of the least profitable premium patterns is one in which the largest premiums are paid, the company can protect its profitability by placing upper limits on premiums paid.

Besides testing different patterns of premiums, credited interest rates, and COI charges, you may also need to test different partial withdrawal patterns. However, if partial withdrawals incur a reasonable surrender charge, they may have little effect on profit margins.

Variable universal life: Most of the issues that apply to UL also apply to VUL. The major difference between the two products is in the investment risk. Because VUL passes much of the investment risk to the buyer, VUL products often have lower capital requirements than UL products have. As a result, a VUL product can often be priced with a lower profit margin than an otherwise similar UL product.

In some countries, VUL products are subject to securities regulations, much like stocks and bonds. Securities regulations may govern the licensing of agents, the maximum allowable commissions and expense charges, and disclosure of relevant information.

VUL products charge a fee as a percentage of assets. This fee has various names, such as a mortality and expense (M&E) charge, risk charge, or asset charge. The insurance company charges this fee in addition to the percentage-of-assets fee typically charged by fund managers. This fee often pays for a good share of the product's expenses and profit margin. This means the company's results will fluctuate with the market value of assets under management. For example, if the funds under management grow quickly in value because of escalating stock prices, the company may end up collecting a much higher level of fees than expected, resulting in higher-than-expected profit margins. Conversely, if the financial markets take a dive, the company may collect lower fees and suffer lower profit margins or even incur a loss.

2.8 Product Implementation

Product implementation actually starts early in the product design process, in connection with the determination of feasibility. During the product development process, discussions are held with representatives from a number of areas of the company. These discussions and supporting documentation serve to keep people throughout the company up to date on the product's design. This communication helps the company identify and resolve the numerous issues and problems that can be created by a new product. For example, a new product feature may require software changes and changes to administrative procedures that affect a number of areas. People from the areas affected will need to be involved to both design the changes and implement them.

Product implementation requires a cooperative effort from a number of areas in the company. The effort may involve people responsible for computer systems, illustrations, investments, policyowner service, underwriting, policy issue, policy filing, legal issues, marketing, and sales. It is important that most, if not all, areas understand the new product. In addition, those responsible for product development need to understand the role and value of each of these areas and involve them early in the process; otherwise, there is the danger of a problem surfacing late in the process. This may require substantial reworking of the product at the last minute. Another possibility is that the product will be left unchanged, with the company adversely affected. For example, a relatively inconsequential and unimportant product feature may be added to a new product, to differentiate it from the previous product. Once that feature is announced to the field force, it may be difficult to remove it from the product. Suppose substantial changes to the company's computer systems are required to support this feature. Had this been known initially, the unimportant feature never would have been included, but once it was announced, it was too late.

Most of the details of product implementation are designed and planned during the final design stage. Once the product design is finalized, product implementation begins in earnest. Rates and values for all issue ages are calculated and loaded into computer systems, product are filed with regulators (where required), sales material and sales illustrations are created, and introduction of the product is planned and executed.

2.8.1   Calculation of Rates for Every Issue Age

During product design and pricing, rates and values are typically created only for every fifth or tenth issue age. We will refer to these as *pivotal issue ages*. The rates associated with pivotal issue ages will be referred to as *pivotal rates*. Once the design is finalized, the next step is to calculate rates and values for every issue age, using interpolation or other formulas. For pre-scheduled products, it may be necessary to calculate premium rates, death benefits, cash values, and dividends for every issue age. For dynamic products, it may be necessary to calculate cost of insurance rates, target premiums, and other rates for every issue age.

A common goal is a smooth progression of rates by issue age. However, discontinuities may sometimes be desirable. For example, the first issue age with separate smoker and nonsmoker rates may have a smoker premium rate that is significantly greater than the rate for the preceding age, as well as a nonsmoker rate that is significantly less. As another example, if the first-year commission rate drops 10% at a certain issue age, you may wish to have a discontinuity in the premium rates that reflects this drop.

Interpolation is the usual method for avoiding discontinuities. The interpolation can be applied to the pivotal rates to produce rates for every issue age. Another approach is to calculate ratios of the pivotal rates to some other set of rates, such as a mortality table. The ratios can be interpolated, and the interpolated ratios can then be multiplied by the other set of rates to determine the rates for each issue age. This more complicated procedure can be helpful when you wish to monitor the relationship between the rates being interpolated and the other set of rates. For example, when interpolating cost of insurance rates, you may wish to interpolate the ratio of COI rates to mortality rates. In the process, you could then ensure that COI rates are never less than mortality rates by allowing no ratios less than one.

When choosing an interpolation formula, you will probably want one that involves second or higher differences. You may also need an extrapolation formula to extend your pivotal rates to the highest and lowest issue ages.

Once you have interpolated rates for all issue ages, genders, risk classes, and policy sizes, the next step is to check for consistency. You may find inconsistencies that are due to data errors or incorrect calculations. A good check for consistency is to calculate first differences of the rates and see how they vary by issue age. You should be able to rationalize increases and decreases in these differences.

It is also helpful to compare different sets of rates to check for consistency. For example, to check a set of female preferred nonsmoker rates for the 250,000 to 999,999 size range, you could compare the rates to any of the following:

- The female preferred nonsmoker rates for the next lower size range
- The female preferred nonsmoker rates for the next higher size range
- The male preferred nonsmoker rates for the 250,000 size range
- The female standard nonsmoker rates for the 250,000 size range
- The corresponding rates for a similar product.

You may also want to compare differences between different sets of rates. For example, the differences from one size range to the next higher size range will usually be about the same for males and females, preferred and standard risks, and smokers and nonsmokers. Similarly, the differences between male preferred nonsmoker and male standard nonsmoker rates should be fairly independent of size range. Sometimes you can check for consistency between products. For example, life paid-up at 65 and 20-pay life should probably share the same rates at issue age 45.

Once rates have been calculated for all issue ages and checked for consistency, they are then loaded into the appropriate computer systems. Testing is needed to ensure that all rates and values have been loaded into the company's computer systems correctly and completely. There is often room for significant process improvement in this area.

Ideally, the process can be automated to use the pivotal rates developed in pricing to calculate and load the rates for all issue ages into the company's computer systems. This can lead to great improvements in the speed and accuracy of product implementation, as well as cost savings and less need for testing.

2.8.2   New Product Filings

Some jurisdictions require that a new life insurance product be filed with insurance regulators before it can be sold. Some go a step further and require regulatory approval before the product can be sold. In the U.S., each of the 50 states has different requirements that make this a long, slow, and difficult process. Not only must different materials be filed with each state, but also the policy form (insurance contract) must be changed for certain states. For some products, it can require more than a year to gain approval from the more difficult states.

In some countries, certain types of products may require approval from a financial regulator other than the insurance regulator. For example, in the U.S., variable products must be filed with and approved by the Securities and Exchange Commission, which regulates the U.S. stock markets.

2.8.3   Sales and Marketing

Deciding how the product will be marketed and sold is an important part of the design process. Early in the implementation phase, the marketing plan should be finalized. As part of implementation, the company may create tools to help the sales force find and contact prospective buyers. For example, by advertising, the company may make potential customers more receptive to buying. In some cases, advertising may motivate customers to contact agents or the company.

At a minimum, sales material will be produced to explain the product to the sales force and customers. This sales material will usually include descriptions of the product and all of its features, rates for all issue ages and risk classes, underwriting requirements, and application forms. Increasingly, this material is given to the sales force in electronic form.

Software is usually provided to enable the agent to illustrate the financial results of buying the product. Because of past abuses, a number of countries have introduced regulations that require full disclosure of the product and, sometimes, the agent's commission. For example, if the company illustrates values it expects or hopes to pay, regulations may require the company to also illustrate the absolute minimum values it guarantees.

Some companies provide software to allow agents to illustrate more sophisticated sales concepts. For example, it may be possible for the employer and employee to split premiums and benefits as follows: The employee pays a small part of the premium, equal to each year's cost of insurance or mortality cost. The employer pays the remainder of the premium, which builds the policy's cash value. The employer is ultimately reimbursed for its portion of the premiums, through either death benefits or cash values. The employee receives the rest of the death benefit and any excess cash value, often at a very attractive price with favorable tax treatment. This is called a *split dollar* plan. There are many specialized sales concepts, such as endowments used to repay mortgages that don't amortize and life insurance used to fund children's education.

How a product is introduced to the sales force may have a lot to do with how well the product sells. For example, if an agent learns about a new product by receiving a package of boring material, it may be hard to get very enthusiastic. The company may be able to improve results by carefully designing the package to catch the agent's interest. Better results are often achieved by personally introducing the product, through agent meetings or one-on-one visits from agent management or company employees. Some companies time new product introductions to coincide with agency conferences. Some go to great lengths to professionally produce video or audio presentations to introduce new products to the sales force.

2.9 Product Management

Product work does not end with the introduction of the product. Managing the product can be just as important to the product's success as the product design. Most manufacturers never again see consumer goods after they are shipped. In contrast, life insurance products never leave the manufacturer. The company must provide administration, accounting, and policyowner service and be subject to insurance risk throughout the product's lifetime. Many consumer goods, such as food, last for days, while some, such as cars, last for years. However, few consumer goods last as long as a life insurance product's lifetime. A whole life product that insures a newborn baby may have a product lifetime of over a century! There are few longer-term commitments than life insurance product management.

Companies organize their product management resources in a number of ways. Product management may be part of the marketing area or the product development area. It may be a part of corporate finance. There are four main purposes behind product management:

1. Manage sales of the product, usually with a goal of maximizing sales or profits

2. Ensure the product is performing as planned, especially in the area of profit margins

3. Develop pricing data that will help in the design of the next generation of products

4. Make ongoing adjustments to keep the product in line with profit goals or commitments made to policyowners.

2.9.1 Manage Sales

Many consumer goods manufacturers have product managers who control all marketing aspects of a product, by managing its design, packaging, advertising, and pricing. One person is responsible for the product's sales and profits. This person carefully tracks the sales of the product and constantly looks for ways to increase sales and profits.

Competitors are also tracked, and their moves are countered by swift reactions.

In contrast, some life insurance companies introduce a product with great fanfare and then seem to forget about it. However, the more successful companies actively manage their products to get the most sales out of them. New sales ideas may be shared with agents to remind them of the product. Special promotions or incentives may feature products the company wishes to emphasize. Product features or underwriting requirements may be fine-tuned to make products more attractive. This kind of active management can stretch the lifetime of a product and delay the need for a replacement.

In some countries, there are strict regulations that guide how products can be sold. The company may need to ensure that proper sales processes are being followed. There may be strict requirements related to sales illustrations. Regulations may also require that adequate disclosure and explanations are given to customers.

2.9.2 Ensure Adequacy of Profits

When a product is developed, many assumptions are made. If actual experience differs from assumptions in a significant way, sales of the product may have to be suspended or a new product may have to be quickly developed as a replacement. For example, if mortality, persistency, or interest margins are materially different from assumptions, the product may be inadequately priced. In some cases, the product can be easily adjusted to reflect actual experience. For example, credited interest rates and cost of insurance rates can usually be adjusted for universal life. This is discussed in Section 2.9.4.

Often, the differences between actual experience and assumptions are not material. For example, a difference in distribution by issue age may not be important if all the issue ages have about the same profit margin. Actual experience is not always credible, such as poor mortality experience resulting from one large death claim.

2.9.3   Develop Pricing Data

A company's existing products are often the best source of information for pricing future products. A company's past mortality and persistency experience is usually a good predictor of future experience for similar products. Underwriting characteristics, such as cholesterol levels and blood pressure, can be studied and used to refine future mortality assumptions and risk classes. The distribution of business between smokers and nonsmokers, males and females, issue age groups, and the percentage of business reinsured for recent products may apply to similar products to be developed in the future.

2.9.4   Make Ongoing Product Adjustments

Many products have features that allow the company to adjust to changes in interest rates, mortality levels, and other factors. Adjustments may be needed to meet the original profit goals or to honor commitments made to policyowners.

Participating products have dividends that are routinely adjusted to reflect changes in interest rates, mortality experience, and expense levels. Universal life products have credited interest rates and cost of insurance rates that can be adjusted. Some products have nonguaranteed elements, such as premiums, cash values, and death benefits that can be adjusted as conditions change.

When faced with adjustments that will negatively affect the policyowner, the company should carefully consider the effect on persistency. For example, when credited interest rates are decreased, many policyowners may decide to terminate their insurance. If this happens in the early policy years, the company may lose the opportunity to recoup its acquisition costs in the future. Because of this, the company may sometimes be better off by not decreasing interest rates.

2.10   Exercises

Exercise 2.1

Using the target market attributes discussed in Section 2.2.1, explain why each of the following would not be considered good target markets:

1. Sales to be made through a variety of distribution channels, including telemarketing, the Internet, and agent solicitation

2. Persons belonging to and employed by a specific religious order

3. Frequent visitors to the Internet site *www.HangGlidein20Minutes.com*

4. Persons residing in the northeastern section of the country of Fredonia.

Exercise 2.2

What core competencies would be most important for the following products or markets?

1. Level term insurance

2. Debit or home insurance sales

3. High-income market

4. Universal life insurance.

Exercise 2.3

How would you organize the product development function? Why would you organize that way?

Exercise 2.4

Explain the buyer-oriented pricing strategy employed by each of the following companies:

1. Company A carefully sells products under a well-recognized name to people with incomes in the top 10%. Similar products, with prices roughly 20% to 25% higher, are sold to a lower-income market by a different distribution system and under a less-recognized name.

2. Company B constantly researches new, emerging trends in the market and is able to design and introduce products with new features, always staying one step ahead of the rest of the market. When competitors catch up and introduce similar products, their prices are always lower.

3. Company C sets its term insurance premiums so that its prices are about average, when compared to other, comparable products.

4. Company D is started from scratch by a wealthy agent. Term products have the lowest price in the market and are fully guaranteed. Investment products have the highest crediting rates in the market and illustrate the best cash values.

Exercise 2.5

Name the competitor-oriented pricing strategy employed in the following situations:

1. Company A is absolutely committed to having the lowest-cost term product on the market. Monitoring of the competition is constant. Changes in price can be made within a matter of weeks. Fifty percent market share is desired.

2. Company B is government-owned and the sole provider of reinsurance to the companies licensed in the country.

3. Country C strictly controls all products and rates. As a result, all companies in Country C offer the same products at the same rates.

4. Company D has spent millions to develop the best and most-efficient underwriting, policy issue, and administration systems. In order to fully utilize the investment in infrastructure it has made, prices are lowered to generate a large increase in sales.

5. Market E is dominated by a small number of companies. They monitor each other's products and rates. Employees of these companies know each other and frequently discuss product and pricing strategies. A move by one company is usually immediately matched by the others.

Exercise 2.6

What types of market research do you think are the most essential? Why?

Exercise 2.7

You are the actuary for a medium-sized company, with sales distribution concentrated in the Northwest. Your company primarily sells term insurance, concentrating on middle-income workers. Your underwriting process is very efficient, and mortality results and profits have been excellent for several years.

Your chief of marketing has noticed an article in the national newspaper. The government desires to spur personal savings in the Northeast, where savings rates have historically been low. A law has been passed that enables those living in the northeastern part of the country to deduct from their taxable income any premiums paid into whole life and universal life insurance programs. The marketing chief sees an opportunity and wants to go after it.

Discuss the feasibility of following the chief of marketing's recommendation.

Exercise 2.8

You have worked with the marketing and sales staff to develop the following grid of premium levels and profit margins. The company has been growing premiums at 15% per year and would like to continue to do so. The company will collect 350 million of total premiums this year. Examine the effect of the three price levels on premium growth and future profits. Which price level would you recommend? Why?

Assume the following:

1. The new product will be the only product sold next year. It will be responsible for all new premiums.
2. Next year's total premium will equal 90% of 350 million (assuming 10% of the current policies will terminate) plus the new premiums shown in the following table.

3. The contribution of the new product to future profit is equal to "PV of premium over product lifetime" times the profit margin shown in the following table.

Price Level	Estimate of New Premium (in millions)	PV of Premium over Product Lifetime (in millions)	Profit Margin
High	80.0	1,000.0	7.0%
Moderate	87.5	1,180.0	5.0
Low	95.0	1,400.0	3.5

Exercise 2.9

Assume that you are the product manager for your company's universal life line of business. One of your junior actuaries has recommended that the cost of insurance charges for a block of UL policies that have been in force for five years be increased 10%. You ask for reasons why they should be increased. You are told that since these policies have been in force a long period of time, the policyowners will not notice the increase, so why not take additional profit. What is your response?

2.11 Answers

Answer 2.1

1. Distribution channels do not define a target market.

2. Although such persons may be a good population to insure, the target market may not be large enough to make it worthwhile. However, those who follow a specific religion may constitute a large enough target market.

3. Although one could argue that these people have the insurance need and a way to be reached (that is, through the web site), people who are interested in dangerous sports may not be a good target market for life insurance.

4. Although concentrating in a specific region may make it easier to serve a target market, this definition is too broad; those living in this region will exhibit a wide range of income levels, education, and insurance needs.

Answer 2.2

The following core competencies would be advantageous for the following products or markets.

1. Level term insurance: operational efficiency, underwriting expertise and discipline, and low-cost distribution

2. Debit or home insurance sales: control of distribution

3. High-income market: financial strength, sophisticated product design, sophisticated distribution, sophisticated home office support, underwriting expertise, superior investment management, and superior service

4. Universal life insurance: efficient and sophisticated home office staff and administration systems, and investment management.

Answer 2.3

There is no single correct answer. There are many valid ways to organize the product development function. The answer will depend on the resources available, the time frame required, the culture and priorities of the company, and the complexity of the product.

Answer 2.4

1. Company A is using segmented pricing for its products. Different brands and approaches are used for different markets.

2. Company B believes it can use skim pricing to maintain profit margins. By always being the first on the street with a new design or feature, it can charge a high price for these features before the competition catches up. Once the competition catches up, the company moves on to a new, more profitable feature or product.

3. Company C is using neutral pricing, since it does not want to be on either extreme of the competitive spectrum.

4. Company D is using penetration pricing, since the profit margins on its products are probably small. This company wants to have an immediate effect and create name recognition by offering extremely competitive products.

Answer 2.5

1. Predatory

2. Independent

3. Cooperative

4. Opportunistic

5. Adaptive

Answer 2.6

Market research in the life insurance industry tends to be overly focused on the distribution system and tracking competitors, which may be a result of the perception that "insurance is sold, not bought." More insights and value may be gained by polling the ultimate buyers of life insurance.

Answer 2.7

An analysis should begin by answering the questions posed under Section 2.6.2.

Does the product fit the company? Your company has had success with term insurance. Although whole life and universal life may be offered, it may not be practical to implement a strong push for products that the company has not had to expend much time to manage in the past. The company seems to pride itself on the underwriting process. When selling cash value life insurance with favorable tax treatment, there may be pressure in the marketplace to issue the business with lower underwriting standards, under the assumption that the buyers are buying primarily to receive the tax benefit and not the insurance protection. Is the company prepared to loosen its underwriting standards in order to meet the demands of the marketplace?

Are there any regulatory barriers? At first glance, there does not seem to be any such barriers. However, the company may not be licensed to do business in all the particular subjurisdictions that may exist in the Northeast.

Are there any implementation barriers? Does the company have administration systems for whole life and universal life that are capable of handling a strong push into cash value life insurance? Does the company have adequate, knowledgeable staff to support the additional cash value business? Does the company have the investment expertise necessary to earn competitive investment returns? With its emphasis on term insurance, this may not be an area of strength for the company. The sales distribution has been concentrated in the Northwest, not the Northeast. This implies a small number of sales associates in the Northeast. Is the company ready to invest in developing sales staff there?

What effect will this product have on sales of the company's other products? The new product will probably not hurt the sales of the existing term business. Since the new product's market focus will be the Northeast, sales there should not cut too much into the sales of the term product, since those sales are concentrated in the Northwest. In fact, sales of the term product might actually increase as the sales force is expanded in the Northeast.

How will the company fare against the likely competition? You can expect that a number of companies will pounce on this opportunity. Those already entrenched in the Northeast and already specializing in cash value life insurance will have a significant competitive advantage over the company. As a result, the company could invest significantly to expand into the Northeast and to strengthen its cash value life insurance capabilities, only to find it is too late and has wasted time, effort, and substantial money. On the other hand, the Northeast cash value life insurance market could be the long-term key to the company's success. To ignore it might result in the company becoming a smaller, less-effective player in the insurance industry and unable to survive long term. This could be a crucial decision for the company. The right answer is unclear.

Answer 2.8

The company can expect the following total premiums, premium growth rates, and present value of future profits for the three different price levels:

Price Level	Total Premium (in millions)	Premium Growth Rate	Present Value of Future Profits (in millions)
High	$(350)(0.9) + 80.0 = 395.0$	12.86%	$(1,000.0)(0.070) = 70.0$
Moderate	$(350)(0.9) + 87.5 = 402.5$	15.00	$(1,180.0)(0.050) = 59.0$
Low	$(350)(0.9) + 95.0 = 410.0$	17.14	$(1,400.0)(0.035) = 49.0$

The company has an interesting choice to make:

1. By choosing high prices, the company could achieve the best present value of profits, but it would slow its growth rate. Slower growth could erode the company's stock price and long-term viability.

2. By choosing moderate prices, the company could achieve premium growth consistent with its recent experience, but with a much-less-than-optimal present value of profits.

3. By choosing low prices, the company could accelerate its premium growth without sacrificing too much in long-term profits, although its profit margin would be low. While this choice may look attractive, the profit margin may be insufficient in light of the risks associated with the product.

Companies are continually faced with decisions like these. Different companies make different choices, depending on their analysis of the conditions and what is valued the most by their owners.

Answer 2.9

For a product sold through an agency sales force, you should never underestimate the ability of the field force to identify unexpected changes in policy values. Agencies and their staffs monitor the performance of their companies' products. An unexpected increase in cost of insurance charges will most certainly be noticed.

Therefore, policyowners, with encouragement from their agents, will be more likely to surrender their policies. Some of the increased profits that may emerge because of higher cost of insurance charges will be offset by higher surrenders, and hence lower profits. In fact, surrender rates could increase high enough to offset the higher profit margins from the increased cost of insurance rates.

If the increase in cost of insurance rates is justifiable and explainable to the agency force, then increased surrenders may be minimized. However, a certain amount of dissatisfaction will occur, so some increased lapses should be expected.

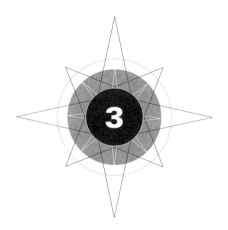

Pricing Assumptions

3.1 Introduction

When pricing a product, you will discover that assumptions are more important than the methods or formulas used. Pricing results are only as valid as the pricing assumptions: garbage in, garbage out. Determining assumptions is the most difficult and financially dangerous aspect of the pricing process. The future is impossible to predict. However, we can often develop a range of assumptions that encompass the most plausible possibilities. Sometimes a plausible range of assumptions is very narrow. Other times it is very wide. By testing such a range of assumptions and designing the product to adjust to future outcomes, you can substantially reduce the financial risk of the product.

The pricing assumptions common to most life insurance products can be divided into the following categories, with the first four usually being the most important:

Mortality

Lapse rates

Interest rates

Expenses

Average size

Sales distribution and volume.

This chapter focuses on this list of assumptions. We have omitted a number of assumptions that relate to specific products. For example, most variable products need assumptions for the customer's choice of investment funds, transfers between investment funds, and the performance of the investment funds. Waiver of premium benefits require disability assumptions. Critical illness benefits require assumptions as to the incidence of various critical illnesses. These are just a few examples of the product-specific assumptions not covered in this chapter. In addition, this chapter does not cover assumptions related to reserves, reinsurance, taxes, and capital requirements. Assumptions for these last four topics are covered in later chapters devoted to each topic.

For each assumption, it is important to understand how and why it may vary. Economic data can sometimes be useful when developing assumptions. Life insurance industry data are often a good source of benchmarks and industry averages. However, for every assumption, the company's own experience is usually the best source of relevant data for pricing. Subtle differences in the ways companies distribute their products and manage their business can translate to important differences in experience and assumptions.

This chapter first addresses each of the assumptions independently. Toward the end of the chapter, we explore interdependencies between different assumptions. For example, high lapse rates can often lead to poor mortality.

When developing assumptions, you should concentrate on the assumptions that are the most critical, the most volatile, or the most unknown. Using sensitivity testing, described in the last section of this chapter, you can determine which assumptions are the most critical to profitability. Sometimes assumptions are unknown. For example, if a company is introducing its first preferred risk product, it will have to rely on the experience of others. In such a case, consultants and reinsurers can be a valuable source of information or second opinions.

The following sections describe life insurance assumptions for mortality, lapse rates, interest rates, expenses, average size, and sale levels. Each section is organized along the following lines, with some exceptions:

1. Why the assumption varies

2. Sources of data

3. General variations

4. Variations by product

5. Trends.

Modifications to these assumptions for annuity products will be discussed in Chapter 13.

3.2 Mortality Assumptions

The most important assumption when pricing a life insurance product is often the mortality assumption. The mortality assumption determines what could potentially be the most costly policyowner benefit to be paid: death benefits. An incorrect assumption for the rate of mortality can have long-term implications for a company because of the long-term nature of most products.

3.2.1 Why Mortality Varies

There are many reasons why mortality experience varies from company to company. Here is a partial list of factors that can affect mortality:

• Personal risk factors: gender, age, medical history, diet, exercise, stress, use of tobacco, alcohol and drugs, family history (genetic tendencies), avocations, occupation, behavior (such as aggressive driving or driving while intoxicated), family (especially presence of a spouse), activity level, social interactions, education, income level, financial condition, and mental condition.

• Environmental risk factors, such as air and water pollution.

- Location risk factors, such as higher exposure to ultraviolet radiation in the Southern Hemisphere (leading to a higher incidence of skin cancer) and exposure to more infectious diseases in certain tropical areas.

- Quality, accessibility, cost, and extent of available medical care, especially preventative care (inoculations, routine testing, and physical exams), emergency care, and medical treatments for major conditions (such as coronary bypass surgery, chemotherapy, and radiation therapy).

- Cultural differences: In some countries, insurance fraud may be more common, suicide may be considered an honorable way to solve a personal problem, guns may be widely available, or violence may be more common.

- Underwriting differences, such as (a) the training of underwriters, (b) the methods and tools used to underwrite, (c) the company's approach to borderline risks (aggressive, balanced, or conservative), (d) the consistency of underwriting, (e) the role played by agents in the underwriting process (whether they tend to bring potential areas of concern to the company's attention or ignore them), and (f) the information collected for underwriting (medical questionnaire, medical examination, blood test, urine sample, and so on).

- Wars, other types of armed conflict, epidemics, and natural disasters, such as typhoons, earthquakes, and floods.

In summary, mortality varies by country, company, and the personal characteristics of each insured.

3.2.2 Mortality Tables

In the major life insurance markets, life insurance industry mortality studies are performed. The results of these studies are large tables of mortality rates, called mortality tables. Usually, separate tables are developed for males and females. Increasingly, separate mortality tables are being developed for smokers and nonsmokers. There are three basic types of mortality tables.

An aggregate table has rates that vary only by the attained age of the insured. If mortality experience for the early or "select" policy years has been excluded, then the table is called an *ultimate table.*

A select table has rates that vary by both issue age and policy year. The word "select" refers to the lower mortality obtained by selecting the best risks through the underwriting process. The effect of selection is often negligible at the younger issue ages and substantial at the older issue ages. The effect of selection wears off over time, although the effect can sometimes be observed 20 or 30 years after issue for some of the higher issue ages.

A select and ultimate table is a combination of the previous two types of mortality tables. Usually the select table is used for the first 15 to 25 policy years, and the ultimate table is used thereafter. Most products in most major life insurance markets use select and ultimate mortality tables for pricing.

Table 3.2.1 illustrates the significant difference between select mortality and ultimate mortality. Mortality rates are generally so small that they are normally expressed as rates per 1,000. For example, rather than expressing a mortality rate as 0.01046 or 1.046%, it is standard practice to express it as 10.46 per 1,000. "Per 1,000" is often omitted. Compare the rates for three insureds, currently 60-year-olds, who were underwritten at different times:

1. A newly underwritten 60-year-old (issue age 60, policy year 1) has a mortality rate of 10.46 per 1,000.

2. A 60-year-old underwritten five years earlier (issue age 55, policy year 6) has a mortality rate of 15.17 per 1,000.

3. A 60-year-old underwritten ten years earlier (attained age 60, policy year 11) has a mortality rate of 19.50, almost double the rate for a newly underwritten 60-year-old.

Table 3.2.1 Mortality Rates Per Thousand

Issue Age	Policy Year											Attained Age
	1	*2*	*3*	*4*	*5*	*6*	*7*	*8*	*9*	*10*	*11+*	
50	4.87	5.51	6.15	6.93	7.83	9.30	10.69	12.06	13.40	14.77	19.50	60
51	5.24	5.95	6.69	7.57	8.61	10.29	11.76	13.24	14.75	16.32	21.47	61
52	5.64	6.45	7.29	8.29	9.48	11.37	12.90	14.53	16.23	18.04	23.65	62
53	6.08	6.99	7.96	9.09	10.43	12.53	14.14	15.93	17.85	19.95	26.05	63
54	6.57	7.60	8.70	9.95	11.44	13.79	15.49	17.47	19.65	22.06	28.69	64
55	7.11	8.27	9.50	10.86	12.54	15.17	16.96	19.16	21.62	24.39	31.57	65
56	7.70	8.91	10.20	11.62	13.44	16.20	18.25	20.69	23.33	26.55	34.68	66
57	8.33	9.58	10.95	12.44	14.41	17.33	19.64	22.34	25.16	28.85	38.00	67
58	8.99	10.29	11.75	13.32	15.46	18.55	21.15	24.12	27.10	31.28	41.60	68
59	9.70	11.06	12.62	14.28	16.61	19.87	22.77	26.00	29.12	33.88	45.54	69
60	10.46	11.89	13.57	15.32	17.85	21.28	24.48	27.97	31.28	36.71	49.90	70

Figure 3.2.1 illustrates mortality rates from Table 3.2.1 for attained ages 60–70 and issue ages 50, 55, and 60. The rates shown for issue age

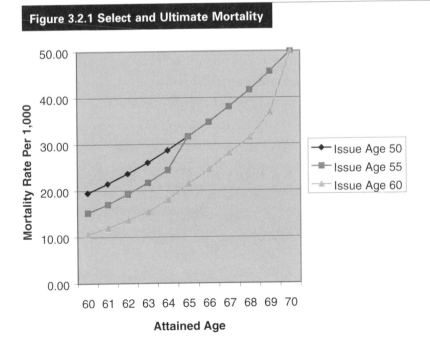

Figure 3.2.1 Select and Ultimate Mortality

50 are all ultimate rates. The first five rates shown for issue age 55 are select; the last six rates are ultimate. The first ten rates shown for issue age 60 are select. Pay particular attention to the discontinuities that occur when select rates give way to ultimate rates at ages 65 and 70. Such discontinuities indicate that a longer select period may be appropriate.

To develop a reliable select and ultimate mortality table, many years of data are needed, and tens of thousands (if not hundreds of thousands) of deaths are needed in the study. As a result, most select and ultimate mortality tables are constructed from industry data obtained by pooling the results of many companies. Larger companies, especially those contributing to the industry mortality table, usually analyze their mortality results as a percentage of the industry table. Some smaller companies may not have the resources to analyze their mortality results. As a result, they may assume that they experience average mortality.

Using the industry average for mortality can be dangerous. Mortality varies widely from company to company because of many factors, such as target markets and underwriting standards. The companies with the lowest mortality may experience half the mortality of the companies with the highest mortality. If the company's mortality results cannot be analyzed, at the very least, the company should analyze the factors that affect mortality before setting mortality assumptions.

In a number of countries, industry mortality tables are developed with aggregate mortality rates instead of select and ultimate mortality rates. This is usually done when insufficient data exist to develop reliable select mortality rates or when the effect of selection is not felt to be significant. Not surprisingly, companies based in countries without select mortality tables tend to base their mortality assumptions solely on aggregate mortality tables. A variation of this approach is to use a reduced percentage of aggregate mortality for the first few policy years. For example, the first-year mortality rate might be 50% of the aggregate rate, and the second-year mortality rate might be 75%. Using the same reduced percentages for all issue ages will tend to overstate the effect of selection at the younger ages and understate the effect at the older ages.

In some countries, no industry studies of insured mortality exist. However, there often are government studies of mortality for the overall population. If large economic disparities exist between the average person in the population and the average insured person, population mortality may be useless as a base for insured mortality. If there are small economic disparities, however, population mortality may be a reasonable starting point for insured mortality. It is difficult to determine how to modify population mortality to reflect the effect of underwriting. If you can find another country with similar conditions affecting mortality and with similar underwriting practices, you may be able to make use of that country's mortality experience. The relationship of insured mortality to population mortality may be similar for both countries.

Figure 3.2.2 illustrates male mortality rates for eight different countries. The use of a logarithmic scale results in a fairly straight line

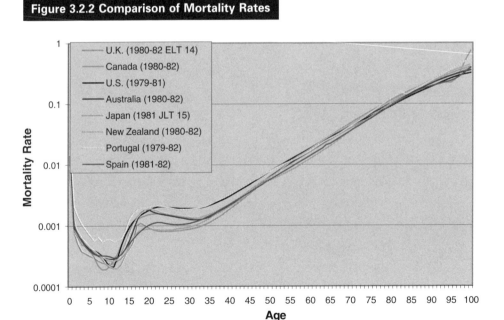

Figure 3.2.2 Comparison of Mortality Rates

Source: The Society of Actuaries (www.soa.org).

from age 35 to age 85. This means that mortality rates increase at an almost-constant percentage over this age range. Were it not for the high rate of accidental deaths experienced by teenagers and young adults, the constant percentage increase in mortality might otherwise start at age 10.

Figure 3.2.3 shows the differences in life expectancies for the same eight countries illustrated in the previous graph. The life expectancy shown is for a newborn male and is calculated by the following formula:

$$\text{Life expectancy} = \sum_{x=1}^{\infty} (x)(\text{Probability of dying at age } x). \qquad (3.2.1)$$

Mortality assumptions are normally expressed as a percentage of a mortality table. In some cases, a company will modify an industry mortality table to reflect additional refinements such as the following:

• A longer select period, so select mortality rates grade smoothly into ultimate mortality rates for the older issue ages

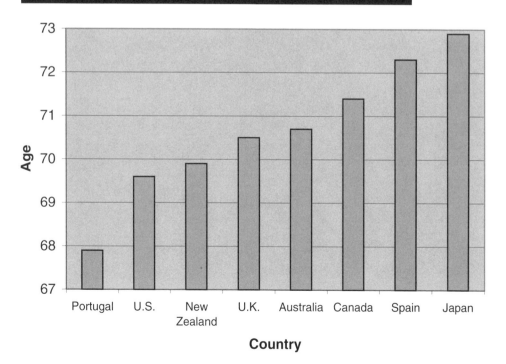

Figure 3.2.3 Newborn Male Life Expectancy (Average Age at Death)

- Interpolation of mortality rates for intermediate issue ages, if the industry mortality table provides rates only for, say, every fifth issue age
- Extension of the mortality table to higher issue ages
- Changes in mortality since the underlying data for the industry table were assembled
- Smoker and nonsmoker versions of the mortality table
- Preferred and residual ("nonpreferred") versions of the mortality table.

When making such modifications, extra care should be taken to avoid unintended distortions. A common technique is to require that a weighted average of the mortality produced by the modified table(s) matches that of the original table. For example, when you review Table 3.2.1, you can observe a significant discontinuity between policy year 10 and policy year 11. This discontinuity could be reduced by extending the select period to 15 years. However, to do so would lower the mortality rates for years 11–15 below the original rates for those years. To compensate, you could raise the ultimate mortality rates (for policy years 16+) until the weighted average of all mortality rates matches that of the original table. The weights used for the weighted average would reflect the company's expected distribution of business by issue age and policy year.

An example of such a modification is shown in Figure 3.2.4. Only policy years 10–20 are shown, since there is no modification to policy years 1–10. The original table has a discontinuity between years 10 and 11. The modified table smoothes this discontinuity by increasing the ultimate rates by 2.65%, and by linearly interpolating the rates between years 10 and 16.

3.2.3 General Mortality Variations

Some variations in mortality are well known:

Females have lower mortality than males, all other factors being equal. While the difference between female and male mortality varies

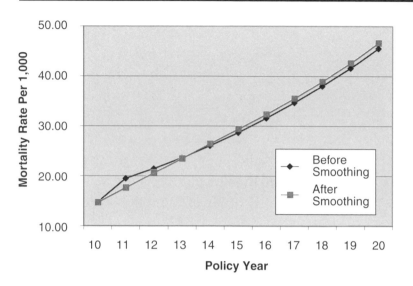

Figure 3.2.4 Smoothing Discontinuities between Select and Ultimate Rates

significantly by age and is changing over time, rough approximations are sometimes used: Female mortality might be set equal to a percentage (usually between 50% and 80%) of male mortality. Alternatively, female mortality rates might be set equal to those for a male three to seven years younger.

Non-tobacco users have lower mortality than tobacco users. The difference varies by age, gender, type of tobacco usage, and the extent of usage. At some ages a heavy smoker may have three times the mortality rate of a lifetime nonsmoker. Light smokers and some pipe and cigar smokers may have only one-and-a-half times the mortality rate of nonsmokers. The overall ratio of smoker to nonsmoker mortality often exceeds two to one. Tobacco usage often has a bigger effect on mortality than gender has.

Education and income level have an effect on mortality. Generally, mortality improves as economic status improves. Economic status can affect the quality and availability of medical care, personal habits (diet, exercise, preventive care), and exposure to risk. In the U.S., those with high incomes have about half the mortality rates of those with low incomes. In some less developed countries, the differences are even more dramatic. There is one interesting anomaly: The working rich, with much less free time on their hands, generally have lower mortality than the idle rich, who sometimes use their free time to engage in riskier behavior.

Size of policy, which is strongly correlated with education and income level, is an important indicator for mortality. It is quite possible for mortality at the smallest policy sizes to be twice as high as mortality for the largest policy sizes. Mortality generally improves as the size of policy increases. However, some studies show mortality increases for the very highest amounts of insurance. In particular, see John M. Bragg and Associates, Inc. (Atlanta, GA), "Bragg Study of Mortality by Policy Size Group."

If the company has had the same underwriting practices in place for a long time, its past mortality experience may be all it needs to develop mortality assumptions. More often, underwriting practices have changed over the years, making it difficult to use past experience to estimate future results. Here are some common changes to underwriting practices:

- The company has added one or more new risk classifications, such as preferred or nonsmoker classes.

- The company has changed its requirements for underwriting information, such as urine specimens, blood tests, or medical examinations. For example, because of the spread of AIDS, many companies began requiring blood tests at much lower policy sizes in the late 1980s. More often, requirements are adjusted to keep pace with competitors' requirements or to reflect changes in the relative costs and benefits of different requirements. For example, as a new test becomes widely used, its cost usually drops, and it becomes cost effective for lower policy sizes.

Industry mortality studies may distinguish between different types of underwriting. For example, the Society of Actuaries has tracked mortality results separately for three different types of underwriting over a period of many years:

1. Medical (examined by a doctor)

2. Paramedical (questions and medical tests administered by a nurse), and

3. Nonmedical (questions about medical history answered by the insured).

Now that some companies are using agents to collect oral fluids and other bodily samples, a fourth category may be needed. This kind of information can be very helpful when a company decides to change the issue ages and policy sizes at which medical and paramedical exams will be required. The medical/paramedical/nonmedical mortality studies can help the company determine whether proposed changes in underwriting requirements make financial sense, as well as help the company develop new mortality assumptions that reflect such changes.

Figure 3.2.5 compares mortality ratios from 1974 to 1991. The ratios shown are ratios of actual mortality to expected mortality, based on the Society of Actuaries' 1965–70 Basic Mortality Table. More detailed information can be obtained from the annual mortality reports

Figure 3.2.5 Select Mortality Ratios

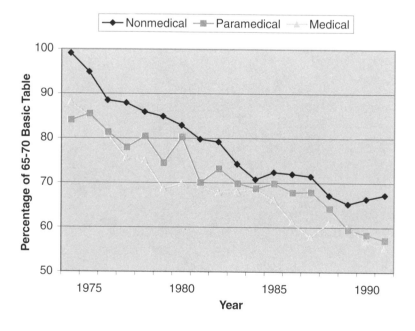

available on the SOA's web site (www.soa.org). Examining this figure we find:

1. Medical mortality ratios showed tremendous improvement between 1974 and 1979 (dropping 22%), very little improvement from 1979 to 1984, and considerable improvement from 1984 to 1991 (dropping 19%). Over these 17 years, medical mortality experienced an average improvement of 2.69% per year.

2. Paramedical mortality ratios fluctuated considerably more than medical mortality, but roughly followed the same trend. Overall, paramedical mortality ratios decreased by an average of 2.24% per year.

3. Nonmedical mortality ratios dropped an average of 2.25% per year.

These mortality ratios dropped much faster than the rate at which U.S. population mortality improved during the same period. The difference is due to a shift in the buying population and improvements in the underwriting process. These factors will be discussed further in Section 3.2.5.

Figure 3.2.6 shows select (policy years 1–15) and ultimate (policy years 16 and later) mortality ratios for the period 1974–91. During this

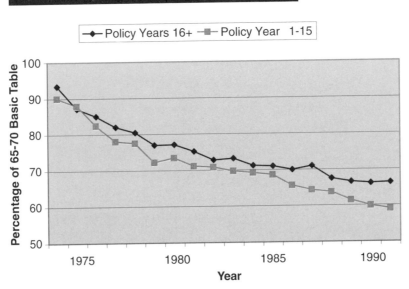

Figure 3.2.6 Select and Ultimate Mortality Ratios

period, select mortality improved an average of 2.46% per year, and ultimate mortality improved an average of 1.99% per year. As with the previous figure, these averages far exceed the underlying rate of mortality improvement for the U.S. population for the same period.

When selling to large groups of insureds, especially employee groups, it is common to use a streamlined approach to underwriting:

Guaranteed issue underwriting usually requires that eligible insureds meet only one underwriting requirement: that they have been actively working a minimum number of hours per week for a certain number of months with no significant medical absences. Eligible employees must become insured when they are first eligible. If they decline insurance and later change their minds, full medical underwriting is usually required. (Otherwise, employees could wait to purchase insurance until they have a serious medical problem.) Guaranteed issue underwriting usually carries with it a number of limits related to the size of the group and the amount of death benefit. Death benefits are often set as a multiple of salary. Any exception to the limits would require full medical underwriting. Guaranteed issue underwriting is commonly used for group life insurance. Group life mortality studies can be useful sources for guaranteed issue mortality data.

Simplified issue underwriting works much the same as guaranteed issue underwriting, with the addition of one or more questions about the insured's medical history. The fewer the number of questions, the longer the questions tend to be. If the questions turn up any significant medical concerns, full medical underwriting may be an option. Some leeway is usually given for minor medical concerns.

Compared to nonmedical underwriting, simplified issue (SI) underwriting involves many fewer medical questions. Therefore, SI underwriting screens out fewer unhealthy risks. As a result, the mortality associated with SI underwriting is generally higher than that associated with nonmedical underwriting. However, compared to guaranteed issue (GI) underwriting, SI underwriting involves more medical questions and screens out more unhealthy risks. Therefore, SI mortality is generally lower than GI mortality.

3.2.3.1 Risk Classes

Over the history of life insurance, the trend has been toward increased risk stratification. The earliest forms of life insurance charged the same premiums for all participants, regardless of age. This often ended in financial disaster, as such schemes tended to attract those more likely to die. As knowledge was gained during the nineteenth century, life insurance programs switched to premiums that varied by issue age, recognizing that mortality varied by age. By the middle of the twentieth century, premiums also varied by gender, although the most common approach was to equate females with males a few years younger, using an age setback.

The latter part of the twentieth century saw the introduction of new risk classifications: smoker/nonsmoker rates in virtually every major life insurance market, and preferred/residual rates in North America and a few other markets. Prior to the advent of nonsmoker and preferred classes, the underwriting process separated risks only between standard risks, multiple levels of substandard risks, and uninsurable risks. Nonsmoker and preferred classes have essentially added "superstandard" risks. Smoker and residual risks can be thought of as mildly substandard risks.

When a group of lives is split into two or more risk classes, it is common practice to tie the new mortality assumptions to the old mortality assumptions. This is accomplished by requiring a match between the weighted averages of the new mortality assumptions for the new risk classes and the original mortality assumptions for the original group of lives.

Example 3.2.1 Reproducing Original Mortality Assumption

For example, suppose the original group of lives has a mortality assumption of 100% of some mortality table. Suppose the group is split into nonsmoker and smoker groups, with smokers expected to be one-third of the total. Suppose smoker mortality ("S") is expected to be double nonsmoker mortality ("NS"). This leads to the following equations:

$$100\% = \frac{1}{3} S + \frac{2}{3} NS,$$

$$S = 2 NS.$$

Solving these two equations, we find NS = 75% and S = 150% of original mortality.

The distribution of the three groups is shown in a simplified fashion in Table 3.2.2. The original group shows the range of mortality ratios for a group of lives before they are split into two new risk classes. The weighted-average mortality ratio for the original group is 100%. The other two distributions represent the range of mortality ratios for the two new risk classes: one for the nonsmokers and one for the smokers. The nonsmokers total two-thirds of the group (95 out of 142.5), and the weighted-average mortality ratio is 75%. The smokers total one-third of the group (47.50 out of 142.5), and the weighted-average mortality ratio is 150%.

Table 3.2.2 Distribution of Insured Risks

Mortality Ratio	Original Group		Nonsmokers		Smokers	
	Weight	*Weight × Ratio*	*Weight*	*Weight × Ratio*	*Weight*	*Weight × Ratio*
25%	15.00	3.75	15.00	3.75	0.00	0.00
50	15.00	7.50	15.00	7.59	0.00	0.00
75	30.00	22.50	30.00	22.50	0.00	0.00
100	32.50	32.50	25.00	25.00	7.50	7.50
125	17.50	21.88	10.00	12.50	7.50	9.38
150	15.00	22.50	0.00	0.00	15.00	22.50
175	12.50	21.88	0.00	0.00	12.50	21.88
200	5.00	10.00	0.00	0.00	5.00	10.00
Total	142.50	142.50	95.00	71.25	47.50	71.25
Weighted-Average Mortality Ratio		100%		75%		150%

When stratifying a group of insureds, one has to be mindful that where you set the dividing line (that is, at what level of mortality) has two basic effects:

1. It determines the average mortality rate for both new groups. The higher the level of mortality at the dividing line, the higher the mortality for *both* groups.

2. Your dividing line interacts with your competitor's dividing lines, unless you sell through agents who never face competition. You can set your dividing lines so you can skim the cream (that is, attract the best risks) away from your competitors, or they can set their dividing lines to do the same to you. The resulting mortality is a mixture of the average mortality you would expect with no competition (some agents and insureds don't shop around) and mortality that reflects the effect of skimming, both pro and con.

As another example, the original group of lives could be nonsmoker risks. The better risks could be preferred nonsmoker risks, and the worse risks could be the residual nonsmoker risks. There are many possible dividing lines between preferred and residual risks. Preferred criteria can be set along a wide spectrum, ranging from only a small percentage qualifying for preferred rates to almost everyone qualifying for preferred rates.

Breaking a group of lives into two groups can affect assumptions beyond mortality:

- Those who qualify for the lowest rates can be expected to have a higher placement rate (that is, the percentage of those who apply for insurance who actually pay for a policy). Those who don't qualify for the lowest rates will tend to be disappointed and have a much lower placement rate. In addition, they may be more apt to shop around for another company that will rate them as a better risk. Placement rates have a big effect on acquisition costs. For example, if only half of the policies applied for and underwritten are ultimately placed, many acquisition costs are effectively doubled.

- Lapse rates are generally lower for those who qualify for the lowest rates, since they tend to feel they have gotten a good deal. Lapse rates are higher for those who don't qualify for the lowest rates, as some feel they have not gotten a good deal.

- The average policy size tends to be higher for those who qualify for the lowest rates. Because of the lower rates, they can afford to purchase more. In addition, they are usually willing to buy more because of the perception of getting a good deal. Conversely, the average policy size is usually lower for those who do not qualify for the lowest rates.

Table 3.2.3 shows sample criteria that might be used to select preferred nonsmoker risks. In practice, there is much diversity in preferred criteria between companies and countries.

Table 3.2.3 Sample Nonsmoker Preferred and Residual Criteria

	Preferred Criteria	*Residual Criteria*
Nonsmoker Definition	No *tobacco* for more than three years	No *cigarettes* for more than one year
Blood Pressure	Lower or equal to 130/80	Lower or equal to 155/95
Total Cholesterol	Lower or equal to 200	Lower or equal to 325
Total Cholesterol to HDL	Lower or equal to 4.5	Lower or equal to 7.5
Build Requirement (for a male 5'10")	Lower or equal to 190 lbs.	Lower or equal to 220 lbs.
Family History	No immediate family member has died of or been diagnosed with cardiovascular disease or diabetes prior to age 65	Not applicable
Personal History	No history of cancer, diabetes, or CVD	No ratable history of cancer, diabetes, or CVD
Motor Vehicle Record	No DWI in last ten years; no moving violations in last three years	No DWI in last three years; no more than three moving violations in last three years
Drugs and Alcohol	No history of excessive use or treatment for drug and alcohol	No excessive use or treatment for drug and alcohol in last five years
Avocation or Occupation	No ratable or modified hazardous sports and no private aviation	No ratable or modified hazardous sports, but some private aviation allowed
Bankruptcy	None in last ten years	Not applicable
Criminal History	None in last ten years	Not applicable
Foreign Residence or Travel	None anticipated and none in last three years	Not applicable

3.2.3.2   Effect of Lying

When a company adds new risk classes, it will often sell a higher percentage of the lower-priced risk classes than a historical analysis of past sales would have predicted. Using basic economic principles, this should be expected. When the price for a product is lowered, sales increase. When the price for a product is raised, sales decrease. By introducing lower rates for healthier lives, the company has lowered the price for those lives and should expect to increase its sales to those lives. Similarly, if the company raises prices for the unhealthier lives, it should expect its sales to those lives to decrease.

When a company introduces a lower-priced risk class, the company should consider the incentive it is creating. Some prospective insureds may lie in order to receive a more favorable risk class and better value. The policy application and underwriting process should be designed to minimize the ability to receive a better value by lying.

The issue of lying can be illustrated by discussing nonsmokers and smokers. The illustration, though, can apply to any significant underwriting criteria, such as drug use, AIDS, or cholesterol levels.

Example 3.2.2 Effect of Lying about Smoking Habits

The discount for being a nonsmoker can be substantial. For some term insurance products, nonsmokers pay roughly half of what smokers must pay. This may create a strong incentive for the applicant to lie about smoking habits, especially if there were no urine specimen or other medical test that would detect nicotine use.

Suppose a company offers voluntary group life insurance with different rates for smokers and nonsmokers. Assume the group is one-third smokers and two-thirds nonsmokers. If one-tenth of the smokers (3.33%) lie about smoking, the company will collect smoker premiums on only 30.0% of the risks. This means the company's premiums will be based on 30% smoker and 70% nonsmoker. If the average smoker premium rate is 4.00 per 1,000 and the average nonsmoker premium rate is 2.00 per 1,000, the company's average premium rate will be 2.60 per 1,000.

Suppose mortality rates are 3.80 per 1,000 for smokers and 1.90 per 1,000 for nonsmokers. On the surface, this would seem to allow a 5% margin between premium rates and mortality rates. If expenses are 3% of premium, this leaves only 2% for profits. Now examine the effect of the liars. The average mortality rate is based on one-third smoker and two-thirds nonsmoker, or 2.53 per 1,000. When compared to the average premium rate of 2.60, this leaves a margin of only 2.7% of premium, which is not even enough to cover expenses! In this example, the liars have turned a thin profit margin into a small expected loss.

It is prudent to determine the extent of lying about smoking habits and other underwriting criteria. This can be determined by checking a random sample of policies. If the percentage lying is acceptably small, this may already be included in industry mortality experience. However, if the percentage lying is unacceptably high, action should be taken. For example, if analyzing smoking habits, the application may need to ask more questions about tobacco use. The company may need to make greater use of nicotine tests, in connection with urine specimens. In some cases, the problem may be corrected by dealing with a small number of agents who may be causing most of the problem.

Significantly lower mortality rates are exhibited by preferred nonsmokers, when compared to residual (also known as nonpreferred or standard) nonsmokers. The same is true for preferred smokers compared to residual smokers. These differences depend on the strictness of the underwriting requirements for a given company. For example, for the nonsmokers, factors may vary by the length of time since cessation of smoking or whether the person never smoked. For smokers, differences can be caused by the amount of tobacco usage, or even the type of tobacco used. For example, cigar smokers may be classified as smokers, but their mortality may be less than that of a heavy cigarette smoker. The percentage difference between preferred and residual mortality may decrease somewhat over time. For example, the residual risk class may exhibit 50% higher mortality in the early years, but the difference may reduce to 40–45% in the later policy years. (Source: John M. Bragg and Associates, Inc. (Atlanta, GA), "New Bragg Preferred/Standard Life Tables and Guides to Underwriting.")

3.2.4   Mortality Variations by Product

Most industry mortality studies present results for all life insurance products combined. However, mortality can vary significantly by product, primarily because of the workings of anti-selection.

3.2.4.1   Anti-selection at Time of Underwriting

Insureds who know or suspect something adverse about their chances of survival tend to buy cheaper forms of life insurance, such as term insurance. For example, some people who suspect they have cancer will buy life insurance before they consult a doctor. In some cases, a person is able to buy life insurance after finding out about a terminal medical condition by concealing it from the insurance company. However, this strategy can backfire when the insurance company investigates an early death and discovers fraud or misrepresentation. Someone contemplating suicide may purchase a large life insurance policy and then kill himself in a way that does not look like suicide, such as by crashing a car or private plane.

In summary, the cheaper forms of life insurance tend to have higher mortality, especially in the early years. The least expensive forms of term insurance may have the highest mortality.

3.2.4.2 Effect of Premium Increases

When a product has a premium increase, some policyowners elect to cancel the insurance rather than pay the increased premium. The larger the percentage increase in premium, the greater the percentage of policyowners who will lapse.

Increasing premium term insurance tends to have the highest lapse rates of any product because of this effect. In addition, since healthier policyowners are more likely to lapse, the mortality of the remaining policyowners tends to worsen over time. Increasing premium term products, with higher than normal lapse rates, often experience mortality deterioration over time, when compared to the normal pattern of select mortality.

Some level term products have a spike in premiums at the end of the level term period that is intended to drive away virtually all remaining policyowners. For example, suppose premiums increase by 300% after ten years of level premiums. Suppose healthy insureds can purchase a replacement policy for a 100% increase in premium. Under such conditions, you can expect a very high lapse rate, with many, if not most, of the continuing insureds being substandard risks, since healthy insureds can purchase new insurance for half the cost. This poses an interesting design dilemma. The higher the premium increase, the higher the mortality of those remaining. It is not clear whether the best strategy is to maximize or minimize the premium increase, or to find some ideal point in between.

3.2.4.3 Effect of Selective Lapses

Those who lapse can be thought of as being in one of two categories:

1. Those who lapse with no thought of whether they continue to be insurable. We will assume that this group has the average mortality of the group that began the policy year. This group includes a mixture of healthy and unhealthy lives. We will refer to these kinds of lapses as "nonselective lapses." These lapses leave the average mortality of the remaining group unchanged.

2. Those who lapse in good health and can qualify for new insurance. We will assume that this group has the same mortality as newly underwritten lives. We will refer to these as "selective lapses." These lapses increase the average mortality of the remaining group by removing those with the lowest mortality rates.

Every insured mortality study has some level of selective lapses built into it. Higher than normal lapse rates will result in more selective lapses and lead to some level of adverse mortality. The big question is: What portion of the extra lapses are selective lapses?

One method of estimating the effect of extra selective lapses on mortality is the "Preservation of Total Deaths" theory. This theory requires you to specify the percentage of extra lapses that are selective lapses, that is, you must answer the "big question" on your own. As its name implies, this theory assumes that the total number of deaths between those who lapse and those who persist remains the same, regardless of the lapse rate.

In the formulas below we will make extensive use of "qd" and "qw." These are used throughout this book to denote mortality rates (qd = probability of *q*uitting due to *d*eath) and lapse rates (qw = probability of *q*uitting due to *w*ithdrawal or lapse).

Let

> qdNorm = Normal mortality rate, that is, the expected mortality rate associated with a normal level of lapse rates.
>
> qdSelect = Select mortality rate for a newly underwritten insured of the same attained age.

qdActual = Actual mortality rate, that is, the rate we are solving for. This will be higher than the normal mortality rate due to extra selective lapses.

qwNorm = Normal lapse rate, that is, the lapse rate associated with a normal level of mortality rates.

qwExtra = Extra lapse rate, equal to the product's lapse rate less the normal lapse rate on which normal mortality rates are based.

SelectPct = The percentage of extra lapses that are selective lapses. This is most often an educated guess or SWAG, a form of scientific guess.

qwSelect = Selective extra lapse rate, equal to the extra lapse rate times the percentage of extra lapses that are assumed to be selective. These lapses are assumed to have a newly select mortality rate, that is, qdSelect.

qwNonsel = Nonselective extra lapse rate, equal to the extra lapse rate minus the selective extra lapse rate. These lapses are assumed to have a normal mortality rate, that is, qdNorm.

From the last two definitions, we have

$$qwSelect = qwExtra\ SelectPct, \tag{3.2.2}$$

$$qwNonsel = qwExtra - qwSelect. \tag{3.2.3}$$

The preservation of total deaths tells us the following: The deaths from those who normally persist (qdNorm) are equal to the deaths from those who actually persist (qdActual) plus the deaths from the extra lapses (a combination of qdNorm and qdSelect). Deaths can be calculated as mortality rates times the probabilities of persisting.

The probability of normally persisting (1 − qwNorm) is equal to the probability of actually persisting (1 − qwNorm − qwExtra) plus the extra lapse probability (qwNonsel + qwSelect). This leads to the following formula for the preservation of total deaths:

$$(1 - \text{qwNorm}) \text{ qdNorm} = (1 - \text{qwNorm} - \text{qwExtra}) \text{ qdActual}$$
$$+ \text{ qwNonsel qdNorm} + \text{qwSelect qdSelect}.$$
$$(3.2.4)$$

Solving for qdActual, we have

$$\text{qdActual}$$
$$= \frac{(1 - \text{qwNorm} - \text{qwNonsel}) \text{ qdNorm} - (\text{qwSelect}) \text{ qdSelect}}{1 - \text{qwNorm} - \text{qwExtra}}.$$
$$(3.2.5)$$

Example 3.2.3 Effect of Selective Lapses

Suppose a group has a normal mortality rate of 2.00 per 1,000, with a normal lapse rate of 5%. Newly underwritten insureds have a mortality rate of 1.00 per 1,000. If the expected lapse rate is 15% (three times normal) and 80% of the extra lapses are assumed to be selective, what is the deteriorated mortality rate of the remaining group?

Answer:

$$\text{qdNorm} = 2.00 \text{ per } 1,000$$
$$\text{qdSelect} = 1.00 \text{ per } 1,000$$
$$\text{qwNorm} = 0.05$$
$$\text{qwExtra} = 0.15 - 0.05 = 0.10$$
$$\text{SelectPct} = 80\%$$
$$\text{qwSelect} = (0.10) \, 80\% = 0.08$$
$$\text{qwNonsel} = 0.10 - 0.08 = 0.02$$
$$\text{qdActual} = \frac{(1 - 0.05 - 0.02) \times 2.00 - (0.08) \, 1.00}{1 - 0.05 - 0.10} = 2.094 \text{ per } 1,000.$$

In other words, a selective extra lapse rate of 8% increases mortality in this case by almost 5%.

3.2.4.4 Effect of Low Lapse Rates

If insureds exhibit some rational behavior, then unhealthy insureds will be more apt than healthy insureds to continue their policies. Similarly, healthy insureds will be more apt than unhealthy insureds to lapse their policies. Over time, the percentage of unhealthy insureds will increase. Higher lapse rates will exaggerate this tendency and increase the percentage of unhealthy insureds.

Conversely, lower lapse rates will tend to decrease the percentage of unhealthy insureds. In other words, lower lapse rates will result in lower mortality than normal. Compared to the industry select mortality table, the effect of selection will wear off more slowly. This results in mortality at the older ages (where the effect of selection is significant) that increases more slowly by policy year.

Products that are purchased with a very long-term goal often exhibit the best persistency and mortality. For example, Term to 100 is only a good value for the consumer if held for many years. A consumer with a shorter-term horizon would be better off buying 10- or 20-year term and paying a lower premium. Not surprisingly, Term to 100 has very low lapse rates, especially at the higher issue ages where the long-term goal is perhaps better understood and implemented. Relative to other products, Term to 100 also has had some of the lowest mortality.

Because of the connection between low lapse rates and low mortality, it is no coincidence that the companies with the best persistency tend to have some of the best mortality experience. In summary, products and companies with higher than average lapse rates tend to have mortality that worsens over time compared to industry averages. Conversely, products and companies with lower than average lapse rates tend to have mortality that improves over time compared to industry averages. This reinforces the importance of satisfied customers.

3.2.5 Mortality Trends

During the twentieth century, medical science advanced much further than it had in all previous centuries combined. Diagnostic tools, preventative measures, drugs, medical treatments, and surgeries combined to lower mortality levels dramatically. At the same time, deaths from accidents in the workplace, pollutants, contaminated water, and infectious diseases were dramatically reduced in the economically advanced countries. The combined effect of all these factors has been a dramatic improvement in life expectancy in the economically advanced countries.

Figure 3.2.7 shows that male Japanese life expectancies increased 73% from 1901 to 1990. The results are even more impressive when we look at changes in mortality rates. For example, the mortality rate for a 45-year-old Japanese male in 1990 was only 19% of the rate in 1901. This translates to a compound annual mortality improvement of 1.8%.

Figure 3.2.8 illustrates the dramatic improvement in the mortality rates underlying the life expectancies of Figure 3.2.7. While mortality rates have dropped, notice how the shape of the curve has not fundamentally changed: There is a minimum at age 10, a relative maximum at age 20, and a constant percentage increase (which shows as a straight line using a logarithmic scale) from age 35 to age 85. In both figures, values are based on the Japanese Life Table, age nearest

Figure 3.2.7 Historic Male Japanese Life Expectancies

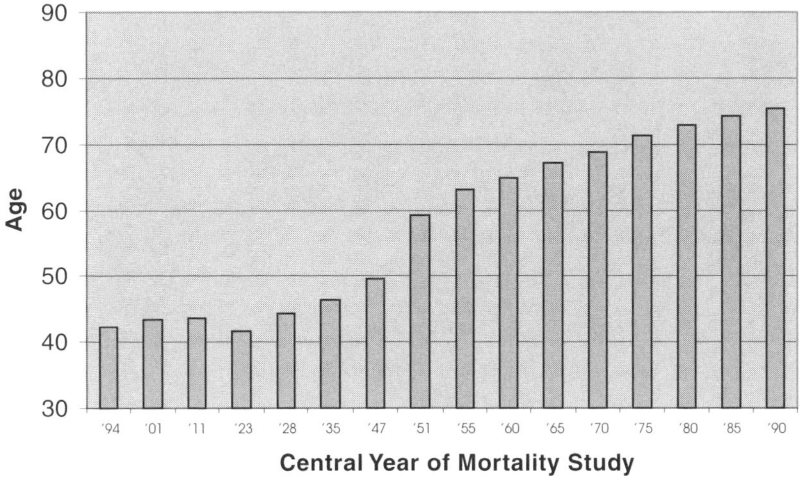

Source: The Society of Actuaries (www.soa.org)

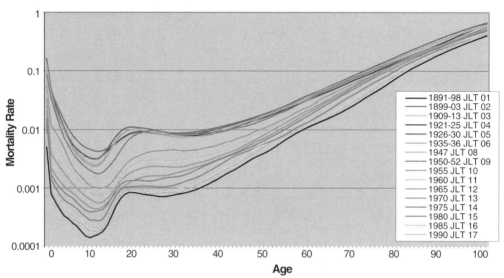

Figure 3.2.8 Historic Male Japanese Mortality Rates

Source: **The Society of Actuaries (www.soa.org).**

birthday, for the year indicated. In some cases, the year shown is the central year of the mortality study.

Although the figures are not shown, female mortality improvement in Japan has been even more dramatic: The mortality rate for a 45-year-old female in 1990 was only 11.66% of the rate in 1894. This translates to a compound annual mortality improvement of 2.4%.

What does the twenty-first century have in store for us? Will mortality improvement accelerate, with the twenty-first century making the medical advances of the twentieth century seem minor? Will mortality improvement slow down because the most important medical advances have already been achieved? Will the human genome project unlock secrets that dramatically improve mortality? Only your reinsurer knows for sure!

Some companies build mortality improvement into their mortality assumptions. Many companies do not. Mortality improvement could be built into the mortality tables used for pricing. Alternatively, if the company wished to vary mortality improvement by product, it could develop separate mortality improvement factors to apply to the mortality rates.

When examining historical mortality trends to develop mortality improvement assumptions, you must be extremely careful when reviewing insured mortality data. Insured mortality trends should be split between true mortality improvement and apparent mortality improvement. Two important trends in the insurance industry contribute to apparent mortality improvement:

1. There has been a gradual movement to more refined risk classes, such as for nonsmokers and preferred risks. The introduction of such risk classes causes those with the lowest mortality to purchase more insurance (because it is less expensive) and those with the highest mortality to purchase less insurance (because it is more expensive). This trend lowers the average mortality of those buying life insurance, even when the underlying mortality rates for the different risk classes remain unchanged. This trend should be backed out of any mortality improvement assumption.

2. There has been a gradual improvement in underwriting information and underwriting decisions, due to developments such as cheaper blood tests and a better understanding of risk factors. Better underwriting results in lower insured mortality. The mortality of the population may not have changed, but the mortality of those accepted for life insurance will improve. This trend, to the extent that it is expected to continue, should affect the initial level of mortality, but probably not long-term mortality. Therefore, it should also be backed out of any mortality improvement factor.

To give you an idea of the significance of these two trends, each of them can exceed the level of true mortality improvement. To make no adjustment for them is dangerous.

Caution should be used with mortality improvement factors, especially when projecting improvements many years into the future. Whether to use them may depend on the design of the product. If the product can be adjusted to reflect actual mortality experience, such as through dividends, cost of insurance charges, or nonguaranteed premiums, then using mortality improvement may be justified. Otherwise, the use of mortality improvements may be too risky.

When used, mortality improvement is reflected in pricing using mortality improvement factors. For example, a 0.5% annual improvement in mortality would translate to a mortality improvement factor of 0.995. A series of three annual mortality improvements of 0.6%, 0.5%, and 0.4% would translate into annual mortality improvement factors of 0.994, 0.995, and 0.996 and a three-year cumulative mortality improvement factor of 0.9851. Mortality rates would be multiplied by cumulative mortality improvement factors to determine the final mortality rates for pricing.

Mortality improvement factors could be designed to vary by age, gender, and risk class. For example, it might be felt that the highest mortality rates have the most room for improvement, while the lowest mortality rates have virtually no room for improvement. Mortality improvement could also vary by calendar year. For example, recent mortality improvement trends might be assumed to continue for a few years and then slow down.

3.3 Lapse Assumptions

Lapse rates are usually critical to a product's profitability and to the long-term viability of the company. High lapse rates cause expenses to be spread over a smaller base of continuing policies. High lapse rates go hand-in-hand with increased anti-selection by policyowners, usually leading to poor mortality results.

Most life insurance products involve large up-front acquisition costs, often in excess of the first-year premium. In order for the company to recoup these costs, the average policy must persist for a number of years. High lapse rates in the early policy years mean that the few who persist will have to pay for most of the acquisition costs. Because of this, high early lapse rates lead to high-cost, often noncompetitive, products. In other words, a company with relatively high lapse rates will have a hard time competing.

On the other hand, companies that are able to achieve low lapse rates have a competitive advantage. Acquisition costs can be spread over a larger base of continuing policies. Low lapse rates are also a sign of satisfied customers and typically lead to more repeat business. A key element of company strategy may be focused on achieving low lapse rates.

A lapse rate measures the percentage of policies or units that are lapsed, surrendered, or otherwise prematurely canceled for any reason other than death. In this book, unless otherwise stated, lapse rates will be annual rates, measuring the lapses during a policy year. Lapses at the very end of the policy year contribute to the lapse rate for the policy year just ended. Lapse rates will be based on units of insurance rather than number of policies. Units will be discussed more fully in Chapter 5, but one unit is often defined as 1,000 of death benefit. For example, $300,000 of death benefit would be 300 units. The persistency rate for a policy year will be calculated as one minus the lapse rate. In some situations (but not in this book), persistency rates reflect all terminations, including deaths.

To be more precise, the lapse rate for a policy year will be calculated as the number of units lapsed during the policy year divided by the number of units in force at the beginning of the policy year. The use of lapse rates will be explored more fully in Chapter 4.

3.3.1 Why Lapse Rates Vary

Lapse rates vary widely from company to company and even within the same company. At the extremes, lapse rates can be higher than 50% or lower than 1%, although most lapse rates fall in the 3–30% range. Many factors can affect lapse rates, such as the following:

The manner in which the policy is sold: If the customer initiates the purchase, lapse rates tend to be low. If the customer is pressured into buying insurance, lapse rates tend to be high.

Perceived value: If the customer believes the policy is a good value, he or she is more likely to continue the policy. The company's reputation can enhance the perceived value. The availability of newer, cheaper products can erode the perceived value or lead policyowners into believing that they were duped. This has often been the case with term insurance, with newer products offering lower premium rates.

The degree of understanding: If the customer clearly understands the benefits of the policy, persistency is enhanced.

Ability to pay: Policyowners with more disposable income are more apt to continue their policies, especially when economic conditions worsen.

The agent's attitude toward persistency: Agents are sometimes motivated to improve persistency, often through the use of chargebacks of commissions on premature lapses and persistency bonuses to reward good persistency. In some situations, agents may actively replace existing policies with newer policies, both to update the customer's coverage (presumably giving the customer a better deal) and to earn additional commissions.

The customer's commitment to the insurance policy: If the policy meets the perceived needs of the insured or if the policy is part of a financial plan or other scheme, persistency is often enhanced.

Ease of premium payments: If premiums are automatically paid through payroll deduction or pre-authorized checks, the customer will not be faced with a periodic choice of whether to continue or discontinue the insurance policy. However, if customers change jobs frequently or routinely overdraw their checking accounts, automatic payments could conceivably hurt persistency.

Figure 3.3.1 shows the average lapse rate for the first two policy years and the average lapse rate for policy years 3 and later. As you can see, a high percentage of policies lapse or surrender during the first two policy years, with a substantial drop thereafter. The higher lapse rates that

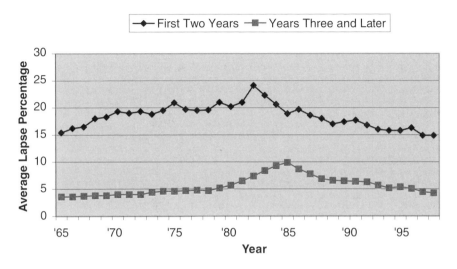

Figure 3.3.1 U.S. Lapse Rates, 1965–1998

Source: **The 1999** *Fact Book* **of the American Council of Life Insurance.**

occurred in the early and mid-1980s can be attributed to a surge of replacement activity (policyowners exchanging their policies for newer policies) brought on by the popularization of term and universal life products.

3.3.2   Sources of Lapse Data

The best source of lapse data is a company's own experience, because lapse rates vary so much from one company to the next. For example, the reputation and financial strength of the company can have a major effect on lapse rates. The training and incentives for agents can have a profound effect on persistency. Unlike mortality, even smaller companies have enough lapses to generate credible lapse studies. Lapse rates can vary by many factors. Larger companies tend to study their lapse rates in more depth and vary their lapse rate assumptions by more factors.

For truly new products (as opposed to updates of existing products), a company's historical lapse rates may not be directly applicable. It may be necessary to look to the experience of other companies. This could be done by using industry lapse studies, engaging consultants, or working with reinsurers. While the lapse experience of other companies can rarely be used directly, it may give the company an idea as to the relative level of lapse rates for a new product.

Lapse assumptions are sometimes based mainly on judgment, such as when developing products for a new company or when developing a product that has very little history. Even so, efforts should be made to collect lapse data that may be partially applicable, such as data from a similar company, market, or product.

Ideally, there will be several studies of your company's lapse experience at your disposal. At worst, you can get some idea of lapse rates by comparing the business in force at consecutive year-ends. Lapse experience will usually need to be adjusted before it can be used. Changes in your products, sales force, company ratings, economic conditions, and many other factors can have an effect on future lapse rates. It may be easy to find reasons for future improvements in persistency. Actually achieving improved persistency may be much more difficult, so care should be taken not to be overly optimistic.

3.3.3 General Lapse Variations

Lapse rates usually vary by type of product, policy year, and issue age. The degree of refinement will depend on the reliability of the data and the degree of sophistication that is desirable or material.

The following general variations in lapse rates often apply:

By policy year: Lapse rates usually decrease rapidly with increasing policy year for the first several years and then decrease very slowly after five or ten years. There are some exceptions: Increasing premium term products often show an increase in lapse rates from the first year to the second year, with little or no drop in lapse rates thereafter.

By issue age: The late teens through the early twenties have the highest lapse rates. Above age 30, lapse rates usually decline with increasing issue age.

By policy size: A larger policy size generally means lower lapse rates. There are some exceptions: Products that are susceptible to replacement, such as increasing premium term, may experience higher lapse rates at the larger policy sizes. The larger the premiums, the more incentive there is to shop for a cheaper price.

By frequency of premium payment: In general, the more frequent the premium payment during the policy year, the higher the lapse rate. This is because the policyowner has more opportunities each year to rethink whether the insurance is necessary and more opportunities to miss a payment.

By method of premium payment: Policies that have premium payments made by pre-authorized withdrawals from checking accounts or by payroll deductions often have lower lapse rates than those that are directly billed.

By standard vs. substandard: Substandard policies (those that must pay higher premium rates because of higher expected mortality) have lapse rates that are generally higher than those for standard policies, with the biggest difference in the first year, declining to almost no difference by the fourth year.

By risk class: This is similar to the differences between standard and substandard lapse rates. Generally, the more preferred or more select risk classes tend to have lower lapse rates.

By gender: When all else is equal, females tend to have somewhat lower lapse rates than males.

By rate of premium increase: In general, when premiums increase, you can expect an increase in lapse rates. The larger the percentage increase in premium, the higher the lapse rate. A rule of thumb that is directionally correct is that a lapse rate for an increasing premium product is roughly equal to (a) plus (b), where (a) is the corresponding lapse rate for an otherwise similar product with level premiums and (b) is the percentage increase in the premium.

3.3.3.1 Effect of Level or Levelized Commissions

Historically, agent compensation on most life insurance products has been *heaped:* The agent received a large first-year commission, followed by much smaller renewal-year commissions. Large up-front commissions are helpful in compensating new agents who do not have the advantage of a stream of renewal commissions and in covering the costs of starting up new agencies. However, this pattern of commissions encourages lapsation of policies in later policy years. Agents may see a stream of small renewal commissions that could potentially be turned into larger first-year commissions by replacing old policies with new policies.

A number of companies have experimented with levelized or level commission patterns, to make the agent just as interested as the company in improving persistency. Example 3.3.1 illustrates possible heaped, levelized, and level commission structures.

Example 3.3.1 Commission Patterns

Policy Year	Heaped	Levelized	Level
1	55.0%	25.0%	16.0%
2–5	6.0	17.5	16.0
6–10	4.0	8.0	16.0
11+	1.5	1.5	1.5

With level and levelized commissions, the agent has more incentive to encourage the policyowner to continue to pay premiums. The agent has less incentive to replace old policies with new policies, in order to generate first-year commissions, which are no longer heaped. As a result, replacement activity should decrease. Level or levelized commissions also give the company more to offer new agents to service the orphaned policies of agents who have left the company.

There are many issues to consider before adopting a levelized or level commission structure:

- At what point will the renewal commissions be vested, so that the agent will receive them even after he or she leaves the company? Once commissions are vested, the agent may be tempted to maximize current income by writing new policies with a company that pays heaped commissions.

- Historical lapse and mortality data are largely based on policies sold with heaped commissions. How much will lapse rates and mortality rates be improved by a change in commission pattern? Will the change in mortality rates even be perceptible? The company will want to closely monitor emerging experience to see if the expected benefits of levelized commissions do in fact emerge.

- How will the company finance new agents if their commissions are largely deferred over a period of many years? How will this affect agent recruiting?

- Should agents be given a choice between heaped and levelized commissions? Should this be a temporary, transitory option or a permanent option?

- To win the agents over to levelized commissions, should the new commission schedules be retroactively applied to both new business and in-force business?

- How will agent retention be affected? The company may lose agents who are opposed to levelized commissions. After the initial defections, the agent group that remains may have a stronger incentive to continue with the company.

- How will agency development costs be affected? With lower commission outlays up front, will the company have to increase agency subsidies?

- If commissions must be disclosed, will level or levelized commissions meet with better customer approval? Will sales increase?

3.3.3.2 Effect of Surrender Charges

Most universal life products have explicit surrender charges that are deducted from the cash value upon surrender or partial withdrawal. Surrender charges are an effective deterrent to premature surrender.

However, as surrender charges grade off, usually over a period of 10 to 20 years, lapse rates may increase. This behavior is more common for products sold primarily as investments.

There is sometimes a spike in the lapse rate in the first year after the surrender charge vanishes. After a spike, lapse rates usually drop and remain at a lower level. This is especially true if the surrender charge exists for a relatively short period, such as less than ten years. For longer surrender charge periods, there is less of a spike in lapse rates.

Here is a rule of thumb that can sometimes be applied to investment-oriented products after the first policy year: Calculate the surrender charge as a percentage of the cash value. Then the surrender charge percentage plus the lapse rate should equal a constant percentage. Example 3.3.2 illustrates this rule of thumb using a constant percentage of 12%, except in years 1 and 10.

Example 3.3.2 Effect of Surrender Charge on Lapse Rate

Policy Year	Surrender Charge	Lapse Rate	Surrender Charge + Lapse Rate
1	9%	15%	24%
2	9	3	12
3	9	3	12
4	9	3	12
5	9	3	12
6	8	4	12
7	7	5	12
8	5	7	12
9	3	9	12
10	0	20*	20
11+	0	12	12

*Assumes a lapse spike occurs in the first year that the surrender charge vanishes.

3.3.3.3   Effect of Interest Bonuses or Return of COI Charges

Some universal life products feature a policyowner bonus that is designed to make the product more competitive and improve persistency. An interest bonus retroactively pays the policyowner an enhanced interest rate if the policy persists to the end of a certain policy year. For example, the interest bonus may retroactively pay interest rates for policy years 1–10 that are 0.25% higher if the policy persists to the end of the tenth policy year.

Another type of bonus refunds all or a portion of COI charges if the policy persists to the end of a certain policy year. For example, all COI charges for the first 20 policy years may be refunded if the policy persists to the end of the twentieth policy year.

By delaying such bonuses until the end of 10 or 20 years, the cost to the company is much reduced, because many policies will lapse before the bonus is paid. While bonuses could also be offered at the end of 30 or 40 years, this is rarely done, since so few policies last that long.

The bonuses may or may not be guaranteed. Either type of bonus could be paid in the form of a lump-sum cash payment or as an addition to the cash value. Such bonuses should result in lower than normal lapse rates, especially in the years just preceding the payment of the bonus. Ignoring the effect of such a bonus on persistency could lead to mispricing. However, after the bonus has been paid, there may well be a spike in lapse rates.

These types of bonuses can create inequities. A policyowner who lapses after 19 years may receive no bonus, while a policyowner who persists one more year may reap a veritable fortune. Besides inequities, such bonuses can also create accounting dilemmas. Unless the company accurately predicts how many policyowners will persist to reap the bonus and sets aside funds accordingly, the pattern of profits could be distorted. For example, by ignoring the bonus, the company could record earnings in the years before the bonus is paid and then incur a substantial loss in the year of the bonus.

3.3.4 Lapse Variations by Product

Lapse rates vary considerably by type of product. Permanent products and other products with a long-term focus tend to have the lowest lapse rates. Term products and other products with a short-term focus tend to have the highest lapse rates. The shorter the term period, the higher the lapse rates tend to be. Increasing premium term products tend to have the highest renewal lapse rates of all, although first-year lapse rates are sometimes lower than average.

3.3.4.1 Term to 100

Term to 100 can exhibit the lowest lapse rates of all, with lapse rates even dropping below 1% in some cases. Term to 100 products are most common in Canada. Term to 100 is one of a group of products commonly referred to as "lapse-supported products." These products, to maintain adequate profitability, actually depend on people to lapse at some point during the life of the product. If lapses are lower than anticipated, profitability will be eroded. In fact, losses have resulted in some cases.

Term to 100 was first introduced in Canada during the mid-1980s. By the end of the decade, a number of companies had introduced Term to 100 products that turned out to be underpriced. This was because actual lapse rates proved to be lower than those priced for. The original expectation was that Term to 100 lapse rates would fall somewhere between the lapse rates for traditional permanent products and the lapse rates for long-duration term products. In actuality, Term to 100 lapse rates turned out to be *lower* than lapse rates for traditional permanent products.

3.3.4.2 Flexible Premium Products

Products with flexible premiums add quite a bit of complexity to lapse rates. Suppose cash values are sufficient to continue the policy for a number of months or years without additional premiums. In that case, the cessation of premium payments does not necessarily cause the policy to lapse right away or even at all. Instead, policy lapsation depends on the history of premium payments and the resulting cash values that have been built up.

Policy lapsation also depends on the extent to which policyowners surrender their policies for cash or leave the cash value in place to continue the policy. For simplicity, you can assume that flexible premium lapses involve both premium cessation and the immediate withdrawal of all available cash value. This is not realistic. To ensure that you are not overlooking something significant, you should do an analysis of the profitability of policies that continue in force after premiums have ceased, with cash values being gradually eroded by mortality and expense charges.

Rather than just perform a lapse study, you also need to study premium payment patterns. You might find that premium payment patterns can be grouped into a number of categories that have similar lapse patterns, such as the following:

- A large single premium sufficient to continue the insurance for many years

- A level premium equal to the target premium, plus an additional single premium in the first policy year

- A level premium equal to the minimum premium required by the company to keep the policy in force during the surrender charge period

- Level premiums sufficient to fund the policy for life, paid over a period of seven to ten years.

By studying your company's experience, you can determine the most common premium patterns experienced by your company. Each pattern may actually be a blend of a large number of different individual patterns that are similar in some way.

You should determine lapse rates separately for each common premium pattern. For example, a pattern with a large single premium will likely result in very low lapse rates. In contrast, a pattern of level minimum premiums will more likely result in lapse rates that fall in between those for permanent and term products. A pattern of level target premiums with an additional first-year premium may result in lower-than-average lapse rates in the early policy years.

When pricing, you should calculate results for each of the most common patterns as well as for a few other patterns. The goal of this is to ensure that the product has no gaping "holes" that could be abused by policyowners and result in unacceptable results for the company. For example, if most of the product's expenses are covered by expense charges that are a percentage of renewal premiums, a single premium pattern may not be profitable.

For each premium payment pattern, you should also determine the corresponding death benefit pattern. Like the premium payment patterns, death benefit patterns will also be a blend of a large number of different individual patterns.

Policy values can then be calculated based on the blended premium payment and death benefit patterns. While this is not entirely accurate, it has the advantage of combining the results of many similar patterns in a single set of calculations. A more accurate approach is to calculate results separately for every significant premium pattern. This is quite possible with many of the common pricing software packages available today. By not combining cells, it is easier to identify unprofitable premium payment patterns.

Many flexible premium products also give the policyowner the option to make partial withdrawals from the cash value. Assumptions for partial withdrawals are often expressed as the percentage of available cash value that is withdrawn in a given policy year. Separate partial withdrawal assumptions should be developed for each common premium payment pattern.

3.3.5 Lapse Trends

Lapse rates sometimes exhibit long-term trends. Attitudes toward particular life insurance products, particular insurance companies, and the life insurance industry in general can change. Economic conditions change. Tax laws change. Competitive alternatives to life insurance may wax or wane.

For example, an event that scandalizes the insurance industry may increase lapse rates for years. Positive press reports may improve persistency for a company. A ratings downgrade may worsen persistency among policyowners sensitive to ratings. New investment or insurance products may trigger mass replacement of less competitive insurance policies. A change in tax law may change the attractiveness of life insurance, as well as public attitudes, resulting in higher or lower persistency, depending on the direction of the change.

A large group of agents may defect to another company and take much of a company's in-force business with them. A competitor's actions, whether by introducing an attractive new product or by actively encouraging its agents to replace your company's business, can cause lapse rates to shoot up.

A company can purposely increase its lapse rates by "cannibalizing" its own business: By replacing its old products with more competitive new products, it can protect its business from competitors and engender policyowner loyalty.

In the worst case, bad press, a ratings downgrade, or insolvency concerns can trigger a "run on the bank." Policyowners, worried that the company may not be able to pay them all, may rush to cancel their insurance and receive their cash values.

Mergers and acquisitions of companies or acquisitions of blocks of business can affect lapse rates. If the agents are not actively involved with the new company, lapse rates can be expected to increase, as the agents are likely to take their business elsewhere. If customer service deteriorates, lapse rates may increase. However, if a stronger, higher-rated company acquires the company or business, lapse rates may actually fall, provided agent relationships and service levels are maintained.

Many forces could cause lapse rates to rise in the future. So it would seem prudent to factor a modest increase in future lapse rates into lapse assumptions. However, for products that are more profitable with higher lapse rates, this would not be advisable.

To better understand the potential effect of a "run on the bank," it would be wise to calculate the results of spikes in lapse rates in various policy years. This might alter the product design to ensure that the level of cash values does not generate large losses when lapse rates are high.

3.4 Interest Rate Assumptions

Insurance companies hold a variety of assets that are used to back insurance policies. The types of assets most commonly held by insurance companies are described in Chapter 15. These assets are used to cover regulatory reserves and capital requirements, which will be fully explained in Chapters 6 and 8. Some assets, such as bonds, preferred stocks, and mortgages, earn interest rates. Stocks and real estate provide some current income but mostly develop capital gains or losses. Computer hardware, software, and furniture provide no investment income. The cost of these assets is spread by gradually reducing their value (that is, by amortizing them) over a number of years.

When pricing a life insurance product, it is necessary to reflect the investment income that will be earned on the various assets backing the product. In this section we will assume that all investment income is converted to interest rates. This assumption works best for products that are supported solely by interest-bearings assets such as bonds and mortgages.

For some companies and some products, a significant portion of the assets is not interest bearing. For example, most variable products are supported by investments in stocks. A better approach for reflecting stock dividends, stock market fluctuations, capital gains, and capital losses is to use stochastic modeling, which will be introduced in Chapter 15. A simplistic treatment would be to assume a fixed pattern of stock dividends, market values, and capital gains and losses. By testing a variety of fixed patterns, such an approach might be useful for preliminary pricing. However, stochastic modeling is highly recommended for final pricing.

This section is structured a little differently from the other sections. After examining why interest rates vary, we review the various facets of investment choices. Once the current investment choices are understood, an investment strategy can be formulated. The strategy may be heavily influenced by the nature of the product. Finally, we review some historical interest rate patterns to better appreciate the futility of trying to predict future interest rates.

3.4.1 Why Interest Rates Vary

Economic conditions are largely defined by interest rates. Economic activity levels and capital gains tend to rise when interest rates and inflation rates are low. Economic downturns are often coupled with capital losses, high interest rates, and high inflation rates, as well as an increase in asset defaults. Governments often manipulate interest rates to achieve economic or political goals. These goals can include protecting the value of their currency, holding down inflation, and helping domestic firms recover from past losses.

Interest rates vary by the duration or maturity of interest-bearing securities. The *yield curve* (see Figure 3.4.1) describes how investment

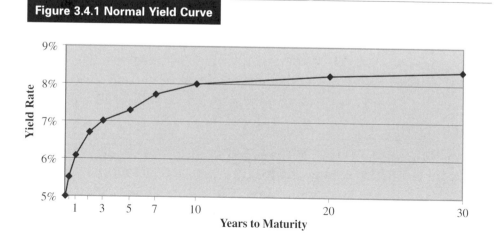

Figure 3.4.1 Normal Yield Curve

yields vary according to the length of the investment. The data points on the curve represent yields for investments that mature in 90 and 180 days, and 1, 2, 3, 5, 7, 10, 20, and 30 years.

Interest rates also vary by the riskiness of the investment and the type of asset. For example, mortgages usually pay higher interest rates than bonds of similar risk, because of the extra expenses associated with mortgages.

Some economic theories link interest rate levels to a country's demographics. To the extent that demographics drive the economy, population projections can be useful predictors of future economic activity. For example, a country with many young people who need to borrow money for their first apartments, furniture, appliances, and cars may create a demand for money that outstrips the supply of money. When this happens, the price of money (the interest rate) rises. This may help explain the high Canadian and U.S. interest rates in the early 1980s, when the highest numbers of baby boomers were starting households of their own. In contrast, a country with an aging population may have relatively more people saving for retirement than young people needing to borrow. This can create a supply of money that exceeds the demand for money, driving interest rates down. This may partially explain the very low interest rates in Japan during most of the 1990s. By using forecasts of increases and decreases in various age groups, you may gain some insight into long-term interest rate tendencies.

Interest rates are unpredictable. In some countries, long-term interest rates tend to change slowly, rarely rising or falling more than 1% in a year or 2% over several years. As a result, some insurance companies confidently predict that current levels of interest rates will continue for a few years, perhaps with some reduction to add a margin of conservatism.

For products with a major investment or savings component, it can be quite dangerous to guarantee current interest levels very far into the future. Over the years, more than a few life insurance companies have become insolvent when interest rates fell and they were no longer able to earn interest rates high enough to support long-term guarantees.

This risk can sometimes be greatly reduced by carefully matching assets with the liabilities they are meant to back. For example, if future product cash flows can be fairly accurately predicted (this may happen if the policyowner has no ability to surrender the policy for a cash value), it may be possible to purchase assets that produce cash flows that closely match the product's cash flows, effectively immunizing the company from future changes in interest rates. This will be covered in Chapter 14.

A simpler way to reduce interest rate risk is through product design. Products that guarantee low interest rates and credit current interest rates based on actual investment performance transfer much of the investment risk from the company to the policyowner. If the product design does not transfer this risk to the policyowner, a proper charge should be assessed, either explicitly through charges or implicitly through higher profit requirements.

3.4.2   Review of Investment Choices

Before an investment strategy and a set of interest rate assumptions can be formulated, you need to review the investment choices that are available. For each investment, perhaps the most important attribute is its net interest rate. However, several other attributes need to be understood: duration, convexity, volatility, liquidity, and callability. These attributes will be covered in Chapters 14 and 15. Generally, the company's investment managers can readily supply all of this information. However, many companies suffer from one or both of the following problems, which limit the successful collaboration of product development and investment staff:

1. The product development staff knows too little about investment choices and investment cash flows and does not attempt to learn all they can from the investment staff.

2. The investment staff knows too little about life insurance products and liability cash flows and does not attempt to learn all they can from the rest of the company.

The result of these problems is often a less than optimal investment strategy, which leads to a more risky, less competitive, or less profitable product.

3.4.2.1 Net Interest Rate

A net interest rate, or net yield, can be calculated for each type of asset, based on the current investment market. In general, the net interest rate is calculated as the gross interest rate net of deductions for investment expenses and the cost of defaults.

3.4.2.2 Gross Interest Rate

We will assume that the interest rate for an investment is constant throughout a policy year. The gross interest rate is the annual effective rate of interest that will be earned during the policy year. The interest rate earned on different assets is often stated differently, depending on the timing of interest payments.

The interest rate for a bond is usually quoted as the semiannual yield rate. For example, a 6% bond may have two semiannual 3% coupon payments. This translates to an annual effective interest rate of 6.09% $(1.03^2 - 1)$.

The interest rate for a mortgage loan with monthly principal and interest payments is typically expressed as a monthly yield rate. For example, a mortgage with a 12% loan interest rate may actually charge 1% interest per month. This translates to an annual effective interest rate of 12.68% $(1.01^{12} - 1)$. No matter how interest rates are traditionally expressed, they must be converted to annual effective interest rates before they can be used for pricing.

3.4.2.3 Investment Expenses

Investment expenses are the expenses incurred by the company's investment staff or charged by an outside investment manager to manage the company's assets. These expenses cover the costs of buying and selling the assets, reviewing and monitoring the assets, collecting investment income, and performing the investment accounting required for the assets. Typically, investment expenses are expressed as an annual percentage of the assets under management, such as 0.15% or 15 basis points. (One basis point is equal to 0.01%.)

Certain types of assets incur higher investment expenses. For example, commercial mortgages may be more expensive to manage than corporate bonds. Typically, companies determine the investment expense rate associated with each asset class. This allows the company to forecast how investment expenses will change as the mix of assets changes.

3.4.2.4 Default Risk

Interest-bearing assets have a risk of default. An asset defaults when the scheduled principal or interest payments are not made. For example, if you do not pay the monthly payment on your home mortgage in time, your mortgage is in default. In some cases, the borrower is ultimately able to repay all overdue principal and interest. However, some percentage of a company's assets typically defaults each year, with the company ultimately receiving a good portion, such as 50%, of the outstanding principal and interest on those assets that default.

For example, if you default on your mortgage, your lender may foreclose on your home and sell it. If your lender can sell it for an amount that equals or exceeds all outstanding principal and interest, then there is no loss on default. However, if property values have dropped, your lender may experience a loss on default.

An annual default cost is the percentage of assets that are expected to default in a year, adjusted for future recoveries of principal and interest on defaulted assets. For example, if 1% of the assets are expected to default and the average default is expected to cost only 40% of the asset, then the annual default cost would be 0.40%.

When buying an interest-bearing security, the investment manager assesses the probability of default, often relying on ratings assigned by rating agencies. These ratings depend on many factors, especially the financial strength and future viability of the issuer of the security. Ratings are typically assigned a letter rating, ranging from AAA, the highest, most secure rating, to BBB, the lowest investment-grade rating, to ratings even lower than BBB. The lower the rating, the higher the expected default rate.

Some assets do not have ratings assigned by rating agencies. In that case, the company would develop a default assumption based on its own experience or based on studies performed by outside firms.

Historical data can be used to calculate expected default costs. However, defaults are highly correlated with economic downturns. Default costs tend to be much lower than average during prosperous times and much higher than average during recessions.

Table 3.4.1 shows average historical default costs for U.S. corporate bonds from 1970 to 1998, expressed as an annual percentage.

Table 3.4.1 Average Annual Cost of Default

Rating	Over 5 Years	Over 10 Years	Over 20 Years
AAA	0.00%	0.00%	0.01%
AA	0.01	0.01	0.04
A	0.04	0.08	0.15
BBB	0.23	0.34	0.45
BB	1.05	1.16	1.22
B	4.11	3.79	3.42
C	4.88	4.40	3.95

While it is typical to use a level default cost, Mr. Keller's research has shown some interesting patterns. While current ratings are a good predictor of the short-term probability of default, ratings change over time. Highly rated securities are more likely to experience rating downgrades than upgrades. At the other end of the spectrum, those poorly rated securities that do not default are more likely to experience rating upgrades than downgrades.

This means that, for highly rated securities, an increasing default cost would more accurately model the financial effect of defaults. For AAA-, AA-, and A-rated securities, default costs are so low that increasing them over time is pointless. However, for BBB-rated securities, the trend may be worth reflecting. For example, a BBB-rated ten-year bond may have an average default cost of 0.34% per year. However, the annual default cost may range from 0.08% in the first year to 0.52% in the tenth year. (These default costs are expressed as a percentage of the original investment.)

Conversely, a decreasing default cost would more accurately model the effect of defaults for poorly rated securities. For example, a C-rated ten-year bond may have an average default cost of 4.40% per year. However, the annual default cost may range from 4.94% in the first year to 1.40% in the tenth year. (Again, these default costs are expressed as a percentage of the original investment. If expressed as a percentage of the nondefaulted investment remaining at the beginning of the tenth year, the tenth-year default cost would be 2.53%.) Clearly, this trend would be material if a large portion of the product's assets were invested in such bonds. However, the volatility of default costs due to changes in the economy may dwarf or obscure such trends.

3.4.2.5   Risk vs. Return

Differences in interest rates earned by various companies are often more a function of the degree of risk-taking than differences in investment acumen. For example, a company that invests in long-duration, riskier, higher-yielding securities may earn higher net interest rates during a boom period. However, during a recession, the same company may find that its net interest rate is depressed because of an increased cost of defaults.

In the U.S. during the 1980s, Executive Life Insurance Company grew impressively, accumulating billions of dollars of assets. Executive Life was publicly praised (by some) as a superior manager of investments, by following a strategy of investing primarily in "junk bonds" (that is, poorly rated bonds with high yields). The interest rates earned by Executive Life exceeded the rates earned by most other companies, even after adjusting for the higher cost of defaults associated with junk bonds. Their returns were aided by the U.S.'s economic boom in the 1980s, which saw fewer defaults on junk bonds than normal. However, an increased number of junk bond defaults in early 1990 caused junk bond market values to tumble to unexpectedly low levels. As a result, Executive Life's assets were suddenly worth less than its liabilities. California regulators seized control of the company and sold its junk bond portfolio at what turned out to be the most unfortunate time. The French group that bought the junk bonds realized in excess of a $1 billion profit within a year, as the market values of junk bonds fully recovered.

In retrospect, Executive Life's mistake was not that it invested in junk bonds, but that it had such a heavy concentration of junk bonds and did not have sufficient capital to withstand an unexpectedly large decline in junk bond market values. Many other companies that had smaller concentrations in junk bonds made it through the early 1990s relatively unscathed, although several did suffer ratings downgrades.

3.4.2.6 Determining Net Interest Rates

A product's net interest rate is needed not only for pricing purposes, but also on a regular basis thereafter, so that results for the product can be tracked. For dynamic products and participating products, the product's net interest rate is needed to update credited interest rates and dividend interest rates, respectively. Table 3.4.2 illustrates the calculation of a weighted average net interest rate for a simple asset portfolio.

Table 3.4.2 Weighted Average Net Interest Rate Calculation

Type of Asset	Rating	Gross Interest Rate	Investment Expense Rate	Annual Default Cost	Net Interest Rate	Weight
Government Securities		5.50%	0.20%	0.00%	5.300%	10%
Corporate Bonds	AAA	6.00	0.20	0.10	5.700	20
	A	6.70	0.20	0.20	6.300	45
	BB	7.75	0.20	1.25	6.300	10
Commercial Mortgages		8.00	0.40	0.35	7.250	15
Weighted Average		6.74	0.23	0.2875	6.2225	100

The initial interest rate assumption for a product can be calculated as a weighted average of the net interest rates for the mix of asset types that will back the product's liabilities, as laid out in the investment strategy. Alternatively, the weighted average net interest rate could be calculated from the weighted averages of gross interest rates, investment expense rates, and annual default costs. Both approaches are illustrated in the Table 3.4.2.

3.4.3 Investment Strategy

There are two fundamentally different approaches to setting interest rates:

1. The segmentation method: Assets are segmented for different lines of business, different products, or different periods of time during which funds were received. Different interest rates are credited to the liabilities backed by each asset segment.

2. The portfolio method: Assets are combined for different lines of business, different products, or different periods of time. A single interest rate is credited to the liabilities backed by the combined assets.

3.4.3.1 Segmentation Method

A company may decide to segment assets for a variety of reasons:

- To allow different lines of business to make independent investment choices and experience the results of those choices.

- To back short-term liabilities with short-term assets and to back long-term liabilities with long-term assets. For example, health insurance liabilities are short term and should be backed by short-term assets. Term to 100 liabilities are long term and should be backed by long-term assets.

- To back products that offer cash surrender values with more liquid and shorter-term assets, while using more illiquid assets to back products with no cash surrender values.

- To credit interest rates to policies based on the interest rates available when funds were received for those policies. This allows the company to be competitive with current "new money" interest rates. Some large companies segment assets as often as every week or every month during times when interest rates are changing significantly.

When segmenting assets, each segment will typically have its own investment strategy. Assets for each segment will be segregated from all other assets, allowing book value, market value, and investment income to be tracked separately for each segment. To make segmentation possible, product cash flows must be tracked separately for each segment. This can add much complexity to administration and accounting.

When developing a new product, you must decide whether the product should share the investment strategy of an existing segment or whether the product has such different investment considerations and will produce sufficient assets to warrant establishing a new asset segment. In the latter case it may be wise to wait and see how well the product sells before establishing a new asset segment.

When the ability to segment assets is subject to regulatory approval, the use of segmentation should be considered even more carefully. Some companies have spent considerable effort gaining regulatory approval to establish a new asset segment for a new product. When actual sales were far below expectations, they had to seek regulatory approval to fold the new segment into an existing segment.

3.4.3.2 Developing a New Investment Strategy

If it is decided that the product warrants a new asset segment, then a new investment strategy is needed. The investment strategy for the product should be developed through discussions between the company's investment managers and those developing the product. The investment managers must gain a thorough understanding of the product, its probable cash flows, and possible variations in cash flows that will need to be accommodated.

The product development staff must gain a good understanding of the various investment alternatives, such as the net interest rates, liquidity, volatility, and callability for each category of assets. Assets may be selected based on their duration and convexity in order to match liability cash flows. It may be necessary to test several possible investment strategies as part of the product development process before a final strategy can be set.

To the extent that the company is willing to mismatch assets and liabilities, it should recognize that this has a cost. If interest rate trends move in the company's favor, there may be no discernible cost or even a benefit. However, if future interest rates result in losses to the company because of the mismatching, there will be a very clear cost. A rational approach may be to calculate an expected cost of mismatching.

As a simple example, the company may estimate that it has a 50% chance of no cost of mismatching and a 50% chance of mismatching with a cost of 1.0%% of assets per year. To reflect the average cost of mismatching, the company could deduct 0.50% from the net interest rate. Asset/liability matching is explored in Chapter 14.

Once the new investment strategy is set, net interest rates should be determined by the company's investment managers, based on a careful analysis of the assets expected to be available to support the investment strategy. This analysis may need to be repeated more than once during the product development process, because of material changes in the investment markets.

3.4.3.3 Portfolio Method

With the portfolio method, one interest rate is calculated for the company's entire investment portfolio. In some cases, a company will use a combination of the segmentation method for some of its business and the portfolio method for the rest of its business.

The portfolio method is most often used by mutual companies in connection with participating products, based on the concept that the entire investment portfolio should benefit all policyowners equally, rather than favoring one generation of policyowners over another. It is also used by some small companies because of its ease and simplicity. Assets are managed in one large portfolio. One interest rate is calculated and applied to all lines of business and all products.

When setting interest rate assumptions for a product using a portfolio method, there are two key items of information: the portfolio interest rate currently being earned on the portfolio, and the new money interest rate currently available on new investments.

Interest rate assumptions generally start with the portfolio rate in the first year. After that, subsequent interest rates may grade toward the new money rate, but this varies greatly by type of product and company philosophy. This will be covered in the next section, which discusses interest rate assumptions for different types of products.

The portfolio method works best with long-duration liabilities with cash flows that are somewhat predictable. If a large portfolio of assets already exists, then, as new money flows in and new investments are purchased, the overall portfolio interest rate will usually move up or down relatively slowly over the years. However, when the interest rate earned on new investments is significantly lower than the portfolio interest rate, the company may experience a surge in new business and new investments, which will drag the portfolio interest rate down more quickly. At the same time, many of the company's highest yielding assets may be prematurely repaid, further accelerating the drop in the portfolio interest rate.

Because of competitive pressures and increased concern about matching assets and liabilities, there has been a long-term trend away from the portfolio method and toward the segmentation method. The segmentation method allows a company to adopt an investment strategy for each product line that better matches the liability pattern. In periods when interest rates on new money are lower than portfolio interest rates, the portfolio method results in more competitive new life insurance products and few companies abandon the portfolio method. However, when interest rates are reversed, with portfolio interest rates lower than new money interest rates, there is significant competitive pressure to switch to a segmentation method, at least for new life insurance business.

Example 3.4.1 Portfolio Interest Rates over Time

Let us examine how a portfolio's interest rate may change from one year to the next. Assume that over the last year, new money net interest rates have fallen from 10% to 8%. We start with a portfolio of $1.0 billion of invested assets earning an average net interest rate of 10.0%, which generates $100 million of net investment income. Individual assets in the portfolio have net interest rates as low as 8.0% and as high as 12.0%.

Many borrowers can now refinance their loans at a lower interest rate, so 40% of the assets ($400 million) will be prematurely repaid in the next year and will be reinvested at the new money interest rate of 8.0%. Borrowers paying high interest rates are much more apt to refinance than those paying low interest rates, so the 40% of assets that will be prematurely repaid will have an average net interest rate of 10.75%. As a result, the assets that will be prematurely repaid will reduce investment income by $43 million ($400 million times 10.75%).

The average interest rate for the $600 million of remaining assets will drop from 10.0% to 9.5%. This is calculated as $100 million of total investment income on the original portfolio less $43 million of lost investment income due to premature repayments, all divided by $600 million of remaining assets.

At the same time, the company is growing. It will increase its invested asset base by $200 million during the next year, growing invested assets to $1.2 billion. This additional $200 million will be invested at 8.0%. At the end of the year, because of all of the preceding assumptions, $600 million of invested assets will be earning 9.5% while $600 million will be earning 8.0%. This will result in an overall average interest rate of 8.75%. In other words, in just one year, the company's portfolio interest rate will have dropped from 10.0% to 8.75%.

Example 3.4.1 illustrates how rapidly a company's average net interest rate can fall when new money interest rates are significantly less than the company's portfolio interest rate. The rate of decrease is affected by how much of the company's existing assets are prepaid and by how much product cash flow is received by the company.

A company's portfolio rate is apt to fall faster toward a lower new money rate and rise slower toward a higher new money rate. Why? There are two main reasons:

1. A lower new money rate means the company's portfolio rate is more competitive, which should attract more new business and cause more new funds to be invested at lower rates. A higher new money rate means the opposite and should result in fewer new funds invested at higher rates.

2. Even more significantly, a lower new money rate will result in the premature repayment of many of the company's higher yielding assets, as borrowers refinance at the new, lower interest rates. This will produce more funds to be reinvested at the lower rates. A higher new money rate will slow down or eliminate the premature repayment of the company's assets, producing less to be reinvested at higher rates.

Example 3.4.2 Interest Rate Earned during the Year

In the Example 3.4.1, we focused on the forward-looking net interest rate for the portfolio at the beginning of two consecutive years. Because of the premature repayment of assets and an increasing asset base, the company's interest rate fell from 10% at the beginning of the year to 8.75% at the end of the year.

In this example, we calculate the net interest rate earned during the year, using three additional assumptions:

(1) Investment income is received in cash twice a year, on July 1 and December 31, (2) all premature repayments and product cash flows other than investment income occur on July 1, and (3) all new investments are purchased on July 1.

Annual effective interest rates of 10.0%, 9.5%, and 8.0% result in semiannual effective interest rates of 4.881%, 4.642%, and 3.923%. The $1 billion of original assets earning 10% will generate $48.81 million ($1 billion times 4.881%) of investment income on July 1. The $600 million of original assets that remain on July 1 will generate $27.85 million ($600 million times 4.642%) of investment income on December 31.

The $600 million of new assets at December 31 will consist of new assets purchased on July 1 plus investment income received on December 31. Investment income received on December 31 consists of $27.85 million from original assets and $21.60 million from $550.55 million of new assets purchased on July 1. 550.55 is calculated as $(600 - 27.85)/(1.03923)$; 21.60 is calculated as $550.55 (0.03923)$. As a check, $550.55 + 21.60 + 27.85 = 600$. Total investment income for the year will be $98.26 million, calculated as $48.81 + 27.85 + 21.60$.

We need a formula to calculate the average net interest rate for the year. Let

A = Invested assets at the beginning of the year

B = Invested assets at the end of the year

I = Investment income for the year, and

i = Average net interest rate for the year.

Assume that (1) beginning assets (A) earn a full year's interest at an interest rate of i and (2) the increase in assets during the year, excluding the increase due to investment income, (that is, $B - A - I$) earns a half-year's interest at an interest rate of $i/2$. From (1) and (2), we have

$$I = Ai + (B - A - I) \frac{i}{2}.$$

Solving for i, we have

$$i = \frac{2I}{A + B - I}. \tag{3.4.1}$$

Returning to our example, this leads to

$$i = \frac{2\ (98.26)}{1{,}000\ +\ 1{,}200\ -\ 98.26} = 9.35\%.$$

Not surprisingly, this rate is approximately the average of the net interest rate at the beginning and end of the year: $(10.0\% + 8.75\%)/2 = 9.375\%$.

Example 3.4.3 Convergence of Portfolio and New Money Rates

If the current new money interest rate is below the portfolio interest rate, common practice is to assume that the portfolio interest rate will decline over the years and eventually grade into the new money interest rate. In the table below, we have assumed that the gap between the portfolio and new money rates narrows by 30% per year. The choice of 30% was purely arbitrary. In addition, a level new money interest rate was assumed. While level and decreasing new money rates are the most common assumptions, increasing new money rates are sometimes projected when the projection begins during a time of relatively low interest rates.

Policy Year	New Money Interest Rate	Portfolio Interest Rate
1	6.50%	7.50%
2	6.50	7.20
3	6.50	6.99
4	6.50	6.84
5	6.50	6.74
6	6.50	6.67
7	6.50	6.62
8	6.50	6.58
9	6.50	6.56
10	6.50	6.54
11 and later	6.50	6.50

3.4.4 Variations in Interest Rate Assumptions by Product

Products handle investment-related risk in different ways. Some products, like universal life and participating permanent products, guarantee a low interest rate and share investment results with the policyowners, effectively transferring much of the investment risk to the policyowners. This greatly simplifies the setting of interest rate assumptions. If you guess wrong, the product can compensate by adjusting credited rates or dividends over the years.

Some products have features that greatly reduce investment risk either by making product cash flows more predictable or by offsetting the effect of adverse cash flows. Here are some features that you might consider as you develop interest assumptions. Many of these are an integral part of the product.

A market value adjustment (MVA) allows the company to reflect the market value of the assets supporting the policy when the policy is surrendered. For example, if assets can be sold for only 90% of their book value, then the policyowner would receive approximately 90% of the policy's cash value. The adjustment works in the policyowner's favor when market values are higher than book values. (Market values and interest rates move in opposite directions. When interest rates increase, you discount using a higher interest rate, so the present value of the asset's cash flows—the market value—is reduced. The opposite is true when interest rates decrease.)

In some jurisdictions, it may be difficult to gain regulatory approval for products with MVAs. In addition, policyowners and even agents may not fully understand the market value adjustment when policies are sold. This can lead to unpleasant surprises if the MVA later reduces the policyowner's surrender value. While the market value adjustment can add equity and stability for both the company and its policyowners, great care must be taken to ensure that the provision is truly understood when policies are sold.

Products that lack any cash surrender value allow the company to invest funds to match the long-term cash flows of the product, with little need for liquidity. Long-term, less liquid investments often carry a higher yield, which should lead to a more competitive or more profitable product.

The existence of a surrender charge can discourage premature surrenders, thereby allowing the company to invest longer term with less need for liquidity. The larger the surrender charge, the bigger the effect on investment strategy. Although surrender charges are primarily designed to recover unamortized acquisition costs upon early surrender, the surrender charge can also help offset capital losses that might result from having to sell assets during a time of high interest rates.

3.4.4.1 Nonparticipating Permanent Products

The alternative to transferring investment risk to the policyowner is not always attractive. Nonpar permanent products, which keep all of the investment risk with the company, can produce results somewhere between the following two extremes:

1. The interest rates assumed in pricing can be set at a low, conservative level. While this approach minimizes the investment risk for the company, it may result in a noncompetitive product and poor consumer value.

2. The interest rates assumed in pricing can be set close to today's interest rate levels. This approach will likely produce a competitive product but may expose the company to enormous risk if interest rates fall significantly. On the other hand, if interest rates rise, the company could enjoy higher than expected profits. However, higher profits could be short-lived if many of the policies are replaced by competitors' products that give credit for higher interest rates.

A compromise solution that falls between these two unattractive extremes may still be unattractive, producing an almost-competitive product with above-average interest rate risk for the company.

Interest rate assumptions for nonpar permanent products usually start with the interest rate currently being earned by the company for the first policy year. Interest rates for subsequent policy years are usually graded down to more conservative interest rates for the later policy years. The slope of the grading should be driven by the degree to which future asset and liability cash flows can be matched.

For example, a nonpar single premium whole life product with no cash values may have liability cash flows consisting only of death benefits. Future death benefits for such products can be accurately projected, since there are no lapses or surrenders. If the company can purchase noncallable assets that closely match the pattern of expected future death benefits, then there is virtually no risk associated with future interest rates. (Callability is discussed in Chapter 15.) In other words, the company can buy all of the assets it needs to support the product on day 1. In this case, very little grading down of future interest rates should be necessary.

However, if only callable assets can be purchased, then you can expect that assets will be called (that is, prematurely repaid) when interest rates fall. This would then put the company in the position of having to reinvest funds under the worst possible conditions: when interest rates are low. To counter this risk, interest rate assumptions should grade down quickly to a safe level. For the rest of this discussion, we will assume that noncallable assets are available.

Now suppose that the same product offers cash values with no explicit or implicit surrender charge. In other words, the policyowner can cash in the policy and move his or her money to another financial institution if interest rates rise. In this case, it will be difficult to match asset and liability cash flows, because the liability cash flows will be extremely unpredictable and dependent on interest rates. This will force the company to invest a good portion of its funds in short-term investments, to be able to manage large cash outflows without having to liquidate investments at a capital loss because of a rise in interest rates. In this case, interest rate assumptions will need to grade down quickly to a level that the company deems very safe.

Finally, suppose that surrender charges are added to the product. If the surrender charges are large enough to cover the likely capital losses associated with having to liquidate long-term assets due to a substantial rise in interest rates, then the company can invest long-term, and a much slower grading down of future interest rates should be supportable. If surrender charges are fairly small and short-term, then interest rates will still need to grade down quickly.

Compared to a single premium product, an annual premium product adds another risk: Annual premiums generally result in net positive cash flows for the product's first ten or more policy years. What will interest rates be when future premiums are received and funds are invested? To counter this additional risk, it is wise to grade down interest rate assumptions more quickly for annual premium products than for otherwise similar single premium products.

3.4.4.2 Participating Permanent Products

The initial dividend scale for a new participating product is based on assumptions as to future interest rates for new money and, if the portfolio method is used, future interest rates to be earned on the existing investment portfolio. The dividend scale can be adjusted to reflect changes in future interest rates, as long as interest rates stay above the level needed to fund guaranteed cash values. This would seem to leave the company free to choose any dividend interest rate that could be rationally justified. However, two competing forces greatly narrow the range of choices:

1. The dividend interest rate should not be too high, because it can be disappointing to policyowners if the company has to lower dividends below the initial dividend scale. Some policyowners base their financial plans on the dividends projected when the policy is purchased. If the initial dividend scale is based on an assumption of high interest rates for an extended period, this can create policyowner expectations that will not be fulfilled if interest rates fall. In the mid- to late 1990s, during a time of relatively low interest rates, many U.S. life insurance companies were sued by their policyowners and subsequently paid large settlements, even though they had justifiably lowered their dividend scales to reflect lower interest rates.

2. On the other hand, basing dividends on future interest rates that are relatively low will result in a noncompetitive product and low sales.

In effect, competition forces a company to base its dividends on future interest rates that are in line with the marketplace. Competition includes not only other life insurance products but also investment products offered by banks, mutual funds, securities firms, and other financial institutions.

Companies may be tempted to raise their dividend interest rates somewhat above the current competitive level in order to capture more new business. If a company's portfolio interest rate has been rising during a period of high new money rates, this would seem to provide perfect justification. However, some competitors will likely react by raising their dividend interest rates. This could lead to an upward spiral of ever more optimistic dividend interest rates.

A portfolio method is often used for par permanent products. As we saw in Section 3.4.3.3, market forces tend to gradually close the gap between new money interest rates and portfolio interest rates. If the portfolio interest rate exceeds the new money interest rate, it would be prudent to assume that the portfolio interest rate moves downward toward the new money interest rate over the next few years. This translates to an initial dividend scale based on declining dividend interest rates.

Let us consider the reversed situation, with the new money interest rate in excess of the portfolio interest rate. A level dividend interest rate based on the current portfolio rate may be both conservative enough and competitive enough to suffice. If the current portfolio rate is not competitive enough, the company may be forced to be less conservative than it would like, in order to match the competition. Another option would be to abandon the portfolio method and embrace the segmentation method, but this is not a decision made lightly.

3.4.4.3 Universal Life

Like par permanent products, UL products have competing forces that drive interest rate assumptions and credited interest rates. The credited interest rate must be set high enough to be competitive with other UL products and investment products. At the same time, the lower the initial credited interest rate can be set, the smaller the chance of disappointing policyowners by having to decrease the credited interest rate in the near future. In addition, the company's profit margins are enhanced by a lower credited interest rate. If a universal life product uses a portfolio method, you can apply the same considerations discussed above for par permanent products.

3.4.4.4   Variable Universal Life

VUL products transfer virtually all investment risk to the policyowners: There is usually no guaranteed interest rate, and cash values have an implicit market value adjustment, due to the nature of VUL. Some VUL products offer investment choices that essentially guarantee principal and credit interest rates, just like UL. Such investment choices can be priced using a UL methodology. Other investment choices require a stochastic modeling approach, which is covered in Chapter 15.

3.4.4.5   Term Insurance

For most forms of term insurance, interest rates are not an important assumption. The importance of interest rates can be determined by calculating results using significantly different interest rates and observing the difference in results. If interest rates are not material, interest rate assumptions may be based on the company's best guess as to future interest rates, perhaps with a little conservatism added. When interest rates are material, interest rate assumptions should be handled like those for nonpar permanent products.

3.4.5   Interest Rate Trends

Figures 3.4.2 and 3.4.3 compare three-month and ten-year interest rates, respectively, for various countries from 1992 through 1999. Three-month interest rates are more volatile and independent from country to country. In contrast, ten-year rates are a little more stable and highly correlated from country to country.

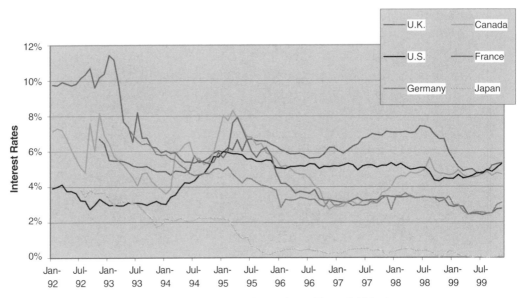

Figure 3.4.2 Comparison of Three-Month Government Bonds

Source: All data are month-end close from Bloomberg Financial Markets.

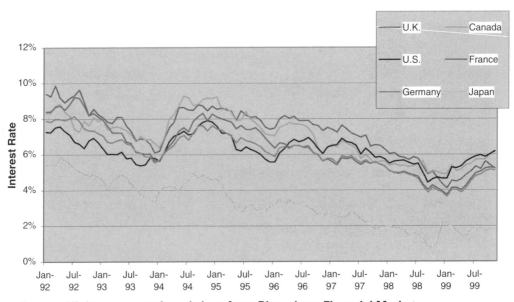

Figure 3.4.3 Comparison of Ten-Year Government Bonds

Source: All data are month-end close from Bloomberg Financial Markets.

Figures 3.4.4 and 3.4.5 show the three-month and ten-year rates for the U.S. and the U.K. on the same graphs, for easier comparison. In most periods the ten-year rate is greater than the 90-day rate. There are a few periods, mainly in the U.K. between July 1997 and July 1999, during which the 90-day rate is higher than the ten-year rate. Such periods are referred to as having an inverted yield curve, which will be discussed further in Chapter 15.

Figure 3.4.6 shows portfolio interest rates for U.S. life insurance companies from 1913 to 1995. These rates showed a fairly smooth upward progression from 1947 through 1985, a period during which new money rates generally exceeded portfolio rates. Portfolio rates dipped in 1986 and 1987, rose slightly in 1988 and 1989, then dropped each year from 1990 to 1995. Many of the bonds and mortgages acquired during the higher interest rate period of the 1980s were called or refinanced during the lower interest rate period of the early 1990s. This added to the downward pressure on portfolio rates.

Figure 3.4.4 Comparison of Three-Month and Ten-Year U.S. Interest Rates

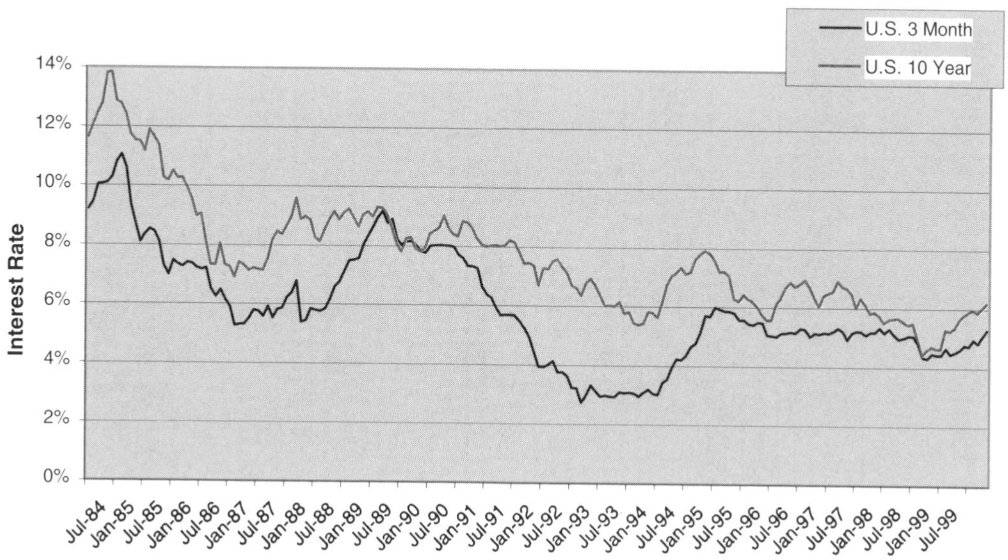

Source: All data are month-end close from Bloomberg Financial Markets.

Figure 3.4.5 Comparison of Three-Month and Ten-Year U.K. Interest Rates

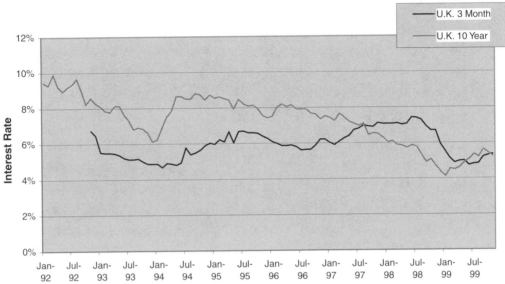

Source: All data are month-end close from Bloomberg Financial Markets.

Figure 3.4.6 Portfolio Interest Rates for U.S. Life Insurance Companies

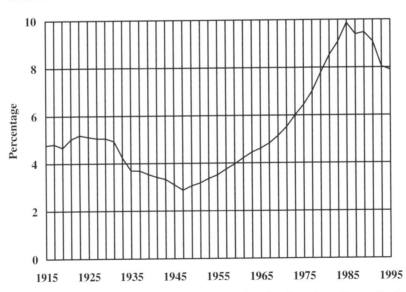

Source: The *Fact Book* published annually by the American Council of Life Insurers.

3.5 **Expense Assumptions**

In this section, besides the usual categories, we will examine an area where there are often conflicting, strongly held points of view: pricing expense philosophy. With assistance from Dr. Thomas Nagle, we will attempt to make a compelling argument for one particular approach.

3.5.1   Why Expenses Vary

Expenses vary tremendously from company to company. In some cases, large companies possess economies of scale that give them a real competitive advantage. Some other large companies seem unable to capitalize on their size to build a cost advantage. Some smaller companies are lean and mean (or anorexic and vicious) to the point that they can successfully compete with much larger companies on an expense basis. Other small companies struggle to cover their costs and make a profit, with little hope of earning a reasonable rate of return.

These kinds of expense differences are due to virtually every factor that helps define a company, from the company culture to its location, employee attributes, employee incentives, salary levels, fringe benefits, cost controls, age of the company, employee turnover, examples set by management, organizational structure, management style, target market, distribution channels, product portfolio, computer systems, company strategy, customer focus, decision-making processes, recruiting and hiring processes, performance management, and so on. The list is endless.

3.5.2 Development of Expense Data

Expenses are company-specific. The expenses used in pricing must be based on company data.

3.5.2.1 Functional Cost Study

The most common source of expense data is a functional cost study, which breaks down all of a company's expenses into functional categories. Typical functional categories would include product development, sales and marketing, policy underwriting and issue, policy maintenance (perhaps split between premium-related, lapse-related, surrender-related, and all other maintenance expenses), claims, premium tax, and overhead. A major part of expenses at most companies would fall into the overhead category. This category would commonly include the expenses of executives, the board of directors, public relations, investor relations, accounting, financial reporting, auditing, and some computer systems. Some expenses, such as those related to policy accounting and valuation, could be allocated more appropriately to policy maintenance or other functions.

A functional cost study often breaks down expenses by analyzing the activities within each department and allocating each department's expenses according to the relative time spent on the various functions it performs. The allocations could be based on precise studies of what each employee does with his or her time. To save time, allocations could be based on rough estimates made by each person as to how much time is spent on each function. Regardless of how a time study is performed, there will be some degree of human error in the results.

Each person's time allocations can be weighted by their salary and grossed up for fringe benefits and other personal expenses, such as personal computers, telephones, furniture, rent, travel, and training costs. Certain expenses may be allocated directly to the related functions, such as the costs of underwriting requirements (medical exams, blood tests, attending physician reports, and so on), premium taxes, commissions, and claim investigations.

Many companies produce functional cost studies on an annual basis. This allows them to track progress in improving productivity or achieving economies of scale. Functional cost studies can also alert the company to adverse trends or can serve as a basis of comparison with other companies.

3.5.2.2 Unit Costs

Functional cost studies are used mainly to determine unit costs. A unit cost is determined by taking the total cost associated with a particular function and dividing by the number of units associated with the function. For example, total product development costs for the year could be divided by the number of products developed during the year to figure the unit cost for developing a single product.

Table 3.5.1 shows the results of a hypothetical functional cost study with associated units and the resulting unit costs. Unit costs can range from simple to extremely complex. A simple underwriting unit cost per policy issued could be calculated as the total costs associated with underwriting (including medical exams, blood tests, inspections, and so on) divided by the number of policies issued. However, because older ages and larger policies require more medical exams, blood tests, inspections, and other requirements, you could develop a complex grid of underwriting unit costs per policy issued that reflected the different costs for each issue age range and death benefit amount range. The cost for each issue age and amount range would be based on the percentage of cases requiring medical exams, blood tests, inspections, and so forth.

Table 3.5.1 Sample Functional Cost Study and Unit Costs

Function	Total Cost	Units	Unit Cost
Overhead	$40 million	One company	$40 million per company
Product Development	2 million	Four products developed	$500,000 per product developed
Sales and Marketing Overhead	5 million	One field force	$5 million per field force
Sales and Marketing	25 million	$100 million of commissions	25.0% of commissions
Underwriting and Issue	30 million	200,000 policies issued	$150 per policy issued
Policy Maintenance:			
Premium-Related	20 million	800,000 premium paying policies	$25 per premium paying policy in force
Lapse-Related	0.1 million	50,000 lapses	$2 per lapse
Surrender-Related	0.1 million	30,000 surrenders	$30 per surrender
All Other	20 million	One million policies	$20 per policy in force
Claims	1 million	$100 million of death benefits paid	1.0% of death benefits paid
Premium Tax	10 million	$500 million of premiums paid	2.0% of premiums paid

For example, assume that medical exams are the only underwriting requirement, exams cost $100 per policy issued, and exams are required only for issue ages 40 and up and death benefits of $250,000 and up. Assume that all other underwriting and policy issue costs amount to $50 per policy issued. The resulting underwriting unit cost grid is shown in Table 3.5.2.

Table 3.5.2 Underwriting Unit Cost Grid

Amount of Death Benefit	Issue Age Range	
	0–39	*40+*
Death Benefits under $250,000	$50	$150
Death Benefits of $250,000+	150	150

Table 3.5.2 is a simplified cost grid. Because underwriting requirements usually vary by issue age and amount of death benefit, cost grids with multiple issue age and death benefit ranges are common.

3.5.2.3   Fixed, Variable, and Mixed Costs

It is important to understand how costs vary as the business grows. Fixed costs are the costs that do not change as the company adds additional business. Many costs fall into this category, such as most of the costs related to the board of directors, company executives, and financial reporting. *Variable costs* are the costs that vary directly with the growth of the business. For example, the cost of mailing to policyowners varies directly with the number of policyowners. The cost of underwriting requirements varies with the number of policies underwritten.

Some expenses are both fixed for a range of growth and variable when certain thresholds are exceeded. For example, most companies can increase the number of policies underwritten to some extent without adding to their underwriting staff. However, there comes a time when one more underwriter must be hired to keep up with the growth of the business. Many expenses within a company fall into this *mixed category* of "fixed to some extent but variable with sufficient growth."

The situation will determine whether these mixed costs are treated as variable or fixed. For example, if a company has two underwriters but only enough business to keep one underwriter busy on a full-time basis, then underwriter costs should probably be considered fixed, unless sales growth of 100% or more is forecast in the near future. However, if a company has 100 underwriters and has been adding underwriters on a regular basis to keep pace with sales growth, then underwriter costs should clearly be considered variable.

For variable or mixed costs, it is important to understand exactly how the costs vary. What can be used to predict changes in costs? For example, is the number of policies underwritten the best predictor of the costs of underwriting requirements? Should the number of policies underwritten be subdivided by issue age and amount group, to better predict the costs of underwriting requirements? Is the number of policies underwritten the best predictor of underwriter costs? Because complex cases with more underwriting requirements require more time to underwrite, would a better predictor include a component for underwriting requirements?

Rather than force an artificial relationship between, say, sales and marketing costs and commissions, it is more important to understand what changes if sales increase. What additional costs are incurred with an increase in sales? For example, agent pension costs, agent bonuses, and agent subsidies may all increase as a percentage of commission when sales increase. However, most sales and marketing expenses are not directly related to commissions. They are related to recruiting, training, and managing the field force, introducing new products, advertising, and developing marketing materials.

Another relevant question is, What is the increase in sales that can be generated by increasing certain sales and marketing expenses, such as those related to the recruiting and training of agents? These are hard questions to answer, but the answers are critical to the company's ability to make informed choices. For example, by understanding the relationship between additional investment in recruiting and training of agents and the resulting long-term profit generated, the company could make informed choices such as the following:

- Because the relationship is so favorable, the company may decide to significantly increase its investment in recruiting and training.

- Because the relationship is so unfavorable, the company may decide to revamp the way it recruits and trains agents, or discontinue recruiting agents altogether.

- Because the relationship is satisfactory, the company may decide to make no major changes.

A good share of a company's maintenance costs may be related to the billing, collecting, and accounting for premiums, as well as the payment of related commissions. For those who pay late, there may be additional costs of late notices and lapse notices and even reinstatement costs. Directly billed policies generally have the highest lapse rate, late payment rate, and expense rate, because of nonautomatic handling of the payment by both the policyowner and the company. Monthly premiums incur 12 times the costs of annual premiums.

For monthly and directly billed policies, premium-related costs can be significant. As a result, many companies transfer a portion of the premium-related costs to the policyowner through higher policy fees or higher expense charges for those who pay more frequently and for those who pay directly rather than through pre-authorized checks (automatic deductions from checking accounts) or payroll deduction. What is then important to pricing is the difference between these policy fees or expense charges and the company's actual costs. If the differences are minor, you may be able to assume that policy fees or expense charges offset such policy expenses, thereby permitting you to ignore both and simplify the pricing process.

3.5.3   Expense Philosophy

There are two diametrically opposed philosophies that guide how a company determines the expenses it includes in pricing. Both of these philosophies are widely used, sometimes in different parts of the same company:

Full cost pricing or *fully allocated expenses:* The company allocates all of its expenses to the various expense rates used for pricing. When multiplied by the proper units, the company's expense rates reproduce the company's total expenses.

Relevant cost pricing or *marginal expense pricing:* The company allocates only those expenses that are relevant to pricing decisions. Only those expenses that would be affected by changes in sales levels would be considered relevant or marginal for pricing decisions.

In most of the remainder of this subsection, we will talk about costs rather than expenses. We will use "cost" to mean the total cost of providing insurance, including the costs of policy benefits, expenses, and capital. Many fine minds have used full cost pricing over the years, as well as some not-so-fine minds (such as the authors). However, experts in pricing almost universally decry full cost pricing. The leading textbook on pricing strategy, *The Strategy and Tactics of Pricing* by Nagle and Holden, makes the case that full cost pricing is less than optimal and is sometimes downright perverse. Because we could not imagine making the case any more eloquently than they do, the remainder of this subsection was adapted from that book in collaboration with Dr. Thomas Nagle, Chairman of Boston-based Strategic Pricing Group Inc.*

3.5.3.1 Full Cost Pricing

The mistake that full cost pricers make is not that they consider costs in their pricing, but that they select the quantities they will sell and the customers they will serve before identifying the prices they can charge. They then try to impose cost-plus prices that may be either more or less than what the customers will pay or the distribution system will sell. In contrast, effective pricers first evaluate what customers will pay and only then choose markets to serve and estimate how much they can sell. For example, when Henry Ford developed the Model T, he began with the customers, asking what they wanted and what they were willing to pay.

A common problem with full cost pricing is an inability to field competitive products. To compensate, some companies price using expense goals or industry benchmarks in place of their current expense levels. These companies often work hard to lower their actual expense levels to match the expenses used in pricing. Many find they are on a treadmill. While they improve their expense levels, so does the competition. Narrowing the gap can be very difficult.

3.5.3.2 Relevant Cost Pricing

One cannot price effectively without understanding costs. To understand one's costs is not simply to know their amounts. Even the least effective

---

*Nagle/Holden, *The Strategy and Tactics of Pricing,* 2nd edition. Copyright 1995, pp. 17–24, 28–32, 40–43. Adapted by permission of Prentice Hall, Upper Saddle River, New Jersey.

pricers, those who mechanically apply cost-plus formulas, know how much they spend on acquisition, maintenance, and overhead. Managers who really understand their costs know more than their levels; they know how their costs will change with the changes in sales that result from pricing decisions. Such knowledge, along with judgment about price sensitivity and competition, are essential factors in pricing strategy.

Not all costs are relevant for every pricing decision. A first step in pricing is to identify the relevant costs, those that actually affect the profits of the pricing decision. In principle, identifying the relevant costs for pricing decisions is actually fairly straightforward. They are the costs that are *incremental* and *avoidable.*

3.5.3.3 Incremental Costs

Pricing decisions affect whether a company will sell less of the product at a higher price or more of the product at a lower price. In either case, some costs remain the same (in total). For example, the expenses of preparing financial statements are probably not affected by the price of the product. Consequently, those costs do not affect the relative profitability of one price versus another. Only costs that rise or fall (in total) when prices change affect the relative profitability of different pricing strategies. We call these costs *incremental* because they represent the increment to costs (positive or negative) that results from the pricing decision.

Incremental costs are the costs associated with changes in pricing and sales levels. The distinction between incremental and nonincremental costs parallels closely, but not exactly, the more familiar distinction between variable and fixed costs. Variable costs, including the costs of policy benefits and the cost of capital, are costs of doing business. Since pricing decisions affect the amount of business that a company does, variable costs are always incremental for pricing. In contrast, fixed costs, such as those of product design, advertising, and overhead, are costs of being in business. They are incremental when deciding whether a price will generate enough revenue to justify being in the business of selling a particular type of product or serving a particular type of customer. Since fixed costs are not affected by how much of the product a company actually sells, most are not incremental when management must decide whether to adopt a simple price change. However, some of these fixed costs are incremental when deciding whether or not to offer a new product. In fact, all fixed costs are incremental at some level of decision making, such as whether or not to discontinue a line of business or sell the company.

Some fixed costs, however, are incremental for pricing decisions, and they must be appropriately identified. Incremental fixed costs are those that directly result from implementing a price change or from offering a version of the product at a different price level. For example, the fixed cost for a company to implement new prices (that is, the costs of calculating the rates, printing new sales material, updating computer files, and gaining regulatory approval) would be incremental when deciding whether or not to change prices.

To further complicate matters, many costs are neither purely fixed nor purely variable. They are fixed over a range of sales but vary when sales go outside that range. You must determine whether such semi-fixed costs are incremental for a particular pricing decision, in order to make that decision correctly.

For example, the company's computer systems may need to be upgraded at significant expense once the number of policies in force exceeds a certain threshold. Prior to reaching that threshold, however, there may be almost no additional computer-related costs for additional policies. Are the costs of the computer upgrade incremental to just the one policy that puts the company over the threshold? Obviously not! But if not, what is the right answer?

If the cost of the upgrade is high enough, the best strategy may be to raise prices to hold the number of policies below the threshold that makes the upgrade necessary. If the cost of the upgrade can be justified by the contribution generated from the additional policies, then it should be made and the sales-constraining price increase avoided. The cost of the upgrade would then, however, be seen as a cost of doing business from that point forward. The cost would not be added as a cost of generating policies since additional policies would not cause the cost to increase. There may be a third possibility: paying a computer service provider to process the additional policies on a cost per policy basis. In that case, the cost would become variable for changes in sales and therefore relevant for pricing.

3.5.3.4   Avoidable Costs

The hardest principle for many business decision makers to accept is that only avoidable costs are relevant for pricing. *Avoidable costs* are those that either have not yet been incurred or that can be reversed. The costs of selling a policy, underwriting it, and delivering it to the customer are avoidable, as is the rental cost of buildings and equipment that are not covered by a long-term lease. The opposite of avoidable costs is *sunk costs:* those costs that a company is irreversibly committed to bear. For example, a company's past expenditures on research and development, or on company-specific software to administer policies, are sunk costs since they cannot be changed regardless of any decisions the company makes in the present. The rent on buildings and equipment within the term of a current lease is a sunk cost, unless the company can avoid the expense by subleasing the property.

The cost of tangible assets (such as computer equipment and furniture) that a company owns may or may not be sunk. If an asset can be sold for an amount equal to its book value, then the asset is not a sunk cost, since the remaining value of the asset can be entirely recovered through resale. In that case, the book value of the asset would represent an avoidable cost. Frequently, the cost of an asset is partially avoidable and partially sunk. For example, new computer equipment could be resold for a substantial portion of its purchase price but would lose some market value immediately after purchase. The portion of the purchase price that cannot be recaptured is sunk and should not be considered in pricing decisions.

From a practical standpoint, the easiest way to identify an avoidable cost is to recognize that it is the *future* cost, not the historical cost, associated with making a sale.

3.5.3.5 Common Mistakes in Estimating Relevant Costs

There are four common errors that managers should avoid when developing useful estimates of relevant costs:

Beware of averaging total variable costs to estimate the cost of a single unit. For example, suppose a company has no room to expand and has adopted a strategy of handling growth by asking employees to work overtime hours at a cost to the company of one-and-a-half times the cost of regular hours. Changes in sales levels will affect overtime costs, not regular costs, so the overtime costs are the incremental and avoidable costs. In contrast, the calculation of average variable costs would be largely based on the cost of regular hours, with some recognition of overtime hours. As a result, average variable costs would significantly understate the incremental cost of additional sales.

Beware of accounting depreciation formulas. Relevant costs should be based on expected changes in market value. Depreciation may or may not be an accurate estimate of the change in market value. In addition, rates of depreciation may vary significantly for tax reporting, regulatory reporting, and stockholder reporting. For most insurance companies, only a small portion of total expense results from depreciation. As a result, variances between depreciation and market value changes are not often material.

Beware of treating a single cost as either all relevant or all irrelevant for pricing. A single cost may have two separate components—one incremental and the other not, or one avoidable and the other sunk—that must be distinguished. Such a cost must be divided into the portion that is relevant to pricing and the portion that is not. For example, the salaries of sales management personnel may be fixed, but their bonuses may be tied to sales levels and therefore incremental.

Beware of overlooking opportunity costs. Opportunity cost is the profit that a company forgoes when it uses assets for one purpose rather than another. They are relevant costs of pricing even though they do not appear on financial statements. They should be assigned hard numbers and managers should incorporate them into their analyses as they would any other cost. For example, the company may own its home office building and carry it on its balance sheet at an amortized cost of $1. As a result, the only costs of occupancy are those related to maintaining the building. However, if the company can sublet all or part of the building that may be unused, there is an opportunity cost of using the space. The opportunity cost is related to what could be earned by leasing the space to someone else. That phantom cost should be charged to the businesses that use the space, even though the company is not actually making an expenditure to retain it.

3.5.3.6   Profit Margin and Pricing Strategy

There are three benefits to determining true unit costs for pricing:

1. It is a necessary first step toward controlling costs.

2. It enables management to determine the minimum price at which the company can profitably accept incremental business that will not affect the pricing of its other products.

3. Most important for our purposes, it enables management to determine the profit margin for each product sold, which is essential for making informed, profitable pricing decisions.

The profit margin has important strategic implications. It is the share of the price that adds to profit or reduces losses. Our concern is not with the average profit, but with the added profit resulting from an additional sale. The profit margin is everything above the portion of the price required to cover the incremental, variable cost of the sale.

We will define the *profit margin* as (a) the present value of profits divided by (b) the present value of premiums. The profit margin tells you the percentage of additional premiums from selling more policies that will be added to profits. For example, the present value of profits may be $500, and the present value of premiums may be $10,000. In this case, the profit margin is 5%.

We will define *premium margin* as (a) the change in the present value of profits caused by a 1% change in the premium level divided by (b) the present value of a 1% change in the premium level. The premium margin tells you the percentage of an increase or decrease in premium that will be added to or subtracted from profits. This measure is based on a change in the premium level. It does not take into account the absolute change in sales that will occur when the premium level is changed. Percentage of premium expenses, including commissions, are the main deductions when calculating premium margin. For example, a 1% increase in the premium level may add $0.70 to the present value of profits and may add $1.00 to the present value of premiums. In this case, the premium margin is 70%. Premium margin is useful for predicting the effect of relatively small changes in the premium level. For large changes in premium level, underlying assumptions such as lapse or mortality rates may change, thereby making the premium margin a poorer predictor of the change in the present value of profits.

Together, profit margin and premium margin enable management to determine the amount by which sales must increase following a price cut (or by how little sales must decline following a price increase) to make the price change profitable. Understanding how changes in sales will affect a product's profitability is the first step in pricing the product effectively.

Consider the effect of an x% change in premium level. Note that x could be positive or negative. Suppose an x% change in price results in a y% change in sales (y could be positive or negative and should be the opposite sign of x). If we let Prem denote the original present value of total premium, then the present value of total premium after the price change will be

$$\text{NewPrem} = \text{Prem}\,(1 + x\%)(1 + y\%). \tag{3.5.1}$$

The revised profit margin will equal the original profit margin plus the amount of profit margin added due to the change in price, divided by the new premium level. The margin added due to the change in premium is equal to the premium margin times the percentage change in price:

$$\text{NewProfitMargin} = \frac{\text{ProfitMargin} + \text{PremiumMargin}\,(x\%)}{1 + x\%}.$$

$$\tag{3.5.2}$$

The revised profit will be the revised profit margin times the new present value of premium:

NewProfit

$$= \frac{\text{Prem } (1 + x\%)(1 + y\%)}{(1 + x\%)} \times [\text{ProfitMargin} + \text{PremiumMargin } (x\%)]$$

$$= \text{Prem } (1 + y\%)[\text{ProfitMargin} + \text{PremiumMargin } (x\%)].$$

$$(3.5.3)$$

Compare Formula 3.5.3 for new total profit to the original total profit:

$$\text{Profit} = \text{Prem} \times \text{ProfitMargin}. \tag{3.5.4}$$

Example 3.5.1

Let Prem = 10,000, ProfitMargin = 5%, and PremiumMargin = 70%. Calculate Profit, NewPrem, NewProfitMargin, and NewProfit for $x = 1$ and $y = -15$ and for $x = 2$ and $y = -20$.

Profit = 10,000 (0.05) = 500.

For $x = 1$ and $y = -15$,

$$\text{NewPrem} = 10{,}000 \ (1.01) \ (0.85) = 8{,}585,$$

$$\text{NewProfitMargin} = \frac{0.05 + 0.70 \ (0.01)}{1.01}$$

$$= 5.644\%,$$

$$\text{NewProfit} = 10{,}000 \ (0.85) \ [0.05 + 0.70 \ (0.01)]$$

$$= 484.50.$$

For $x = 2$ and $y = -20$,

$$\text{NewPrem} = 10{,}000 \ (1.02) \ (0.80) = 8{,}160,$$

$$\text{NewProfitMargin} = \frac{0.05 + 0.70(0.02)}{1.02}$$

$$= 6.2745\%,$$

$$\text{NewProfit} = 10{,}000 \ (0.80)[0.05 + 0.70 \ (0.02)]$$

$$= 512.00.$$

3.5.3.7 Breakeven Sales Change

Now suppose that we wish to find the breakeven sales change, that is, the increase in sales that would exactly offset the effect of an $x\%$ decrease in price. We can accomplish this by setting the original total profit equal to the new total profit and solving for $y\%$:

$$
\begin{aligned}
\text{Prem} \times \text{ProfitMargin} = \text{Prem}\,(1 + y\%) \\
\times\, [\text{ProfitMargin} \\
+ \text{PremiumMargin}\,(x\%)].
\end{aligned}
\tag{3.5.5}
$$

Solving for $y\%$, we obtain the breakeven sales change:

$$
y\% = \frac{\text{ProfitMargin}}{\text{ProfitMargin} + \text{PremiumMargin}\,(x\%)} - 1.
\tag{3.5.6}
$$

The breakeven sales change can be used to evaluate a possible premium decrease. If the premium decrease is expected to increase sales by more than the breakeven sales change, then it should be considered. The same formula can be used to evaluate a possible premium increase. In that case, if the premium increase is expected to decrease sales by less than the breakeven sales change, then it should be considered. The operation of Formula 3.5.6 is illustrated in Table 3.5.3.

Table 3.5.3 Effect of Profit and Premium Margins on Breakeven Sales Changes

	Product A	Product B
ProfitMargin	5.0%	10.0%
PremiumMargin	70.0	80.0
Breakeven Sales Percentage Change Needed to Offset a		
1.0% Price Increase ($x\% = 1.0\%$)	-12.3%	-7.4%
0.5% Price Increase ($x\% = 0.5\%$)	-6.5	-3.8
0.5% Price Reduction ($x\% = -0.5\%$)	7.5	4.2
1.0% Price Reduction ($x\% = -1.0\%$)	16.3	8.7

3.5.3.8 Summary of Relevant Cost Pricing

When we consider only the incremental, avoidable costs in making pricing decisions, we are not saying that other costs are unimportant.

We are saying only that the level of those costs is irrelevant to decisions about which price will generate the most money to cover them and to earn a profit. Since nonincremental fixed and sunk costs are unaffected by a pricing decision, consideration of them clouds the issue of which price changes and levels will generate the most profit to cover them.

If you are still nervous about ignoring some costs, you should be. All costs are obviously important to profitability since they all, regardless of how they are classified, have to be covered before profits are earned. At some point, all costs must be considered. What distinguishes relevant cost pricing from full cost pricing is when they are considered.

A major reason that relevant cost pricing is more profitable than full cost pricing is that it encourages managers to think about costs when they can still do something about them. Every cost is incremental and avoidable at some time. For example, even the cost of product development and design, although it will be fixed and sunk by the time the first policy is sold, is incremental and avoidable before the design process begins. The same is true for other costs. The key to profitable pricing is to recognize that customers in the marketplace, not your costs, determine your prices. Consequently, before you incur any costs, you need to estimate what customers will pay for the product that you intend to offer. Then you can decide what costs you can profitably incur, given the revenue that you expect to earn.

Of course, no one has perfect foresight. Managers must make decisions to incur costs without knowing how the market will respond. When their expectations are accurate, the market rewards them with sales at the prices they expected, enabling them to cover all costs and to earn a profit. When they overestimate a product's value, the resulting profit margin may prove inadequate to cover all the costs incurred.

Both full cost and relevant cost pricers must worry about covering all costs, but they do so in completely different ways. Full cost pricers incur costs first, then worry about how to get prices and sales volumes that will cover them. Relevant cost pricers estimate probable prices and sales volumes first, then think about how they can offer products at costs low enough to make a good profit. Relevant cost pricing begins when all costs considered are incremental and avoidable, but does not stop there. It involves constantly reevaluating potential prices along a product's path to development, asking the question, Does the potential contribution to profits from this product justify bearing the additional incremental, avoidable costs remaining to bring it to market?

After the product is launched, relevant cost pricing involves periodically reevaluating the price level to see if any changes would add to the product's contribution to profits. Such a regular evaluation of price from a product's inception through its replacement will not guarantee profits. However, relevant cost pricing, based on proper analyses and sound managerial judgment, is far more likely to produce profits than is full cost pricing, based on unrealistic assumptions.

Every future cost is relevant to one or more decisions. Table 3.5.4 contains examples of costs and the decisions for which they are relevant.

Table 3.5.4 Examples of Relevant Costs and Associated Decisions

Relevant Cost	Decision
Costs that vary with the number of policies issued or in force, premium payments, commission payments, death benefits, lapses, and surrenders	What prices should be charged for products?
Costs related to maintaining a distribution channel	Should the distribution channel be continued?
Costs related to developing and introducing a new product	Should the new product be developed?
Costs related to maintaining a certain product line or line of business	Should the company continue the product line or line of business? Can it compete?
Costs related to remaining an independent company	Sould the company remain independent? Is it viable?

3.5.4 General Expense Variations

Once a functional cost study has been performed and costs have been studied to understand how they vary (fixed, variable, or mixed) and what causes them to vary, the final step is to develop unit costs for pricing. Unit costs will be heavily influenced by the expense philosophy employed, be it full cost pricing, relevant cost pricing, or something in between. With full cost pricing, the emphasis is on developing unit costs that will reproduce the company's total expenses when unit costs are applied to the current number of units in each category. With relevant cost pricing, it is most important to develop unit costs that accurately reflect how expenses will change with changes in sales levels.

Table 3.5.1 illustrated how unit costs might be structured for pricing purposes. With relevant cost pricing, overhead expenses would be omitted. With full cost pricing, overhead expenses would be arbitrarily allocated to one or more bases, such as policies in force, death benefits in force, or premiums paid. This arbitrary choice can have a major effect on the company's competitiveness in different situations.

For example, using Table 3.5.1, if $45 million of overhead (including sales and marketing overhead) is spread over one million policies, it increases per policy expenses by $45 per year. This would make the company much less competitive in the small policy market (where premiums average, say, $200 per policy) while having only a minor effect in the large policy market (where premiums average, say, $5,000 per policy). Now suppose that the $45 million of overhead were allocated instead as a percentage of the $500 million in premium the company has on its books. That would increase the percentage of premium expenses by 9%, which would have a relatively small effect on the small policy market ($18 of extra expenses on a premium of $200) and a disastrous effect on the highly competitive large policy market ($450 of extra expenses on a premium of $5,000). The arbitrary nature of overhead expense allocations and the resulting effect on competitiveness is a strong indication that full cost pricing is flawed.

3.5.5 Expense Variations by Product

Few companies are able to track the expenses associated with different products. However, using a little common sense, we can figure out that some products and product features have additional complications and must cost more to administer. With some ingenuity and perhaps some interviews or time and motion studies, we can estimate the additional costs.

3.5.5.1 Term Products

Term insurance tends to be the simplest and cheapest product to administer. Typically, term insurance has no cash values and no dividends. In many cases it has level premiums. Some term products have two sets of premiums: current and guaranteed. This can add some complications to sales illustrations, policy issue, and valuation.

3.5.5.2 Permanent Products

Cash values can add considerable complexity to policy administration. Cash values must be shown in sales illustrations and policy forms. They must be considered in valuation. Some companies send annual reports to policyowners to inform them of their current cash value. Cash values must be calculated for policyowner inquiries and cash surrenders, and they can often be loaned. Many companies allow products with cash values to be changed through a complex procedure into other products with cash values. This might be done for a variety of reasons, such as to shorten the premium-paying period, to exchange a previous insured for a new insured, or to modify the premium or death benefit without changing the cash value. In summary, the complexities associated with cash values can add considerable expense over the lifetime of the policy.

3.5.5.3 Participating Products

Annual dividends can add even more complexity than cash values add. Dividends must be recalculated and updated periodically (often every year or two) to reflect the company's recent experience. Because dividends vary by issue year, issue age, policy year, gender, risk class, and perhaps other parameters, the recalculation of dividends can be almost as complicated as the original pricing of the product.

Many companies offer numerous dividend options, which in turn may develop cash values and dividends themselves. Dividend options can complicate many processes, such as annual policyowner reports, policy loans, surrender processing, and valuation. Depending on the degree of automation, dividends can add more administration expense than cash values add.

3.5.5.4 Dynamic Products

On the surface, the accumulation of premium payments, the crediting of interest rates, and the deduction of mortality and expense charges seems like a simple way to calculate cash values. However, it can be complicated by a number of factors:

- Policies can lapse and reinstate, requiring historical calculations to be reversed and catch-up calculations to be performed.

- Mistakes can be made, such as crediting premiums to the wrong policy or increasing the policy's death benefit as of the wrong point in time. Fixing a simple mistake often requires a complex process to undo past calculations and redo new calculations.

- The ability to re-create past calculations means that the entire history of credited interest rates, mortality charges, and expense charges must be accessible.

- Products that segment assets (in order to credit different interest rates to different premiums according to when the premiums were received) add enormous administrative complexity. To maintain multiple segments within a single policy, business rules and software must govern the creation of new segments, the crediting of premiums to the proper segment, the crediting of interest by segment, and the allocation of withdrawals and mortality and expense charges by segment.

The expense and difficulty of undo/redo and segmentation capabilities should not be underestimated. If the company has no experience with these kinds of expenses, outside advice should be sought.

3.5.5.5 Flexible Premium Products

Flexible premiums are more prone to human error than are fixed premium dynamic products, because fixed premiums can be recognized as the right or wrong amount. This means the undo/redo capability will be used more often for flexible premium products.

The most difficult additional complication for flexible premium products is related to commissions, which often are calculated as a high commission rate on first-year premiums up to the amount of a target premium and a much lower commission rate on any excess over the target premium. Most companies further complicate this by paying the high commission rate only on continuing planned premiums. In other words, if the agent received a full commission on a first-year target premium of $1,000 but the subsequent year's premium was only $400, the agent's first-year commission would be recalculated so that the high commission rate was paid on only $400.

This means that the company must not only calculate more complex commissions based on target premiums, but also track the next year's premium and be prepared to retroactively recalculate the first-year commission and charge a portion of the original commission back to the agent. This not only adds expense and complexity, but it also can be unpleasant for both the company and the agent.

3.5.6 Expense Trends

A company's expenses can be divided into three major categories: (1) overhead expenses, (2) expenses related to the acquisition of new business, and (3) expenses related to the servicing and maintenance of in-force business.

3.5.6.1 Overhead Expenses

Almost all companies seek to grow their overhead expenses more slowly than the company grows. If overhead expenses were allocated as part of a full cost pricing philosophy, it would be rare to assume that overhead expenses per unit increase over time. One of the following assumptions is more likely:

1. Overhead expenses will grow slower than inflation (and perhaps will decrease because of automation and other expense improvement measures), and the company will grow faster than inflation, so overhead expenses per unit will decrease over time.

2. Overhead expenses per unit will remain constant. This may be done either to be conservative or because the company has had trouble growing.

3.5.6.2 Acquisition Expenses

Because expenses related to the acquisition of new business are almost all current expenses, there is no need to consider long-term expense trends for them. Current unit costs can be used for pricing, perhaps with some adjustment for upcoming, known changes.

3.5.6.3 Maintenance Expenses

A number of factors will interact to change a company's maintenance expenses over time: The company will likely grow, inflation will increase salaries and other costs, automation and new processes will improve efficiency and productivity, and business changes will raise service standards.

As the company grows, costs can be spread over a bigger base, potentially reducing unit costs. This is often referred to as "building economies of scale." This is especially true for full cost pricing, since much of the expense base is fixed. For relevant cost pricing, the growth of the company will have much less effect on unit costs, since relevant costs are virtually all variable.

Inflation and productivity improvements work in opposite directions. In a country with historically high inflation rates, inflation may be only slightly moderated by productivity improvements. However, in a country with very low inflation, productivity improvements may offset most of the effect of inflation.

Increasing service standards may affect a company's costs over time. Some examples of service standards that may become the norm include

- A toll-free long distance number for policyowner service
- A policyowner service center that is open for customer calls in the evenings and on weekends
- The ability for customers to determine their policy values over the phone using push-button technology, with no human intervention required, 24 hours a day, 7 days a week ("24 × 7")
- The ability for customers to view policy information and perform certain policy transactions over the Internet, 24 × 7
- The ability for customers to write checks against their cash values, automatically generating either policy loans or withdrawals.

As service standards increase, there will be multiple effects: (1) the costs of developing and maintaining a higher level of service, (2) the costs savings resulting from more efficient ways of delivering service, and (3) increased customer satisfaction, resulting in improved persistency and profitability. Some economists estimate that customer service provided over the telephone can be provided for as little as 10% of the cost of service provided through the mail. Similarly, some estimate that service provided via the Internet, where the policyowner serves him- or herself, may cost as little as 10% as much as telephone service.

The net effect of company growth, inflation, productivity improvements, and increasing service standards often results in an assumption that maintenance expenses will stay about the same or slowly increase or decrease. The main exception to this would be a situation where inflation is significant, in which case the unit costs would be increased with inflation less an adjustment for productivity improvements and, in the case of full cost pricing, increasing economies of scale.

3.6 Average Size Assumptions

The product's average size, measured by number of units or death benefit, is used primarily in connection with expenses and policy fees. All pricing calculations are performed on a unit basis. To convert per policy expenses and policy fees to a unit basis, we divide by the average number of units per policy, or average size.

Average size is most important when the policy has a wide range of possible sizes and prices do not vary by size. For example, if the same premium rates applied to all policy sizes from $10,000 to $1,000,000 or more, the average size would be a very important assumption. If annual per policy expenses were $100, consider the effect of two different average sizes: With an average size of $25,000 or 25 units, per policy expenses would amount to $4.00 per unit, which would be a very heavy expense load to add to per unit premiums. With an average size of $100,000 or 100 units, per policy expenses would amount to only $1.00 per unit. A $3.00 difference in premiums per unit could make an immense difference in the ability to field a competitive product.

Policy fees are a good way to pay for per policy expenses. In the previous example, by charging a $100 noncommissionable policy fee, per policy expenses could be removed from per unit premiums. This approach would allow every policy to cover its fair share of expenses. On the other hand, a large policy fee may not be attractive to the company's agents and customers. They may view a large policy fee as a sign of inefficiency and high expenses. It may be easier to sell products with lower policy fees and higher per unit premiums.

When prices do not vary by size of policy, large policies end up subsidizing small policies. When per policy expenses are relatively small, this may be acceptable. Otherwise you may be ignoring the principles of relevant cost pricing and making much less than optimal pricing decisions.

It is common to charge lower per unit prices as policy size increases for two reasons:

1. Per policy expenses, once converted to a per unit basis, decrease as policy size increases. It is equitable to charge lower per unit prices to larger policies.

2. Price sensitivity increases as policy size increases. In other words, larger policies are more apt to be sold in a competitive environment, because there is more at stake. On the other hand, small policies tend to face less competition. A company often needs to charge lower prices for its larger policies in order to be competitive.

Policy fees and per policy expense charges have a similar effect to reducing per unit prices as policy size increases. Instead of reducing the per unit price at just a few key policy sizes such as $100,000, $250,000, and $1,000,000, policy fees reduce the unit price more continuously. For example, every 10% increase in policy size reduces the policy fee per unit by 9.09%.

Example 3.6.1 Prices Varying by Size of Policy

When prices vary by size of policy, there are usually several break points at which prices drop, as in the following table:

Policy Size Range	Premium Rate	Average Size
$25,000–49,999	$20.00	$30,000
50,000–99,999	18.50	60,000
100,000–249,999	17.60	150,000
250,000–499,999	17.30	300,000
500,000–999,999	17.15	600,000
1,000,000+	17.06	1,500,000

Given an annual per policy expense of $90 and the average sizes shown above, see if you can reproduce the differences in premium rates from one size range to the next. Hint: The premium rates equal $17.00 plus $90 divided by the average size.

3.6.1 Sources of Average Size Data

Average size varies mainly by the size of the customer's insurance need and ability to pay. Average size data are very easy for a company to develop. All that needs to be done is add up the units or death benefits for a homogenous group of policies and divide by the number of policies in the group. The more recent the data, the better they will reflect current conditions. When prices for a product vary by policy size, care must be taken to compute average size separately for each size range.

When average size assumptions are needed for a new product that is not replacing an existing product, you should use average size results for the most similar product with prices that vary by the same size ranges. If no such product exists or a new size range is being introduced for the first time, you may have to make some estimates. Outside advice is rarely needed, as good estimates can usually be made. For example, the average size for most size ranges is usually close to the minimum size and no more than one-third of the way between the minimum size and maximum size.

Grouping existing data in a different way can help you estimate the average size for new size ranges. A new size range will cause more policies to be sold at the minimum size of the new range, because some customers will increase the amount they buy in order to get the price discount for the new size range.

3.6.2 General Average Size Variations and Size Variations by Product

In general, younger customers have less ability to pay and therefore have smaller policy sizes. Because the price of life insurance increases rapidly with advancing age, the oldest issue ages often exhibit smaller policy sizes as well. Smokers tend to buy smaller policies than nonsmokers do, probably because of the price differential. In general, those who are placed in the risk classes with the lowest mortality and lowest prices tend to buy larger policies, perhaps because the price is lower and perhaps because they feel they are getting a good deal and should buy more in order to get more of a good deal.

Term insurance has the highest average size. Generally, the lower the product's premium rates, the higher the average size. If the product has lower prices, customers will buy more of it. Permanent products have premium rates that are several to many times higher than term insurance premium rates. Not surprisingly, permanent product average sizes are often several times smaller than term product average sizes.

Some products are used to provide for large insurance needs. For example, joint second-to-die products are sold to pay the estate taxes of wealthy couples. At the other extreme, some products are sold to provide only enough money for the cost of a funeral. The targeted market or need has a large effect on average size.

3.7 Sales Assumptions

How much of the product will be sold combined with the product's profit margin will determine whether it is worthwhile to develop the product. Unfortunately, a fair amount of product development time and effort must be invested before you have a sense of the effect of different price levels on expected sales levels and the product's profit margins. Once you have this sense, however, you can estimate sales levels and profit margins for different price levels. This information, together with estimates of the remaining costs of product development, implementation, and introduction, will help determine whether the product development project should be completed or immediately terminated.

3.7.1 Why Sales Levels Vary

Sales levels are very difficult to predict because there are so many variables outside the company's control. Even with a stable economy and a controlled distribution system that sells only for the company, it is difficult to predict what a price change or new product will do to sales levels. Results depend on how the product or price change is introduced and explained, whether the company supports the new product with advertising or improved marketing tools, how it compares to competitors' recent moves, and so on. Add to these variables the effect of changing preferences and shifting attitudes among consumers and the distribution force.

If the company does not control its distribution, a major driver will be how the new product compares to every other similar product available to its agents or customers, especially those products still on the drawing board that will be introduced around the same time as the company's new product. It is difficult to perform competitive comparisons to products that have yet to be designed, much less introduced! Even so, the likely moves of competitors should be anticipated, in both the short term and longer term.

Over the long term, the portfolio of products a company offers is only one of many variables that affect sales levels. The company's reputation, ratings, service, support, agent relationships, customer relationships, and other attributes will affect sales. What the company does to expand its distribution channels will have a major effect. A number of actions, such as discontinuing an ancillary product line or being the first to raise premiums, lower dividends, or lower interest rates, can cause agents to move to another company and can reduce sales of unrelated products.

3.7.2   Sources of Sales Data

Most new products simply replace sales of older products, either intentionally or unintentionally, and have no significant effect on the company's overall level of sales. When this is the case, the company should examine why it is introducing a new product that is presumably more competitive and has lower profit margins. Does it really want to lower profits while expecting no significant gain in sales levels? The answer may be that, to keep the loyalty of agents and customers over the long term, the company simply must periodically introduce products that are more competitive.

When a new product is expected mainly to replace sales of older products, the company should start with its current sales mix by product and estimate what the sales mix will look like after the new product has been fully introduced. The effect of recent new product introductions could be used as a guide. The company should also estimate its future overall level of sales, which may be increased somewhat by the new product. Again, recent new product introductions could be used as a guide. The overall sales level times the new product's share of sales should give you a fair estimate of the new product's expected sales. By using a disciplined approach, reviewing the results, and learning from experience, you should be able to refine the process to develop better sales estimates over time.

Occasionally, a new product will cause a company's sales to skyrocket. For example, if one of the major players in the U.S. brokerage term market introduces a new term product with the lowest premium rates in the market, its sales will soar until a major competitor introduces even lower prices. Past experience in the brokerage term market can be used to help estimate sales increases. However, without knowing what all the other major players are planning, sales estimates can be far off.

Rather than try to lead the pack, some companies instead aim at maintaining a reputation for being competitive. They achieve this by frequently updating their products to be within a reasonable range of the market leaders. Such a philosophy makes it easier to estimate future sales levels, which should rise and fall more modestly as the company introduces lower rates and then is leapfrogged by its competitors. This philosophy may include thinking along the following lines: If an agent or customer will abandon the company to save a modest amount, then let a competitor have the business, as such business is more apt to be lapsed and moved to another company in a year or two anyway.

As another example, some companies have field forces that are loyal only to a point. They will sell the company's products as long as they are somewhat competitive. In this case, replacing a noncompetitive product with a competitive product may dramatically increase sales. By comparing the company's sales mix by product to that for other companies, the company may be able to develop a fair estimate of the volume of business for each product that is going to competitors and that could probably be recaptured.

As yet another example, a company may be slow to introduce a new type of product, such as VUL, preferred term, or joint last-to-die UL. Therefore, it may find that its agents increasingly are selling those products for other companies. By introducing a missing product, the company may be able to recapture part of its agents' business and increase the company's overall sales. Industry statistics should be available that show the mix of new business by type of product. This should give the company a good sense as to how much additional business it could write by capturing part of its agents' sales on a product it does not currently offer.

On the other hand, agents' habits can be hard to break. In addition, agents may prefer to place specialized products with companies they believe are the experts for those products. Just because a company introduces a missing product doesn't mean it will automatically replace the other companies its agents have been using.

3.8   Sensitivity Testing and Scenario Testing

Because of the uncertainty present in all assumptions, it is useful to test more than one set of assumptions. This can be done in two general ways: sensitivity testing and scenario testing.

3.8.1   Sensitivity Testing

Sensitivity testing involves varying key assumptions (such as mortality, lapse, interest, expense, sales levels, or tax rates) and observing the effect on profit margins. When testing more than one assumption for sensitivity, it is common to vary one assumption at a time. For example, you might test a 10% increase in mortality, a 20% increase in lapse rates, and a 2% decrease in interest rates. The amount of variation that you test should relate to the degree of uncertainty you feel in each assumption.

For example, if mortality were based on a conservative interpretation of highly credible company mortality studies, you would likely skip sensitivity testing for mortality. However, if lapse rates are based on just three years of credible experience from a similar product, you may want to do sensitivity testing for lapse rates in policy years 4 and later. If you are reasonably sure that those lapse rates will fall within a certain corridor, you may want to sensitivity test both ends of that corridor. If profit margins vary considerably, you may wish to build a little extra conservatism into the lapse assumptions used for pricing. Another solution may be to change the product design to reduce the sensitivity to lapses by, for example, increasing surrender charges in the later policy years.

One area should always be explored with sensitivity testing: the effect of policyowners behaving in ways that maximize the value they obtain from the life insurance product. For example, consider a ten-year level term product that assumes that 50% of the policyowners who persist to the end of the tenth year will then pay a greatly increased premium starting in the eleventh year, while the other 50% lapse. Assume further that the eleventh-year premium would be much higher than the premium that would be available for a newly issued policy. In this case, a wise policyowner would lapse and purchase a new policy, unless the insured is unhealthy and unlikely to qualify for a new policy. Because of this, it would be wise to test the effect of a tenth-year lapse rate much higher than 50%, combined with the resulting increase in mortality anti-selection.

For some products, the situation is reversed: The product's profitability may depend on policyowners lapsing when to do so would be to their disadvantage. This is the case for Term to 100 and other lapse-supported products. In this case, the effect of lower lapse rates must be tested.

The type of sensitivity testing performed varies by the type of product. For example, interest rate sensitivity testing can be omitted for short-duration term products. Lapse rate sensitivity testing may be unnecessary for a product with sufficiently high surrender charges. Mortality sensitivity testing may not be required for products with death benefits that only slightly exceed cash values. Sensitivity testing of assumptions such as mortality, expenses, or taxes may be skipped if the company feels these are well known and unlikely to change. Products with relatively minor implementation and introduction expenses may not need to be sensitivity tested for lower than expected sales levels.

Sensitivity testing can have several results: It can lead to (1) changes in product design, (2) cancellation of the product, (3) changes in assumptions, (4) a better understanding of the product's risks, and

(5) the establishment of mechanisms for timely monitoring and management of a product's most important risks.

3.8.2 Scenario Testing

Scenario testing is sometimes used as a synonym for sensitivity testing. However, we will use it to mean something a little different. We will define a scenario as a plausible set of consistent assumptions. For example, one scenario might consist of an upward spike in interest rates, coupled with an increase in lapse rates (caused by policyowners surrendering their policies to take advantage of high interest rates available elsewhere) and a slight increase in mortality rates (caused by increased anti-selection). Scenario testing estimates the effect of various scenarios on a product, a block of business, or an entire company.

Scenarios are constructed in every way imaginable. Often, the driving assumption in the scenario relates to the economy or interest rates. The economy may go through boom and bust cycles or experience a prolonged boom or bust (that is, a recession). Interest rates may cycle up and down, randomly fluctuate, jump up and stay up, drop down and stay down, gradually drift downward, gradually drift upward, or remain relatively constant. The driving assumption then guides the choice of other assumptions. For example, if interest rates are the driving assumption, they could directly affect lapse rates and the inflation rate used for maintenance expenses. Lapse rates, in turn, could affect mortality rates.

Scenarios are also constructed to examine the effect of certain combinations of assumptions that are of concern to the company. For example, for a single-pay nonpar whole life product, the company may want to examine the effect of a slow decline in interest rates, coupled with slowly increasing lapse and mortality rates, over a period of many years. No matter what assumptions are chosen for a scenario, it is common to start from current levels of interest, mortality, sales, expenses, and so on and grade into the scenario over a period of several years.

3.9 Exercises

Exercise 3.1

Describe the differences between aggregate, select, ultimate, and select and ultimate mortality tables. Which type of mortality table is usually the most appropriate for use in developing life insurance products?

Exercise 3.2

Mortality can vary significantly by gender, tobacco usage, and size of policy. Which factor is generally the most and least significant?

Exercise 3.3

You are given the following information:

- A group is composed of 75% nonsmokers and 25% smokers
- The mortality of the overall group is 37.5% of Table XXX, an old, decrepit, but still widely used mortality table
- Smokers have twice the mortality rate of nonsmokers.

Suppose the company offers 50% discounts for nonsmokers for the first time. As a result, while 75% of the buyers are still nonsmokers, nonsmokers now buy twice as much insurance as smokers buy. What is the mortality of nonsmokers, smokers, and the new overall group, reflecting nonsmokers buying twice as much as smokers? Express your answers as a percentage of Table XXX.

Exercise 3.4

Suppose everyone in a group of 51 insureds has a different expected mortality percentage. These 51 different percentages are spread evenly from 75% to 125% (that is, one person at every whole percentage). Initially this entire group is placed in the "standard" risk class. You are asked to split this group into two groups: a preferred, lower-mortality group, and a select, higher-mortality group. (In this case, "select" is a clever marketing name you have chosen for the non-preferred risks.)

Where would you draw the line so that the average mortality of the preferred group would be 90%? What would the average mortality of the select group be in this case?

Where would you draw the line so that the average mortality of the preferred group would be 85%? What would the average mortality of the select group be in this case?

Exercise 3.5

Building on Exercise 3.4, suppose you just discovered that a competitor has a super-preferred category that you think is skimming half of the people with mortality of 85% or less out of your preferred group. What effect has this had on the average mortality of the first preferred group (originally targeted to achieve 90% mortality) from Exercise 3.4?

Exercise 3.6

Refer to Example 3.2.3 at the end of Section 3.2.4.3.

a. Recalculate qdActual assuming the expected lapse rate is 25% instead of 15%.

b. Recalculate qdActual assuming only 50% of the extra lapses are selective.

c. Finally, recalculate qdActual assuming both of the previous changes.

Exercise 3.7

Suppose a block of $1 billion of life insurance issued on December 31, 1999 has the following experience over the next three years:

Year	Amount Lapsed	Death Benefits Paid
2000	$99,000,000	$1,000,000
2001	89,000,000	1,000,000
2002	80,000,000	1,000,000

Calculate the lapse rate, mortality rate, and persistency rate for each year. What are the two ways in which the persistency rate can be calculated?

Exercise 3.8

Which of each of the following pairs tend to have higher lapse rates?

First year/renewal year

Issue age 25/issue age 55

$10,000 policy/$1,000,000 policy

Quarterly premiums/annual premiums

Directly billed/pre-authorized checks

Substandard risk/standard risk

Smoker/nonsmoker

Nonpreferred (residual) risk/Preferred risk

Male/female

Increasing premiums/level premiums

Heaped commissions/level commissions

No surrender charge/surrender charge

10-year term/Term to 100

Whole life/Term to 100

Exercise 3.9

Describe five different events that could cause a company's lapse rates to soar.

Exercise 3.10

If ages 25 to 30 are the peak ages for borrowing money and increasing personal debt and ages 55 to 60 are the peak ages for saving money, explain how demographics might be used to predict the supply and demand for money, decades in advance. What effect would changes in the supply and demand for money have on interest rates?

Exercise 3.11

Suppose you have the following investment choices for constructing a new asset portfolio:

Asset Class	Gross Yield	Annual Default Cost	Investment Expenses	Maturity (years)
Government Bonds	6.00%	0.00%	0.05%	3
Corporate Bonds	7.25	0.02	0.10	10
Junk Bonds	15.00	5.00	0.20	5

To limit its risk in a declining economy, the company has decided to limit the investment in junk bonds to no more than 20%. In addition, the company wishes to keep the average maturity of its assets at six years. How would you allocate investments among the asset classes to maximize yield within the constraints given? What is the resulting portfolio's net yield?

Exercise 3.12

Comparing the segmentation and portfolio methods of crediting interest, which is generally more competitive in a rising interest rate environment? Why? Which is more competitive in a falling interest rate environment?

Exercise 3.13

To derive Formula 3.4.1, we assumed that the increase in assets during the year, excluding the portion of the increase due to investment income (equal to $B - A - I$), earns a half-year's *simple* interest ($i/2$). Show how to develop a more refined version of Formula 3.4.1 using compound interest in place of simple interest, that is, using "$(1 + i)^{1/2} - 1$" in place of "$i/2$." Feel free to stop short of solving the quadratic equation. Which formula would you rather use as an approximation of the average net interest rate?

Exercise 3.14

A new blood test has become available that will allow the company to screen out prospective insureds with the newly discovered biathlon deficiency (BAD) condition. The laboratory your company uses for blood testing can now perform a BAD screen. You are given the following information:

- By screening out those with the BAD condition, the present value of the resulting mortality savings over the life of a policy issued to a 45-year-old are equal to $0.50 per 1,000 of death benefit.

- The BAD screen will cost an extra $10 if you are already collecting a blood sample.

- Collecting a blood sample costs $25. Performing the usual blood tests costs $15.

- The usual blood tests generate mortality savings with a present value of $0.50 per 1,000 of death benefit for a 45-year-old, over the life of a policy.

At what policy size should you require a blood sample for 45-year-olds? Which blood tests (the usual and/or the BAD screen) should you perform on each blood sample?

Exercise 3.15

A company currently sells only UL business. It is considering whether to develop and sell a ten-year term product. The company expects the term product to reduce the sales of its UL products. This will allow one UL underwriter to be transferred to underwriting term products. However, the company believes it will need three underwriters for the term product. The company's administrative system will have to be modified to support term products, since the current system was designed to support only universal life.

Focusing only on the above information, determine the relevant costs for each of the following decisions:

1. Whether to enter the term insurance business and develop a term product

2. What prices to charge for the term product.

Remember, for a cost to be relevant to a decision, it must be both incremental and avoidable.

Exercise 3.16

Recalculate the breakeven sales changes in Table 3.5.3 after reducing the premium margins from 70% and 80% to 50% and 60%, respectively.

3.10   Answers

Answer 3.1

Refer to Section 3.2.2. Select and ultimate mortality tables are usually the most appropriate.

Answer 3.2

There is no universal answer to this question. The answer varies significantly by country and target market. In the North American middle- and upper-income markets, tobacco usage would be the most significant and size of policy would be the least significant.

Answer 3.3

First, determine separate mortality assumptions for nonsmokers (NS) and smokers (S). We know that

$$0.75 \text{ NS} + 0.25 \text{ S} = 37.5\%,$$
$$\text{S} = 2 \text{ NS}.$$

Solving for NS and S,

$$1.25 \text{ NS} = 37.5\%,$$
$$\text{NS} = 30\%,$$
$$\text{S} = 60\%.$$

The new amount of insurance sold will be $(0.75)(2) + (0.25)(1) = 1.75$.

Therefore, the new overall mortality will be

$$\frac{1.50 \text{ NS} + 0.25 \text{ S}}{1.75} = \frac{45.0\% + 15.0\%}{1.75} = 34.3\%.$$

Answer 3.4

To average 90%, the cutoff for the preferred group should be up to and including 105%:

$$\sum_{x=75}^{105} \frac{x\%}{31} = 90\%.$$

The mortality for the select group would then be

$$\sum_{x=106}^{125} \frac{x\%}{20} = 115.5\%.$$

To average 85%, the cutoff for the preferred group should be up to and including 95%:

$$\sum_{x=75}^{95} \frac{x\%}{21} = 85\%.$$

The mortality for the select group would then be

$$\sum_{x=96}^{125} \frac{x\%}{30} = 110.5\%.$$

Answer 3.5

The preferred group had a cutoff at 105%, with 31 people. If a competitor takes half of the prospective insureds with mortality of 85% or better, that leaves 5.5 people with mortality of 75–85% (with an average of 80%) and 20 people with mortality of 86–105% (with an average of 95.5%). This will cause the average mortality of the preferred group to rise from 90% to

$$\frac{(5.5 \text{ people})(80.0\%) + (20 \text{ people})(95.5\%)}{25.5 \text{ people}}$$

$$= 92.2\%.$$

Answer 3.6

a. qwExtra = 0.20, SelectPct = 80%
   qwSelect = (0.20) 80% = 0.16
   qwNonsel = 0.20 − 0.16 = 0.04
   qdActual = ((1 − 0.05 − 0.04) 2.00 − (0.16) 1.00)/0.75 = 2.2133
   Anti-selection increases mortality by 10.7%.

b. qwExtra = 0.10, SelectPct = 50%
   qwSelect = (0.10) 50% = 0.05
   qwNonsel = 0.10 − 0.05 = 0.05
   qdActual = ((1 − 0.05 − 0.05) 2.00 − (0.05) 1.00)/0.85 = 2.0588
   Anti-selection increases mortality by 2.9%.

c. qwExtra = 0.20, SelectPct = 50%
   qwSelect = (0.20) 50% = 0.10
   qwNonsel = 0.20 − 0.10 = 0.10
   qdActual = ((1 − 0.05 − 0.10) 2.00 − (0.10) 1.00)/0.75 = 2.1333
   Anti-selection increases mortality by 6.7%.

Answer 3.7

Year	Amount in Force at the Beginning of the Year	Lapse Rate	Mortality Rate (per 1,000)	Persistency Rate
2000	$1,000,000,000	9.90%	1.00	90.10%
2001	900,000,000	9.89	1.11	90.11
2002	810,000,000	9.88	1.25	90.12

The persistency rate in the table was calculated as "one minus the lapse rate," which is the method used in this book. The other way of calculating persistency is the amount in force at the end of the year divided by the amount in force at the beginning of the year, which results in 90% persistency for all three years in this exercise.

Answer 3.8

The first of each pair tends to have higher lapse rates.

Answer 3.9

1. A ratings downgrade could lead to mass lapsation among rating-sensitive customers.

2. If a large group of agents defected to another company, much of their business may follow them.

3. If the company allows its products to become very uncompetitive (for example, UL credited interest rates 2% below rates available elsewhere), savvy policyowners will find a better deal.

4. If the company decides to replace an old series of policies with an updated product, almost all of the policies being replaced may appear to lapse.

5. If the company suffers a public-relations fiasco, lapse rates may shoot up.

Answer 3.10

Based on those already born, you can accurately predict those reaching the prime borrowing ages of 25 to 30 over the next 25 years. Similarly, you can predict the number of people who will attain the prime savings years of 55 to 60 for many years to come. When the number of prime borrowers peaks, you can expect the demand for money to be at a relative maximum. When the number of prime savers peaks, you would expect the supply of money to be at a relative maximum. Increases in demand will tend to drive up interest rates, while increases in supply will tend to drive down interest rates.

Answer 3.11

Since junk bonds provide the highest net yield after the deduction of default costs and investment expenses, the percentage invested in junk bonds should be maximized at the limit of 20%. The percentage invested in each of the other assets is then solved for based on the constraint that the average maturity be six years:

$$(Gov\%)(3 \text{ years}) + (Corp\%)(10 \text{ years}) + (Junk\%)(5 \text{ years})$$
$$= 6 \text{ years}.$$

Junk% = 20%, so Gov% = 80% − Corp%. This leads to:

$$(80\% − \text{Corp}\%)(3 \text{ years}) + (\text{Corp}\%)(10 \text{ years}) + (20\%)(5 \text{ years})$$
$$= 6 \text{ years}.$$

Solving for Corp%, we find Corp% = 37%, so Gov% = 43%.

Calculating the net yield using these allocations, we have

Government bonds:	$(43\%)(0.06 − 0.00 − 0.0005)$
Corporate bonds:	$+ (37\%)(0.0725 − 0.0002 − 0.001)$
Junk bonds:	$+ (20\%)(0.15 − 0.05 − 0.002)$
Total:	$= 7.1566\%.$

Answer 3.12

The segmentation method is more competitive in a rising interest rate environment because the interest rates credited on new money are not dragged down by the returns currently being earned on old money, as is the case for the portfolio method. Conversely, in a falling interest rate environment, the interest rate credited by the portfolio method is subsidized by the higher returns currently being earned on old money.

Answer 3.13

In place of $I = A\,i + (B − A − I)\,i/2$, we have

$$I = A\,i + (B − A − I)((1 + i)^{1/2} − 1).$$

Letting $x = (1 + i)^{1/2}$, we can convert this into a quadratic equation and solve for x:

$$I = A\,(x^2 − 1) + (B − A − I)(x − 1).$$

Rearranging terms, we have

$$Ax^2 + (B − A − I)x − B = 0.$$

This can be solved using the quadratic formula.

Note that A is the cash flow at time 0, $(B − A − I)$ is the cash flow at time $\frac{1}{2}$, and $−B$ is the cash flow at time 1. These cash flows plus investment income add up to zero. This is not a coincidence!

Answer 3.14

You can double the mortality savings by performing the BAD screen, which adds just 25% ($10) to the cost of performing only the usual blood tests ($40). Similarly, you can double the mortality savings by performing the usual blood tests, which adds just 43% ($15) to the cost of performing only the BAD screen ($35). Therefore, you will always perform both the BAD screen and the usual blood tests whenever you collect blood. The question then becomes: At what policy size is it worthwhile to spend $50 to collect blood and perform all the tests in order to save $1.00 per thousand? The answer: $50,000.

Answer 3.15

The cost or lost profit associated with a decline in UL business due to the introduction of term insurance is relevant to the decision as to whether to enter the term insurance business. This cost is fixed and incremental: The damage will be done, or it won't be. It is definitely an avoidable cost.

The costs of the underwriters needed to support the term product are relevant to the pricing of the term product. The need for additional underwriters will vary with the sales of the term product. Their costs will be incremental as sales grow beyond the capacity of one or two underwriters. Their costs are avoidable if sales do not grow sufficiently.

The cost of modifying the administrative system to support term products is relevant to the decision as to whether to enter the term insurance business. In terms of that decision, this cost is both incremental and avoidable.

Answer 3.16

	Product A	Product B
ProfitMargin	50%	10.0%
PremiumMargin	50.0	60.0
Breakeven Sales Percentage Change Needed to Offset a		
1.0% Price Increase ($x\% = 1.0\%$)	−9.1%	−5.7%
0.5% Price Increase ($x\% = 0.5\%$)	−4.8	−2.9
0.5% Price Reduction ($x\% = -0.5\%$)	5.3	3.1
1.0% Price Reduction ($x\% = -1.0\%$)	11.1	6.4

Part II
Product Pricing

Product pricing is also known as profit testing, modeling, or pricing. Life insurance pricing is one of the more sophisticated and complicated processes in the financial world. For most people in the life insurance business, it is a mystery, and justifiably so.

The goal of Part II is to introduce you to the components of product pricing one step at a time, in as simple and straightforward a way as possible. Anyone with mathematical aptitude and a basic knowledge of insurance should be able to master the elements of pricing by studying these chapters. Your goal should not be to memorize variables and formulas, but rather to understand them. You should focus on developing your ability to derive formulas from basic principles and craft new formulas to fit new situations. Such abilities are quite valuable in the workplace.

Part II is organized around building each of the components of distributable earnings, which are the earnings that can be distributed to the owners of the company. Distributable earnings take into account not only the basic cash flows and reserve requirements of the business, but also the capital required for the company to withstand financial fluctuations and economic downturns.

Distributable earnings are calculated as (a) product cash flows (premiums less benefits less expenses) plus (b) investment income less (c) taxes and less (d) the increase in reserves and required capital. When distributable earnings are negative, they represent additional capital contributions that the owners must make to support the company.

The chapters of Part II are organized as follows:

- Chapter 4, "Basic Actuarial Mathematics," develops formulas for interest, discounting, survivorship, deaths, and lapses.

- Chapter 5, "Life Insurance Cash Flows," explains and develops formulas for the cash flows associated with life insurance products, including premiums and many types of insurance benefits and expenses.

- Chapter 6, "Reserves," explains and develops formulas for many different types of reserves and for increases in reserves.

- Chapter 7, "Reinsurance," explains the most common forms of reinsurance and develops adjustments to the formulas presented in Chapters 5 and 6 to reflect the impact of reinsurance.

- Chapter 8, "Investment Income," develops formulas for the investment income earned on the assets backing reserves, including policy loans.

- Chapter 9, "Taxes," explains the various types of taxes payable by life insurance companies and develops formulas for these taxes. In addition, deferred taxes are addressed.

- Chapter 10, "Required Capital," explains the associated risks and components of required capital and develops formulas for these components, as well as for the overall increase in required capital. Required capital frameworks are presented for several countries.

- Chapter 11, "Profit Measurement and Analysis," develops formulas for various types of earnings, including distributable earnings. Many different profit measures are introduced.

- Chapter 12, "Quarterly Calculations," develops adjustments to the formulas presented in Chapters 4 through 11 to convert the formulas from annual to quarterly calculations, in order to model the patterns of cash flows and earnings more accurately.

- Chapter 13, "Annuity and Investment Products," starts by describing annuity and investment products in some detail. Next, special design issues, assumptions, and pricing issues are addressed. Finally, modifications to the life insurance pricing formulas presented in Chapters 4 through 12 are developed, to adapt them to annuity and investment products.

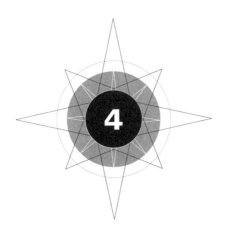

Basic Actuarial Mathematics

4.1 Introduction

This chapter serves two purposes: For the more experienced reader, it introduces the basic actuarial notation that will be used in subsequent chapters. A quick review of the notation introduced in this chapter is all that is needed for the experienced reader.

For the less experienced reader, it serves as an introduction to basic actuarial mathematics. This chapter is designed especially for nonactuaries, although a basic knowledge of algebra, probability, and finance is helpful in understanding the material.

Unlike traditional actuarial notation, which was designed to minimize calculations before the advent of computers, the notation and formulas in this book are designed for use in spreadsheets and computer programs.

4.2 Notation Methodology

It is important for the student to read and understand this section to see how the notation for time and policy years will be used in the upcoming chapters.

4.2.1 General Rule

This book will make extensive use of the value t in variable names when referring to values that vary by policy year. You may be accustomed to using the variable t as a measure of time. For example, $t = 0$ may denote the current time, $t = 1$ may denote one year from now, and $t = 1.5$ may denote a year and a half from now.

For insurance policies, the concept of a policy year confuses the issue somewhat. A policy year is a one-year-long period of time rather than a single point in time. Policy year 1 runs from the policy issue date until just before the first policy anniversary. Policy year 2 runs from the first policy anniversary until just before the second policy anniversary, and so on.

The following time line illustrates the differences between time and policy year:

```
Time:           0           1           2           3           4
Policy year:         1           2           3           4
                |--------------|--------------|--------------|--------------|
```

The following notation rules are used throughout this book. Although you may believe these rules were established solely to confuse you, that is not the case. They were also intended to confuse the authors!

- t will be used to denote policy year, as well as time.
- Policy year t covers the time interval $[t - 1, t)$. (Note: "[" or "]" includes the beginning or ending end point of the time interval; "(" or ")" excludes the beginning or end point of the time interval.)

- The use of (*t*) in a variable's name will usually denote a variable as of the *end* of policy year *t*; for example, Div(*t*) will denote a policyholder dividend payable at the end of policy year *t*.

- When a policy year of zero is used, represented by (0) in the variable name, it denotes the moment just before the policy is issued and just before the first premium is paid.

4.2.2 Exceptions

For every rule, there must be at least one exception. Whenever there is an exception, one or both of the following will occur:

- The exception will be clearly stated in the text. For example, one naturally thinks of premium flows as occurring at the beginning of a policy year. In the section discussing premiums, this fact is clearly stated.

- To clearly distinguish the timing of certain items, the use of "Beg," "Mid," and "End" will occur at the end of the variable name. For example, CashFlowBeg(*t*), CashFlowMid(*t*), and CashFlowEnd(*t*) indicate, respectively, cash flows occurring at the beginning, middle, and end of policy year *t*.

4.3 Interest

When someone borrows money, they are required to repay the amount they borrow plus interest. Interest is the charge for the loan. Interest makes the lender willing to loan the money. The rate of interest is essentially the price of borrowed money. The interest rate depends on the riskiness of the borrower and supply versus demand for money.

For example, if Bob borrows $100 for one year with an interest rate of 10%, Bob will have to repay $100 plus 10% of $100, for a total repayment of $110 at the end of the year.

4.3.1 Compound Interest

If money is borrowed for more than one year with no repayments until the end of the loan, interest is typically compounded, which means you must pay interest on any unpaid interest. For example, if Bob borrows $100 for two years with an interest rate of 10%, Bob will have to repay $121 at the end of two years. The first year's interest is 10% of $100. The next year's interest is 10% of $110. The $121 repayment consists of $100 of principal repayment and $21 of interest.

4.3.2 Accumulation

The same principle of compound interest applies to money invested at a given interest rate for a number of years. For example, if Bob deposits $100 with a bank that agrees to pay him 10% interest for two years, Bob's account will grow from $100 to $110 to $121 in two years. In effect, Bob is lending money to the bank. Borrowing and investing are two sides of the same coin.

In general, to accumulate an amount with interest for one year at interest rate i, multiply the amount by $(1 + i)$. To accumulate an amount for t years, multiply by $(1 + i)^t$. In fact, this formula applies even if t is not a whole number: t can be any positive number. To accumulate an amount for m months, multiply by $(1 + i)^{m/12}$. To accumulate for d days, multiply by $(1 + i)^{d/365}$.

Let

$$\text{InitInv} = \text{Amount of the initial investment}$$
$$\text{AccumInv} = \text{Amount of the accumulated investment after } t \text{ years at interest rate } i.$$

Then,

$$\text{AccumInv} = \text{InitInv} \, (1 + i)^t. \tag{4.3.1}$$

In insurance calculations, interest rates often vary from year to year, in which case the accumulation factor $(1 + i)^t$ does not apply. To handle varying interest rates, we need some additional notation:

$$n = \text{The final policy year for calculations; the maximum value of } t$$

$$i(t) = \text{Interest rate for policy year } t$$

$$\text{AccumFactor}(t) = \text{Factor that is applied to accumulate an investment from time 0 to time } t, \text{ applying } t \text{ years of varying interest rates: this is the accumulation factor.}$$

The accumulation factor, AccumFactor(t), is used to accumulate amounts starting at time 0 and ending at time t. In policy year terms, AccumFactor(t) accumulates amounts starting at the issue date and ending at the *end* of policy year t. The interest rate for policy year 1, $i(1)$, applies from time 0 to time 1, as shown in the following time line:

Time:	0	1	2	3	4
Policy year:		1	2	3	4
		---------------	---------------	---------------	---------------	
Interest rate:		$i(1)$	$i(2)$	$i(3)$	$i(4)$

When interest rates vary from year to year, the accumulation factor for a period of n years is calculated iteratively, starting with AccumFactor(0) = 1:

$$\text{AccumFactor}(t) = \text{AccumFactor}(t - 1)\,(1 + i(t)), \text{ for } t = 1 \text{ to } n. \tag{4.3.2}$$

Alternatively, the previous formula can be stated as

$$\text{AccumFactor}(n) = \prod_{t=1}^{n} (1 + i(t)). \tag{4.3.3}$$

These formulas presume that interest rates change annually. Similar formulas can be developed for interest rates that change daily, monthly, or quarterly.

Example 4.3.1

Given $i(1) = 10\%$ and $i(2) = 9\%$, calculate AccumFactor(1) and AccumFactor(2).

Solution: AccumFactor(1) = 1.100, and AccumFactor(2) = $(1.100)(1.090) = 1.199$.

4.3.3 Discounting

Up to this point, we have started with a known current amount and determined a future accumulated amount. Often it is necessary to do the reverse of this: to work backward from a known future amount to determine the required current amount. This "backward accumulation" process is called discounting. Accumulation works interest rates forward in time. Discounting works interest rates backward in time.

For example, how much should Bob invest now at 10% interest in order to accumulate $121 at the end of two years? We determine the answer by discounting $121 for two years' interest at 10%. To do this we divide by 1.10 twice: By dividing $121 by 1.10, we determine that Bob needs $110 after one year in order to have $121 after two years. By dividing $110 by 1.10, we determine that Bob needs $100 now to accumulate $121 in two years.

Discount factors are used to perform discounting, just as accumulation factors are used to perform accumulation. The discount factor for t years is the amount required today to accumulate to one dollar in t years. Alternatively, it can be defined as the present value (or current value) of one dollar payable t years in the future:

DiscFactor(t) = Present value at time 0 of $1 that is payable at time t, discounting using t years of varying interest rates. This is the discount factor.

DiscFactor(t) is used to discount amounts from time t back to time 0. In policy year terms, DiscFactor(t) discounts amounts from the *end* of policy year t back to the issue date.

In general, the discount factor for a period of time is equal to 1 divided by the accumulation factor for the same period of time:

$$\text{DiscFactor}(t) = \frac{1}{\text{AccumFactor}(t)}. \qquad (4.3.4)$$

Because the one-year discount factor is used so frequently, it is given its own symbol, v:

v = One-year discount factor,

$$v = \frac{1}{1 + i} = (1 + i)^{-1}. \qquad (4.3.5)$$

If the interest rate remains constant for t years, then v^t is the discount factor for t years:

$$\text{DiscFactor}(t) = v^t = \frac{1}{(1 + i)^t} = (1 + i)^{-t}. \qquad (4.3.6)$$

If the discount factor varies from year to year, DiscFactor(n) can be calculated iteratively, starting with DiscFactor(0) = 1:

$$\text{DiscFactor}(t) = \frac{\text{DiscFactor}(t - 1)}{1 + i(t)}, \quad \text{for } t = 1 \text{ to } n. \qquad (4.3.7)$$

Alternatively, this can be stated as

$$\text{DiscFactor}(n) = \prod_{t=1}^{n} \frac{1}{1 + i(t)}. \qquad (4.3.8)$$

Example 4.3.2

Given $i(t)$ shown below, calculate $v(t)$ and DiscFactor(t).

t	$i(t)$	$v(t)$	*DiscFactor(t)*
1	0.10	0.90909	0.90909
2	0.10	0.90909	0.82645
3	0.10	0.90909	0.75131

A time line may help you see this process more clearly:

Time:	0		1		2		3
Policy year:		1		2		3	

```
|--------------|--------------|--------------|
```

$i(t)$:		0.10		0.10		0.10	
$v(t)$:		0.90909		0.90909		0.90909	
DiscFactor(t):	1.00000		0.90909		0.82645		0.75131

Example 4.3.3

Given $i(t)$ shown below, calculate $v(t)$ and DiscFactor(t).

t	$i(t)$	$v(t)$	*DiscFactor(t)*
1	0.10	0.90909	0.90909
2	0.09	0.91743	0.83403
3	0.08	0.92593	0.77225

A time line may help you see this process more clearly:

Time:	0		1		2		3
Policy year:		1		2		3	

```
|--------------|--------------|---------------|
```

$i(t)$:		0.10		0.09		0.08	
$v(t)$:		0.90909		0.91743		0.92593	
DiscFactor(t):	1.00000		0.90909		0.83403		0.77225

4.3.4 Present Values

In financial calculations, it is very common to calculate a series of future payments. To assess the value of a series of future payments, the present value of each future payment is calculated, and the results are summed. This gives us a way to determine how much we would be willing to pay today for a given series of future cash flows. Converting future cash flows into one present value also makes it possible to compare different financial arrangements: If everything else were equal, you would prefer the arrangement that paid you the greatest present value.

Let

$\mathrm{Cash}(t)$ = Cash flow at time t. Cash flows can be positive (to be received by you) or negative (to be paid by you).

$\mathrm{PV}(t)$ = Present value at time 0 of future cash flows occurring between time 0 and time t. $\mathrm{PV}(t)$ could be defined to include or exclude $\mathrm{Cash}(0)$. We have chosen to include $\mathrm{Cash}(0)$.

In policy year terms, $\mathrm{PV}(t)$ discounts future cash flows occurring at the *end* of policy years 0 through t back to the issue date.

The present value of each future cash flow can be calculated and summed to determine $\mathrm{PV}(n)$, the basic present value, by starting with $\mathrm{PV}(0) = \mathrm{Cash}(0)$:

$$\mathrm{PV}(t) = \mathrm{PV}(t-1) + \mathrm{Cash}(t)\, \mathrm{DiscFactor}(t), \quad \text{for } t = 1 \text{ to } n.$$

$$(4.3.9)$$

Alternatively, this can be stated as

$$\mathrm{PV}(n) = \sum_{t=0}^{n} \mathrm{Cash}(t)\, \mathrm{DiscFactor}(t).$$

$$(4.3.10)$$

Example 4.3.4

Given $i(t)$ and Cash(t) shown below, calculate DiscFactor(t), Cash(t) DiscFactor(t), and PV(t).

t	$i(t)$	$v(t)$	*DiscFactor(t)*	*Cash(t)*	*Cash(t) DiscFactor(t)*	*PV(t)*
0			1.00000	1,000	1,000.00	1,000.00
1	0.10	0.90909	0.90909	−350	−318.18	681.82
2	0.09	0.91743	0.83403	−350	−291.91	389.91
3	0.08	0.92593	0.77225	−350	−270.29	119.62

4.4 Mortality

Life insurance starts with a simple concept: In return for a series of premium payments, the insurance company agrees to pay a death benefit if the insured dies. At a minimum, the pricing actuary's job is to ensure that the present value of expected premium payments is more than the present value of expected death benefits.

Mortality rates (the probabilities of death) obviously help determine the present value of death benefits. Mortality rates also impact the present value of premiums, because the tendency to pay life insurance premiums drops dramatically after death.

A mortality rate is usually defined as an annual probability: It is the probability that a person who starts the year alive will die within the next year. The symbols q and p are used to denote the probabilities of dying (*quitting*) and not dying (*persisting*) during the next year:

q = Mortality rate, or probability of dying during the next year, for a life starting the year

p = Persistency rate, or probability of not dying during the next year, for a life starting the year.

Although mortality rates vary by many underwriting factors, such as issue age, sex, and use of tobacco, the following formulas will apply to just one set of underwriting factors (issue age, sex, and risk class) at a time, so the only variation we will reflect is mortality changing over time. It is common for mortality to increase as people age and as the screening effect of underwriting wears off over time:

$q(t)$ = Mortality rate, or probability of dying during policy year t, for a life starting the year

$p(t)$ = Persistency rate, or probability of not dying during policy year t, for a life starting the year.

Since everyone starting policy year t will either die or not die during the year, we have

$q(t) + p(t) = 1$, which leads to
$q(t) = 1 - p(t)$ and
$p(t) = 1 - q(t)$. $\qquad$ (4.4.1)

Actuaries supply the mortality rates, $q(t)$, to be used for each policy year. Each $p(t)$ is then calculated as $1 - q(t)$. For example, if $q(t) = 0.1$, then $p(t) = 1 - 0.1 = 0.9$. Using traditional actuarial notation, $q(t)$ would be written as $q_{[x]+t-1}$.

4.4.1 Survival (Using Only Mortality)

In order to determine the present value of a stream of expected payments of any type, we first must determine the probability of living from the issue date to the time of each payment, as illustrated by the following time line:

Time:	0		1		2		3
Policy year:		1		2		3	
	|--------------|--------------|--------------|						
Mortality rate:		$q(1)$		$q(2)$		$q(3)$	
Persistency rate:		$p(1)$		$p(2)$		$p(3)$	
Payment:			Payment(1)	Payment(2)	Payment(3)		

Let

SurvFactor(*t*) = Probability of surviving from time 0 to time *t*. This is the basic survivorship factor. This factor has traditionally been written as $_tp_x$, where *x* is the age at inception (issue age). SurvFactor(*t*) has been used in place of $_tp_x$ so there will be no confusion with *p*(*t*).

In policy year terms, SurvFactor(*t*) is the probability of surviving from policy issue to the *end* of policy year *t*.

To survive from time 0 to time *t*, you must survive each of policy years 1 through *t*. The probability of survival from time 0 to time *t* is therefore

The probability of surviving policy year 1

Times the probability of surviving policy year 2

Times the probability of surviving policy year 3

Times . . .

Times the probability of surviving policy year *t* − 1

Times the probability of surviving policy year *t*.

SurvFactor(*n*) can be calculated iteratively, starting with SurvFactor(0) = 1:

$$\text{SurvFactor}(t) = \text{SurvFactor}(t-1)\, p(t), \quad \text{for } t = 1 \text{ to } n. \quad (4.4.2)$$

Alternatively, this can be stated as

$$\text{SurvFactor}(n) = \prod_{t=1}^{n} p(t). \quad (4.4.3)$$

Example 4.4.1

Given $q(t)$ below, calculate $p(t)$ and SurvFactor(t).

t	$q(t)$	$p(t)$	SurvFactor(t)
1	0.003	0.997	0.99700
2	0.004	0.996	0.99301
3	0.005	0.995	0.98805

4.4.2   Present Value of a Series of Payments (Using Mortality and Interest Only)

In insurance calculations, it is often necessary to calculate the present value of a series of future payments.

Let

$\text{Pmt}(t)$ = Payment due at the end of policy year t (which is t years after the issue date)

$\text{PVPmt}(n)$ = The present value at time 0 of the payments for policy years 1 to n; this is the basic present value of payments.

The present value of each individual payment can be calculated and summed to determine PVPmt(n), by starting with PVPmt(0) = 0:

$$\text{PVPmt}(t) = \text{PVPmt}(t-1) + \text{Pmt}(t)\,\text{SurvFactor}(t)\,\text{DiscFactor}(t),$$
$$\text{for } t = 1 \text{ to } n. \tag{4.4.4}$$

Future payments are adjusted for the probability of being paid, using SurvFactor(t), and are also discounted for interest, using DiscFactor(t). A time line may make this clearer:

Time: 0   1   2   3

Policy year: 1   2   3

```
|---------------|---------------|---------------|
```

Payment: Pmt(1)   Pmt(2)   Pmt(3)

SurvFactor(0) SurvFactor(1) SurvFactor(2) SurvFactor(3)

DiscFactor(0) DiscFactor(1) DiscFactor(2) DiscFactor(3)

Alternatively, the previous formula can be stated as

$$PVPmt(n) = \sum_{t=1}^{n} Pmt(t)\ SurvFactor(t)\ DiscFactor(t). \qquad (4.4.5)$$

Example 4.4.2

Given $q(t) = 0.003$, 0.004, and 0.005 for $t = 1$ to 3, $i = 10\%$, and $Pmt(n) = 100$, calculate $PVPmt(t)$.

t	$Pmt(n)$	$SurvFactor(t)$	$DiscFactor(t)$	$PVPmt(t)$
1	100	0.99700	0.90909	90.636
2	100	0.99301	0.82645	172.703
3	100	0.98805	0.75131	246.936

As stated, the calculations above assume that payments occur at the end of the policy year. Certain types of payments, such as premiums, occur at the beginning of the policy year. In this case, the formulas for $PVPmt(n)$ would have to be adjusted to reflect payments occurring at the beginning of the policy year. Such adjustments to the formulas are left as an exercise (see Exercise 4.4).

4.5 Lapses

In the previous section, we assumed that mortality was the only force reducing the number of insureds from year to year. In reality, a significant percentage of insureds voluntarily cancel their life insurance each year, either by lapsing (that is, not paying premiums) or by surrendering the policy for its cash value. We will refer to both lapses and surrenders as lapses, for simplicity.

We will use qd and qw for the probabilities of death and lapse, in place of q (for death only). We chose qw (w for withdrawal) rather than ql (l for lapse) because the letter l looks too much like the number 1. The probability of persisting, p, will take on a slightly different meaning:

$qd(t)$ = Mortality rate or probability of dying during policy year t, for a life starting the year

$qw(t)$ = Lapse rate or probability of lapsing during policy year t, for a life starting the year

$p(t)$ = Persistency rate or probability of not dying or lapsing during policy year t, for a life starting the year.

There is some interplay between qd and qw. To be counted as a death claim, the policy must not have lapsed. To be counted as lapsed, the insured must not have died. This is a circular relationship, making it hard to determine one without first determining the other.

The simplest case occurs if lapses can happen only at the end of the policy year. This will be the assumption used in most of this book. (Chapter 12 will refine the formulas to reflect surrenders throughout the policy year.) Under this assumption, lapse rates have no impact on deaths during the policy year. To survive from one policy year to the next, the insured first must not die during the policy year and then must not lapse at the end of the policy year. This translates to

$$p(t) = (1 - qd(t))\,(1 - qw(t)). \tag{4.5.1}$$

This revised formula for $p(t)$ can be used with the previous formulas for SurvFactor(t) and PVPmt(n) to reflect the combined impact of mortality and lapses.

Given the mortality and lapse rates shown below, calculate persistency rates and survival factors.

t	$qd(t)$	$qw(t)$	$p(t)$	$SurvFactor(t)$
0				1.00000
1	0.003	0.12	0.87736	0.87736
2	0.004	0.07	0.92628	0.81268
3	0.005	0.05	0.94525	0.76819

4.6 Factors for Pricing

For pricing purposes we need a few more factors related to interest, deaths, and lapses.

4.6.1 Midyear Discount Factor

We will assume that deaths occur at the middle of the policy year, so we will need to be able to discount for both whole years and half years of interest. We therefore add to the notation previously defined for discount factors to adjust for half years:

DiscFactorMid(t) = Discount factor that is applied to an amount in the middle of policy year t to determine the present value of the amount, using $t - \frac{1}{2}$ years of varying interest rates.

The discount factor for the middle of policy year t ($t - \frac{1}{2}$ years) is equal to the discount factor for $t - 1$ years divided by a factor that discounts for half a year's interest at $i(t)$:

$$\text{DiscFactorMid}(t) = \frac{\text{DiscFactor}(t - 1)}{(1 + i(t))^{1/2}}. \qquad (4.6.1)$$

4.6.2 Lapses and Deaths

The following formulas calculate the number of lapses and deaths that occur during policy year t.

Let

$$\text{Deaths}(t) = \text{The probability of surviving through } t - 1 \text{ policy}$$
$$\text{years and then dying during policy year } t$$
$$\text{Lapses}(t) = \text{The probability of surviving through } t - 1 \text{ policy}$$
$$\text{years and then lapsing at the end of policy year } t.$$

To calculate the probability of dying during policy year t, multiply the probability of surviving from time 0 to time $t - 1$ by the mortality rate for policy year t:

$$\text{Deaths}(t) = \text{SurvFactor}(t - 1) \, qd(t). \tag{4.6.2}$$

To calculate the probability of lapsing at the end of policy year t, multiply the probability of surviving from time 0 to time $t - 1$ by the probability of not dying during policy year t and then multiply by the probability of lapsing during policy year t:

$$\text{Lapses}(t) = \text{SurvFactor}(t - 1) \, (1 - qd(t)) \, qw(t). \tag{4.6.3}$$

Collectively Deaths(t) and Lapses(t) add up to the probability of surviving to the end of policy year $t - 1$ and terminating before the end of policy year t. In other words,

$$\text{Deaths}(t) + \text{Lapses}(t) = \text{SurvFactor}(t - 1) - \text{SurvFactor}(t). \tag{4.6.4}$$

To ensure your understanding of the above relationships, use Formulas 4.6.2–4.6.4 to reproduce the following formula for SurvFactor(t), which states that the probability of surviving from one year to the next is equal to the probability of not dying times the probability of not lapsing:

$$\text{SurvFactor}(t) = \text{SurvFactor}(t - 1) \, (1 - qd(t)) \, (1 - qw(t)). \tag{4.6.5}$$

Example 4.6.1

Given the mortality and lapse rates shown below, calculate $p(t)$, SurvFactor(t), Deaths(t), and Lapses(t).

t	$qd(t)$	$qw(t)$	$p(t)$	SurvFactor(t)	Deaths(t)	Lapses(t)
0				1.00000		
1	0.003	0.12	0.87736	0.87736	0.00300	0.11964
2	0.004	0.07	0.92628	0.81268	0.00351	0.06117
3	0.005	0.05	0.94525	0.76819	0.00406	0.04043

4.7 Joint Life Mortality

Most life insurance policies insure a single life. This chapter has focused on single life policies up to this point, although many of the same formulas apply equally well to joint life policies, which insure multiple lives. Although policy designs are not necessarily restricted to the following, there are generally two kinds of multiple life policies: those that pay death benefits on the first death, and those that pay death benefits on the last death.

4.7.1 Joint First-to-Die

Joint first-to-die policies pay a death benefit when the first of multiple lives dies. This section addresses only joint first-to-die policies that cover two lives. Some variations of first-to-die policies pay double the death benefit if the two lives die within a short time of each other. We will focus on the more normal first-to-die variation that pays the same death benefit whether one or two lives die.

In order to apply the formulas introduced in this chapter to joint first-to-die products, we will develop a joint first-to-die mortality rate that subsequently can be used just like a single life mortality rate.

All of the following probabilities vary by policy year but, for simplicity, (t) has been omitted (that is, qx should read $qx(t)$, qy should read $qy(t)$, and so on). All of the following probabilities are based on both insureds being alive at the beginning of the policy year:

qx = Probability that the first life, life x, dies during the policy year, given that life x is alive at the beginning of the policy year

qy = Probability that the second life, life y, dies during the policy year, given that life y is alive at the beginning of the policy year

px = Probability that life x does not die during the policy year, given that life x is alive at the beginning of the policy year

py = Probability that life y does not die during the policy year, given that life y is alive at the beginning of the policy year

qxy = Probability that life x or life y or both die during the policy year, given that both lives are alive at the beginning of the policy year

pxy = Probability that neither life x nor life y dies during the policy year, given that both lives are alive at the beginning of the policy year.

By definition, we know

$$px = 1 - qx,$$
$$py = 1 - qy,$$
$$pxy = 1 - qxy.$$

The probability of both lives not dying can be calculated as the probability of life x not dying times the probability of life y not dying:

$$pxy = px\, py,$$
$$pxy = (1 - qx)(1 - qy).$$

This results in

$$1 - qxy = (1 - qx)(1 - qy), \text{ or}$$
$$qxy = qx + qy - qx\, qy. \tag{4.7.1}$$

We can also calculate qxy by noting that there are three possible ways for the first death to occur during a policy year:

1. *x* dies, *y* lives

2. *y* dies, *x* lives

3. Both die.

Therefore, the probability of at least one life dying is equal to the sum of three probabilities:

1. The probability of life *x* dying times the probability of life *y* not dying

2. The probability of life *y* dying times the probability of life *x* not dying

3. The probability of both lives dying during the year.

This translates into the following formula:

$$qxy = qx\,py + qy\,px + qx\,qy$$
$$= qx\,(1 - qy) + qy\,(1 - qx) + qx\,qy$$
$$= qx + qy - qx\,qy.$$

This is the same as Formula 4.7.1. You can rationalize this result by observing that both *qx* and *qy* include the probability that both lives die, so *qx* + *qy* double counts the probability that both die. Therefore, it is necessary to deduct *qx qy* to correct this double counting.

To apply the formulas previously introduced in this chapter to joint first-to-die products, simply substitute *qxy* for *qd* or *q*.

Example 4.7.1

Given the various mortality rates *qx* and *qy* shown below, calculate the joint first-to-die mortality rate *qxy*:

qx	*qy*	*qxy*
0.001	0.001	0.001999
0.001	0.010	0.010990
0.010	0.010	0.019900
0.010	0.100	0.109000
0.100	0.100	0.190000

4.7.2   Joint Last-to-Die

Joint last-to-die policies pay a death benefit when the last of multiple lives dies. This section addresses only joint last-to-die policies that cover two lives.

In order to apply the formulas introduced in this chapter to joint last-to-die products, we will develop a joint last-to-die mortality rate that can be used just like a single life mortality rate. We will use much of the same notation we defined for joint first-to-die, but we will change the definitions of qxy and pxy to reflect the second death. "LTD" (for last-to-die) will be added to the beginning of the variable names for qxy and pxy to distinguish them from the first-to-die qxy and pxy:

$$qx(t) = \text{Probability that life } x \text{ dies during policy year } t,$$

given that life x is alive at the beginning of the policy year

$$qy(t) = \text{Probability that life } y \text{ dies during policy year } t,$$

given that life y is alive at the beginning of the policy year

$$px(t) = \text{Probability that life } x \text{ does not die during}$$

policy year t, given that life x is alive at the beginning of the policy year

$$py(t) = \text{Probability that life } y \text{ does not die during}$$

policy year t, given that life y is alive at the beginning of the policy year

$$\text{SurvFactor}x(t) = \text{Probability of life } x \text{ surviving from issue to the}$$

end of policy year t, with survival based only on mortality, ignoring lapses

$$\text{SurvFactor}y(t) = \text{Probability of life } y \text{ surviving from issue to the}$$

end of policy year t, with survival based only on mortality, ignoring lapses

SurvFactor*xy*(*t*) = Probability of at least one of life *x* and life *y* surviving from issue to the end of policy year *t*, with survival based only on mortality. This is often referred to as the probability that the joint "status" *xy* survives from issue to the end of policy year *t*. A joint status survives when at least one of the persons *x* and *y* survives to the end of policy year *t*.

LTD*pxy*(*t*) = Probability of the second death not occurring during policy year *t*, given that at least one life is alive at the beginning of the policy year

LTD*qxy*(*t*) = Probability of the second death occurring during policy year *t*, given that at least one life is alive at the beginning of the policy year.

The following approach to calculating joint last-to-die mortality rates is often referred to as "Frasierization" or "Frasierized mortality rates." It is named after Bill Frasier, who first published and popularized this approach in the U.S. in the late 1980s.

We start with values for $qx(t)$ and $qy(t)$, which we can use to calculate $px(t)$ and $py(t)$ (as always, $p + q = 1$):

$$px(t) = 1 - qx(t),$$
$$py(t) = 1 - qy(t).$$

The probability of life *x* surviving *t* years is equal to the probability of surviving $t - 1$ years times the probability of surviving one more year. This relationship allows us to calculate SurvFactor*x*(*n*) iteratively, starting with SurvFactor*x*(0) = 1:

$$\text{SurvFactor}x(t) = \text{SurvFactor}x(t - 1)\, px(t), \quad \text{for } t = 1 \text{ to } n.$$
(4.7.2)

This is equivalent to

$$\text{SurvFactor}x(n) = \prod_{t=1}^{n} px(t).$$
(4.7.3)

SurvFactor$y(n)$ can be calculated using formulas similar to Formulas 4.7.2 or 4.7.3.

The probability of both lives dying by the end of policy year t is equal to the probability of life x dying by the end of policy year t times the probability of life y dying by the end of policy year t. This translates to the following relationship:

$$1 - \text{SurvFactor}xy(t) = (1 - \text{SurvFactor}x(t))\,(1 - \text{SurvFactor}y(t)).$$

Solving for SurvFactor$xy(t)$, we have

$$\text{SurvFactor}xy(t) = \text{SurvFactor}x(t) + \text{SurvFactor}y(t) \\ - \text{SurvFactor}x(t)\,\text{SurvFactor}y(t). \qquad (4.7.4)$$

You can rationalize this result by observing that both SurvFactor$x(t)$ and SurvFactor$y(t)$ include the probability that both lives survive, so SurvFactor$x(t)$ + SurvFactor$y(t)$ double counts the probability that both survive. Therefore, it is necessary to deduct "SurvFactor$x(t)$ SurvFactor$y(t)$" to correct this double counting.

The probability of at least one life surviving to the end of policy year t is equal to the probability of surviving to the end of policy year $t - 1$ and then surviving from the end of policy year $t - 1$ to the end of policy year t. This kind of iterative formula for survival should be familiar to you by now:

$$\text{SurvFactor}xy(t) = \text{SurvFactor}xy(t - 1)\,\text{LTD}pxy(t).$$

We now can calculate LTD$pxy(t)$:

$$\text{LTD}pxy(t) = \frac{\text{SurvFactor}xy(t)}{\text{SurvFactor}xy(t - 1)}. \qquad (4.7.5)$$

We can finally determine LTD$qxy(t)$:

$$\text{LTD}qxy(t) = 1 - \text{LTD}pxy(t). \qquad (4.7.6)$$

To apply the formulas introduced in this chapter to joint last-to-die products, simply substitute LTDqxy for qd or q.

Example 4.7.2

To test your understanding of these concepts, work through the following somewhat simplified example, where lives x and y have the same mortality rates.

t	$qx(t)$ $(=qy(t))$	$px(t)$ $(=py(t))$	$SurvFactorx(t)$ $(=SurvFactory(t))$	$SurvFactorxy(t)$	$LTDpxy(t)$	$LTDqxy(t)$
1	0.010	0.990	0.990000	0.999900	0.999900	0.000100
2	0.011	0.989	0.979110	0.999564	0.999664	0.000336
3	0.012	0.988	0.967361	0.998935	0.999371	0.000629

For those of you familiar with mortality rates, you will notice that, even though qx and qy are relatively high mortality rates, qxy starts out incredibly small and grows very fast.

For the first policy year, $qxy = qx\,qy$. If qx and qy were both 0.001 (one in a thousand, an approximate mortality rate for people under 40 years old), qxy would be 0.000001, or one in a million! Such a low joint last-to-die mortality rate may make no sense for two young married people who often travel together. The chance of both dying in an automobile or airplane accident would seem to be much more than one in a million! Therefore, it is common to increase qxy for the probability of joint accidental death, which probably ranges from a low of 0.00001 to a high of 0.0001 (0.01 per thousand to 0.10 per thousand), depending on the exposure to joint accidental death.

4.8 Pricing Example

A pricing example is developed in Chapters 4 through 11 that builds on each chapter's formulas. Tables 4.8.1 and 4.8.2 are this chapter's contribution to that pricing example, which spans and ties together Chapters 4 through 11.

Table 4.8.1 Accumulation and Discount Factors; Survivorship Assumptions

t	AccumFactor	DiscFactor	DiscFactorMid	qd	qw	p
1	1.07000	0.93458	0.96674	0.00117	0.12	0.87897
2	1.14490	0.87344	0.90349	0.00172	0.07	0.92840
3	1.22504	0.81630	0.84439	0.00231	0.05	0.94781
4	1.31080	0.76290	0.78914	0.00275	0.05	0.94379
5	1.40255	0.71299	0.73752	0.00313	0.05	0.94703
6	1.50073	0.66634	0.68927	0.00347	0.03	0.96663
7	1.60578	0.62275	0.64418	0.00379	0.03	0.96632
8	1.71819	0.58201	0.60203	0.00414	0.03	0.96598
9	1.83846	0.54393	0.56265	0.00456	0.03	0.96558
10	1.96715	0.50835	0.52584	0.00508	1.00	0.00000

Note: $i = 0.07$ for all t.

Table 4.8.2 Survivorship Factors

t	SurvFactor	Deaths	Lapses
0	1.00000		
1	0.87897	0.00117	0.11986
2	0.81604	0.00151	0.06142
3	0.77344	0.00189	0.04071
4	0.73275	0.00213	0.03857
5	0.69393	0.00229	0.03652
6	0.67078	0.00241	0.02075
7	0.64819	0.00254	0.02005
8	0.62614	0.00268	0.01937
9	0.60459	0.00286	0.01870
10	0.00000	0.00307	0.60152

4.9   Exercises

Exercise 4.1

Using the following interest rates, calculate five years of accumulation factors and discount factors.

t	i(t)	AccumFactor(t)	DiscFactor(t)
0		1.00000	1.00000
1	0.080		
2	0.075		
3	0.070		
4	0.065		
5	0.060		

Exercise 4.2

Using the factors developed in the previous exercise, calculate the present value of each of the following three sets of cash flows (A, B, and C).

t	Cash Flows		
	A	B	C
0	−1,000	100	−100
1	80	100	40
2	80	100	35
3	80	100	30
4	80	100	25
5	1,080	0	20

Exercise 4.3

Given the following mortality rates, calculate persistency rates and survival factors.

t	q(t)	p(t)	SurvFactor(t)
0			1.00000
1	0.0020		
2	0.0025		
3	0.0030		
4	0.0035		
5	0.0040		

Exercise 4.4

Adjust the formulas for PVPmt(n) in Formula 4.4.4 to reflect payments that occur at the beginning of the policy year.

Exercise 4.5

Given the following mortality rates and lapse rates, calculate persistency rates and survival factors.

t	$qd(t)$	$qw(t)$	$p(t)$	$SurvFactor(t)$
0				1.00000
1	0.0020	0.15		
2	0.0025	0.10		
3	0.0030	0.07		
4	0.0035	0.06		
5	0.0040	0.05		

Exercise 4.6

Using the discount factors from Exercise 4.1 and the survival factors from the previous exercise, complete the following table.

t	$DiscFactor(t)$	$SurvFactor(t)$	$DiscFactor(t) \times SurvFactor(t)$
0	1.00000	1.00000	1.00000
1			
2			
3			
4			
5			

Using the above results, calculate the present value of annual premiums of 300 per year payable at the beginning of policy years 1–5. (Hint: Use Exercise 4.4.)

Exercise 4.7

Building on Exercise 4.6, calculate the probability of surviving to the beginning of the policy year and then either dying or lapsing during the policy year.

t	$Deaths(t)$	$Lapses(t)$
1		
2		
3		
4		
5		

Exercise 4.8

Building on Exercises 4.1 and 4.7, calculate midyear discount factors and the product of the midyear discount factors times Deaths(t).

t	$DiscFactorMid(t)$	$DiscFactorMid(t) \times Deaths(t)$
1		
2		
3		
4		
5		

Use the above factors to calculate the present value of a death benefit of 100,000 payable at the middle of the policy year of death for years 1–5.

Exercise 4.9

Using the following single life mortality rates for lives x and y, calculate joint first-to-die and joint last-to-die mortality rates.

t	$qx(t)$	$qy(t)$	$FTDqxy(t)$	$LTDqxy(t)$
1	0.0100	0.0050		
2	0.0150	0.0070		
3	0.0200	0.0090		
4	0.0250	0.0110		
5	0.0300	0.0130		

4.10 Answers

Answer 4.1

t	$i(t)$	$AccumFactor(t)$	$DiscFactor(t)$
0		1.00000	1.00000
1	0.080	1.08000	0.92593
2	0.075	1.16100	0.86133
3	0.070	1.24227	0.80498
4	0.065	1.32302	0.75585
5	0.060	1.40240	0.71306

Answer 4.2

	A		B		C	
t	Cash Flow	PV	Cash Flow	PV	Cash Flow	PV
0	−1,000.00	−1,000.00	100.00	100.00	−100.00	−100.00
1	80.00	74.07	100.00	92.59	40.00	37.04
2	80.00	68.91	100.00	86.13	35.00	30.15
3	80.00	64.40	100.00	80.50	30.00	24.15
4	80.00	60.47	100.00	75.58	25.00	18.90
5	1,080.00	770.11	0.00	0.00	20.00	14.26
Total Present Value:		37.96		434.81		24.49

Answer 4.3

t	q(t)	p(t)	SurvFactor(t)
0			1.00000
1	0.00200	0.99800	0.998000
2	0.00250	0.99750	0.995505
3	0.00300	0.99700	0.992518
4	0.00350	0.99650	0.989045
5	0.00400	0.99600	0.985088

Answer 4.4

Let

> $\mathrm{Pmt}(t)$ = Payment due at the *beginning* of policy year t (which is $t-1$ years after the issue date)
>
> $\mathrm{PVPmt}(n)$ = The present value at time 0 of the payments for policy years 1 to n. This is the basic present value of payments.

The present value of each individual payment can be calculated and summed to determine $\mathrm{PVPmt}(n)$, by starting with $\mathrm{PVPmt}(0) = 0$:

> $\mathrm{PVPmt}(t) = \mathrm{PVPmt}(t-1)$
> $+ \mathrm{Pmt}(t)\,\mathrm{SurvFactor}(t-1)\,\mathrm{DiscFactor}(t-1),$
> for $t = 1$ to n.

Answer 4.5

t	qd(t)	qw(t)	p(t)	SurvFactor(t)
0				1.00000
1	0.00200	0.150	0.84830	0.84830
2	0.00250	0.100	0.89775	0.76156
3	0.00300	0.070	0.92721	0.70613
4	0.00350	0.060	0.93671	0.66144
5	0.00400	0.050	0.94620	0.62585

Answer 4.6

t	DiscFactor(t)	SurvFactor(t)	DiscFactor(t) × SurvFactor(t)
0	1.00000	1.00000	1.00000
1	0.92593	0.84830	0.78546
2	0.86133	0.76156	0.65595
3	0.80498	0.70613	0.56842
4	0.75585	0.66144	0.49995
5	0.71306	0.62585	0.44627

The present value of annual premiums of 300 per year payable at the beginning of policy years 1–5 is 300(1.00000 + 0.78546 + 0.65595 + 0.56842 + 0.49995) = 1052.93.

Answer 4.7

t	Deaths(t)	Lapses(t)
1	0.00200	0.14970
2	0.00212	0.08462
3	0.00228	0.05315
4	0.00247	0.04222
5	0.00265	0.03294

The present value of a death benefit of 100,000 payable at the middle of the policy year of death for years 1–5 is 100,000 (0.00192 + 0.00189 + 0.00190 + 0.00193 + 0.00194) = 958.00

Answer 4.8

t	DiscFactorMid(t)	DiscFactorMid(t) × Deaths(t)
1	0.96225	0.00192
2	0.89304	0.00189
3	0.83268	0.00190
4	0.78003	0.00193
5	0.73414	0.00194

Answer 4.9

FTD*qxy* can be calculated from Formula 4.7.1.

t	qx(t)	qy(t)	FTDqxy(t)
1	0.0100	0.0050	0.01495
2	0.0150	0.0070	0.02190
3	0.0200	0.0090	0.02882
4	0.0250	0.0110	0.03573
5	0.0300	0.0130	0.04261

To calculate LTD*qxy*, a few more details are shown that follow Formulas 4.7.2–4.7.6.

t	px	py	SurvFactorx	SurvFactory	SurvFactorxy	LTDpxy	LTDqxy
0			1.00000	1.00000	1.00000		
1	0.99000	0.99500	0.99000	0.99500	0.99995	0.99995	0.00005
2	0.98500	0.99300	0.97515	0.98804	0.99970	0.99975	0.00025
3	0.98000	0.99100	0.95565	0.97914	0.99907	0.99937	0.00063
4	0.97500	0.98900	0.93176	0.96837	0.99784	0.99877	0.00123
5	0.97000	0.98700	0.90380	0.95578	0.99575	0.99790	0.00210

Life Insurance Cash Flows

5.1 Introduction

This chapter presents formulas for calculating the basic life insurance cash flows: premiums, expenses, death benefits, surrender benefits, dividends, endowments, and partial withdrawal benefits. Premiums are received by the insurance company. All of the other cash flows are paid out by the insurance company. These cash flows are the fundamental building blocks of any pricing model. They are independent of how you measure financial results.

To promote understanding of the underlying concepts, the formulas in Chapters 5 through 11 use annual calculations for a single issue age and risk class. Formulas in later chapters will address modes other than annual and the simultaneous modeling of a variety of issue ages and risk classes.

In Sections 5.2 through 5.7, we will develop formulas for the life insurance cash flows of pre-scheduled products. "Pre-scheduled products" are products with premiums and benefits that are known well in advance. Premiums and benefits are either set at issue or, in the case of dividends or nonguaranteed premiums, are recalculated from time to time and reset for future use.

"Dynamic products" form the counterpart to pre-scheduled products. Dynamic product calculations are presented in Section 5.8. Dynamic product cash flows are covered in Section 5.9. Cash flows for both pre-scheduled and dynamic products are summarized in Section 5.10.

5.1.1 "Per Unit" Definitions

Calculations will be presented on a "per unit" basis. Typically, for life insurance, a unit is defined as 1,000 of death benefit in all policy years. However, the death benefit for some plans of life insurance is not level in all years. Increasing and decreasing death benefit patterns are not uncommon. In such instances, the unit is defined to incorporate the death benefit pattern. For example, an increasing term plan that doubles its death benefit in ten years may define one unit as a death benefit pattern of 1,000 in the first year, 1,100 in the second year, 1,200 in the third year, and so on. The death benefit per unit would be 2,000 in the eleventh and later years.

It is important to understand the difference between "per unit in force" and "per unit issued:"

- Many policy-related values, such as premiums, death benefits, cash values, and account values, are defined or calculated on a "per unit in force" basis. For example, a policy might have a constant premium per unit of 8.00 and a constant death benefit per unit of 1,000. In general, use of the phrase "per unit" will mean "per unit in force."

- In order to calculate the projected amounts for each policy year for each unit issued, results are adjusted for survivorship. The result is then expressed as a "per unit issued" amount.

For example, if the probability of survival to the beginning of year 7 is 0.60, then, in year 7, an 8.00 premium per unit in force converts to 4.80 of premium per unit issued. In other words, for each unit issued with an annual premium rate of 8.00 per unit, it is expected that 4.80 will be collected in year 7. When referring to per unit issued, we will always use the phrase "per unit issued."

As we discussed in Chapter 4, insurance present values can be calculated by adjusting for survivorship and discounting for interest. By calculating results on a "per unit issued" basis, we have already adjusted for survivorship and all that remains to calculate present values is to discount for interest.

Another example may help clarify the difference between "per unit in force" and "per unit issued." Referring to the following table, the death benefit per unit in force in policy year 3 is 1,200. However, the death benefit *per unit issued* in policy year 3 is 4.7808. This is equal to the death benefit per unit in force times Deaths(3), which is the probability of surviving to the beginning of policy year 3 and then dying during policy year 3.

t	Death Benefit per Unit in Force	Deaths(t)	Death Benefit per Unit Issued	DiscFactorMid(t)
1	1,000	0.002860	2.8600	0.96225
2	1,100	0.003414	3.7554	0.89097
3	1,200	0.003984	4.7808	0.82497

The present value of death benefits is calculated by discounting the stream of death benefits per unit issued and summing them:

$$\text{PV of Death Benefit} = (2.8600)(0.96225) + (3.7554)(0.89097)$$
$$+ (4.7808)(0.82497)$$
$$= 10.0420.$$

5.1.2 Notation

As mentioned in Chapter 4, a subscript of (t) will, in general, indicate a value as of the end of policy year t. When timing is not as of the end of the period, "Beg" and "Mid" will occur in the variable name, and occasionally "End" will occur.

In addition, you will see many variable names that end in "_pu". These variable names are meant to distinguish "per unit in force" from "per unit issued." Therefore, "_pu" will denote "per unit in force"; for example, "Prem(*t*)" represents premiums paid per unit issued. "Prem_pu(*t*)" represents premium paid per unit in force.

5.2 Premiums for Pre-Scheduled Products

We will assume that premiums are paid annually at the beginning of the policy year.

Let

$$\text{Prem}(t) = \text{Premium per unit issued}$$

$$\text{Prem\_pu}(t) = \text{Premium per unit in force}$$

PolicyFee = Flat amount paid each year per policy, usually designed to cover per policy expenses; this policy fee could be a weighted average of the policy fees for the various modes of payment, such as annual, quarterly, and monthly.

AvgSize = Average number of units per policy sold.

Prem_pu(*t*) reflects the anticipated premium pattern. The policy fee is converted to a policy fee per unit by dividing by the average size. Premiums per unit issued are calculated by adding the premium per unit and the policy fee per unit and adjusting for survivorship:

$$\text{Prem}(t) = \left(\text{Prem\_pu}(t) + \frac{\text{PolicyFee}}{\text{AvgSize}} \right) \text{SurvFactor}(t - 1).$$

$$(5.2.1)$$

Since premiums are assumed to be paid at the *beginning* of the policy year, the survivorship factor used is SurvFactor(*t* − 1).

5.3 Expenses

Expenses are broken into three major categories: acquisition expenses, commission and related expenses, and maintenance expenses.

5.3.1 Acquisition Expenses

Acquisition expenses are the expenses related to acquiring new business, such as selling, underwriting, and issuing new policies. Acquisition expenses can be allocated in many ways: per unit, as a percentage of premium, or per policy, to name the most common. Many companies use more than one of these allocation bases for acquisition expenses.

Note the scope of the definition of "acquisition expenses" as used in this book. The term "acquisition expenses" will exclude commissions, even though commissions are truly acquisition expenses. For example, in U.S. GAAP accounting, commissions are normally included with other first-year expenses to calculate deferred acquisition costs. However, as you will see in Chapter 6, not all commissions are included in deferred acquisition costs. The choice of which commissions to defer can vary by the type of product and the overall commission pattern. Therefore, we have chosen to separate commissions from acquisition expenses.

Let

$$
\begin{aligned}
\text{AcqExp}(t) =\ & \text{Total acquisition expenses per unit issued;} \\
& \text{acquisition expenses are assumed to occur only} \\
& \text{at the issue date, that is, } \text{AcqExp}(t) = 0 \\
& \text{for } t > 1 \\
\text{AcqExp\_pu} =\ & \text{Acquisition expense per unit issued} \\
\text{AcqExpPrem} =\ & \text{Acquisition expense as a percentage of first-year} \\
& \text{premium} \\
\text{AcqExpPerPol} =\ & \text{Acquisition expense per policy issued.}
\end{aligned}
$$

Then,

$$
\begin{aligned}
\text{AcqExp}(1) &= \text{AcqExp\_pu} + \text{AcqExpPrem Prem}(1) \\
&\quad + \frac{\text{AcqExpPerPol}}{\text{AvgSize}}, \quad \text{for } t = 1, \\
\text{AcqExp}(t) &= 0, \quad \text{for } t > 1.
\end{aligned}
\tag{5.3.1}
$$

To convert components to a per unit issued basis, AcqExpPrem is multiplied by first-year premiums and AcqExpPerPol is divided by average size.

5.3.2 Commissions and Sales Expenses for Pre-Scheduled Products

Commissions and other forms of agent compensation for pre-scheduled products are paid to agents when premiums are paid, which we will assume is at the beginning of the policy year.

Most companies have a department that services its agents, sales force, or field force. This department is sometimes called the "Agency Department," "Field Services," or "Sales Support." The expense of this department and other sales expenses (agent bonuses, agent pension costs, contests, conferences, etc.) are frequently expressed as a percentage of commissions. We will assume sales expenses are paid at the same time as commissions. To reduce the number of variables, sales expenses will be included in the calculation of commissions.

Let

$$\text{Comm}(t) = \text{Commissions and other agent compensation paid as a percentage of premium, per unit issued}$$

$$\text{CommPct}(t) = \text{The percentage of premiums used to calculate commissions and other agent compensation}$$

$$\text{SalesExpPct}(t) = \text{Sales expenses, expressed as a percentage of commissions and other agent compensation.}$$

Then,

$$\text{Comm}(t) = \text{CommPct}(t)\,\text{Prem}(t)\,(1 + \text{SalesExpPct}(t)). \qquad (5.3.2)$$

5.3.3 Maintenance Expenses

Maintenance expenses usually include the expenses of billing, collecting premiums, paying premium tax, maintaining policy records, performing accounting and valuation, providing annual reports to policyowners, handling policyowner inquiries, and other policyowner services.

Maintenance expenses can be allocated in many ways: per unit, as a percentage of premium, or per policy, to name the most common.

Many companies use more than one of these allocation bases for maintenance expenses.

For simplicity, we will assume that all maintenance expenses occur at the *beginning* of the policy year.

Let

$$\text{MaintExp}(t) = \text{Total maintenance expenses incurred at the}$$
$$\text{\textit{beginning} of policy year } t, \text{ per unit issued}$$
$$\text{ExpPrem}(t) = \text{Maintenance expense as a percentage of premium}$$
$$\text{Exp\_pu}(t) = \text{Maintenance expense per unit in force}$$
$$\text{ExpPerPol}(t) = \text{Maintenance expense per policy in force}$$

Then,

$$\text{MaintExp}(t) = \left(\text{Exp\_pu}(t) + \frac{\text{ExpPerPol}(t)}{\text{AvgSize}} \right) \text{SurvFactor}(t - 1)$$
$$+ \text{ExpPrem}(t)\, \text{Prem}(t). \qquad (5.3.3)$$

In the above calculations, all components are converted to a per unit issued basis:

- $\text{Exp\_pu}(t)$ is multiplied by a $\text{SurvFactor}(t - 1)$
- ExpPerPol is divided by average size and multiplied by $\text{SurvFactor}(t - 1)$
- $\text{ExpPrem}(t)$ is multiplied by $\text{Prem}(t)$. $\text{Prem}(t)$ is already adjusted for survivorship to the beginning of policy year t.

5.4 Death Benefits and Claim Expenses

The death benefit is the amount payable upon the death of the person insured. Sometimes there is a difference between the original or guaranteed death benefit pattern and the actual death benefit paid upon death. The actual death benefit paid may exceed the original or guaranteed death benefits for various reasons. For example, some dynamic policies build cash surrender values that eventually exceed the death benefit pattern. In such a case, the death benefit is increased to be no less than the cash surrender value.

Participating plans that pay dividends to policyowners often pay an additional dividend upon death. This additional dividend can be a function of the dividends paid to persisting policyowners, or it can be a separate dividend scale paid only to policies terminated by death.

5.4.1 Death Benefits

Let

> $DeathBen(t)$ = Death benefits paid in policy year t, per unit issued. Death benefits are assumed paid at the *middle* of the policy year, on average. This is financially equivalent to death benefits being evenly spread throughout the policy year.
>
> $DB\_puMid(t)$ = Death benefit per unit in force at the middle of the policy year, including any dividends payable on death. This is assumed to be the average death benefit for the policy year.
>
> $ROPFactor$ = Return of premium factor, which is the average percentage of current year annual premiums returned on death.

Death benefits are calculated as the average death benefit times the probability of death, plus a return of "unearned" premium at time of death:

$$DeathBen(t) = \left(DB\_puMid(t) + \frac{ROPFactor\ Prem(t)}{SurvFactor(t-1)} \right) Deaths(t).$$

$$(5.4.1)$$

"ROPFactor" adjusts for any return of premium upon death. Several approaches are commonly used to determine the premium to be returned at death:

- No premiums paid beyond the date of death are refunded. This would translate to ROPFactor = 0.

- All premiums paid beyond the date of death are refunded. Because we assume deaths occur halfway through the policy year on average, this would translate to ROPFactor = ½.

- All premiums paid beyond the month of death are refunded. Because the company would, on average, retain an extra half-month of premium compared to the previous case, this would translate to ROPFactor = 11/24.

We divide by SurvFactor$(t - 1)$ in the ROPFactor portion of the formula because both Prem(t) and Deaths(t) have already been adjusted for survivorship. If we did not divide by SurvFactor$(t - 1)$, we would be double counting the effect of survivorship in that portion of the formula.

Returning premiums paid beyond the date or month of death requires the company to charge slightly higher premiums than if such premiums were not returned. However, this consumer-friendly feature is increasingly the norm.

5.4.2 Claim Expenses

Claim expenses include the costs of verifying claims, investigating problem claims, and processing claim payments. Claim expenses are assumed to occur at the same time death benefits are paid, in the middle of policy year t.

Claim expenses could be included in maintenance expenses. However, claim expenses can be substantial, particularly if claims can be contested because of misrepresentation by the applicant. Some countries limit the period during which a company may contest claims. For example, the U.S. limits contestability to the first two policy years. If the expenses related to contestable claims are significant, it may be advisable to have an explicit claim expense during the contestable period. After the contestable period, claim expenses may be immaterial and could easily be included with maintenance expenses.

Let

$$\text{ClaimExp}(t) = \text{Claim expenses per unit issued}$$
$$\text{ClaimExp\_pu}(t) = \text{Claim expenses per unit ``dying''}$$
$$\text{ClaimExpPerPol}(t) = \text{Claim per policy ``dying.''}$$

Then,

$$\text{ClaimExp}(t) = \left(\text{ClaimExp\_pu}(t) + \frac{\text{ClaimExpPerPol}(t)}{\text{AvgSize}} \right) \text{Deaths}(t).$$

$$(5.4.2)$$

5.5 Surrender Benefits

Surrender benefits are also known as termination benefits. However, since "termination" could also include death, we have chosen to use "surrender benefits" to denote amounts paid to the policyowner upon termination of the policy for any reason other than death.

Similar to claim expenses, a separate expense factor could be developed for surrender expenses. However, surrender expenses are normally not significant and are therefore included with maintenance expenses.

In some countries, notably the U.S., the product may offer the policyowner one or more alternatives to cash surrender; for example, the cash surrender value could be used to purchase extended term insurance or paid-up insurance. For pricing purposes these alternatives are almost always treated as if they were cash surrenders. This implicitly assumes that the single premiums charged for these alternatives are cost neutral. Some companies track the mortality experience of these alternatives to ensure they are charging adequate single premiums for them. Lapse studies generally count those who select alternatives to cash surrender as lapsed.

Surrender benefits are assumed to be paid only at the end of the policy year.

Let

> SurrBen(t) = Surrender benefits paid per unit issued
>
> CV_pu(t) = Cash value per unit in force, including any additional dividend payable to lapsing policyowners, in excess of any annual dividend.

Surrender benefits are calculated as the cash value times the probability of lapse:

SurrBen(t) = CV_pu(t) Lapses(t). (5.5.1)

5.6 Dividends

Some companies pay annual policyowner dividends only to policies that are in force on their anniversaries or have premiums paid beyond their anniversaries. Other companies pay pro-rated dividends to policies that lapse during the policy year. For companies that pay an additional dividend on surrender or death, such dividends should be calculated as part of death benefits or surrender benefits.

If pro-rated dividends are paid to lapsing policies, then partial dividends have to be calculated for lapsing policies. Since we have assumed that lapses do not occur until the end of the policy year, the formulas below do not take into account pro-rated dividends. However, the formula does allow for whether or not dividends are paid to those who lapse at the end of the policy year.

Let

$$\text{Div}(t) = \text{Dividends paid, per unit issued}$$
$$\text{Div\_pu}(t) = \text{Dividend per unit in force}$$
$$\text{DivRule} = \text{Dividend rule, which equals 1 if dividends are paid to policies lapsing at the end of the policy year and 0 if dividends are not paid to policies lapsing at the end of the policy year.}$$

Then,

$$\text{Div}(t) = \text{Div\_pu}(t) (\text{SurvFactor}(t) + \text{Lapses}(t) \, \text{DivRule}).$$
(5.6.1)

5.7 Pure Endowment Benefits

Pure endowment benefits pay the pure endowment amount to all policyowners that survive to a given attained age or a given duration. Whole life plans typically pay a pure endowment benefit upon reaching a maximum age, such as age 100. Plans such as Endowment at Age 85 or 20-Year Endowment provide death benefits until the end of the policy is reached, at which time an endowment benefit (usually equal to the death benefit) is paid to the policyowner. Still other plans may offer a periodic endowment benefit, such as $3 per unit in force at the end of every third year.

Let

$$\text{PureEndow}(t) = \text{Pure endowment benefit per unit issued}$$
$$\text{PureEndow\_pu}(t) = \text{Pure endowment benefit per unit in force.}$$

Then,

$$\text{PureEndow}(t) = \text{PureEndow\_pu}(t)\,\text{SurvFactor}(t). \qquad (5.7.1)$$

5.8 Dynamic Product Calculations

In this section, we develop formulas for the life insurance cash flows of dynamic products. "Dynamic products" are products with premiums and benefits that can fluctuate from month to month, depending on the premiums the policyowner pays, the withdrawals the policyowner makes, the investment returns credited to the policy, and the mortality and expenses charges deducted from the policy.

Some common names for dynamic products include universal life, variable universal life, unit-linked life, and adjustable life. Most dynamic products offer flexible premiums, but some have premiums that are fixed at issue.

5.8.1 Common Features of Dynamic Products

The following are some of the most common features of dynamic products:

- Premiums are flexible, often subject to a minimum premium for a number of years.

- Commissions are a high percentage of premiums up to an amount called a "target premium" and a low percentage of premiums for amounts over the target premium. Additional commissions may be paid each year as a small percentage of the account value.

- The account value (also called policy value, fund value, and many other names) is increased by premiums paid and interest credited and decreased by withdrawals, mortality charges, and expense charges. For variable products replace "interest credited" with "investment returns," which could be positive or negative. The account value is usually updated at least once a month on the policy's "monthiversary."

- The cash value is equal to the account value less a surrender charge. The surrender charge is usually at its maximum at issue and gradually declines to zero over a number of years.

- A bonus is sometimes added to the account value if the policy persists to a certain policy year. For example, if the policy is in force on its twentieth anniversary, the company may retroactively credit a slightly higher interest rate or retroactively refund some percentage of mortality or expense charges.

- The death benefit is usually determined by one of the following methods and is decreased by partial withdrawals. The death benefit is equal to one of the following:

  a. A fixed amount (often referred to as "Option A" or "Option 1")

  b. A fixed amount plus the account value (often referred to as "Option B" or "Option 2")

  c. A fixed amount plus the sum of premiums paid.

  In addition, the death benefit is usually never less than a percentage (equal to 100% or more) of the account value. In the U.S., the percentage would vary by age to conform with the tax rules for a policy to qualify as life insurance.

- Mortality charges are usually deducted monthly and calculated as a monthly cost of insurance (COI) rate times the net amount at risk. The net amount at risk is generally the death benefit less the account value. The COI rates vary just as mortality rates do, that is, by age, sex, risk class, and so on.

- Expense charges are usually a percentage of premiums (with a reduced percentage applied to premiums paid in excess of the target premium) and a flat amount per month. Sometimes expense charges are a percentage of account value, especially for variable products. Occasionally, expense charges are per thousand of fixed amount or death benefit.

The above list is not an exhaustive inventory of the hundreds of variations of dynamic product features. However, the features listed do cover the majority of dynamic products issued to date.

5.8.2 Dynamic Product Calculations

To calculate the cash flows associated with dynamic products, we first need to develop a method of calculating the elements that make up the typical dynamic product. We will develop an approach that works for most dynamic products while keeping it as simple as possible.

5.8.2.1 Notation

To handle monthly calculations, some new notation is needed:

- M will be used to denote policy month. M will equal 0 to 12.
- (t, M) will refer to month M, policy year t. Unless otherwise noted, variables will be as of the end of month M, policy year t.
- "Month M, policy year t" covers the interval from time $t - 1 + (M - 1)/12$ to time $t - 1 + M/12$.
- When a policy month of zero is used, represented by $(t, 0)$ in the variable name, it denotes the beginning of the policy year, which is equivalent to the end of the previous policy year. In other words, $(t, 0)$ denotes the same point in time as $(t - 1, 12)$. This will prove useful in connection with recursive calculations.

The following time line illustrates the first few months of policy year t:

Time:	$t-1$	$t-1+\dfrac{1}{12}$	$t-1+\dfrac{2}{12}$	$t-1+\dfrac{3}{12}$	$t-1+\dfrac{4}{12}$
Policy year, month:	$t,0$	$t,1$	$t,2$	$t,3$	$t,4$

|----------------|----------------|----------------|----------------|

The variables defined here fall into several groups:

- Assumptions, such as premium per unit and partial withdrawal rate
- Product features, such as surrender charges, COI rates, and expense charge rates, that can be solved for or adjusted as part of the pricing process
- Results, such as account value, cash value, and death benefit.

5.8.2.2   Premiums, Policy Values, and Partial Withdrawals

The calculation of the policy values is partially dependent on partial withdrawal assumptions. Many dynamic products allow part of the account value to be withdrawn as a partial withdrawal. Partial withdrawals usually have a pro-rata surrender charge applied. Some products allow the policyowner to withdraw up to a certain percentage of the account value each year with no surrender charge applied—a so-called penalty-free partial withdrawal. Death benefits are reduced by partial withdrawals. Otherwise, someone aware of their imminent death would have the incentive to withdraw the maximum in order to receive that amount in addition to the death benefit.

There are two assumptions related to the partial withdrawal benefit that are needed for pricing:

The percentage of account value that is withdrawn each year through partial withdrawals. This is sometimes referred to as a cash value lapse rate.

The percentage of withdrawals each year that are penalty-free, if any.

For simplicity, we will assume that partial withdrawals occur only at the end of the policy month. Because of partial withdrawals, the death benefit per unit, cash value per unit, and account value per unit may be lower at the beginning of month M, policy year t than they were at the end of month $M - 1$, policy year t.

Let

$$\text{Prem\_pu}(t, M) =$$ Premium per unit in force paid at the *beginning* of month M, policy year t. This variable specifies the expected level and pattern of premium payments. It is normal to test many different levels and patterns of premiums to ensure the product has no significant loopholes.

$$\text{AV\_pu}(t, M) =$$ The account value per unit in force

$$\text{CV\_pu}(t, M) =$$ The cash value per unit in force

$$\text{SC\_pu}(t, M) =$$ The surrender charge per unit in force

$$\text{GrossPW\_pu}(t, M) =$$ The gross amount of partial withdrawals per unit in force, equal to the deduction from the account value related to partial withdrawals

$$\text{PWCharge\_pu}(t, M) =$$ Partial withdrawal charge per unit in force, equal to the amount deducted from the gross partial withdrawal before paying the policyowner

$$\text{PWBen\_pu}(t, M) =$$ Partial withdrawal benefit per unit in force, equal to the amount paid to the policyowner net of any partial withdrawal charge

$$\text{CumPWBen\_pu}(t, M) =$$ Cumulative partial withdrawal benefit per unit

$$\text{PartWithRate}(t, M) =$$ The percentage of account value that is withdrawn. We will assume that $\text{PartWithRate}(t, M)$ has already been converted from an annual withdrawal rate to a monthly rate using a formula of the form $\text{MonthlyRate} = 1 - (1 - \text{AnnualRate})^{1/12}$.

FreeWithPct(t) = The average percentage of account value withdrawn during policy year t that is not subject to surrender charges

Bonus_pu(t) = The persistency or other bonus per unit in force that is added to the account value at the end of policy year t.

The cash value is equal to the account value less the surrender charge:

$$\text{CV\_pu}(t, M) = \text{AV\_pu}(t, M) - \text{SC\_pu}(t, M). \tag{5.8.1}$$

The gross partial withdrawal is equal to the monthly partial withdrawal rate times the end of the month account value (to avoid circular formulas):

$$\text{GrossPW\_pu}(t, M) = \text{PartWithRate}(t, M)\,\text{AV\_pu}(t, M). \tag{5.8.2}$$

The partial withdrawal charge is equal to the gross partial withdrawal times the portion subject to surrender charges times the current surrender charge (converted to a percentage by dividing by AV_pu):

PWCharge_pu(t, M)

$$= \text{GrossPW\_pu}(t, M)\,(1 - \text{FreeWithPct}(t))\,\frac{\text{SC\_pu}(t, M)}{\text{AV\_pu}(t, M)}. \tag{5.8.3}$$

Note that FreeWithPct(t) assumes that a study of a company's experience has been performed, so that it represents the *average* percentage of account value that is not subject to surrender charges.

The partial withdrawal benefit is the gross partial withdrawal less the partial withdrawal charge:

$$\text{PWBen\_pu}(t, M) = \text{GrossPW\_pu}(t, M) - \text{PWCharge\_pu}(t, M). \tag{5.8.4}$$

The cumulative partial withdrawal benefit is calculated for use in determining death benefits. It could be based on withdrawal benefits that are gross or net of withdrawal charges. We have chosen to base it on net withdrawal benefits:

CumPWBen_pu(t, M)

$$= \text{CumPWBen\_pu}(t, M - 1) + \text{PWBen\_pu}(t, M). \tag{5.8.5}$$

5.8.2.3 Death Benefits, COI Charges, and Expense Charges

Let

$$\text{DB\_puEnd}(t, M) = \text{Death benefit per unit in force at the } end$$
of month M, policy year t

$$\text{FixedAmt\_pu} = \text{The average fixed amount per unit in}$$
force that is used to calculate death
benefits, usually in connection with
Option A and Option B

$$\text{DBPctAV}(t) = \text{The percentage multiplied by the account}$$
value per unit in force to determine the
minimum death benefit per unit in force.
This percentage equals 100% or more.

$$\text{COICharge\_pu}(t, M) = \text{Cost of insurance charge per unit in}$$
force, equal to the COI rate times the net
amount at risk per unit in force

$$\text{COIRate}(t) = \text{Monthly cost of insurance rate. } \text{COI}(t)$$
has already been converted from an
annual rate to a monthly rate
using a formula of the form
$\text{MonthlyRate} = \text{AnnualRate}/12$.

$$\text{ExpCharge\_pu}(t, M) = \text{Total expense charge per unit in force,}$$
consisting of the following expense
charges

$$\text{PremCharge}(t) = \text{Percentage of premium expense charge}$$

$$\text{FlatCharge}(t) = \text{Flat monthly per policy charge}$$

$$\text{AVCharge}(t, M) = \text{Percentage of account value expense}$$
charge.

We will assume that death benefits are calculated using Option A or Option B, subject to a minimum death benefit of a percentage (of 100% or more) of the account value.

For Option A, the death benefit is reduced by cumulative partial withdrawals. The death benefit is then subject to a minimum death benefit based on a percentage of the account value.

DB_puEnd(t, M) equals the greater of the following:

1. FixedAmt_pu $-$ CumPWBen_pu(t, M), and
2. DBPctAV(t) AV_pu(t, M). (5.8.6)

For Option B, there is no need to reduce the death benefit explicitly for partial withdrawals, since partial withdrawals already reduce the account value, which is part of the death benefit calculation. As with Option A, the death benefit is then subject to a minimum death benefit based on a percentage of the account value.

DB_puEnd(t, M) equals the greater of the following:

1. FixedAmt_pu $+$ AV_pu(t, M), and
2. DBPctAV(t) AV_pu(t, M). (5.8.7)

Note that a common variation of these formulas substitutes cash value for account value.

The COI charge is equal to the COI rate times the net amount at risk, which is calculated as the death benefit less the account value:

COICharge_pu(t, M)
$$= \text{COIRate}(t) \, (\text{DB\_puEnd}(t, M - 1) - \text{AV\_pu}(t, M - 1)).$$
(5.8.8)

We will assume the expense charge per unit is calculated at the beginning of the month. It is composed of a percentage of the current month's premium, a flat amount, and a percentage of the account value at the end of the previous month. In practice there are many different ways of calculating these charges. They could be deducted before or after the various other deductions and additions to the account value during the month:

ExpCharge_pu(t, M)
$$= \text{Prem\_pu}(t, M) \, \text{PremCharge}(t) + \frac{\text{FlatCharge}(t)}{\text{AvgSize}}$$
$$+ \text{AV\_pu}(t, M - 1) \, \text{AVCharge}(t, M).$$
(5.8.9)

5.8.2.4 Account Value Calculation

Let

$\text{IntCred\_pu}(t, M)$ = Interest credited to the account value, per unit in force

$\text{CredIntRate}(t, M)$ = The monthly credited interest rate. We will assume that this rate has already been converted from an annual effective interest rate to a monthly rate using a formula of the form: $i(t, M) = (1 + i)^{1/12} - 1$.

To accommodate variable or unit-linked products, we can redefine $\text{CredIntRate}(t, M)$ to be the investment performance for the month, positive or negative, as a percentage of the funds invested. Because of the volatility in monthly investment performance, variable products are better handled using a stochastic modeling approach, which is discussed in Chapter 15. For now, we will keep things simple and use $\text{CredIntRate}(t, M)$ for both fixed and variable products.

The account value can be calculated in many ways, with the results dependent on the order in which items are added to or deducted from the account value. We have chosen the following approach, which is rarely used in practice but greatly simplifies the formulas:

- All calculations for the current month are based on the account value and death benefit at the end of the previous month

- All current month activity is added to or deducted from the account value at the end of the month.

A full month's interest is earned on the previous month's account value:

$$\text{IntCred\_pu}(t, M) = \text{AV\_pu}(t, M - 1)\, \text{CredIntRate}(t, M).$$

$$(5.8.10)$$

By basing all earlier calculations on the previous month's account value and death benefit, all the components of the current month's account value have been precalculated. All that remains is to add and subtract these components from the prior month's account value:

$$
\begin{aligned}
\text{Av\_pu}(t, M) = {} & \text{AV\_pu}(t, M - 1) + \text{IntCred\_pu}(t, M) \\
& + \text{Prem\_pu}(t, M) + \text{Bonus\_pu}(t, M) \\
& - \text{ExpCharge\_pu}(t, M) - \text{COICharge\_pu}(t, M) \\
& - \text{GrossPW\_pu}(t, M).
\end{aligned} \tag{5.8.11}
$$

5.9 Life Insurance Cash Flows for Dynamic Products

In this section, we will develop formulas for the life insurance cash flows of dynamic products such as universal life and variable universal life. These formulas will build on the formulas already presented for pre-scheduled products in the following way:

1. Premiums: Separate formulas for dynamic
2. Acquisition expenses: Use pre-scheduled formulas
3. Commissions and sales expenses: Separate formulas for dynamic
4. Maintenance expenses: Use pre-scheduled formulas
5. Death benefits: Separate formulas for dynamic
6. Claim expenses: Use pre-scheduled formulas
7. Surrender benefits: Use pre-scheduled formulas
8. Dividends: Not applicable to dynamic
9. Pure endowment benefits: Not applicable to dynamic
10. Partial withdrawal benefits: Applies only to dynamic.

To summarize, this section presents formulas only for premiums, commissions and sales expenses, death benefits, and partial withdrawal benefits. Whenever possible, notation already defined for pre-scheduled products will be reused for dynamic products.

5.9.1 Premiums for Dynamic Products

Policy fees are assumed not to apply to dynamic products. Instead, any premium paid is added to the account value. We will assume all premiums are paid at the beginning of the first month of the policy year and that none of the premiums paid are refunded in the event of death during the policy year. Let

$$\text{Prem\_pu}(t) = \text{Premium per unit in force, paid at the beginning of the first month of the policy year.}$$

Premiums per unit issued equal the premium per unit for the first month times the beginning-of-the-year survivorship factor:

$$\text{Prem}(t) = \text{Prem\_pu}(t) \, \text{SurvFactor}(t - 1). \tag{5.9.1}$$

5.9.2 Commissions and Sales Expenses for Dynamic Products

Commissions for dynamic products are usually calculated for each policy year as a higher percentage of premiums up to an amount called a "target premium" and a lower percentage of premiums for amounts in excess of the target premium. Additional commissions may be paid as a small percentage of the account value:

$$\text{TargetPrem\_pu}(t) = \text{Annual target premium per unit in force}$$
$$\text{HighCommPct}(t) = \text{The higher commission rate that applies to premiums paid up to the amount of the target premium}$$
$$\text{LowCommPct}(t) = \text{The lower commission rate that applies to premiums paid in excess of the amount of the target premium}$$
$$\text{HighCommPrem}(t) = \text{The premium per unit in force that is subject to the high commission rate}$$
$$\text{LowCommPrem}(t) = \text{The premium per unit in force that is subject to the low commission rate}$$
$$\text{AVComm}(t) = \text{Commissions and other agent compensation paid as a percent of the account value, per unit issued}$$
$$\text{AVCommPct}(t) = \text{The percentage of account value paid as a commissions and other agent compensation}$$
$$\text{AV\_pu}(t) = \text{The account value per unit in force, equal to AV\_pu}(t, 12).$$

The "high commission" premium is equal to the lesser of the target premium per unit and the premium per unit:

$$\text{HighCommPrem}(t) = \min\ (\text{Prem\_pu}(t),\ \text{TargetPrem\_pu}(t)).$$

$$(5.9.2)$$

The "low commission" premium plus the "high commission" premium equals the premium per unit; therefore,

$$\text{LowCommPrem}(t) = \text{Prem\_pu}(t) - \text{HighCommPrem}(t). \quad (5.9.3)$$

Commissions and related expenses are calculated by applying the higher and lower commission rates to the appropriate premiums and then adjusting the result for distribution expenses and survivorship:

$$\begin{aligned}
\text{Comm}(t) = {}&(\text{HighCommPrem}(t)\ \text{HighCommPct}(t) \\
&+ \text{LowCommPrem}(t)\ \text{LowCommPct}(t)) \\
&(1 + \text{SalesExpPct}(t))\ \text{SurvFactor}(t - 1). \quad (5.9.4)
\end{aligned}$$

We will assume that commissions and other agent compensation paid as a percentage of the account value are paid only at the end of the policy year, although payments more often than once per year are possible:

$$\begin{aligned}
\text{AVComm}(t) = {}&\text{AVCommPct}(t)\ \text{AV\_pu}(t) \\
&(1 + \text{SalesExpPct}(t))\ \text{SurvFactor}(t). \quad (5.9.5)
\end{aligned}$$

5.9.3   Death Benefits for Dynamic Products

The formula for death benefits for dynamic products is very similar to that for pre-scheduled products. The only difference is related to the amount of premium returned upon death. In general, fixed premium dynamic products return unearned premium upon death and flexible premium products do not.

The death benefit per unit at the middle of the policy year is the death benefit at the end of policy month 6:

$$\text{DB\_puMid}(t) = \text{DB\_puEnd}(t, 6). \qquad (5.9.6)$$

If premium payments are fixed, then

$$\text{DeathBen}(t) = \left(\text{DB\_puMid}(t) + \frac{\text{ROPFactor Prem}(t)}{\text{SurvFactor}(t - 1)}\right)\text{Deaths}(t).$$

$$(5.9.7)$$

If premium payments are flexible, then

$$\text{DeathBen}(t) = \text{DB\_puMid}(t)\ \text{Deaths}(t). \tag{5.9.8}$$

Note: Some dynamic products return unearned cost of insurance charges upon death. However, since cost of insurance charges are normally deducted monthly, the average amount returned on death equals one-half of one month's cost of insurance charge. This is normally a small amount compared to the overall death benefit and will be ignored.

5.9.4 Partial Withdrawal Benefits for Dynamic Products

Let

$\text{PartWithBen}(t)$ = Partial withdrawal benefits paid per unit issued

$\text{PWBen\_pu}(t)$ = Partial withdrawal benefit per unit in force. When calculating monthly partial withdrawal benefits, you can force them to occur only at the end of the policy year. In that case, $\text{PWBen\_pu}(t) = \text{PWBen\_pu}(t, 12)$.

We will assume that partial withdrawals are made only at the end of the policy year:

$$\text{PartWithBen}(t) = \text{PWBen\_pu}(t)\ \text{SurvFactor}(t). \tag{5.9.9}$$

5.10 Cash Flow Summaries

Cash flows can be summarized by timing and by type of cash flow. This section applies to both pre-scheduled and dynamic products.

5.10.1 Summary of Cash Flows by Timing

All of the cash flows presented in this chapter can be segregated into three groups, based on their timing:

- Beginning-of-the-policy-year cash flows
- Middle-of-the-policy-year cash flows and
- End-of-the-policy-year cash flows.

The cash flows in this chapter can be thought of as product cash flows, that is, cash flows generated by the inner workings of the policy. By adding up the product cash flows for each of these groups, we can prepare for investment income and tax calculations in later chapters.

Let

$$\text{CashFlowBeg}(t) = \text{Beginning-of-the-year cash flows per unit issued}$$
$$\text{CashFlowMid}(t) = \text{Middle-of-the-year cash flows per unit issued}$$
$$\text{CashFlowEnd}(t) = \text{End-of-the-year cash flows per unit issued}$$
$$\text{ProdCashFlow}(t) = \text{Total product cash flow per unit issued.}$$

Then,

$$\text{CashFlowBeg}(t) = \text{Prem}(t) - \text{AcqExp}(t) - \text{Comm}(t) - \text{MaintExp}(t), \tag{5.10.1}$$
$$\text{CashFlowMid}(t) = -\text{DeathBen}(t) - \text{ClaimExp}(t), \tag{5.10.2}$$
$$\text{CashFlowEnd}(t) = -\text{AVComm}(t) - \text{SurrBen}(t) - \text{Div}(t) - \text{PureEndow}(t) - \text{PartWithBen}(t), \tag{5.10.3}$$
$$\text{ProdCashFlow}(t) = \text{CashFlowBeg}(t) + \text{CashFlowMid}(t) + \text{CashFlowEnd}(t). \tag{5.10.4}$$

ProdCashFlow(t) can be positive or negative in any given policy year.

5.10.2   Summary of Cash Flows by Type

For use in later chapters, we will summarize cash flows by type: premiums, benefits, and expenses. Premiums are already "summarized" by Prem(t). To summarize benefits and expenses, let

$$\text{Ben}(t) = \text{Total policy benefits per unit issued,}$$
$$\text{Exp}(t) = \text{Total expenses per unit issued.}$$

Then,

$$\text{Ben}(t) = \text{DeathBen}(t) + \text{SurrBen}(t) + \text{Div}(t) + \text{PureEndow}(t) + \text{PartWithBen}(t), \tag{5.10.5}$$
$$\text{Exp}(t) = \text{AcqExp}(t) + \text{Comm}(t) + \text{AVComm}(t) + \text{MaintExp}(t) + \text{ClaimExp}(t). \tag{5.10.6}$$

Total product cash flow can also be calculated as

$$\text{ProdCashFlow}(t) = \text{Prem}(t) - \text{Ben}(t) - \text{Exp}(t). \qquad (5.10.7)$$

5.11 Pricing Model

This chapter's contribution to the Chapters 4–11 pricing example is given in Tables 5.11.1 through 5.11.5.

Table 5.11.1 Premium and Acquisition Expense Factors

t	AcqExp_pu	AcqExpPrem	AcqExpPerPol
1	1.50	0.25	50.00
2–10	0.00	0.00	0.00

Note: For all t, Prem_pu = 6.20, PolicyFee = 30.00, and AvgSize = 100.00.

Table 5.11.2 Maintenance Expense and Premium Expense Factors

t	CommPct	SalesExpPct
1	1.100	0.250
2	0.100	0.050
3	0.100	0.050
4	0.050	0.050
5	0.050	0.050
6–10	0.030	0.050

Note: For all t, CV_pu(t) = 0, Div_put(t) = 0, Exp_pu = 0.15, ExpPrem = 0.0250, and ExpPerPol = 25.00.

Table 5.11.3 Death Benefit Factors

t	ClaimExp_pu	ClaimExpPerPol
1	100.00	200.00
2	100.00	200.00
3–10	0.00	0.00

Note: For all t, DB_puMid = 1,000.00 and ROPFactor = 0.50.

Table 5.11.4 Product Cash Flows

t	Prem	AcqExp	Comm	MaintExp	DeathBen	ClaimExp
1	6.50000	3.62500	8.93750	0.56250	1.17380	0.11934
2	5.71331	0.00000	0.59990	0.49442	1.51674	0.15421
3	5.30424	0.00000	0.55694	0.45902	1.89117	0.00000
4	5.02739	0.00000	0.26394	0.43506	2.13388	0.00000
5	4.76288	0.00000	0.25005	0.41217	2.30096	0.00000
6	4.51058	0.00000	0.14208	0.39034	2.41578	0.00000
7	4.36008	0.00000	0.13734	0.37731	2.55052	0.00000
8	4.21324	0.00000	0.13272	0.36461	2.69223	0.00000
9	4.06993	0.00000	0.12820	0.35221	2.86449	0.00000
10	3.92983	0.00000	0.12379	0.34008	3.08129	0.00000

Table 5.11.5 Pre-Reinsurance Cash Flow Summary

t	CashFlowBeg	CashFlowMid	Ben	Exp	ProdCashFlow
1	−6.62500	−1.29314	1.17380	13.24434	−7.91814
2	4.61899	−1.67095	1.51674	1.24852	2.94804
3	4.28827	−1.89117	1.89117	1.01597	2.39710
4	4.32839	−2.13388	2.13388	0.69900	2.19450
5	4.10066	−2.30096	2.30096	0.66222	1.79969
6	3.97815	−2.41578	2.41578	0.53242	1.56237
7	3.84542	−2.55052	2.55052	0.51466	1.29490
8	3.71592	−2.69223	2.69223	0.49732	1.02369
9	3.58952	−2.86449	2.86449	0.48041	0.72503
10	3.46596	−3.08129	3.08129	0.46387	0.38466

Note: The pricing model does not have any cash flow items that occur at the end of the year. Therefore CashFlowEnd(t) = 0.00 for all t.

5.12 Exercises

Many of the following exercises build on the exercises preceding them. Spreadsheets will reduce the data entry required.

Exercise 5.1 Annual Premiums

Given a policy fee of 100 per year, an average size policy with 200,000 of death benefit, a unit defined as 1,000 of death benefit, and the following values for premiums per unit in force and survival factors, calculate the premium per unit issued.

t	*Prem_pu(t)*	*SurvFactor(t − 1)*
1	10.00	1.00
2	10.00	0.90
3	10.00	0.85

Exercise 5.2

Suppose that half (call this "AnnualPct") of the policies will be issued with an annual mode of payment (as in Exercise 5.1) and half (call this "SemiAnnualPct") of the policies will be issued with a semiannual mode of payment. Next suppose that the semiannual mode of payment has the following characteristics: The policy fee for the semiannual mode (call this the "SemiAnnualPolicyFee") is 60 every six months, and 51% (call this the "SemiAnnualFactor") of the premium per unit in force must be paid every six months. Finally, we will define SurvFactorMid(t) to be the probability of surviving from issue to the middle of policy year t. (Assume that one-half of the deaths occur during the first half of the policy year, and the other half occur during the second half of the policy year.)

a. Develop a revised formula for Prem(t) that reflects a mixture of annual and semiannual modes of payments, using AnnualPct, SemiAnnualPct, SemiAnnualPolicyFee, SemiAnnualFactor, and SurvFactorMid(t).

b. Apply the revised formula for Prem(t) to the data from Exercise 5.1 and the semiannual data given above to complete the following table.

t	Semiannual Prem_pu[a]	SurvFactorMid(t)	Semiannual Prem(t)[b]	Prem(t)[c]
1		0.95		
2		0.87		
3		0.83		

[a] Include the semiannual policy fee, converted to a per unit in force basis.
[b] Before applying SemiAnnualPct, that is, assume 100% semiannual.
[c] Assume 50% annual and 50% semiannual.

Exercise 5.3

Building on Exercise 5.1, calculate acquisition expense and commissions per unit issued given the following information:

- Acquisition expenses of 100 per policy and 50% of first-year premium
- Commissions of 80% of first-year premiums and 10% of renewal premiums, and
- Sales expenses of 25% of first-year commissions and 10% of renewal commissions.

t	AcqExp(t)	Comm(t)
1		
2	0.0000	
3	0.0000	

Exercise 5.4

Building on Exercises 5.1 through 5.3, calculate maintenance expenses per unit issued, given maintenance expenses of 60 per policy in force at the beginning of the policy year and 2% of premium.

t	ExpPerPol(t) /AvgSize	ExpPrem(t) × Prem(t)	MaintExp(t)
1			
2			
3			

Exercise 5.5

Building on Exercises 5.1 through 5.4, calculate death benefits per unit issued, given a level death benefit per unit in force of 1,000, return of premiums paid beyond the month of death, and the following probabilities of death.

t	$DB\_puMid(t)$	$ROPFactor\ Prem(t)$ $/SurvFactor(t-1)$	$Deaths(t)$	$DeathBen(t)$
1	1,000		0.0010	
2	1,000		0.0011	
3	1,000		0.0012	

Exercise 5.6

Building on Exercise 5.5, calculate claim expenses, given that contestable death claims, which are defined as claims occurring during the first two policy years, cost the company an average of 1,000 per claim, and incontestable death claims (those that occur after the first two policy years) cost 100 per claim.

t	$ClaimExpPerPol(t)$	$ClaimExp(t)$
1	1,000	
2	1,000	
3	100	

Exercise 5.7

Given the following probabilities of lapse and cash values per unit in force, calculate surrender benefits per unit issued.

t	$Lapses(t)$	$CV\_pu(t)$	$SurrBen(t)$
1	0.0990	0.00	
2	0.0489	2.00	
3	0.0238	8.00	

Exercise 5.8

Calculate dividends per unit issued, given that dividends are *not* paid to policies lapsing during the policy year and given the following data.

t	Div_pu(t)	SurvFactor(t)	Lapses(t)	Div(t)
1	0.00	0.9000	0.0990	
2	0.50	0.8500	0.0489	
3	1.00	0.8250	0.0238	

Exercise 5.9

Calculate the pure endowment benefit per unit issued, given that a 1,000 endowment benefit per unit is payable to those policies still in force at the end of 20 policy years and given the following survival factors.

t	SurvFactor(t)	PureEndow(t)
18	0.400	
19	0.372	
20	0.350	

Exercise 5.10

Using the results of all the preceding exercises in this chapter *except* Exercise 5.2 (Semiannual Premiums) and Exercise 5.9 (Endowment Benefits), calculate cash flows at the beginning, middle, and end of the policy year, on a per unit issued basis.

t	CashFlowBeg(t)	CashFlowMid(t)	CashFlowEnd(t)
1			
2			
3			

Exercise 5.11

Using the results of all the preceding exercises in this chapter *except* Exercise 5.2 (Semiannual Premiums) and Exercise 5.9 (Endowment Benefits), summarize cash flows by premiums, expenses, benefits, and total (product) on a per unit issued basis.

t	$Prem(t)$	$Exp(t)$	$Ben(t)$	$ProdCashFlow(t)$
1				
2				
3				

5.13 Answers

Answer 5.1

t	$Prem\_pu(t)$	$PolicyFee$ $/AvgSize$	$SurvFactor(t-1)$	$Prem(t)$
1	10.00	0.50	1.00	10.5000
2	10.00	0.50	0.90	9.4500
3	10.00	0.50	0.85	8.9250

Answer 5.2

a.

$SurvFactorMid(t) = SurvFactor(t-1) \times (1 - 0.5 \times qd(t))$.

$Prem(t)$

$= AnnualPct\ (Prem\_pu(t) + PolicyFee/AvgSize)\ SurvFactor(t-1)$

$\quad + SemiAnnualPct\ (Prem\_pu(t)\ SemiAnnualFactor$

$\quad + SemiAnnualPolicyFee/AvgSize)$

$\quad \times (SurvFactor(t-1)$

$\quad + SurvFactorMid(t))$.

b.

t	Semiannual Prem_pu	SurvFactorMid(t)	Semiannual Prem(t)	Prem(t)
1	5.40	0.95	10.530	10.5150
2	5.40	0.87	9.558	9.5040
3	5.40	0.83	9.072	8.9985

Answer 5.3

t	AcqExp(t)	Comm(t)
1	5.7500	10.5000
2	0.0000	1.0395
3	0.0000	0.9818

Answer 5.4

t	ExpPerPol(t) /AvgSize	ExpPrem(t) × Prem(t)	MaintExp(t)
1	0.30	0.2100	0.5100
2	0.30	0.1890	0.4590
3	0.30	0.1785	0.4335

Answer 5.5

t	DB_puMid(t)	ROPFactor Prem(t) /SurvFactor(t − 1)	Deaths(t)	DeathBen(t)
1	1,000	4.8125	0.0010	1.0048
2	1,000	4.8125	0.0011	1.1053
3	1,000	4.8125	0.0012	1.2058

Answer 5.6

t	ClaimExpPerPol(t)	ClaimExp(t)
1	1,000	0.0050
2	1,000	0.0055
3	100	0.0006

Answer 5.7

t	Lapses(t)	CV_pu(t)	SurrBen(t)
1	0.0990	0.00	0.0000
2	0.0489	2.00	0.0978
3	0.0238	8.00	0.1904

Answer 5.8

t	Div_pu(t)	SurvFactor(t)	Lapses(t)	Div(t)
1	0.00	0.9000	0.0990	0.0000
2	0.50	0.8500	0.0489	0.4250
3	1.00	0.8250	0.0238	0.8250

Answer 5.9

t	SurvFactor(t)	PureEndow(t)
18	0.400	0.0000
19	0.372	0.0000
20	0.350	350.0000

Answer 5.10

t	CashFlowBeg(t)	CashFlowMid(t)	CashFlowEnd(t)
1	−6.2600	−1.0098	0.0000
2	7.9515	−1.1108	−0.5228
3	7.5098	−1.2064	−1.0154

Answer 5.11

t	$Prem(t)$	$Exp(t)$	$Ben(t)$	$ProdCashFlow(t)$
1	10.5000	16.7650	1.0048	-7.2698
2	9.4500	1.5040	1.6281	6.3179
3	8.9250	1.4159	2.2212	5.2880

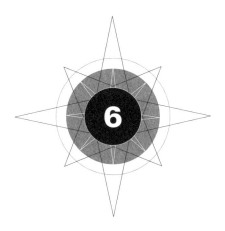

Reserves

Introduction

This chapter serves two purposes. For some readers it serves as an introduction to reserves and valuation. You may wish to focus on the reserve methods that are most applicable to your situation. For all readers it explains the impact of various types of reserves on pricing and develops some pricing formulas for use in later chapters.

The dictionary defines a *reserve* as "something kept back or saved for future use." In life insurance reserves are necessary when premiums are designed and expected to be more than sufficient to pay benefits in the early policy years and less than sufficient in the later policy years. Something must be kept back and saved for future use, in order for the insurance company to be able to pay benefits in the later policy years.

Insurance companies must maintain assets at least equal to reserve and capital requirements, to make provision for their promise to pay all future claims and expenses. Generally, reserves can be thought of as the amount by which future benefits and expenses are expected to exceed future premiums, on a present value basis. Together, reserves and future premiums must be sufficient to cover future benefits and expenses.

To better understand reserves, consider the following example.

Example 6.1.1

Policy Year	Premium	Expected Benefits	End-of-Year Reserve
0			0
1	100	50	50
2	100	100	50
3	100	150	0
Total	300	300	

To keep this example simple, we will ignore interest, survivorship and expenses. Over the three-year period, total premiums of 300 are exactly enough to cover total expected benefits of 300, so no reserve is needed at issue (policy year 0). At the end of the first-year, however, future premiums are only 200 and future benefits are expected to be 250.

To cover this deficit of 50, the insurance company must establish a reserve of 50, which is funded from the excess of first-year premium over first-year benefit. After two years, the future deficit will again be 50, which means the company must continue to hold a reserve of 50. After three years, there are no future premiums or benefits, so no reserve is needed.

Many forms of life insurance have level premiums and increasing mortality rates, as in the above example. As a result, the insurance company must retain a portion of premiums collected when insureds are younger to help it pay claims when insureds are older. The portion of premiums that must be retained is determined by reserve methods. Insurance laws, regulations, or accounting practices govern the reserve method used. Generally, reserves plus the present value of future premiums must be sufficient to cover the present value of future benefits and expenses.

In practice, reserves help ensure that insurance companies can fulfill the promises they have made. Without reserve requirements, an overly optimistic, naive, or unscrupulous insurance company could sell a lot of insurance by promising benefits that were unsupportable by premiums. The insurance company could even pay the promised benefits for some period of time, perhaps years, by collecting more and more premiums to pay more and more benefits. (This is similar to the famous Ponzi scheme, named after Charles Ponzi, who organized an investment swindle in 1919–20. The swindle promised high returns from fictitious sources and used funds raised from later investors to pay off early investors.) Without reserve requirements, there is a significant danger that the insurance company will not be able to honor its promises to policyowners.

Reserves help prevent this problem by forcing a periodic comparison of future benefits and expenses with future premiums and investment returns. This periodic comparison is called a valuation of liabilities or, simply, a valuation. If unsupportable promises are being made, a qualified actuary will usually be able to spot and report the problem before it grows too large.

Reserve requirements indirectly give the general public a level of confidence that insurance companies can and will honor their commitments. Without confidence in insurance companies, people will buy much less insurance.

6.2   Purpose of Reserves

So far, we have discussed the fundamental purpose for reserves: To help the insurance company honor its commitments to policyowners, that is, to promote the company's solvency. Reserves calculated for this purpose will be referred to as *solvency reserves*. Reserves are often used for two other important purposes: (1) To help determine the company's earnings for financial reporting to stockholders and stock markets (*earnings reserves*); and (2) to help determine the company's taxable earnings (*tax reserves*).

It is not unusual for a company to have to calculate three different sets of reserves: one set for solvency, one set for earnings, and one set for taxes. Why? Let us examine the motives behind each set of reserves.

6.2.1 Solvency Reserves

The purpose of solvency reserves is to help ensure that the insurance company will meet all of its obligations to policyowners. Solvency reserves are often higher than earnings reserves and sometimes higher than tax reserves. This is because solvency reserve regulations and standards are usually biased toward overestimating future benefits and expenses and underestimating future interest rates, in order to strengthen the likelihood of companies remaining solvent. For the same reason, solvency reserve standards often require insurance companies to immediately expense a significant share of acquisition costs, rather than spread them over time. Thus, a block of policies that are profitable in the long run may generate losses in the year of issue.

As a result of these conservative measures, it is fairly common for new business to produce initial solvency reserves well in excess of the initial assets generated by initial net cash flows. This is referred to as *new business strain*. Because of new business strain, an insurance company can actually become insolvent by writing too much profitable business. This is quite unlike other industries, where excess sales usually improve a company's earnings and solvency.

6.2.2 Earnings Reserves

The purpose of earnings reserves is to help calculate earnings on a fair and consistent basis over time, thereby giving stockholders and stock markets an accurate and dependable measure of the company's progress.

When earnings are measured using solvency reserves, earnings are often distorted. A big jump in new business can depress earnings because of increased new business strain. On the other hand, a big reduction in new business can cause a big increase in earnings. Earnings based on solvency reserves can send the misguided message that growth is bad. It is not surprising, therefore, that there is a trend toward measuring earnings using a more realistic, less conservative approach to reserves than that used for solvency reserves.

Compared to solvency reserves, earnings reserves typically have less conservatism built in. For example, the assumptions for future mortality rates and interest rates might be much closer to realistic estimates. Earnings reserves usually defer most acquisition costs, spreading the costs over many policy years rather than expensing them at issue.

It is fairly common for new business to produce initial earnings reserves that are roughly equal to initial assets. In other words, earnings reserves usually reduce or eliminate the distortion of new business strain that is commonly associated with solvency reserves. With earnings reserves, when an insurance company writes higher than expected amounts of profitable business, it may actually increase its earnings. However, solvency reserves would typically not allow such earnings to be distributed to policyowners and shareholders.

As shown in Figure 6.2.1, when solvency reserves are used to determine earnings, a representative pattern of earnings would be a loss of 100 in the first year followed by a stream of positive earnings in future years. When earnings reserves are used instead, the corresponding pattern would be positive earnings in all years. The reasons for these patterns will become more apparent later in this chapter when initial expenses are discussed.

Notice that, even when earnings reserves are used, the vast majority of earnings emerge over many future years, not just in the first year. These future earnings provide an additional buffer against the possibility of unfavorable future experience. By spreading earnings over many years, earnings reserves based on more realistic assumptions still retain a significant element of conservatism.

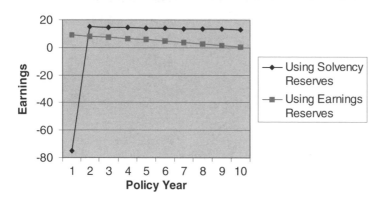

Figure 6.2.1 Representative Earnings Patterns

6.2.3 Tax Reserves

The purpose of tax reserves is to help calculate taxable earnings or taxable income. In the calculation of taxable income, tax reserves are used in place of solvency or earnings reserves.

In most countries, tax reserves are identical to solvency reserves. This approach is advantageous for several reasons:

- It promotes solvency by only taxing earnings in excess of the amounts needed to maintain solvency.
- Because solvency reserves are usually the largest possible choice for tax reserves, it provides the largest tax deductions for insurance companies.
- It is simple and easy to administer.

In some countries tax reserves are set at a lower level than solvency reserves, thereby eliminating the above advantages. This is usually done to increase the government's tax revenue from life insurance companies.

6.3 Reserve Methods

There are a number of basic methods that are used to calculate reserves. The particular reserve method to be used is determined by insurance laws or regulations, actuarial or accounting practices, or tax laws or regulations. Reserve methods differ in their answers to the following questions:

- Are reserve calculations prospective (discounting future amounts back to the present time) or retrospective (accumulating past amounts up to the present time)?

- For prospective calculations, are gross or net future premiums reflected?

- What is the source of assumptions used to calculate reserves? Simplified assumptions spelled out in regulations? More realistic assumptions based on experience? Or realistic assumptions with provisions for adverse deviation?

- When using realistic assumptions, are assumptions locked in at issue (*static assumptions*), or are the latest available data used (dynamic assumptions)?

- What is the treatment of nonguaranteed elements, such as dividends, premiums, or death benefits that can be adjusted from time to time? Are reserves based on current values of the nonguaranteed elements or on guaranteed values? What is the impact of a change in current values?

- What is the treatment of acquisition costs?

  Are acquisition costs ignored, fixed or limited by formula, or based on company statistics?

  Are acquisition costs spread out over time by being incorporated into the reserve calculation or through the capitalization and amortization of an asset (*deferred acquisition cost* or DAC) separate from the reserve?

  Against what revenue stream are acquisition costs matched and expensed? Are they matched with premiums, other sources of revenue, or benefits?

  Over what period of time are acquisition costs amortized? Over the full premium-paying period (if matched with premiums) or over the full benefit period (if matched with other sources of revenue or benefits)? Or over some shorter period of time?

- Are earnings reserves calculated for the entire lifetime of the policy, or are they graded into solvency reserves at the end of, say, 20 or 30 years?

Theoretically, a large number of combinations of answers to the above questions are possible. However, relatively few combinations are widely used. We will examine four widely used reserve methods:

- The simplified net premium method
- The realistic net premium method
- The gross premium method
- The accumulation method.

6.3.1 Overview of Prospective Reserve Methods

The simplified net premium method, realistic net premium method, and gross premium method are all *prospective reserve methods:* They discount future amounts back to the present time in order to calculate reserves.

When an insurance company retains a portion of premiums to build reserves, the amounts retained are invested mainly in interest-bearing assets like bonds and mortgages. The interest income earned on these assets is anticipated in the reserve calculation through the use of present values.

This is the prospective reserve formula:

Reserve = Present value of future benefits and expenses
       − Present value of future premiums.   (6.3.1)

The premiums in Formula 6.3.1 could be net premiums or gross premiums (that is, the premiums paid by the policyowner). Net premiums are typically calculated as a level percentage of gross premiums, sufficient to cover all future benefits and expenses. The following formula would typically be used to determine the ratio of net premiums to gross premiums:

NetPremRatio

$$= \frac{\text{Present value at issue of all future benefits and expenses}}{\text{Present value at issue of all future gross premiums}}.$$

(6.3.2)

This results in the present value of all net premiums equal to the present value of all benefits and expenses.

The prospective reserve calculations can be defined more rigorously. Note that similar to the "(t)" notation, "(s)" implies end of policy year s, unless otherwise noted. Let

$n =$ The last policy year for policy benefits, that is, the final policy year

$\text{PVFP}(s) =$ Present value of future premiums (for policy years $s + 1$ through n), per unit in force

$\text{PVFB}(s) =$ Present value of future benefits and expenses (for policy years $s + 1$ through n), per unit in force

$\text{NetPrem\_pu}(s) =$ Net premium for policy year s, per unit in force at the *beginning* of policy year s

$\text{NetPremRatio} =$ Ratio of net premium to gross premium in all policy years; for the gross premium method, NetPremRatio is set equal to 1

$\text{Res\_pu}(s) =$ Reserve per unit in force.

The assumptions used to calculate reserves are usually different from those used for pricing purposes. Also, certain benefits and expenses used in pricing may be omitted from reserve calculations. For example, the simplified net premium method usually ignores lapses and, therefore, surrender benefits. However, the formulas already developed in Chapters 4 and 5 can still be used to help calculate simplified net premium reserves, with the appropriate benefits and expenses omitted, and reserve assumptions substituted for pricing assumptions.

In Chapter 5, cash flows are calculated on a "per unit issued" basis, which means they are adjusted for the probability of surviving from time 0 (the issue date) to the time of the cash flow. Because the above present values (PVFP and PVFB) are calculated on a "per unit in force at the end of policy year s" basis, we want to reflect survivorship only from the end of policy year s to the time of the cash flow. Therefore, we will have to adjust Chapter 5 cash flows for the probability of surviving from time 0 to the end of policy year s. This adjustment is made by dividing the cash flow by SurvFactor(s). In other words,

$$\begin{aligned}&\text{Cash flow at time } t \text{ per unit in force at end of policy year } s\\&= \frac{\text{Cash flow at time } t \text{ per unit issued}}{\text{SurvFactor}(s)}.\end{aligned} \quad (6.3.3)$$

We have a similar obstacle in using the discount factors developed in Chapter 4, which discount from the time of the cash flow back to time 0. We want to discount only from the time of the cash flow back to the end of policy year s. Therefore, we will have to adjust for discounting from the end of policy year s back to time 0. This adjustment is made by dividing DiscFactor(t) by DiscFactor(s). In other words,

$$\begin{aligned}&\text{Present value at time } s \text{ of \$1 payable at time } t\\&= \frac{\text{DiscFactor}(t)}{\text{DiscFactor}(s)}.\end{aligned} \quad (6.3.4)$$

The present value of future premiums as of the end of policy year s can now be calculated using Formulas 6.3.3 and 6.3.4:

$$\text{PVFP}(s) = \frac{\displaystyle\sum_{t=s+1}^{n} \text{Prem}(t)\,\text{DiscFactor}(t-1)}{\text{SurvFactor}(s)\,\text{DiscFactor}(s)}. \quad (6.3.5)$$

All of the cash flows summarized at the end of Chapter 5 are benefits and expenses, with one exception: Prem(t) is contained in CashFlowBeg(t). So, by deducting Prem(t) from CashFlowBeg(t), we can use Chapter 5 cash flows to calculate benefits and expenses for policy year t. Using this fact along with Formulas 6.3.3 and 6.3.4, we can now calculate the present value of future benefits and expenses as of the end of policy year s:

$$\text{PVFB}(s)$$

$$
= \sum_{t=s+1}^{n} \big[-(\text{CashFlowBeg}(t) - \text{Prem}(t))\, \text{DiscFactor}(t-1)
$$
$$
- \text{CashFlowMid}(t)\, \text{DiscFactorMid}(t)
$$
$$
- \text{CashFlowEnd}(t)\, \text{DiscFactor}(t) \big]
$$
$$
/(\text{SurvFactor}(s)\, \text{DiscFactor}(s)). \tag{6.3.6}
$$

The major difference between the formulas for PVFP and PVFB is that there are three benefit and expense cash flows per year, each with its own discount factor. Because benefits and expenses are negative cash flows, we have subtracted them in order to calculate a positive PVFB. The ratio of net premiums to gross premiums can now be calculated as

$$
\text{NetPremRatio} = \frac{\text{PVFB}(0)}{\text{PVFP}(0)} \text{ for the net premium methods, and}
$$
$$
= 1 \text{ for the gross premium method.} \tag{6.3.7}
$$

Net premiums can then be calculated from gross premiums:

$$
\text{NetPrem\_pu}(s) = \frac{\text{NetPremRatio}\,\text{Prem}(s)}{\text{SurvFactor}(s-1)}, \text{ for } s = 1 \text{ to } n. \tag{6.3.8}
$$

Finally, the reserve per unit in force at the end of policy year s can be calculated:

$$
\text{Res\_pu}(s) = \text{PVFB}(s) - \text{NetPremRatio}\,\text{PVFP}(s). \tag{6.3.9}
$$

6.3.2 Simplified Net Premium Method

The simplified net premium method is the original method of calculating reserves, developed when "calculator" referred to a person, not a machine. This was almost the only reserve method used until the 1970s, when electronic life insurance data and computing power were finally sufficient to support more refined methods. Even today, many countries still use simplified net premium methods, especially for solvency reserves.

Here are the usual simplifications that most simplified net premium methods share:

- Mortality is the only decrement. Lapses are ignored.
- Death and endowment benefits are the only benefits reflected. Surrender benefits, dividends, and other benefits are ignored.
- The mortality rates and interest rates for reserve calculations are dictated by regulations. Reserve mortality rates are often much higher than pricing mortality rates. Reserve interest rates are typically lower than current and pricing interest rates.
- Deaths are assumed to occur at the end of the policy year. A common variation assumes a uniform distribution of deaths (UDD) throughout the policy year.
- Actual acquisition expenses are ignored. Instead, a formula defines the maximum initial expenses that can be incorporated in the reserve calculations.
- Maintenance expenses are ignored. The difference between gross and net premiums or the conservatism built into the reserve assumptions is assumed to be sufficient to provide for future maintenance expenses.

Conservative mortality and interest assumptions usually produce conservative reserves. However, because the simplified net premium method ignores so many important factors, it can produce nonsensical results. For example, the reserve could be much less than cash surrender values, since these are ignored. To overcome this particular problem, some countries require that solvency reserves be increased so that they are no less than cash surrender values.

If the resulting reserves are viewed as unduly conservative, the simplified approach lends itself to manipulation of the product design to overcome excess conservatism. In the figures below, you will see how the premium slope can be used to produce zero or negative reserves.

6.3.2.1 Relative Slope of Premiums and Benefits: Impact on Reserves

The magnitude of net premium reserves is largely determined by whether the slope of premiums is roughly equal to, less than, or greater than the slope of expected benefits. Figures 6.3.1–6.3.3 illustrate these possibilities and are based on examples that are presented later in this section.

As a general rule, when premiums and benefits have the same slope, net premium reserves tend to be quite small, because current year premiums are used to pay current year benefits, as in Figure 6.3.1.

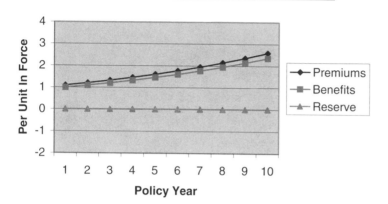

Figure 6.3.1 Premiums and Benefits with Same Slope

When benefits have a much steeper slope than premiums, significant net premium reserves develop because a significant portion of early year premiums must be accumulated to pay later year benefits, as in Figure 6.3.2.

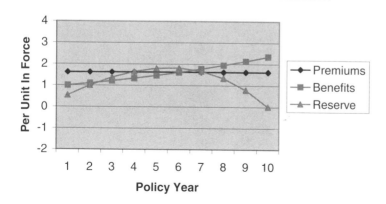

Figure 6.3.2 Benefits Increase Faster Than Premiums

When premiums have a much steeper slope than benefits, the opposite is true: Net premium reserves turn negative and grow to significant negative values. Why? In the early policy years, net premiums are much less than benefits. Because of the steeper premium slope, however, net premiums eventually "cross over" the benefits and eventually, in the later policy years, become much greater than benefits. Since reserves are calculated as the present value of future benefits less future net premiums, reserves become increasingly negative as the policy approaches the *crossover* year, as in Figure 6.3.3.

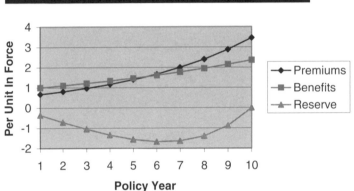

Figure 6.3.3 Premiums Increase Faster Than Benefits

Negative reserves could be a problem if the company is counting on policyowners to pay steeply increasing premiums while their expected benefits are not increasing nearly as fast. This is a common problem with level-premium decreasing-term policies. A common solution to this problem is to shorten the premium paying period to eliminate the negative reserves. Unless there is a good reason for policyowners to continue their insurance (such as ongoing perceived value, tax incentives, or contractual obligations with a third party), negative reserves may not be appropriate. For solvency purposes, negative reserves are usually not allowed.

6.3.2.2 Initial Expense

Including an initial or acquisition expense in the reserve calculation results in lower reserves, especially in the early policy years, because the net premium is calculated to cover death benefits and the initial expense. The higher the initial expense, the higher the net premium. Since the present value of future net premiums is deducted from the present value of future benefits when computing reserves, the higher the initial expense, the more net premium is deducted and the lower the reserve.

In practice, the initial expense is often netted against the first-year net premium. This practice eliminates the need for an explicit initial expense and results in a reduced first-year net premium. The reserve method with no initial expense is referred to as the *net level premium reserve method,* since there is no reduction in the first-year net premium. Methods that employ an initial expense (either explicitly or by reducing the first-year net premium) are referred to as *modified premium reserve methods.*

The practice of netting the initial expense against the first-year net premium has an advantage that will not be evident until later in this chapter. When calculating reserves at the beginning of the first policy year, it is necessary to deduct the initial expense from the first-year net premium. In spite of this advantage, the authors prefer the explicit approach of stating the initial expense.

Reserves can also be thought of as an accumulation of past net premiums less an accumulation of past benefits and expenses (see Exercise 6.1). Therefore, the higher the initial expense, the more expenses are deducted in the reserve accumulation process and the lower the reserve.

Three simplified net premium methods have been used in more than one country: net level, full preliminary term, and Zillmer. These methods differ only in their initial expense. *Net level* (NL) has no initial expense. *Full preliminary term* (FPT) has an initial expense that is just enough to force the reserve at the end of policy year 1 to equal zero. Some countries use a variation of FPT called the *Commissioners reserve valuation method* (CRVM), which limits the FPT initial expense in rare situations, resulting in a reserve at the end of the first policy year that is greater than zero in those rare situations. *Zillmer* has an initial expense equal to 3.5% of death benefit.

6.3.2.3 Back to the Basics

Using the simplified net premium method, it is instructive to go back to the basics and develop a simplified formula for PVFB in terms of mortality rates, death benefits, endowment benefits, survival factors, discount factors, and an initial expense factor. Because lapses are ignored, we will use $q(t)$ for the mortality rate. We will assume that deaths occur only at the end of the policy year. SurvFactor(t) and DiscFactor(t) will be as defined in Chapter 4.

The calculation of the present value of future benefits and expenses is greatly simplified, compared to Formula 6.3.6, since death and endowment benefits at the end of each policy year are the only benefits and because no expenses are included. Let

DB_pu(t) = Death benefit per unit in force at the *end* of policy year t.

Then,

$$\text{PVFB}(s) = \sum_{t=s+1}^{n} [q(t)\ \text{DB\_pu}(t)\ \text{SurvFactor}(t-1) + \text{Endow\_pu}(t)\ \text{SurvFactor}(t)]\ \text{DiscFactor}(t) / \text{SurvFactor}(s)\ \text{DiscFactor}(s). \tag{6.3.10}$$

When PVFB(0) is calculated, the initial expense per unit issued, as defined by the simplified net premium reserve method being used, should be added to Formula 6.3.10.

In Formula 6.3.10, "$q(t)$ DB_pu(t) SurvFactor($t-1$) + Endow_pu(t) SurvFactor(t)" is used in place of "CashFlowEnd(t)." This represents:

1. The probability of surviving from issue to the end of policy year $t - 1$ times the probability of dying during policy year t times the death benefit per unit, plus

2. The probability of surviving to the end of policy year t times the amount of any endowment benefit payable at that point in time.

The other discount and survivorship factors serve the same purpose in Formulas 6.3.6 and 6.3.10.

Combining Formula 6.3.10 with Formulas 6.3.5 (PVFP) and 6.3.9 (Res_pu), we have the following formula for simplified net premium reserves:

$$
\begin{aligned}
\text{Res\_pu}(s) \\
= \sum_{t=s+1}^{n} [q(t)\ \text{DB\_pu}(t)\ \text{SurvFactor}(t - 1)\ \text{DiscFactor}(t) \\
+ \text{Endow\_pu}(t)\ \text{SurvFactor}(t)\ \text{DiscFactor}(t) \\
- \text{NetPrem\_pu}(t)\ \text{SurvFactor}(t - 1) \\
\text{DiscFactor}(t - 1)]/(\text{SurvFactor}(s)\ \text{DiscFactor}(s)).
\end{aligned}
$$

$$(6.3.11)$$

This formula is complicated because of the different survivorship and discount factors that apply to each of the three components. If we factor out $\text{SurvFactor}(t - 1)$ and $\text{DiscFactor}(t - 1)$ from all three components, we can simplify Formula 6.3.11:

$$
\begin{aligned}
\text{Res\_pu}(s) \\
= \sum_{t=s+1}^{n} [(q(t)\ \text{DB\_pu}(t) + \text{Endow\_pu}(t))\ p(t)/(1 + i(t)) \\
- \text{NetPrem\_pu}(t)]\ \text{SurvFactor}(t - 1)\ \text{DiscFactor}(t - 1) \\
/(\text{SurvFactor}(s)\ \text{DiscFactor}(s)).
\end{aligned}
$$

$$(6.3.12)$$

By factoring out $\text{SurvFactor}(t - 1)$ and $\text{DiscFactor}(t - 1)$, all values are being discounted with interest and survivorship from the *beginning* of the policy year. Because death benefits and endowment benefits are paid at the end of the policy year, they must be discounted for a year's interest. Since endowment benefits are paid only to those who survive to the end of the policy year, they must be discounted for a year's survivorship.

6.3.2.4   Fackler Reserve Accumulation Formula

The *Fackler reserve accumulation formula,* named for its developer, David Parks Fackler, allows you to calculate the reserve for the next policy year given the current reserve and the net premium, death benefit, mortality rate, and interest rate for the next year. This can be handy when you want to project future reserves from current reserves quickly and easily. The Fackler formula is useful for analyzing changes in reserves from one period to the next. By using average mortality and interest rates, the formula can be applied on an aggregate basis to a large number of policies at once. It also can be used as a spot check on the internal consistency of reserve calculations, although reserves could be both consistent and wrong.

The Fackler reserve accumulation formula is developed from a simple observation: The reserves for two consecutive policy years are calculated by discounting most of the same future benefits and future net premiums. Comparing Res_pu($s - 1$) and Res_pu(s) using Formula 6.3.12 and ignoring endowment benefits (which typically do not apply until the final policy year, if ever), we notice two differences:

1. Res_pu($s - 1$) includes death benefits and net premiums for policy year s while Res_pu(s) does not.

2. Res_pu($s - 1$) discounts (for both interest and survivorship) to a time that is one year earlier than does Res_pu(s).

These two differences are captured in the following formula:

$$\text{Res\_pu}(s - 1) - \frac{q(s)\ \text{DB\_pu}(s)}{1 + i(s))} + \text{NetPrem\_pu}(s)$$
$$= \frac{\text{Res\_pu}(s)p(s)}{1 + i(s)}. \tag{6.3.13}$$

Rearranging terms, we obtain the Fackler reserve accumulation formula:

$$\text{Res\_pu}(s) = [(\text{Res\_pu}(s - 1) + \text{NetPrem\_pu}(s))\,(1 + i(s))$$
$$- \text{DB\_pu}(s)\,q(s)]/p(s). \tag{6.3.14}$$

The above formula can be thought of as a four-step process for converting Res_pu($s - 1$) into Res_pu(s):

Step 1: Add NetPrem_pu(s) to Res_pu($s - 1$). This is the reserve at the beginning of policy year s. Note that both amounts are per unit in force at the end of year $s - 1$ and can therefore be added together without adjustment.

Step 2: Multiply the result of Step 1 by $(1 + i(s))$ to accumulate the amount with interest to the end of policy year s.

Step 3: Deduct the death benefits payable at the end of policy year s from the result of Step 2. Note that both amounts are per unit in force at the end of year $s - 1$ but have been accumulated with interest to the end of policy year s.

Step 4: The result of Step 3 is divided by $p(s)$, to "accumulate" for survivorship from the end of policy year $s - 1$ to the end of policy year s. (Since we would multiply by $p(s)$ to discount for survivorship from the end of policy year s back to the end of policy year $s - 1$, dividing by $p(s)$ allows us to move in the opposite direction.) At this point, the final result, Res_pu(s), has been accumulated with both interest and survivorship to the end of policy year s and is therefore per unit in force at the end of policy year s.

6.3.2.5   Examples

You should reinforce your understanding of the simplified net premium method by reproducing the following examples with a spreadsheet. These examples are the source of the graphs presented earlier in this section. All of the following examples share the following interest and survivorship assumptions. DB_pu is a level 1,000.

Example 6.3.1 Discount and Survival Factors

The following data are used in Examples 6.3.2–6.3.4.

t	DiscFactor	q	p	SurvFactor	DeathBen
0	1.000000	0.000000	0.000000	1.000000	0.000000
1	0.952381	0.001000	0.999000	0.999000	1.000000
2	0.907029	0.001100	0.998900	0.997901	1.100000
3	0.863838	0.001210	0.998790	0.996694	1.210000
4	0.822702	0.001331	0.998669	0.995367	1.331000
5	0.783526	0.001464	0.998536	0.993910	1.464100
6	0.746215	0.001611	0.998389	0.992309	1.610510
7	0.710681	0.001772	0.998228	0.990551	1.771561
8	0.676839	0.001949	0.998051	0.988621	1.948717
9	0.644609	0.002144	0.997856	0.986502	2.143589
10	0.613913	0.002358	0.997642	0.984175	2.357948

For all t, $i = 5.0\%$. The result of these assumptions is PVFB(0) = 11.769802.

Example 6.3.2 Premiums and Benefits with the Same Slope; Zero Reserves

t	Prem_pu	Prem	NetPrem_pu
1	1.100000	1.100000	0.952381
2	1.210000	1.208790	1.047619
3	1.331000	1.328206	1.152381
4	1.464100	1.459259	1.267619
5	1.610510	1.603049	1.394381
6	1.771561	1.760772	1.533819
7	1.948717	1.933730	1.687201
8	2.143589	2.123334	1.855921
9	2.357948	2.331116	2.041513
10	2.593742	2.558731	2.245664

Note: PVFP(0) = 13.5941213. Ratio = PVFB(0)/PVFP(0) = 0.8658. For all t, Res_pu = 0.

Example 6.3.3 Level Premiums with Increasing Benefits; Positive Reserves

t	Prem	Res_pu
1	1.620000	0.532932
2	1.618380	0.993070
3	1.616600	1.366777
4	1.614644	1.638696
5	1.612495	1.791553
6	1.610134	1.805929
7	1.607541	1.660004
8	1.604693	1.329277
9	1.601566	0.786237
10	1.598133	0.000000

Note: PVFP(0) = 13.0648. Ratio = PVFB(0)/PVFP(0) = 0.9009.
For all t, Prem_pu = 1.62 and NetPrem_pu = 1.459428.

Example 6.3.4 Premiums Increasing Faster Than Benefits; Negative Reserves

t	Prem_pu	Prem	NetPrem_pu	Res_pu
1	0.670000	0.670000	0.604804	−0.365321
2	0.804000	0.803196	0.725765	−0.722328
3	0.964800	0.962775	0.870918	−1.055257
4	1.157760	1.153932	1.045102	−1.343451
5	1.389312	1.382875	1.254122	−1.560180
6	1.667174	1.657021	1.504947	−1.671197
7	2.000609	1.985223	1.805936	−1.632978
8	2.400731	2.378047	2.167123	−1.390574
9	2.880877	2.848095	2.600548	−0.874993
10	3.457053	3.410388	3.120657	0.000000

Note: PVFP(0) = 13.03854. Ratio = PVFB(0)/PVFP(0) = 0.9027.

6.3.3 Realistic Net Premium Method

The realistic net premium method is a natural evolution of the simplified net premium method, made possible by the growth in computing power. When used for solvency reserves, there is less need for conservative assumptions, because the realistic net premium method does not ignore important factors such as lapse rates, cash surrender values, and maintenance expenses.

The realistic net premium method is a good choice for earnings reserves. By incorporating all of the important factors, this method is less apt to distort earnings. To the extent that actual experience matches reserve assumptions, pre-tax earnings will emerge as a level percentage of premiums. Why? If net premiums exactly cover all benefits and expenses, the remainder of the gross premium contributes to earnings. Earnings will equal a level percentage of premiums, where the percentage is one minus the ratio of net premiums to gross premiums. For example, if net premiums are 90% of the gross premiums, then pre-tax earnings should be 10% of gross premiums, provided actual experience exactly matches the reserve assumptions.

This relationship between the realistic net premium method and earnings is useful for validating pricing software. If identical assumptions are used for reserves and pricing, then earnings should be a level percentage of premiums. (If you try this, be sure to zero out income taxes. Also, invested assets must equal the net premium reserve.) If earnings do not emerge as a level percentage of premiums, there is a difference in the formulas that could be either a mistake or an added refinement. Even for pricing software that has been validated, this exercise can be very instructive for someone new to pricing, because it points out the differences between pricing and reserves, in both assumptions and formulas used.

The realistic net premium method would typically include all of the benefits and expenses presented in Chapter 5. However, some of the assumptions, especially expenses, may be less refined for reserves than for pricing. Why is this? Are accurate reserves not as important as accurate product design and pricing?

First, reserves are self-correcting. All policies start with a zero reserve before the policy is issued and end with a zero reserve after the policy is terminated. A reserve inaccuracy is therefore only temporary (if you call a period of up to 100 years "temporary") and causes what accountants refer to as a *timing difference*. With different reserves the same cumulative earnings eventually emerge, but at different times.

Second, an inaccuracy that impacts all policy years may have little or no impact on reserves. However, the same inaccuracy may have a significant impact on profitability if ignored in pricing. For example, in Exercise 6.2 you will see that adding a 2% of premium expense to all policy years has no impact on net premium reserves at the end of each policy year. This is because net premiums are increased by the amount of the additional expense. The increased net premiums and increased expenses cancel each other out in the reserve calculation. However, increasing expenses by 2% of premiums would significantly reduce profitability.

6.3.4 Gross Premium Method

The gross premium method can be derived from the realistic net premium method simply by setting NetPremRatio equal to one. In other words, gross premium reserves are calculated by deducting 100% of gross premiums from PVFB:

$$\text{Res\_pu}(s) = \text{PVFB}(s) - \text{PVFP}(s). \tag{6.3.15}$$

With net premium methods, the difference between gross and net premiums is a source of annual earnings. Net premium methods tend to spread earnings over the lifetime of the policy as a level percentage of premiums. In contrast, the gross premium method tends to recognize all the earnings at issue, at least when realistic assumptions are used. The only source of earnings after issue comes from conservatism, intentional or otherwise, in the reserve assumptions. For example, if mortality assumptions used for gross premium reserves were 10% higher than expected mortality, you would expect future earnings to equal 10% of expected claims each year.

In practice, the gross premium method rarely recognizes all the earnings at issue because of the conservatism or provisions for adverse deviations (PADs) built into the reserve assumptions. In fact, with sufficiently large PADs it is quite possible to generate an excessively large reserve at issue and thereby cause a first-year loss. This means that, if the PADs were truly needed, gross premiums would not be sufficient to pay benefits and expenses, so a reserve is required at issue to cover this theoretical deficiency.

When the gross premium method is used, regulations or actuarial guidelines usually control the PADs that must be built into reserve assumptions. The magnitude of the PADs will determine whether there is a first-year profit or loss. Renewal earnings will emerge to the extent actual experience is better than the reserve assumptions. This approach of releasing earnings as actual experience unfolds is sometimes called the *release from risk approach* of recognizing earnings. Net premium methods recognize earnings both as a percentage of premium and, if there is conservatism in the reserve assumptions, as risk is released. The more conservative the assumptions, the more earnings emerge as risk is released.

Gross premium reserves are very sensitive to changes in benefits and expenses. For example, adding a 2% of premium expense to all policy years would increase gross premium reserves by 2% of the present value of future premiums. This is very different from the effect of such a change on net premium reserves, which is zero.

When the gross premium method is applied to a block of business using best estimates of future experience (that is, zero PADs), this is called a *gross premium valuation*. A gross premium valuation can be used to determine the present value of future pre-tax cash flows from the block of business. This can be useful information when the block of business is being sold or other significant changes are being contemplated. The gross premium reserve in this case is the minimum reserve needed to meet future obligations (ignoring income taxes) and provides for no future earnings.

By comparing gross premium reserves to solvency or earnings reserves, you can determine the adequacy or conservatism of those reserves. The difference between those reserves and gross premium reserves is a rough estimate of the present value of future pre-tax earnings. This is only a rough estimate because future solvency or earnings reserves, which help determine the incidence of earnings, have been ignored.

6.3.5   Accumulation Method

The three prospective reserve methods just discussed work best with products that have pre-scheduled premiums and benefits, such as traditional whole life, endowment, and term insurance products. For most dynamic products, such as universal life (UL) and variable universal life (VUL), premiums are flexible. Future death benefits and cash values depend on premiums paid, withdrawals made, investment experience, and deductions for benefits and expenses.

Prospective reserves are based on the calculation of PVFP and PVFB. How can you calculate prospective reserves when future premiums and future benefits are largely unknown? It is possible to make a number of assumptions as to future premiums and benefits to permit the calculation of PVFP and PVFB. In fact, U.S. solvency reserves use just such an approach to calculate simplified net premium reserves for UL, but it is very complicated and beyond the scope of this book.

A simpler approach for dynamic products is to use the account value as a basis for reserves.

6.3.5.1   Solvency Reserves

In countries that use the simplified net premium method for solvency reserves, the account value should be adequate for solvency reserve purposes if certain conditions are met:

- For UL, future guaranteed interest rates must be no more than the maximum interest rate allowed for reserves. For VUL, this is not an issue, since actual investment returns less investment management fees are credited to the account value.

- Future guaranteed cost of insurance (COI) rates must be sufficient to cover the cost of future death claims, based on reserve mortality rates. When reserve mortality rates are too conservative, it is common to have guaranteed maximum COI rates that equal or exceed reserve mortality rates coupled with current COI rates that are competitive.

- Future expense charges must be sufficient to cover future maintenance expenses.

If one or more of the above conditions are not met, the account value plus an additional reserve could be used for solvency purposes. The additional reserve would cover excess guaranteed interest rates or insufficient cost of insurance charges.

6.3.5.2 Initial Expense

Some policies employ surrender charges to help recoup acquisition costs on policies that lapse, especially in the early policy years. When a policy has (1) surrender charges, (2) guaranteed interest rates less than the maximum valuation interest rates, and (3) sufficient COI rates, something less than the account value may be a more appropriate solvency reserve. The difference between maximum valuation interest rates and guaranteed interest rates provide future interest margins that can be used to amortize an initial expense. Future COI margins can also be used to amortize an initial expense. The solvency reserve could then be calculated as

Account value − Present value of future interest and COI margins.

In practice, the solvency reserve is usually not allowed to be less than the cash surrender value, to protect against lapses. Because the cash surrender value is equal to the account value less a surrender charge, a surrender charge roughly equal to "the present value of future interest and COI margins" can help bring solvency reserves and cash surrender values closer together.

The initial expense may be prescribed by formula, as in the full preliminary term and Zillmer reserve methods. If there is a maximum initial expense, it could be used to calculate a ratio, as follows:

$$\text{Max ratio} = \text{the lesser of}$$
$$\left[1, \frac{\text{maximum initial expense}}{\text{PV of future interest and COI margins at issue}} \right]. \quad (6.3.16)$$

Then the solvency reserve could be calculated as

$$\text{Account value} - (\text{Max ratio})$$
$$\times (\text{PV of future interest and COI margins}). \quad (6.3.17)$$

6.3.6   Treatment of Acquisition Costs

When reserve methods use realistic assumptions, acquisition costs are treated in one of three different but equivalent ways:

- Acquisition costs are combined with all other expenses and benefits, and one reserve is calculated. This is the approach preferred by many actuaries: Acquisition costs are accorded no special treatment and are not separated from other expenses and benefits.

- Acquisition costs are treated separately from benefits and other expenses. A separate "expense reserve" and "expense net premium" is calculated just for acquisition costs. (Likewise, a separate "benefit reserve" and "benefit net premium" is calculated for benefits and maintenance expenses.) Expense reserves after issue are usually negative. This can be seen by reviewing the formula: present value of future acquisition expenses minus the present value of future net premiums. Since the present value of future acquisition expenses is usually zero (because most acquisition costs are incurred at issue) and the present value of future net premiums is greater than zero, then the expense reserves after issue are negative. At issue, the expense reserve equals the first net premium minus the acquisition costs. Thereafter, the expense reserve declines as the present value of future net premiums declines.

- Acquisition costs are treated just like the previous case for expense reserves, except the negative expense reserves are switched to positive

(DAC) assets. This is the approach preferred by many accountants. Many industries have acquisition-type costs that are capitalized (that is, counted as an asset) when the costs are paid, and then the asset is amortized to spread the cost over the useful future lifetime of the items acquired.

Example 6.3.4 Treatment of Acquisition Costs

The following example illustrates the three different approaches for the treatment of deferred acquisition costs.

End of Policy Year	One Combined Reserve	Separate Reserves		Reserve with DAC Asset	
		Expense Reserve	Benefit Reserve	DAC	Benefit Reserve
1	−1.00	−1.50	0.50	1.50	0.50
2	−0.35	−1.35	1.00	1.35	1.00
3	0.20	−1.20	1.40	1.20	1.40
4	0.60	−1.05	1.65	1.05	1.65
5	0.90	−0.90	1.80	0.90	1.80
6	1.05	−0.75	1.80	0.75	1.80
7	1.10	−0.55	1.65	0.55	1.65
8	0.90	−0.40	1.30	0.40	1.30
9	0.60	−0.20	0.80	0.20	0.80
10	0.00	0.00	0.00	0.00	0.00

6.3.6.1 "Renewal" Acquisition Costs

What if acquisition costs are incurred over several policy years instead of only at issue? For example, instead of paying a 55% first-year commission followed by 5% commissions for the next nine years and zero thereafter, a company might level out commissions by paying 20% for the first five years followed by 5% for the next five years and zero thereafter. In this example, a case could be made for splitting the commissions between acquisition costs and maintenance expenses in one of several different ways:

Example 6.3.5

Policy Year	Commission Rate	Acquisition Costs		
		Case 1	Case 2	Case 3
1	20%	20%	15%	20%
2	20	20	15	0
3	20	20	15	0
4	20	20	15	0
5	20	20	15	0
6	5	5	0	0
7	5	5	0	0
8	5	5	0	0
9	5	5	0	0
10	5	5	0	0
11+	0	0	0	0

Case 1: All commissions are considered acquisition costs, regardless of when they are paid.

Case 2: Only commissions in excess of 5% of premium are considered acquisition costs. Five percent of premium is considered a service fee to agents, to reimburse them for servicing policyowners.

Case 3: Only the first-year commission is considered an acquisition cost.

Accounting practices usually dictate which of the three cases must be applied. Accounting practices also govern whether or not the commissions excluded from acquisition costs are included in maintenance costs.

If renewal year commissions must be immediately expensed as in Case 3 (that is, if renewal commissions are excluded from both DAC and benefit reserve calculations), this can have a detrimental impact on the pattern of earnings. Instead of spreading earnings over all policy years as a level percentage of premiums, the realistic net premium method will be forced to distort earnings: Earnings will be depressed during the years when significant renewal commissions are being immediately expensed. Earnings will be inflated in other years.

6.3.6.2 Acquisition Costs and the Accumulation Method

The accumulation method is used primarily for dynamic products, such as UL and VUL. (The accumulation method is also used for accumulation annuities, which will be discussed in Chapter 13. However, income annuities generally use a prospective method.)

Benefit reserves and expense reserves typically follow the following approach: (1) The account value functions as the benefit reserve, covering all future benefits and maintenance expenses. (2) A DAC asset is calculated to capitalize and amortize acquisition costs. The account value will function adequately as a benefit reserve if the following conditions are met:

1. For UL, future credited interest rates must not be expected to exceed future interest rates earned by the company. For VUL, this is not an issue.

2. Future expected mortality rates must not be expected to exceed future COI charges.

3. Future expenses must not be expected to exceed future expense charges.

Using a prospective reserve method, a portion of the premium is implicitly or explicitly (when there is a separate expense reserve or DAC) used to amortize acquisition expenses. Under the accumulation method, the entire premium is credited to the account value, leaving no premium to amortize acquisition expenses.

This means we must find some new sources to amortize acquisition expenses, such as

- Income from surrender charges on surrendering policies
- Interest margins: the expected difference between interest rates to be earned by the company and interest rates to be credited to the account value
- COI margins: the expected difference between COI charges to be deducted and death claims to be paid, and
- Expense margins: the expected difference between expense charges to be deducted and expenses to be paid.

Accounting procedures will determine which of these types of revenue can be used, how much acquisition expense can be capitalized, and how it is to be amortized. Here is an example of how this might work when all acquisition costs are incurred at issue:

1. Let the present value at time t of all future profit margins, consisting of future expected surrender charge income, interest margins, COI margins, and expense margins, be denoted by

$$\text{PVFM}(t) = \text{PV of future profit margins at time } t. \quad (6.3.18)$$

2. Calculate the ratio of acquisition costs to PVFM(0):

$$\text{DAC ratio} = \frac{\text{Acquisition costs}}{\text{PVFM}(0)}, \text{ but not more than 1.} \quad (6.3.19)$$

3. Calculate the DAC asset at time t as

$$\text{DAC}(t) = (\text{DAC ratio})\,\text{PVFM}(t). \quad (6.3.20)$$

A variation on the above theme is to solve for the discount rate that results in

$$\text{PV of acquisition costs} = \text{PVFM}(0). \quad (6.3.21)$$

This approach answers the sometimes difficult question of the proper rate to use for discounting. Deferred acquisition costs can then be calculated as

$$\text{DAC}(t) = \text{PVFM}(t). \quad (6.3.22)$$

This is similar to what is done when a bond is purchased at a premium or discount, that is,

1. The effective interest rate that equates the purchase price of the bond with the present value of future coupons and the maturity value is solved for.

2. The difference between the effective interest rate and the coupon rate is used to amortize the bond's premium or discount over the lifetime of the bond.

6.4 Valuation

Valuation refers to the process of calculating reserves for all of a company's policies at the end of a financial reporting period.

6.4.1 Valuation Processes

A number of different processes are used for valuation. The process used depends on accuracy desired, information available, computer hardware available, valuation software available, valuation methods, the number of policies that must be valued, and the time available to complete the process. Valuation processes differ mainly in their degree of accuracy and efficiency. For example, when a company must value many millions of policies, the efficiency of the process may be the prime consideration. A slow process could run for days or even weeks. For a company with 10,000 policies, the goal may be to complete the valuation at the lowest possible cost, since just about any valuation process will be fast enough.

6.4.1.1 Traditional Valuation Process before Computers

Just in case you think you have it tough, consider how valuation was performed before computers were widely available. (We will refer to this as the traditional valuation process.) Many of today's valuation processes still bear some resemblance to this ancient process.

Before the advent of the computer, the technology used by insurance companies was based on punched cards that could record up to 80 characters, basically the same characters found on today's keyboards. These punched cards were first used in the 1890 U.S. Census. Insurance companies used these cards for decades to record basic life insurance policy data, such as the data needed for valuation.

Two big, powerful machines were available to process these cards. A card sorter allowed you to sort on any one of the 80 columns. To sort on ten columns, you fed the same cards through the sorter ten times, each time sorting on a different column. Great care was taken to stack the cards up properly after each sort. One slip and you had to start over. The card sorter was typically used to sort the company's policies into order by plan of insurance, issue age, and issue year.

A tabulator allowed you to add up numbers from all cards with matching characteristics and print the results. The total amount of insurance and number of policies in force was typically printed for all policies with the same plan of insurance, issue age, and issue year.

Armed with a summary of all of the company's policies, sorted by plan of insurance, issue age, and issue year, valuation clerks took over. Using published tables of reserve factors, each amount of insurance was multiplied by the appropriate reserve factor, either by hand or using a mechanical calculator, once calculators were invented. Every calculation was done a second time to ensure accuracy.

Finally, the reserves for all plans of insurance, issue ages, and issue years were totaled (twice, of course). Grand totals for amount of insurance and number of policies were also calculated. For many companies, valuation could take a month or more.

6.4.1.2 Traditional Valuation Process after Computers

Many companies today use a valuation process that is simply an automated version of the traditional valuation process. Cards have been replaced with files of policy data stored on hard disks. Reserve factors are also stored on hard disks. Policy data are sorted into reserve factor order, and totals for each valuation cell (policies that share the same plan of insurance, issue age, issue year, sex, underwriting class, and other factors) are calculated. A program multiplies the total amount of insurance for each valuation cell by the appropriate reserve factor to calculate reserves for each cell. Reserves for all the cells are summed to calculate the grand total reserve.

6.4.1.3 Grouping

To the extent that many policies share the same reserve factors, the traditional valuation process may be an efficient choice. If there are too many valuation cells, some grouping of similar policies can be done to reduce the number of valuation cells. For example, instead of calculating reserves for every combination of plan of insurance and issue age, reserve factors could be calculated for every fifth age and for only the most significant or unique plans of insurance. Each policy would be assigned to the valuation cell for the nearest issue age and the most similar plan of insurance. In some jurisdictions, grouping may not be permissible.

6.4.1.4 Seriatim Valuation Process

When few policies share the same reserve factors, the seriatim (one policy at a time) valuation process is more appropriate. The seriatim process simply multiplies each policy's amount of insurance by the appropriate reserve factor. No sorting and summarizing by valuation cell is done. However, because most companies desire more information than simply a grand total reserve, some sorting and summarization of the results is normally done. For example, reserves could be summarized by plan of insurance or issue year.

There are two variations to the seriatim valuation process: (1) Rather than precalculating reserve factors for each valuation cell, precalculate reserves for each policy. (2) Rather than precalculating anything, calculate the reserve for each policy as needed.

6.4.1.5 Modeling

When sufficient data are not available to calculate reserves, it may be necessary to use a modeling process to estimate reserves. Life insurance modeling software can be used to project future reserves, premiums, and in-force amounts of insurance, given an initial distribution of business. The ratio of actual premiums or amounts in force to projected premiums or amounts in force could be use to "true up" the projected reserve, as follows:

$$\text{Estimated reserve} = (\text{Projected reserve})\,\frac{(\text{Actual premium})}{(\text{Projected premium})}.$$

6.4.2 Reserves throughout the Policy Year

Up to this point, all of our discussions have applied to reserves at the end of the policy year, also known as *terminal reserves*. At the end of any financial reporting period, only a small percentage of policies are at the end of a policy year. We need to address reserves at other times of the policy year.

6.4.2.1 Initial Reserve

The reserve per unit in force at the beginning of the policy year is called the *initial reserve*. At the beginning of the policy year, two things can occur:

1. A premium may become due.

2. Expenses may be incurred. Because premiums can be paid other than annually, we will split expenses between those that are incurred when premiums are paid (mainly commissions) and other expenses that are incurred at the beginning of the policy year.

   These two factors lead to the formula for the initial reserve, which equals the previous year's terminal reserve plus the net premium less beginning of the year expenses. Let

Exp_puPrem(t) = Expense for policy year t that is incurred when premiums are paid, per unit in force. This consists of commissions and other percent-of-premium expenses.

Exp_puBeg(t) = Expense that is incurred at the *beginning* of policy year t, per unit in force at the beginning of policy year t. This excludes premium-related expenses.

Res_puBeg(t) = The initial reserve for policy year t, per unit in force at the *beginning* of policy year t.

Percent of premium expenses consist of acquisition, commission, and maintenance expense components. SurvFactor is used to convert from a "per unit issued" basis to a "per unit in force" basis:

$$\text{Exp\_puPrem}(t) = \frac{\text{AcqExpPrem}(t) + \text{Comm}(t) + \text{MaintExpPrem}(t)}{\text{SurvFactor}(t-1)}. \quad (6.4.1)$$

Other beginning-of-the-year expenses are calculated as total expense less percent of premium expenses:

$$\text{Exp\_puBeg}(t) = \frac{\text{AcqExp}(t) - \text{AcqExpPrem}(t) + \text{MaintExp}(t) - \text{MaintExpPrem}(t)}{\text{SurvFactor}(t-1)}. \quad (6.4.2)$$

The initial reserve can now be calculated from the previous year's terminal reserve by adding the net premium per unit and deducting the beginning of the year expenses included in the reserve assumptions:

$$\text{Res\_puBeg}(t) = \text{Res\_pu}(t-1) + \text{NetPrem\_pu}(t) - \text{Exp\_puPrem}(t) - \text{Exp\_puBeg}(t). \quad (6.4.3)$$

6.4.2.2 Mean Reserve

The reserve per unit in force at the middle of the policy year, also called the *mean reserve* per unit, is calculated as the average of the initial and terminal reserves. Let

$$\text{Res\_puMid}(t) = \text{The mean reserve for policy year } t, \text{ per unit in force at the middle of policy year } t.$$

Then,

$$\text{Res\_puMid}(t) = \frac{\text{Res\_puBeg}(t) + \text{Res\_pu}(t)}{2}. \tag{6.4.4}$$

Substituting using Formula 6.4.3 and rearranging terms, we have

$$\text{Res\_puMid}(t) = \frac{\text{Res\_pu}(t-1) + \text{Res\_pu}(t)}{2}$$
$$+ \frac{\text{NetPrem\_pu}(t) - \text{Exp\_puPrem}(t) - \text{Exp\_puBeg}(t)}{2}. \tag{6.4.5}$$

Formula 6.4.5 shows that the mean reserve is the average of two terminal reserves plus half of a net premium less expenses that occur at the beginning of the year.

Many valuations are done using the mean reserve for the current policy year for each policy. Assuming a uniform distribution of issue dates throughout the year, the average policy is halfway through the policy year at any valuation date. Policies that are more than halfway are offset by policies that are less than halfway.

6.4.2.3 Relationship of Initial to Terminal Reserve

The initial reserve grows or shrinks into the terminal reserve during the policy year through the operation of two opposing forces: (1) The accumulation of interest causes the reserve to increase during the policy year. (2) Expected policy benefits are paid out of the reserve and cause the reserve to decrease during the policy year.

When reserves are relatively small (say, in the early policy years and for most term insurance), interest is a much smaller force than expected policy benefits. In this case, the reserve jumps up on the anniversary by the amount of the net premium and then declines during the policy year, as shown in Figure 6.4.1, which illustrates reserves for four policy years. For each policy year, three values are shown: initial reserve, mean reserve, and terminal reserve.

Figure 6.4.1 Reserves throughout the Policy Year

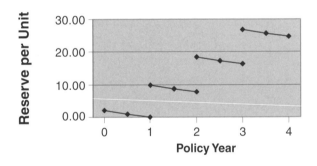

Policy Year	NetPrem_pu	Initial Reserve	Mean Reserve	Terminal Reserve
1	2.00	2.00	1.00	0.00
2	10.00	10.00	9.00	8.00
3	10.00	18.00	17.25	16.50
4	10.00	26.50	26.00	25.50

When reserves are relatively large (say, in the later policy years for a permanent product), interest is a larger force than expected policy benefits. In this case the reserve jumps up on the anniversary by the amount of the net premium and then increases further during the policy year, as shown in Figure 6.4.2.

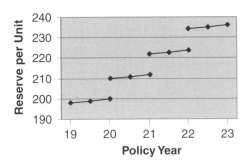

Figure 6.4.2 Reserves throughout the Year; Relatively Large Terminal Reserves

Policy Year	NetPrem_pu	Initial Reserve	Mean Reserve	Terminal Reserve
20	10.00	198.00	199.00	200.00
21	10.00	210.00	211.00	212.00
22	10.00	222.00	223.00	224.00
23	10.00	234.00	235.00	236.00

6.4.2.4   Interpolated Reserves

Sometimes mean reserves are not appropriate. For example, if a company has historically issued 20% of its policies during the month of December, the average policy will not be halfway through the policy year at the valuation date. In this case *interpolated reserves* will provide a more accurate result.

Interpolated reserves calculate a current reserve that is interpolated between the initial reserve and the terminal reserve. Let

Frac = The fraction of a year from the previous policy anniversary to the valuation date

Res_puInt(t, Frac) = The interpolated reserve for policy year t, per unit in force at a date that is a fraction of a year equal to "Frac" from the previous anniversary.

Then,

$$\text{Res\_puInt}(t, \text{Frac}) = \text{Res\_puBeg}(t)\,(1 - \text{Frac}) + \text{Res\_pu}(t)\,\text{Frac}.$$
(6.4.6)

This formula assumes that all interim reserves fall on a straight line between the initial and terminal reserves, as illustrated in Figures 6.4.1 and 6.4.2. This linear (that is, straight line) interpolation is consistent with an assumption of a uniform distribution of deaths, which would result in death claims being uniformly deducted from the reserve throughout the policy year.

Linear interpolation is *not* consistent with compound interest, which is exponential, not linear. Linear interpolation overstates the interest earned early in the policy year and understates the interest earned later in the policy year. However, using a relatively high interest rate of 10%, the mean reserve would be overstated by only 0.12% by using linear interpolation. With an interest rate of 4%, the overstatement caused by using linear interpolation is just 0.02%. For most purposes the slight conservatism associated with linear interpolation is acceptable.

Formula 6.4.6 can be rewritten in terms of terminal reserves, net premiums, and beginning-of-the-year expenses as follows:

$$\begin{aligned}
\text{Res\_puInt}&(t, \text{Frac}) \\
&= (\text{Res\_pu}(t - 1) - \text{Exp\_puBeg}(t)) (1 - \text{Frac}) \\
&\quad + (\text{NetPrem\_pu}(t) - \text{Exp\_puPrem}(t)) (1 - \text{Frac}) \\
&\quad + \text{Res\_pu}(t) \, \text{Frac} \tag{6.4.7}
\end{aligned}$$

Formula 6.4.7 separates the portion of the interpolated reserve related to premiums. This will be useful when we interpolate reserves for nonannual premiums in Chapter 12.

6.4.3   Static or Dynamic Reserve Assumptions

Static reserve assumptions are set when the policy is issued and are not subsequently changed, even if actual experience turns out to be far different from the assumptions. Static reserve assumptions are referred to as being "locked in," since they cannot be changed. For products with pre-scheduled premiums and benefits, static reserve assumptions allow reserves to be precalculated years in advance.

In contrast, dynamic reserve assumptions are reviewed every year or every few years for appropriateness. Reserve assumptions are updated based on recent experience and the current outlook for the future. When reserve assumptions are updated, reserves can change. There are two basic approaches to handling the impact of a change in reserve assumptions: freeze the current reserve, or allow the current reserve to change. These same two approaches also apply when nonguaranteed elements are changed.

6.4.3.1   Freeze the Current Reserve

"Freeze the current reserve" means to use the current reserve as a new starting point, with the new assumptions (or new values for nonguaranteed elements) affecting only future years. To use Res_pu(t) as the new starting point, we must first calculate new net premiums for future policy years based on the following ratio:

$$\text{NetPremRatio}(t) = \frac{\text{PVFB}(t) - \text{Res\_pu}(t)}{\text{PVFP}(t)}. \tag{6.4.8}$$

"NetPremRatio(t)" denotes the new ratio of net premiums to gross premiums to be used to calculate future reserves following a change in assumptions at the end of policy year t. In Formula 6.4.8, both PVFB(t) and PVFP(t) should be calculated using the new assumptions. Future net premiums can then be calculated using a variation of Formula 6.3.8:

$$\text{NetPrem\_pu}(s) = \frac{\text{NetPremRatio}(t)\ \text{Prem}(s)}{\text{SurvFactor}(s-1)},$$

for $s = t + 1$ to n. $\tag{6.4.9}$

Future reserves are calculated using a variation of Formula 6.3.9 with NetPremRatio(t) substituted for NetPremRatio:

$$\text{Res\_pu}(s) = \text{PVFB}(s) - \text{NetPremRatio}(t)\ \text{PVFP}(s), \quad \text{for } s = t \text{ to } n. \tag{6.4.10}$$

When $s = t$ and Formula 6.4.8 is used to substitute for NetPremRatio(t) in Formula 6.4.10, we have

$$\text{Res\_pu}(t) = \text{PVFB}(t) - \frac{\text{PVFB}(t) - \text{Res\_pu}(t)}{\text{PVFP}(t)}\ \text{PVFP}(t)$$

$$= \text{Res\_pu}(t).$$

This demonstrates that Formula 6.4.8 does indeed "freeze" Res_pu(t).

6.4.3.2   Allow the Current Reserve to Change

If the current reserve is *not* frozen, it is normal to calculate the reserve before and after the change in assumptions, so the impact of the change can be reported to regulators, stockholders, or tax authorities. For example, if a company significantly impacted its earnings by changing reserve assumptions, stockholders and stock markets would want to know what the company's earnings would have been without the change in assumptions, since that may be more predictive of future earnings.

When updating assumptions, should you update the assumptions only for future policy years, or should you also update past policy years to reflect actual experience? Regulations and accounting procedures will likely answer this question. Either way, new net premiums and reserves would be recalculated for all policy years, starting at time 0. The new net premiums and reserves would be calculated in exactly the same fashion as the original net premiums and reserves, with new assumptions substituted for the original assumptions.

6.4.4   Nonguaranteed Elements

As we saw in Chapter 1, there are a number of products with nonguaranteed elements. For example, premium rates, dividend rates, cost of insurance rates, interest rates, and expense charges may be subject to periodic updates to reflect actual experience. Account values, cash values, and even death benefits may be determined by formulas that reflect investment experience.

When a company changes nonguaranteed elements, there are questions as to how reserves will be impacted:

- Should we freeze the current reserve and only allow the change in nonguaranteed elements to impact future reserves?

- Should we recalculate reserves from inception, perhaps causing a significant change in the current reserve?

- If the current reserve is allowed to change, how do we calculate and report the amount of the reserve change?

Regulations and accounting procedures will determine the answers to these questions. Because the same issues and techniques apply to changes in nonguaranteed elements and changes in reserve assumptions, you should refer to the previous section to see how to freeze the current reserve when nonguaranteed elements change.

When a policy has both guaranteed and nonguaranteed elements, another question arises: Should reserves be calculated using guaranteed values or current values? For example, consider a policy that charges current premiums that are less than guaranteed maximum premiums. Which premiums should be used to calculate reserves? Other possible elements that could have both guaranteed and current values include dividends, cash surrender values, endowment benefits, surrender charges, expense charges, cost of insurance charges, and interest rates.

For the realistic net premium method, current values are normally used to calculate reserves, since current values are more realistic than guaranteed values and are more consistent with the realistic assumptions. However, for the simplified net premium method, guaranteed values are sometimes used, especially when they are more consistent with the simplified (and often unrealistic) assumptions.

It is common for nonguaranteed elements and reserve assumptions to change at the same time. For example, improved mortality could trigger a reduction in both mortality assumptions and nonguaranteed premium rates. An increase in interest rate assumptions could trigger an increase in dividend rates. Such changes may be offsetting, thereby causing little change in reserves.

6.5 Impact of Reserves on Pricing

Reserves impact the timing of earnings and the present value of earnings, but not the ultimate cumulative total of earnings. This is because all reserves start and finish at zero.

Conservative reserves can cause large early losses, especially in the first policy year. However, the situation is reversed in the later policy years: Large earnings are generated as conservative reserves are released. Solvency reserves typically range from conservative to very conservative. Earnings reserves typically range from moderately conservative to slightly conservative.

Insufficient reserves can have the opposite impact. Artificially high earnings can be generated in the early policy years. Losses may emerge in the later policy years. Reserves are never intended to be insufficient, but it does happen from time to time.

6.5.1   Reserves Used to Determine Results

Solvency reserves, earnings reserves, and tax reserves can all play a role in pricing. When a company is taxed on its income or earnings, tax reserves are used to calculate taxable income.

In most cases, solvency reserves are important because they impact how much capital must be invested in the business and when the returns on that capital can be realized. The more conservative the solvency reserves, the more capital must be invested and the later the returns on that capital can be withdrawn from the business. Solvency reserves almost always have a significant impact on pricing. Few companies can afford to ignore them.

Earnings reserves play an important part in pricing for insurance companies that have publicly traded stock. These "public companies" typically have goals such as increasing revenue and earnings by 15% per year and achieving a 15% return on equity. Achieving such goals can help a company drive its stock price upwards, thereby satisfying its stockholders. While such goals can be difficult to reflect when pricing a single product, a company can build a model of its in-force and new business and see whether its current pricing strategy is likely to achieve its stockholder goals.

Earnings reserves may also come into play when a foreign parent owns an insurance company. The capital tied up in the insurance company may count as part of the parent company's capital, receiving accounting treatment similar to an investment in common stock. As long as the parent company's investment in the insurance company appreciates at an attractive rate, it may not care whether it can withdraw the earnings. In other words, solvency reserves may be a secondary concern to the parent. Earnings reserves on the parent company's basis may become the main driver of earnings measurement. In certain circumstances this can give an insurance company with a foreign parent a significant competitive advantage over locally owned insurance companies. The same advantage can exist for a foreign company that operates a local branch (that is, a foreign company that is licensed to transact insurance directly rather than through a local subsidiary).

6.5.2 Pricing Problems with Terminal Reserves

When conservative assumptions are used in the reserve calculation, reserves can cause significant losses in the early policy years. This is not unusual when the simplified net premium method is used.

6.5.2.1 Conservatism Missing from Terminal Reserves

Many forms of term insurance have very low or even zero terminal reserves that do not reflect the degree of conservatism that shows through when mean reserves are used for valuation.

It is possible for reserves to be very conservative, because of reserve mortality rates that may be two or three times pricing mortality rates. This conservatism is at its maximum at the beginning of the policy year, because the initial reserve must cover expected death benefits for the full policy year based on reserve mortality. This conservatism is cut in half at the middle of the policy year and is at its minimum at the end of the policy year. An example will help illustrate this.

Example 6.5.1 Conservatism Missing from Terminal Reserves

Consider an annually renewable term insurance policy with the following premiums, death benefits, pricing mortality rates, reserve mortality rates, net premiums, terminal reserves, and mean reserves, all per 1,000 of death benefit in force at the beginning of the policy year.

For purposes of this example, pricing and reserve mortality rates have been set at 60% and 150% of premium rates. Net premiums have been calculated as reserve mortality rates divided by 1.04, assuming a 4% valuation interest rate with all death benefits assumed to be paid at the end of the policy year. Because premium rates and reserve mortality rates share the same slope, terminal reserves are zero and mean reserves are half the net premium. Amounts have been rounded and are per 1,000 of death benefit.

t	Premium	Mortality Rates		Net Premium	Mean Reserve
		Pricing	Reserves		
1	1.00	0.60	1.50	1.44	0.72
2	1.10	0.66	1.65	1.59	0.79
3	1.21	0.73	1.82	1.75	0.87
4	1.33	0.80	2.00	1.92	0.96

Note: For all t, Terminal Reserve = 0.

This example shows an initial reserve (equal to the net premium) that is very conservative, equal to 2.4 (1.44/0.60 in the first policy year) times the amount needed to pay death benefits based on pricing mortality. At the same time, the terminal reserve has no conservatism, being equal to zero. The mean reserve is only half the initial reserve, but it is still 2.4 times the amount needed to pay death benefits for the second half of the policy year, based on pricing mortality.

6.5.2.2   Reserve Adjustment for Missing Conservatism

In pricing, we measure results from the end of one policy year to the end of the next policy year, so nonconservative terminal reserves are naturally used. In financial reporting we measure results from the end of one fiscal year to the end of the next fiscal year. Conservative mean reserves are used, since policies are halfway between anniversaries on the average at the end of any financial reporting period. This means that pricing on a policy year basis will produce results that are out of touch with reality.

The impact of this pricing distortion can be enormous. When terminal reserves are used, the pricing results may show relatively little first-year strain, leading the company to think it can issue large volumes of the new product with little impact on its capital position. However, the actual first-year strain that flows through the company's financial statements may be many times larger than that anticipated. This means the rates of return on the product will be far less than those expected. As a result of this distortion, the pricing performed would have to be deemed a failure.

To rectify the situation, it is necessary to add an adjustment to terminal reserves that reflects the extra conservatism in mean reserves that is missing from terminal reserves. Here we will assume the primary source of this extra conservatism is the difference between reserve and pricing mortality rates.

The extra conservatism will be based on the difference between reserve and pricing mortality rates multiplied by the net amount at risk, which is equal to the death benefit less the reserve. The result is divided by two, since mean reserves provide for only half of the current policy year's death benefits.

Let

$$qr(t) = \text{Reserve mortality rate}$$
$$qp(t) = \text{Pricing mortality rate}$$

ExtraCon(t) = The extra conservatism contained in mean reserves that is not contained in terminal reserves. This amount is per unit in force and is not allowed to be less than zero. It is equal to the difference between reserve and pricing mortality rates times the net amount at risk per unit in force.

Then,

$$\text{ExtraCon}(t) = \frac{(\text{qr}(t) - \text{qp}(t))\,(\text{DB\_pu}(t) - \text{Res\_pu}(t))}{2},$$

but not less than zero.   (6.5.1)

When a group of policies issued in the same year have been in force for an average of one year, half of the policies will still be in their first policy year while the other half will be in their second policy year. For example, suppose policies issued throughout the year 2001 were issued on 1 July 2001, on the average. On 1 July 2002, these policies would be one year old on the average, but only half of them would have crossed their first policy anniversary and would have entered their second policy year.

If we wish to reflect this kind of distribution of issue dates, the first-year terminal reserve should be adjusted by the average of the extra conservatism in the first and second policy years' mean reserves. In general, the reserve adjustment for policy year t should be an average of the extra conservatism in the mean reserves for policy years t and $t + 1$:

$$\text{Res\_puAdj}(t) = \frac{\text{ExtraCon}(t) + \text{ExtraCon}(t + 1)}{2}.$$ (6.5.2)

Res_puAdj(t) is per unit in force at the end of policy year t. Res_puAdj(t) should be added to Res_pu(t) for pricing purposes, to approximate the extra conservatism that is found in mean reserves.

Example 6.5.2 Impact of Missing Conservatism

Let us examine the impact of overlooking the conservatism that is missing from terminal reserves. The first two columns are calculated based on the results of Example 6.5.1. The third and fourth columns are pre-tax earnings per unit issued and cannot be calculated directly. They are given purely to illustrate the impact of the missing conservatism. As you will see in Chapter 11, the change in reserves, per unit issued, is deducted when calculating earnings.

t	Extra Conservatism	Reserve Adjustment	Pre-tax Earnings with Terminal Reserves = 0	Pre-tax Earnings with Adjusted Terminal Reserves
1	0.90	0.945	−0.500	−1.300
2	0.99	1.004	0.500	0.520
3	1.09	1.145	0.500	0.510
4	1.20			

In this example, the actual first-year strain is 2.6 times the strain resulting from zero terminal reserves. Also, notice how renewal profits are only slightly increased by the higher reserves released when policies lapse. The extra loss of (0.80) in the first year is very slowly reversed over the lifetime of the policies insured.

6.5.3 Impact of Reserves on Earnings

When calculating earnings, the increase in reserves is deducted. Because there are potentially three different kinds of earnings, we will calculate three different increases in reserves:

1. The increase in solvency reserves will be used in the calculation of distributable earnings.

2. The increase in earnings reserves will be used in the calculation of stockholder earnings, that is, earnings reported to stockholders and stock markets.

3. The increase in tax reserves will be used in the calculation of taxable earnings.

The earnings reserve will be broken into two parts for illustrative purposes: (1) a benefit reserve, which covers all benefits and maintenance expenses, and (2) a DAC asset, which covers only acquisition expenses. A DAC asset will be used rather than a negative expense reserve.

We will need some additional notation for the five reserves (both per unit in force and per unit issued) and the five increases in reserves:

$SolvRes\_pu(t)$ = Solvency reserve per unit in force

$EarnRes\_pu(t)$ = Earnings reserve per unit in force. This is equal to the benefit reserve per unit in force less the DAC per unit in force. Earnings reserve per unit in force can be used in place of its two components.

$BenRes\_pu(t)$ = Benefit reserve per unit in force

$DAC\_pu(t)$ = Deferred acquisition cost asset per unit in force

$TaxRes\_pu(t)$ = Tax reserve per unit in force.

$SolvRes(t)$ = Solvency reserve per unit issued

$EarnRes(t)$ = Earnings reserve per unit issued, equal to benefit reserve per unit issued less DAC per unit issued. This reserve can be used in place of its two components.

$$\text{BenRes}(t) = \text{Benefit reserve per unit issued}$$
$$\text{DAC}(t) = \text{Deferred acquisition cost asset per unit issued}$$
$$\text{TaxRes}(t) = \text{Tax reserve per unit issued}$$
$$\text{SolvResIncr}(t) = \text{Solvency reserve increase per unit issued}$$
$$\text{EarnResIncr}(t) = \text{Earnings reserve increase per unit issued, equal}$$

to benefit reserve increase *plus* DAC amortization. This reserve increase can be used in place of its two components.

$$\text{BenResIncr}(t) = \text{Benefit reserve increase per unit issued}$$
$$\text{DACAmort}(t) = \text{DAC asset amortization (that is, decrease) per}$$

unit issued

$$\text{TaxResIncr}(t) = \text{Tax reserve increase per unit issued.}$$

Each of the four "per unit issued" reserves is calculated using a formula of the form

$$\text{Res}(t) = \text{Res\_pu}(t) \; \text{SurvFactor}(t). \tag{6.5.3}$$

Each of the four reserve increases is calculated using a formula of the form

$$\text{ResIncr}(t) = \text{Res}(t) - \text{Res}(t - 1). \tag{6.5.4}$$

The deferred acquisition cost asset per unit issued is calculated as

$$\text{DAC}(t) = \text{DAC\_pu}(t) \; \text{SurvFactor}(t). \tag{6.5.5}$$

Because amortization is a decrease in an asset, $\text{DACAmort}(t)$ is calculated as the DAC in year $t - 1$ minus the DAC in year t:

$$\text{DACAmort}(t) = \text{DAC}(t - 1) - \text{DAC}(t). \tag{6.5.6}$$

Why would $\text{BenResIncr}(t)$ and $\text{DACAmort}(t)$ be calculated as two separate items rather than one combined $\text{EarnResIncr}(t)$? This separate treatment is required by certain accounting practices, such as U.S. GAAP. In the income statement, which presents the components of net income or earnings, the benefit reserve increase is grouped with benefits paid, while DAC amortization is grouped with expenses paid. This grouping helps stock analysts and stockholders to better understand the company's results.

For certain policy designs and features, it is important to realize that Res(t) occurs the moment after any end-of-the-policy-year benefits have been paid out, such as endowment benefits and dividends. This affects the value of Res(t).

For example, a 20-year endowment policy would pay an endowment benefit at the end of year 20. Res(19) would have a value that approaches the value of the endowment benefit to be paid at the end of year 20. Res(20) would be the reserve immediately following the payment of the endowment benefit. Therefore, Res(20) would be zero.

6.6 International Survey of Reserve Methods

This section contains historical information as of January 1, 2000. At that time, there were efforts underway in a number of countries to modernize insurance regulation and reserving standards. There is a clear movement away from the use of simplified net premium methods. Table 6.6.1 summarizes the methods used in selected countries for solvency reserves.

6.6.1 Earnings Reserves

Most of the countries listed in Table 6.6.1 use solvency reserves to calculate stockholder earnings. Here are the exceptions.

Table 6.6.1 Solvency Reserve Method Used in Selected Countries

Country	Solvency Reserve Method Used
Argentina	Simplified net premium
Australia	Gross premium. Uses best-estimate assumptions with prescribed PADs. However, solvency reserves include a provision for future shareholder profits, which makes this method a little like a realistic net premium method.
Brazil	Simplified net premium
Canada	Gross premium. Uses best-estimate assumptions with PADs.
Chile	Simplified net premium
France	Gross premium, with limitations on assumptions. Reserves cannot be negative or less than cash values.
Germany	Simplified net premium
Hong Kong	Realistic net premium
Italy	Simplified net premium
Japan	Simplified net premium
Malaysia	Simplified net premium
Mexico	Simplified net premium
The Netherlands	Realistic net premium with conservative interest rate
Singapore	Semirealistic net premium. Ignores lapse rates and maintenance expenses. Based on U.K. method.
South Africa	Simplified net premium. In addition, gross premium reserves are calculated using best-estimate assumptions to provide a more realistic picture of financial position.
Spain	Simplified net premium
Taiwan	Simplified net premium
United Kingdom	Semirealistic net premium. Ignores lapse rates and maintenance expenses.
United States	Simplified net premium

In Australia, *margin on services* (MoS) reserves are used to calculate earnings. MoS reserves are similar to the solvency reserves described in Table 6.6.1, but without PADs.

In the United Kingdom, two methods are used for earnings reserves:

1. A modified solvency reserve, which is essentially the solvency reserve with a deferred acquisition cost asset.

2. A gross premium reserve using best-estimate assumptions with PADs. This is also described as an *embedded value method,* with present values based on an investment earnings rate in place of a discount rate. *Embedded value* usually refers to the present value of future earnings, discounted using the company's desired rate of return.

In the United States, earnings reserves are governed by U.S. GAAP, which varies by type of product:

- For dynamic products, earnings reserves are calculated using the accumulation method, with deferred acquisition costs based on Formula 6.3.22. Reserve assumptions are dynamic.

- For all pre-scheduled products, earnings reserves are based on a realistic net premium method with a separate deferred acquisition cost asset. Reserve assumptions are static.

In both cases, best-estimate assumptions with modest PADs are used.

Earnings reserves are becoming a factor in more countries because of the following developments:

- The increased tendency among multinational corporations based outside the U.S. to list their stock on the New York Stock Exchange. This choice gives these companies access to additional capital but requires them to calculate quarterly earnings on a U.S. GAAP basis.

- The *Euro,* the common currency for the European Union, will link the major European stock markets more closely. This will open up new sources of capital to European companies, but at a likely price of increased disclosure. Without a more realistic determination of earnings, stock prices will be understated.

- The international wave of demutualizations has increased the number of publicly traded life insurance companies, although consolidation has worked in the opposite direction. The realistic reporting of earnings is much more important to stockholders than it is to mutual policyowners.

- The increasing use of stock options as part of management compensation outside the U.S. will place pressure on senior management to increase their company's stock price. Because stock prices are closely tied to earnings levels and growth rates, this adds importance to the determination of earnings and the use of earnings reserves.

6.6.2 Tax Reserves

At this time, only U.S. life insurers are unfortunate enough to have tax reserves that are significantly less than solvency reserves. Canadian companies, in some cases, have tax reserves that exceed solvency reserves. All other countries that tax life insurance companies on earnings use solvency reserves for tax reserves, with minor adjustments in a few countries.

6.7 Pricing Example

Here are this chapter's additions to the pricing example. Table 6.7.1 shows the basic solvency reserve calculation factors. The solvency reserve interest rate is equal to 5% in all years.

Table 6.7.1 Solvency Reserve Calculation Factors

t	DiscFactor	q	p	SurvFactor
0	1.00000			1.00000
1	0.95238	0.00455	0.99545	0.99545
2	0.90703	0.00492	0.99508	0.99055
3	0.86384	0.00532	0.99468	0.98528
4	0.82270	0.00574	0.99426	0.97963
5	0.78353	0.00621	0.99379	0.97354
6	0.74622	0.00671	0.99329	0.96701
7	0.71068	0.00730	0.99270	0.95995
8	0.67684	0.00796	0.99204	0.95231
9	0.64461	0.00871	0.99129	0.94402
10	0.61391	0.00956	0.99044	0.93499

Table 6.7.2 shows the calculation of the premium and benefit discount factors used to calculate the various present values. These

values assume premiums are paid at the beginning of the year and death occurs at the end of the year. The premium discount factor is simply the present value of gross premiums (including policy fees) payable at the beginning of each remaining premium period. Gross premium per unit and policy fees are shown in Table 5.11.1.

Table 6.7.2 Calculation of Solvency Reserves

t	Discounting Factors for		PVFP(t)	PVFB(t)	SolvRes_pu	SolvRes
	Premiums	Benefits				
0	51.50127	48.69777				
1	45.00127	44.36443	47.46731	46.79557	1.91218	1.68075
2	38.83896	39.92215	43.22836	44.43397	3.55877	2.90409
3	32.99897	35.36995	38.77103	41.55675	4.89624	3.78696
4	27.46666	30.71714	34.08021	38.11336	5.88832	4.31468
5	22.22804	25.95057	29.14018	34.02029	6.46637	4.48724
6	17.26986	21.07594	23.93278	29.20729	6.57730	4.41193
7	12.57947	16.05911	18.43902	23.53949	6.10421	3.95670
8	8.14504	10.88723	12.63656	16.89091	4.94223	3.09454
9	3.95539	5.54044	6.50000	9.10476	2.95859	1.78873
10	0.00000	0.00000	0.00000	0.00000	0.00000	0.00000

Note: NetPremRatio: 0.94556.

The net premium ratio in the solvency reserve calculation is equal to the present value of benefits at issue divided by the present value of gross premiums at issue:

$$\text{NetPremRatio} = \frac{48.69777}{51.50127} = 0.94556.$$

The "discount factors" represent the present value of future premiums or benefits beyond year t, but discounted back to time 0. These values were used to calculate PVFP(t) and PVFB(t). For example, PVFP(5) is calculated as

$$\begin{aligned}
\text{PVFP}(5) &= \frac{\text{Premium Discount Factor}(5)}{\text{DiscFactor}(5)\ \text{SurvFactor}(5)} \\
&= \frac{22.22804}{0.78353 \times 0.97354} \\
&= 29.14015.
\end{aligned}$$

(There is a slight rounding error compared to the accuracy of the underlying spreadsheet used to do the calculations.) Similarly, PVFB(5) is calculated as

$$\begin{aligned}
\text{PVFB}(5) &= \frac{\text{Benefit Discount Factor}(5)}{\text{DiscFactor}(5)\ \text{SurvFactor}(5)} \\
&= \frac{25.95057}{0.78353 \times 0.97354} \\
&= 34.02025 \text{ (again, a slight rounding error).}
\end{aligned}$$

The reserve per unit in year 5 is then

$$\begin{aligned}
\text{Res\_pu}(5) &= \text{PVFB}(5) - \text{NetPremRatio PVFP}(5) \\
&= 34.02029 - 0.94556 \times 29.14018 \\
&= 6.46650 \text{ (again, a slight rounding error).}
\end{aligned}$$

Tables 6.7.3 through 6.7.6 show the development of earnings reserves. Table 6.7.3 shows the earnings reserve calculation factors. The earnings reserves are developed with PADs for mortality, lapses, and interest. For earnings reserves the following assumptions apply:

- Mortality is 110% of the mortality in Table 4.8.1
- Lapses are 105% of the lapse rates in Table 4.8.1
- Interest rate is 6.5% (versus 7.0% as you will see in Table 8.5.1).

Table 6.7.3 Earnings Reserve Calculation Factors

t	DiscFactor(t)	DiscFactor Mid(t)	qd(t)	qw(t)	p(t)	Surv Factor(t)	Deaths(t)	Lapses(t)
0	1.00000					1.00000		
1	0.93897	0.96900	0.00129	0.12600	0.87288	0.87288	0.00129	0.12584
2	0.88166	0.90986	0.00189	0.07350	0.92475	0.80719	0.00165	0.06403
3	0.82785	0.85433	0.00254	0.05250	0.94509	0.76287	0.00205	0.04227
4	0.77732	0.80219	0.00303	0.05250	0.94463	0.72063	0.00231	0.03993
5	0.72988	0.75323	0.00344	0.05250	0.94424	0.68045	0.00248	0.03770
6	0.68533	0.70726	0.00382	0.03150	0.96480	0.65650	0.00260	0.02135
7	0.64351	0.66409	0.00417	0.03150	0.96446	0.63317	0.00274	0.02059
8	0.60423	0.62356	0.00455	0.03150	0.96409	0.61043	0.00288	0.01985
9	0.56735	0.58550	0.00502	0.03150	0.96364	0.58824	0.00306	0.01913
10	0.53273	0.54977	0.00559	0.03150	0.96309	0.56652	0.00329	0.01843

Table 6.7.4 details the per unit in force amortizable expenses from Chapter 5. In general, these are the expenses that are assumed to be "deferrable" in the earnings reserve calculation.

Table 6.7.4 Earnings Reserves Amortizable Expense Factors

t	AcqExp_pu	AcqExpPrem	AcqExpPerPol	CommPct(t)	DisExpPct(t)
1	1.500	0.250	50.000	1.070	0.200
2	0.000	0.000	0.000	0.070	0.000
3	0.000	0.000	0.000	0.070	0.000
4	0.000	0.000	0.000	0.020	0.000
5	0.000	0.000	0.000	0.020	0.000
6–10	0.000	0.000	0.000	0.000	0.000

Table 6.7.5 calculates the key factors to be used in the earnings reserve calculations, per unit issued. These factors are the premiums, acquisition expenses, commissions, and death benefits. These factors are calculated using the mortality and lapse assumptions found in Table 6.7.3.

Table 6.7.5 Earnings Reserves Calculation Values

t	Prem(t)	AcqExp(t)	Comm(t)	DeathBen(t)
1	6.500	3.625	8.346	1.291
2	5.674	0.000	0.397	1.657
3	5.247	0.000	0.367	2.058
4	4.959	0.000	0.099	2.315
5	4.684	0.000	0.094	2.489
6	4.423	0.000	0.000	2.606
7	4.267	0.000	0.000	2.746
8	4.116	0.000	0.000	2.893
9	3.968	0.000	0.000	3.072
10	3.824	0.000	0.000	3.298

Table 6.7.6 details the calculation of benefit and expense reserves. The first part of the table shows the calculation of the premium, benefit, and expense discount factors. These discount factors have the same definition and use as those explained on Page 52 for Table 6.7.2. These values assume premiums and expense occur at the beginning of the year and deaths occur at the middle of the year. The premium discount factor reflects the present value of future gross premiums, using the earnings reserve discount and survivorship factors.

Table 6.7.6 Calculation of Earnings Reserves

t	Discounting Factors for			PVFP	PVFB	PVFE	Benefit Reserve per Unit	Expense Reserve per Unit
	Premiums	Benefits	Acquisition Expenses					
0	37.56713	17.33059	12.82265	37.56713	17.33059	12.82265		
1	31.06713	16.07943	0.85165	37.90519	19.61860	1.03910	2.13206	−11.89893
2	25.73973	14.57193	0.47873	36.16830	20.47581	0.67269	3.79054	−11.67250
3	21.11390	12.81394	0.15492	33.43243	20.29001	0.24531	4.86685	−11.16606
4	17.00889	10.95674	0.07282	30.36419	19.55991	0.13000	5.55220	−10.23409
5	13.36783	9.08180	0.00000	26.91627	18.28630	0.00000	5.86920	−9.18723
6	10.13964	7.23890	0.00000	22.53654	16.08930	0.00000	5.69267	−7.69231
7	7.21516	5.41542	0.00000	17.70823	13.29110	0.00000	5.12188	−6.04428
8	4.56676	3.61157	0.00000	12.38138	9.79169	0.00000	4.07988	−4.22609
9	2.16929	1.81299	0.00000	6.50000	5.43239	0.00000	2.43379	−2.21862
10	0.00000	0.00000	0.00000	0.00000	0.00000	0.00000	0.00000	0.00000

Benefit net premium ratio = 46.132%

Expense net premium ratio = 34.133%

Total net premium ratio = 80.265%

Two key values are shown at the bottom of Table 6.7.6: the benefit net premium ratio and the expense net premium ratio. These percentages show that, using earnings reserve assumptions (110% of pricing mortality, 105% of pricing lapses, and 6.50% investment income), the present value at issue of benefits and expenses as a percentage of premiums are 46.132% and 34.133%, respectively. If the sum of the two values were to exceed 100%, then, under the earnings reserve assumptions, there would be insufficient premiums anticipated to cover benefits and pay for expenses.

The benefit reserve net premium paid at the beginning of each year is equal to gross premium times the benefit net premium ratio. The expense reserve net premium paid at the beginning of each year is equal to gross premium times the expense net premium ratio. The benefit reserve is equal to the present value of future benefits minus the present value of future benefit reserve net premiums. The expense reserve is equal to the present value of future expenses minus the present value of future expense reserve net premiums.

For example, at the end of year 5, the benefit reserve per unit is calculated as

$$\text{BenRes\_pu}(5) = \text{PVFB}(5) - \text{BenResNetPremRatio}(5)\,\text{PVFP}(5)$$
$$= 18.28630 - 0.46132 \times 26.91627$$
$$= 5.86929 \text{ (again, a slight rounding error).}$$

Similarly, at the end of year 5, the expense reserve per unit is calculated as

$$\text{ExpRes\_pu}(5) = \text{PVFE}(5) - \text{ExpResNetPremRatio}(5)\,\text{PVFP}(5)$$
$$= 0.00000 - 0.34133 \times 26.91627$$
$$= -9.18733 \text{ (again, a slight rounding error).}$$

6.8 Exercises

Exercise 6.1

In the discussion of initial expense allowances, it was stated that reserves can be calculated as an accumulation of past net premiums less an accumulation of past benefits and expenses. Using the definitions of net premiums and reserves, develop such a formula. Hint: $0 = \text{PVFB}(0) - \text{PVFP}(0)$. Find a way to combine this with $\text{Res\_pu}(t) = \text{PVFB}(t) - \text{PVFP}(t)$.

Exercise 6.2

Show that adding a 2% of premium expense to all policy years has no effect on reserves at the end of each policy year. Hint: You can calculate the net premium and reserve for this additional expense separately and add it to the net premium and reserve for the benefits and other expenses.

Exercise 6.3

Explain the reserve pattern for a 30-year term policy that would result from benefits that increased faster than premiums increased for the first ten policy years and then increased at the same rate as premiums increased for the next 20 policy years. Construct and graph an example.

Exercise 6.4

A whole life policy uses the simplified net premium method with

1. An annual gross premium per unit of Prem_pu
2. A level death benefit of 1,000 per unit in force
3. A first-year reserve mortality rate of q
4. A first-year reserve interest rate of i
5. Death benefits assumed paid at the end of the policy year
6. No maintenance expenses
7. Present value of future benefits at issue equal to PVFB(0), and
8. Present value of future premiums at issue equal to PVFP(0).

Do the following:

a. Calculate the net premium ratio for the net level premium method.

b. Calculate the net premium ratio and the initial expense for the full preliminary term method. Hints:

  NetPremRatio = (PVFB(0) + initial expense)/PVFP(0),
  Res_pu(1) = 0 (from the definition of FPT), and
  Res_pu(1) = (0 + NetPrem_pu(1) − initial expense)$(1 + i)/p$
   − 1,000q/p (from a modification of the Fackler reserve
accumulation formula 6.3.14).

c. Calculate the net premium ratio and the initial expense for the Zillmer method.

d. Under what condition would the full preliminary term and Zillmer methods produce the same results?

Exercise 6.5

How would you change the Fackler reserve accumulation formula to reflect death benefits payable at the middle of the policy year instead of at the end of the policy year?

Exercise 6.6

How would you change the Fackler reserve accumulation formula to reflect lapse rates and surrender benefits payable at the end of the policy year?

Exercise 6.7

Given the same realistic reserve assumptions, does the realistic net premium method or the gross premium method generally produces larger reserves? Why?

Exercise 6.8

For a ten-year level premium policy with acquisition costs of $5 per unit issued, calculate the acquisition cost net premium and deferred acquisition cost per unit in force at the end of each policy year using the following assumptions:

a. 100% survivorship and no discounting (that is, $p(t) = 1$ and $i(t) = 0$ for all t).

b. 100% survivorship and 7% interest.

c. 90% survivorship and 7% interest (that is, $p(t) = 0.90$ and $i(t) = 0.07$ for all t).

Hints: Assume Prem_pu $= 1.00$ for all t and then calculate PVFP(t) for all t. Use PVFB(0) $= 5.000$ and PVFB(t) $= 0$ for $t > 0$. Apply Formulas 6.3.7–6.3.9.

Exercise 6.9

Given the following information and assuming annual premiums, calculate the initial reserve, mean reserve, and interpolated reserves as of the end of the third and ninth policy months for policy year t:

$$\text{Res\_pu}(t - 1) = 10.00$$
$$\text{NetPrem\_pu}(t) = 6.00$$
$$\text{Exp\_puPrem}(t) = 0.60$$
$$\text{Exp\_puBeg}(t) = 0.40$$
$$\text{Res\_pu}(t) = 14.00.$$

6.9   Answers

Answer 6.1

Let

$$\text{Ben}(t) = \text{Benefits and expenses in year } t, \text{ discounted to the beginning of the year}$$
$$\text{DF}(t) = \text{DiscFactor}(t), \text{ and}$$
$$\text{SF}(t) = \text{SurvFactor}(t).$$

For ease of manipulation, let us restate NetPrem, PVFB and PVFP:

$$\text{NetPrem}(t) = \text{Prem}(t) \, \text{NetPremRatio}$$
$$\text{PVFP}(s) = \sum_{t=s+1}^{n} \frac{\text{NetPrem}(t) \, \text{DF}(t-1)}{\text{SF}(s) \, \text{DF}(s)},$$
$$\text{PVFB}(s) = \sum_{t=s+1}^{n} \frac{\text{Ben}(t) \, \text{DF}(t-1)}{\text{SF}(s) \, \text{DF}(s)},$$

Because net premiums are calculated so that the reserve at time 0 is zero, we know that $0 = \text{PVFB}(0) - \text{PVFP}(0)$. This can be rewritten as

$$0 = \sum_{t=1}^{n} \frac{(\text{Ben}(t) - \text{NetPrem}(t)) \, \text{DF}(t-1)}{\text{SF}(0) \, \text{DF}(0)}. \tag{6.9.1}$$

Multiplying Formula 6.9.1 by $(\text{SF}(0) \, \text{DF}(0))/(\text{SF}(s) \, \text{DF}(s))$, we have

$$0 = \sum_{t=1}^{n} \frac{(\text{Ben}(t) - \text{NetPrem}(t)) \, \text{DF}(t-1)}{\text{SF}(s) \, \text{DF}(s)}. \tag{6.9.2}$$

From the definition of reserves, we know that

$$\text{Res\_pu}(s) = \sum_{t=s+1}^{n} \frac{(\text{Ben}(t) - \text{NetPrem}(t)) \, \text{DF}(t-1)}{\text{SF}(s) \, \text{DF}(s)}. \tag{6.9.3}$$

Subtracting Formula 6.9.2 from Formula 6.9.3, we have

$$\text{Res\_pu}(s) = \sum_{t=1}^{s} \frac{(\text{NetPrem}(t) - \text{Ben}(t)) \, \text{DF}(t-1)}{\text{SF}(s) \, \text{DF}(s)}. \tag{6.9.4}$$

Now let us analyze each term in Formula 6.9.4.

"$(\text{NetPrem}(t) - \text{Ben}(t)) \, \text{DF}(t-1)$" is the net premium less benefits and expenses for policy year t on a per unit issued basis and discounted back to time 0. By dividing this term by "(SF(s) DF(s))," we are accumulating it with survivorship and interest to the end of policy year s. In other words, we have shown that a net premium reserve can also be calculated as an accumulation of past net premiums net of past benefits and expenses.

Answer 6.2

Calculate the net premium and reserve for an expense equal to 2% of premiums:

$$PVFB(t) = 2\% \ PVFP(t)$$
$$NetPremRatio = PVFB(0)/PVFP(0)$$
$$= 2\% \ PVFP(0)/PVFP(0) = 2\%$$
$$Res\_pu(t) = PVFB(t) - NetPremRatio \ PVFP(t)$$
$$= 2\% \ PVFP(t) - 2\% \ PVFP(t) = 0.$$

This shows that the additional reserve for an expense equal to 2% of premiums is zero.

Answer 6.3

Case 1:

The ratio of the present value of benefits to the present value of premiums for the first ten years is equal to the corresponding ratio for the last 20 years, that is, both ratios are equal to NetPremRatio. This means the tenth-year reserve is equal to zero. As a result, reserves for the first ten years and the last 20 years can be calculated independently, since both periods have the same ratio of benefits to premiums. Reserves for the first ten years will follow a humpback pattern, starting and ending at zero with the reserve at a maximum somewhere around policy year 5. Reserves for the last 20 years will be zero, since the "initial" reserve at policy year 10 is zero, and premiums and benefits have the same slope.

Case 2:

The ratio of the present value of benefits to the present value of premiums for the first ten years is greater than the corresponding ratio for the last 20 years. This means that premiums are relatively insufficient in the first ten years, compared to the last 20 years. As a result, the tenth-year reserve will be negative. Reserves will follow a modified humpback pattern during the first ten years, starting at zero, ending negative, and probably hitting a maximum no later than the fifth policy year. Reserves after the tenth year will also be negative, but will slowly increase towards zero, which will be reached at the end of the thirtieth year.

Case 3:

The ratio of the present value of benefits to the present value of premiums for the first ten years is less than the corresponding ratio for the last 20 years. This means that premiums are excessive during the first ten years, when compared to the last 20 years. As a result, the tenth-year reserve will be positive. Reserves will follow a modified humpback pattern during the first ten years, starting at zero, ending positive, and probably hitting a maximum after the fifth policy year. Reserves after the tenth year will also be positive, but will slowly decrease toward zero, which will be reached at the end of the thirtieth year. The last 20 years may exhibit a slight humpback of its own.

Figure 6.9.1 Reserves for 30-Year Term, with Ten Years of Increasing Premiums followed by 20 Years of Level Premiums

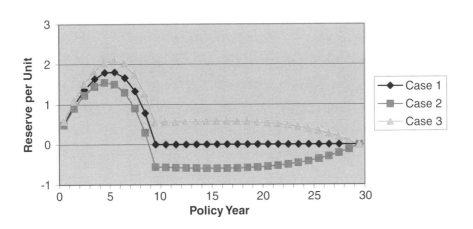

Answer 6.4

a. PVFB(0)/PVFP(0).

b. Because the reserve at the end of the first year is zero for FPT, we know that

$$0 = \text{PVFB}(1) - \text{NetPremRatio PVFP}(1).$$

This leads to $\text{NetPremRatio} = \dfrac{\text{PVFB}(1)}{\text{PVFP}(1)}$, where $p = 1 - q$,

$$\text{PVFB}(1) = \frac{\text{PVFB}(0)(1 + i) - 1{,}000q}{p}, \text{ and}$$

$$\text{PVFP}(1) = \frac{(\text{PVFP}(0) - \text{Prem\_pu})(1 + i)}{p}.$$

NetPrem_pu(1) = NetPremRatio Prem_pu, where NetPremRatio is calculated as above. Solving for initial expense using the Fackler formula, we have

$$\text{Initial expense} = \text{NetPrem\_pu}(1) - \frac{1{,}000q}{1 + i}.$$

c. $\text{NetPremRatio} = \dfrac{\text{PVFB}(0) + 35}{\text{PVFP}(0)}$

Initial expense = (3.5%)(1,000) = 35.

d. The net premiums and reserves for the FPT and Zillmer methods will be equal if and only if the initial expenses for the two methods are equal. This is the case if

$$\frac{\text{Prem\_pu PVFB}(1)}{\text{PVFP}(1)} - \frac{1{,}000q}{1 + i} = 35.$$

Answer 6.5

Multiply DB_pu(s) by $(1 + i)^{1/2}$.

Answer 6.6

$p(s)$ should be calculated based on both lapses and deaths. In other words,

$$p(s) = (1 - qd(s))(1 - qw(s)).$$

Formula 6.3.14 can then be replaced with the following expanded version of the Fackler reserve accumulation formula:

$$Res\_pu(s) = [(Res\_pu(s - 1) + NetPrem\_pu(s))(1 + i(s))$$
$$- DB\_pu(s) \, qd(s) - CV\_pu(s)(1 - qd(s))qw(s)]/$$
$$p(s).$$

Answer 6.7

Generally, net premiums based on realistic assumptions are less than gross premiums because gross premiums are usually sufficient to cover realistic benefits and expenses and produce a profit margin. Since reserves are calculated as the present value of future benefits less the present value of future premiums, the lower the premiums, the higher the reserves. Therefore, realistic net premium reserves are generally higher than gross premium reserves.

Answer 6.8

End of Policy Year	$p(t) = 1, i(t) = 0$		$p(t) = 1, i(t) = 7\%$		$p(t) = 0.90, i(t) = 7\%$	
	PVP(t)	DAC(t)	PVP(t)	DAC(t)	PVP(t)	DAC(t)
0	10.000	5.000	7.515	5.000	5.178	5.000
1	9.000	4.500	6.971	4.638	4.968	4.797
2	8.000	4.000	6.389	4.251	4.717	4.555
3	7.000	3.500	5.767	3.837	4.419	4.267
4	6.000	3.000	5.100	3.393	4.065	3.925
5	5.000	2.500	4.387	2.919	3.644	3.519
6	4.000	2.000	3.624	2.411	3.144	3.035
7	3.000	1.500	2.808	1.868	2.549	2.461
8	2.000	1.000	1.935	1.287	1.841	1.778
9	1.000	0.500	1.000	0.665	1.000	0.966
10	0.000	0.000	0.000	0.000	0.000	0.000
NetPremRatio		0.50000		0.66532		0.96553

Answer 6.9

$$\text{Res\_puBeg}(t) = 10.00 + 6.00 - 0.60 - 0.40 = 15.00$$

$$\text{Res\_puMid}(t) = \frac{15.00 + 14.00}{2} = 14.50$$

$$\begin{aligned}\text{Res\_puInt}(t, 0.25) &= (10.00 + 6.00 - 0.60 - 0.40)(1 - 0.25) \\ &\quad + 14.00(0.25) = 14.75\end{aligned}$$

$$\begin{aligned}\text{Res\_puInt}(t, 0.75) &= (10.00 + 6.00 - 0.60 - 0.40)(1 - 0.75) \\ &\quad + 14.00(0.75) = 14.25.\end{aligned}$$

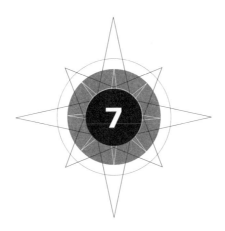

Reinsurance

7.1 Introduction

This chapter develops an approach for fully reflecting the impact of reinsurance in pricing. Methods for approximating the impact of reinsurance are not presented. Such methods are limited only by your imagination. For example, you might determine that the impact of reinsurance could be fairly approximated as a percentage of premium expense or a percentage increase in the death benefit. However, when developing an approximate method, it is wise to validate it by comparing its results to the results from fully reflecting reinsurance.

This chapter will

- Define reinsurance and commonly used reinsurance terms
- Explain why reinsurance is used
- Describe only the most common reinsurance methods (Yearly Renewable Term [YRT] and coinsurance), and
- Develop formulas to reflect the impact of reinsurance on cash flows and reserves.

Although there are many methods of reinsuring risks, the two primary ones to understand for pricing life insurance are YRT and coinsurance. There are several variations on these basic forms, such as modified coinsurance, coinsurance with funds withheld, or a combination of coinsurance and modified coinsurance. However, by concentrating on only YRT and coinsurance in this chapter, the basics behind reinsurance are developed. Once these methods are understood, the groundwork is established to move on to those modifications, although those other methods are beyond the scope of this book.

It follows that reinsurance, by affecting cash flows and reserves, also affects investment income, taxes, required capital, and financial results. We will focus on the effect of reinsurance on cash flows and reserves, from which all of the other effects will automatically flow. This approach allows us to limit the discussion of reinsurance to this one chapter.

7.2 Reinsurance Defined

Reinsurance is insurance for insurance companies. The primary insurance risks inherent in a life insurance product are mortality, investment, persistency, and expense risk. Reinsurance allows one insurance company to pass some or all of these insurance risks to another insurance company. The company passing or *ceding* the risk is called the ceding company. In this chapter, we will refer to the ceding company as simply "the company." The company accepting or *assuming* the risk will be called the reinsurer.

The following paragraphs define some of the common reinsurance terms used in this chapter.

7.2.1 Net Amount at Risk

When an insured dies, the company's loss is equal to the death benefit paid less the reserve being held at the time of death. For old, permanent policies, the reserve can make a significant difference. For example, a policy in force for 30 years might have a death benefit of 100,000 and a reserve of 40,000. If the insured dies after 30 years, the company will pay out 100,000 in cash but also will release a reserve of 40,000, for a net loss of only 60,000. The net loss on death, equal to the death benefit less the reserve, is referred to as the net amount at risk.

7.2.2 Retention Limit

Every company has a maximum amount that it is willing to lose when one insured dies. This maximum amount is called the retention limit. The retention limit normally applies to all policies a particular company may have in force on any one insured; that is, it normally applies to the total net amount at risk on all policies in force for each insured. (In some circumstances, for administrative reasons, the retention limit may apply to the total death benefits in force, rather than the total net amounts at risk in force.) Since insureds may have multiple policies in force, retention limit management can be difficult.

Some companies reduce their retention limit for the older issue ages or high substandard ratings. In addition, it is common for a company to increase its retention limit as the company grows, although there may be many years between retention increases.

Besides retention limits for death benefits, companies also have retention limits for other benefits such as accidental death benefits, waiver of premium benefits, disability benefits, critical illness benefits, and so on. Sometimes retention limits for various benefits are integrated. For example, the death benefit retention limit could apply to all death benefits, including accidental death benefits. More often, to keep things easy to administer, different retention limits are independently applied to each different type of benefit. For example, a company might have a retention limit of 1 million for death benefits and an additional retention limit of 250,000 for accidental death benefits.

7.2.3 Reinsurance Treaty

A reinsurance treaty or reinsurance agreement is the contract between the company and the reinsurer that documents how the reinsurance will work. For example, the treaty defines which business is to be reinsured, how it will be reinsured, what premiums must be paid to the reinsurer, what benefits the reinsurer must pay, and how to handle some common problems that may occur.

There are a number of ways to define which policies are to be reinsured, but there are two primary approaches used in reinsurance treaties:

- The treaty defines which products or classes of business are to be automatically reinsured. This is called *automatic* reinsurance.

- The treaty defines which policies can be selectively reinsured, one policy at a time. This is called *facultative* reinsurance.

7.2.4 Automatic

Under the terms of an automatic treaty, the ceding company cannot selectively decide which policies are to be reinsured, and the reinsurer must reinsure all covered policies, as long as the terms of the treaty are met. Automatic reinsurance is typically handled on an excess or first dollar basis.

7.2.4.1 Excess of Retention or *Excess*

Excess refers to the portion of the net amount at risk for an insured that is in excess of the company's retention limit. For example, if the retention limit were 1 million and a policy were issued with 1.5 million of net amount at risk, then 0.5 million would be automatically reinsured on an "excess" basis.

For most plans of insurance, there is very little difference between the initial death benefit and the initial net amount at risk. Because of this, the initial death benefit is sometimes used in place of the initial amount at risk to determine whether a policy exceeds the retention limit.

7.2.4.2 First Dollar Quota Share or *First Dollar*

First dollar refers to the practice of reinsuring a percentage of every risk from the very first dollar of death benefit, as opposed to reinsuring only risks in excess of retention. For example, when a company reinsures 50% of each policy, it is reinsuring on a first dollar basis.

First dollar quota share is another name for "first dollar." *Quota share* refers to the percentage that is reinsured with a particular reinsurer. For example, if a company retains 20% of every risk and reinsures 40% with Reinsurer A, 20% with Reinsurer B, and 20% with Reinsurer C, then the reinsurers' quota shares are 40%, 20%, and 20%, respectively.

Because the company's retention limit must be enforced, it is normal for first dollar reinsurance to also require excess reinsurance. Example 7.2.1 illustrates this. For Policy 1, with a net amount at risk of 1,250,000 and 50% reinsured, the ceding company's 1,000,000 retention limit is not exceeded, so no reinsurance on an excess basis is needed. For Policy 2, with a net amount at risk of 3,000,000 and only 50% reinsured, however, the ceding company's retention limit is exceeded, so reinsurance on an excess basis is needed. The company will reinsure 1.5 million on a first dollar quota share basis and 0.5 million on an excess basis, in order to satisfy the retention limit. If the insured has other policies with the company, even more will have to be reinsured on an excess basis.

Example 7.2.1

In this example, the retention limit is 1,000,000, the quota share reinsured on a first dollar basis is 50%, and the quota share retained is 50%.

	Policy 1	*Policy 2*
Net Amount at Risk	1,250,000	3,000,000
Amount Retained	625,000	1,000,000
Amount Reinsured on a First Dollar Basis	625,000	1,500,000
Amount Reinsured on an Excess Basis	0	500,000

7.2.5 Facultative

Facultative reinsurance involves three steps:

- The company decides it would like to reinsure a particular policy. The company may decide to reinsure because the policy is too big or because the insured has complicating factors, such as poor health. It sends underwriting information to one or more reinsurers for their review.

- Each reinsurer reviews the underwriting material and decides whether or not it wants to offer to reinsure the risk and, if so, at what price.

- The company reviews the offers from the various reinsurers and decides which reinsurer will receive the risk, if the policy is placed. This decision is usually governed by company rules to ensure fairness. For example, most companies award the reinsurance to the reinsurer with the best price, with the first offer received winning in the event of a tie. This is referred to as *first in, best offer.*

7.2.6 Recapture

In some cases, the treaty may give the company the right to pull back or *recapture* some of the risk it originally reinsured. In less developed reinsurance markets, many treaties give the company an annual right to recapture all business reinsured. Such a liberal recapture provision greatly restricts the use of reinsurance, as the reinsurer must view the treaty as a one-year agreement.

Because life insurance is a long-term business, reinsurance in more developed markets also tends to be long term, with very restrictive recapture provisions. For example, some typical restrictions on recapture include the following:

- Recapture is not allowed at all or only after a number of years, such as ten or 20 years

- Recapture of a risk is not allowed unless the company kept its full retention at issue

- The amount that can be recaptured is limited to the increase in the company's retention limit since the policy was issued

Recapture provisions give the company a valuable option. If reinsurance on the original terms is still desired, the business need not be recaptured. However, if the original terms are no longer attractive, the recapture provision can be used to terminate all of the reinsurance eligible for recapture.

Although recapture can have a significant effect on the net cost of reinsurance, the formulas developed in this chapter ignore recapture. However, Exercises 7.1, 7.2, and 7.3 will help you develop an approach for reflecting recapture in pricing.

7.2.7 Expense Allowance

An *expense allowance* is often paid by the reinsurer to reimburse the company for expenses on the business reinsured. For example, suppose the company has expenses equal to 150% of first-year premiums and 10% of renewal premiums. The reinsurer might pay an expense allowance equal to 150% of first-year reinsurance premiums and 10% of renewal reinsurance premiums to cover its fair share of the company's expenses. Many reinsurers are averse to offering first-year expense allowances in excess of 100%, because of the increased risk and capital strain. Therefore, the expense allowances might be adjusted to, say, 100% in the first year and 20% in renewal years.

In many cases, the company tells the reinsurer the reinsurance premium rates it wishes to pay and asks the reinsurer to quote in terms of the maximum expense allowances it is willing to pay to receive those premium rates. In other words, reinsurers are often asked to compete on expense allowances instead of reinsurance premium rates. Since expense allowances are deducted from reinsurance premium rates to arrive at net reinsurance premium rates, these are two sides of the same coin.

Occasionally, expense allowances are expressed per thousand of death benefit or per policy. However, in this chapter, we will assume all expense allowances are expressed as percentages of reinsurance premiums.

7.3 Reflecting Reinsurance

When a large percentage of a new product is to be reinsured, reinsurance can have an important impact on the design and pricing of the product. In such a case, to ignore reinsurance can lead to a poorly designed or mispriced product. At the other extreme, when a very small percentage of a product is to be reinsured, reinsurance can have an immaterial impact on product design and pricing. When this is the case, reinsurance can be safely ignored.

What should you do when a small but significant portion of a product is to be reinsured? If the expected cost of reinsurance is very close to the expected benefit from reinsurance, you may be able to ignore reinsurance. If in doubt, it is best to reflect reinsurance in pricing and measure its effect. As you gain experience and insight, you will be better able to gauge when to fully reflect reinsurance, when to approximate its effect, and when to ignore its effect.

There are a number of reasons a company may wish to reinsure its business:

- First, the obvious reason: Every company has a limit on how much it is willing to lose due to one death. All companies reinsure amounts in excess of their retention limits. Some companies with high retention limits purchase very little excess reinsurance.

- Rather than turn away business or make conservative underwriting offers, most companies use facultative reinsurance. When underwriters are uncertain how to assess a potential insured, they send the case to their facultative reinsurers to assess. The reinsurer stands behind its advice by taking all or a large part of the risk.

- A company may partner with a reinsurer when entering a new line of business, adopting a new form of underwriting, or developing a new type of product. A reinsurance partner can help the company establish proper design, pricing, and underwriting standards. Better yet, the reinsurer stands behind its advice by taking a share of the risk.

- A company's field force may demand a particular product with which the company is not comfortable. A reinsurer may be willing to take the majority of the risk and, over time, help the company get more comfortable with the risk.

- A company may be writing new business at a faster pace than its capital will allow. Expense allowances can be structured so that reinsurance can help finance the new business by, in effect, using the reinsurer's capital to augment the company's capital. This is usually far more appealing than the alternative of temporarily shutting down new business. Shutting down will force the company's agents to sell another insurance company's products. Once they are working with another company, it may be very difficult to bring all the agents back.

- There are many ways that reinsurance can affect taxes. For example, a company may have started operations within the past few years, incurring significant losses as it built its infrastructure and economies of scale. These tax losses may be deductible in the future only if the company earns profits that exceed those losses within, say, five years after those losses have occurred (a five-year tax loss carryforward). If the company does not expect to earn sufficient profits to use the tax losses before they expire, reinsurance can accelerate current profits for the company in exchange for a share of future profits on business already written.

- A company may find that the rate of return acceptable to the reinsurer is lower than the rate of return earned by the product being reinsured. By reinsuring a portion of the business, the company can earn a higher rate of return on the business it retains. For example, suppose a competitive product produces a 15% rate of return while the company's shareholders demand an 18% rate of return. If reinsurance is secured with a rate of return of only 12%, then the company could leverage its return from 15% to 18% by reinsuring half of the business.

- A company may not wish to keep the risk of period-by-period swings that can occur with mortality results. By reinsuring a large part of the business on a first dollar basis, the mortality results become extremely predictable. In essence, predictable reinsurance rates are substituted for unpredictable actual mortality results.

Handwritten margin notes:

50,000
× .18
———
400000
50000
———
9000.00

ALL earns
100,000
earns 15%
Split it up:
Stockhldr Reiny
50,000 50,000
15%   3%
= 7,500 1500
1,500
———
9,000

Ceding Co
keeps
the assets.

It earns
15% on the
assets,
pays the
reinsurer
only 12%.

Then the
remaining
3% is tossed
in with the
assets earn-
ing 15%.

- The reinsurance market may offer prices that make it more attractive to reinsure rather than retain business, especially considering all of the factors discussed above. The company may conclude that it can improve its financial position through reinsurance, by changing the timing, stability, or level of its earnings, as well as by using the reinsurer's capital instead of its own.

7.4 Yearly Renewable Term

Yearly Renewable Term is the most common reinsurance method. In its simplest form, it has two elements:

- The company pays the reinsurer a reinsurance premium once a year, on each policy's anniversary
- The reinsurer pays the company a reinsured death benefit if and when the insured dies.

Each letter of the acronym YRT can be examined to better understand its true meaning:

- *Yearly* means that premiums are paid once per year and that underlying reinsurance premium rates change once per year. The reinsurance premium rates often are based on a table of mortality rates. YRT premiums are sometimes paid more often than once per year, such as on a monthly basis.

- *Renewable* means that this is *not* a one-year contract. It is ongoing. "Renewable" is misleading, however, because no action is required to renew. In fact, reinsurance premiums must be paid. The company can terminate the reinsurance only in accordance with recapture provisions in the treaty. Failure to pay reinsurance premiums will result in nonpayment of reinsured claims. "Renewable" means the reinsurer cannot terminate the reinsurance.

- *Term* means that only the mortality risk is reinsured (although we will see how the reinsurer can also assume persistency risk with YRT). The policy being reinsured can be any kind of life insurance; it does not have to be term insurance. YRT premiums often bear no relation to the premiums of the policy being reinsured.

7.4.1 Net Amount at Risk Formulas

YRT death benefits are based on net amounts at risk. The net amount at risk per unit can be calculated by subtracting one of three different amounts from the death benefit: solvency reserves, cash values, or, in the case of term insurance or products with insignificant cash values, nothing. YRT premiums and YRT death benefits are based on the same net amounts at risk.

The net amount at risk calculation varies by company and treaty. It may depend on the type of product and administrative capabilities of the company. For pre-scheduled products, the net amount at risk is typically calculated based on values at the end of the policy year, with that amount applied to the entire policy year. For dynamic products, the net amount at risk may be calculated as often as monthly. In this book, we will assume that the net amount at risk is based on end-of-policy-year values and stays constant throughout the policy year.

Let

$$\text{Naar\_pu}(t) = \text{Net amount at risk per unit in force.}$$

The following formula is used when solvency reserves are deducted from policy death benefits to determine the net amount at risk:

$$\text{Naar\_pu}(t) = \text{DB\_pu}(t) - \text{SolvRes\_pu}(t). \qquad (7.4.1)$$

Compared to solvency reserves, cash values are often more readily available to company personnel through published material and computer systems. Because of their availability and because cash values are often a fair approximation for solvency reserves, at least in the long term, it is quite common to use cash values in place of solvency reserves when calculating net amount at risk. The following formula is used when cash values are deducted from policy death benefits to determine the net amount at risk:

$$\text{Naar\_pu}(t) = \text{DB\_pu}(t) - \text{CV\_pu}(t). \qquad (7.4.2)$$

A common variation for Formulas 7.4.1 and 7.4.2 is to calculate every tenth year using the above formulas (that is, policy years 0 or 1, 10, 20, 30, and so on) and then use linear interpolation for the intermediate years (that is, policy years 1–9, 11–19, 21–29, and so on). For example, if the tenth-year net amount at risk is 900 and the twentieth-year net amount at risk is 800, the intervening net amounts at risk would be interpolated as 890, 880, 870, and so on.

For term insurance, reserves and cash values are usually insignificant, so a net amount at risk equal to the death benefit would typically be used:

$$\text{Naar\_pu}(t) = \text{DB\_pu}(t). \tag{7.4.3}$$

7.4.2   YRT on a First Dollar Basis

Let

$$\text{ReinsDB\_pu}(t) = \text{The average reinsured amount per unit in force}$$
$$\text{ReinsPct}(t) = \text{The percentage of total units in force that is reinsured during policy year } t.$$

When reinsuring on a first dollar basis, the YRT death benefit is simply the percentage reinsured times the net amount at risk:

$$\text{ReinsDB\_pu}(t) = \text{ReinsPct}(t) \, \text{Naar\_pu}(t). \tag{7.4.4}$$

For first dollar reinsurance, the same reinsured percentage applies to every policy, regardless of size. Also, the reinsured percentage does not change over time. Compared to the procedure discussed in the next section, this is simple and straightforward.

7.4.3   YRT on an Excess Basis

Estimating YRT death benefits that will be reinsured on an excess basis can be quite a bit more complicated. The portion of a policy's death benefit that is reinsured can range from 0% (when totally within the company's retention limit) to 100% (when the company's retention limit has already been filled by other policies on the same life). When pricing a new product, there are several methods used to determine the average percentage that will be reinsured:

- *Brute force method:* Develop a distribution of policy sizes for the product, perhaps separately for each age group. Figure the percentages reinsured for every size policy and then develop a weighted average percentage reinsured for all sizes combined, with the weights based on the distribution by policy size.

- *Straightforward method:* Use the percentage reinsured by age group for a similar product with a similar average size and the same retention limit. Age group is important, because younger people tend to buy smaller policies. The percentage reinsured may increase dramatically for the middle or older age groups.

- *Finesse method:* Review your company's existing business and develop a relationship between percentage reinsured and the ratio of average size to retention limit. For example, where average size is 10% of retention limit, you may find that only 1% of the business is reinsured. Where average size is half of the retention limit, you may find that 10% of the business is reinsured. Where average size equals retention limit, you may find that 25% of the business is reinsured. Warning: These numbers are made-up examples; you should perform a study to determine the appropriate relationships for your company. With this method, once you know the average size, you can estimate the percentage reinsured.

A second complication for excess YRT death benefits is how the percentage reinsured varies by policy year. If a constant amount is retained and net
amounts at risk decrease over time, then the percentage reinsured will gradually decrease over time. However, if net amounts at risk increase, the percentage reinsured will gradually increase over time. In some countries, the standard practice is to hold the percentage reinsured constant. This reduces the complexity of administration and pricing.

Policies with unlimited potential increases in net amount at risk can pose significant problems. In such cases, it is common for the reinsurer to limit its risk to a flat amount or a percentage of the policy's original net amount at risk. This can leave the company with a net retained risk that may ultimately exceed its retention limit by a wide margin.

We will assume that the percentage reinsured can vary by policy year. Formula 7.4.4 will be used to determine reinsured death benefits for YRT on an excess basis.

7.4.4 YRT Premium Rates

YRT premium rates can be expressed in a number of ways. The pricing department and the administrative capabilities of the company influence the basis used for YRT rates.

The most common methods of expressing YRT premium rates are the following:

- As a percentage of the company's mortality table used for pricing. This basis makes it easier to estimate the effect of reinsurance on pricing. However, the company may be reluctant to share its mortality table with others.

- As a percentage of a standard industry mortality table. Often, a company will develop its mortality assumptions as a percentage of an industry mortality table, so this basis can also make it easier to estimate the effect of reinsurance on pricing.

- For a term insurance product, as a percentage of the term insurance premium rates.

- For a universal life product, as a percentage of the cost of insurance rates.

In recent years, there has been a trend to increase the number of risk classes. Premium rates vary not only by male and female, but increasingly by smoker and nonsmoker, preferred and standard. Multiple preferred classes are becoming more common. YRT premium rates often vary by the same risk classes that apply to the underlying product. Where YRT rates are not aligned with the underlying risk classes, you should examine the effect on profits if the expected distribution by risk class does not materialize.

In some cases, YRT premium rates are set equal to 100% of a mortality table or set of term insurance premium rates. Expense allowances are then determined. For example, suppose a company wishes its YRT premium rates to be based on T-2000, an imaginary industry mortality table. The following two approaches are equivalent:

- Premiums equal to 80% of T-2000 with no expense allowances
- Premiums equal to 100% of T-2000 with expense allowances equal to 20% of T-2000.

7.4.4.1   Zero First-Year YRT Premium Rates

When YRT premium rates have the same slope by policy year as expected mortality rates do, only the mortality risk is transferred; that is, the year-by-year YRT premium rates are expected to cover the year-by-year mortality costs. To the extent that lapses differ from expected, the year-by-year ratio of YRT premiums to expected claims does not change.

To help the company with the strain of writing new business, reinsurers will often provide YRT premium rates of zero in the first year. The same effect can be accomplished with an expense allowance of 100% of first-year reinsurance premiums. By helping the company with new business strain, the reinsurer also participates in the lapse risk. Zero first-year reinsurance premium rates are balanced by higher reinsurance premium rates in renewal years. If lapses are higher than expected, there will not be sufficient renewal reinsurance premium to cover the lack of reinsurance premium in the first year.

Table 7.4.1 illustrates two sets of YRT premium rates that are roughly equivalent, one with and one without zero first-year premium rates expressed as a percentage of T-2000, a fictitious mortality table:

Table 7.4.1 YRT Premium Rates as Percentage of T-2000

Policy Year	Set 1	Set 2
1	50%	0%
2+	50	58

7.4.4.2 Monthly and Quarterly Premiums

The term *yearly renewable term* implies that reinsurance premiums are paid annually. This is not always the case.

Most YRT treaties are administered on a monthly or quarterly basis, even when premiums are paid annually. When premiums are paid annually, annual YRT premiums are paid to the reinsurer on all policies that cross policy anniversaries during a given month or quarter. For example, if administration were done on a monthly basis, then, at the end of September, annual YRT premiums would be paid for all reinsured policies that have policy anniversaries in September. If administration were done on a quarterly basis, then, at the end of September, annual YRT premiums would be paid for all reinsured policies with policy anniversaries in July, August, and September.

Because of the flexibility of premium payments and potential death benefit changes, UL and VUL policies are subject to more unpredictable changes in net amount at risk than are most products. Because of this, it is common for the YRT death benefit to be recalculated every month, with YRT premiums paid monthly. In other words, reinsured UL and VUL policies often have 12 YRT premiums per year, with each premium covering just one month. This adds greatly to the administrative burden.

Companies that have studied monthly net amount at risk patterns for dynamic products have generally found that significant changes in net amount at risk from month to month are extremely rare. In other words, changing the reinsured net amount at risk every month is rarely cost justifiable. Rather than deal with the extra complexity of monthly premiums, some companies choose to reinsure their UL and VUL policies using just one YRT death benefit amount per year, which permits an annual premium. While this may result in more or less reinsurance than is needed, the difference may not be significant. In addition, as long as the same YRT death benefit is used to compute both premiums and death benefits, the result should be equitable for both the company and the reinsurer.

Understanding how your company administers YRT reinsurance premium payments is important because it affects both cash flows and reserves held. By paying annual YRT premiums, more cash flows out of the company early in the policy year, resulting in some loss of investment income. On the other hand, paying annual YRT premiums usually results in a bigger reinsurance reserve credit (that is, a bigger reduction in reserves due to reinsurance).

7.4.4.3 Calendar Year Premiums

Rather than changing premium rates and paying annual premiums on the policy anniversary, some treaties use January 1 as the date all premiums are due. This might be done for accounting reasons (no unearned premiums and no reserve credits at the end of the calendar year) or for administrative reasons. Although this would seem like a simple, convenient approach, with all premiums on all policies due only on January 1, there are some complications: Partial year, pro-rated premiums must be paid for new business, policy changes, and terminations.

A variation of this approach is *calendar month* premiums, with premium rates changing on January 1 and monthly premiums due on all policies on the first day of every month. This approach has the accounting benefit of no unearned premiums and no reserve credits at the end of every calendar month. Because premiums are paid monthly, there may be no need to pro-rate premiums for reinsured business issued, changed or terminated during the preceding month. On the other hand, paying premiums 12 times per year can add greatly to the cost of administration.

7.4.5 YRT Cash Flows

There are three cash flows related to YRT reinsurance: premiums, death benefits, and expense allowances.

7.4.5.1 Premiums

We will assume that the company pays reinsurance premiums at the beginning of each policy year. Let

ReinsPrem_pu(t) = Reinsurance premium rate, per unit of
reinsured death benefit

ReinsPrem(t) = Reinsurance premium paid to the reinsurer,
per unit issued.

The reinsured premium paid to the reinsurer at the beginning of the policy year is calculated by multiplying the reinsured death benefit per unit by the reinsurance premium rate and then adjusting for survivorship:

$$\text{ReinsPrem}(t) = \text{ReinsDB\_pu}(t)\ \text{ReinsPrem\_pu}(t)\ \text{SurvFactor}(t-1).$$
(7.4.5)

7.4.5.2 Death Benefits

In Chapter 5, death benefits were assumed to be paid in the middle of the policy year. We will assume that the reinsurer incurs its share of death claims at the same point in time. In practice, the reinsurer usually pays its share of death claims one to two months after the date of death. However, since the company usually pays its reinsurance premiums one to two months after the policy anniversary, these timing differences largely cancel each other. Let

ReinsDeathBen(t) = Reinsured death benefits received from the
reinsurer, per unit issued.

The reinsured death benefit received from the reinsurer at the middle of the year is equal to the average reinsured amount times the probability of dying during the year:

$$\text{ReinsDeathBen}(t) = \text{ReinsDB\_pu}(t)\ \text{Deaths}(t).$$
(7.4.6)

7.4.5.3 Expense Allowances

Expense allowances are not common with YRT reinsurance. When they are provided, they are usually calculated as a percentage of the reinsurance premiums. They are then deducted from the amount due the reinsurer when the reinsurance premiums are paid. Let

$$\text{ExpAllowPct}(t) = \text{Expense allowance percentage that applies to reinsurance premiums paid}$$

$$\text{ExpAllow}(t) = \text{Expense allowances received from the reinsurer, per unit issued.}$$

The expense allowance is calculated by applying the expense allowance percentage to the reinsurance premium:

$$\text{ExpAllow}(t) = \text{ReinsPrem}(t)\ \text{ExpAllowPct}(t). \tag{7.4.7}$$

7.4.5.4 Adjusting Gross Cash Flows

The gross cash flows (that is, before deduction for reinsurance) calculated in Chapter 5 should be adjusted by deducting the related reinsurance cash flows. For YRT only three cash flow adjustments are needed: The formulas below and others to follow are iterative formulas of the form $A = A - B$. This approach is used as a simple way to express the adjustment for the effect of reinsurance. A more rigorous approach would be to define separate values for "pre-reinsurance" and "post-reinsurance."

$$\text{Prem}(t) = \text{Prem}(t) - \text{ReinsPrem}(t), \tag{7.4.8}$$
$$\text{DeathBen}(t) = \text{DeathBen}(t) - \text{ReinsDeathBen}(t), \tag{7.4.9}$$
$$\text{Comm}(t) = \text{Comm}(t) - \text{ExpAllow}(t). \tag{7.4.10}$$

7.4.6 YRT Reserve Credits

When a company transfers risk to a reinsurer through reinsurance, the company's reserves are usually reduced. We will refer to this reduction in reserves as a *reserve credit*. The amount of the reinsurance reserve credit is governed by valuation and accounting rules. Different rules can have dramatically different effects on the amount of the reserve credit. The following methods for calculating reinsurance reserve credits may apply to solvency, earnings, or tax reserves.

7.4.6.1 One-Year Term Method

The simplest reserve credit for YRT is based on the one-year term (OYT) method, the method used for U.S. solvency reserves. Under this approach, YRT reinsurance is treated as a series of one-year contracts. Reserve credits are based on OYT reserves, with terminal reserves equal to zero and mean reserves equal to one-half the OYT net valuation premiums. OYT net valuation premiums are equal to the valuation mortality rate discounted for a full or half year's interest.

When reserves are calculated at the end of the policy year, the one-year term method results in zero YRT reserve credits, since YRT terminal reserves equal zero. In practice, though, reserve credits between policy anniversaries are greater than zero, so a reserve credit of one-half the net valuation premium is normally reflected, as illustrated below. More precise ways to incorporate YRT reserve credits will be reflected in quarterly calculations in Chapter 12.

Let

$$\text{OYTRes\_puMid}(t) = \text{One-year term mean reserve, per unit in force; this is equal to half the OYT net valuation premium}$$

$$\text{ResCredit}(t) = \text{Reserve credit, per unit issued}$$

$$\text{ResCreditIncr}(t) = \text{Increase in reserve credit, per unit issued.}$$

The reserve credit is calculated as the OYT mean reserve per unit in force times the reinsured death benefit, adjusted for survivorship:

$$\text{ResCredit}(t)$$
$$= \text{ReinsDB\_pu}(t) \; \text{OYTRes\_puMid}(t) \; \text{SurvFactor}(t), \qquad (7.4.11)$$

$$\text{ResCreditIncr}(t) = \text{ResCredit}(t) - \text{ResCredit}(t-1). \qquad (7.4.12)$$

7.4.6.2 Stand-Alone Method

The stand-alone method calculates reinsurance reserves independently of the underlying product's cash flows. Reinsurance reserves are calculated as if the reinsurance terms stood alone. The reserve method and related assumptions are applied to reinsurance premiums, reinsured death benefits, and expense allowances to calculate reinsurance reserves or reserve credits. The reserve credit increase is calculated using Formula 7.4.12.

The stand-alone method allows a company to apply independently the same reserve methods and reserve assumptions to both gross business (that is, before deduction of reinsurance) and reinsured business. The net reserve held by the company is then calculated as gross reserves less reinsurance reserves or reserve credits. This is the primary method used for U.S. GAAP reserves.

7.4.6.3   Net Cash Flow Method

A more sophisticated approach, such as that used in Canada, does not directly calculate a reserve credit. Instead, reserves are based on the company's future cash flows, calculated net of reinsurance. Projected premium cash flows are net of reinsurance premiums, projected death benefit cash flows are net of reinsured death benefits, and projected expense cash flows are net of expense allowances. All other projected cash flows are unaffected by reinsurance.

For the net cash flow method, the impact of YRT reinsurance on reserves depends on the relationship between YRT premium rates (net of expense allowances) and valuation mortality rates:

- If YRT premium rates are less than valuation mortality rates, then reinsurance will reduce reserves, effectively creating a reinsurance reserve credit.
- If YRT premium rates roughly match valuation mortality rates, there may be little or no reserve credit.
- If YRT premium rates significantly exceed valuation mortality rates, reinsurance will *increase* reserves, thereby generating, in effect, a negative reserve credit.

The reserve credit for the net cash flow method is calculated as (1) less (2), where (1) is the reserve based on cash flows ignoring reinsurance and (2) is the reserve based on cash flows that are net of reinsurance.

7.4.6.4   Adjustments to Reserve Increases

Once the reserve credit is determined, the reserve credit increase can be calculated using Formula 7.4.12. The reserve increases calculated in

Chapter 6 should be adjusted by deducting the appropriate reinsurance reserve credit increase. Solvency, earnings, and tax reserve increases should be adjusted using a formula of the following form:

$$\text{ResIncr}(t) = \text{ResIncr}(t) - \text{ResCreditIncr}(t). \qquad (7.4.13)$$
$$\text{(Adjusted)}$$

7.5 Coinsurance

Coinsurance is the simplest and purest form of reinsurance. In return for a share of the premiums paid to the reinsurer, the company receives from the reinsurer that same share of all policy benefits and also receives an expense allowance for the reinsurer's share of its projected expenses. The reinsurer holds its share of the policy reserves, with the company taking a matching reserve credit. Coinsurance normally transfers mortality, investment, and persistency risk to the reinsurer. Expense risk may remain with the company, because the company may absorb any deviations between actual expenses and expense allowances.

Two common variations of coinsurance are used when the company desires to retain control of invested assets:

- *Modified coinsurance:* The ceding company retains the reinsurer's share of reserves and related assets. The reinsurer periodically pays the company an amount equal to its share of reserve increases. The company pays the reinsurer an amount equal to its share of any reserve decreases. The company also reimburses the reinsurer for interest on reserves, since the company earns interest on assets backing the reinsurer's share of reserves.

- *Coinsurance with funds withheld:* The company takes a reserve credit and the reinsurer sets up its share of reserves, but the assets backing the reinsurer's reserve are withheld by and remain with the company. These assets are often held by the company in a trust established for the benefit of the reinsurer. The reinsurer shows the amount of funds withheld by the company as an asset on the reinsurer's balance sheet. Investment income earned on the funds withheld is paid to the reinsurer.

Table 7.5.1 summarizes the three types of coinsurance described above. In all three cases, mortality, investment, and persistency risk is passed to the reinsurer.

Table 7.5.1 Types of Coinsurance

Transaction Type	Reinsured Invested Assets Held by	Reinsured Reserves Held by
Coinsurance	Reinsurer	Reinsurer
Modified Coinsurance	Company	Company
Coinsurance with Funds Withheld	Company	Reinsurer

7.5.1   Credited Interest Rates

Under coinsurance, the reinsurer assumes and manages its own investment risk. Assets are transferred to the reinsurer who is then responsible for investing and earning an adequate return on the assets backing its share of the reserves.

The setting of credited interest rates can become complicated when a dynamic product is coinsured. For participating products, the setting of the dividend interest rate poses the same issues.

Even if investment strategies are aligned, investment returns will rarely be the same for the company and its reinsurers. Reaching a consensus can be difficult, for example, if the company wishes to subsidize current interest rates and its reinsurers do not. These kinds of potential conflicts should be addressed ahead of time in treaty language, with clear procedures for setting credited interest rates and resolving differences. The compromises reached with reinsurers may change the expected interest spreads and the pricing of the product.

7.5.2   Coinsurance Premiums and Benefits

With coinsurance, the ceding company and reinsurer share premiums and policy benefits proportionately.

Because the policy fee is often designed to cover per policy expenses, the company may want to retain the policy fee. It is common for coinsurance to exclude the policy fee from the premium paid to the reinsurer.

7.5.3 Coinsurance Expense Allowances

Expense allowance percentages are usually negotiated. If there are multiple reinsurers with different expense allowances, then a weighted average of the expense allowances will be needed for pricing.

For example, Table 7.5.2 below illustrates three reinsurers with different expense allowances that result in a weighted average expense allowance of 22.8%, with 50% of the business coinsured.

Table 7.5.2 Weighted Average Expense Allowance

Reinsurer	Quota Share	Expense Allowance (as Percentage of Premium)
1	25.0%	25.0%
2	15.0	21.0
3	10.0	20.0
Total	50.0	
Weighted average		22.8

7.5.4 Coinsurance Cash Flows

Coinsurance cash flows fall into three categories: premiums, policy benefits, and expense allowances.

7.5.4.1 Premiums

Reinsurance premiums will depend on whether or not policy fees are included. If the reinsurance premium includes the policy fee, then the reinsurance premium is simply the reinsured percentage times the gross premium:

$$\text{ReinsPrem}(t) = \text{ReinsPct}(t)\,\text{Prem}(t).$$ (7.5.1)

If policy fees are excluded from reinsurance premiums, then the reinsurance premium is calculated as the reinsured percentage times the premium per unit, adjusted for survivorship:

$$\text{ReinsPrem}(t) = \text{ReinsPct}(t)\,\text{Prem\_pu}(t)\,\text{SurvFactor}(t-1).$$ (7.5.2)

7.5.4.2 Policy Benefits

Each reinsured policy benefit is equal to the reinsured percentage times the policy benefit:

$$\text{ReinsDeathBen}(t) = \text{ReinsPct}(t)\,\text{DeathBen}(t),$$ (7.5.3)
$$\text{ReinsSurrBen}(t) = \text{ReinsPct}(t)\,\text{SurrBen}(t),$$ (7.5.4)
$$\text{ReinsDiv}(t) = \text{ReinsPct}(t)\,\text{Div}(t),$$ (7.5.5)
$$\text{ReinsPartWithBen}(t) = \text{ReinsPct}(t)\,\text{PartWithBen}(t),$$ (7.5.6)
$$\text{ReinsPureEndow}(t) = \text{ReinsPct}(t)\,\text{PureEndow}(t).$$ (7.5.7)

Death benefits are assumed paid at the middle of the policy year. All other policy benefits are assumed paid at the end of the policy year.

Not all coinsurance agreements reimburse policyholder dividends directly. Instead, the reinsurer's share of the dividend may be built into the expense allowances. If this is the case, then $\text{ReinsDiv}(t)$ should be set to zero.

If all benefits are reinsured, then total reinsured policy benefits are equal to the reinsured percentage times total policy benefits:

$$\text{ReinsBen}(t) = \text{ReinsPct}(t)\,\text{Ben}(t).$$ (7.5.8)

7.5.4.3 Expense Allowances

Coinsurance expense allowances can be expressed in a variety of ways. Most often, the expense allowances are expressed as a percentage of reinsurance premiums.

Sometimes expense allowances are expressed per unit in force or per policy, but these are not covered here (see Exercise 7.4). If the company excludes the policy fee from the reinsurance premium, the retained policy fee is equivalent to a per policy expense allowance.

Expense allowances expressed as a percentage of reinsurance premiums are calculated using a formula identical to Formula 7.4.7 for YRT:

$$\text{ExpAllow}(t) = \text{ReinsPrem}(t) \, \text{ExpAllowPct}(t). \tag{7.5.9}$$

When the company pays a commission based on account values at the end of the policy year, the reinsurer would normally pay a matching expense allowance based on account values. Let

$\text{AVExpAllowPct}(t)$ = Expense allowance percentage, applied to account values at the end of policy year t

$\text{AVExpAllow}(t)$ = Expense allowances based on account values at the end of policy year t, per unit issued.

Expense allowances based on account values are calculated as

(a) The reinsured percentage times

(b) The account value expense allowance percentage times

(c) The account value per unit in force at the end of the policy year times

(d) An adjustment for survivorship:

$$\text{AVExpAllow}(t)$$
$$= \text{ReinsPct}(t) \, \text{AVExpAllowPct}(t) \, \text{AV\_pu}(t) \, \text{SurvFactor}(t). \tag{7.5.10}$$

7.5.4.4 Adjusting Gross Cash Flows

The gross cash flows calculated in Chapter 5 should be adjusted by deducting the related reinsurance cash flows. For coinsurance, numerous cash flow adjustments are needed. Again, these adjustments are in the form $\acute{A} = A - B$ for simplicity.

$A_{adjusted}$

$$\text{Prem}(t) = \text{Prem}(t) - \text{ReinsPrem}(t), \qquad (7.5.11)$$

$$\text{DeathBen}(t) = \text{DeathBen}(t) - \text{ReinsDeathBen}(t), \qquad (7.5.12)$$

$$\text{SurrBen}(t) = \text{SurrBen}(t) - \text{ReinsSurrBen}(t), \qquad (7.5.13)$$

$$\text{Div}(t) = \text{Div}(t) - \text{ReinsDiv}(t), \qquad (7.5.14)$$

$$\text{PartWithBen}(t) = \text{PartWithBen}(t) \\ - \text{ReinsPartWithBen}(t), \qquad (7.5.15)$$

$$\text{PureEndow}(t) = \text{PureEndow}(t) - \text{ReinsPureEndow}(t), \qquad (7.5.16)$$

$$\text{Comm}(t) = \text{Comm}(t) - \text{ExpAllow}(t), \qquad (7.5.17)$$

$$\text{AVComm}(t) = \text{AVComm}(t) - \text{AVExpAllow}(t). \qquad (7.5.18)$$

7.5.5   Coinsurance Reserve Credits

Much of the discussion of YRT reserve credits in Subsection 7.4.6 also applies to coinsurance. The main exception is the OYT method, which only applies to YRT. The stand-alone and net cash flows methods can be adapted to coinsurance simply by substituting "coinsured policy benefits" for "reinsured death benefits." When applying the net cash flow method to coinsurance, ignore the discussion of the relationship of YRT premium rates to valuation mortality rates; it does not apply to coinsurance.

If expense allowances and retained policy fees closely match projected expenses (or if expenses are not part of the reserve calculation), then all components of the reserve calculation, namely, premiums, policy benefits, and expenses, are shared between the company and the reinsurer. If the same mortality rates, lapse rates, and interest rates are used to calculate both gross reserves and coinsured reserves, then the resulting coinsurance reserves should approximate the reinsured percentage times the gross reserve:

$$\text{ResCredit}(t) = \text{ReinsPct}(t)\,\text{Res}(t). \qquad (7.5.19)$$

Reserve increases are adjusted identically for YRT and coinsurance reserve credits. Refer to the discussion for YRT at the end of Section 7.4.6.

7.6 Pricing Model

The following material presents the reinsurance adjustments to the Chapters 4–11 pricing example. Table 7.6.1 develops the reinsurance premiums and reinsured death benefits under a YRT structure. The reinsurance percentage is constant in all years, and a zero first-year YRT rate structure is utilized.

Table 7.6.2 develops reserve credits based on Table 7.6.1. The OYT reserve credit is equal to the valuation rate in Table 6.7.1, discounted for one year's valuation interest (also shown in Table 6.7.1) and divided by two.

Table 7.6.1 YRT Reinsurance Premiums and Death Benefits

t	$Naar\_pu(t-1)$	$ReinsDB\_pu$	$ReinsPrem\_pu$	$ReinsPrem$	$ReinsDeathBen$
1	998.09	249.52	0.00000	0.00000	0.29194
2	996.44	249.11	0.00187	0.41051	0.37661
3	995.10	248.78	0.00252	0.51116	0.46895
4	994.11	248.53	0.00300	0.57619	0.52861
5	993.53	248.38	0.00341	0.62094	0.56967
6	993.42	248.36	0.00378	0.65185	0.59803
7	993.90	248.47	0.00413	0.68854	0.63169
8	995.06	248.76	0.00451	0.72764	0.66756
9	997.04	249.26	0.00497	0.77574	0.71169
10	1,000.00	250.00	0.00554	0.83693	0.76783

Note: For all t, ReinsPct $= 0.25$.

Table 7.6.2 Calculation of Reserve Credits

t	OYTRes_puMid	ResCredit	ResCreditIncr
1	0.00217	0.47520	0.47520
2	0.00234	0.47626	0.00106
3	0.00253	0.48745	0.01119
4	0.00273	0.49776	0.01032
5	0.00296	0.50970	0.01193
6	0.00320	0.53230	0.02260
7	0.00348	0.55987	0.02757
8	0.00379	0.59041	0.03054
9	0.00415	0.62505	0.03463
10	0.00455	0.00000	-0.62505

7.7 Exercises

Exercise 7.1

Develop revised formulas for YRT premiums and death benefits (Formulas 7.4.4, 7.4.5, and 7.4.6) to reflect the impact of recapture. Assume that, except for the impact of recapture, a constant percentage equal to ReinsPct is reinsured. Use the following additional notation:

$\text{RecapPct}(t)$ = The percentage of the original reinsurance that is recaptured at the end of policy year t

$\text{CumRecapPct}(t)$ = The cumulative percentage of reinsurance that has been recaptured through the end of policy year t.

Develop a formula for $\text{CumRecapPct}(t)$ in terms of $\text{RecapPct}(t)$ and $\text{CumRecapPct}(t-1)$.

Exercise 7.2

Building on Exercise 7.1, explain how to revise formulas for coinsurance premiums, policy benefits, and reserve credits using the stand-alone method (Formulas 7.5.1 through 7.5.8 and 7.5.19).

Exercise 7.3

Building on Exercise 7.2, assume that the treaty states that the reinsurer must pay an amount to the company equal to the reserve credit on the portion of the reinsurance recaptured at the end of the policy year. Assume the reserve credit is equal to the gross reserves times the percentage currently reinsured. Develop a formula for the recaptured reserve credit (call it "RecapRes(t)") in terms of Res(t).

Exercise 7.4

Assume that expense allowances are not a percentage of premiums but instead are equal to an amount per unit in force plus an amount per policy in force. Develop a formula for expense allowances to replace Formula 7.5.9. Use the following additional notation:

$$\text{ExpAllow\_pu}(t) = \text{Expense allowance per unit reinsured}$$
$$\text{ExpAllowPerPol}(t) = \text{Expense allowance per policy.}$$

The expense allowance per policy could be a flat amount per policy reinsured or could be adjusted to reflect the percentage reinsured. Develop formulas for each possibility.

Exercise 7.5

Some reinsurance treaties provide for an experience refund that causes the reinsurer to return a portion of its profits if experience is favorable. Typically, the reinsurer is allowed to accumulate past losses and net them against any current profits when calculating an experience refund.

For a YRT treaty, assume that the reinsurer must return 50% of profits, where profits are calculated as 90% of reinsurance premiums less 100% of reinsurance death benefits. (The factor of 90% provides the reinsurer with a 10% margin for profit and expense.) Assume losses are accumulated with 8% interest, with the accumulation beginning at the end of the year of loss. Losses are simply negative profits, calculated using the same formula as profits.

Develop formulas for loss carryforwards and experience refunds, using the following additional notation:

$$\text{Result}(t) = \text{Profit or loss}$$

$\text{Profit}(t) = $ Profit, equal to Result(t), if Result(t) is greater than zero

$\text{Loss}(t) = $ Loss, equal to $-$Result(t), if Result(t) is less than zero

$\text{LossCarryForward}(t) = $ The accumulation of past losses, net of profits not eligible for an experience refund, accumulated with 8% interest, as of the end of year t

$\text{IneligibleProfit}(t) = $ Portion of profit not eligible for an experience refund, because of accumulated past losses

$\text{EligibleProfit}(t) = $ Portion of profit eligible for an experience refund; the profit in excess of accumulated past losses

$\text{ExperienceRefund}(t) = $ Experience refund payable.

Hint: The loss carryforward must equal zero before any profit is eligible for experience refunds.

Exercise 7.6

Modified coinsurance ("modco") treaties require the reinsurer to pay the company a modified coinsurance adjustment calculated as (a) less (b), where (a) is the increase in the modco reserve, and (b) is modco interest, equal to the interest earned by the company on the modco reserve.

To keep things simple, we will assume the following:

- Modco reserves are equal to solvency reserves times the percentage reinsured.

- Modco adjustments are paid at the end of the policy year. (In practice, modco adjustments are normally paid at the end of each calendar quarter.)

- Modco interest for the year is calculated as a modco interest rate times the modco reserve at the end of the previous policy year.

Let

$$\text{ModcoRes}(t) = \text{Modified coinsurance reserve at the end of year } t.$$

$$\text{iModco}(t) = \text{Modco interest rate for year } t, \text{ that is, the interest rate paid by the company to the reinsurer on the modco reserve.}$$

$$\text{ModcoInt}(t) = \text{Modco interest to be paid by the company to the reinsurer.}$$

$$\text{ModcoAdj}(t) = \text{Modified coinsurance adjustment payable to the company at the end of policy year } t.$$

Develop formulas for ModcoRes(t), ModcoInt(t), and ModcoAdj(t). How would product cash flows and solvency reserve increases be adjusted to move from coinsurance to modified coinsurance?

7.8 Answers

Answer 7.1

Cumulative recapture percentages are calculated as follows:

$$\text{CumRecapPct}(0) = 0,$$
$$\text{CumRecapPct}(t) = \text{CumRecapPct}(t - 1) + \text{RecapPct}(t)).$$

Change Formula 7.4.4 to reflect a constant ReinsPct and the cumulative impact of recapture through the end of the previous policy year:

$$\text{ReinsDB\_pu}(t) = \text{ReinsPct Naar\_pu}(t) \, (1 - \text{CumRecapPct}(t - 1)).$$

With this change to Formula 7.4.4, no change is needed to Formulas 7.4.5 or 7.4.6, since the impact of recapture is already reflected in ReinsDB_pu.

Answer 7.2

Multiply all but reserve credits by $(1 - \text{CumRecapPct}(t - 1))$. Multiply reserve credits by $(1 - \text{CumRecapPct}(t))$.

Answer 7.3

$$\text{RecapRes}(t) = \text{Res}(t) \ \text{ReinsPct}(t) \ \text{RecapPct}(t).$$

Answer 7.4

If the expense allowance per policy is a flat amount per policy reinsured, then

$$\text{ExpAllow}(t) = \left(\text{ExpAllow\_pu}(t) \ \text{ReinsPct}(t) + \frac{\text{ExpAllowPerPol}(t)}{\text{AvgSize}} \right)$$
$$\times \ \text{SurvFactor}(t - 1).$$

If the expense allowance per policy is adjusted to reflect the percentage reinsured, then

$$\text{ExpAllow}(t) = \left(\text{ExpAllow\_pu}(t) + \frac{\text{ExpAllowPerPol}(t)}{\text{AvgSize}} \right)$$
$$\times \ \text{ReinsPct}(t) \ \text{SurvFactor}(t - 1).$$

Answer 7.5

$$\text{Result}(t) = (0.90) \ \text{ReinsPrem}(t) - \text{ReinsDeathBen}(t)$$
$$\text{Profit}(t) = \max(0, \text{Result}(t))$$
$$\text{Loss}(t) = \max(0, -\text{Result}(t))$$
$$\text{IneligibleProfit}(t) = \min(\text{Profit}(t),$$
$$\text{LossCarryforward}(t - 1)(1.08))$$
$$\text{EligibleProfit}(t) = \text{Profit}(t) - \text{IneligibleProfit}(t)$$
$$\text{ExperienceRefund}(t) = \text{EligibleProfit}(t) \ (0.50)$$
$$\text{LossCarryforward}(0) = 0$$
$$\text{LossCarryforward}(t) = \text{LossCarryforward}(t - 1)(1.08) + \text{Loss}(t)$$
$$- \text{IneligibleProfit} \ (t.)$$

Answer 7.6

$$\text{ModcoRes}(t) = \text{SolvRes}(t) \ \text{ReinsPct}(t)$$
$$\text{ModcoInt}(t) = \text{ModcoRes}(t - 1) \ \text{iModco}(t)$$
$$\text{ModcoAdj}(t) = \text{ModcoRes}(t) - \text{ModcoRes}(t - 1)$$
$$- \text{ModcoInt}(t.)$$

Product cash flows would be adjusted to reflect ModcoAdj(t) as an additional cash flow received from the reinsurer at the end of the year. ModcoAdj(t) would be added to CashFlowEnd(t) and either added to Prem(t) or subtracted from Ben(t).

By definition, modified coinsurance results in all solvency reserves being held by the company and none being held by the reinsurer. Compared to coinsurance, solvency reserve increases should be adjusted to reflect no reinsurance reserve credits.

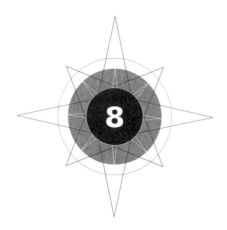

Investment Income

8.1 Introduction

This chapter discusses the investment income earned on cash flows that occur during the policy year and investment income earned on assets supporting policy reserves.

8.1.1 Investment Income Based on Assets Supporting the Product

In this book, investment income is calculated based on the assets needed to support the product and *not* the assets developed from the product's cumulative cash flows. To support a product, the company must have assets equal to solvency reserves plus required capital. For purposes of this chapter, we will assume that a company must have assets equal only to solvency reserves. The discussion of assets supporting required capital and the investment income earned on those assets will be covered in Chapter 10.

To achieve the requirement that assets equal solvency reserves, it is assumed that the company's owners contribute additional capital when it is needed and withdraw excess capital when it is available.

This point is best illustrated with an example. Assume a company issues a group of policies with the following results for the first policy year:

- 1,000,000 of premiums
- 750,000 of expenses
- 200,000 of policy benefits
- 400,000 of solvency reserves at the end of the first policy year.

The net cash flow on this business is 50,000, equal to the premiums less expenses and policy benefits. A capital contribution of 350,000 is needed in addition to the net cash flow to fund the solvency reserves. At the end of the first year, the company needs to have 400,000 of assets supporting the group of policies, not just the initial 50,000 of cash flows. The company will earn interest during the year on the cash flows and the capital contribution. Taxes may be positive or negative for this group of policies, depending on how taxes are calculated. The amount of interest earned and taxes paid will impact the amount of the capital contribution that is needed.

8.1.2 Investment Income Based on Cumulative Cash Flows

There is another way to calculate the asset base for investment income. This method does not take into account capital contributions and distributions. We will refer to this alternative as "investment income based on cumulative cash flows." This method accumulates insurance cash flows with interest, net of taxes. If there are negative cumulative cash flows in the early years, they accumulate negative interest. You can think of negative interest as borrowing from the company's owners and paying them interest. In the later years, assets typically exceed solvency reserves and required capital. The interest earned on excess assets adds even more to the excess. Although this approach does not seem appropriate for calculating profits for a company with stockholders, it may be useful for a mutual company that has no outside source of capital and no one but policyowners to receive excess capital. Also, certain regulatory tests may use cumulative cash flow methods.

Investment income on cumulative cash flows is used to calculate *asset shares*. Asset shares are equal to insurance cash flows accumulated with interest and net of taxes, calculated on a per unit in force basis, and assuming no capital contributions or distributions. Asset shares are useful for determining the share of a company's assets that resulted from a certain group of policies. Asset shares can be useful for allocating assets or investment income between different groups of policies, for setting dividend scales, and for calculating policyowner equity in connection with demutualization.

Calculating investment income based on cumulative cash flows is not necessarily wrong, but it can produce misleading results. For example, suppose the balance sheet items in Table 8.1.1 resulted from calculating investment income based on cumulative cash flows instead of assets supporting the product.

Table 8.1.1 Apparent versus True Earnings

Policy Year	Assets	Solvency Reserves	Required Capital	Excess Capital	Apparent Earnings	True Earnings
1	−9	0	1	−10	−10	−10
2	−1	6	1	−8	2	2.5
3	6	11	1	−6	2	2.4
4	12	15	1	−4	2	2.3
5	17	18	1	−2	2	2.2
6	21	20	1	0	2	2.1
7	24	21	1	2	2	2.0
8	26	21	1	4	2	1.9
9	27	20	1	6	2	1.8
10	27	18	1	8	2	1.7

In Table 8.1.1, these formulas apply:

Excess Capital = Assets − Reserves − Required Capital
Apparent Earnings = change in Excess Capital
True Earnings = Apparent Earnings − 5% after-tax interest on previous year's Excess Capital.

There is a natural but flawed tendency to interpret the annual change in excess capital as the required capital contribution or available distributable earnings. *This is wrong!* True distributable earnings are based on maintaining zero excess capital. The error is equal to the interest earned on the prior year's excess (or shortage of) capital.

For simplicity, we have assumed that all capital contributions and distributions occur at the end of the year. However, capital contributions should be made *before* they are needed, not after. A more accurate approach would have been to reflect a capital contribution of 9.5 at the beginning of year 1. Here 9.5 is calculated as 10/1.05, which discounts for one year of after-tax interest at 5%.

8.2 Policy Loans

Some policies allow the policyowner to borrow money from the company, using the policy's cash value as collateral. This is called a policy loan. The company charges interest on the policy loan that is either paid by the policyowner or added to the loan balance. If the loan is not repaid, the outstanding loan principal is deducted from the cash surrender value if the policy is surrendered or from the death benefits if the insured dies. This feature results in policy loans being the most secure assets that a life insurance company can have.

The impact of policy loans on pricing can be underestimated. For example, suppose a Universal Life product requires a 1.50% spread between the earned and credited rates to achieve its profit objectives. Next, suppose the product allows policyowners to take out policy loans and be credited interest on loaned cash values at a rate equal to the policy loan interest rate less 0.75%. In other words, the company earns a spread of only 0.75% on loaned cash values. Combine this lower spread with the high transaction costs often associated with small policy loans, and you can see how ignoring policy loans can lead to misleading results.

However, a lower spread on policy loans may be acceptable, since capital requirements for policy loans are typically lower (for example, zero) than for invested assets. These differences should be understood when setting policy loan interest rate provisions.

8.2.1   Balance Sheet Treatment of Policy Loans

Policy loans are typically shown as an asset on the balance sheet. However, policy loans can be viewed as an early distribution of the cash value, thereby reducing the company's ultimate liability. Because of this, some accounting procedures require that policy loans be shown as an offset to liabilities rather than as an asset. Tables 8.2.1 and 8.2.2 show the two ways policy loans are treated on the balance sheet.

Table 8.2.1 Policy Loans Shown as an Asset

Assets		Liabilities	
Invested Assets	800	Reserves	1,000
Policy Loans	200		
Total Assets	1,000	Total Liabilities	1,000

Note: Invested assets refer to all assets other than policy loans.

Table 8.2.2 Policy Loans Shown as a Reduction in Liabilities

Assets		Liabilities	
Invested Assets	800	Reserves	1,000
		(Less Policy Loans)	(200)
Total Assets	800	Total Liabilities	800

Regardless of the accounting treatment, the amount of other invested assets supporting the reserves is reduced when policy loans are made, because cash is paid out to the policyowner.

8.2.2   Income Statement Treatment of Policy Loans

Policy loan interest can impact the income statement in two different ways. Policy loan interest can be an addition to investment income, or it can be a deduction from policy benefits, as shown in Table 8.2.3.

Table 8.2.3 Policy Loan Interest Treatment in Income Statement

	Policy loans shown as an asset	Policy loans shown as a reduction in liability
Balance Sheet Treatment		
Income Statement Treatment	Policy loan interest shown as an addition to investment income	Policy loan interest shown as a reduction in benefits
Premiums	100	100
Investment Income		
Interest on Invested Assets	40	40
Interest on Policy Loans	10	
Total Income	150	140
Policy Benefits		
Benefits Paid	(70)	(70)
Increase in Reserves	(40)	(40)
Interest on Policy Loans		10
Expenses	(25)	(25)
Total Benefits and Expenses	(135)	(125)
Income before Taxes	15	15
Taxes	(5)	(5)
Net Income	10	10

8.2.3   Impact of Policy Loans on Pricing

There are two basic ways to handle policy loans in pricing:

- Combine policy loans with invested assets and use a weighted-average earned interest rate that is applied to total assets. This approach works well if the interest rates for policy loans and invested assets are not materially different and if there is no need or desire to track policy loans separately.

- Track policy loans and invested assets separately and apply separate interest rates to each. This is the more general approach, and the one we will develop in this chapter.

Because a policy loan cannot exceed the cash surrender value, it is common to study policy loan activity as a percentage of available cash surrender value. This percentage is referred to as the *policy loan utilization rate*. Depending on the statistical studies available, this rate could be a function of issue age, policy year, product type, economic conditions, and other variables.

Let

$$\text{PolLoanUtilRate}(t) = \text{Policy loan utilization rate; the percentage of the available cash surrender value that is loaned at the end of year } t$$

$$\text{PolLoan}(t) = \text{Policy loan outstanding at the end of year } t, \text{ per unit issued}$$

$$\text{PolLoanIntRate}(t) = \text{The annual effective policy loan interest rate, usually defined in the policy}$$

$$\text{PolLoanInt}(t) = \text{The amount of policy loan interest, per unit issued.}$$

Then,

$$\text{PolLoan}(t) = \text{PolLoanUtilRate}(t) \ \text{CV\_pu}(t) \ \text{SurvFactor}(t),$$
(8.2.1)

$$\text{PolLoanInt}(t) = \text{PolLoan}(t - 1) \ \text{PolLoanIntRate}(t).$$
(8.2.2)

In Formula 8.2.1 SurvFactor(t) converts the cash value from per unit in force to per unit issued. In Formula 8.2.2 the policy loan at the end of the previous year earns a full year's interest during the current year. For simplicity, these formulas assume that all policy loan activity (that is, new loans and repayment of principal and interest) occurs at the end of the year.

8.3 Invested Assets

This section addresses assets other than policy loans, which we will refer to as *invested assets*. In practice, invested assets will consist mainly of interest-bearing assets such as bonds and mortgages.

8.3.1 Interest Rates for Invested Assets

Interest rate assumptions for invested assets are discussed in Chapter 3. Here we will assume that interest rates have been developed that are net of investment expenses and asset default costs. We will further assume that these interest rates result from an investment strategy that ensures assets of appropriate quality, duration, and liquidity are purchased each year. Finally, we will assume that these interest rates reflect that a small portion of a company's assets, such as goodwill, furniture, computer hardware, and software, do not earn any investment income.

In this chapter, we will assume that one constant interest rate is earned on invested assets during a given policy year. In many situations, using one interest rate is neither accurate nor appropriate. It is quite common for a company to be earning an average rate on existing investments (that is, the portfolio rate) that is significantly different from the average rate that can be earned on new investments (that is, the new money rate). The impact of this difference is explained more fully in Chapter 3.

We need an equivalent semiannual interest rate to apply to cash flows that occur in the middle of the policy year, so let

$$\text{InvIntRate}(t) = \text{Interest rate earned on invested assets, net of investment expenses and asset default rates}$$
$$\text{InvIntRateMid}(t) = \text{Semiannual interest rate equivalent to InvIntRate}(t), \text{ on an annual effective basis.}$$

Then,

$$\text{InvIntRateMid}(t) = (1 + \text{InvIntRate}(t))^{1/2} - 1. \qquad (8.3.1)$$

8.3.2   Interest Earned on Invested Assets

Actuaries and others often talk about "investment income on reserves" as a component of profit. Technically this is not correct. A company does *not* earn investment income on reserves. Instead, a company earns investment income on the assets supporting the reserves.

In practice, assets have to be at least equal to solvency reserves at any point in time. We will assume that investment income is earned on assets that are invested at the beginning of the policy year. The amount of those invested assets is equal to the solvency reserves at the end of the previous year. Chapter 12 refines the formulas to reflect the fact that invested assets change throughout the policy year rather than remaining fixed for an entire year.

We leave the discussion of taxes for Chapter 9, but it is important to recognize that, in some countries, insurance companies must pay estimated taxes during the fiscal year, not after the close of the year. The actual timing of these tax payments affects the amount of investment income earned, and the amount of investment income affects the amount of taxes. To remove this circularity, this book assumes that taxes are paid at the end of the policy year.

An exercise at the end of Chapter 9 explores the revised formulas needed to reflect taxes payable at the middle of the policy year.

Interest earned on invested assets is made up of two components for each year:

- Interest earned on invested assets already in place at the end of the previous policy year. These assets, along with policy loans, support solvency reserves.

- Interest earned on insurance cash flows occurring during the policy year.

8.3.2.1   Interest Earned on Invested Assets at the End of the Previous Year

Total assets at the end of the year are assumed to be equal to solvency reserves. Invested assets are equal to total assets less policy loans.

Invested assets at the end of the previous year earn a full year's interest during the current year.

Let

$$\text{Assets}(t) = \text{Total assets at the end of year } t, \text{ per unit issued}$$

$$\text{InvAssets}(t) = \text{All assets other than policy loans at the end of year } t, \text{ per unit issued}$$

$$\text{InvInt}(t) = \text{Interest earned during year } t \text{ on all assets other than policy loans at the end of year } t - 1, \text{ per unit issued.}$$

Then,

$$\text{Assets}(t) = \text{SolvRes}(t), \tag{8.3.2}$$

$$\text{InvAssets}(t) = \text{Assets}(t) - \text{PolLoan}(t), \tag{8.3.3}$$

$$\text{InvInt}(t) = \text{InvAssets}(t - 1)\,\text{InvIntRate}(t). \tag{8.3.4}$$

Recall from Chapter 7 that certain reserve credits may be taken for reinsurance. If reinsurance is modeled, then the amount of assets is affected. Formula 8.3.2 would then be adjusted as follows, with the adjustment affecting the results for Formulas 8.3.3 and 8.3.4:

$$\text{Assets}(t) = \text{SolvRes}(t) - \text{ResCredit}(t).$$

Also, reinsurance may transfer a portion of the policy loans and policy loan interest to the reinsurer. If so, Formula 8.3.3 should be adjusted to reflect the impact of reinsurance.

8.3.2.2 Interest Earned on Insurance Cash Flows

In Chapters 5 and 7, we assumed that insurance cash flows occur at three different points in the policy year. Premiums, acquisition expenses, and maintenance expenses are assumed to occur at the beginning of the year. Death benefits are assumed to occur at the middle of the year. Policyowner dividends, surrender benefits, and other benefits are assumed to occur at the end of the year.

The calculation of investment income on cash flows during the policy year takes into account the assumed timing of those cash flows.

Cash flows at the beginning of the year earn a full year's interest. Cash flows at the middle of the year earn a half-year's interest. Cash flows at the end of the year do not impact investment income in the current year.

Let

$$\text{CashFlowInt}(t) = \text{Interest earned on insurance cash flows generated during the year, per policy issued.}$$

Then,

$$\text{CashFlowInt}(t) = \text{CashFlowBeg}(t)\ \text{InvIntRate}(t)$$
$$+ \text{CashFlowMid}(t)\ \text{InvIntRateMid}(t). \qquad (8.3.5)$$

8.4 Total Investment Income

Total investment income consists of policy loan interest and the two components of interest earned on invested assets. Let

$$\text{InvIncome}(t) = \text{Total investment income, per unit issued.}$$

Then,

$$\text{InvIncome}(t) = \text{PolLoanInt}(t) + \text{InvInt}(t) + \text{CashFlowInt}(t).$$
$$(8.4.1)$$

8.5 Pricing Model

Here is this chapter's contribution to the Chapters 4–11 pricing example. Table 8.5.1 develops the investment income for the invested assets. The invested assets are net of reinsurance reserve credits. Since the examples assume no policy loans, the invested assets equal the solvency reserves, and investment income is based on the end of the previous year's invested assets. The cash flows come from the pricing example tables in Chapters 5 and 7.

Table 8.5.1 Investment Income

t	InvAssets	InvInt	CashFlowBeg	CashFlowMid	CashFlowInt	InvIncome
1	1.20555	0.00000	−6.62500	−1.00120	−0.49820	−0.49820
2	2.42783	0.08439	4.20848	−1.29434	0.25006	0.33445
3	3.29951	0.16995	3.77711	−1.42222	0.21546	0.38541
4	3.81691	0.23097	3.75220	−1.60527	0.20742	0.43839
5	3.97754	0.26718	3.47972	−1.73129	0.18401	0.45119
6	3.87963	0.27843	3.32630	−1.81775	0.17030	0.44872
7	3.39682	0.27157	3.15688	−1.91884	0.15496	0.42653
8	2.50413	0.23778	2.98828	−2.02467	0.13951	0.37729
9	1.16369	0.17529	2.81378	−2.15280	0.12289	0.29818
10	0.00000	0.08146	2.62902	−2.31347	0.10443	0.18589

Note: For all t, InvIntRate = 7.00%, InvIntRateMid = 3.441%.

8.6 Exercises

Exercise 8.1

Let CumCashFlow(t) = Cumulative cash flows as of the end of policy year t, per unit issued.

Develop a formula for CumCashFlow(t) based on CumCashFlow($t − 1$), CashFlowBeg(t), CashFlowMid(t), CashFlowEnd(t), InvIntRate(t), and InvIntRateMid(t). Ignore taxes.

Exercise 8.2

Let AssetShare(t) = Asset share per unit in force at the end of policy year t.

Develop a formula for AssetShare(t) in terms of CumCashFlow(t) and SurvFactor(t).

Exercise 8.3

In Table 8.1.1, what impact would a doubling of required capital have on excess capital, apparent earnings, and true earnings?

Exercise 8.4

Suppose a Universal Life policy is expected to be supported by invested assets that earn 7% interest (net of investment expenses and asset defaults), with a credited interest rate 1.5% below the earned rate. Suppose further that (1) policy loans are charged an interest rate of only 4%, (2) annual policy loan expenses amount to 0.5% of outstanding policy loans, and (3) the portion of the cash value that is loaned is credited with an interest rate of only 3%. Develop a formula for the average interest spread being earned on all assets at the end of policy year t, in terms of PolLoan(t), InvAssets(t), and Assets(t).

Exercise 8.5

Suppose a reinsurance agreement reduces solvency reserves and policy loans by a percentage equal to ReinsPct. How would Formulas 8.3.2 and 8.3.3 be adjusted to reflect this reinsurance agreement?

Exercise 8.6

In any given year, the funds that are available for investment at the new money rate come from several sources:

- Insurance cash flows
- Investment income cash flows (such as bond coupons and mortgage payments)
- Capital cash flows (that is, capital contributions or distributed earnings), and
- Reinvestment of assets purchased in prior years that mature, repay, or are sold during the current year.

Let

RolloverRate(s, t) = The percentage of investments made during year s that are available for reinvestment during year t. Assume that no assets roll over during the policy year in which they are purchased, that is, RolloverRate(s, s) = 0

InvAssets(s, t) = Invested assets that were purchased during year s that are still invested at the end of year t

InvIntRate(s, t) = Interest rate earned during year t on invested assets that were purchased during year s.

Develop formulas for the following and explain the meaning of each:

a. A formula for InvAssets(t) in terms of InvAssets(s, t) for $s = 1$ to t.

b. A formula for InvAssets(t, t), assuming InvAssets(t) = SolvRes(t).

c. A formula for InvAssets(s, t) in terms of InvAssets(s, $t - 1$), InvAssets(s, s), and RolloverRate(s, t).

d. A formula for InvInt(t) in terms of InvAssets(s, $t - 1$) and InvIntRate(s, t) for $s = 1$ to $t - 1$.

e. A formula for InvIntRate(t), the average interest rate earned on investments during year t, in terms of InvInt(t) and InvAssets($t - 1$).

Exercise 8.7

In Exercise 8.6, it is theoretically possible for InvAssets(t, t) to be negative. How could this happen? What would it mean? How could a negative result be avoided?

Exercise 8.8

In Exercise 8.6, which interest rate would apply to insurance cash flows occurring during year t?

8.7 Answers

Answer 8.1

$$\text{CumCashFlow}(t)$$
$$= (\text{CumCashFlow}(t-1)$$
$$+ \text{CashFlowBeg}(t))(1 + \text{InvIntRate}(t))$$
$$+ \text{CashFlowMid}(t)(1 + \text{InvIntRateMid}(t))$$
$$+ \text{CashFlowEnd}(t).$$

Answer 8.2

$$\text{AssetShare}(t) = \frac{\text{CumCashFlow}(t)}{\text{SurvFactor}(t)}.$$

Answer 8.3

Excess capital would be lowered by 1 in every policy year.

Apparent earnings would be reduced from -10 to -11 in the first policy year and would not be impacted thereafter.

True earnings would also be reduced from -10 to -11 in the first policy year. Thereafter, true earnings would be increased by 0.05, equal to -5% times the reduction in the previous year's excess capital.

Answer 8.4

The average spread earned on nonloaned assets is 1.5% (given). The average spread earned on policy loans is 0.5%, equal to 4% less 0.5% expense and less 3% credited. The average spread earned on all assets is

$$\frac{1.5\% \ \text{InvAssets}(t) + 0.5\% \ \text{PolLoan}(t)}{\text{Assets}(t)}.$$

Answer 8.5

$$\text{Assets}(t) = \text{SolvRes}(t) \, (1 - \text{ReinsPct})$$
$$\text{InvAssets}(t) = \text{Assets}(t) - \text{PolLoan}(t) \, (1 - \text{ReinsPct})$$
$$= (\text{SolvRes}(t) - \text{PolLoan}(t)) \, (1 - \text{ReinsPct}).$$

Answer 8.6

a. $\text{InvAssets}(t) = \sum_{s=1}^{t} \text{InvAssets}(s, t).$

This formula shows that current invested assets are equal to the sum of the assets purchased in each year that are still invested. It allows you to break down current invested assets by the year in which assets were purchased.

b. $\text{InvAssets}(t, t) = \text{SolvRes}(t) - \sum_{s=1}^{t-1} \text{InvAssets}(s, t).$

This formula shows that the assets to be purchased during policy year t will equal the solvency reserve less the assets purchased in prior years that are still invested.

c. $\text{InvAssets}(s, t) = \text{InvAssets}(s, t - 1) - \text{InvAssets}(s, s) \, \text{RolloverRate}(s, t).$
This formula shows how to track the assets purchased in year s from one year to the next, by deducting the rollover rate times the assets originally purchased.

d. $\text{InvInt}(t) = \Sigma \, \text{InvAssets}(s, t - 1) \, \text{InvIntRate}(s, t).$
Investment income for year t is the sum of investment income earned in year t on the assets purchased in each year that are still invested in year t.

e. $\text{InvIntRate}(t) = \dfrac{\text{InvInt}(t)}{\text{InvAssets}(t - 1)}.$
The average interest rate can be determined by dividing investment income by beginning assets.

Answer 8.7

Yes, $\text{InvAssets}(t, t)$ can be negative. For this to happen, solvency reserves would have to decrease by more than the sum of rollovers for the year.

This means that insufficient assets will be liquidated to cover outbound cash flows. The investment strategy could be changed to provide more asset maturities or sales of assets in year t.

Answer 8.8

InvIntRate(t, t).

Taxes

Introduction

"Nothing in life is sure but death and taxes." This saying applies equally well to our business: "Nothing in life *insurance* is sure but death and taxes."

This chapter develops formulas that reflect the effect of taxes on pricing. Many jurisdictions have rules for calculating taxable earnings that differ from the calculation of pre-tax earnings. This means that, in many cases, taxes *cannot* be calculated simply by applying a tax rate to pre-tax earnings.

Insurance company taxation varies significantly by jurisdiction. Almost all countries tax life insurance companies at the national level. In addition, some countries tax insurance at the state, provincial, or other levels. The taxation of life insurance is often balanced with the taxation of other financial products, such as savings accounts, bonds, stocks, and mutual funds.

Life insurance companies are taxed by applying a tax rate to a taxable amount. There are four general types of *insurance company taxes*:

- Tax on earnings
- Tax on investment income less expenses $(I - E)$
- Tax on capital, and
- Premium tax. Premium taxes are usually included with percent of premium expenses and are not addressed in this chapter.

It is possible for an insurance company to be subject to two or more of the above types of taxes at the same time, each with its own tax rate and complex set of rules. A thorough knowledge of insurance company taxation for the jurisdictions in which the company operates is crucial to the proper pricing of an insurance product.

As in Chapter 8, the formulas in this chapter do not take into account the effect of required capital. Chapter 10 discusses required capital and its effect on taxes.

9.2 Tax on Earnings

The tax on earnings is calculated as taxable earnings times a tax rate. Instead of a single tax rate, a series of tax rates may apply to different levels of taxable earnings or to different situations. Taxable earnings may be simply calculated as pre-tax solvency earnings (that is, premiums plus investment income less benefits, expenses, and solvency reserve increases). Unfortunately, taxable earnings are not always so simple. There can be numerous adjustments to pre-tax solvency earnings to arrive at taxable earnings. These adjustments fall into two major categories: timing differences and permanent differences.

Timing differences, also known as *temporary differences,* refer to differences that reverse themselves over time. For example, basing taxable earnings on tax reserves instead of solvency reserves produces a timing difference. Cumulative taxable earnings will eventually equal cumulative pre-tax earnings because tax reserves will eventually equal solvency reserves (both eventually equal zero), although it may take until the last policy terminates for this to happen.

Permanent differences refer to differences that do not reverse themselves over time. For example, certain types of investment income may be nontaxable. Also, certain types of expenses may be nondeductible when figuring taxable earnings.

9.2.1 Pre-Tax Earnings

Before calculating taxable earnings, pre-tax earnings must be calculated. Pre-tax solvency earnings are equal to premiums plus investment income, less benefits, expenses, and increase in solvency reserves. Similarly, pre-tax stockholders earnings are equal to premiums plus investment income less benefits, expenses, increase in benefit reserves, and amortization of deferred acquisition costs.

If reinsurance is reflected in pricing, all of the values used in the formulas below would be adjusted for reinsurance, using adjustments similar to those presented in Chapter 7.

Let

$$\text{PreTaxSolvEarn}(t) = \text{Total pre-tax solvency earnings, per unit issued}$$

$$\text{PreTaxStockEarn}(t) = \text{Total pre-tax stockholder earnings, per unit issued.}$$

Then

$$\begin{aligned}
\text{PreTaxSolvEarn}(t) = {} & \text{Prem}(t) + \text{InvIncome}(t) - \text{Ben}(t) \\
& - \text{Exp}(t) - \text{SolvResIncr}(t), \quad (9.2.1)
\end{aligned}$$

$$\begin{aligned}
\text{PreTaxStockEarn}(t) = {} & \text{Prem}(t) + \text{InvIncome}(t) \\
& - \text{Ben}(t) - \text{Exp}(t) \\
& - \text{BenResIncr}(t) - \text{DACAmort}(t). \quad (9.2.2)
\end{aligned}$$

By substituting using Formula 5.10.7, we can simplify these formulas:

$$\begin{aligned}
\text{PreTaxSolvEarn}(t) = {} & \text{ProdCashFlow}(t) \\
& + \text{InvIncome}(t) - \text{SolvResIncr}(t), \quad (9.2.3)
\end{aligned}$$

$$\begin{aligned}
\text{PreTaxStockEarn}(t) = {} & \text{ProdCashFlow}(t) + \text{InvIncome}(t) \\
& - \text{BenResIncr}(t) - \text{DACAmort}(t). \quad (9.2.4)
\end{aligned}$$

9.2.2 Taxable Earnings

Taxable earnings are calculated as pre-tax solvency earnings plus adjustments for timing differences and permanent differences.

9.2.2.1 Timing Differences

This book illustrates only those timing differences due to differences between tax, solvency, and earnings reserves. However, this does not mean that other timing differences, such as those mentioned below, are not significant. Ignoring them could result in inadequate pricing.

In general, any difference between solvency standards and tax standards for the current value of an asset or liability results in a timing difference, because every asset is eventually sold or written off and every liability is eventually extinguished. Insurance regulators tend toward conservatism, which results in asset values somewhat understated and liability values somewhat overstated for solvency purposes. Tax authorities are sometimes more interested in increasing tax revenue, which may result in asset values somewhat overstated and liability values somewhat understated for tax purposes. This can result in numerous differences between solvency and tax values for assets and liabilities, such as some of the following:

- Different treatment of unrealized and realized capital gains and losses
- Different carrying values for bonds, mortgages, real estate, and other assets
- Different amortization schedules for goodwill, deferred acquisition costs, and other assets
- Different treatment of uncollected amounts
- Different calculations for reserves
  - Different interest rates
  - Different mortality rates
  - Different reserve methods

- Different calculations for claim liabilities
  - Discounting of future claim payments on known claims
  - Expense of handling future claim payments on known claims
  - Estimation of incurred but not reported claims
  - Treatment of contested claim liabilities
- Different timing for incurring policyowner dividend liabilities
- Liabilities not recognized for tax purposes such as
  - Reserve to stabilize investment returns
  - Reserve to offset future capital losses
  - Other contingency reserve
  - Required capital.

Timing differences vary significantly from country to country.

To understand which of a company's timing differences are significant for pricing, it is helpful to convert a company's solvency balance sheet to a tax balance sheet. The solvency basis and tax basis for every asset and liability should be examined. The differences that are significant, ongoing, and relevant to the product being developed should be reflected in pricing. For example, if the difference in treatment for bonds is significant and the product being developed will produce significant investments in bonds, then this difference should be incorporated in pricing.

Formulas for timing differences, other than tax reserves, will not be presented. They are beyond the scope of this book because they vary so much from country to country and change over time. However, the following treatment of tax reserves should serve as a guide for how to treat other timing differences. Be sure to treat asset differences in the opposite way you treat liability differences.

As you will see below, the calculation of taxable income differs from the calculation of pre-tax solvency earnings. Often, much of the difference is due to the use of tax reserves in place of solvency reserves. Table 9.2.1 illustrates that, if initial and final reserves for the period are zero, then total earnings over the entire period will be the same, although the pattern of earnings will depend on the pattern of reserves.

Table 9.2.1 Solvency Earnings Pattern Versus Taxable Earnings Pattern

	TotalCashFlow Plus InvIncome	Solvency Reserve Increase	Pre-Tax Solvency Earnings[a]	Tax Reserve Increase	Taxable Earnings[b]
1	1,000	1,200	−200	1,000	0
2	900	−300	1,200	−250	1,150
3	800	−300	1,100	−250	1,050
4	700	−300	1,000	−250	950
5	600	−300	900	−250	850
Total	4,000		4,000		4,000

[a] Pre-Tax Solvency Earnings = ProdCashFlow(t) + InvIncome(t) − SolvResIncr(t)
[b] Taxable Earnings = ProdCashFlow(t) + InvIncome(t) − TaxResIncr(t)

Note that, over the lifetime of a policy, the overall change in solvency reserve is always equal to the overall change in tax reserve. Both sets of reserves begin with a value of zero at time zero. Likewise, both sets of reserves end with a value of zero upon termination or expiration of the last policy.

9.2.2.2 Permanent Differences

This book illustrates permanent differences that are due to nontaxable investment income. This does not mean that other permanent differences are not significant. Ignoring them could result in inadequate pricing. Here are some examples of permanent differences:

- Investment income from certain kinds of investments may be nontaxable or taxed at a lower rate, such as stock dividends, capital gains, or interest on certain types of government bonds, such as municipal bonds in the U.S.

- Tax credits may be available for certain expenditures such as research and development.

- Certain expenses that are politically unpopular may not be deductible, such as business entertainment expenses.

For nontaxable investment income, we will assume we can precalculate the portion of each year's investment income that will be nontaxable. Investment income that is taxed at a lower rate can be handled by treating a portion of the investment income as fully taxable and the remainder as nontaxable.

For nondeductible expenses, a similar approach could be taken: The nondeductible portion of each year's expenses could be precalculated, and expenses could be adjusted. This is left as an exercise at the end of the chapter.

9.2.2.3 Capital Gains and Losses

Some taxing jurisdictions have unique items in their tax laws and regulations. In many instances, these items can be ignored when pricing a product. However, to the extent these items are significant for the product being priced or from an overall company perspective, you may want to reflect the impact of these items. One such example might be the taxation of capital gains and losses.

Under certain situations, capital gains and losses can create both timing differences and permanent differences. For example, in the U.S. realized capital gains are immediately taxable, but capital losses are deductible only against capital gains. If a company incurs large capital losses in a year, it may not receive a tax deduction for the capital losses if there are not sufficient capital gains to offset the capital losses. However, the company can carry forward any unused capital losses to offset taxes on capital gains over the next three years. If the unused capital losses are used within three years, then we have a timing difference, as illustrated in Table 9.2.2. However, if the unused capital losses expire before they can be used, then a permanent difference is created.

Table 9.2.2 Tax Treatment of Capital Losses

Year	Capital Gains	Capital Losses	Loss CarryFwd[a]	Taxable Income[b]	Taxes Paid[c]	After-Tax Income[d]
		Assuming Tax Losses Must Be Carried Forward				
1	0.00	50.00	50.00	0.00	0.00	−50.00
2	40.00	0.00	10.00	0.00	0.00	40.00
3	75.00	0.00	0.00	65.00	26.00	49.00
Sum	115.00	50.00		65.00	26.00	39.00
PV at 8%					20.64	26.90
		Assuming Tax Losses Are Immediately Deductible				
1	0.00	50.00		−50.00	−20.00	−30.00
2	40.00	0.00		40.00	16.00	24.00
3	75.00	0.00		75.00	30.00	45.00
Sum	115.00	50.00		65.00	26.00	39.00
PV at 8%					19.01	28.52

Note: Tax rate = 40%
[a] Loss CarryFwd = max (0, Previous Loss Carryforward − Capital Gains + Capital Losses)
[b] Taxable Income = Capital Gains − Capital Losses + Change in Loss Carryforward
[c] Taxes Paid = Taxable Income × Tax Rate
[d] After-tax Income = Capital Gains − Capital Losses − Taxes Paid

The impact of deferring the deductibility of capital losses is illustrated in Table 9.2.2. The first example in the table illustrates capital losses being carried forward and then offset by future capital gains. The second example illustrates capital losses that are fully deductible in the year incurred. Although total taxes and after-tax earnings over the three-year period are the same, the deferred deductibility of capital losses results in a loss of investment income.

In Table 9.2.2 the first section shows capital losses that are not immediately deductible. They are not fully deducted until the third year, producing a present value of after-tax income of 26.90. The second section shows capital losses that are immediately deductible, resulting in a present value of after-tax income of 28.52, which is 6% higher than 26.90. If some of the capital losses expired before they could be deducted, the difference would be more dramatic.

9.2.2.4 Formulas for Taxable Earnings

Taxable earnings will be calculated as pre-tax solvency earnings plus permanent and timing differences. Permanent differences will be calculated as nontaxable investment income. Timing differences will be calculated as the difference between the increase in tax reserves and the increase in solvency reserves.

Let

$$
\begin{aligned}
\text{TimingDiff}(t) = {}& \text{Timing difference between solvency earnings} \\
& \text{and taxable earnings in year } t, \text{ per unit issued} \\
\text{NonTaxInvPct}(t) = {}& \text{Percentage of investment income that is} \\
& \text{nontaxable} \\
\text{PermDiff}(t) = {}& \text{Permanent difference between solvency} \\
& \text{earnings and taxable earnings in year } t, \text{ per} \\
& \text{unit issued} \\
\text{TaxableEarn}(t) = {}& \text{Taxable earnings, per unit issued} \\
\text{EarnTaxRate}(t) = {}& \text{Tax rate applied to taxable earnings.}
\end{aligned}
$$

Then,

$$
\text{TimingDiff}(t) = \text{SolvResIncr}(t) - \text{TaxResIncr}(t), \tag{9.2.5}
$$
$$
\text{PermDiff}(t) = -\text{InvIncome}(t)\,\text{NonTaxInvPct}(t), \tag{9.2.6}
$$
$$
\begin{aligned}
\text{TaxableEarn}(t) = {}& \text{PreTaxSolvEarn}(t) + \text{TimingDiff}(t) \\
& + \text{PermDiff}(t).
\end{aligned} \tag{9.2.7}
$$

Substituting using Formulas 9.2.5, 9.2.1, and 9.2.3 produces two alternative formulas for taxable earnings:

$$
\begin{aligned}
\text{TaxableEarn}(t) = {}& \text{Prem}(t) + \text{InvIncome}(t) - \text{Ben}(t) - \text{Exp}(t) \\
& - \text{TaxResIncr}(t) + \text{PermDiff}(t),
\end{aligned} \tag{9.2.8}
$$
$$
\begin{aligned}
\text{TaxableEarn}(t) = {}& \text{ProdCashFlow}(t) + \text{InvIncome}(t) \\
& - \text{TaxResIncr}(t) + \text{PermDiff}(t).
\end{aligned} \tag{9.2.9}
$$

Note the similarity between the formulas for taxable earnings and pre-tax earnings. There is no adjustment to investment income (other than permanent differences) as we move from pre-tax earnings to taxable earnings. This is because investment income is earned on assets that are based on the amount of solvency reserves, not tax reserves.

9.2.2.5 Earnings Tax Rate

Earnings taxes can be levied at more than one level of government. For example, a company may be taxed on earnings at both the national level and the state or provincial level. If the calculation of taxable earnings is the same or similar at both levels, the two tax rates can be combined. If taxable earnings are sufficiently different, it may be necessary to perform separate tax calculations for each level.

Some jurisdictions have progressive tax rates that increase with the size of the company. Assets, taxable earnings, or other measures may determine the size of the company. Some jurisdictions have tax rates that vary by product type.

When more than one tax rate can apply to taxable earnings, you should use the tax rate that is most likely to apply to the additional taxable earnings that the product is expected to generate.

9.2.2.6 Tax on Earnings

Let

$$\text{TaxOnEarn}(t) = \text{Tax on earnings, per unit issued}$$
$$\text{EarnTaxRate}(t) = \text{Tax rate applied to earnings.}$$

The tax on earnings is calculated by applying the appropriate tax rate to taxable earnings:

$$\text{TaxOnEarn}(t) = \text{TaxableEarn}(t)\ \text{EarnTaxRate}(t). \tag{9.2.10}$$

From the insurance company's perspective, it is desirable for taxable earnings to be as low as possible, in order to minimize taxes. However, the best that usually can be hoped for is for taxable earnings to be no greater than pre-tax solvency earnings. This is the case when there are no timing differences or permanent differences.

9.2.2.7 Tax Losses

In the first policy year, most insurance products generate a pre-tax loss, that is, negative pre-tax solvency earnings. This usually results in a tax loss (negative taxable earnings). Generally, tax losses are immediately deductible only to the extent that they offset taxable gains (positive taxable earnings). For example, suppose a company is pricing a new product, with anticipated tax losses in the first year of 25 million. The full 25 million will not be deductible unless the company has at least 25 million of taxable gains from other business. For a large, established company with a strong and steady flow of earnings, this may not be a concern. However, for small, fast-growing, or new companies, there often will not be enough taxable gains to offset all of the tax losses.

Table 9.2.3 illustrates two different treatments of tax losses. Both illustrations have the same pattern of taxable earnings.

Table 9.2.3 Tax Impact of Deductibility of Losses

Year	Preliminary Taxable Income	TaxLoss Carry Forward[a]	Taxable Income	Taxes Paid
\multicolumn{5}{Assuming No Immediate Deductibility of Losses}
1	−35	35	0	0
2	5	30	0	0
3	15	15	0	0
4	20	0	5	2.00
5	25	0	25	10.00
Sum	30		30	12.00
PV at 8%				8.28
\multicolumn{5}{Assuming Immediate Deductibility of Losses}
1	−35		−35	−14.00
2	5		5	2.00
3	15		15	6.00
4	20		20	8.00
5	25		25	10.00
Sum			30	12.00
PV at 8%			30	6.20

Note: Tax rate = 40%
[a] TaxLoss CarryForward = max (0, Previous TaxLoss CarryForward − Preliminary Taxable Income)

The first illustration assumes that initial tax losses *are not* immediately deductible. The initial tax losses are carried forward and offset against future taxable gains. In this case taxes are not paid until year 4, which is preceded by three years of zero taxes. The present value of the entire stream of taxes at 8% is 8.28.

The second illustration assumes that initial tax losses *are* immediately deductible, generating a negative tax of (14.00) in the first year. The present value at 8% of the entire stream of taxes is 6.20, significantly lower than the present value of 8.28 when tax losses were not immediately deductible.

When tax losses are not immediately deductible, the investment in the business will be greater. A higher investment leads to lower returns on the business. While this discussion of tax losses has focused on the earnings tax, the same principles often apply to other forms of tax, such as tax on $I - E$ (discussed below) and tax on capital.

9.3 Tax on Investment Income Less Expenses $(I - E)$

Taxation of insurance companies based on investment income less expenses $(I - E)$ is the oldest basis for taxing insurance companies. Taxing an insurance company on $I - E$ is a way to indirectly tax the policyowner as the cash values build up within an insurance contract. Here is how the tax on $I - E$ accomplishes this:

Rearranging the terms of Formula 9.2.1, we find that $I - E$ equals:

$$\text{InvIncome}(t) - \text{Exp}(t) = \text{Ben}(t) + \text{SolvResIncr}(t) \\ - \text{Prem}(t) + \text{PreTaxSolvEarn}(t).$$

$$(9.3.1)$$

The solvency reserve increase can be thought of as future policyowner benefits. Collectively, then, "benefits plus reserve increases less premiums" represents the net amount of value created for all policyowners during the year. From this we see that taxing the insurance company on $I - E$ is equivalent to taxing policyowners on their increase in value *and* taxing the insurance company on its pre-tax solvency earnings.

There is a worldwide movement away from the $I - E$ method in order to make life insurance taxation more comparable to taxation of other financial institutions. Australia, Canada, and the United States have all moved from taxing $I - E$ to taxing earnings.

Other than term insurance, most life insurance contracts build cash values for the policyowner. In most countries, the policyowner is not taxed as cash values build up. The tax on $I - E$ is intended to indirectly tax this cash value buildup.

When insurance companies are taxed on earnings and not $I - E$, the policyowner often is taxed when the policy is surrendered. The amount taxed at surrender is usually the amount, if any, by which the cash surrender value exceeds cumulative premiums paid. While the cash value remains within the policy, the policyowner is not taxed. The cash value buildup and unrealized capital gains on stocks are not taxed for a similar reason: To tax an unrealized gain can force the owner to sell the stock or surrender the policy in order to pay the tax. Forcing people to terminate their insurance would not be in the public's best interest.

When insurance companies are taxed on $I - E$ and not earnings, the policyowner is usually not taxed on cash value in excess of premiums paid when the policy is surrendered. This is because the insurance company has already paid the tax on the increase in value through the tax on $I - E$. For the same reason the policyholder is not taxed as the cash value builds up.

The tax on $I - E$ is governed by detailed rules that define which forms of investment income are taxable and which expenses are deductible. We will assume that we can precalculate the percentage of investment income that is taxable each year, as well as the percentage of expenses that are deductible each year. In some jurisdictions, only investment-related expenses are deductible in the calculation of $I - E$, which is a much more onerous approach to indirectly taxing policyowners.

Let

$$IETaxInvIncPct(t) = \text{Percentage of investment income subject to the tax on } I - E$$

$$IETaxInvInc(t) = \text{Investment income subject to the tax on } I - E, \text{ per unit issued}$$

$$IEDeductExpPct(t) = \text{The percentage of expenses deductible in the tax on } I - E$$

$$IEDeductExp(t) = \text{Expenses deductible in the tax on } I - E, \text{ per unit issued}$$

$$IETaxRate(t) = \text{Tax rate applicable to } I - E$$

$$TaxOnIE(t) = \text{Tax on } I - E, \text{ per unit issued.}$$

Investment income subject to the tax on $I - E$ can be computed in a number of different ways:

- Equal to 100% of investment income
- Equal to investment income times the ratio of solvency reserves to total assets
- Equal to investment income times the ratio of tax reserves to total assets
- Equal to investment income times the ratio of cash values to total assets.

Also, the ratio could be based on invested assets instead of total assets. We will assume that taxable investment income can be calculated as a ratio times investment income:

$$IETaxInvInc(t) = InvIncome(t) \ IETaxInvIncPct(t). \qquad (9.3.2)$$

If only investment-related expenses are deductible, then $IEDeductExpPct(t)$ equals zero. This is because investment income is already calculated net of investment-related expenses, since interest rates are net of investment-related expenses. We will assume that deductible expenses can be calculated as a percentage of total expenses:

$$IEDeductExp(t) = Exp(t) \ IEDeductExpPct(t) \qquad (9.3.3)$$

$$TaxOnIE(t) = (IETaxInvInc(t) - IEDeductExp(t)) \ IETaxRate(t). \qquad (9.3.4)$$

9.4 Tax on Capital

A company's capital may be taxed as a form of minimum tax, an additional tax or, in the case of mutual companies in the U.S., as a tax on imputed stockholder dividends. In any case, such a tax is calculated as a percentage of capital and is usually in the form of a permanent difference. In the U.S., this tax is popularly referred to as the *mutual company surplus tax.*

There may be special rules within the tax code to define capital for tax purposes. We will refer to this as *tax capital.* When pricing a particular product, one must understand these rules and be prepared to adjust the pricing formulas to approximate this capital. In this way the proper amount of tax will be charged to the particular product being priced.

Tax capital may bear little resemblance to required capital or actual capital.

Let

$$\text{CapTaxRate}(t) = \text{The tax rate on capital}$$
$$\text{TaxCapital}(t) = \text{Tax capital, per unit issued}$$
$$\text{TaxOnCap}(t) = \text{The tax on capital, per unit issued.}$$

Then

$$\text{TaxOnCap}(t) = \text{TaxCapital}(t)\,\text{CapTaxRate}(t). \tag{9.4.1}$$

9.5 Total Tax

Other financial institutions are quick to point out any tax advantage that life insurance products enjoy over their products. In particular, if life insurance products can build up cash values with no current taxation and other types of financials products do not escape current taxation, pressure to change the tax system may be brought to bear. As a result, some countries that have adopted a tax on earnings have not totally abandoned the tax on $I - E$. This is done by setting the total tax equal to the greater of the tax on earnings or the tax on $I - E$.

To summarize, most jurisdictions use one of the following three bases for insurance company taxes:

- Tax on earnings
- Tax on $I - E$
- Greater of tax on earnings or tax on $I - E$

If there is a tax on capital, it may be in addition to the above tax or act as a minimum tax.

Let

Tax(t) = Total tax, per unit issued.

Tax(t) is calculated using the formula that corresponds to one of the above three bases for insurance company taxes:

$$\text{Tax}(t) = \text{TaxOnEarn}(t), \tag{9.5.1}$$
$$\text{Tax}(t) = \text{TaxOnIE}(t), \tag{9.5.2}$$
$$\text{Tax}(t) = \max(\text{TaxOnEarn}(t), \text{TaxOnIE}(t)). \tag{9.5.3}$$

If there is a tax on capital, Tax(t) is adjusted in one of two ways. If the tax on capital is an additional tax, then

$$\text{Tax}(t) = \text{Tax}(t) + \text{TaxOnCap}(t). \tag{9.5.4}$$

If the tax on capital is a minimum tax, then

$$\text{Tax}(t) = \max(\text{Tax}(t), \text{TaxOnCap}(t)). \tag{9.5.5}$$

Some jurisdictions do not levy corporate taxes. Instead, annual corporate licensing fees are usually assessed. If a company sets up a subsidiary in a jurisdiction that has no corporate taxes, care should be taken: The company's home country may impute tax on the earnings of the subsidiary.

9.6 Deferred Taxes

When there are significant differences between taxable earnings and stockholder earnings, some financial reporting accounting principles (such as U.S. GAAP) require the insurance company to accrue taxes that are based on stockholder earnings rather than the tax it actually pays. Consider Example 9.6.1:

Example 9.6.1

The insurance company is taxed on its solvency earnings at a rate of 40%. In the early years, stockholder earnings significantly exceed solvency earnings because of the deferral of significant acquisition costs, which is purely a timing difference. In the later years, the situation is reversed, and solvency earnings significantly exceed stockholder earnings.

GAAP

Year	Pre-Tax Solvency Earnings	Taxable Earnings	Taxes Currently Payable	Pre-Tax Stockholder Earnings	Taxes as a Percentage of Stockholder Earnings
1	100	100	40	300	13%
2	200	200	80	350	23
3	300	300	120	400	30
4	400	400	160	450	36
5	500	500	200	500	40
6	600	600	240	550	44
7	700	700	280	600	47
8	800	800	320	650	49
9	900	900	360	700	51
Sum	4,500	4,500	1,800	4,500	40

Note: Tax rate = 40%

You can see that taxes paid as a percentage of stockholder earnings range from 13% to 51%. Does this make sense? For some financial reporting accounting principles, the answer is "No."

Solvency earnings (low, take out all acq. costs)
Taxable Earnings (Solv. earnings + Δ Solv Rsvs$_{INCR}$ – Δ Tax Rsvs$_{INCR}$
   – Investment Income (% of Inv. Inc. that is not taxable)
Stockholder earnings (higher, some acq. costs are deferred, not as conservative mortality)

To correct the nonsensical situation in Example 9.6.1, some accounting principles apply the income tax rate to pre-tax stockholder earnings (adjusted for any permanent differences) to determine the taxes to be accrued. The amount of accrued taxes for the accounting period less the taxes currently payable is referred to as the *provision for deferred taxes.* In other words, if actual taxes paid are less than pre-tax stockholder earnings times the tax rate, the difference is accounted for as tax to be paid later, that is, a deferred tax.

The *deferred tax liability* is the cumulative sum of all past provisions for deferred taxes, if that amount is positive. The *deferred tax asset*, which is less common, is the cumulative sum of all past provisions for deferred taxes, if that amount is negative, with the sign changed from negative to positive, to change from a liability to an asset.

If accrued taxes exceed taxes currently payable, then the provision for deferred taxes increases the deferred tax liability or reduces the deferred tax asset. If taxes currently payable exceed accrued taxes, then the provision for deferred taxes is negative, and it decreases the deferred tax liability or increases the deferred tax asset.

Example 9.6.2 builds on Example 9.6.1 to illustrate the provision for deferred taxes and the deferred tax liability.

Example 9.6.2

actually.
s/b paid

Year	Pre-Tax Stockholder Earnings	Taxes Currently Payable	Accrued Taxes	Provision for Deferred Taxes (Liability)	Deferred Tax Liability
1	300	40	120	80	80
2	350	80	140	60	140
3	400	120	160	40	180
4	450	160	180	20	200
5	500	200	200	0	200
6	550	240	220	−20	180
7	600	280	240	−40	140
8	650	320	260	−60	80
9	700	360	280	−80	0
Sum	4,500	1,800	1,800	0	

Note: Tax rate = 40%; accrued tax as a percentage of stockholder earnings in all cases is 40%.

By using accrued taxes and deferred taxes, the tax rate on pre-tax stockholder earnings becomes a level 40%.

The following definitions and formulas assume that deferred taxes apply only to taxes on earnings and not to taxes on $I - E$ or capital. This is done for simplicity. Accounting for taxes can be much more complex than the following presentation.

Let

$$\text{AccruedTax}(t) = \text{Taxes accrued, equal to the tax rate on earnings}$$
times pre-tax stockholder earnings adjusted for permanent differences

$$\text{DefTaxProv}(t) = \text{Provision for deferred taxes, equal to accrued}$$
taxes less taxes currently payable

$\qquad$ DefTaxLiab(t) = Deferred tax liability, equal to the cumulative sum of past and current year provisions for deferred taxes. If the cumulative sum is negative, we will allow the deferred tax liability to be negative and not bother to change it to a positive deferred tax asset.

Then

$$\text{AccruedTax}(t) = (\text{PreTaxStockEarn}(t) \\ + \text{PermDiff}(t))\, \text{EarnTaxRate}(t), \qquad (9.6.1)$$

$$\text{DefTaxProv}(t) = \text{AccruedTax}(t) - \text{TaxOnEarn}(t), \qquad (9.6.2)$$

$$\text{DefTaxLiab}(t) = \text{DefTaxLiab}(t - 1) + \text{DefTaxProv}(t). \qquad (9.6.3)$$

In the formulas above, the provision for deferred taxes is calculated first, with the calculation of the deferred tax liability following. It is possible and, in some cases, preferable to calculate the deferred tax liability first.

Using Formulas 9.2.7, 9.2.10, and 9.6.1, we can rearrange Formula 9.6.2 to better understand the provision for deferred taxes:

$$\begin{aligned} \text{DefTaxProv}(t) \\ = (\text{PreTaxStockEarn}(t) &+ \text{PermDiff}(t))\, \text{EarnTaxRate}(t) \\ - (\text{PreTaxSolvEarn}(t) &+ \text{PermDiff}(t) \\ + \text{TimingDiff}(t))\, &\text{EarnTaxRate}(t) \\ = (\text{PreTaxStockEarn}(t) &- \text{PreTaxSolvEarn}(t) \\ - \text{TimingDiff}(t))\, &\text{EarnTaxRate}(t). \qquad (9.6.4) \end{aligned}$$

If the difference between pre-tax stockholder and pre-tax solvency earnings is due solely to reserve differences and the timing difference is entirely the difference between increases in solvency and tax reserves (as we assumed in Formula 9.2.5), then we have

$$\begin{aligned} \text{DefTaxProv}(t) \\ = (-\text{EarnResIncr}(t) &+ \text{SolvResIncr}(t) - \text{SolvResIncr}(t) \\ + \text{TaxResIncr}(t))\, &\text{EarnTaxRate}(t), \text{ or} \\ \text{DefTaxProv}(t) \\ = (\text{TaxResIncr}(t) &- \text{EarnResIncr}(t))\, \text{EarnTaxRate}(t). \qquad (9.6.5) \end{aligned}$$

Because the cumulative sum of reserve increases is equal to the reserve at the end of the year, the deferred tax liability can be calculated directly as the tax rate times the current difference between tax and earnings reserves:

$$\text{DefTaxLiab}(t) = (\text{TaxRes}(t) - \text{EarnRes}(t))\ \text{EarnTaxRate}(t).$$

$$(9.6.6)$$

More generally, the deferred tax liability can be calculated as the sum of all future timing differences times the tax rate to be paid going forward. (Note that past timing differences will generally equal future timing differences, since all reserves and other timing differences eventually go to zero.) In fact, some accounting principles (such as U.S. GAAP) define the deferred tax liability in this way. When the deferred tax liability is calculated directly like this, the provision for deferred taxes is calculated as the increase in deferred tax liability from one year to the next. In other words, the provision is calculated from the change in liability rather than the other way around (as Formulas 9.6.1 through 9.6.3 do).

Calculating the deferred tax liability first has the strong advantage of keeping the deferred tax liability in line with current reality. For example, if future tax rates were changed to zero (as they should be for life insurance companies), the deferred tax liability would be calculated as zero using Formula 9.6.6. When the deferred tax liability is calculated as cumulative timing differences times the future tax rate (or, equivalently, future timing differences times the future tax rate), a change in tax rate is immediately reflected.

However, if the deferred tax liability is calculated as the sum of *past* provisions for deferred tax, this logical connection does not exist. In this case a company could end up with a deferred tax liability that has no relation to the future taxes it expects to pay. This is exactly what happened in the early 1980s in the U.S., when the top corporate tax rate was lowered from 48% to 35%. Up until that time, U.S. GAAP specified that the deferred tax liability was to be calculated as the accumulation of past provisions for deferred taxes. With future tax rates reduced from 48% to 35%, existing deferred tax liabilities no longer made sense. This prompted the change in U.S. GAAP to calculate deferred tax liabilities based on future differences times future tax rates.

If future changes in tax rates are known at the time of pricing, then Formulas 9.6.1, 9.6.2, and 9.6.3 would not be appropriate. Instead, the correct approach would be to calculate deferred tax liabilities first and use them to back into the provision for deferred tax. This is done in Exercise 9.6. However, in most cases, future changes in tax rates cannot be anticipated at the time of pricing, so Formulas 9.6.1, 9.6.2, and 9.6.3 will usually suffice.

9.7 Pricing Example

The following tables are this chapter's contribution to the Chapters 4–11 pricing example. Tables 9.7.1 and 9.7.2 are similar to Tables 6.7.1 and 6.7.2, showing the calculation of tax reserves. In the pricing example, the tax reserves differ from the solvency reserves only by the valuation interest rate. Solvency reserves were calculated assuming a 5% interest rate, while the tax reserves assumed a 7.50% interest rate.

Table 9.7.1 Tax Reserve Calculation Factors

t	DiscFactor	q	p	SurvFactor
0	1.00000			1.00000
1	0.93023	0.00455	0.99545	0.99545
2	0.86533	0.00492	0.99508	0.99055
3	0.80496	0.00532	0.99468	0.98528
4	0.74880	0.00574	0.99426	0.97963
5	0.69656	0.00621	0.99379	0.97354
6	0.64796	0.00671	0.99329	0.96701
7	0.60275	0.00730	0.99270	0.95995
8	0.56070	0.00796	0.99204	0.95231
9	0.52158	0.00871	0.99129	0.94402
10	0.48519	0.00956	0.99044	0.93499

Note: For all *t*, Tax Reserve Interest Rate = 7.50%.

Table 9.7.2 Calculation of Tax Reserves

Duration	Discounting Factors for		PVFP	PVFB	TaxRes_pu	TaxRes
	Premiums	Benefits				
0	46.92671	42.66223				
1	40.42671	38.42967	43.65736	41.50073	1.81075	1.59159
2	34.40771	34.19161	40.14166	39.88954	3.39577	2.77107
3	28.83619	29.94968	36.35821	37.76215	4.70801	3.64138
4	23.68095	25.71482	32.28287	35.05553	5.70637	4.18135
5	18.91291	21.47731	27.88979	31.67137	6.31608	4.38295
6	14.50506	17.24452	23.14935	27.52139	6.47575	4.34381
7	10.43225	12.98956	18.02967	22.44938	6.05816	3.92685
8	6.67125	8.70512	12.49385	16.30285	4.94439	3.09589
9	3.20049	4.37878	6.50000	8.89302	2.98371	1.80392
10	0.00000	0.00000	0.00000	0.00000	0.00000	0.00000

Note: NetPremRatio $= 0.90912$.

Taxable earnings are calculated after pre-tax earnings. Table 9.7.3 calculates pre-tax solvency earnings, using solvency reserves as the basis for the calculation. Prem(t), Ben(t), and Exp(t) are from Chapter 5, adjusted for reinsurance in Chapter 7. InvIncome(t) is from Chapter 8, and SolvResIncr(t) is from Chapter 6, with adjustments for reinsurance reserves from Chapter 7.

Table 9.7.3 Calculation of Pre-Tax Solvency Earnings

t	Prem	InvIncome	Ben	Exp	SolvRes	SolvResIncr	PreTaxSolvEarn
1	6.50000	-0.49820	0.88186	13.24434	1.20555	1.20555	-9.32995
2	5.30280	0.33445	1.14013	1.24852	2.42783	1.22228	2.02632
3	4.79308	0.38541	1.42222	1.01597	3.29951	0.87169	1.86862
4	4.45120	0.43839	1.60527	0.69900	3.81691	0.51740	2.06792
5	4.14194	0.45119	1.73129	0.66222	3.97754	0.16063	2.03899
6	3.85872	0.44872	1.81775	0.53242	3.87963	-0.09791	2.05519
7	3.67154	0.42653	1.91884	0.51466	3.39682	-0.48280	2.14738
8	3.48560	0.37729	2.02467	0.49732	2.50413	-0.89269	2.23359
9	3.29418	0.29818	2.15280	0.48401	1.16369	-1.34045	2.29960
10	3.09290	0.18589	2.31347	0.46387	0.00000	-1.16369	1.66513

Table 9.7.4 follows the formulas derived in this chapter to convert pre-tax solvency earnings into taxable earnings, and then calculates tax on those earnings using a 38% tax rate. For simplicity, we assume that the reinsurance tax reserve is the same as the reinsurance solvency reserve.

Table 9.7.4 Calculation of Tax on Earnings

t	SolvResIncr	TaxRes	TaxResIncr	TimingDiff	TaxableEarn	TaxOnEarn
1	1.20555	1.11639	1.11639	0.08915	−9.24080	−3.51150
2	1.22228	2.29481	1.17841	0.04386	2.07018	0.78667
3	0.87169	3.15393	0.85912	0.01257	1.88118	0.71485
4	0.51740	3.68358	0.52965	−0.01226	2.05566	0.78115
5	0.16063	3.87325	0.18966	−0.02903	2.00995	0.76378
6	−0.09791	3.81150	−0.06174	−0.03617	2.01902	0.76723
7	−0.48280	3.36698	−0.44453	−0.03828	2.10911	0.80146
8	−0.89269	2.50548	−0.86150	−0.03120	2.20239	0.83691
9	−1.34045	1.17887	−1.32661	−0.01384	2.28576	0.86859
10	−1.16369	0.00000	−1.17887	0.01519	1.68032	0.63852

Note: For all t, EarnTaxRate $= 0.38$.

9.8 Exercises

Exercise 9.1

Explain what is meant by "timing differences" and "permanent differences." Which type of difference has a greater impact on taxes over the life of a policy? Which is more important?

Exercise 9.2

If a country enacted new legislation that significantly decreased the tax rate on life insurance company earnings in five years, what impact would you expect this to have on life insurance product design?

Exercise 9.3

If your company has cumulative tax losses that are in danger of expiring in a few years, what impact should this have on the design of the products your company sells?

Exercise 9.4

Assuming the nondeductible percentage of each year's expenses is NonDedExpPct(t), expand Formula 9.2.6 for permanent differences to reflect nondeductible expenses.

Exercise 9.5

If a company is taxed on total investment income less total expenses, what impact will this have on how the company is run and the types of products sold?

Exercise 9.6

As explained at the end of Section 9.6, deferred taxes are best handled by calculating the deferred tax liability directly (as in Formula 9.6.6) and then calculating the provision for deferred taxes as the change in deferred tax liability. Using this approach in combination with Examples 9.6.1 and 9.6.2, and the fact that past timing differences also equal future timing differences to be released, what impact would the following occurrences have on the provision for deferred taxes and the deferred tax liability for year 5?

a. A reduction in the tax rate to 20% for years 5 and later.

b. A reduction in the tax rate to 35% for year 5, 30% for year 6, 25% for year 7, and 20% for years 8 and later, with all of these tax rates first becoming known at the beginning of year 5.

Exercise 9.7

The formulas in this chapter assume taxes are payable at the end of the policy year. Develop revised formulas for InvIncome(t) (from Chapter 8) that reflect taxes payable at the middle of the policy year, in terms of the following notation:

TaxRate(t) = The tax rate that applies to a small change in investment income. This will equal either EarnTaxRate(t) or IETaxRate(t), depending on the tax base that applies to the company.

InvIncDecr(t) = The decrease in investment income caused by Taxes(t) being paid at the middle of the policy year

TaxDecr(t) = The decrease in taxes caused by InvIncDecr(t).

Assume the decrease in investment income is equal to a half-year's interest times (a) less (b) where (a) equals taxes calculated before reflecting any decrease in investment income due to taxes and (b) equals the decrease in investment income due to taxes being paid at the middle of the policy year.

Assume that taxes are decreased by the lost investment income times the applicable tax rate.

There is a circular relationship here. By paying taxes earlier, investment income is lost. Lost investment income leads to lower taxes. Lower taxes result in increased investment income. Increased investment income leads to higher taxes.

Hint: Develop formulas for InvIncDecr(t) and TaxDecr(t) in terms of each other and Taxes(t), InvIntRateMid(t), and TaxRate(t). You can then solve the two equations for the two unknowns, InvIncDecr(t) and TaxDecr(t). Once you have isolated the impacts of the circular relationship, you can finalize Taxes(t) and InvIncome(t) by making the following adjustments:

$$\text{Taxes}(t) = \text{Taxes}(t) - \text{TaxDecr}(t)$$
$$\text{InvIncome}(t) = \text{InvIncome}(t) - \text{InvIncDecr}(t).$$

9.9 Answers

Answer 9.1

Timing differences are differences between taxable earnings and reported earnings that eventually reverse themselves over time. They are normally caused by a difference in the valuation of assets and liabilities between tax standards and solvency or earnings standards. Permanent differences are differences between taxable earnings and reported earnings that will not reverse themselves over time.

The last two questions have no general answer. The answer is highly dependent on the tax regime of the country. For example, in the U.S. in 1999, timing differences for individual life insurance tended to be massive compared to permanent differences.

Answer 9.2

You could expect new product designs to reduce profits in the early policy years and shift them to later years. For example, commissions might be increased or accelerated to help sell more policies while tax rates are still high. This would allow acquisition costs to be deducted at a high tax rate and most renewal earnings to be taxed at a lower rate. Also, early year cash values might be improved to help sales and to increase reserves in the early years.

Answer 9.3

Generally, your company should offer products with low new business strain and the highest possible profits in the early policy years, in order to make use of the cumulative tax losses before they expire. However, the answer can best be determined by projecting the entire company's results for several years into the future. This will allow you to see the interaction of the company's tax losses being carried forward with overhead expenses, profits from business already in force, and the impact of various new business strategies.

Answer 9.4

$$\text{PermDiff}(t) = \text{Exp}(t)\ \text{NonDedExpPct}(t)$$
$$- \text{InvIncome}(t)\ \text{NonTaxInvPct}(t).$$

Answer 9.5

As much as is feasible, the company will attempt to keep investment income in balance with expenses. If investment income is much greater than expenses, there will be a tendency to encourage more high-expense and low-investment-income types of products, such as term insurance or health insurance. If expenses are much greater than investment income, there will be a tendency to sell more products with high investment income and low expenses, such as investment and pension products.

Answer 9.6

a. Future timing differences are equal to 500, based on the future differences between taxable earnings and pre-tax stockholders earnings in Example 9.6.1. Therefore, the deferred tax liability at the end of year 5 is equal to 20% of 500, or 100. This means the provision for deferred taxes for year 5 should be $100 - 200 = -100$. In other words, half of the previous deferred tax liability is released because of the tax rate being cut in half.

b. Looking at Example 9.6.1, we see future timing differences of 50, 100, 150, and 200 for years 6, 7, 8, and 9. Applying the tax rates of 30%, 25%, 20%, and 20% for these four years to these timing differences, we obtain a deferred tax liability at the end of year 5 equal to $50(30\%) + 100(25\%) + 350(20\%) = 110$. The provision for deferred taxes for year 5 is $110 - 200 = -90$.

Answer 9.7

$$\text{InvIncDecr}(t) = (\text{Taxes}(t) - \text{TaxDecr}(t))\,\text{InvIntRateMid}(t),$$
$$\text{TaxDecr}(t) = \text{InvIncDecr}(t)\,\text{TaxRate}(t).$$

We can solve the above two formulas for $\text{InvIncDecr}(t)$ and $\text{TaxDecr}(t)$ in terms of $\text{Taxes}(t)$, $\text{InvIntRateMid}(t)$, and $\text{TaxRate}(t)$, as follows:

$$\text{InvIncDecr}(t) = \frac{\text{Taxes}(t)}{\text{TaxRate}(t) + 1/\text{InvIntRateMid}(t)},$$
$$\text{TaxDecr}(t) = \frac{\text{Taxes}(t)}{1 + 1/(\text{InvIntRateMid}(t)\,\text{TaxRate}(t))}.$$

9.10 Appendix

Calculation of DAC Taxes

In certain countries, in particular the U.S., the taxing authorities have recognized the often large difference between solvency and stockholder earnings. This difference is sometimes cited as one reason for additional taxes on insurance companies, to help raise tax revenues.

In the U.S., such revenue-raising goals have resulted in the so-called *DAC Tax*. (Section 848 of the Internal Revenue Code, "Capitalization of Certain Policy Acquisition Expenses," is the actual section and name of the code.) The DAC Tax regulation reduces the amount of expenses that can be deducted. The limitation is defined as a percentage of premium, and varies by product type (see Table 9.10.1). In effect, the company pays an additional tax on each premium collected. The percentage is recovered in renewal years by amortizing the percentage out of taxable earnings over either five or ten years, depending on the size of the company.

Table 9.10.1 Percentage of Premium Subject to DAC Tax

Type of Business	Percentage of Premium
Individual Life and Individual Disability Income	7.70%
Group Life	2.05
Annuities	1.75
All Qualified Plans	0.00

The methodology used to incorporate this into pricing can best be illustrated through an example.

Although the DAC Tax regulation limits the amount of expenses that can be deducted, the calculation is normally handled by adding a percentage of premium to taxable earnings. For example, for an individual life insurance product in any given tax year, 7.70% of the gross premiums received would be added to taxable earnings. However, if the company is large enough to have to use the ten-year amortization schedule, 5% of 7.70% would be deducted from taxable earnings in the year the gross premiums were paid. Ten percent of 7.70% would be deducted for each of the next nine years, and 5% of 7.70% would be deducted ten years after the gross premiums were paid, as shown in Table 9.10.2.

Table 9.10.2 Effect of DAC Tax on Taxable Earnings*

Year	Added into Taxable Earnings	Deducted from Taxable Earnings
1	7.70%	5% of 7.70%
2–10	0.00	10% of 7.70%
11	0.00	5% of 7.70%

*As a percentage of gross premiums paid in year 1, assuming individual life business.

As you can see from Table 9.10.2, the total amount of DAC Tax added to taxable earnings over the entire period for a given year's gross premiums is zero. However, the DAC Tax accelerates taxes, which are then reversed over the next ten years. The net effect is that the company loses investment income by having to pay taxes earlier.

Although the DAC Tax concept seems simple enough, it is cumbersome to track. Each calendar year's gross premiums produces its own array of additions to taxable earnings and subtractions from taxable earnings that must be tracked. At any one time in the pricing process, up to 11 arrays of DAC Tax premium amounts have to be tracked and run through the taxable earnings formula. The calculation becomes even more cumbersome when quarterly profit calculations are performed.

DAC Tax amounts are added into taxable earnings as follows.

Let

$$\text{DACTaxAmount}(t) = \text{Amount added into taxable earnings, per unit issued}$$

$$\text{DACTaxPct} = \text{Applicable DAC Tax rate, as determined by the product type and by size of company.}$$

Then

$$\begin{aligned}
\text{DACTaxAmount}(t) = \ & \text{DACTaxPct Prem}(t) \\
& + \text{DACTaxPct Prem}(t)\ (-5\%) \\
& + \text{DACTaxPct} \sum_{r=-1}^{-9} \text{Prem}(t + r)\ (-10\%) \\
& + \text{DACTaxPct Prem}(t - 10)\ (-5\%).
\end{aligned}$$

$$(9.10.1)$$

Taxable earnings is then calculated as

$$\begin{aligned}
\text{TaxableEarn}(t) = \ & \text{PreTaxSolvEarn}(t) + \text{TimingDiff}(t) \\
& + \text{PermDiff}(t) + \text{DACTaxAmount}(t).
\end{aligned} \quad (9.10.2)$$

Note that the DAC Tax is really just a timing difference, and conceptually, is just an adjustment to the tax reserve. However, the unique aspect is that the adjustment is not based on the amount in force at a given duration (one normally thinks of the reserve as an amount per unit at a given duration), but is instead based on the amount of premium paid in the current and prior ten years.

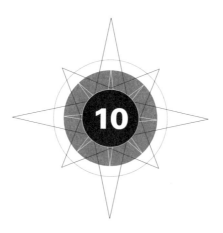

Required Capital

10.1 Introduction

What is the minimum capital necessary for an insurance company to remain solvent? The answer to this question seems simple: Assets should at least equal liabilities. This may be true in some jurisdictions, but, in general, a company needs assets to exceed liabilities by some margin in order to be a healthy, ongoing entity.

The difference between assets and liabilities is commonly referred to as *capital, equity,* or *surplus.* We will refer to it as "capital" throughout this book. Capital is available to invest in new business or to pay dividends to policyholders or stockholders of the company. However, companies are careful not to let capital levels drop below a target or minimum level, which we will refer to as *required capital.* Other names for required capital are *risk-based capital, minimum capital, minimum surplus, required surplus, capital adequacy reserve,* and *solvency margin.* Required capital is the amount of capital a company needs to withstand reasonable fluctuations in results.

The required capital formula used in pricing may come from solvency regulations, rating agencies, or a solvency model developed by the company. Most companies target a percentage of these requirements in their pricing. For example, a company might target 250% of minimum regulatory requirements. Or a company might target 150% of a rating agency's capital requirement standard. The target percentage of minimum capital requirements typically would be close to the average for the industry, unless the company wanted to be substantially better or worse than average.

When a company develops its own required capital formula, it may use sophisticated techniques to model the various risks. For example, the model could reflect the degree of asset-liability matching and project results under a variety of different scenarios. The formula may be set so that the company can withstand the various risks with, say, a 99% probability of remaining solvent.

The components of distributable earnings covered up to this part of the book have resulted purely from the cash flows and reserves for the insurance product. Premiums, expenses, and benefits are those anticipated by pricing, reserves are those established according to regulations and company standards, investment income is calculated based on the assets backing the reserves, and taxes follow from all the preceding items.

A typical insurance product produces losses in the early policy years, followed by a stream of profits in subsequent years. The losses in the early policy years can be thought of as the investment in the business. The subsequent stream of profits can be thought of as repayment of the initial investment, with interest.

The buildup of required capital in the early policy years is another part of the investment in the business. The gradual release of required capital in later policy years adds to the distributable earnings from the business. Regardless of how a company chooses to calculate required capital, the required capital standards must be understood and accurately incorporated into the pricing.

There are a variety of ways to calculate required capital. Methods vary from country to country and company to company. In general, though, most required capital formulas cover several of the following risks associated with operating an insurance company:

- Asset default risk

- Insurance risk

- Interest rate risk

- Interest spread risk

- Other risk.

This list is derived primarily from the risks that are detailed in a variety of regulatory capital formulas, as you will see in Section 10.8. The list is not exhaustive. Each company should determine the required capital formula that best applies to its situation. For example, a company may decide that the risk of increasing expenses is important enough to designate a separate expense risk component in the company's required capital formula.

10.2 Asset Default Risk

Asset default occurs when an asset permanently loses value. For example, if the issuer of a bond becomes insolvent and can no longer make payments, then the bond may be worth only a fraction of its book value. If a mortgagee can no longer make payments, then the mortgage may be worth only the value of its collateral, net of the expenses of foreclosure. When an asset defaults, the company must reduce the value of the asset shown on its books. This directly reduces capital and may also reduce earnings, depending on the accounting treatment for losses due to asset defaults.

An insurance company's assets are made up of a variety of invested assets. These assets can range from cash and government securities to corporate bonds, commercial mortgages, residential mortgages, preferred stock, common stock, and real estate. Each of these types of assets has a different default risk. In addition, each type of asset has many categories, each with its own probability of default. For example, corporate bonds on a company's balance sheet will consist of bonds ranging from low to high quality, each with a different probability of default.

Asset default risk may also include risks such as the nonpayment of reinsurance receivables, as well as guarantees and contingencies that are not included in the balance sheet.

10.2.1 Asset Default Probabilities

Asset default risk is normally measured by assigning one-year asset default probabilities to different categories of assets. The weighted average asset default probability is then obtained by summing the percentage of the company's assets in each category times the corresponding default probability for that category.

Asset default probability for a product depends on the mix of assets supporting that product. The asset default probability is normally expressed as a percentage of assets and is equal to the one-year asset default probability. The mix of assets will determine the asset default probability to be deducted when establishing the interest assumptions. For example, the mix of assets and risk probabilities in Table 10.2.1 may apply.

Recall from Chapter 8 that investment yield assumptions are normally net of investment expenses and the cost of asset defaults. The cost of default is usually only a portion of the probability of default, because not all of the defaulting asset's value is typically lost. In Table 10.2.1 a portion of 0.83%, such as 50% of 0.83%, would be deducted from the annual investment yield to reflect the impact of asset default on interest assumptions.

Table 10.2.1 Weighted Average Asset Default Probability

Asset Category	Portfolio Weight	Annual Default Probability	Weight × Probability
Government Bonds	10%	0.0%	0.00%
Corporate Bonds Rated A or Better	60	0.3	0.18
Corporate Bonds Rated BBB	10	1.5	0.15
Commercial Mortgages	20	2.5	0.50
Weighted Average Asset Default Probability			0.83%

10.2.2   Asset Default Factors

When calculating asset default risk for required capital purposes, asset default factors are used in place of asset default probabilities. These factors may be dictated by regulation, suggested by rating agencies, or adopted by company policy. Often, asset default factors are related to asset default probabilities; for example, the factors may be two times the probabilities. Weighted average asset default factors are calculated just like weighted average asset default probabilities.

When assets are assumed to equal reserves, the weighted average asset default factor can be applied to the reserves for each policy year to determine the contribution to each policy year's required capital. In Chapters 14 and 15, we will explore the dynamic modeling of assets. When assets are dynamically modeled by asset category, it is more common to apply asset default factors to each asset category. The dynamic asset model can then calculate the weighted average asset default factor based on the mix of assets at any given point of time.

There is no asset default risk associated with policy loans, because policy loans are fully collateralized by cash values and death benefits; policy loans are always repaid in full when policies are surrendered or death claims are paid. The average asset default risk is reduced by policy loans outstanding.

Let

$$\text{AssetDefRisk}(t) = \text{The asset default component of required capital, per unit issued}$$

$$\text{AssetDefFactor}(t) = \text{The weighted average asset default risk factor, expressed as a percentage of reserves net of policy loans.}$$

Then,

$$\text{AssetDefRisk}(t) = \text{AssetDefFactor}(t)\,(\text{SolvRes}(t) - \text{PolLoan}(t)).$$
$$(10.2.1)$$

Solvency reserves and policy loans would be adjusted to be net of any reinsurance impact.

10.3 Insurance Risk

Insurance risk is primarily the risk that mortality or morbidity experience exceeds the levels anticipated in pricing. This risk can result from random fluctuations or from incorrect assumptions used in pricing. The law of large numbers means that random fluctuations usually become less significant as the size of the company increases. Actually, the size of absolute fluctuations increases as company size increases, but fluctuations tend to decrease as a percentage of total claims.

Insurance risk may also include the risk of pricing assumptions for persistency, expenses, and investment income being wrong. Alternatively, these could be included with "other risk" or ignored.

Pricing assumptions are always wrong. It's a question of how wrong and in which direction. Historical studies may give you an indication of the stability or volatility of the mortality or morbidity risk. Recent changes in underwriting standards, claims practices, or policy definitions may make past experience less relevant. Changes in economic conditions, medical practices, and lifestyles may also add to the uncertainty of your pricing assumptions.

10.3.1 Mortality Risk

For required capital purposes, mortality risk is often expressed as a percentage of the company's total death benefits, net of reserves, which is the company's total net amount at risk. Because of the law of large numbers, the percentage is sometimes reduced as total net amount at risk increases. Consider this list of mortality risk factors that vary by amount:

First 500 million of amount at risk: 0.20% of amount at risk

Next 1 billion of amount at risk: 0.18% of amount at risk

Next 2.5 billion of amount at risk: 0.15% of amount at risk

Next 6 billion of amount at risk: 0.11% of amount at risk

Excess over 10 billion of amount at risk: 0.06% of amount at risk.

When mortality risk factors vary by amount as in this example, you should reflect the company's current and projected total amounts at risk when determining the appropriate mortality risk factors to use for pricing.

Let

$$\text{MortRisk}(t) = \text{The mortality risk component of required capital, per unit issued}$$
$$\text{MortFactor}(t) = \text{The mortality risk factor, expressed as a percentage of net amount at risk.}$$

Then,

$$\text{MortRisk}(t) = \text{MortFactor}(t)\,(\text{DB\_pu}(t) - \text{SolvRes\_pu}(t)) \\ \times \text{SurvFactor}(t). \tag{10.3.1}$$

Death benefits and solvency reserves would be adjusted to be net of any reinsurance impact.

10.3.2 Morbidity Risk

For required capital purposes, morbidity risk is often expressed as a percentage of premiums. This may follow from a presumption that morbidity claims will be a fairly level percentage of premiums.

Let

> MorbRisk(t) = The morbidity risk component of required
> capital, per unit issued
>
> MorbFactor(t) = The morbidity risk factor, expressed as a
> percentage of premium.

Then,

$$\text{MorbRisk}(t) = \text{MorbFactor}(t)\ \text{Prem}(t). \tag{10.3.2}$$

The premium used in the calculation would be net of any premiums reinsured.

10.4 Interest Rate Risk

Interest rate risk has three main components:

- Disintermediation risk, which is the risk of having to sell assets at a loss to fund substantial cash outflows

- Guarantee risk, which is the risk that interest rate guarantees will exceed interest rates earned, and

- Liquidity risk, which is the risk that assets cannot be sold fast enough to cover cash demands on liabilities.

10.4.1 Disintermediation Risk

Disintermediation risk is the risk of loss due to having to sell assets at depressed prices to cover cash outflows—such as surrenders, withdrawals, and policy loans—at a time when interest rates have increased and asset values have therefore decreased.

In order to credit competitive interest rates to policyowners, insurance companies will often invest in long-term investments, which typically earn higher yields than short-term investments. If policyowners can loan from, withdraw from, or surrender their policies with little or no penalty, the company may be exposed to significant interest rate risk. If interest rates rise significantly, the following could happen:

- Policyowners will be able to earn significantly higher interest rates on new life insurance policies or new investments.

- Because the company has invested long-term, it will not be able to match the higher interest rates available on new life insurance policies or new investments.

- As a result, many policyowners will decide to loan from, withdraw from, or surrender their policies in order to earn higher interest rates elsewhere.

- This will create a large, unexpected cash outflow that may force the company to sell long-term investments to generate the needed cash.

- Because interest rates are higher, the market value of long-term investments will have dropped significantly.

- The company will experience large losses when it sells large amounts of long-term investments at depressed market values to fund the cash outflows.

- Large losses may result in ratings downgrades and a general loss of confidence in the company's ability to meet its obligations, triggering further surrenders and more losses. This could lead to a downward spiral, perhaps ending in insolvency.

A well-run company will limit interest rate risk by (1) investing in assets with cash flows that closely match its liability cash flows and (2) limiting its exposure to products that allow unplanned cash flows with little or no penalty.

Since interest rate risk is closely tied to the amount of cash value available upon surrender, interest rate risk is normally expressed as a percentage of cash values or, as a close proxy, a percentage of reserves. Interest rate risk factors sometimes vary by the nature of the withdrawal options given to policyowners.

Products that allow full withdrawal without any market value adjustment are assigned the highest interest rate risk factor. Products that adjust the policyowner's available value based on current interest rates (that is, market value-adjusted products) are usually assigned lower interest rate risk factors. Here are some interest rate risk factors that vary by withdrawal and surrender charge features:

Withdrawal with no market value adjustment or surrender charge: 0.50%

Withdrawal with partial market value adjustment and no surrender charge: 0.25%

Withdrawal with partial market value adjustment and surrender charge: 0.20%

Withdrawal with full market value adjustment: 0.10%.

Interest rate risk factors may also be reduced if a significant surrender charge applies to funds withdrawn. Products that do not allow any form of withdrawal have the lowest interest rate risk factors.

10.4.2 Guarantee Risk

Another form of interest rate risk occurs when a product implicitly or explicitly guarantees interest rates. If a significant portion of the product's cash flows will be invested months or years after the guarantee is set, there is a chance that the company will not be able to earn the interest rate guaranteed. For example, in the late 1990s when current interest rates were very low in Japan, many Japanese life insurance companies earned interest rates well below their guarantees to policyholders, resulting in substantial losses throughout the industry.

10.4.3 Liquidity Risk

Liquidity risk is the risk that a company will not be able to raise the cash it needs to meet its obligations on time. This is an important risk for most life insurance companies, because most liabilities are payable on demand and most assets are invested long-term. In other words, most insurance companies are invested long but have liabilities that are potentially very short. If there is a "run on the bank," assets may have to be sold at discounted prices in order to raise cash quickly enough to fund substantial cash outflows. If the company were not able to sell assets quickly enough to meet its obligations, the company would likely be placed under regulatory supervision.

Assets are normally valued on a company's books assuming an orderly, efficient sale of those assets, or assuming they will be held to maturity. However, if a company were to attempt to sell a large portion of its assets within a short period of time, the prices that the company would receive for those assets would likely be severely depressed. This may occur because potential buyers of the assets will sense that the company is in a desperate situation and will therefore offer artificially low prices for the assets. During a liquidity crisis, a company would have little chance of being able to sell its more illiquid assets—those that require weeks or even months of time to sell at a fair price.

10.4.4   Interest Rate Risk Component

Cash values that are already loaned are not subject to further withdrawal. Also, policy loan interest rates would not normally fall below guaranteed interest rates. Therefore, interest rate risk is calculated net of policy loans. Reserves are normally used as a proxy for cash values.

Let

$\text{IntRateRisk}(t)$ = The interest rate risk component of required capital, per unit issued

$\text{IntRateFactor}(t)$ = The interest rate risk factor, expressed as a percentage of reserves net of policy loans. This factor will usually be higher if there are no penalties on unplanned cash withdrawals. If no unplanned cash withdrawals are allowed, this factor will usually be zero or close to zero.

Then,

$$\text{IntRateRisk}(t) = \text{IntRateFactor}(t)\,(\text{SolvRes}(t) - \text{PolLoan}(t)).$$

$$(10.4.1)$$

Solvency reserves and policy loans would be adjusted to be net of any reinsurance impact.

10.5 Interest Spread Risk

Interest spread risk is the risk of insufficient interest spreads due to investment and pricing decisions. This risk is in addition to asset default risk and interest rate risk.

Many insurance products are priced with an assumed spread or margin between the interest rate earned on assets backing the product and the interest rate credited (either explicitly or implicitly) to policyholders. The profitability of such products is often highly dependent on achieving the priced-for spread.

Many factors can prevent the company from meeting its priced-for spread, such as

- Communication or coordination problems between the company's investment, pricing, and administration areas
- Insufficient availability of the investment opportunities that were assumed in pricing
- Changes in the interest spread relationships between different categories of investments; for example, ten-year corporate bond interest rates may initially exceed government bond interest rates by 100 basis points (1.00%) and later exceed them by only 75 basis points (0.75%)
- Minimum interest rate guarantees in the product that may prevent a company from earning the priced-for spread if interest rates drop sufficiently
- Similar, competing products that offer attractive credited rates. The company may be forced to accept a lower spread to match competitor's credited rates, in order to minimize lapses.

Interest spread risk is normally expressed as a percentage of reserves, with reserves used as a proxy for cash values. Since products with a priced-for spread usually have a fixed spread on policy loans, interest spread risk is normally calculated net of policy loans.

Let

$$\begin{aligned}\text{IntSpreadRisk}(t) = \ &\text{The interest spread risk component of} \\ &\text{required capital, per unit issued}\end{aligned}$$

$$\begin{aligned}\text{IntSpreadFactor}(t) = \ &\text{The interest spread risk factor, as a} \\ &\text{percentage of reserves net of policy loans.} \\ &\text{The factor typically is lower for products} \\ &\text{that can adjust dividends, premiums, or} \\ &\text{other elements to compensate for reduced} \\ &\text{interest spreads.}\end{aligned}$$

Then,

$$\text{IntSpreadRisk}(t) = \text{IntSpreadFactor}(t)\,(\text{SolvRes}(t) - \text{PolLoan}(t)).$$
$$(10.5.1)$$

Solvency reserves and policy loans would be adjusted to be net of any reinsurance impact.

10.6   Other Risk

An insurance company is subject to a variety of other risks that are difficult to quantify. "Other risk" might include some of the following:

- The risk that products are mispriced (presumably because someone did not read this book!)

- The risk of lawsuits against the company (especially in the U.S.)

- The risk of a change in tax law that causes many in-force policies to lapse or causes the company to pay higher taxes than expected

- The risk of adverse publicity that causes many in-force policies to lapse

- The risk of a change in accounting or valuation regulations that diminishes the company's capital

- The risk of expenses growing faster than provided for in pricing, because of excessive inflation or the expenses of complying with onerous new regulations

- The risk of poor management or company fraud. "Poor management" can encompass a wide variety of items. In some sense, all insurance company insolvencies are due to poor management.

"Other risk" is very subjective and can be estimated in many ways. For required capital purposes, "other risk" is often expressed as a percentage of premiums. It also can be expressed in other ways, such as a percentage of assets or reserves. We will use simply a percentage of premium.

Let

$\text{OtherRisk}(t)$ = The "other risk" component of required capital, per unit issued

$\text{OtherFactor}(t)$ = The "other risk" factor, expressed as a percentage of premium.

Then,

$$\text{OtherRisk}(t) = \text{OtherFactor}(t)\,\text{Prem}(t). \qquad (10.6.1)$$

The premium used in the calculation would be net of any premium reinsured.

10.7 Impact of Required Capital on Distributable Earnings

The risk components need to be added to determine total required capital. Also, investment income needs to be calculated on the invested assets that back required capital. Therefore, an assumed interest rate must be set for the assets backing the required capital. Often, this rate is the same interest rate earned on the assets backing reserves, but this is not always the case. For example, companies may invest assets backing reserves more conservatively and take a more aggressive posture with assets backing required capital.

The change in required capital from year to year is an important part of the distributable earnings formula. Although required capital is integral to proper pricing and maintenance of a strong, healthy company, taxing authorities usually allow no tax deductions for required capital. Taxes are normally a function of the product cash flows, reserve changes, and investment income. The change in required capital is neither taxable nor tax deductible. However, the investment income earned on assets backing required capital is normally taxable.

Let

$$\text{ReqCap}(t) = \text{The total required capital, per unit issued}$$
$$\text{RCIntRate}(t) = \text{Interest rate earned on assets backing required capital}$$
$$\text{InvIncRC}(t) = \text{Investment income earned on assets backing required capital, per unit issued}$$
$$\text{TaxRate}(t) = \text{The tax rate applied to investment income earned on assets backing required capital}$$
$$\text{TaxInvIncRC}(t) = \text{Taxes on investment income earned on assets backing required capital, per unit issued.}$$

Then,

$$\text{ReqCap}(t) = \text{AssetDefRisk}(t) + \text{MortRisk}(t) + \text{MorbRisk}(t)$$
$$+ \text{IntRateRisk}(t) + \text{IntSpreadRisk}(t)$$
$$+ \text{OtherRisk}(t). \tag{10.7.1}$$

The assets that back required capital will also have an asset default risk. In other words, setting up required capital creates a need for additional required capital, because of the asset default risk. To correct for this omission, we can divide by $(1 - \text{AssetDefFactor}(t))$, as follows:

$$\text{ReqCap}(t) = [\text{AssetDefRisk}(t) + \text{MortRisk}(t) + \text{MorbRisk}(t)$$
$$+ \text{IntRateRisk}(t) + \text{IntSpreadRisk}(t)$$
$$+ \text{OtherRisk}(t)]/(1 - \text{AssetDefFactor}(t)). \tag{10.7.2}$$

There is a simple alternative to Formula 10.7.2: Increase the asset default risk factor by the ratio of the company's assets to its liabilities. While this may not be accurate for a particular product, it should be accurate for the company as a whole. For example, if a company's assets are 110% of its liabilities, the company could increase its asset default risk factor by 10% to adjust for "required capital on required capital."

Investment income on required capital and the tax thereon are calculated as follows:

$$\text{InvIncRC}(t) = \text{ReqCap}(t - 1) \ \text{RCIntRate}(t), \quad\quad (10.7.3)$$
$$\text{TaxInvIncRC}(t) = \text{InvIncRC}(t) \ \text{TaxRate}(t). \quad\quad (10.7.4)$$

Note that capital is required at the beginning of the first year, the moment the policy is issued. This is because most early cash flows are negative, and reserves and required capital have to be established at issue. As you will see in the next chapter, this book assumes that the first capital contribution is made at the *end* of the first year. This means that there is no capital in place at the beginning of the first year, that is, ReqCap(0) = 0 and, therefore, InvIncRC(1) = 0. This approach has been taken to keep the formulas a little simpler. It is not realistic. In actual practice, you will want to more accurately reflect the timing of capital contributions. (Exercises at the end of Chapter 11 address this issue.)

10.8 Survey of Required Capital for Selected Countries

Required capital formulas vary widely from country to country and are continually evolving. Descriptions of regulatory required capital for the U.S., Canada, Australia, and the European Union are presented to provide you with a glimpse of the wide diversity in this area. The formulas for the EU are relatively simple and practical but can result in very conservative required capital in certain situations, such as for a company specializing in term insurance sold to young, healthy people. In contrast, the formulas for the other three countries are wildly complicated but produce more balanced results over a range of different situations.

10.8.1 U.S. Risk-Based Capital

In the United States, solvency regulations specify a risk-based capital (RBC) formula. In 2000, most U.S. companies were targeting required capital of 200% to 250% of the regulatory minimum RBC. The RBC formula specifies the required amount of capital to be maintained in relation to the following categories of risk:

- Asset default risk

- Insurance risk

- Interest rate risk, and

- Other risk.

A bewildering number of factors are provided in the formulas for these risks.

Asset default factors are applied to a company's assets, with different factors for different types of assets. Asset classes include bonds, mortgages, real estate, and stocks (differentiated between affiliated and unaffiliated). Factors are given for reinsurance receivables and off-balance-sheet items, such as guarantees and contingencies.

For bonds, the factors are adjusted depending on the number of bonds on a company's books (the more bonds, the lower the factor, since default risk is spread among a larger number of borrowers). Finally, under variable products, since the risk of asset default is passed directly to policyowners, asset default risk factors are lower for assets backing variable products.

Insurance risk factors are applied for mortality risk and morbidity risk. Mortality risk factors are applied to the company's total net amount at risk. Mortality risk factors are tiered, with the factors depending on the company's total amount at risk.

Morbidity risk factors are expressed as a percentage of premium and differ between individual, group, and credit accident and health business. A second morbidity risk factor is expressed as a percentage of claim reserves on both individual and group accident and health business.

Interest rate risk factors are applied to policy reserves (net of policy loans), with factors varying depending on the risk characteristics and withdrawal provisions of the underlying products. Products are classified as low, medium, and high risk, depending on the extent to which changes in interest rates may affect disintermediation risk. Variable products receive favorable treatment since changes in asset values are passed directly to policyowners.

In general, life insurance is classified as low risk. Annuities, however, are not so clearly defined. Deferred annuities that are not subject to discretionary withdrawal are considered low risk. Deferred annuities that are subject to discretionary withdrawal, but with surrender charges of 5% or more of the account value, are considered medium risks. Deferred annuities that are subject to discretionary withdrawal at book value, with a surrender charge of less than 5% of account value, are considered high risk. (Annuities will be discussed further in Chapter 13.)

Other risk factors are applied as a percentage of premium collected. Factors vary for life, annuity, and accident and health premiums.

The four risk components are referred to in the RBC formula as follows:

Asset default risk: C1 risk

Insurance risk: C2 risk

Interest rate risk: C3 risk

Other risk: C4 risk.

The RBC formula does not simply sum the individual risk components. Instead, the formula assumes that the C2 risk is totally independent of the C1 and C3 risks. To reflect this independence, a company's final risk-based capital is calculated by applying a "covariance adjustment" to the four components:

$$\text{Risk-Based Capital} = [(\text{C2 risk})^2 + (\text{C1 risk} + \text{C3 risk})^2]^{1/2} + \text{C4 risk.}$$

Table 10.8.1 illustrates the effect of the covariance adjustment. Companies 1 and 2 have the same individual components, except for C1 risk. For Company 1, the impact of the covariance adjustment is to reduce RBC by 18%. However, for Company 2, the impact is to reduce RBC by only 5%.

Table 10.8.1 Impact of Covariance Adjustment

RBC Components	Company 1	Company 2
C1 Risk	90,000,000	10,000,000
C2 Risk	400,000,000	400,000,000
C3 Risk	10,000,000	10,000,000
C4 Risk	1,000,000	1,000,000
Sum of Components	501,000,000	421,000,000
RBC, Reflecting the Covariance Adjustment	413,310,563	401,499,688
Ratio of RBC to Sum	0.82	0.95

Risk-based capital is compared to the company's total capital, after adjustment for a number of miscellaneous liabilities. If the ratio of adjusted capital to RBC is less than a certain percentage, then various levels of regulatory intervention apply, depending on the ratio.

10.8.2   Canadian MCCSR

Minimum capital standards in Canada are defined by minimum continuing capital and surplus requirements (MCCSR). The minimum capital requirement is determined by applying factors for the following risk factors:

- Asset default risk
- Insurance risk
- Interest margin pricing risk, and
- Interest rate risk.

The MCCSR is calculated by summing the results of each of the four components. Then it is compared to the company's capital, which is composed of two tiers.

Asset default factors are applied to the book value of a company's assets, with different factors for different types of assets. Asset classes include bonds, mortgages, real estate, equity investments, limited partnerships, and leases. Also, factors are given for off-balance sheet exposures, interest-rate–related contracts (such as interest rate swaps), and foreign-exchange-rate–related contracts.

Insurance risk factors are given for life insurance (including accidental death and dismemberment), disability risks, annuities involving life contingencies, and morbidity risks:

- The life insurance factors vary depending on whether the business is participating or nonparticipating, individual or group, and by the years remaining during which the mortality cost can be changed. In addition, the factors are tiered, depending on the company's total net amount at risk.

- The morbidity risk component for disability income insurance is calculated for new claim risk and for continuing claim risk. The new claim risk is calculated by applying factors to premiums, with the factors varying by the years of premium guarantee remaining. The continuing claim risk is calculated by applying factors to the disability income claim reserves. These factors depend on the years of benefits remaining.

- The morbidity risk component for accident and sickness benefits is also calculated for new claim risk and for continuing claim risk. The new claim risk is calculated by applying factors to annual earned premiums. The continuing claim risk is calculated by applying factors to incurred but unpaid claims relating to prior years.

Interest margin pricing risk is calculated by applying a factor to the policy liabilities. One set of factors applies to all participating contracts and nonparticipating contracts with adjustable premiums or adjustable interest credits. Different factors apply to all other business. No factors apply to guaranteed interest contracts that offer renewal only at the same interest rate used for new business. Finally, no factor is required for business where there is no repricing risk (such as paid-up business not receiving dividends) or for business where the policy liabilities are not discounted for interest.

Interest rate risk is calculated by applying a factor to the policy liabilities. Factors are given for life and health insurance, endowment insurance, single premium immediate annuities, and disability claims payable in installments. In addition, these factors vary depending on the guarantee period remaining on premium rates or credited interest rates. Separate factors are used for accumulation funds, deferred annuities, retirement income policies, and universal life products. The factors vary with the remaining term of the guarantee. Also, the factors vary according to when funds can be withdrawn and whether the funds are available at book value or with a market value adjustment.

The MCCSR is calculated by summing the four components. The MCCSR is then compared to the company's capital, which is defined as the sum of Tier 1 capital (core capital) and Tier 2 capital (supplementary capital). The calculation of the two tiers can be summarized as follows:

• Tier 1 capital includes common equity, contributed capital, retained earnings, capital invested in the company's participating and nonparticipating accounts, and noncumulative perpetual preferred shares. Deductions are made in Tier 1 capital for goodwill, reserves for cash value deficiencies (that is, any excess of cash value over reserve, calculated policy by policy), 55% of unrealized amortized net gains and losses, and 100% of negative reserves.

• Tier 2 capital consists of preferred shares, subordinated debt, minority interest, other debentures, 50% of negative reserves, 50% of reserves for cash value deficiencies, and 45% of unrealized unamortized net gains and losses on widely traded stocks.

In general, negative reserves increase capital. However, for the purpose of calculating capital for the MCCSR comparison, Tier 1 capital is reduced by the amount of negative reserves. Tier 2 capital then adds back 50% of those negative reserves. The net effect is that only half of negative reserves are counted as capital for the MCCSR comparison.

10.8.3   Australian Liabilities: Three Levels of Requirements

Capital adequacy standards in Australia are not driven by formulas, as they are in the United States and Canada. Instead, assets and liabilities are valued on a current basis. Total assets are compared to different levels of liability, with each level being dynamically calculated. An Australian life insurance company's assets are divided between one or more *statutory funds* and a *shareholders fund*. You can think of a "statutory fund" as being the assets held for the benefit of a certain group of policyowners. Not shown below is the "shareholders fund," which are assets held for the benefit of shareholders.

Table 10.8.2 organizes the different levels of liabilities required in Australia.

Table 10.8.2 Australian "Required Capital"

Assets	Allocation of Liabilities		
	Excess Assets		
Total Assets of Statutory Fund (SF), at Net Realizable Value	Capital Adequacy Reserve (CAR)	Capital Adequacy Requirement	
	Solvency Margin (SM)	Solvency Requirement	
	Present Value of Planned Future Profit Margins	MoS Liability	
	Best Estimate of Policy Liabilities (BEL)		

Failure to have assets at least equal to the capital adequacy reserve (CAR) level means that assets cannot be transferred out of the statutory fund (SF) to pay stockholder dividends. If total assets are below the CAR level, the company must produce a business plan showing how it plans to remedy the situation.

If total assets are below the solvency margin (SM) level, the regulators will intervene in the operations of the company. Note that the term "solvency margin" has been substituted for the Australian term "solvency reserve" to avoid confusion with the solvency reserve defined in Chapter 6.

10.8.3.1 Margin on Services: Earnings Reserves

Margin on Services (MoS) is the method used for earnings reserves in Australia and is analogous to U.S. GAAP. In Table 10.8.2, the "MoS Liability" equals the best estimate policy liability (BEL) plus the present value (PV) of planned future profit margins. Using the MoS valuation basis, PV of income will equal PV of outgo plus PV of profit margins.

The underlying philosophy of MoS is

- Profit is from services provided or risks borne
- Profit is to be recognized when earned
- Acquisition is not a service
- Profit margin must be linked to a *profit carrier,* such as a percentage of premiums or claims; a product can have more than one profit carrier
- Negative margins result in immediate loss recognition
- Liabilities are recalculated each year, based on current best estimates.

MoS is based on forward-looking reserve calculations. However, MoS also allows a retrospective accumulation, provided it produces a liability that is no less than that produced by the forward-looking reserve calculation. Australia's MoS reserves are fairly similar to U.S. GAAP benefit reserves net of DAC.

10.8.3.2 Solvency Requirement

The solvency requirement prescribes the minimum total assets to ensure that the company will be in a position to meet its guaranteed obligations to policyowners and other creditors under a range of adverse circumstances. In Table 10.8.2 the solvency requirement is shown equal to the MoS Liability plus the solvency margin. In practice, the solvency requirement is calculated directly. The solvency margin is then calculated as the difference between the solvency requirement and the MoS Liability.

The solvency requirement consists of the following components:

- Solvency liability
- Expense reserve
- Other liabilities
- Resilience reserve
- Inadmissible asset reserve.

The *solvency liability* is a calculation of the company's liabilities on a basis that is more conservative than the BEL and at least as strong as the minimum prescribed basis. The solvency liability for each policy must equal or exceed both the BEL and any cash surrender value.

The *expense reserve* provides for the run-out of acquisition costs that can occur upon closing a statutory fund to new business and that are not included in the solvency liability. The solvency liability and expense reserve must exceed the cash surrender value. There is a prescribed basis for calculation of the expense reserve. Shareholder capital can be used to offset this reserve.

Other liabilities include all amounts owed to creditors.

To the extent changes in asset values will not be matched by a corresponding change in liability values when there are adverse movements in interest rates, a *resilience reserve* is required. There is a prescribed basis that involves recalculating the value of assets and liabilities given the prescribed change in interest rates.

Finally, the *inadmissible asset reserve* provides for asset risks associated with assets whose value depends upon the ongoing conduct of business, holdings in associated financial entities, and concentration of asset exposures. This reserve is calculated on a prescribed basis and essentially places limits on the value of assets that can be taken into account.

10.8.3.3   Capital Adequacy Requirement

The capital adequacy requirement addresses the financial strength of the statutory fund on an ongoing basis. Total assets must be sufficient to ensure the ongoing solvency of the fund for the next three years, assuming experience in line with that assumed in the BEL, including best estimate levels of new business. In practice, the capital adequacy requirement is calculated directly. The capital adequacy reserve (CAR) is then calculated as the difference between the capital adequacy requirement and the solvency requirement.

The capital adequacy requirement consists of the following components:

- Capital adequacy liability
- Other liabilities
- Resilience reserve
- Inadmissible asset reserve
- New business reserve.

The *capital adequacy liability* is calculated on a basis more conservative than that used for the BEL. For each assumption, there is a prescribed range of values or margins. For example, interest rates must be 0.4% to 3.0% below those used for the BEL. The appointed actuary determines the assumptions based on prescribed qualitative factors. Each assumption must meet prescribed standards and may be more conservative than the corresponding assumption used in calculating the solvency liability. The assumption may be less conservative than the prescribed standard only in exceptional circumstances.

Other liabilities are calculated the same as for solvency. The *resilience reserve* is calculated the same as for solvency, but with higher interest rate margins (roughly double the level for solvency). The *inadmissible asset reserve* is calculated the same as for solvency, except that "assets whose value depends upon the ongoing conduct of business" count toward capital adequacy.

The *new business reserve*, which cannot be negative, is determined as the additional amount required to ensure that the solvency requirement of the fund will be met over the next three years. Credit can be taken for capital emerging over that period from the existing business of the fund and also for any "new business capital," which consists of (1) existing binding arrangements for the external raising of capital designed to finance new business, and (2) existing shareholder capital to the extent it is not already committed to meeting the expense reserve of the solvency standard.

10.8.4 European Union Solvency Margin

Compared to the preceding required capital methods, the European Union standards are refreshingly simple and straightforward, at least as of 2000. The EU regulations require companies to maintain a solvency margin of assets over liabilities. This solvency margin differs for direct companies and reinsurers.

10.8.4.1 Solvency Margin for Direct Companies

The solvency margin calculation varies by class of business and is calculated as the sum of parts 1 and 2.

For Class I (life and annuity/pensions business that is not investment-linked):

1. 4% of solvency reserves, except for unit-linked products where the investment risk is passed to the policyowner, in which case the requirement is 1%. Reinsurance credit can be taken up to a maximum of 15% of gross aggregate reserves.

2. A percentage of the net amount at risk for life products, depending on the duration of the product:

    Less than three years: 0.10%

    Three to five years: 0.15%

    More than five years: 0.30%.

    Reinsurance credit can be taken up to a maximum of 50% of the gross aggregate amount at risk.

For Class II (accidental death and other supplementary insurance):

1. Based on premium-based solvency margin calculation for non-life insurance.

2. Not applicable.

For Class III (life and annuity/pensions business that is investment-linked):

1. The 4% requirement for Class I above becomes 0%, provided that the business has no investment or expense charge guarantees.

2. Same as Class I.

For Class IV (permanent health and critical illness business):

1. Same as Class I if not investment-linked, or Class III if investment-linked.

2. Not applicable.

10.8.4.2 Solvency Margin for Reinsurers

The solvency margin for reinsurers is the same as for direct companies under section 1, except the maximum reinsurance credit that can be taken is 50%, and under section 2, the requirement is 0.1% for all durations.

10.8.4.3 Guarantee Fund

One-third of the solvency margin constitutes the guarantee fund, which must not be less than 800,000 Euros.

10.8.4.4 Admissible Assets

Unusual assets that may, with the agreement of the home state regulator, count toward the solvency margin include profit reserves (amounts voluntarily held in reserve to offset possible future losses, such as losses from catastrophes), hidden reserves, and deferred acquisition costs.

10.9 Pricing Model

Tables 10.9.1 and 10.9.2 are this chapter's contribution to the pricing example that spans and ties together Chapters 4 through 11. Table 10.9.1 details the required capital factors. Notice that RCIntRate is higher than the interest rate earned on reserves and cash flows. It is not uncommon to assume that the assets backing required capital earn a different interest rate than those backing cash flows and reserves.

Table 10.9.1 Required Capital Risk Factors

t	AssetDefFactor	MortFactor	IntRateFactor	IntSpreadFactor	OtherFactor	RCIntRate
1–10	0.0200	0.0012	0.0100	0.0075	0.0300	0.0800

Table 10.9.2 Required Capital Components

t	AssetDefRisk	MortRisk	IntRateRisk	IntSpreadRisk	OtherRisk	ReqCap*	InvIncRC	TaxInvIncRC
1	0.02411	0.78956	0.01206	0.00904	0.19500	1.02977	0.00000	0.00000
2	0.04856	0.73182	0.02428	0.01821	0.15908	0.98195	0.08238	0.03131
3	0.06599	0.69269	0.03300	0.02475	0.14379	0.96022	0.07856	0.02985
4	0.07634	0.65560	0.03817	0.02863	0.13354	0.93227	0.07682	0.02919
5	0.07955	0.62051	0.03978	0.02983	0.12426	0.89392	0.07458	0.02834
6	0.07759	0.59973	0.03880	0.02910	0.11576	0.86098	0.07151	0.02718
7	0.06794	0.57981	0.03397	0.02548	0.11015	0.81734	0.06888	0.02617
8	0.05008	0.56075	0.02504	0.01878	0.10457	0.75922	0.06539	0.02485
9	0.02327	0.54252	0.01164	0.00873	0.09883	0.68499	0.06074	0.02308
10	0.00000	0.00000	0.00000	0.00000	0.00000	0.00000	0.05480	0.02082

*Uses Formula 10.7.1; assumes *AssetDefFactor* includes a provision for required capital on required capital.

Note: For all *t*, EarnTaxRate = 0.38.

10.10 Exercises

Exercise 10.1

a. If a company earns an interest rate of 10% on all of its assets and a tax rate of 40% applies to investment income, what is the rate of return earned on assets backing required capital? (Note: Rates of return are *always* after tax.)

b. If the rate of return on capital other than required capital is 18% and required capital represents one-third of total capital, what is the rate of return on total capital?

Exercise 10.2

Building on the previous exercise, assume the company reinsures 50% of its business, with the following results: 50% of the company's required capital is shifted to the reinsurer, the reinsurer provides allowances that cover 60% of new business strain, and the reinsurer retains 50% of future earnings, as shown below.

	Capital to Cover New Business Strain	Required Capital	Total Capital	Pre-Tax Earnings, Excluding Interest on RC
Before Reinsurance	400	200	600	120
Impact of Reinsurance	−240	−100	−340	−60
After Reinsurance	160	100	260	60

a. What are the company's after-tax earnings, including interest on required capital?

b. What is the company's rate of return on the business it retains?

Exercise 10.3

Using the mortality risk factors in Section 10.3.1, calculate the average mortality risk factor for a company with 4 billion of net amount at risk. If the company expects to double its net amount at risk over the next ten years, how will this impact its average mortality risk factor?

Exercise 10.4

A company has 100 million of universal life account value on its books. This business is supported by total capital of 5,000,000, on which the company is currently earning 15%, after tax. These universal life policies currently have no surrender charges. If the company offers an exchange program to convert these policies to policies with surrender charges, what is the maximum commission rate, as a percentage of account value, that the company can pay its agents and still maintain the same after-tax rate of return during the year of the exchange? Use the following interest rate risk factors, assume that the exchange has no impact on after-tax earnings other than the after-tax cost of commissions, and use a 40% tax rate:

Universal life policies without surrender charges: 1.00%

Universal life policies with surrender charges: 0.25%.

Exercise 10.5

If a company has 1 billion of required capital and an asset default factor of 1%, how much of the company's required capital is related to the asset default risk on required capital, the so-called *required capital on required capital?*

Exercise 10.6

Referring to Table 10.8.1, assume Company 1 and Company 2 enter into two different reinsurance transactions:

Company 1 transfers 40 million of C1 risk to Company 2.

At the same time, Company 2 transfers 6 million of C2 risk to Company 1.

Which company's risk-based capital position is improved, after taking into account the covariance adjustment?

10.11 Answers

Answer 10.1

a. $10\% (1 - 40\%) = 6\%$.

b. $\frac{2}{3} (18\%) + \frac{1}{3} (6\%) = 14\%$.

Answer 10.2

a. After-tax earnings = 60 (1 − 40%) + 100 (6%) = 42.

b. Rate of return = $\dfrac{42}{260}$ = 16.15%.

Answer 10.3

The total mortality risk component for 4 billion of net amount at risk is

$$(500)\ 0.20\% + (1,000)\ 0.18\% + (2,500)\ 0.15\%$$
$$= 1 + 1.8 + 3.75$$
$$= 6.55 \text{ million.}$$

Dividing by 4 billion, we obtain the average mortality risk factor

$$\frac{6.55}{4,000} = 0.1638\%.$$

If the company were to double, its mortality risk component would become

$$6.55 + (4,000)\ 0.11\% = 10.95 \text{ million.}$$

Its average mortality risk factor would fall to

$$\frac{10.95}{8,000} = 0.1369\%, \text{ which represents a 16\% decrease.}$$

Answer 10.4

After-tax income/5,000,000 = 15%, so, after-tax income = 750,000.

Other capital + Interest-rate-risk capital = 5,000,000,
Other capital + (0.01)(100,000,000) = 5,000,000,
so, Other capital = 4,000,000.

After the exchange program,

$$\frac{750,000 - \text{Commissions}\ (1 - \text{TaxRate})}{\text{Other capital} + (0.0025)(100,000,000)} = 15\%,$$

$$\frac{750,000 - \text{Commissions}\ (1 - 0.40)}{4,250,000} = 15\%,$$

Commissions = 187,500, or 0.1875% of account values.

Answer 10.5

Using Formula 10.7.2,

$$1 \text{ billion} = \frac{\text{Components of required capital}}{1 - 0.01}.$$

This leads to

Components of required capital = 990 million.

Required capital on required capital is the difference between these two:

RC on RC = 1 billion − 990 million = 10 million.

Answer 10.6

Surprisingly, both companies lower their RBC by about 2 million. The reinsurance transactions allow both companies to achieve a better balance of risk, thereby lowering their RBC through the operation of the covariance adjustment. Company 1's RBC falls from 413.3 million to 411.4 million. Company 2's RBC falls from 401.5 million to 399.5 million.

RBC Component	Company 1	Company 2
C1 Risk	50,000,000	50,000,000
C2 Risk	406,000,000	394,000,000
C3 Risk	10,000,000	10,000,000
C4 Risk	1,000,000	1,000,000
Sum of Components	467,000,000	455,000,000
RBC, Reflecting the Covariance Adjustment	411,409,552	399,542,344
Ratio of RBC to Sum	0.88	0.88

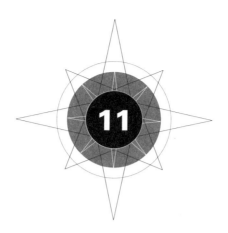

Profit Measurement and Analysis

11.1 Introduction

This chapter brings together all of the concepts introduced in Chapters 4 through 10. We will first develop the calculation of distributable earnings, followed by stockholder earnings. Distributable earnings are based on solvency earnings, which are the earnings that result from the use of solvency reserves (also known as statutory or regulatory reserves). In contrast, stockholder earnings result from the use of earnings reserves, such as U.S. GAAP reserves.

We will then discuss considerations for selecting profit measures, such as which accounting basis to employ, how risk should be reflected, and how future values should be discounted. Finally, we will discuss and develop formulas for measuring and analyzing profits.

11.2 Distributable Earnings

Chapters 4 through 10 developed concepts and formulas that are all needed in the calculation of distributable earnings. We will calculate distributable earnings in three steps:

1. First, we will calculate pre-tax solvency earnings.

2. Next, we will deduct taxes to determine after-tax solvency earnings.

3. Finally, we will adjust after-tax solvency earnings for the increase in required capital and add after-tax investment income on the assets backing required capital.

11.2.1   Pre-Tax Solvency Earnings

Pre-tax solvency earnings for each policy year are calculated as product cash flows plus investment income minus the increase in solvency reserves. For your convenience, we repeat some formulas from Chapters 5–8.

Product cash flows equal premiums less benefits and expenses:

$$\text{ProdCashFlow}(t) = \text{Prem}(t) - \text{Ben}(t) - \text{Exp}(t). \qquad (5.10.7)$$

If reinsurance is reflected in pricing, then premiums, benefits, and expenses are adjusted as follows. While these formulas are not mathematically correct, they are a simple way to show how pre-reinsurance values are adjusted to reflect any reinsurance.

Premiums:

$$\text{Prem}(t) = \text{Prem}(t) \qquad - \text{ReinsPrem}(t). \qquad (7.5.11)$$

Benefits:

$$
\begin{aligned}
\text{DeathBen}(t) &= \text{DeathBen}(t) & - \text{ReinsDeathBen}(t), && (7.5.12)\\
\text{SurrBen}(t) &= \text{SurrBen}(t) & - \text{ReinsSurrBen}(t), && (7.5.13)\\
\text{Div}(t) &= \text{Div}(t) & - \text{ReinsDiv}(t), && (7.5.14)\\
\text{PartWithBen}(t) &= \text{PartWithBen}(t) & - \text{ReinsPartWithBen}(t), && (7.5.15)\\
\text{PureEndow}(t) &= \text{PureEndow}(t) & - \text{ReinsPureEndow}(t). && (7.5.16)
\end{aligned}
$$

Expenses:

$$
\begin{aligned}
\text{Comm}(t) &= \text{Comm}(t) & - \text{ExpAllow}(t), && (7.5.17)\\
\text{AVComm}(t) &= \text{AVComm}(t) & - \text{AVExpAllow}(t). && (7.5.18)
\end{aligned}
$$

The increase in solvency reserves is calculated as

$$\text{SolvResIncr}(t) = \text{SolvRes}(t) - \text{SolvRes}(t-1). \qquad (6.5.4)$$

If reinsurance is reflected in pricing, the increase in solvency reserves is adjusted:

$$\text{SolvResIncr}(t) = \text{SolvResIncr}(t) - \text{ResCreditIncr}(t). \qquad (7.4.13)$$

Investment income is calculated as the sum of policy loan interest, interest on other assets, and interest on current year cash flows:

$$\text{InvIncome}(t) = \text{PolLoanInt}(t) + \text{InvInt}(t) + \text{CashFlowInt}(t). \qquad (8.4.1)$$

If reinsurance is reflected in pricing, then solvency reserves and cash flows will be adjusted, so investment income will automatically be calculated net of the impact of reinsurance.

Let

$\text{PreTaxSolvEarn}(t) = $ Pre-tax solvency earnings, per unit issued.

Then,

$$\text{PreTaxSolvEarn}(t) = \text{ProdCashFlow}(t) + \text{InvIncome}(t) - \text{SolvResIncr}(t). \qquad (11.2.1)$$

11.2.2   After-Tax Solvency Earnings

Taxes to be deducted from pre-tax solvency earnings are calculated using the appropriate formulas from Section 9.5 of Chapter 9. After-tax solvency earnings are then calculated as

$$\text{AfterTaxSolvEarn}(t) = \text{PreTaxSolvEarn}(t) - \text{Tax}(t). \qquad (11.2.2)$$

11.2.3   Adjustment for Required Capital

To determine distributable earnings, after-tax solvency earnings are (1) reduced for the increase in required capital, and (2) increased by after-tax investment income on assets backing required capital.

Let

$\text{ReqCapIncr}(t) = $ Increase in required capital, per unit issued

$\text{ATInvIncRC}(t) = $ After-tax investment income on assets backing required capital, per unit issued

$\text{DistrEarn}(t) = $ Distributable earnings, per unit issued.

Then,

$$\text{ReqCapIncr}(t) = \text{ReqCap}(t) - \text{ReqCap}(t-1), \quad\quad (11.2.3)$$

$$\text{ATInvIncRC}(t) = \text{InvIncRC}(t) - \text{TaxInvIncRC}(t), \quad\quad (11.2.4)$$

$$\text{DistrEarn}(t) = \text{AfterTaxSolvEarn}(t) - \text{ReqCapIncr}(t)$$
$$+ \text{ATInvIncRC}(t). \quad\quad (11.2.5)$$

Although it is preferable to price a product over the lifetime of the policies, it may not always be practical. Therefore, the pricing horizon may be shortened to perhaps 10, 20, or 30 years. We will define n to be the final policy year for pricing calculations.

When n is less than the policy's final policy year, not all future profits or losses will be included in the profit stream. A large amount of capital may be tied up in required capital at the end of year n as well. One common method to compensate for not taking all future years of profit into account is to release the required capital at the end of the pricing horizon, so that $\text{ReqCap}(n) = 0$. For some components of the required capital formula, this can be done by explicitly releasing the nth year required capital into the final year of distributable earnings; for other components, this can be accomplished by setting the lapse rate equal to 100% at the end of year n. Note that both approaches are used in year 10 of Table 10.9.2. If the lapse rate is set to 100%, the difference between reserves and cash values will also be released into the profit calculation (reserves will drop to zero, and cash value will be paid out as surrender benefits).

You should be aware of items that may affect profits even if all policies were to lapse at once. For example, the effect of the DAC tax (explained in the Appendix to Chapter 9) will continue for up to ten years after the last policy has lapsed. At the end of year n, the present value of all future events should flow through the profit calculation for year n.

11.3 Stockholder Earnings

The profit measurements up to this point have been based on solvency reserves and required capital. However, as mentioned in Chapter 6, it is often useful or necessary to calculate profits based on earnings reserves. Whereas solvency reserves often distort profit by causing significant new business strain, earnings reserves typically produce a smoother pattern of earnings, often with no loss in the first policy year.

11.3.1 Pre-Tax Stockholder Earnings

Pre-tax stockholder earnings are calculated very much like pre-tax solvency earnings, with three similar components:

- Product cash flows are identical for solvency and stockholder earnings. Cash is cash.
- The main difference between stockholder earnings and solvency earnings is the subtraction of the increase in earnings reserves (net of deferred acquisition costs) in place of the subtraction of the increase in solvency reserves.
- When calculating stockholder earnings, we will assume that invested assets equal solvency reserves plus required capital. This means that investment income will include investment income on assets backing both solvency reserves and required capital.

Let

$$PreTaxStockEarn(t) = \text{Pre-tax stockholder earnings, per unit issued.}$$

Then,

$$\begin{aligned} PreTaxStockEarn(t) = {} & ProdCashFlow(t) - BenResIncr(t) \\ & - DACAmort(t) + InvIncome(t) \\ & + InvIncRC(t). \end{aligned} \tag{11.3.1}$$

Remember that the increase in earnings reserves is composed of two parts: the increase in benefit reserve, and the amortization of deferred acquisition costs.

Recall from Chapter 6 that

$$DACAmort(t) = DAC(t-1) - DAC(t). \tag{6.5.6}$$

In the first policy year, acquisition costs are usually capitalized, and DAC helps boost earnings by offsetting most acquisition costs. Since $DAC(0)$ equals 0, $DACAmort(1)$ will almost always be negative. Therefore, subtracting it in Formula 11.3.1 increases pre-tax stockholder earnings. After year 1, DAC will generally decrease, so $DACAmort(t)$ will usually be positive. Therefore, subtracting $DACAmort(t)$ will generally reduce pre-tax stockholder earnings after the first year.

We can also calculate pre-tax stockholder earnings from pre-tax solvency earnings by making two adjustments:

1. Adding back the increase in solvency reserves and subtracting the increase in earnings reserves (net of DAC), and

2. Adding investment income on required capital.

This translates to

$$
\begin{aligned}
\text{PreTaxStockEarn}(t) = {} & \text{PreTaxSolvEarn}(t) + \text{SolvResIncr}(t) \\
& - \text{BenResIncr}(t) - \text{DACAmort}(t) \\
& + \text{InvIncRC}(t).
\end{aligned}
\tag{11.3.2}
$$

11.3.2 After-Tax Stockholder Earnings

To calculate after-tax stockholder earnings, three components of tax must be deducted from pre-tax stockholder earnings:

- Tax on pre-tax solvency earnings, or $\text{Tax}(t)$

- Tax on investment income earned on assets backing required capital, or $\text{TaxInvIncRC}(t)$

- Tax on the difference between shareholder and solvency earnings, excluding investment income on required capital. This is the provision for deferred taxes, or $\text{DefTaxProv}(t)$. This additional tax is not paid in cash, but instead is added to the deferred tax liability. This is explained more fully in Chapter 9.

Let

$$
\text{AfterTaxStockEarn}(t) = \text{After-tax stockholder earnings, per unit issued.}
$$

Then,

$$
\begin{aligned}
\text{AfterTaxStockEarn}(t) = {} & \text{PreTaxStockEarn}(t) - \text{Tax}(t) \\
& - \text{TaxInvIncRC}(t) - \text{DefTaxProv}(t).
\end{aligned}
\tag{11.3.3}
$$

Both distributable earnings and after-tax stockholder earnings are very important to stockholders, but they serve very different purposes:

Positive distributable earnings represent the maximum amount that can be paid to stockholders. *Negative distributable earnings* represent capital contributions that stockholders must pay into the company to keep it financially strong.

After-tax stockholder earnings represent earnings that are reported to stockholders. For a growing company, stockholder earnings usually exceed distributable earnings. For a company that is not growing, the opposite is true.

Comparing Formula 11.3.3 for after-tax stockholder earnings to Formula 11.2.5 for distributable earnings, you will notice that Formula 11.3.3 does not subtract the increase in required capital. In other words, required capital has no bearing on stockholder earnings, except for investment income earned on the assets backing required capital. However, required capital *is* part of the equity base used to calculate return on equity, as you will soon see.

11.3.3 Return on Equity

Return on equity (ROE) is calculated as after-tax stockholder earnings divided by the stockholder equity base. There are two common ways to calculate the stockholder equity base: (1) stockholder equity at the beginning of the policy year, and (2) the average of stockholder equity at the beginning and end of the policy year.

Stockholder equity can be calculated as assets minus liabilities at any point in time. In our simplified pricing model, assets consist of DAC plus the invested assets backing solvency reserves and required capital. Liabilities consist of benefit reserves and the deferred tax liability.

Let

$$\text{StockAssets}(t) = \text{Stockholder assets at the end of the year, per unit issued}$$

$$\text{StockLiabilities}(t) = \text{Stockholder liabilities at the end of the year, per unit issued}$$

$$\text{StockEquity}(t) = \text{Stockholder equity at the end of the year, per unit issued}$$

$$\text{EquityBase}(t) = \text{Either beginning of the year or average}$$
$$\text{stockholder equity, depending on the choice}$$
$$\text{of equity base, per unit issued}$$
$$\text{ROE}(t) = \text{Return on equity for year } t.$$

Then,

$$\text{StockAssets}(t) = \text{SolvRes}(t) + \text{ReqCap}(t) + \text{DAC}(t), \quad (11.3.4)$$
$$\text{StockLiabilities}(t) = \text{BenRes}(t) + \text{DefTaxLiab}(t), \quad (11.3.5)$$
$$\text{StockEquity}(t) = \text{StockAssets}(t) - \text{StockLiabilities}(t), \quad (11.3.6)$$
$$\text{EquityBase}(t) = \text{StockEquity}(t - 1), \text{ if ROE is based}$$
$$\text{on beginning of the year stockholder}$$
$$\text{equity, or}$$
$$= \tfrac{1}{2} \, (\text{StockEquity}(t - 1)$$
$$+ \text{StockEquity}(t)), \text{ if ROE is based}$$
$$\text{on the average}$$
$$\text{equity for the year}, \quad (11.3.7)$$
$$\text{ROE}(t) = \frac{\text{AfterTaxStockEarn}(t)}{\text{EquityBase}(t)}. \quad (11.3.8)$$

One important point needs to made about Formula 11.3.4. Recall from Chapters 8 and 10 that there must be assets backing solvency reserves and required capital. A company does *not* earn investment income on reserves. Instead, a company earns investment income on the assets that back the reserves. Therefore, the first two terms of Formula 11.3.4 are meant to represent the *assets that back* solvency reserves and required capital.

Formula 11.3.8 produces one ROE for each policy year. The fact that the ROE varies from policy year to policy year makes it very difficult to determine whether or not the company's ROE goal will be met over the lifetime of the product. In a later section, we will develop a weighted-average approach to ROE that will allow us to compare a weighted-average result to the company's ROE goal. The weighted-average ROE and the pattern of ROEs by policy year may be important targets when developing and pricing a product.

11.4 Selection of Profit Goals

Before profit goals can be selected, some basic questions need to be answered:

- Which accounting basis should be used to calculate profits?
- How should the product's degree of risk be reflected in the profit goals?
- What rate should be used to discount future values or as a targeted rate of return?

After covering each of these questions, we will examine some commonly used profit measures.

There is sometimes one more question: Should the impact of required capital be reflected? We assume the answer is always "yes." However, there may be obscure situations where there is less need to reflect required capital. For example, in a country with conservative solvency reserves and minimal capital requirements, a company with ready access to capital (say, from a parent company with an abundance of capital) may not need to reflect required capital in pricing.

11.4.1 Choice of Accounting Basis

Many companies must report one set of earnings to regulators, based on solvency reserves, and another set of earnings to stockholders and stock markets, based on earnings reserves. To distinguish between these two types of earnings, we will refer to them as solvency earnings and stockholder earnings. We will use the words "earnings" and "profits" interchangeably.

In situations where earnings are reported on two different bases, there is no absolute standard as to which basis should be used for pricing. However, because solvency reserves and capital requirements drive shareholders' investments in and returns from the business, there is a strong tendency to favor solvency earnings as the primary driver of pricing.

Some companies price using solvency earnings rather than stockholder earnings because solvency results are more important to insurance rating organizations and regulators. For example, a company that needs to conserve its capital by limiting the sale of new business would probably price using solvency earnings.

A company that places heavy emphasis on stockholder earnings would be more likely to price using stockholder earnings. Such a company would typically use an approach that involves earnings reserves, solvency reserves, and required capital. The primary profit goal may be a certain return on stockholder equity, where equity consists mainly of required capital plus the difference between earnings reserves and solvency reserves.

Some companies have considered and rejected stockholder earnings as a basis for pricing, because of the added difficulty. When developing a new product, almost every change in product design or assumptions requires a recalculation of earnings reserves. For pricing based on stockholder earnings to be feasible, you need pricing software that automatically recalculates earnings reserves every time a product feature or assumption is changed; such software is commercially available.

11.4.2 Reflecting Risk in Profit Goals

There are a variety of ways to reflect risk when pricing a product. A realistic approach is recommended, using best-estimate assumptions with profit goals related to the degree of risk. The alternative, using conservative or padded assumptions, produces results that are difficult to interpret.

Groundbreaking products or other risky products would seem to demand higher profit margins. Here are a few examples of ways to reflect the degree of risk when pricing a product:

- A formula could be devised to determine the profit margin as a function of the degree of risk. This approach might reflect lapse, mortality, expense, and investment risks.

- The profit margin for a product could be set to reflect the estimated degree of risk. This approach requires much judgment, but also allows much flexibility.

- Sensitivity analysis could be used to estimate the degree of risk and set profit margins. The more volatile the profits, especially on the downside, the greater the targeted profit margin.

Regardless of the approach used, examining the product design and the origin of the assumptions used could identify certain risks that require special treatment. For example, extra mortality margins should probably be included for products using a new approach to underwriting. It may be possible to make adjustments in product design to reduce risk. For example, if large losses are sustained on lapses in the early policy years, then early duration cash values could be reduced to compensate.

When choosing a mortality table, you are likely to select a table based on the experience of the company over the past few years or a table based on recent industry experience. Such mortality tables are usually free from unusual, unpredictable occurrences such as wars or epidemics. Therefore, some consideration should be given to the unexpected occurrences not built into the mortality table. Although we cannot predict when catastrophes will happen or how severe they will be, we can expect that they will occur. It may be difficult to develop an explicit assumption to take these unexpected occurrences into account. Instead, such occurrences could contribute to certain adverse scenarios to be tested.

Some allowance should also be made for risks related to assumptions other than mortality. These risks may be subtler, because the experience of the past is not as easily understood and is less useful for predictions. For example, past interest rates and trends are not good predictors of future interest rates. Chapter 14 will introduce a better way of dealing with the seeming randomness of interest rates.

11.4.3 Choice of Discount Rates and Rates of Return

The decision to offer a new life insurance product is an investment decision, with returns on that investment expected over a very long period of time. To analyze this investment decision, it is necessary to discount future results.

The decision as to what rate to use for discounting future values is influenced by a number of factors:

- What is the company's cost of capital, on both a weighted average and marginal basis? In general, a company would not normally accept a rate of return that is less than its cost of capital. The cost of capital is a weighted average of a company's various sources of capital. These sources and their associated costs could include the return on equity expected by stockholders, the after-tax cost of debt (in general, interest paid on debt is tax-deductible), and the net cost of capital obtained through reinsurance. Because a particular product may make greater or lesser use of one of these sources of capital (especially reinsurance), the marginal cost of capital for that product may differ from the company's weighted-average cost of capital.

- What range of returns can the company expect to earn on alternative investments in other, similarly risky ventures? This is the "opportunity cost" of capital. If other business units or products with similar risks provided higher rates of return, you would need a good reason to accept a lower rate of return for the product being priced: for example, the product is strategically important, providing significant value beyond its direct financial results, or the opportunities to invest at higher rates of return are limited and will not use all of the company's available capital.

- What is the company's current capital position, and what is it expected to be over the next few years? If the company has more capital than it can use over the next few years, then it should be receptive to short-term investment opportunities that earn a better rate of return than what the company expects to earn on its idle capital. However, very few life insurance products fall into the category of "short-term investment opportunities," since life insurance returns are typically earned over a few decades, not a few years.

- How will discounting be used? Generally, if discounting is used to determine whether a product produces an acceptable rate of return, the discount rate will be based on the company's cost of capital or the opportunity cost of alternative investments. However, when discounting is used simply to give more weight to the early policy years and less weight to the later policy years, there are many different approaches used to determine the discount rate. Besides cost of capital and opportunity cost, other common choices for discount rates are the pre-tax or after-tax yields on the invested assets supporting the product.

Discounting using after-tax interest rates employs the returns available on very safe investments (that is, the investments backing the product). Such low discount rates would never be used as targeted rates of return. Instead, they would be used to compare different streams of amounts, such as the present value of profits and the present value of premiums.

Discounting using before-tax interest rates has no theoretical basis. The practical motivation for this approach is that only one set of interest rates is needed for both investment returns and discounting.

Basing the discount rate on the company's cost of capital or opportunity cost has perhaps the greatest appeal. However, such a discount rate may be hard to determine for a mutual company. A company may require all of its business units or products to produce a targeted rate of return. Alternatively, a company may set different targets based on the riskiness of the business unit or product.

There is a common misperception about the relationship between pre-tax and after-tax rates of return: It would seem natural that the after-tax rate of return is simply the pre-tax rate times "one minus the tax rate." Instead, the two rates of return are often quite close. In the following discussion, "profits" can be interpreted as either "distributable earnings" or "solvency earnings."

- The pre-tax rate of return is the rate that discounts the stream of pre-tax profits to zero (assuming that pre-tax profits consist of a first-year loss followed by a stream of positive profits).

- Taxes are often close to a level percentage of pre-tax profits. For the sake of argument, let us assume taxes are *exactly* a level percentage of pre-tax profits.

- This means that after-tax profits will follow exactly the same pattern as pre-tax profits, which means they are discounted to zero by using the pre-tax rate of return. (As explained in Section 9.2.2, this assumes that all first-year losses are immediately deductible against renewal-year gains from old business.)

- In this case, the pre-tax and after-tax rates of return are identical.

For companies that have developed effective strategies for minimizing taxes and for countries with constantly changing tax laws, a case can be made for pricing on a pre-tax basis. An alternative might be to add an additional margin to the profit measure to cover anticipated tax changes. However, if the pattern of income taxes by policy year is significantly different from the pattern of pre-tax earnings, it is important to price on an after-tax basis.

When tax reserves are significantly less than solvency reserves, it is quite possible for a product to have a positive present value of pre-tax profits and a negative present value of after-tax profits. In the U.S. in the early 1980s, tax loopholes made the opposite situation possible: Some products actually had a negative present value of pre-tax profits with a positive present value of after-tax profits. The tax loopholes, which allowed tax reserves well in excess of solvency reserves, were quickly closed.

11.5 Present Values

In the rest of this chapter, we will use a number of present value calculations. Rather than present a different formula for each present value, we will define one present value calculation that we can use repeatedly.

Let

$$\text{PV(Variable, } n) = \text{The present value of } n \text{ years of Variable}(t);$$
$$\text{``Variable}(t)\text{'' could be PreTaxSolvEarn}(t),$$
$$\text{AfterTaxSolvEarn}(t), \text{DistrEarn}(t), \text{ and so on.}$$
$$\text{PVPrem}(n) = \text{The present value of } n \text{ years of premiums}$$

$n =$ The final policy year for calculations. To ensure that the release of final reserves and final required capital is reflected in pricing, it is wise to set n equal to the last policy year plus one.

Then,

$$PV(\text{Variable}, n) = \sum_{t=1}^{n} \text{Variable}(t) \, \text{DiscFactor}(t). \qquad (11.5.1)$$

This formula may not be appropriate for use with profits that are negative for one or more policy years after the first policy year. At the end of this section, an alternative formula for the present value of profits (Formula 11.5.3) is presented that overcomes the deficiencies in this formula.

Because premiums are paid as of the beginning of the policy year, we will need a special formula for the present value of premiums:

$$PVPrem(n) = \sum_{t=1}^{n} \text{Prem}(t) \, \text{DiscFactor}(t - 1). \qquad (11.5.2)$$

Thus far in this chapter, we have presented formulas for five different kinds of profits:

1. Pre-tax solvency earnings

2. After-tax solvency earnings

3. Distributable earnings

4. Pre-tax stockholder earnings

5. After-tax stockholder earnings.

For simplicity, we will refer to the present value of all of the above as "PVProfit."

Let

$PVProfit(n) = PV(\text{Profit}, n)$, where Profit is one of the five kinds of profit listed above.

When you discount future losses using a high discount rate, you may be effectively assuming that you can earn interest at the high discount rate on earlier profits in order to offset later losses. A discount rate applied to future losses is essentially the interest rate the company must pay on a loan from its policyowners. A company seeking to make a 15% rate of return may not be happy when the cash flows are reversed and it turns out the company is actually *paying* 15% interest to its policyowners. That is exactly what occurs when you discount future losses at 15%.

To solve this problem, the following approach will allow you to use your targeted discount rate except when the present value of future profits is negative, in which case you will discount using a lower rate. Let

$i(t)$ = The discount rate to be applied to year t when the present value of future profits is positive. This is the company's normal discount rate.

$j(t)$ = The discount rate to be applied to year t when the present value of future profits is negative. This may be equal to the company's after-tax interest rate earned on invested assets or some other rate the company can earn on its investments.

PVFP(t) = The present value of future profits as of the end of year t, including Profit(t), per unit issued.

To calculate the present value of future profits at time zero, we will start with the last policy year and work backwards one year at a time, using the following iterative procedure:

If PVFP is positive, then discount using the normal discount rate $i(t)$.

If PVFP is negative, then discount using the lower discount rate $j(t)$.

In mathematical terms this translates to the following:

Set PVFP(n) = Profit(n),

For $t = n, n - 1, \ldots, 2, 1$:

If PVFP(t) > 0, then

$$\text{PVFP}(t-1) = \frac{\text{PVFP}(t)}{1+i(t)} + \text{Profit}(t-1),$$

otherwise

$$\text{PVFP}(t-1) = \frac{\text{PVFP}(t)}{1+j(t)} + \text{Profit}(t-1). \tag{11.5.3}$$

When done, set PVProfit(n) = PVFP(0). Note: If Profit(1) is the first profit calculated, then use Profit(0) = 0.

11.6 Profit Measures

This section discusses the following profit measures:

> Embedded value
>
> Return on investment (ROI)
>
> Weighted-average return on equity (ROE)
>
> Profit as a percentage of premium
>
> Profit as a percentage of assets
>
> Profit as a percentage of revenue
>
> Profit as a percentage of risk charges
>
> Accumulated profit as a percentage of reserves
>
> Breakeven year
>
> New business strain.

These are the profit measures used by most life insurance companies today. The majority of companies use two profit measures. A common combination is ROI or ROE combined with profit as a percentage of premium. In such a case, the company would typically set a minimum ROI or ROE goal, but would also require that profit be at least a minimum percentage of premium.

Publicly traded stock companies tend to use embedded value, ROI, or ROE as one of their profit goals. Each of these goals involves a targeted rate of return. Most publicly traded companies disclose this rate of return to investment analysts, stockholders, and potential stockholders. In addition, these companies typically disclose their targeted growth rate, because growth in earnings is a key driver of stock price. The higher the growth rate of earnings, the higher the stock price as a multiple of earnings per share.

Mutual companies tend to use other profit measures. In addition, mutual companies are careful to choose profit targets that will internally generate sufficient capital to support new sales, since their access to outside capital is limited.

11.6.1 Embedded Value

Embedded value, also known as value added, is used both to price new business and to manage a company's financial results. In this chapter, we will focus on embedded value's use in pricing. Embedded value is just about the simplest profit measure because there is essentially only one decision to make regarding the profit criteria: the hurdle rate.

The embedded value of a block of business is simply its present value of future profits, calculated using a discount rate equal to the company's *hurdle rate*. The hurdle rate is the rate of return the company's owners expect. For a stock company, the hurdle rate should be in line with the company's weighted average cost of capital, discussed in Chapter 16.

The hurdle rate should be consistent with the return available on investments of comparable risk. Theoretically, the hurdle rate should vary by product, market, and other factors, when the degree of risk also varies by these factors. However, in practice, one hurdle rate is often used for all of a company's products.

The pricing goal is to maximize the embedded value generated by the new product. This is accomplished by adjusting prices to maximize embedded value per unit times units sold. A company using embedded value typically would scuttle a new product that produced negative embedded value. This happens when the rate of return of the product is less than the hurdle rate.

When calculating embedded value, it is normal to base profits on either after-tax solvency earnings or distributable earnings. Distributable earnings better reflect the owners' expected cash flows and are therefore preferable.

Let

EmbeddedValue(n) = Embedded value, equal to the present value of profits over n policy years, discounted using the hurdle rate.

Then,

$$\text{EmbeddedValue}(n) = \text{PV}(\text{Profit}, n). \tag{11.6.1}$$

As noted in the previous section, Formula 11.5.3 should be used for discounting, in order to handle situations where the present value of future profits in some policy years is negative. If Formula 11.5.3 is *not* used and a first-year profit is followed by nothing but losses, an embedded value of zero means the company has borrowed money at an interest rate equal to the hurdle rate. While owners are happy to earn the hurdle rate, they may be irate if they have effectively borrowed money at that same rate, because of a pricing blunder.

11.6.2   Return on Investment

The return on investment (ROI) is a solved-for discount rate that causes the present value of profits to equal zero. When calculating ROI, it is normal to base profits on either after-tax solvency earnings or distributable earnings. Since distributable earnings better reflect the owners' expected cash flows, they are preferable to after-tax solvency earnings.

As a profit goal, ROI can be a primary or a secondary profit goal. For example, a company might have the following profit goals: profit equal to 10% of premiums, subject to a minimum ROI of 15%. Another example might be ROI of 15%, subject to a minimum profit equal to 5% of premiums.

There are some practical problems related to ROI calculations. The calculations "blow up" when all policy years are profitable, since it is impossible to find an interest rate that causes the present value of profits to equal zero. A similar problem occurs when the first-year loss is small compared to renewal year profits. A meaningless ROI of, say, 1,000% may result. To overcome this problem, the ROI could be calculated in aggregate for all the cells for a product, for a group of products, or for the company's entire new product portfolio. Meaningless or nonexistent ROIs are very common when profits are based on stockholder earnings, since first-year stockholder earnings are usually positive.

Losses in later policy years can also produce meaningless ROIs, as we will see. Because the investor is paying out rather than receiving cash flows, losses in later policy years can change the interpretation of an ROI. Rather than a rate of return being earned, it can become a rate of return being paid. In such a case, a high ROI may be undesirable. The generalized ROI approach deals with situations such as these.

11.6.2.1 Simple ROI

The simple ROI is found by solving the following formula for i:

$$0 = \sum_{t=1}^{n} \text{Profit}(t)\,(1 + i)^{-t}. \tag{11.6.2}$$

Substituting v for $(1 + 1)^{-1}$, we can see that finding the ROI is equivalent to finding the roots of the following polynomial:

$$0 = \sum_{t=1}^{n} \text{Profit}(t)\,v^{t}. \tag{11.6.3}$$

Example 11.6.1 Simple ROI

Let us examine ROIs for two simple cases, each with an initial investment of 1,000. In the table below the annual profit and present value of profit (calculated using the ROI) are shown.

	Case 1		Case 2	
t	*Profit(t)*	*Profit(t) v^t, with i = 5%*	*Profit(t)*	*Profit(t) v^t, with i = 6%*
1	−1,000	−952.38	−1,000	−943.40
2	50	45.35	310	275.90
3	50	43.19	295	247.69
4	1,050	863.84	530	419.81
Total	150	0.00	135	0.00

The ROI for Case 1 is 5%, as demonstrated by the total of the third column. The ROI for Case 2 is 6%, as demonstrated by the total of the fifth column. Based on its higher ROI, it appears that Case 2 would be preferred by an investor. However, if 6% is below the investor's hurdle rate, then alternative investments should be sought.

11.6.2.2   Multiple ROIs

Drawing on mathematics, we know that the number of positive roots of the polynomial (Formula 11.6.3) is equal to the number of sign changes of Profit(t). In other words, if profits start negative, then turn positive, then turn negative, and then turn positive and stay positive, there are three sign changes, so there must be three positive roots for such a polynomial. When v is positive, we know i must be greater than −100%.

Example 11.6.2 Multiple ROIs

Consider the following example, which has four roots: $v = 0.9$, 1.0, 0.0, and -1.0, which translate to ROIs of 11.11%, 0.0%, 100%, and -200%. Which is the correct ROI?

t	$Profit(t)$	$Profit(t)\ v^t$, with $i = 11.11\%$	$Profit(t)\ v^t$, with $i = 100\%$
1	-45	-40.500	-22.500
2	140	113.400	35.000
3	-55	-40.095	-6.875
4	-140	-91.854	-8.750
5	100	59.049	3.125
Total	0	0.000	0.000

This table demonstrates that both $i = 11.11\%$ ($v = 0.9$) and $i = 100\%$ ($v = 0.5$) are possible ROIs. Also, since the sum of the profits equals zero, $i = 0.0\%$ ($v = 1.0$) is a possible ROI. The demonstration of the fourth possible ROI, $i = -200\%$ ($v = -1.0$), is left as an exercise.

Example 11.6.3 Analyzing the Cash Flows

Once again, which is the correct ROI? Surprisingly, the correct answer is "none of the above." Let us dig a little deeper into this example to see why. To make it a little more dramatic, assume that all of the above numbers are in millions. Further assume that you are a multimillionaire with 45 million that you are looking to invest. At the present time and into the future, you expect to be able to safely earn 7% interest on your 45 million (so 7% is your hurdle rate). Finally, for simplicity, assume there are no taxes and the profits in the above example are fully guaranteed. Would you make this investment? If you can earn an ROI of 11.11% or 100%, of course you would. But if you earn an ROI of 0% or -100%, you wouldn't. So which is it?

Walk through this investment, one year at a time:

- At the end of the first year, you invest your 45 million.

- At the end of the second year, you receive 140 million, which you accumulate at your hurdle rate of 7%.

- The 140 million accumulates to 149.8 million by the end of the third year, at which time you must pay 55 million, leaving you with 94.8 million.

- The 94.8 million accumulates at the 7% hurdle rate to 101.436 million by the end of the fourth year, at which time you must pay 140 million. You are 38.564 million short, which you are able to borrow from yourself at 7%.

- Your 38.564 million of debt accumulates at the 7% hurdle rate to 41,263,480 by the end of the fifth year, at which time you receive the final payment of 100 million, leaving you with a net of 58,736,520. Over four years, your effective rate of return was only 6.89%.

Had you left the 45 million to earn 7% interest for the last four years, you would have ended up with 58,985,820, so you are better off leaving your money where it is and declining this investment opportunity.

How did we end up with an ROI of 6.89% instead of one of the four ROIs we expected? The answer, as you have probably already observed, is that we had to invest some of the cash flows at a rate of 7%, and we had to borrow some money at a rate of 7%. These realities brought our rate of return back to Earth.

11.6.2.3 Generalized ROI

The purpose of Example 11.6.3 is to point out the dangerous flaws in using a simple ROI calculation (such as Formula 11.6.2 or 11.6.3) when there is more than one sign change in profits. The resulting ROIs will typically *all* be wrong. When profits start negative and then turn positive and stay positive, the simple ROI calculation works fine. When profits start positive and then turn negative and stay negative, the simple ROI calculation still works fine, but the result is not a rate of return or ROI. Instead, it is the rate of interest at which you are *borrowing* money. As mentioned in Section 11.5, present value calculations are also erroneous when there is more than one sign change in profits.

A more generalized approach to calculating ROI has been developed, using Formula 11.5.3. First you select *j*, the rate you are willing to pay for borrowed money. Then you solve for the value of *i* that results in the present value of profits equal to zero. If there is such a value of *i*, it is the ROI. Generally, if the first-year profit is negative and the sum of all years' profits is positive, there will be one and only one ROI.

Example 11.6.4 Generalized ROI

Let us calculate the generalized ROI for the previous example. We will solve for the ROI using a trial and error approach. In the previous analysis, we developed an ROI of 6.89%, but this was based on borrowing 38,564,000 at the end of the fourth year. This was wrong. The investment should have been sufficient to avoid having to borrow money. Still, 6.89% may be a good first guess for the ROI.

The following table shows the PVFPs resulting from several ROI guesses. Positive PVFPs are discounted using i and negative PVFPs are discounted using $j = 7\%$.

t	$Profit(t)$	$PVFP(t)$, using $i = 6.89\%$	$PVFP(t)$, using $i = 6.83\%$	$PVFP(t)$, using $i = 6.8324\%$
5	100	100.000	100.000	100.000
4	-140	-46.446	-46.393	-46.395
3	-55	-98.407	-98.358	-98.360
2	140	48.031	48.076	48.075
1	-45	-0.065	0.003	0.000
0	0	-0.061	0.003	0.000

The correct ROI, at long last, is 6.8324%, although 6.83% is close enough.

11.6.3 Weighted-Average Return on Equity

At the end of Section 11.3, we developed an annual formula for ROE. While the pattern of ROEs by policy year may be illuminating and point out potential problems or opportunities, a weighted-average ROE is more useful as an overall profit measure.

To properly calculate a weighted-average ROE, you must calculate a weighted-average return (based on after-tax stockholder earnings) and divide by a weighted-average equity base. One way to weight the policy year results is to discount them using the company's ROI goal or hurdle rate.

Another way to weight policy year results is to link them with the company's targeted growth rate. For example, if the company's goal is to grow by 10% per year, then you could calculate what the ultimate ROE would be if the company grew by 10% forever and sold only the product being priced. Such an approach gives more weight to the early policy years and less weight to the later policy years.

Continuing our example, a ten-year term product would develop weights of 1.00 for the tenth year, 1.10 for the ninth year, 1.21 for the eighth year, . . . , and $(1.10)^9$ for the first year. These weights may seem backwards, but remember that, after nine years of sales increasing by 10% per year, the first-year results associated with the most recent issue year deserve much more weight than the tenth-year results associated with business issued ten years earlier. Table 11.6.1 illustrates the weights and the policy years they apply to.

Table 11.6.1 Weights for Weighted-Average ROE

Weight	*Applied to Profit and Equity Base for Year*
$(1.10)^9$	1
$(1.10)^8$	2
$(1.10)^7$	3
. . .	. . .
$(1.10)^1$	9
$(1.10)^0$	10

What if we were to divide all of the weights in the preceding example by $(1.10)^{10}$? The resulting weights would be $(1.10)^{-1}$ for the first year, $(1.10)^{-2}$ for the second year, $(1.10)^{-3}$ for the third year, . . . , and $(1.10)^{-10}$ for the tenth year. In other words, using a targeted growth rate of 10% to develop weights is equivalent to discounting using an interest rate of 10%. In general, growth rates can be directly converted to interest rates. This means we can use discount factors and present values, no matter whether we weight using growth rates or discount using an ROI goal or hurdle rate.

Let

WtdAvgROE(n) = The weighted average return on equity, calculated by dividing the present value of after-tax stockholder earnings by the present value of the equity base, over a period of n policy years.

Then,

$$\text{WtdAvgROE}(n) \quad = \frac{\text{PV(AfterTaxStockEarn, } n)}{\text{PV(EquityBase, } n)}. \qquad (11.6.4)$$

Ideally, each policy year's ROE will be within a few percent of the weighted-average ROE. The ROE pattern may point out potential problems or opportunities. For example, the ROE pattern for the first few years may be well in excess of the company's weighted-average ROE, followed by ROEs that are lower than the weighted average. If the company's performance and management's compensation is linked to ROE, such a pattern may please current investors and management. However, careful consideration should be given to the ROE shortfalls that will develop in later years. Such a pattern may not be in the long-term best interests of the company. By understanding what causes the pattern of ROEs to be skewed, you may find some ways to level or smooth the pattern.

11.6.4   Profit as a Percentage of Premium

Profit as a percentage of premium is one of the most commonly used profit measures. It is calculated as the present value of profits divided by the present value of premiums. This measure has the advantage of being fairly concrete and easy to explain.

For this profit measure, it is common to use the pre-tax or after-tax interest rates earned on assets for discounting purposes. This generally produces a positive present value of profits. In contrast, if you were to discount using the product's ROI or the company's hurdle rate, the present value of profits would likely be zero or close to zero, and this profit measure would be rendered meaningless. This comment regarding discount rates applies to all profit measures that compare the present value of profits to the present value of another measure (such as premiums, revenue, assets, or risk charges).

Let

$\text{Profit\%Prem}(n)$ = Profit as a percentage of premium, calculated as the present value of profits divided by the present value of premiums over a period of n years.

Then,

$$\text{Profit\%Prem}(n) = \frac{\text{PVProfit}(n)}{\text{PVPrem}(n)}. \tag{11.6.5}$$

11.6.5 Profit as a Percentage of Assets

Profit as a percentage of assets is often referred to as *return on assets* (ROA) or profit spread. ROA can be calculated for each policy year as profit divided by assets. However, when a different ROA is calculated for each policy year, the results are hard to interpret and use. Therefore, we will calculate a return on assets that is equal to the present value of profits divided by the present value of assets.

Many products are priced with a targeted spread between the rate earned on company investments and the interest rate credited to policyowners. It is useful to know how much of that spread is retained as profits, on the average. For example, suppose a product priced with a

2.00% spread between the earned rate and the credited rate has an ROA of 0.35%, or 35 basis points. This means that, after taking expenses, mortality, and lapses into account, only 0.35% of the targeted 2.00% spread is retained as profits.

ROA is a function of profits and assets. There are three choices for ROA profits and the corresponding ROA assets, as shown in Table 11.6.2.

Table 11.6.2 ROA Numerators and Denominators

ROA Profits	ROA Assets
After-tax solvency earnings	Solvency reserves
Distributable earnings	Solvency reserves plus required capital
After-tax stockholder earnings	Solvency reserves plus required capital plus deferred acquisition costs (that is, stockholder assets)

Let

$\text{ROA}(n)$ = Return on assets for the first n policy years, calculated as the present value of profits divided by the present value of assets.

Then,

$$\text{ROA}(n) = \frac{\text{PVProfit}(n)}{\text{PV(Assets, } n)}. \tag{11.6.6}$$

11.6.6 Profit as a Percentage of Revenue

Profit as a percentage of revenue is a generalization of profit as a percentage of premium. While premium is often the most important revenue item, there are other choices that may make more sense for certain types of products, as shown in Table 11.6.3.

Table 11.6.3 Revenue Measures	
Type of Product	*Important Sources of Revenue*
Investment-Oriented	Investment income and perhaps expense and surrender charges
Universal Life	Investment income (or targeted interest spread), mortality charges, expense charges, and surrender charges
Variable Universal Life	Investment charges (as a percentage of account value), mortality charges, expense charges, and surrender charges
Term Insurance	Premiums
Whole Life Insurance	Premiums and perhaps investment income

Profit as a percentage of revenue is calculated as the present value of profits divided by the present value of revenue. Profits can be any of the five different kinds of profits developed earlier in this chapter. Revenue can be anything that makes sense, such as some of the choices in Table 11.6.3.

In summary, profit as a percentage of revenue has no standard approaches or benchmarks to compare to. It is useful mainly as a way to compare the relative profitability of similar types of products. For example, it may be useful in comparing a new universal life product to the old one it is replacing. It is *not* useful in comparing the profitability of two very different types of products, such as universal life and term insurance, especially when different revenue measures are involved.

11.6.7 Profit as a Percentage of Risk Charges

Risk charges are an attempt to quantify the degree of risk inherent in a product. There are no standard approaches to calculating risk charges, but here are two possible approaches:

- Risk charges may consist of mortality, lapse, and investment components. The mortality risk charge may be a function of the net amount of risk and the uncertainty in the mortality rate. The lapse risk charge may be a function of the accumulated loss, if any, and the uncertainty in the lapse rate. The investment risk charge may be a function of the funds invested and many other considerations: the interest sensitivity of the product, the uncertainty in the interest rate, the possibility of disintermediation, and the likelihood of asset default.

- A simpler approach would be to calculate risk charges as a percentage of required capital. This presumes that required capital is an accurate measure of the degree of risk, which may not be the case.

Profit as a percent of risk charges is calculated as the present value of profits divided by the present value of risk charges. This profit measure has the attraction of directly comparing profit to risk. However, because risk charges are arbitrary, the attraction may be based more on illusion than reality. Also, risk charges are a fairly abstract concept. It is difficult to interpret the results of this profit measure and even more difficult to explain them. One solution would be to convert the results to another profit measure, such as profit as a percentage of premium, before presenting them to others.

11.6.7.1 Risk-Free Rates and Risk Charges

In one financial theory, investors demand rates of return that rise with the increasing riskiness of the underlying investment. In addition, investors demand a minimum rate of return for a risk-free investment. Using profit as a percentage of risk charges may give us a way to adapt this theory to life insurance investments. The key would be to develop risk charges that are fairly compatible with the rates of return associated with a number of products, ranging from low risk to high risk. For example, consider Table 11.6.4.

Table 11.6.4 Risk and Rate of Return

Product	Level of Risk	Industry-Average Rate of Return
Risk-Free Investment	None	5.0%
Product A	Low	8.0
Product B	Medium	12.0
Product C	High	20.0

The goal for developing meaningful risk charges would be to produce profits *net of risk charges* that earn the risk-free rate of return. In Table 11.6.4, subtracting meaningful risk charges from profits would reduce the rate of return for each product to 5%. Another way of saying this is that, with present values based on the risk-free rate of 5%, the present value of profits should equal the present value of risk charges.

By using industry-average rates of return to establish the appropriate level of risk charges, you can ensure that your pricing will be roughly in line with the rest of the market. Other approaches to developing risk charges can be taken, but they run the risk of being out of touch with the market. If your risk charges are too high, your company's products will be noncompetitive. If your risk charges are too low, your pricing may be overly competitive, resulting in increased sales but lower profit margins. In this case, your competitors are apt to react by lowering their prices, causing your increased sales to return to prior levels and locking in your lower profit margin.

11.6.7.2 Summary

As with profit as a percentage of revenue, there are no standard approaches to profit as a percentage of risk charges. There is a wide range of choices to be made as to which type of profit to use and how to calculate risk charges. The main attraction of this kind of profit measure is the ability to tie profitability to the riskiness of the business. While this is a laudable theoretical goal, most measures of risk are fairly arbitrary.

However, developing risk charges that reproduce the risk-free rate of return for a range of products has both theoretical and practical appeal. In this case, the profit goal would be present value of profits equal to present value of risk charges. Present values would be calculated using the risk-free rate of return. Profits would be based on distributable earnings, since these best represent the investors' cash flows.

11.6.8   Accumulated Profit as a Percentage of Reserves

One of the earliest profit goals, especially for mutual companies, was to accumulate profits equal to a certain percentage of reserves (or cash values) by the end of a certain policy year. For example, the goal could be to accumulate profits equal to 10% of reserves by the end of the twentieth policy year. With such a goal, it was intended that one generation of policyowners would provide the capital needed to fund the next generation of policyowners. Today this profit goal is rarely used when pricing new products, although it is still used by some companies for setting policyowner dividend scales.

This profit measure and breakeven year (defined in the next section) are both based on the accumulation of profits. Accumulated profits are usually based on after-tax solvency earnings and are usually accumulated using after-tax interest rates. Occasionally, distributable earnings or stockholder earnings are accumulated.

Let

AccumProfit(n) = Accumulated profit at the end of policy year n.

Then,

$$\text{AccumProfit}(n) = \sum_{t=0}^{n} \text{Profit}(t)\,\text{AccumFactor}(t). \qquad (11.6.7)$$

Another approach to determining accumulated profit is to calculate it iteratively, starting with AccumProfit(0) = 0 and using $i(t)$ as the interest rate for accumulation. As noted above, $i(t)$ is usually set equal to the after-tax interest rate:

$$\text{AccumProfit}(t) = \text{AccumProfit}(t - 1)(1 + i(t)) + \text{Profit}(t),$$
$$\text{for } t = 1 \text{ to } n. \tag{11.6.8}$$

To calculate accumulated profit as a percentage of reserves at the end of n years, we will need to divide accumulated profit by reserves, with both calculated on a per unit issued basis. If profit is based on solvency earnings or distributable earnings, then solvency reserves would be used in the following formula. If profit is based on stockholder earnings, then earnings reserves would be used.

Let

$\text{AccumProfitPct}(n) = $ Accumulated profit as a percentage of reserves, with both factors calculated per unit issued at the end of year n.

Then,

$$\text{AccumProfitPct}(n) = \frac{\text{AccumProfit}(n)}{\text{Res}(n)}. \tag{11.6.9}$$

A similar formula could be developed for accumulated profit as a percentage of cash values, making sure to convert the cash values at the end of year n to a per unit issued basis.

11.6.9 Breakeven Year

Breakeven year can be defined as the policy year in which accumulated profits first turn positive. A better definition would be the first policy year in which accumulated profits turn positive and remain positive thereafter. The breakeven year is used more as an indicator or danger sign than as a profit measure. A product that does not break even for many years may involve undue lapse risk or may require too much capital for too long. It may be better to redesign the product or not offer it at all, rather than settle for a late breakeven year.

For example, if a product does not break even for 20 years but eventually achieves acceptable rates of return, there may be a flaw in the pricing. To rely on the profits that accrue after 20 years to provide most of the product's earnings may be a dangerous gamble. By testing the sensitivity of profits to changes in long-term lapse rates, you can determine the extent of such a gamble.

A *modified breakeven year* could be determined by assuming that all policies lapse at the end of a given year, releasing required capital and excess reserves into the profit calculation. Using this approach, the first year that produces accumulated profits, including the release of required capital and excess reserves, would be the modified breakeven year. Reflecting the release of these items will give you a better picture of the effect of all policies lapsing at once. The modified breakeven year is often several years earlier than the breakeven year.

In the case of a mutual company, a late breakeven year may be acceptable, because the ultimate goal may be to return all or most profits to policyowners. For example, a mutual company may have two goals:

1. To accumulate profits to a certain level by a certain policy year and then

2. To return those accumulated profits over the remaining lifetime of the product.

In practice, returning all the accumulated profits is not often feasible. Instead, a mutual company uses a portion of accumulated profits to fund new business.

Breakeven year analysis has become more important in the U.S. because of an *illustration regulation*. This regulation requires an actuary to calculate the breakeven year as a method of ensuring that the product's illustrations are supportable.

11.6.10 New Business Strain

Although not truly a profit measure, new business strain is often evaluated as part of the pricing process. If strain is unacceptably high, the product may be redesigned to lower the strain. Strain is often converted to a percentage of first-year premium. This allows strain to be easily coupled with premium projections to estimate how much capital will be needed to finance new business.

Let

NBStrain = The financial strain (that is, capital contribution) associated with writing new business, expressed as a percentage of first-year premium.

Then,

$$\text{NBStrain} = \frac{\text{DistrEarn}(1)}{\text{Prem}(1)}. \qquad (11.6.10)$$

(handwritten annotation:) Solv Earnings − All takes + Inv Inc RC − ARC
↘ PCF + Inv Inc − Δ Solv Rsv

If distributable earnings remain negative beyond the first year, this formula should be extended to include the present value of additional years of new business strain.

11.6.11 Summary of Profit Measures

The choice of profit goals is one of the most important decisions a company can make. Profit goals must fit the company's strategy, allow the company to successfully compete, and provide long-term financial results that allow the company to grow and appropriately reward its owners. It is vital that the company be able to track its results at meaningful levels for the profit goals chosen.

For example, if ROE is the major pricing objective, a company must be able to calculate ROE at levels below the total company, such as for each business unit, each market, and each product group. This requires that both stockholder earnings and stockholder equity be split by business unit, market, and product group. If a company cannot break its results down to such levels, then it will not be able to determine which business units, markets, and products to grow and which to de-emphasize.

11.7 Pricing Model

Here is this chapter's contribution to the pricing example that spans and ties together Chapters 4 through 11. Table 11.7.1 builds on calculations from previous pricing examples to calculate distributable earnings.

Table 11.7.1 Calculation of Distributable Earnings

t	PreTaxSolvEarn	Tax	AfterTaxSolvEarn	ReqCapIncr	ATInvIncRC	DistrEarn
1	−9.32995	−3.51150	−5.81845	1.02977	0.00000	−6.84822
2	2.02632	0.78667	1.23965	−0.04782	0.05108	1.33855
3	1.86862	0.71485	1.15377	−0.02173	0.04870	1.22420
4	2.06792	0.78115	1.28677	−0.02795	0.04763	1.36235
5	2.03899	0.76378	1.27520	−0.03834	0.04624	1.35979
6	2.05519	0.76723	1.28796	−0.03294	0.04434	1.36524
7	2.14738	0.80146	1.34592	−0.04364	0.04270	1.43227
8	2.23359	0.83691	1.39668	−0.05812	0.04054	1.49534
9	2.29960	0.86859	1.43101	−0.07423	0.03766	1.54290
10	1.66513	0.63852	1.02661	−0.68499	0.03398	1.74557

Table 11.7.2 shows the calculations for various profit measures. The ROI for our sample product is calculated as 14.11%. Note that all the required surplus is released at the end of the pricing horizon, as suggested in Section 11.2.3. This is accomplished by setting qw in the final year equal to 1.00 in Table 4.8.1.

Table 11.7.2 Various Profit Measures

Discount Rate	PV of Premium[d]	PV of DistrEarn	Profit as a Percentage of Premium
7.00%	33.4037	2.1756	6.51%
4.34[a]	36.4077	3.3732	9.27%
12.00[b]	28.9284	0.5233	1.81%
14.11[c]	27.3948	0.0000	0.00%

[a]After-tax interest rate.
[b]Using a hurdle rate of 12%, embedded value is 0.5233.
[c]The ROI is 14.11%.
[d]PV of premium is net of YRT reinsurance premiums paid.

Tables 11.7.3–11.7.6 develop stockholder earnings for the sample product. We have chosen to show the earnings reserves in two parts (a benefit reserve and a deferred acquisition cost), similar to how reserves are shown under U.S. GAAP. If the earnings reserve were shown as one number, it would equal the Benefit Reserve minus the DAC.

Table 11.7.3 Calculation of Pre-Tax Stockholder Earnings

t	*PreTaxSolvEarn*	*SolvResIncr*	*BenResIncr*	*DACAmort*	*InvIncRC*	*PreTaxStockEarn*
1	−9.32995	1.20555	1.87402	−10.45881	0.00000	0.46039
2	2.02632	1.22228	1.21920	0.93363	0.08238	1.17815
3	1.86862	0.87169	0.67102	0.88887	0.07856	1.25897
4	2.06792	0.51740	0.30414	1.13728	0.07682	1.22071
5	2.03899	0.16063	0.00446	1.12371	0.07458	1.14603
6	2.05519	−0.09791	−0.25431	1.21548	0.07151	1.06762
7	2.14738	−0.48280	−0.49857	1.24200	0.06888	0.99003
8	2.23359	−0.89269	−0.76538	1.27172	0.06539	0.89994
9	2.29960	−1.34045	−1.08314	1.30478	0.06074	0.79826
10	1.66513	−1.16369	−1.47144	1.34135	0.05480	0.68633

Table 11.7.4 Calculation of After-Tax Stockholder Earnings

t	*PreTaxStockEarn*	*Tax*	*TaxInvIncRC*	*AccruedTax*	*DefTaxProv*	*AfterTaxStockEarn*
1	0.46039	−3.51150	0.00000	0.17495	3.68645	0.28544
2	1.17815	0.78667	0.03131	0.44770	−0.37028	0.73045
3	1.25897	0.71485	0.02985	0.47841	−0.26629	0.78056
4	1.22071	0.78115	0.02919	0.46387	−0.34647	0.75684
5	1.14603	0.76378	0.02834	0.43549	−0.35663	0.71054
6	1.06762	0.76723	0.02718	0.40569	−0.38871	0.66192
7	0.99003	0.80146	0.02617	0.37621	−0.45142	0.61382
8	0.89994	0.83691	0.02485	0.34198	−0.51978	0.55797
9	0.79826	0.86859	0.02308	0.30334	−0.58833	0.49492
10	0.68633	0.63852	0.02082	0.26081	−0.39854	0.42553

Table 11.7.5 Calculation of Stockholder Assets and Liabilities

t	SolvRes	ReqCap	DAC	StockAssets	BenRes	DefTaxLiab	StockLiabilities
1	1.20555	1.02977	10.45881	12.69413	1.87402	3.68645	5.56047
2	2.42783	0.98195	9.52519	12.93496	3.09322	3.31618	6.40939
3	3.29951	0.96022	8.63632	12.89605	3.76424	3.04988	6.81412
4	3.81691	0.93227	7.49904	12.24822	4.06838	2.70341	6.77179
5	3.97754	0.89392	6.37534	11.24680	4.07284	2.34678	6.41962
6	3.87963	0.86098	5.15986	9.90047	3.81854	1.95807	5.77661
7	3.39682	0.81734	3.91785	8.13202	3.31996	1.50665	4.82661
8	2.50413	0.75922	2.64614	5.90949	2.55458	0.98687	3.54146
9	1.16369	0.68499	1.34135	3.19003	1.47144	0.39854	1.86998
10	0.00000	0.00000	0.00000	0.00000	0.00000	0.00000	0.00000

Table 11.7.6 Calculation of Equity Base and ROE

t	AfterTaxStockEarn	StockEquity	Beginning of Year		Average Equity	
			EquityBase	ROE	EquityBase	ROE
1	0.28544	7.13366	0.00000	N/A	3.56683	8.00%
2	0.73045	6.52557	7.13366	10.24%	6.82961	10.70%
3	0.78056	6.08193	6.52557	11.96%	6.30375	12.38%
4	0.75684	5.47642	6.08193	12.44%	5.77918	13.10%
5	0.71054	4.82718	5.47642	12.97%	5.15180	13.79%
6	0.66192	4.12386	4.82718	13.71%	4.47552	14.79%
7	0.61382	3.30541	4.12386	14.88%	3.71463	16.52%
8	0.55797	2.36803	3.30541	16.88%	2.83672	19.67%
9	0.49492	1.32005	2.36803	20.90%	1.84404	26.84%
10	0.42553	0.00000	1.32005	32.24%	0.66002	64.47%

11.8   Exercises

Exercise 11.1

Calculate the weighted-average cost of capital for a company that wishes to maintain a capital structure of 85% equity and 15% debt. Assume that stockholders demand a 15% after-tax ROE. The pre-tax cost of debt is 8%. The company pays a tax rate of 40%.

Exercise 11.2

Given the following data, calculate investment income on assets backing required capital, the tax on it, after-tax solvency earnings, and distributable earnings.

The assets backing required capital earn a pre-tax interest rate of 6%. A tax rate of 30% applies to investment income earned on required capital.

t	Pre-Tax SolvEarn	Tax	ReqCap
1	−10.00	−3.00	3.00
2	2.50	0.75	4.00
3	2.00	0.60	5.00

Exercise 11.3

Demonstrate that one of the possible ROIs for the following stream of profits is −200%.

t	Profit(t)
1	−45
2	140
3	−55
4	−140
5	100
Total	0

Table 11.8.1 Data for Exercises 11.4–11.8

t	Prem	SolvRes	PreTaxSolvEarn	ReqCap	InvIncRC	EarnRes
1	229.86	111.64	−342.09	55.72	3.90	−257.21
2	211.78	119.27	157.47	51.82	3.90	−142.57
3	193.50	126.36	129.27	47.80	3.63	−47.06
4	176.46	134.13	105.78	44.15	3.35	33.82
5	162.46	134.44	96.25	40.97	3.09	104.44
6	150.26	144.58	71.98	38.42	2.87	166.98
7	139.82	154.55	60.01	36.21	2.69	222.25
8	130.07	157.87	55.15	34.08	2.53	270.32
9	121.74	162.70	42.87	32.29	2.39	311.73
10	114.45	168.78	31.19	30.79	2.26	346.11
11	108.21	211.40	−16.00	30.20	2.16	372.56
12	102.47	220.36	8.47	29.08	2.11	389.34
13	97.21	229.46	−2.64	28.06	2.04	396.33
14	92.35	238.65	−15.05	27.15	1.96	391.39
15	87.84	248.61	−28.00	26.34	1.90	373.83
16	83.68	259.35	−41.29	25.61	1.84	342.30
17	79.62	270.97	−55.07	24.93	1.79	295.40
18	75.69	283.80	−68.11	24.31	1.75	233.02
19	71.86	297.75	−80.68	23.73	1.70	154.37
20	68.15	240.14	−13.14	18.14	1.66	65.66
21	0.00	0.00	186.69	0.00	1.27	0.00
PV at:						
3.85%	1,929.91	2,527.38	220.09	490.00	36.78	2,401.54
5.00	1,804.24	2,243.82	203.39	451.02	33.78	2,064.34
7.00	1,619.81	1,846.74	176.17	394.43	29.45	1,589.13
9.00	1,469.75	1,542.61	151.07	349.01	25.99	1,223.51
12.00	1,292.39	1,208.47	117.05	296.10	21.99	822.25
15.00	1,156.42	973.68	87.09	256.18	18.99	543.37
20.00	990.82	716.57	45.28	208.38	15.41	247.55

Use Table 11.8.1 with Exercises 11.4–11.8. It will be easiest to solve the exercises if you type the columns into an electronic spreadsheet.

Exercise 11.4

Assuming no timing or permanent differences between solvency and tax reserves, calculate Distributable Earnings (DistrEarn), using Table 11.8.1 and a tax rate of 45%.

Exercise 11.5

Using Table 11.8.1, calculate simple ROI and generalized ROI. For generalized ROI, negative values should be discounted at the after-tax interest rate. The pre-tax interest rate is 7.00%. Also, calculate embedded value assuming a 15% hurdle rate.

Exercise 11.6

Calculate pre-tax and after-tax stockholder earnings, using Table 11.8.1 and a tax rate of 45%.

Exercise 11.7

Using Table 11.8.1 and the results of Exercise 11.6, calculate stockholder equity and year-by-year return on equity, based on average equity.

Exercise 11.8

Review the patterns for solvency earnings, distributable earnings, and stockholder earnings from Exercises 11.4 and 11.6 and compare them to the pattern for premiums. Other than the first-year strain associated with solvency and distributable earnings, we expect earnings to roughly follow the pattern of premiums. It looks like something unusual is going on.

a. What is causing solvency earnings and distributable earnings to turn negative in the later years?

b. Why aren't stockholder earnings closer to a level percentage of premiums?

c. Why does ROE turn negative?

Exercise 11.9

Capital contributions are mainly required to provide the initial required capital and cover the strain of writing new business. Capital contributions are most common in the first policy year but sometimes occur after the first policy year as well.

We calculate distributable earnings as of the end of the policy year, but when distributable earnings are negative, capital contributions are needed at the beginning of the year. Likewise, when distributable earnings are positive, capital could be released at the beginning of the year, consistent with the timing of capital contributions.

Let

$$\text{CapRel}(t) = \text{Capital released at the beginning of the policy year in anticipation of positive distributable earnings at the end of the policy year}$$

$$\text{CapContr}(t) = \text{Capital contribution made at the beginning of the policy year to counter negative distributable earnings at the end of the policy year.}$$

In effect, we are moving distributable earnings from the end of the policy year to the beginning of the year. To accomplish this, you need to perform the following steps:

a. Develop formulas for $\text{CapRel}(t)$ and $\text{CapContr}(t)$ in terms of $\text{DistrEarn}(t)$, $\text{RCIntRate}(t)$, and $\text{TaxRate}(t)$.

b. Modify Formula 10.7.3 for $\text{InvIncRC}(t)$ to take into account the interest on change in assets represented by $\text{CapRel}(t)$ and $\text{CapContr}(t)$.

c. Recalculate $\text{DistrEarn}(t-1)$ to reflect $\text{CapRel}(t)$ and $\text{CapContr}(t)$, since these cash flows to and from owners happen at the same point in time.

When you finish this process, you will have created a cash flow for owners at time 0, namely, $\text{DistrEarn}(0)$. The formulas for all profit measures will need to be changed to start with $t = 0$.

Exercise 11.10

Now let us apply the formulas developed in the previous exercise. Repeat Exercises 11.4 and 11.5 to recalculate distributable earnings and ROIs, reflecting capital contributions made at the beginning of the year. What effect did this change have on the ROIs? Why?

Distributable earnings can be recalculated very quickly, using the following simple procedure:

1. Calculate CapContr(t) and CapRel(t) for all t.
2. Recalculate DistrEarn*($t - 1$) = CapRel(t) − CapContr(t) for all t.

Calculate CapContr(t), CapRel(t), and DistrEarn*($t - 1$) using RCIntRate = 7.0% and TaxRate = 45%, for all t. (The asterisk distinguishes the recalculated DistrEarn* from the original DistrEarn.)

11.9 Answers

Answer 11.1

Weighted-average cost of capital

$$= 85\% \times 15\% + 15\% \times 8\% \times (1 - 40\%)$$
$$= 12.75\% + 0.72\% = 13.47\%.$$

Answer 11.2

t	$InvIncRC(t)$	$TaxInvIncRC(t)$	$AfterTaxSolvEarn(t)$	$DistrEarn(t)$
1	0.00	0.000	−7.00	−10.000
2	0.18	0.054	1.75	0.876
3	0.24	0.072	1.40	0.568

Answer 11.3

t	Profit(t)	PV of Profit (t) with $i = -200\%$
1	-45	45
2	140	140
3	-55	55
4	-140	-140
5	100	-100
Total	0	0

With $i = -200\%$, $v = 1/(1 + -2) = -1$, which is a meaningless discount factor.

Answers 11.4 and 11.5

Table 11.9.1 shows the calculation of DistrEarn, which leads to the calculation of simple ROI and generalized ROI.

Table 11.9.1 Distributable Earnings and ROIs

t	DistrEarn(t)	PVFP(t)
1	−241.73	**0.00**
2	92.65	286.13
3	77.12	229.01
4	63.67	179.79
5	57.81	137.45
6	43.72	94.27
7	36.70	59.84
8	33.85	27.39
9	26.68	−6.71
10	19.90	−34.68
11	−7.03	−56.68
12	6.95	−51.57
13	0.68	−60.77
14	−6.28	−63.81
15	−13.54	−59.74
16	−20.97	−47.98
17	−28.62	−28.05
18	−35.88	0.67
19	−42.86	43.26
20	−0.72	101.94
21	121.52	121.52
ROI:	19.71%	18.3676%
	(Simple)	(Generalized)
PV at:		
3.85%	123.11	
5.00	108.97	
7.00	87.29	
9.00	68.56	
12.00	44.74	
15.00	24.93	
20.00	−1.35	

Note: After-tax Interest Rate $= 3.85\%$

Since there are no timing or permanent tax differences, after-tax earnings are calculated as PreTaxSolvEarn (1 − TaxRate). DistrEarn is calculated as

$$\text{PreTaxSolvEarn } (1 - \text{TaxRate}) - \text{ReqCapIncr}$$
$$+ \text{ InvIncRC } (1 - \text{TaxRate}).$$

For example, in year 8:

$$\text{DistrEarn}(8) = 55.15\,(1 - 0.45) - (34.08 - 36.21)$$
$$+ 2.53\,(1 - 0.45) = 33.85.$$

The simple ROI is calculated by solving for the rate of return that causes DistrEarn to equal zero. With an electronic spreadsheet, you can probably use the software's "IRR" function to calculate the simple ROI. Looking at the bottom section of Table 11.9.1, you can conclude that the ROI is between 15% and 20%, since the present value at 15% is greater than zero and the present value at 20% is less than zero. Linear interpolation between the present values at 15% and 20% results in an estimated ROI of 19.74%, which is very close to the actual result of 19.71%.

To calculate generalized ROI, start with the year 21 and work upwards through the table. Discount any negative values of PVFP using the after-tax interest rate of 3.85% (calculated as 7.00% (1 − 0.45)). Discount positive values of PVFP using the trial ROI. When you find a trial ROI that results in PVFP(1) = 0, you have found the generalized ROI.

For example, PVFP for year 19 is calculated as

$$\text{PVFP}(19) = \frac{101.94}{1 + 0.183676} + -42.86 = 43.26.$$

PVFP for year 10 is calculated as

$$\text{PVFP}(10) = \frac{-56.68}{1 + 0.0385} + 19.90 = -34.68.$$

There are several ways to evaluate embedded value. If embedded value includes the effect of both taxes and required capital, then the embedded value based on a hurdle rate of 15% is shown at the bottom of Table 11.9.1 as 24.93. If embedded value is based on pre-tax solvency earnings, it is shown at the bottom of Table 11.8.1 as 87.09. If embedded value is after taxes, but ignoring required capital, then embedded value can be calculated as the pre-tax embedded value times one minus the tax rate: 87.09 $(1 - 0.45) = 47.90$. This shortcut is only possible when taxes are a level percentage of pre-tax earnings. This is only true when there are no material differences between taxable earnings and pre-tax earnings.

Answers 11.6 and 11.7

Table 11.9.2 uses Formula 11.3.2 to calculate pre-tax stockholder earnings, with EarnRes(t) from Table 11.8.1 used to calculate "$- \text{BenResIncr}(t) - \text{DACAmort}(t)$" :

$$\begin{aligned} \text{PreTaxStockEarn}(t) = \; & \text{PreTaxSolvEarn}(t) + \text{SolvResIncr}(t) \\ & - \text{BenResIncr}(t) - \text{DACAmort}(t) \\ & + \text{InvIncRC}(t). \end{aligned} \tag{11.3.2}$$

For example, in year 7:

$$\begin{aligned} \text{PreTaxStockEarn}(7) = \; & 60.01 + (154.55 - 144.58) \\ & - (222.25 - 166.98) \\ & + 2.69 = 17.40. \end{aligned}$$

Accrued tax is simply PreTaxStockEarn times the tax rate of 45%. This allows us to calculate after-tax stockholder earnings using the formula (omitting subscript for simplicity)

$$\text{AfterTaxStockEarn} = \text{PreTaxStockEarn} - \text{AccruedTax}.$$

The calculation of equity is tedious, since you must first calculate the deferred tax liability (DefTaxLiab). But to calculate DefTaxLiab, you first need to calculate the deferred tax provision using the formula

DefTaxProv = AccruedTax − Tax.

For example, in year 9:

DefTaxProv(9) = 3.91 − 45% (42.87 + 2.39) = −16.46,

where the values in parentheses are pre-tax solvency earnings and investment income on required capital.

DefTaxLiab can then be calculated as the previous year's deferred tax liability plus the provision for deferred tax. Finally, equity can be calculated as

StockEquity = Assets Backing Solvency Reserves + Assets Backing Required Capital − Earnings Reserves − Deferred Tax Liability.

For example, in year 12:

StockEquity(12) = 220.36 + 29.08 − 389.34 − (−76.04)
= −63.86.

Average equity is easily calculated. Finally, ROE can be calculated as AfterTaxStockEarn divided by average equity.

Table 11.9.2 Stockholder Earnings, Taxs, Equity, and ROE

t	PreTax StockEarn	Accrued Tax	AfterTax StockEarn	DefTaxProv	DefTaxLiab	Equity	Mean Equity	ROE
1	30.65	13.79	16.86	165.98	165.98	258.59	129.29	13.0%
2	54.37	24.46	29.90	−48.15	117.83	195.83	227.21	13.2
3	44.48	20.01	24.46	−39.79	78.04	143.18	169.51	14.4
4	36.02	16.21	19.81	−32.90	45.14	99.32	121.25	16.3
5	29.02	13.06	15.96	−31.64	13.50	57.47	78.40	20.4
6	22.45	10.10	12.35	−23.58	−10.08	26.10	41.79	29.6
7	17.39	7.83	9.57	−20.39	−30.47	−1.03	12.54	76.3
8	12.93	5.82	7.11	−20.14	−50.60	−27.77	−14.40	−49.4
9	8.68	3.91	4.77	−16.46	−67.06	−49.68	−38.72	−12.3
10	5.15	2.32	2.83	−12.74	−79.80	−66.75	−58.21	−4.9
11	2.34	1.05	1.28	7.28	−72.52	−58.44	−62.59	−2.1
12	2.76	1.24	1.52	−3.52	−76.04	−63.87	−61.15	−2.5
13	1.52	0.68	0.84	0.95	−75.09	−63.71	−63.79	−1.3
14	1.03	0.46	0.57	6.35	−68.74	−56.86	−60.29	−0.9
15	1.43	0.64	0.79	12.39	−56.35	−42.53	−49.70	−1.6
16	2.82	1.27	1.55	19.02	−37.33	−20.02	−31.27	−5.0
17	5.25	2.36	2.89	26.34	−10.99	11.49	−4.26	−67.8
18	8.84	3.98	4.86	33.84	22.85	52.23	31.86	15.3
19	13.62	6.13	7.49	41.67	64.52	102.59	77.41	9.7
20	19.63	8.83	10.80	14.00	78.51	114.11	108.35	10.0
21	13.48	6.07	7.42	−78.51	0.00	0.00	57.05	13.0
PV at:								
3.85%	261.54	117.69	143.84	2.10	56.63	559.22	548.85	
5.00	245.72	110.57	135.15	3.85	80.77	549.73	536.64	
7.00	222.48	100.11	122.36	7.58	115.93	536.12	518.58	
9.00	203.40	91.53	111.87	11.86	143.59	524.51	502.86	
12.00	180.42	81.19	99.23	18.62	173.80	508.52	481.28	
15.00	162.20	72.99	89.21	25.26	193.64	492.85	460.71	
20.00	138.86	62.48	76.37	35.18	211.06	466.34	427.48	

Answer 11.8

Compare the pattern of solvency reserves to the pattern of earnings reserves. You can see a visual comparison below in Figure 11.9.1.

Earnings reserves are based on realistic assumptions, with some margin for adverse deviation. Solvency reserves, on the other hand, are usually meant to be conservative, so they are normally well in excess of that needed to meet future obligations under expected assumptions. However, this is not the case in all policy years of our example.

Solvency reserves are actually less than earnings reserves in years 6 through 17. Therefore, there are not enough assets allocated to the product in the later years. Now we can answer the questions:

a. Solvency earnings and distributable earnings turn negative in the later years because solvency reserves are insufficient.

b. The calculation of earnings reserves implicitly assumes the product will have assets at least equal to earnings reserves. In this unusual case, this is a faulty assumption. The product is not allocated the assets and therefore the investment income it needs in the later years. This is why stockholder earnings are not close to a level percentage

Figure 11.9.1

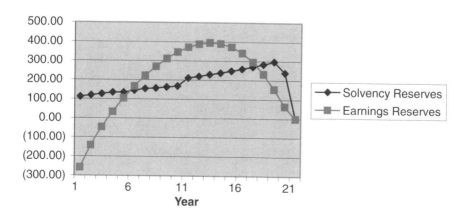

Comparison of Reserves

of premiums. However, because earnings reserves better reflect the reality of the product, the pattern of stockholder earnings is better behaved than the pattern of solvency earnings.

c. Because the product does not have sufficient assets in the later policy years, stockholder equity actually turns negative, causing ROE to also turn negative.

Answer 11.9

a. If $\text{DistrEarn}(t) \geq 0$, then calculate $\text{CapRel}(t)$ as

$$\text{CapRel}(t) = \frac{\text{DistrEarn}(t)}{1 + \text{RCIntRate}(t)\,(1 - \text{TaxRate}(t))};$$

otherwise $\text{CapRel}(t) = 0$.

If $\text{DistrEarn}(t) < 0$, then calculate $\text{CapContr}(t)$ as

$$\text{CapContr}(t) = \frac{-\,\text{DistrEarn}(t)}{1 + \text{RCIntRate}(t)\,(1 - \text{TaxRate}(t))};$$

otherwise $\text{CapContr}(t) = 0$.

b. At the beginning of year t, additional assets equal to $\text{CapContr}(t)$ are allocated by the owners to back the business, or assets equal to $\text{CapRel}(t)$ can be released to the owners to support other businesses. These assets earn, or lose, interest at a rate of $\text{RCIntRate}(t)$:

$$\text{InvIncRC}(t) = (\text{ReqCap}(t - 1) + \text{CapContr}(t) - \text{CapRel}(t)) \times \text{RCIntRate}(t).$$

c. $\text{DistrEarn}^*(t - 1)$ is recalculated by adding $\text{CapRel}(t)$ and subtracting $\text{CapContr}(t)$:

$$\text{DistrEarn}^*(t - 1) = \text{CapRel}(t) - \text{CapContr}(t).$$

Answer 11.10

The results of the procedure developed in Exercise 11.9 are shown in Table 11.9.3. Notice that an extra time period (time 0) has been added to the calculation. This reflects the capital contribution made at the issue date of the policies to fund the new business strain and initial required capital.

ROI and Generalized ROI remain the same as in Exercise 11.4 because capital contributed or released at the beginning of each year is discounted using the same after tax interest rate. If these amounts were discounted at two different interest rates, then different ROIs would develop.

Table 11.9.3 Recalculated Distributable Earnings

t	DistrEarn	CapRel	CapContr	DistrEarn*	Gen ROI
0				−232.77	0.00
1	−241.73	0.00	232.77	89.22	275.52
2	92.65	89.22	0.00	74.26	220.52
3	77.12	74.26	0.00	61.31	173.13
4	63.67	61.31	0.00	55.66	132.36
5	57.81	55.66	0.00	42.10	90.78
6	43.72	42.10	0.00	35.34	57.62
7	36.70	35.34	0.00	32.60	26.38
8	33.85	32.60	0.00	25.69	−6.46
9	26.68	25.69	0.00	19.16	−33.39
10	19.90	19.16	0.00	−6.76	−54.58
11	−7.03	0.00	6.76	6.69	−49.65
12	6.95	6.69	0.00	0.66	−58.51
13	0.68	0.66	0.00	−6.05	−61.45
14	−6.28	0.00	6.05	−13.04	−57.53
15	−13.54	0.00	13.04	−20.19	−46.20
16	−20.97	0.00	20.19	−27.56	−27.01
17	−28.62	0.00	27.56	−34.55	0.65
18	−35.88	0.00	34.55	−41.28	41.65
19	−42.86	0.00	41.28	−0.70	98.16
20	−0.72	0.00	0.70	117.02	117.02
21	121.52	117.02	0.00	0.00	0.00
ROI:	19.71%			19.71%	18.3676%
		RCIntRate:		7.00%	
		TaxRate:		45.00	
		AT Int Rate:		3.85	

Quarterly Calculations

In order to keep Chapters 4 through 11 simpler, we concentrated on annual formulas. For many purposes, annual formulas are accurate enough. However, there are some areas, such as lapses, acquisition costs, reserve increases, taxes, and earnings, where more refinement may be necessary. For example, an annual model could significantly understate the capital required to fund a block of new business.

When pricing results are calculated more often than annually, they are often calculated on a quarterly basis. This is partially because many life insurance companies report financial results on a quarterly basis to regulators, shareholders, or both. Because of the monthly product calculations associated with most dynamic products, a monthly pricing basis is also common. Whether monthly or quarterly calculations are performed, many of the results are summarized on an annual basis to make them easier to review.

In this chapter, we will revisit many of the formulas presented in earlier chapters. For pre-scheduled products, we will convert the formulas to a quarterly basis. For dynamic products, we will convert the formulas to a monthly basis but summarize results on a quarterly basis.

The ultimate goal will be to calculate all the profit measures on a quarterly basis.

12.2 Notation and Expense Rates

Monthly notation was defined in Section 5.8. To handle quarterly calculations, we will need some new notation:

- Q will be used to denote "quarter." We will use the uppercase Q for quarter to distinguish from the lower case q used for mortality and lapse rates. Q will equal 0, 1, 2, 3, and 4. $Q = 0$ will denote the beginning of the policy year. $Q = 4$ will denote the end of the policy year.

- (t, Q) will refer to policy year t, quarter Q. Unless otherwise noted, variables will be as of the end of policy year t, quarter Q.

- "Policy year t, quarter Q" covers the period from time $[t - 1 + (Q - 1)/4$ to time $t - 1 + Q/4$.

- When a policy quarter of zero is used, represented by $(t, 0)$ in the variable name, it denotes the beginning of the policy year, which is equivalent to the end of the previous policy year. So $(t, 0)$ denotes the same point in time as $(t - 1, 4)$. This is very useful for recursive calculations.

The following time line illustrates the four quarters of policy year t:

```
Time:                 t − 1         t − 3/4        t − 1/2       t − 1/4        t
Policy year, quarter:        t, 1          t, 2           t, 3          t, 4
                      |--------------|----------------|----------------|--------------|----
```

Whenever possible, we will use the notation defined in previous chapters. We will define quarterly versions of variables only when needed, in order to keep this long chapter a little shorter. For example, because annual commission rates are the norm, CommPercent(t) will be used as is, rather than defining a quarterly commission rate such as CommPercent(t, Q).

An area of confusion when converting annual formulas to quarterly formulas is whether the expense rates should be expressed as an annual rate or a quarterly rate. To maintain consistency, this chapter will assume that *all expense rates are expressed as annual rates.* Therefore, some expense formulas will divide by four when calculating quarterly expenses.

In other expense formulas, it is not necessary to divide by four, because the expense rate is being applied to a base that is already on a quarterly basis. For example, because $\text{Prem}(t, Q)$ includes only one quarter's premium, it can be multiplied by $\text{ExpPrem}(t)$ to calculate quarterly percent of premium expenses, with no need to divide by four.

12.3 Basic Actuarial Mathematics

In this section, we develop monthly and quarterly formulas for discounting, survivorship, deaths, and lapses. For monthly calculations, we will assume that interest rates and lapse rates can vary by month. For quarterly calculations, we will assume that interest rates and lapse rates can vary by quarter.

Because the formulas in this section are almost identical for monthly and quarterly, we will present only the quarterly formulas. Monthly formulas are addressed in Exercise 12.1.

12.3.1 Discounting

We will assume that monthly and quarterly interest rates are derived from annual effective rates.

Let

$$i\text{Annual}(t, M) = \text{Annual interest rate for } (t, M)$$
$$i(t, M) = \text{Monthly interest rate for } (t, M)$$
$$\text{DiscFactor}(t, M) = \text{Discount factor for the } end \text{ of } (t, M), \text{ equal to}$$

the present value at time 0 of 1 payable at time $t - 1 + M/12$

$$\text{DiscFactorMid}(t, M) = \text{Discount factor for the } \textit{middle} \text{ of } (t, M),$$
equal to the present value at time 0 of 1
payable at time $t - 1 + M/12 - 1/24$

$$i\text{Annual}(t, Q) = \text{Annual interest rate for } (t, Q)$$

$$i(t, Q) = \text{Quarterly interest rate for } (t, Q)$$

$$\text{DiscFactor}(t, Q) = \text{Discount factor for the } \textit{end} \text{ of } (t, Q), \text{ equal to}$$
the present value at time 0 of 1 payable at
time $t - 1 + Q/4$

$$\text{DiscFactorMid}(t, Q) = \text{Discount factor for the } \textit{middle} \text{ of } (t, Q), \text{ equal}$$
to the present value at time 0 of 1 payable at
time $t - 1 + Q/4 - 1/8$

The annual interest rate must first be converted to a quarterly interest rate:

$$i(t, Q) = (1 + i\text{Annual}(t, Q))^{1/4} - 1. \qquad (12.3.1)$$

DiscFactor(t, Q) can be calculated using the following iterative formula, starting with DiscFactor$(0, 0) = 1$ and remembering that DiscFactor$(t, 0) = $ DiscFactor$(t - 1, 4)$, because of the way notation was defined at the beginning of this chapter:

$$\text{DiscFactor}(t, Q) = \frac{\text{DiscFactor}(t, Q - 1)}{1 + i(t, Q)}. \qquad (12.3.2)$$

Alternatively, the discount factor at time (n, R) can be calculated as the product of many quarterly discount factors:

$$\text{DiscFactor}(n, R) = \left[\prod_{t=1}^{n-1} \prod_{Q=1}^{4} \frac{1}{1 + i(t, Q)} \right] \prod_{Q=1}^{R} \frac{1}{1 + i(n, Q)}. \qquad (12.3.3)$$

The third product, $\prod_{Q=1}^{R}$, is necessary to capture the final fractional year of discounting.

We will assume that deaths occur at the middle of the policy quarter, so we will need to discount for both whole and half quarters of interest. The discount factor for the middle of (t, Q), is equal to the discount factor for $(t, Q - 1)$, divided by a factor that discounts for half a quarter's interest at $i(t, Q)$:

$$DiscFactorMid(t, Q) = \frac{DiscFactor(t, Q - 1)}{(1 + i(t, Q))^{1/2}}. \tag{12.3.4}$$

Example 12.3.1 Discounting

Given Annual$i(t, Q)$ shown below, calculate DiscFactor(t, Q) and DiscFactorMid(t, Q).

t, Q	$iAnnual(t, Q)$	$i(t, Q)$	$DiscFactor(t, Q)$	$DiscFactorMid(t, Q)$
1,1	0.10	0.02411	0.97645	0.98816
1,2	0.10	0.02411	0.95346	0.96489
1,3	0.10	0.02411	0.93101	0.94217
1,4	0.10	0.02411	0.90909	0.91999
2,1	0.09	0.02178	0.88971	0.89935
2,2	0.08	0.01943	0.87276	0.88120
2,3	0.07	0.01706	0.85812	0.86541
2,4	0.06	0.01467	0.84571	0.85189

12.3.2   Survivorship

We will assume that mortality rates *do not* vary by month or quarter. While there is theoretical support for varying mortality rates by month or quarter, we have very little data to tell us how mortality rates vary by month or quarter. In contrast, many companies have lapse studies that track lapse rates by policy month. Let

$qdM(t) =$ Monthly mortality rate for policy year t. We will assume that $qdM(t)$ has already been converted from an annual mortality rate to a monthly rate using a formula of the form $qdM(t) = 1 - (1 - qd(t))^{1/12}$

Annual$qw(t, M) =$ Annual rate of lapse for (t, M)

$qw(t, M) =$ Monthly lapse rate for (t, M)

SurvFactor$(t, M) =$ Survivorship factor for the *end* of year t, month M, equal to the probability of surviving from issue to time $t - 1 + M/12$

$qdQ(t)$ = Quarterly mortality rate for policy year t. We will assume that $qdQ(t)$ has already been converted from an annual mortality rate to a quarterly rate using a formula of the form $qdQ(t) = 1 - (1 - qd(t))^{1/4}$

$\text{Annual}qw(t, Q)$ = Annual rate of lapse for (t, Q)

$qw(t, Q)$ = Quarterly lapse rate for (t, Q)

$\text{SurvFactor}(t, Q)$ = Survivorship factor for the *end* of year t, quarter Q, equal to the probability of surviving from issue to time $t - 1 + Q/4$

The quarterly lapse rate is calculated from the annual lapse rate for each quarter:

$$qw(t, Q) = 1 - (1 - \text{Annual}qw(t, Q))^{1/4}. \tag{12.3.5}$$

$\text{SurvFactor}(t, Q)$ can be calculated using the following iterative formula, starting with $\text{SurvFactor}(0, 0) = 1$ and remembering that $\text{SurvFactor}(t, 0) = \text{SurvFactor}(t - 1, 4)$:

$$\begin{aligned}
&\text{SurvFactor}(t, Q) \\
&\quad = \text{SurvFactor}(t, Q - 1)(1 - qdQ(t))(1 - qw(t, Q)).
\end{aligned} \tag{12.3.6}$$

Alternatively, the survivorship factor at time (n, R) can be calculated as the product of many quarterly survivorship factors:

$$\begin{aligned}
\text{SurvFactor}(n, R) = &\left[\prod_{t=1}^{n-1} \prod_{Q=1}^{4} (1 - qdQ(t))(1 - qw(t, Q)) \right] \\
&\times \prod_{Q=1}^{R} (1 - qdQ(n))(1 - qw(n, Q)).
\end{aligned}$$

$$\tag{12.3.7}$$

The third product, $\prod\limits_{Q=1}^{R}$, is necessary to capture the final fractional year of survivorship.

Example 12.3.2 Survivorship

Given $qd(t)$ and Annual$qw(t)$, calculate SurvFactor(t, Q).

t, Q	$qd(t)$	$qdQ(t)$	Annual$qw(t, Q)$	$qw(t, Q)$	SurvFactor(t, Q)
1,1	0.003	0.00075085	0.12	0.03145307	0.96782
1,2	"	"	"	"	0.93667
1,3	"	"	"	"	0.90653
1,4	"	"	"	"	0.87736
2,1	0.004	0.00100150	0.07	0.01797909	0.86072
2,2	"	"	"	"	0.84440
2,3	"	"	"	"	0.82839
2,4	"	"	"	"	0.81268
3,1	0.005	0.00125235	0.05	0.01274146	0.80132
3,2	"	"	0.04	0.01015360	0.79219
3,3	"	"	0.03	0.00758588	0.78520
3,4	"	"	0.02	0.00503794	0.78026

12.3.3   Lapses and Deaths

The following formulas calculate the probability of lapsing or dying during (t, M) or (t, Q). Let

Deaths(t, M) = The probability of surviving $t - 1$ policy years and $M - 1$ months and then dying during year t, month M

Lapses(t, M) = The probability of surviving $t - 1$ policy years and M months and then lapsing at the end of year t, month M

$$
\begin{aligned}
\text{Deaths}(t, Q) = \ &\text{The probability of surviving } t - 1 \text{ policy years} \\
&\text{and } Q - 1 \text{ quarters and then dying during year } t, \\
&\text{quarter } Q \\
\text{Lapses}(t, Q) = \ &\text{The probability of surviving } t - 1 \text{ policy years} \\
&\text{and } Q \text{ quarters and then lapsing at the end of} \\
&\text{year } t, \text{ quarter } Q.
\end{aligned}
$$

To calculate the probability of dying during (t, Q), multiply the probability of surviving to the end of $(t, Q - 1)$ by the mortality rate for (t, Q):

$$
\text{Deaths}(t, Q) = \text{SurvFactor}(t, Q - 1) \; qdQ(t). \tag{12.3.8}
$$

To calculate the probability of lapsing at the end of policy year t, multiply the probability of surviving to the end of $(t, Q - 1)$ by the probability of not dying during (t, Q). Then multiply by the probability of lapsing during (t, Q):

$$
\text{Lapses}(t, Q) = \text{SurvFactor}(t, Q - 1) \; (1 - qdQ(t)) \; qw(t, Q). \tag{12.3.9}
$$

Collectively, Deaths(t, Q) and Lapses(t, Q) add up to the probability of surviving to the end of $(t, Q - 1)$ and terminating before the end of (t, Q). In other words,

$$
\begin{aligned}
\text{Deaths}(t, Q) + \text{Lapses}(t, Q) = \ &\text{SurvFactor}(t, Q - 1) \\
&- \text{SurvFactor}(t, Q).
\end{aligned} \tag{12.3.10}
$$

Example 12.3.3 Calculation of Quarterly Deaths, Lapses, and Survivorship

Given quarterly mortality and lapse rates, calculate the probabilities of death, lapse, and survivorship for the years and quarters shown.

t, Q	$qdQ(t)$	$qw(t, Q)$	$Deaths(t, Q)$	$Lapses(t, Q)$	$SurvFactor(t, Q)$
1,1	0.00075085	0.03145307	0.00075085	0.0314295	0.96782
1,2	0.00075085	0.03145307	0.00072668	0.0304180	0.93667
1,3	0.00075085	0.03145307	0.00070330	0.0294392	0.90653
1,4	0.00075085	0.03145307	0.00068067	0.0284918	0.87736
2,1	0.00100150	0.01797909	0.00087868	0.0157583	0.86072
2,2	0.00100150	0.01797909	0.00086202	0.0154595	0.84440
2,3	0.00100150	0.01797909	0.00084567	0.0151664	0.82839
2,4	0.00100150	0.01797909	0.00082963	0.0148788	0.81268
3.1	0.00125235	0.01274146	0.00101776	0.0103418	0.80132
3,2	0.00125235	0.01015360	0.00100354	0.0081261	0.79219
3,3	0.00125235	0.00758588	0.00099210	0.0060019	0.78520
3,4	0.00125235	0.00503794	0.00098334	0.0039508	0.78026

The formulas for monthly probabilities of death and lapse, that is, $Deaths(t, M)$ and $Lapses(t, M)$, can be derived by substituting M for Q in the preceding formulas.

12.4   Cash Flows for Pre-scheduled Products

In this section, we develop quarterly formulas for the life insurance cash flows of pre-scheduled products. Dynamic product cash flows are presented in the next section.

12.4.1 Premiums

In Chapter 5, we dealt only with annual premiums. In this chapter, we will address annual, semiannual, quarterly, and monthly premiums, which we will refer to as "modal premiums." We will assume that all premiums due for the quarter are paid at the beginning of the quarter. This is obviously not correct for monthly premiums, but it does simplify the formulas.

Modal premiums present two complications:

1. Modal premiums per unit are not usually a simple fraction of the annual premiums per unit. For example, quarterly premiums per unit may be 26% of annual premiums per unit.

2. Modal policy fees are not usually a simple fraction of the annual policy fee. For example, a quarterly policy fee may be 15.00 while the annual policy fee is 50.00.

To handle these complications in as simple a manner as possible, we will number the modes of payment and define a number of new variables. Let

$$m = \text{Mode of payment, used as a subscript,}$$
$$\text{with}$$
$$m = 1 \text{ for annual}$$
$$m = 2 \text{ for semiannual}$$
$$m = 3 \text{ for quarterly and}$$
$$m = 4 \text{ for monthly}$$

$$\text{ModalFactor}(m, Q) = \text{Factor that is used to convert the}$$
$$\text{annual premium per unit into the}$$
$$\text{modal premium per unit for mode } m \text{ in}$$
$$\text{quarter } Q; \text{ see Example 12.4.1}$$

$\text{ModalPolicyFee}(m, Q)$ = Policy fee that is payable for mode m in quarter Q; see Example 12.4.2

$\text{ModalDist}(m)$ = The percentage of business issued with premium paid under mode m. In other words, this is the percentage of business issued with annual premiums, semiannual premiums, quarterly premiums, or monthly premiums, depending on the value of m.

$\text{Prem\_pu}(m, t, Q)$ = Premium for mode m paid during the period (t, Q), including the modal policy fee, per unit in force

$\text{AnnlzdPrem\_pu}(m, t)$ = Annualized premium for mode m and policy year t, equal to the sum of modal premiums over the four quarters of the policy year, per unit in force

$\text{Prem}(t, Q)$ = Total premium for the period (t, Q), per unit issued; see Example 12.4.3.

Example 12.4.1 Modal Factors

A product has semiannual premium rates that are 51% of annual premium rates, quarterly premium rates that are 26% of annual premium rates, and monthly premium rates that are 8.75% of annual premium rates. These produce annualized premium rates equal to 102%, 104%, and 105% of annual premium rates. These percentages exceed 100% in order to compensate for lost interest and other costs associated with collecting nonannual premiums. The following modal factors would apply to the four quarters:

ModalFactor(m, Q)

Q	Annual Modal Factor	Semiannual Modal Factor
1	1.00	0.51
2	0.00	0.00
3	"	0.51
4	"	0.00

For all Q, the modal factors for quarterly = 0.26 and for monthly = 0.2625.

For the monthly mode, the monthly modal factor is 0.0875, but, since we are calculating quarterly premiums, the monthly factor is multiplied by three.

Example 12.4.2 Modal Policy Fees

A product has an annual policy fee of 50.00, a semiannual policy fee of 27.00, a quarterly policy fee of 15.00, and a monthly policy fee of 6.00. The annualized policy fees of 54.00, 60.00, and 72.00 are in excess of the 50.00 annual policy fee in order to cover the extra costs of billing, collecting, and accounting for the additional nonannual premiums. The following modal policy fees would apply:

$ModalPolicyFee(m, Q)$

Q	Annual Modal Policy Fee	Semiannual Modal Policy Fee
1	50.00	27.00
2	0.00	0.00
3	"	27.00
4	"	0.00

For all Q, the modal policy fees quarterly $= 15$ and for monthly $= 18$.

For monthly mode, we multiply the monthly policy fee by three, since we are calculating quarterly premiums.

The per unit premium paid for mode m during quarter Q is equal to the annual premium per unit in force times the modal factor for mode m, plus the modal policy fee divided by the average size:

$$Prem\_pu(m, t, Q) = Prem\_pu(t) \; ModalFactor(m, Q)$$
$$+ \frac{ModalPolicyFee(m, Q)}{AvgSize}. \qquad (12.4.1)$$

Premium income for the monthly mode can be modeled more precisely by developing a minor adjustment to the above premium formula. For those dying in the first month of the quarter, only one month of premium is paid for the quarter. For those dying in the second month, two months of premiums are paid. For those dying in the third month of the quarter, all three months of premiums are paid. On average, those dying in the quarter pay two months of premiums. In other words, one-third of the premium for the quarter is lost for those who die. Therefore, Formula 12.4.1 could be modified for the monthly mode of payment ($m = 4$) as follows:

$$\text{Prem\_pu}(4, t, Q) = \left(\text{Prem\_pu}(t) \text{ ModalFactor}(4, Q) \right.$$
$$\left. + \frac{\text{ModalPolicyFee}(4, Q)}{\text{AvgSize}} \right) \left(1 - \frac{qdQ(t)}{3} \right)$$
$$(12.4.2)$$

Annualized premiums per unit are calculated by summing modal premiums per unit over the four quarters:

$$\text{AnnlzdPrem\_pu}(m, t) = \sum_{Q=1}^{4} \text{Prem\_pu}(m, t, Q). \qquad (12.4.3)$$

$\text{Prem}(t, Q)$ is calculated as the weighted average for all modes (weighted by the modal distribution) of modal premium per unit in force, adjusted for survivorship:

$$\text{Prem}(t, Q) = \sum_{m=1}^{4} \text{ModalDist}(m) \text{ Prem\_pu}(m, t, Q)$$
$$\times \text{SurvFactor}(t, Q - 1). \qquad (12.4.4)$$

Example 12.4.3 Modal Premiums

Using the modal factors and modal policy fees in Examples 12.4.1 and 12.4.2, and the modal distribution below, calculate $\text{Prem\_pu}(m, t, Q)$ and $\text{Prem}(t, Q)$. Assume $\text{SurvFactor}(t, Q) = 1.00$ for all (t, Q), $\text{Prem\_pu}(t) = 5.50$ for all t, and $\text{AvgSize} = 125$.

Q	m	ModalDist	ModalFactor	ModalPolicyFee	Prem_pu	ModalDist × Prem_pu
1	1	0.50	1.0000	50.0000	5.9000	2.9500
	2	0.10	0.5100	27.0000	3.0210	0.3021
	3	0.15	0.2600	15.0000	1.5500	0.2325
	4	0.25	0.2625	18.0000	1.5878	0.3969

$$\text{Prem}(t, 1) = 3.8815$$

Q	m	ModalDist	ModalFactor	ModalPolicyFee	Prem_pu	ModalDist × Prem_pu
2	1	0.50	0.0000	0.0000	0.0000	0.0000
	2	0.10	0.0000	0.0000	0.0000	0.0000
	3	0.15	0.2600	15.0000	1.5500	0.2325
	4	0.25	0.2625	18.0000	1.5878	0.3969

$$\text{Prem}(t, 2) = 0.6294$$

Q	m	ModalDist	ModalFactor	ModalPolicyFee	Prem_pu	ModalDist × Prem_pu
3	1	0.50	0.0000	0.0000	0.0000	0.0000
	2	0.10	0.5100	27.0000	3.0210	0.3021
	3	0.15	0.2600	15.0000	1.5500	0.2325
	4	0.25	0.2625	18.0000	1.5878	0.3969

$$\text{Prem}(t, 3) = 0.9315$$

Q	m	ModalDist	ModalFactor	ModalPolicyFee	Prem_pu	ModalDist × Prem_pu
4	1	0.50	0.0000	0.0000	0.0000	0.0000
	2	0.10	0.0000	0.0000	0.0000	0.0000
	3	0.15	0.2600	15.0000	1.5500	0.2325
	4	0.25	0.2625	18.0000	1.5878	0.3969

$$\text{Prem}(t, 4) = 0.6294$$

12.4.2 Acquisition Expenses

Let

$\text{AcqExp}(t, Q) = $ Total acquisition expenses for (t, Q), per unit issued. Acquisition expenses are assumed to occur only in the first policy year, that is, $\text{AcqExp}(t, Q) = 0$ for $t > 1$.

Acquisition expenses, other than the first-year percentage of premium expenses, are assumed to be incurred only in the first quarter of the first policy year:

$$\text{AcqExp}(1, 1) = \text{AcqExp\_pu} + \text{AcqExpPrem} \, \text{Prem}(1, 1)$$
$$+ \frac{\text{AcqExpPerPol}}{\text{AvgSize}},$$
$$\text{AcqExp}(1, Q) = \text{AcqExpPrem} \, \text{Prem}(1, Q) \text{ for } Q = 2, 3, \text{ and } 4,$$
$$\text{AcqExp}(t, Q) = 0 \text{ for } t > 1. \tag{12.4.5}$$

12.4.3 Commissions and Sales Expenses

Let

$$\text{Comm}(t, Q) = \text{Commissions and other agent compensation paid as a percentage of premium at the beginning of } (t, Q), \text{ per unit issued.}$$

Commissions and distribution expenses are assumed paid when premiums are paid:

$$\text{Comm}(t, Q) = \text{CommPercent}(t)\,\text{Prem}(t, Q)\,(1 + \text{DistExpPercent}(t)). \tag{12.4.6}$$

12.4.4 Maintenance Expenses

We will assume that all maintenance expenses occur at the beginning of the quarter. Maintenance expenses expressed as a percentage of premiums are paid as premiums are paid. We will assume that per unit and per policy maintenance expenses are incurred evenly in each quarter throughout the policy year. Let

$$\text{MaintExp}(t, Q) = \text{Total maintenance expenses incurred at the beginning of } (t, Q), \text{ per unit issued.}$$

Then,

$$\begin{aligned}
\text{MaintExp}(t, Q) \\
= \frac{1}{4}\left(\text{Exp\_pu}(t) + \frac{\text{ExpPerPol}(t)}{\text{AvgSize}}\right)\text{SurvFactor}(t, Q - 1) \\
+ \text{ExpPrem}(t)\,\text{Prem}(t, Q).
\end{aligned} \tag{12.4.7}$$

Note that we divide by four for the per unit and per policy expenses, but not for percent of premium expenses, since $\text{Prem}(t, Q)$ is a quarterly premium, not an annual premium.

12.4.5   Death Benefits

Let

$$\text{DeathBen}(t, Q) =$$ Death benefits paid in (t, Q), per unit issued. Death benefits are assumed paid at the middle of the quarter, on average.

$$\text{DB\_puMid}(t, Q) =$$ Death benefit per unit in force at the middle of (t, Q), including any dividends payable on death. This is assumed to be the average death benefit for the quarter. For products whose pre-scheduled death benefits change throughout the policy year, intermediate death benefits per unit are usually obtained by linear interpolation between end-of-policy-year values.

$$\text{ROPFactor}(m, Q) =$$ Return of premium factor, which is the average percentage of annualized premiums for mode m that will be returned if death occurs in quarter Q; see Example 12.4.4

$$\text{ROP\_pu}(m, t, Q) =$$ Average premium per unit in force returned on death in (t, Q) for mode m

$$\text{ROP\_pu}(t, Q) =$$ Average premium per unit in force returned on death in (t, Q) for all modes combined.

The average amount of premium returned on death depends on both the mode of payment and the quarter in which the death occurs. See Example 12.4.4.

For each mode, the average premium per unit returned on deaths in (t, Q) is calculated as the annualized premium per unit times the appropriate return of premium factor:

$$\text{ROP\_pu}(m, t, Q) = \text{AnnlzdPrem\_pu}(m, t) \, \text{ROPFactor}(m, Q). \tag{12.4.8}$$

The average premium returned on death in quarter Q for all modes combined is calculated as the weighted average of premium returned on death for each mode:

$$\text{ROP\_pu}(t, Q) = \sum_{m=1}^{4} \text{ModalDist}(m) \ \text{ROP\_pu}(m, t, Q). \quad (12.4.9)$$

Death benefits are calculated as the death benefit per unit in force plus the return of premium per unit in force, all times the probability of death:

$$\text{DeathBen}(t, Q)$$
$$= (\text{DB\_puMid}(t, Q) + \text{ROP\_pu}(t, Q)) \ \text{Deaths}(t, Q). \quad (12.4.10)$$

Example 12.4.4 Modal Return of Premium Factors

Return of premium factors depend on the company's practice for returning premiums on death (for example, whether to return premiums paid beyond the *date* of death or the *month* of death), the mode of payment, and the quarter in which death occurs. The following table shows modal return of premium factors assuming premiums paid beyond the *month* of death are returned:

Q	Annual ROP Factor	Semiannual ROP Factor
1	0.8333	0.3333
2	0.5833	0.0833
3	0.3333	0.3333
4	0.0833	0.0833

For all Q, ROP Factor for quarterly = 0.0833 and for monthly = 0.

If death occurs in the first quarter, there will be zero, one, or two full months remaining in the quarter at the time of death. On average, there will be one full month remaining in the quarter and one month's premium to be refunded if death occurs in the current quarter. For annual premiums, an average of ten months of premiums will be refunded if death occurs in the first quarter. For semiannual premiums, four months of premiums will be refunded. For quarterly premiums, one month will be refunded. For monthly premiums, there are never any refunds.

12.4.6 Claim Expenses

Let

$$\text{ClaimExp}(t, Q) = \text{Claim expenses per unit issued in } (t, Q).$$

Then,

$$\text{ClaimExp}(t, Q)$$
$$= \left(\text{ClaimExp\_pu}(t) + \frac{\text{ClaimExpPerPol}(t)}{\text{AvgSize}} \right) \text{Deaths}(t, Q).$$

$$(12.4.11)$$

Note that it is not necessary to divide by four, since $\text{Deaths}(t, Q)$ is a quarterly value, not an annual value.

12.4.7 Surrender Benefits

Let

$$\text{SurrBen}(t, Q) = \text{Surrender benefits paid at the end of } (t, Q),$$
per unit issued

$$\text{UEPFactor}(m, Q) = \text{Unearned premium factor, equal to the}$$
percentage of annualized premium that must be returned on lapses for mode m occurring at the end of quarter Q; see Example 12.4.5

$$\text{CV\_pu}(t, Q) = \text{Cash value per unit in force at the end of}$$
(t, Q), including any additional dividend payable to lapsing policyholders, in excess of any annual dividend.

For pre-scheduled products, cash values at the end of each quarter are usually obtained by linear interpolation between end-of-policy-year cash values, plus a return of any unearned premiums (see Example 12.4.5):

$$CV\_pu(t, Q) = \left(1 - \frac{Q}{4}\right) CV\_pu(t - 1) + \left(\frac{Q}{4}\right) CV\_pu(t)$$

$$+ \sum_{m=1}^{4} ModalDist(m) \ UEPFactor(m, Q)$$

$$\times AnnlzdPrem\_pu(m, t). \qquad (12.4.12)$$

We will assume that surrender benefits are paid only at the end of the quarter. Surrender benefits are calculated as the cash value times the probability of lapse.

$$SurrBen(t, Q) = CV\_pu(t, Q) \ Lapses(t, Q). \qquad (12.4.13)$$

Example 12.4.5 Unearned Premium Factors

The following factors represent the portion of the annualized premium that is unearned at the end of each quarter:

Q	Annual UEP Factor	Semiannual UEP Factor
1	0.75	0.25
2	0.50	0.00
3	0.25	0.25
4	0.00	0.00

For all Q, UEP Factor for both quarterly and monthly modes equals 0.

Premiums are considered gradually earned between premium due dates. For example, semiannual premiums are earned gradually over a six-month period. At the end of the first and third quarters, three months worth of semiannual premiums are unearned, which translates to 25% of the annualized premium.

12.4.8 Dividends

Let

> $Div(t, Q)$ = Dividends paid at the end of (t, Q), per unit issued.

Dividends for the first three quarters of the year are zero, since dividends are paid only at the end of the policy year. Therefore,

$$Div(t, 4) = Div\_pu(t) \, (SurvFactor(t, 4) + Lapses(t, 4) \, DivRule),$$
$$Div(t, Q) = 0 \quad \text{for } Q = 1, 2, \text{ and } 3. \tag{12.4.14}$$

12.4.9   Pure Endowment Benefits

Let

> $PureEndow(t, Q)$ = Pure endowment benefit paid at the end of (t, Q), per unit issued.

Pure endowment benefits are rarely paid at any point in time other than on policy anniversaries, so

$$PureEndow(t, 4) = PureEndow\_pu(t) \, SurvFactor(t, 4),$$
$$PureEndow(t, Q) = 0 \quad \text{for } Q = 1, 2, \text{ and } 3. \tag{12.4.15}$$

12.5   Cash Flows for Dynamic Products

This section presents formulas for selected dynamic product cash flows: premiums, commissions and related expenses, death benefits, surrender benefits, and partial withdrawal benefits. Formulas for acquisition expenses, maintenance expenses, and claim expenses are not presented, since the expense formulas for pre-scheduled products can be used as is or with minor modifications for dynamic products. This section will build on the notation, variable names, definitions, and formulas presented in Section 5.8. Before proceeding, you may want to reacquaint yourself with that section.

Because dynamic products calculate account values and other product variables on a monthly basis, we will calculate dynamic product cash flows on a monthly basis. The resulting monthly cash flows can then be summed to determine quarterly cash flows. For example, the results for $M = 1, 2,$ and 3 can be added together to obtain the results for $Q = 1$.

Many of the formulas for pre-scheduled products combined the results of several modes of payment. This is not possible for dynamic products. Each mode of payment produces a unique pattern of account values. Therefore, all of the formulas for dynamic products will be for a single mode of payment. To combine the results for several modes of payments, you will have to go through a process similar to combining the results for different issue ages or different risk classes.

The mode of payment will be reflected in the pattern of premiums contained in the monthly premium per unit variable, Prem_pu(t, M). For example, quarterly premiums can be tested by using positive values of Prem_pu(t, M) for $M = 1, 4, 7,$ and 10, and zero values for the other months. If the product allows flexible premiums, any irregular premium payment patterns will also be reflected in Prem_pu(t, M).

12.5.1 Premiums

Premiums are calculated as the premium per unit for the month times the probability of surviving to the beginning of the month:

$$\text{Prem}(t, M) = \text{Prem\_pu}(t, M)\, \text{SurvFactor}(t, M - 1). \qquad (12.5.1)$$

12.5.2 Commissions and Sales Expenses

Commissions for dynamic products are usually calculated for each policy year as a higher percentage of premiums up to an amount called a "target premium" and a lower percentage of premiums for amounts in excess of the target premium. Because the target premium could be exceeded at any point during the year, it will be necessary to track year-to-date premiums. Some dynamic products pay additional commissions as a small percentage of the end-of-year account value. Let

$$\text{YTDPrem\_pu}(t, M) = \text{Policy year-to-date premium per unit in force through month } M; \text{ this is needed to compare to the target premium when calculating commissions}$$

$$\text{HighCommPrem}(t, M) = \text{The premium per unit in force in month } M \text{ that is subject to the high commission rate}$$

$$\text{LowCommPrem}(t, M) = \text{The premium per unit in force in month } M \text{ that is subject to the low commission rate}$$

$$\text{Comm}(t, M) = \text{Commissions and other agent compensation paid as a percentage of premium at the beginning of month } M, \text{ per unit issued}$$

$$\text{AVComm}(t, M) = \text{Commissions and other agent compensation paid as a percentage of the end-of-year account value, per unit issued.}$$

Year-to-date premiums must be accumulated and compared to the target premium to determine the proper commission rate to be applied to the premium. Year-to-date premiums are calculated by adding one month's premium to the prior year-to-date total:

$$\text{YTDPrem\_pu}(t, 0) = 0,$$
$$\text{YTDPrem\_pu}(t, M) = \text{YTDPrem\_pu}(t, M - 1) + \text{Prem\_pu}(t, M).$$
$$(12.5.2)$$

The "high commission" premium for the month is equal to the excess of the target premium over the prior month's YTD premium, but not less than zero and not more than the current month's premium. This ensures that high commissions are paid only on premiums up to the amount of the target premium:

$$
\begin{aligned}
\text{HighCommPrem}(t, M) \\
= \max\{0, \min[\text{Prem\_pu}(t, M), \text{TargetPrem\_pu}(t) \\
- \text{YTDPrem\_pu}(t, M)]\}.
\end{aligned} \tag{12.5.3}
$$

The "low commission" premium for the month plus the "high commission" premium for the month equal the total premium per unit for the month. In other words,

$$
\begin{aligned}
\text{LowCommPrem}(t, M) = \text{Prem\_pu}(t, M) \\
- \text{HighCommPrem}(t, M).
\end{aligned} \tag{12.5.4}
$$

Commissions and related expenses for the month are calculated by applying the higher and lower commission rates to the appropriate premiums and then adjusting the result for distribution expenses and survivorship:

$$
\begin{aligned}
\text{Comm}(t, M) = (\text{HighCommPrem}(t, M) \ \text{HighCommPercent}(t) \\
+ \text{LowCommPrem}(t, M) \ \text{LowCommPercent}(t)) \\
(1 + \text{DistExpPercent}(t)) \ \text{SurvFactor}(t, M - 1).
\end{aligned} \tag{12.5.5}
$$

We will assume that commissions paid as a percentage of the account value are paid only at the end of the policy year, though payments more often than once a year are possible:

$$
\begin{aligned}
\text{AVComm}(t, M) = 0 \quad \text{for } M = 1 \text{ to } 11, \\
\text{AVComm}(t, 12) = \text{AVCommPct}(t) \ \text{AV\_pu}(t, 12) \\
(1 + \text{DistExpPercent}(t)) \ \text{SurvFactor}(t, 12).
\end{aligned} \tag{12.5.6}
$$

Example 12.5.1

The target premium per unit is 7.50, and the monthly premium per unit (Prem_pu(t, M) is 1.00. Calculate YTDPrem_pu, HighCommPrem, and LowCommPrem for all 12 months. If the high commission rate is 80% and the low commission rate is 3%, what is the average commission rate for month 8?

Month	YTDPrem_pu	HighCommPrem	LowCommPrem
1	1.00	1.00	0.00
2	2.00	1.00	0.00
3	3.00	1.00	0.00
4	4.00	1.00	0.00
5	5.00	1.00	0.00
6	6.00	1.00	0.00
7	7.00	1.00	0.00
8	8.00	0.50	0.50
9	9.00	0.00	1.00
10	10.00	0.00	1.00
11	11.00	0.00	1.00
12	12.00	0.00	1.00

The average commission rate for month 8 is ($0.50 \times 80\%$ + $0.50 \times 3\%$)/($0.50 + 0.50$) = 41.5%.

12.5.3   Death Benefits for Dynamic Products

In general, fixed premium products return unearned premiums upon death, even if policy values are determined dynamically. Flexible premium products do not return premiums on death.

ROPFactor(*m*, *M*) = Return of premium factor, which is the percentage of annualized premiums for mode m that will be returned if death occurs in month *M*; see Example 12.5.2

ROP_pu(*t*, *M*) = Average premium per unit in force returned on death in month *M* for the premium mode being calculated.

Example 12.5.2 Return of Premium Factors

The following table shows return of premium factors for various modes of payment assuming premiums paid beyond the *month* of death (rather than the *date* of death) are returned.

Month of Death (M)	Annual ROP Factor	Semiannual ROP Factor	Quarterly ROP Factor
1	0.9167	0.4167	0.1667
2	0.8333	0.3333	0.0833
3	0.7500	0.2500	0.0000
4	0.6667	0.1667	0.1667
5	0.5833	0.0833	0.0833
6	0.5000	0.0000	0.0000
7	0.4167	0.4167	0.1667
8	0.3333	0.3333	0.0833
9	0.2500	0.2500	0.0000
10	0.1667	0.1667	0.1667
11	0.0833	0.0833	0.0833
12	0.0000	0.0000	0.0000

For all *M*, the monthly ROP factor = 0.

Death benefits for dynamic products with fixed premiums: If premium payments are fixed, then return of premium per unit is calculated as annualized premium times the appropriate return of premium factor. Annualized premium is calculated as in Section 12.4.1:

$$\text{ROP\_pu}(t, M) = \text{AnnlzdPrem\_pu}(m, t) \ \text{ROPFactor}(m, M).$$

$$(12.5.7)$$

Death benefits are calculated as death benefits per unit, as of the end of the prior month, plus return of premium per unit, all multiplied by the probability of death:

$$\text{DeathBen}(t, M) = (\text{DB\_puEnd}(t, M - 1)$$
$$+ \ \text{ROP\_pu}(t, M)) \ \text{Deaths}(t, M). \qquad (12.5.8)$$

Death benefits for dynamic products with flexible premiums: If premium payments are flexible, then

$$\text{DeathBen}(t, M) = \text{DB\_puEnd}(t, M - 1) \ \text{Deaths}(t, M). \qquad (12.5.9)$$

12.5.4   Surrender Benefits

We will assume that surrenders can occur at the end of any policy month. Because all premiums are added to the account value, there is no need for return of unearned premium:

$$\text{SurrBen}(t, M) = \text{CV\_pu}(t, M) \ \text{Lapses}(t, M). \qquad (12.5.10)$$

12.5.5   Partial Withdrawal Benefits

We will assume that partial withdrawals can occur at the end of any policy month:

$$\text{PartWithBen}(t, M) = \text{PWBen\_pu}(t, M) \ \text{SurvFactor}(t, M).$$

$$(12.5.11)$$

It is assumed that all of the preceding monthly cash flows for dynamic products are summarized into quarterly cash flows for use in the remainder of this chapter.

12.6   Summary of Cash Flows

This section summarizes life insurance cash flows for both pre-scheduled and dynamic products. The same groupings presented in

Section 5.10 for annual cash flows are used for quarterly cash flows. The only significant differences between this section and Section 5.10 are the use of "(t, Q)" and "quarterly" in place of "(t)" and "annual."

12.6.1 Summary of Cash Flows by Timing

It is useful to segregate the quarterly cash flows into three groups, based on their timing: beginning of the quarter, middle of the quarter, and end of the quarter.

Let

$$\text{CashFlowBeg}(t, Q) = \text{Beginning of the quarter cash flows for } (t, Q), \text{ per unit issued}$$

$$\text{CashFlowMid}(t, Q) = \text{Middle of the quarter cash flows for } (t, Q), \text{ per unit issued}$$

$$\text{CashFlowEnd}(t, Q) = \text{End of the quarter cash flows for } (t, Q), \text{ per unit issued}$$

$$\text{ProdCashFlow}(t, Q) = \text{Total product cash flow for } (t, Q), \text{ per unit issued.}$$

The same groupings apply for annual and quarterly calculations:

$$\text{CashFlowBeg}(t, Q) = \text{Prem}(t, Q) - \text{AcqExp}(t, Q) - \text{Comm}(t, Q) - \text{MaintExp}(t, Q), \tag{12.6.1}$$

$$\text{CashFlowMid}(t, Q) = -\text{DeathBen}(t, Q) - \text{ClaimExp}(t, Q), \tag{12.6.2}$$

$$\text{CashFlowEnd}(t, Q) = -\text{AVComm}(t, Q) - \text{SurrBen}(t, Q) - \text{Div}(t, Q) - \text{PureEndow}(t, Q) - \text{PartWithBen}(t, Q), \tag{12.6.3}$$

$$\text{ProdCashFlow}(t, Q) = \text{CashFlowBeg}(t, Q) + \text{CashFlowMid}(t, Q) + \text{CashFlowEnd}(t, Q). \tag{12.6.4}$$

$\text{ProdCashFlow}(t, Q)$ could be positive or negative in any given quarter.

These formulas could be further refined for monthly premiums, for example, by shifting premiums and related commissions for the second and third months of each quarter from CashFlowBeg(t, Q) to

CashFlowMid(t, Q). This is supportable by noting that the average due date for the second and third month's premiums is at the middle of the quarter.

The monthly premium refinement developed for pre-scheduled products is also applicable to dynamic products. In addition, dynamic products have surrender benefits and partial withdrawal benefits that are paid at the end of the first and second months of each quarter. These benefits could be shifted from CashFlowEnd(t, Q) to CashFlowMid(t, Q). This is supportable by noting that the average payment date for these benefits (that is, at the end of the first and second months) is at the middle of the quarter. Exercise 12.7 explores this further.

12.6.2   Summary of Cash Flows by Type

It is useful to summarize cash flows by type: premiums, benefits, and expenses. Premiums are already "summarized" by Prem(t, Q). To summarize benefits and expenses, let

Ben(t, Q) = Total policy benefits paid in (t, Q), per unit issued
Exp(t, Q) = Total expenses paid in (t, Q), per unit issued.

Then,

$$\text{Ben}(t, Q) = \text{DeathBen}(t, Q) + \text{SurrBen}(t, Q) + \text{Div}(t, Q)$$
$$\qquad + \text{PureEndow}(t, Q) + \text{PartWithBen}(t, Q), \quad (12.6.5)$$
$$\text{Exp}(t, Q) = \text{AcqExp}(t, Q) + \text{Comm}(t, Q) + \text{AVComm}(t, Q)$$
$$\qquad + \text{MaintExp}(t, Q) + \text{ClaimExp}(t, Q). \quad (12.6.6)$$

Total product cash flow can also be calculated as

$$\text{ProdCashFlow}(t, Q) = \text{Prem}(t, Q) - \text{Ben}(t, Q) - \text{Exp}(t, Q).$$
$$(12.6.7)$$

12.7   Reserves

In Chapter 5, we discussed initial, mean, and terminal reserves with annual premiums. In this chapter, we will develop quarterly reserves and reserves for nonannual premiums. The discussions in Sections 12.7.1–12.7.4 apply only to pre-scheduled products. By their nature, dynamic products with monthly calculations lend themselves more easily to quarterly calculations of reserves.

12.7.1 Reserves for Nonannual Premiums

When premiums are paid annually, the reserve during each year looks like a sawtooth. A sharp increase in reserve when the premium is paid at the beginning of the year is followed by a gradual decrease throughout the year, until the terminal reserve is reached at the end of the policy year. In later policy years, the "gradual decrease" may become a "gradual increase," if the effect of interest accumulation outweighs mortality costs. When premiums are paid more often than annually, reserves exhibit the same basic "sawtooth" pattern, but the pattern is repeated multiple times per year. Each time a premium is paid, there is a sharp increase in reserve followed by a gradual decrease until the next premium is paid.

For example, for quarterly premiums, there are four sawtooth periods each year. In effect, there is an initial reserve and a terminal reserve for each quarter, with intermediate reserves interpolated between the beginning and end of each quarter. This is best explained with an illustration (see Figure 12.7.1).

Figure 12.7.1 exhibits the same kind of pattern shown in Figure 6.4.1. The main difference is that we have substituted quarter-years for full years. Similarly, for monthly premiums, the reserves would follow a monthly pattern, with 12 sawtooth periods each year.

Figure 12.7.1 Reserve Pattern for Quarterly Premiums

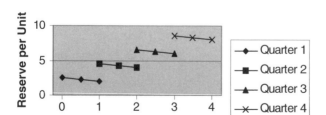

For nonannual premiums, there are two basic ways to calculate the terminal reserves for each premium due date:

- The calculation of PVFP and PVFB can be switched to a nonannual basis, so that the terminal reserve can be directly calculated for each premium due date. For example, for a quarterly paying ten-year term policy, the reserve three months after issue would reflect 39 future quarterly premiums and 9.75 years of future benefits and expenses. To switch reserve calculations to a nonannual basis, discounting and survivorship must be switched to the same frequency as the premiums. While this approach has some theoretical appeal, it is rarely used in practice.

- The terminal reserves for each premium due date can be interpolated from the terminal reserves for annual premium policies. This assumes that the terminal reserves for each premium due date fall on a straight line between annual terminal reserves. This is actually a good approximation. Because of the reliance on simple annual premium reserves, this is the more commonly used approach. In Figure 12.7.2, notice how the reserves for quarterly premiums match the interpolated annual premium reserves at the end of each quarter.

Figure 12.7.2 Comparison of Reserves for Quarterly and Annual Premiums

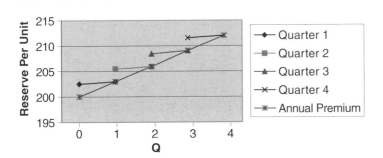

12.7.2 Interpolated Reserves for Nonannual Premiums

Before we can develop an interpolated reserve formula for nonannual premiums, we need some additional notation. Remember that "Frac" is the fraction of a year from the previous policy anniversary to the valuation date:

$\text{Freq}(m)$ = Frequency: how many times per year premiums are due for mode m, equal to 1, 2, 4, and 12 for annual, semiannual, quarterly, and monthly modes of payment, respectively

$\text{Period}(m)$ = Fraction of a year between premium due dates for mode m, equal to one divided by the frequency, or 1, ½, ¼, and ¹⁄₁₂ for annual, semiannual, quarterly, and monthly modes of payment, respectively

$\text{FracDef}(m, \text{Frac})$ = As of the valuation date, the fraction of the policy year for which premium payments for the current policy year are still deferred (that is, not yet due), for mode m. Annual premiums for the current year are never deferred. Quarterly premiums beyond the current policy quarter are deferred. Monthly premiums beyond the current policy month are deferred.

$\text{FracDue}(m, \text{Frac})$ = As of the valuation date, the fraction of the policy year for which premium payments for the current policy year are due (that is, no longer deferred), for mode m. Annual premiums for the current year are always due. Quarterly premiums through the current policy quarter are due. Monthly premiums through the current policy month are due.

$\text{FracPrem}(m, \text{Frac})$ = The fraction of a year from the previous premium due date to the valuation date, for mode m.

Examples 12.7.1 and 12.7.2 help to clarify and illustrate these definitions.

Example 12.7.1 Fractional Premium Timeline

The following timeline example may help to clarify the above time periods, with quarterly frequency ($m = 3$, Freq(m) = 4), Period(m) equal to one-fourth of a year, and the valuation date falling $\frac{5}{8}$ of the way through the policy year (Frac = 0.625):

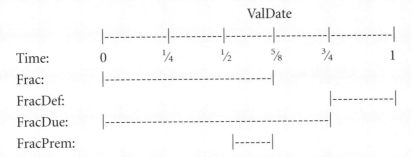

One quarterly premium is deferred, so FracDef is $\frac{1}{4}$. Three quarterly premiums are due, so FracDue is $\frac{3}{4}$. There is half of a quarter between the previous premium due date (at time $\frac{1}{2}$) and the valuation date, so FracPrem is one-eighth of a year.

Example 12.7.2 Fractional Premium Table

The following table shows values of Frac, FracDef, and FracPrem for quarterly and monthly modes of payment.

Beginning of Policy Month	Frac	Quarterly		Monthly	
		FracDef	FracPrem	FracDef	Frac Prem
1	0.0000	0.7500	0.0000	0.9167	0.0000
2	0.0833	"	0.0833	0.8333	"
3	0.1667	"	0.1667	0.7500	"
4	0.2500	0.5000	0.0000	0.6667	"
5	0.3333	"	0.0833	0.5833	"
6	0.4167	"	0.1667	0.5000	"
7	0.5000	0.2500	0.0000	0.4167	"
8	0.5833	"	0.0833	0.3333	"
9	0.6667	"	0.1667	0.2500	"
10	0.7500	0.0000	0.0000	0.1667	"
11	0.8333	"	0.0833	0.0833	"
12	0.9167	"	0.1667	0.0000	"

Period is equal to one divided by the frequency:

$$\text{Period}(m) = \frac{1}{\text{Freq}(m)}. \tag{12.7.1}$$

For example, for the quarterly mode, the period is equal to $\frac{1}{4}$, and the frequency is equal to 4.

Because every premium is either due or deferred, it follows that

$$\text{FracDef}(m, \text{Frac}) + \text{FracDue}(m, \text{Frac}) = 1. \tag{12.7.2}$$

For Frac < 1.0, the fraction of the policy year for which premium payments are due can be calculated in terms of the period and how far into the policy year you are:

$$\text{FracDue}(m, \text{Frac}) = \left(\text{INT} \left[\frac{\text{Frac}}{\text{Period}(m)} \right] + 1 \right) \text{Period}(m). \tag{12.7.3}$$

INT[x] is a function that rounds x down to the nearest integer. INT[Frac/Period(m)] represents the number of premium payments due so far for the policy year, excluding the first premium payment, which is why one is added to the result. Multiplying by Period(m) converts the number of premium payments due to the fraction of the year's premiums that are due.

Example 12.7.3

If you are five-eighths of a year from the last anniversary (that is, Frac = 0.625) and the frequency is quarterly (that is, Period = 0.25), then three-quarters of the year's premiums are due:

$$FracDue(3, 0.625) = \left(INT \left[\frac{0.625}{0.25} \right] + 1 \right) 0.25$$
$$= (2 + 1)\, 0.25 = 0.75.$$

From their definitions, Frac − FracPrem(m, Frac) equals the portion of the policy year up to the previous premium due date. FracDue(m, Frac) equals the portion of the policy year up to the next premium due date. By subtracting one period from this, we see that FracDue(m, Frac) − Period(m) also equals the portion of the policy year up to the previous premium due date. Therefore,

$$Frac - FracPrem(m, Frac) = FracDue(m, Frac) - Period(m).$$
$$(12.7.4)$$

Annual premium reserves and nonannual premium reserves are based on identical policy benefits. There often are additional collection expenses for nonannual premiums, because it costs more to process several premiums than it does to process one annual premium. Less interest is earned on nonannual premiums, since premiums are paid later in the policy year, on average. However, nonannual premiums are usually increased to cover these differences in expenses and interest. Assuming the differences between annual and nonannual premiums are fairly constant from year to year as a percentage of premiums, we can use annual premium reserves as an accurate starting point for nonannual premium reserves. Let

$$\text{Res\_puInt}(m, t, \text{Frac}) = \text{Reserve per unit in force at time Frac}$$
during year t, for mode m

$$\text{NetPrem\_pu}(m, t) = \text{Annualized net premium per unit in}$$
force for year t, mode m. We will assume that modal net premiums per unit do not change within the policy year.

$$\text{Exp\_puPrem}(m, t) = \text{Annualized expense for year } t, \text{ mode } m$$
that is incurred when premiums are paid, per unit in force at the beginning of policy year t. This consists of commissions and other percentage-of-premium expenses.

There are two ways to calculate annualized net premiums. The simple, less precise, but more often used approach is to set annualized net premiums per unit equal to annual net premiums per unit:

$$\text{NetPrem\_pu}(m, t) = \text{NetPrem\_pu}(t). \tag{12.7.5}$$

Alternatively, annualized net premiums per unit can be calculated as annualized gross premium per unit times the ratio of net annual premiums to gross annual premiums. This ratio was defined in Chapter 6:

$$\text{NetPrem\_pu}(m, t) = \text{Ratio} \sum_{Q=1}^{4} \text{Prem\_pu}(m, t, Q). \tag{12.7.6}$$

Annualized percentage-of-premium expenses should be calculated in a manner that is consistent with the calculation of annualized net premiums per unit. An easy way to ensure this is to maintain the same ratio of percentage-of-premium expenses to net premiums:

$$\text{Exp\_puPrem}(m, t) = \text{NetPrem\_pu}(m, t) \frac{\text{Exp\_puPrem}(t)}{\text{NetPrem\_pu}(t)}. \tag{12.7.7}$$

Assuming that the only other significant difference between annual premium and nonannual premium reserves is the timing of premiums, the formula for nonannual premium interpolated reserves is

$$
\begin{aligned}
\text{Res\_puInt}&(m, t, \text{Frac}) \\
&= (\text{Res\_pu}(t-1) - \text{Exp\_puBeg}(t))\,(1 - \text{Frac}) \\
&\quad + \text{Res\_pu}(t)\,\text{Frac} \\
&\quad + (\text{NetPrem\_pu}(m, t) - \text{Exp\_puPrem}(m, t)) \\
&\quad \times (\text{Period}(m) - \text{FracPrem}(m, \text{Frac})). \qquad (12.7.8)
\end{aligned}
$$

"Frac" is used to interpolate the end-of-year values. "Period − FracPrem" is used to pro-rate the net premium less related expenses. The difference between this formula and Formula 6.4.7 for interpolated annual premium reserves is the factor applied to net premium less related expenses. "Period − FracPrem" represents the unearned portion of the most recently due payment. For example, if the valuation date is halfway between quarterly premium due dates, then the unearned premium will be one-eighth of a year's premium. (A premium is said to be gradually "earned" over the period to which it applies.)

Formula 12.7.8 produces the sawtooth pattern of reserves illustrated in Figure 12.7.2, with one sawtooth for each period of the year. For annual premiums, Period = 1 and FracPrem = Frac, so Formula 6.4.7 for annual premium interpolated reserves is merely a special case of Formula 12.7.8 for nonannual premiums.

12.7.3 Deferred Premiums

Deferred premiums are the premiums for the current policy year that are not yet due. For example, 7.5 months after the anniversary, three quarterly premiums would be due and one quarterly premium would be deferred. If premiums were paid monthly, eight monthly premiums would be due and four monthly premiums would be deferred.

A common approach to calculating reserves for nonannual premiums is to use annual premium reserves. This purposely overstates reserves, but something called a deferred premium asset can be developed to offset the overstatement. If we subtract Formula 12.7.8 for nonannual premium reserves from Formula 6.4.7 for annual premium reserves, we can determine the overstatement and therefore the amount of such a deferred premium asset:

$$\text{DefPrem}(t, \text{Frac}) = (\text{NetPrem\_pu}(m, t) - \text{Exp\_puPrem}(m, t))$$
$$\times (1 - \text{Frac} - \text{Period}(m) + \text{FracPrem}(m, \text{Frac})).$$

Substituting using Formula 12.7.4, we obtain

$$\text{DefPrem}(t, \text{Frac}) = (\text{NetPrem\_pu}(m, t) - \text{Exp\_puPrem}(m, t))$$
$$\times (1 - \text{FracDue}(m, \text{Frac})).$$

Finally, substituting using Formula 12.7.2, we obtain

$$\text{DefPrem}(t, \text{Frac}) = (\text{NetPrem\_pu}(t) - \text{Exp\_puPrem}(t))$$
$$\times \text{FracDef}(m, \text{Frac}). \tag{12.7.9}$$

In other words, to convert an annual premium reserve into a nonannual premium reserve, all we need do is deduct the deferred fraction of the net premium less related expenses. The use of a deferred premium asset is a simple solution to the problem of calculating different reserves for annual and nonannual premiums. Before the advent of computers, this simple approach was widely used, either as an adjustment to reserves or to determine a separate deferred premium asset.

12.7.4 Comparison of Mean Reserves to Interpolated Reserves

When performing valuations, it is quite common to use mean reserves in combination with deferred premium assets. How does this practice compare to using interpolated reserves for nonannual premiums? In other words, what is the difference between (1) mean reserves with deferred premium assets and (2) interpolated reserves for nonannual premiums?

Because of the way we determined the deferred premium asset, we know that (2) interpolated reserves for nonannual premiums are equal to (3) annual premium interpolated reserves with deferred premium assets. Therefore, the difference between (1) and (2) is the same as the difference between (1) and (3).

The difference between (1) and (3) is equal to the difference between mean reserves and annual premium interpolated reserves. Examining Formula 6.4.5 for mean reserves and Formula 6.4.7 for interpolated reserves, we see that this difference amounts to mean reserves using factors of "$\frac{1}{2}$" and "$\frac{1}{2}$" in place of the interpolation factors "$(1 - \text{Frac})$" and "Frac."

12.7.5 Quarterly Reserves

In this section, we will define quarterly reserve calculations for reserves in general. We will leave it for the reader to apply the general quarterly reserve formulas to solvency reserves, earnings reserves, benefit reserves, deferred acquisition costs, and tax reserves. Let

$$\text{Res\_pu}(t, Q) = \text{Reserve per unit in force at the end of } (t, Q)$$
$$\text{Res}(t, Q) = \text{Reserve at the end of } (t, Q), \text{ per unit issued}$$
$$\text{ResIncr}(t, Q) = \text{Reserve increase during } (t, Q), \text{ per unit issued.}$$

12.7.5.1 Pre-Scheduled Products

Reserves at the end of each quarter can be calculated in a variety of ways, as discussed in Sections 12.7.1–12.7.4. In order to accurately predict financial results, it is imperative that the calculation method used in pricing match the method that will be used in valuation. Here are the major choices for pre-scheduled products:

- Reserves can directly reflect modal premiums and be interpolated to the end of the quarter, as in Formula 12.7.8.
- Reserves can be calculated by using Formula 6.4.7 for interpolated annual premium reserves and deducting a deferred premium asset calculated using Formula 12.7.9. This is mathematically equivalent to the previous choice, so it will not be discussed further.
- Reserves can be calculated by using Formula 6.4.5 for mean annual premium reserves and deducting a deferred premium asset calculated using Formula 12.7.9.

If reserves are calculated using Formula 12.7.8 for interpolated nonannual premium reserves, then

$$Res\_pu(t, Q) = (Res\_pu(t - 1) - Exp\_puBeg(t)) \left(1 - \frac{Q}{4}\right)$$

$$+ Res\_pu(t) \frac{Q}{4} + \sum_{m=1}^{4} \bigg(ModalDist(m)$$

$$\times (NetPrem\_pu(m, t) - Exp\_puPrem(m, t))$$

$$\times \left(Period(m) - FracPrem\left(m, \frac{Q}{4}\right)\right)\bigg). \quad (12.7.10)$$

If reserves are calculated using Formula 6.4.5 for mean annual premium reserves with a deduction for a deferred premium asset calculated using Formula 12.7.9, then

$$Res\_pu(t, Q)$$

$$= \tfrac{1}{2} (Res\_pu(t - 1) - Exp\_puBeg(t)) + \tfrac{1}{2} Res\_pu(t)$$

$$- \sum_{m=1}^{4} \bigg(ModalDist(m) \ (NetPrem\_pu(m, t)$$

$$- Exp\_puPrem(m, t)) \ FracDef\left(m, \frac{Q}{4}\right)\bigg). \quad (12.7.11)$$

12.7.5.2 Dynamic Products

Reserves for dynamic products are typically based on the account value, perhaps with an adjustment for initial expenses or additional reserves. Let

$AV\_pu(t, Q)$ = The account value per unit in force at the end of (t, Q)

$ResAdj\_pu(t)$ = The reserve adjustment per unit in force at the end of policy year t. This is equal to the difference between the reserve and account value per unit in force at the end of policy year t. We will assume this difference is pre-scheduled or recalculated from time to time.

The reserve at the end of quarter Q can be calculated as the account value at the end of quarter Q plus the reserve adjustment:

$$\text{Res\_pu}(t, Q) = \text{AV\_pu}(t, Q) + \text{ResAdj\_pu}(t - 1)\left(1 - \frac{Q}{4}\right)$$

$$+ \text{ResAdj\_pu}(t)\,\frac{Q}{4}. \tag{12.7.12}$$

To calculate deferred acquisition costs, $\text{AV\_pu}(t, Q)$ should be omitted from the preceding formula, and the signs should be reversed to switch from a liability to an asset.

12.7.5.3 Reserve and Increase in Reserve

The reserve per unit issued is calculated by adjusting the reserve per unit in force for survivorship:

$$\text{Res}(t, Q) = \text{Res\_pu}(t, Q)\,\text{SurvFactor}(t, Q). \tag{12.7.13}$$

The increase in reserve is calculated as the reserve at the end of the quarter less the reserve at the beginning of the quarter:

$$\text{ResIncr}(t, Q) = \text{Res}(t, Q) - \text{Res}(t, Q - 1). \tag{12.7.14}$$

12.8 Reinsurance

12.8.1 Yearly Renewable Term

We will examine several methods of paying YRT reinsurance premiums:

- Formulas for annual reinsurance premiums will be developed for both pre-scheduled and dynamic products
- Formulas for quarterly reinsurance premiums will be developed for pre-scheduled products
- Formulas for monthly reinsurance premiums will be developed for dynamic products.

Sometimes a substantial percentage of a block of business is reinsured, and a significant percentage of the policyholders pay monthly or quarterly premiums. If reinsurance premiums are paid on annual basis, reinsurance premiums can exceed policyholder premiums at the beginning of the policy year. When this occurs, it may be especially important to accurately reflect the impact of reinsurance.

12.8.1.1 Annual Reinsurance Premiums

YRT reinsured amounts are normally calculated only once per year and remain constant for the entire policy year. Reinsurance premiums are usually paid annually, during the month following the policy anniversary. Annual reinsurance premiums are pro-rated for policies that lapse before their next anniversary. This results in refunds of unearned reinsurance premium.

For annual reinsurance premiums, net amounts at risk, reinsured death benefits, and reinsurance premiums per unit in force are calculated as presented in Section 7.4. Reinsurance premiums must be adjusted for refund of unearned premium on lapses. Let

ReinsPrem(t, Q) = Reinsurance premium paid at the beginning of year t, quarter Q: This is used for pre-scheduled products

ReinsPrem(t, M) = Reinsurance premium paid at the beginning of year t, month M: This is used for dynamic products.

Pre-scheduled Products: For pre-scheduled products, the first quarter's premium is the annual premium:

$$\text{ReinsPrem}(t, 1)$$
$$= \text{ReinsDB\_pu}(t)\ \text{ReinsPrem\_pu}(t)\ \text{SurvFactor}(t, 0).$$

$$(12.8.1)$$

Subsequent quarters' premiums are refunds of unearned premiums on lapses:

$$\text{ReinsPrem}(t, Q) = \text{ReinsDB\_pu}(t)\left(\frac{Q-1}{4} - 1\right)$$
$$\times\ \text{ReinsPrem\_pu}(t)\ \text{Lapses}(t, Q-1).$$

$$(12.8.2)$$

For example, for $Q = 2$, the first quarter in which a refund is paid, 75% of a year's premium is refunded for lapses in the prior quarter.

Dynamic Products: For dynamic products, the first month's premium is the annual premium:

$$\text{ReinsPrem}(t, 1)$$
$$= \text{ReinsDB\_pu}(t)\ \text{ReinsPrem\_pu}(t)\ \text{SurvFactor}(t, 0). \quad (12.8.3)$$

Subsequent months' premiums are refunds of unearned premiums on lapses:

$$\text{ReinsPrem}(t, M) = \text{ReinsDB\_pu}(t) \left(\frac{M - 1}{12} - 1 \right)$$
$$\text{ReinsPrem\_pu}(t)\ \text{Lapses}(t, M - 1). \quad (12.8.4)$$

For example, for $M = 2$, the first month in which a refund is paid, 91.67% of a year's premium is refunded for lapses in the prior month.

12.8.1.2 Quarterly Reinsurance Premiums

Reinsurance premiums are sometimes paid quarterly. A *quarterly reinsurance premium* refers to the practice of paying a reinsurance premium four times per year for each reinsured policy. Be careful not to confuse this with the common practice of paying annual reinsurance premiums once a quarter for policies that cross their policy anniversaries during the quarter. This common practice results in one annual reinsurance premium per policy per year, not four quarterly premiums.

For pre-scheduled products, we assume that lapses occur only at the end of the quarter. Therefore, quarterly reinsurance premiums theoretically result in no premium refunds. In actuality, one quarterly premium is often paid before it is realized a policy has lapsed, so such premiums must be refunded. We will ignore this minor timing difference and assume that there are no overpayments and no refunds of quarterly reinsurance premiums.

Let

$$\text{Naar\_pu}(t, Q) = \text{Net amount at risk per unit in force at}$$
$$\text{the end } (t, Q)$$
$$\text{ReinsDB\_pu}(t, Q) = \text{The average reinsured amount per unit in}$$
$$\text{force at the beginning of } (t, Q)$$

> ReinsPrem_pu(t, Q) = Annualized reinsurance premium per unit in force, *not* per thousand of reinsured death benefit.

Net Amount at Risk Level through the Year: When reinsurance premiums are paid quarterly, net amounts at risk, reinsured death benefits, and reinsurance premium per unit in force are usually calculated only once a year, using the formulas in Section 7.4. In this case, the following formulas apply:

$$\text{Naar\_pu}(t, Q) = \text{Naar\_pu}(t), \tag{12.8.5}$$

$$\text{ReinsDB\_pu}(t, Q) = \text{ReinsDB\_pu}(t), \tag{12.8.6}$$

$$\text{ReinsPrem\_pu}(t, Q) = \text{ReinsPrem\_pu}(t). \tag{12.8.7}$$

Net Amount at Risk Changes Quarterly: In some cases, the above variables are recalculated each quarter, and the following formulas would be used:

Net amount at risk is calculated by deducting solvency reserves, cash values, or nothing (for most term insurance):

$$\text{Naar\_pu}(t, Q) = \text{DB\_pu}(t, Q) - \text{SolvRes\_pu}(t, Q), \tag{12.8.8}$$

$$\text{Naar\_pu}(t, Q) = \text{DB\_pu}(t, Q) - \text{CV\_pu}(t, Q), \tag{12.8.9}$$

$$\text{Naar\_pu}(t, Q) = \text{DB\_pu}(t, Q). \tag{12.8.10}$$

The YRT death benefit is the percentage reinsured times the net amount at risk:

$$\text{ReinsDB\_pu}(t, Q) = \text{ReinsPct}(t)\,\text{Naar\_pu}(t, Q - 1). \tag{12.8.11}$$

The annualized reinsurance premium per unit in force is equal to the reinsured death benefit per unit in force times the reinsurance premium per 1,000 of reinsured death benefit:

$$\text{ReinsPrem\_pu}(t, Q) = \text{ReinsDB\_pu}(t, Q)\,\frac{\text{ReinsPremPer1000}(t)}{1,000} \tag{12.8.12}$$

Reinsurance Premium Calculation: Whether the preceding variables change monthly or annually, the quarterly reinsurance premium is equal to one-fourth of the annualized reinsurance premium per unit in force divided by four and adjusted for survivorship:

ReinsPrem(t, Q)

$$= \frac{1}{4} \, \text{ReinsDB\_pu}(t, Q) \, \text{ReinPrem\_pu}(t, Q) \, \text{SurvFactor}(t, Q - 1).$$

(12.8.13)

12.8.1.3 Monthly Reinsurance Premiums

Reinsurance premiums are sometimes paid monthly, usually in connection with dynamic products. A *monthly reinsurance premium* refers to the practice of paying a reinsurance premium 12 times per year for each reinsured policy. Be careful not to confuse this with the common practice of paying annual reinsurance premiums once a month for policies that cross their policy anniversaries during the month.

For dynamic products, we assume that lapses occur at the end of each month. Therefore, monthly reinsurance premiums theoretically result in no premium refunds. Dynamic products often have monthly reinsurance premiums, so that reinsured amounts can be closely coordinated with amounts at risk that change monthly. In practice, this closer coordination is rarely worth the administrative complexity of changing reinsured amounts every month. More companies are realizing this and switching to annual reinsurance premiums for dynamic products, coupled with a special adjustment as needed for any exceptionally large change in amount at risk.

Let

$$\text{Naar\_pu}(t, M) = \text{Net amount at risk per unit in force at the end } (t, M)$$

$$\text{ReinsDB\_pu}(t, M) = \text{The average reinsured amount per unit in force at the beginning of } (t, M)$$

$$\text{ReinsPrem\_pu}(t, M) = \text{Annualized reinsurance premium per unit in force, } not \text{ per thousand of reinsured death benefit.}$$

Net Amount at Risk Level through the Year

When reinsurance premiums are paid monthly, net amounts at risk, reinsured death benefits, and reinsurance premium per unit in force are usually calculated only once a year, using the formulas in Section 7.4. In this case, the following formulas apply:

$$\text{Naar\_pu}(t, M) = \text{Naar\_pu}(t), \qquad (12.8.14)$$

$$\text{ReinsDB\_pu}(t, M) = \text{ReinsDB\_pu}(t), \qquad (12.8.15)$$

$$\text{ReinsPrem\_pu}(t, M) = \text{ReinsPrem\_pu}(t). \qquad (12.8.16)$$

Net Amount at Risk Changes Monthly

In some cases, these variables are recalculated each month, and the following formulas would be used:

Net amount at risk is calculated by deducting solvency reserves, cash values, or nothing (for most term insurance):

$$\text{Naar\_pu}(t, M) = \text{DB\_pu}(t, M) - \text{SolvRes\_pu}(t, M), \qquad (12.8.17)$$

$$\text{Naar\_pu}(t, M) = \text{DB\_pu}(t, M) - \text{CV\_pu}(t, M), \qquad (12.8.18)$$

$$\text{Naar\_pu}(t, M) = \text{DB\_pu}(t, M). \qquad (12.8.19)$$

The YRT death benefit is the percentage reinsured times the net amount at risk:

$$\text{ReinsDB\_pu}(t, M) = \text{ReinsPct}(t)\,\text{Naar\_pu}(t, M - 1). \qquad (12.8.20)$$

The annualized reinsurance premium per unit in force is equal to the reinsured death benefit per unit in force times the reinsurance premium per 1,000 of reinsured death benefit:

$$\text{ReinsPrem\_pu}(t, M) = \text{ReinsDB\_pu}(t, M)\,\frac{\text{ReinsPremPer1000}(t)}{1,000}.$$

$$(12.8.21)$$

Reinsurance Premium Calculation

Whether the preceding variables change monthly or annually, the monthly reinsurance premium is calculated as one-twelfth of the annualized reinsurance premium per unit in force, adjusted for survivorship:

$$\text{ReinsPrem}(t, M) = \frac{1}{12}\,\text{ReinsDB\_pu}(t, M)\,\text{ReinsPrem\_pu}(t, M)$$

$$\times \text{SurvFactor}(t, M - 1). \qquad (12.8.22)$$

12.8.1.4   Reinsured Death Benefits

For pre-scheduled products, we will assume that reinsured death benefits are reimbursed at the same time death benefits are paid to the beneficiary, that is, at the middle of the quarter, on average. Let

$$\text{ReinsDeathBen}(t, Q) = \text{Reinsured death benefits received from the reinsurer in } (t, Q), \text{ per unit issued.}$$

The reinsured death benefit received from the reinsurer is equal to the average reinsured amount times the probability of dying in policy year t, quarter Q:

$$\text{ReinsDeathBen}(t, Q) = \text{ReinsDB\_pu}(t, Q) \ \text{Deaths}(t, Q). \quad (12.8.23)$$

For dynamic products, we will assume that reinsured death benefits are reimbursed at the same time death benefits are paid to the beneficiary, that is, at the middle of the month, on average. Let

$$\text{ReinsDeathBen}(t, M) = \text{Reinsured death benefits received from the reinsurer in } (t, M), \text{ per unit issued.}$$

The reinsured death benefit received from the reinsurer is equal to the average reinsured amount times the probability of dying in policy year t, quarter M:

$$\text{ReinsDeathBen}(t, M) = \text{ReinsDB\_pu}(t, M) \ \text{Deaths}(t, M). \quad (12.8.24)$$

12.8.1.5   Expense Allowances

For pre-scheduled products, we will assume that the company receives an expense allowance from the reinsurer at the beginning of each quarter, calculated as a percentage of the reinsurance premium. If reinsurance premiums are paid annually, then the allowance is paid on the first quarterly premium. The next three quarters result in premium refunds and allowance refunds on lapses. Let

$$\text{ExpAllow}(t, Q) = \text{Expense allowances received from the reinsurer in } (t, Q).$$

The expense allowance is calculated by applying the expense allowance percentage to the reinsurance premium:

$$\text{ExpAllow}(t,\, Q) = \text{ReinsPrem}(t,\, Q)\, \text{ExpAllowPct}(t). \qquad (12.8.25)$$

For dynamic products, we will assume that the company receives an expense allowance from the reinsurer at the beginning of each month, calculated as a percentage of the reinsurance premium. If reinsurance premiums are paid annually, then the allowance is paid on the first monthly premium. The next 11 months result in premium refunds and allowance refunds on lapses. Let

$\text{ExpAllow}(t,\, M)$

  $= $ Expense allowances received from the reinsurer in $(t,\, M)$.

The expense allowance is calculated by applying the expense allowance percentage to the reinsurance premium:

$$\text{ExpAllow}(t,\, M) = \text{ReinsPrem}(t,\, M)\, \text{ExpAllowPct}(t). \qquad (12.8.26)$$

12.8.1.6 Adjusting Gross Cash Flows

The gross cash flows (that is, before deduction for reinsurance) calculated in Sections 12.4 and 12.5 should be adjusted by deducting the related reinsurance cash flows. While these formulas and many to follow are not mathematically correct, they are a simple way to show how pre-reinsurance values are adjusted to reflect any reinsurance. For YRT, only three cash flow adjustments are needed. For dynamic products, the monthly reinsurance cash flows should be summarized into quarterly cash flows in order to use the following formulas:

$$\text{Prem}(t,\, Q) = \text{Prem}(t,\, Q) - \text{ReinsPrem}(t,\, Q), \qquad (12.8.27)$$
$$\text{DeathBen}(t,\, Q) = \text{DeathBen}(t,\, Q) - \text{ReinsDeathBen}(t,\, Q),$$
$$(12.8.28)$$
$$\text{Comm}(t,\, Q) = \text{Comm}(t,\, Q) - \text{ExpAllow}(t,\, Q). \qquad (12.8.29)$$

12.8.1.7 YRT Reserve Credits

We will focus our discussion on the one-year term (OYT) method of calculating reinsurance reserve credits. The stand-alone and net cash flow methods of calculating reinsurance reserves can be converted to a quarterly basis by using the methods presented in Section 12.7.

Quarterly reserve credits will be presented for annual, quarterly, and monthly reinsurance premiums. Because results will be summarized on a quarterly basis, there is no need to calculate monthly reserve credits. Let

OYTNetPrem_pu(t) = One-year term net premium, per unit in force. This is equal to the valuation mortality rate discounted for a full or half year's valuation interest.

OYTRes_pu(t, Q) = One-year term reserve, per unit in force at the end of (t, Q). This will be calculated differently for annual, quarterly, and monthly reinsurance premiums.

ResCredit(t, Q) = Reserve credit at the end of (t, Q), per unit issued

ResCreditIncr(t, Q) = Increase in reserve credit during (t, Q), per unit issued.

Regardless of reinsurance premium frequency, the following formulas apply. The reserve credit is calculated as the one-year term reserve per unit in force times the reinsured death benefit, adjusted for survivorship:

$$\text{ResCredit}(t, Q) = \text{ReinsDB\_pu}(t, Q)\ \text{OYTRes\_pu}(t, Q)$$
$$\text{SurvFactor}(t, Q), \tag{12.8.30}$$
$$\text{ResCreditIncr}(t, Q) = \text{ResCredit}(t, Q) - \text{ResCredit}(t, Q - 1). \tag{12.8.31}$$

Annual Reinsurance Premiums: OYT reserve credits for annual reinsurance premiums can take one of two forms: a level mean reserve that is held throughout the policy year, and an interpolated reserve.

If a level mean reserve is held throughout the policy year, then the OYT reserve per unit is calculated as half the OYT net premium:

$$\text{OYTRes\_pu}(t, Q) = \tfrac{1}{2}\ \text{OYTNetPrem\_pu}(t). \tag{12.8.32}$$

Mean reserves are calculated as the average of the initial and terminal reserves. In this case, the initial reserve is the net premium and the terminal reserve is zero.

Interpolated OYT reserves are equal to the OYT net premium at the beginning of the policy year and gradually decline to zero by the end of the policy year:

$$\text{OYTRes\_pu}(t, Q) = \left(1 - \frac{Q}{4}\right) \text{OYTNetPrem\_pu}(t). \qquad (12.8.33)$$

For $Q = 0$, reserves equal the full net premium. For $Q = 4$, reserves equal zero. In other words, there is a big discontinuity in reserves, depending on whether you calculate them just before or just after the anniversary. This is the same problem identified in Section 6.5.2. A similar "reserve adjustment for missing conservatism" may be warranted for OYT reserves.

Quarterly Reinsurance Premiums: OYT reserve credits for quarterly reinsurance premiums can take one of two forms: a level mean reserve that is held throughout the policy year, and an interpolated quarterly reserve, which is rarely used.

If a level mean reserve is held throughout the policy year, then the OYT reserve per unit is calculated as half the quarterly net premium (the quarterly net premium is one-fourth of the annual net premium):

$$\text{OYTRes\_pu}(t, Q) = \frac{1}{8} \text{OYTNetPrem\_pu}(t). \qquad (12.8.34)$$

Interpolated quarterly reserves are equal to the quarterly net premium at the beginning of quarter and gradually decline to zero by the end of the quarter. However, because we are calculating all reserves as of the end of the quarter, this results in zero reserve credits. As a result, most companies use the mean reserve approach for modeling.

Monthly Reinsurance Premiums: OYT reserve credits for monthly reinsurance premiums are usually calculated as a level mean reserve that is held throughout the policy year. The OYT reserve per unit is calculated as half the monthly net premium (the monthly net premium is one-twelfth of the annual net premium):

$$\text{OYTRes\_pu}(t, Q) = \frac{1}{24} \text{OYTNetPrem\_pu}(t). \qquad (12.8.35)$$

12.8.1.8   Adjustment to Reserve Increase

Once the increase in reserve credit has been calculated, the reserve increase can be adjusted as follows:

$$\text{ResIncr}(t, Q) = \text{ResIncr}(t, Q) - \text{ResCreditIncr}(t, Q). \qquad (12.8.36)$$

12.8.2   Coinsurance

Quarterly calculations for coinsurance are virtually the same as annual calculations. The main difference is the substitution of (t, Q) for (t).

12.8.2.1   Coinsurance Premiums

Reinsurance premiums will depend on whether or not policy fees are included. If the reinsurance premium includes the policy fee, then the reinsurance premium is simply the reinsured percentage times the direct premium:

$$\text{ReinsPrem}(t, Q) = \text{ReinsPct}(t)\,\text{Prem}(t, Q). \qquad (12.8.37)$$

If policy fees are excluded from reinsurance premiums, then the reinsurance premium is calculated as the reinsured percentage times the premium per unit, adjusted for survivorship:

$$\begin{aligned}\text{ReinsPrem}(t, Q) = {}& \text{ReinsPct}(t)\,\text{PremPerUnit}(t, Q) \\ & \times \text{SurvFactor}(t, Q - 1). \qquad (12.8.38)\end{aligned}$$

12.8.2.2   Policy Benefits

Each reinsured policy benefit is equal to the reinsured percentage times the policy benefit:

$$\begin{aligned}\text{ReinsDeathBen}(t, Q) &= \text{ReinsPct}(t)\,\text{DeathBen}(t, Q). & (12.8.39) \\ \text{ReinsSurrBen}(t, Q) &= \text{ReinsPct}(t)\,\text{SurrBen}(t, Q). & (12.8.40) \\ \text{ReinsDiv}(t, Q) &= \text{ReinsPct}(t)\,\text{Div}(t, Q). & (12.8.41) \\ \text{ReinsPartWithBen}(t, Q) &= \text{ReinsPct}(t)\,\text{PartWithBen}(t, Q). & \\ & & (12.8.42) \\ \text{ReinsPureEndow}(t, Q) &= \text{ReinsPct}(t)\,\text{PureEndow}(t, Q). & (12.8.43)\end{aligned}$$

Total reinsured policy benefits are equal to the reinsured percentage times total policy benefits:

$$\text{ReinsBen}(t, Q) = \text{ReinsPct}(t) \text{ Ben}(t, Q). \tag{12.8.44}$$

12.8.2.3 Expense Allowances

Most expense allowances are calculated as a percentage of reinsurance premiums:

$$\text{ExpAllow}(t, Q) = \text{ExpAllowPct}(t) \text{ ReinsPrem}(t, Q). \tag{12.8.45}$$

When the company pays a commission based on account values at the end of the policy year, the reinsurer would normally pay a matching expense allowance. Expense allowances based on account values are paid at the same time account value commissions are paid, at the end of the year:

$$
\begin{aligned}
\text{AVExpAllow}(t, 4) &= \text{ReinsPct}(t) \text{ AVExpAllowPct}(t) \text{ AV\_pu}(t) \\
&\quad \times \text{SurvFactor}(t, 4), \\
\text{AVExpAllow}(t, Q) &= 0 \quad \text{for } Q = 1, 2, \text{ and } 3.
\end{aligned}
\tag{12.8.46}
$$

12.8.2.4 Adjusting Gross Cash Flows

The gross cash flows calculated in Chapter 5 should be adjusted by deducting the related reinsurance cash flows. For coinsurance, numerous cash flow adjustments are needed:

$$\text{Prem}(t, Q) = \text{Prem}(t, Q) - \text{ReinsPrem}(t, Q), \tag{12.8.47}$$

$$\text{DeathBen}(t, Q) = \text{DeathBen}(t, Q) - \text{ReinsDeathBen}(t, Q), \tag{12.8.48}$$

$$\text{SurrBen}(t, Q) = \text{SurrBen}(t, Q) - \text{ReinsSurrBen}(t, Q), \tag{12.8.49}$$

$$\text{Div}(t, Q) = \text{Div}(t, Q) - \text{ReinsDiv}(t, Q), \tag{12.8.50}$$

$$
\begin{aligned}
\text{PartWithBen}(t, Q) &= \text{PartWithBen}(t, Q) \\
&\quad - \text{ReinsPartWithBen}(t, Q),
\end{aligned}
\tag{12.8.51}
$$

$$\text{PureEndow}(t, Q) = \text{PureEndow}(t, Q) - \text{ReinsPureEndow}(t, Q), \tag{12.8.52}$$

$$\text{Comm}(t, Q) = \text{Comm}(t, Q) - \text{ExpAllow}(t, Q), \tag{12.8.53}$$

$$\text{AVComm}(t, Q) = \text{AVComm}(t, Q) - \text{AVExpAllow}(t, Q). \tag{12.8.54}$$

12.8.2.5 Coinsurance Reserve Credits

If the same valuation assumptions and methods are used to calculate both gross reserves and coinsured reserves, then the reserve credit is the reinsured percentage of the gross reserve:

$$\text{ResCredit}(t, Q) = \text{ReinsPct}(t)\,\text{Res}(t, Q). \tag{12.8.55}$$

The same formulas for increase in reserve credit and adjustment of reserve increase apply for YRT and coinsurance. Refer to Formulas 12.8.31 and 12.8.36.

12.9 Investment Income

Quarterly investment income is calculated much the same as investment income for annual calculations. Assets and cash flows vary from quarter to quarter and are accumulated with quarterly interest rates. However, we will assume that the amount of outstanding policy loan can change only at the end of the policy year. In other words, we will assume that the amount of outstanding policy loan is constant from quarter to quarter during the policy year, except for the compounding of interest. Let

$$\text{PolLoan}(t, Q) = \text{Policy loan outstanding at the end of } (t, Q), \text{ per unit issued}$$

$$\text{PolLoanIntRateQ}(t) = \text{The quarterly policy loan interest rate for } (t, Q), \text{ equivalent to PolLoanIntRate}(t) \text{ on an annual effective basis}$$

$$\text{PolLoanInt}(t, Q) = \text{The amount of policy loan interest earned during } (t, Q), \text{ per unit issued}$$

$$\text{AnnualInvIntRate}(t, Q) = \text{Annual effective interest rate earned on invested assets during } (t, Q), \text{ net of investment expenses and asset default costs}$$

$$\text{InvIntRate}(t, Q) = \text{Quarterly interest rate earned on invested assets during } (t, Q), \text{ net of investment expenses and asset default costs}$$

$$\text{InvIntRateMid}(t, Q) = \text{Semiquarterly interest rate equivalent to InvIntRate}(t, Q), \text{ on an annual effective basis}$$

$$\text{Assets}(t, Q) = \text{Total assets at the end of } (t, Q), \text{ per unit issued}$$

$$\text{InvAssets}(t, Q) = \text{All assets other than policy loans at the end of } (t, Q), \text{ per unit issued}$$

$$\text{InvInt}(t, Q) = \text{Interest earned during } (t, Q) \text{ on all assets other than policy loans at the end of } (t, Q - 1), \text{ per unit issued}$$

$$\text{CashFlowInt}(t, Q) = \text{Interest earned during } (t, Q), \text{ on insurance cash flows generated during the quarter, per policy issued}$$

$$\text{InvIncome}(t, Q) = \text{Total investment income earned during } (t, Q), \text{ per unit issued}$$

The policy loan outstanding at the end of the year is calculated using Formula 8.2.1 for PolLoan(t). The policy loan outstanding is accumulated with interest during the year:

$$\text{PolLoan}(t, 4) = \text{PolLoan}(t),$$
$$\text{PolLoan}(t, Q) = \text{PolLoan}(t, Q - 1) + \text{PolLoanInt}(t). \quad (12.9.1)$$

The quarterly policy loan interest rate is calculated from the annual rate:

$$\text{PolLoanIntRateQ}(t) = (1 + \text{PolLoanIntRate}(t))^{1/4} - 1. \quad (12.9.2)$$

Policy loan interest for the quarter is calculated as

$$\text{PolLoanInt}(t, Q) = \text{PolLoan}(t, Q - 1) \, \text{PolLoanIntRateQ}(t). \quad (12.9.3)$$

The quarterly interest rate earned on invested assets is calculated from the annual rate:

$$\text{InvIntRate}(t, Q) = (1 + \text{AnnualInvIntRate}(t, Q))^{1/4} - 1. \quad (12.9.4)$$

The interest rate for half a quarter is calculated from the quarterly rate:

$$\text{InvIntRateMid}(t, Q) = (1 + \text{InvIntRate}(t, Q))^{1/2} - 1. \quad (12.9.5)$$

Assets at the end of each quarter are set equal to the solvency reserve:

$$\text{Assets}(t, Q) = \text{SolvRes}(t, Q). \tag{12.9.6}$$

If reinsurance is modeled, then assets are affected. The above formula would be adjusted to reflect the effect of reinsurance reserve credits:

$$\text{Assets}(t, Q) = \text{SolvRes}(t, Q) - \text{ResCredit}(t, Q). \tag{12.9.7}$$

Invested assets at the end of each quarter are equal to total assets less policy loans:

$$\text{InvAssets}(t, Q) = \text{Assets}(t, Q) - \text{PolLoan}(t, Q). \tag{12.9.8}$$

Quarterly investment income on invested assets is equal to invested assets times the quarterly interest rate:

$$\text{InvInt}(t, Q) = \text{InvAssets}(t, Q - 1)\,\text{InvIntRate}(t, Q). \tag{12.9.9}$$

Interest on cash flows occurring during the quarter is equal to cash flows at the beginning of the quarter times a quarterly interest rate plus cash flows at the middle of the quarter times an interest rate for half of the quarter:

$$\begin{aligned}\text{CashFlowInt}(t, Q) = {}& \text{CashFlowBeg}(t, Q)\,\text{InvIntRate}(t, Q) \\ & + \text{CashFlowMid}(t, Q)\,\text{InvIntRateMid}(t, Q). \end{aligned} \tag{12.9.10}$$

Total investment income for the quarter is equal to policy loan interest plus interest on invested assets plus interest on cash flows occurring during the quarter:

$$\begin{aligned}\text{InvIncome}(t, Q) = {}& \text{PolLoanInt}(t, Q) + \text{InvInt}(t, Q) \\ & + \text{CashFlowInt}(t, Q). \end{aligned} \tag{12.9.11}$$

12.10 Taxes

Let

$$\begin{aligned}\text{PreTaxSolvEarn}(t, Q) = {}& \text{Pre-tax solvency earnings, per unit issued} \\ \text{TimingDiff}(t, Q) = {}& \text{Timing difference between solvency} \\ & \text{earnings and taxable earnings for } (t, Q), \\ & \text{per unit issued} \end{aligned}$$

$$\text{PermDiff}(t, Q) = \text{Permanent difference between solvency earnings and taxable earnings for } (t, Q), \text{ per unit issued}$$

$$\text{TaxableEarn}(t, Q) = \text{Taxable earnings for } (t, Q), \text{ per unit issued}$$

$$\text{TaxOnEarn}(t, Q) = \text{The tax on earnings for } (t, Q), \text{ per unit issued}$$

$$\text{IETaxableInvInc}(t, Q) = \text{Investment income for } (t, Q) \text{ that is subject to the tax on } I - E, \text{ per unit issued.}$$

$$\text{IEDeductExp}(t, Q) = \text{Expenses for } (t, Q) \text{ that are deductible in the tax on } I - E, \text{ per unit issued}$$

$$\text{TaxOnIE}(t, Q) = \text{Tax on } I - E \text{ for } (t, Q), \text{ per unit issued}$$

$$\text{TaxCapital}(t, Q) = \text{Taxable capital for } (t, Q), \text{ per unit issued}$$

$$\text{TaxOnCap}(t, Q) = \text{The tax on capital for } (t, Q), \text{ per unit issued}$$

$$\text{Tax}(t, Q) = \text{Total tax for } (t, Q), \text{ per unit issued}$$

$$\text{AccruedTax}(t, Q) = \text{Taxes accrued for } (t, Q), \text{ per unit issued}$$

$$\text{DefTaxProv}(t, Q) = \text{Provision for deferred taxes for } (t, Q), \text{ per unit issued}$$

$$\text{DefTaxLiab}(t, Q) = \text{Deferred tax liability at the end of } (t, Q), \text{ per unit issued.}$$

12.10.1 Tax on Earnings

Pre-tax solvency earnings are calculated as product cash flows plus investment income minus the increase in solvency reserves:

$$\text{PreTaxSolvEarn}(t, Q) = \text{ProdCashFlow}(t, Q) + \text{InvIncome}(t, Q) - \text{SolvResIncr}(t, Q). \quad (12.10.1)$$

We will assume the only timing difference is due to the difference between the quarterly increase in solvency reserves and the quarterly increase in tax reserves:

$$\text{TimingDiff}(t, Q) = \text{SolvResIncr}(t, Q) - \text{TaxResIncr}(t, Q).$$
$$(12.10.2)$$

We will assume that the only permanent difference is due to a percentage of investment income being nontaxable:

$$\text{PermDiff}(t, Q) = -\text{InvIncome}(t, Q) \, \text{NonTaxInvPct}(t). \quad (12.10.3)$$

Taxable earnings are calculated as pre-tax solvency earnings plus permanent and temporary differences:

$$\begin{aligned}\text{TaxableEarn}(t, Q) = \text{PreTaxSolvEarn}(t, Q) + \text{TimingDiff}(t, Q) \\ + \text{PermDiff}(t, Q). \quad (12.10.4)\end{aligned}$$

The tax on earnings is calculated by applying the appropriate tax rate to taxable earnings. It is assumed that the tax rate does not vary by quarter within a tax year:

$$\text{TaxOnEarn}(t, Q) = \text{TaxableEarn}(t, Q) \, \text{EarnTaxRate}(t). \quad (12.10.5)$$

12.10.2   Tax on $I - E$

Consistent with our approach in Chapter 9, we will assume that taxable investment income can be calculated as a ratio times investment income:

$$\text{IETaxableInvInc}(t, Q) = \text{InvIncome}(t, Q) \, \text{IETaxableInvIncPct}(t).$$
$$(12.10.6)$$

We will assume that deductible expenses can be calculated as a percentage of total expenses:

$$\text{IEDeductExp}(t, Q) = \text{Exp}(t, Q) \, \text{IEDeductExpPct}(t). \quad (12.10.7)$$

Tax on $I - E$ is then calculated as taxable investment income net of deductible expenses times the appropriate tax rate:

$$\begin{aligned}\text{TaxOnIE}(t, Q) = (\text{IETaxableInvInc}(t, Q) \\ - \text{IEDeductExp}(t, Q)) \, \text{IETaxRate}(t). \quad (12.10.8)\end{aligned}$$

12.10.3 Tax on Capital

We will assume that tax on capital is calculated as taxable capital at the end of the quarter times one-quarter of the annual tax rate that is applied to capital:

$$\text{TaxOnCap}(t, Q) = \text{TaxCapital}(t, Q) \, \frac{\text{CapTaxRate}(t)}{4}. \qquad (12.10.9)$$

12.10.4 Total Taxes

Tax(t, Q) is calculated using the formula that corresponds to the proper base for insurance company taxes:

$$\text{Tax}(t, Q) = \text{TaxOnEarn}(t, Q), \qquad (12.10.10)$$
$$\text{Tax}(t, Q) = \text{TaxOnIE}(t, Q), \qquad (12.10.11)$$
$$\text{Tax}(t, Q) = \max(\text{TaxOnEarn}(t, Q), \text{TaxOnIE}(t, Q)). \qquad (12.10.12)$$

If there is a tax on capital, Tax(t, Q) is adjusted in one of two ways. If the tax on capital is an additional tax, then

$$\text{Tax}(t, Q) = \text{Tax}(t, Q) + \text{TaxOnCap}(t, Q). \qquad (12.10.13)$$

If the tax on capital is a minimum tax, then

$$\text{Tax}(t, Q) = \max(\text{Tax}(t, Q), \text{TaxOnCap}(t, Q)). \qquad (12.10.14)$$

12.10.5 Deferred Taxes

Accrued taxes are equal to pre-tax stockholder earnings (calculated in Section 12.12), adjusted for permanent differences, times the tax rate on earnings:

$$\text{AccruedTax}(t, Q) = (\text{PreTaxStockEarn}(t, Q) + \text{PermDiff}(t, Q))$$
$$\times \text{EarnTaxRate}(t). \qquad (12.10.15)$$

The provision for deferred taxes for is equal to accrued taxes less taxes currently payable:

$$\text{DefTaxProv}(t, Q) = \text{AccruedTax}(t, Q) - \text{TaxOnEarn}(t, Q). \qquad (12.10.16)$$

The deferred tax liability is equal to the deferred tax liability at the end of the prior quarter plus the current quarter's provision for deferred taxes:

$$DefTaxLiab(t, Q) = DefTaxLiab(t, Q - 1) + DefTaxProv(t, Q).$$

$$(12.10.17)$$

12.11 Required Capital

Quarterly calculations for required capital mirror the annual calculations for required capital, with annual risk factors applied to quarterly values. Let

$$
\begin{aligned}
AssetDefRisk(t, Q) &= \text{Asset default component of required} \\
&\quad \text{capital, per unit issued} \\
MortRisk(t, Q) &= \text{Mortality risk component of required} \\
&\quad \text{capital, per unit issued} \\
MorbRisk(t, Q) &= \text{Morbidity risk component of required} \\
&\quad \text{capital, per unit issued} \\
IntRateRisk(t, Q) &= \text{Interest rate risk component of required} \\
&\quad \text{capital, per unit issued} \\
IntSpreadRisk(t, Q) &= \text{Interest spread risk component of required} \\
&\quad \text{capital, per unit issued} \\
OtherRisk(t, Q) &= \text{The ``other risk'' component of required} \\
&\quad \text{capital, per unit issued} \\
ReqCap(t, Q) &= \text{Total required capital at the end of } (t, Q), \\
&\quad \text{per unit issued.}
\end{aligned}
$$

The components of required capital are determined by applying annual required capital factors to the appropriate quarterly values. The values should be adjusted for the impact of reinsurance:

$$
\begin{aligned}
AssetDefRisk(t, Q) &= AssetDefFactor(t)\,(SolvRes(t, Q) \\
&\quad - PolLoan(t, Q)), \quad\quad (12.11.1) \\
MortRisk(t, Q) &= MortFactor(t)\,(DB\_pu(t, Q) \\
&\quad - SolvRes\_pu(t, Q)) \\
&\quad \times SurvFactor(t, Q), \quad\quad (12.11.2) \\
MorbRisk(t, Q) &= MorbFactor(t)\,Prem(t, Q), \quad (12.11.3) \\
IntRateRisk(t, Q) &= IntRateFactor(t)\,(SolvRes(t, Q) \\
&\quad - PolLoan(t, Q)), \quad\quad (12.11.4)
\end{aligned}
$$

$$\text{IntSpreadRisk}(t, Q) = \text{IntSpreadFactor}(t) \, (\text{SolvRes}(t, Q)$$
$$- \text{PolLoan}(t, Q)), \tag{12.11.5}$$
$$\text{OtherRisk}(t, Q) = \text{OtherFactor}(t) \, \text{Prem}(t, Q). \tag{12.11.6}$$

The components of required capital are added together to determine total required capital. The result is divided by "$1 - \text{AssetDefFactor}(t)$" in order to provide for required capital on required capital:

$$\text{ReqCap}(t, Q) = [\text{AssetDefRisk}(t, Q) + \text{MortRisk}(t, Q)$$
$$+ \text{MorbRisk}(t, Q) + \text{IntRateRisk}(t, Q)$$
$$+ \text{IntSpreadRisk}(t, Q) + \text{OtherRisk}(t, Q)]$$
$$/ (1 - \text{AssetDefFactor}(t)). \tag{12.11.7}$$

Let

$$\text{RCIntRate}(t, Q) = \text{Quarterly interest rate earned on assets}$$
backing required capital during (t, Q), equal to $(1 + \text{RCIntRate}(t))^{1/4} - 1$

$$\text{InvIncRC}(t, Q) = \text{Investment income earned on assets}$$
backing required capital during (t, Q), per unit issued

$$\text{TaxInvIncRC}(t, Q) = \text{Taxes on investment income earned on}$$
assets backing required capital, per unit issued

Investment income on required capital and the tax thereon are calculated as follows:

$$\text{InvIncRC}(t, Q) = \text{ReqCap}(t, Q - 1) \, \text{RCIntRate}(t, Q), \tag{12.11.8}$$
$$\text{TaxInvIncRC}(t, Q) = \text{InvIncRC}(t, Q) \, \text{TaxRate}(t). \tag{12.11.9}$$

12.12 Profit Measures

The following additional variables are needed to calculate quarterly profit measures:

$$\text{AfterTaxSolvEarn}(t, Q) = \text{After-tax solvency earnings, per unit issued}$$

$$\text{ReqCapIncr}(t, Q) = \text{Increase in required capital, per unit issued}$$

$$\text{ATInvIncRC}(t, Q) = \text{After-tax investment income on assets backing required capital, per unit issued}$$

$$\text{DistrEarn}(t, Q) = \text{Distributable earnings, per unit issued}$$

$$\text{PreTaxStockEarn}(t, Q) = \text{Pre-tax stockholder earnings, per unit issued}$$

$$\text{AfterTaxStockEarn}(t, Q) = \text{After-tax stockholder earnings, per unit issued}$$

$$\text{StockAssets}(t, Q) = \text{Stockholder assets at the end of } (t, Q), \text{ per unit issued}$$

$$\text{StockLiabilities}(t, Q) = \text{Stockholder liabilities at the end of } (t, Q), \text{ per unit issued}$$

$$\text{StockEquity}(t, Q) = \text{Stockholders equity at the end of } (t, Q), \text{ per unit issued}$$

12.12.1 Distributable Earnings

When distributable earnings are calculated quarterly, odd patterns of earnings can result. Losses can occur for a given quarter within a policy year, even though total earnings for the year are positive. The formula for pre-tax solvency earnings was presented in Section 12.10. After-tax solvency earnings are calculated as

$$\text{AfterTaxSolvEarn}(t, Q) = \text{PreTaxSolvEarn}(t, Q) - \text{Tax}(t, Q).$$

$$(12.12.1)$$

The increase in required capital during the quarter is calculated as

$$\text{ReqCapIncr}(t, Q) = \text{ReqCap}(t, Q) - \text{ReqCap}(t, Q - 1).$$

$$(12.12.2)$$

After-tax investment income on the assets backing required capital is calculated as

$$\text{ATInvIncRC}(t, Q) = \text{InvIncRC}(t, Q) - \text{TaxInvIncRC}(t, Q).$$
$$(12.12.3)$$

Distributable earnings are calculated as after-tax solvency earnings less the increase in required capital plus after-tax investment income on the assets backing required capital:

$$\text{DistrEarn}(t, Q) = \text{AfterTaxSolvEarn}(t, Q) - \text{ReqCapIncr}(t, Q)$$
$$+ \text{ATInvIncRC}(t, Q). \qquad (12.12.4)$$

12.12.2 Stockholder Earnings

When interpolated reserves are used quarterly stockholder earnings typically show a smoother pattern of earnings, often with no loss in any quarter. Pre-tax stockholder earnings are calculated as product cash flows less the increase in earnings reserves (consisting of benefit reserve increase and DAC amortization) plus investment income, including investment income on required capital:

$$\text{PreTaxStockEarn}(t, Q) = \text{ProdCashFlow}(t, Q) - \text{BenResIncr}(t, Q)$$
$$- \text{DACAmort}(t, Q) + \text{InvIncome}(t, Q)$$
$$+ \text{InvIncRC}(t, Q). \qquad (12.12.5)$$

After-tax stockholder earnings are calculated as pre-tax earnings less taxes, including the provision for deferred taxes:

$$\text{AfterTaxStockEarn}(t, Q) = \text{PreTaxStockEarn}(t, Q) - \text{Tax}(t, Q)$$
$$- \text{TaxInvIncRC}(t, Q)$$
$$- \text{DefTaxProv}(t, Q). \qquad (12.12.6)$$

12.12.3 Return on Equity

Calculating ROE on a quarterly basis will often give meaningless results. Depending on the reserving pattern, stockholder earnings can be erratic. Therefore, ROE is best calculated by using four successive quarters, rather than calculating quarter-by-quarter ROEs. Stockholder assets are calculated as the assets used for solvency purposes plus DAC:

$$\text{StockAssets}(t, Q) = \text{Assets}(t, Q) + \text{DAC}(t, Q). \qquad (12.12.7)$$

Stockholder liabilities are calculated as benefit reserves plus the deferred tax liability:

$$\text{StockLiabilities}(t, Q) = \text{BenRes}(t, Q) + \text{DefTaxLiab}(t, Q).$$
$$(12.12.8)$$

Stockholder equity is calculated as the difference between stockholder assets and liabilities:

$$\text{StockEquity}(t, Q) = \text{StockAssets}(t, Q) - \text{StockLiabilities}(t, Q).$$
$$(12.12.9)$$

There are two common ways to calculate the stockholder equity base:

1. Stockholder equity at the beginning of the policy year:

$$\text{EquityBase}(t) = \text{StockEquity}(t, 0). \qquad (12.12.10)$$

2. A five-point weighted average stockholder equity, based on stockholder equity at the beginning of the policy year and the end of each of the next four quarters:

$$\text{EquityBase}(t) = \frac{\text{StockEquity}(t, 0) + \text{StockEquity}(t, 4)}{8}$$
$$+ \frac{\sum_{Q=1}^{3} \text{StockEquity}(t, Q)}{4}. \qquad (12.12.11)$$

Most often, ROE is calculated as annual stockholder earnings divided by the equity base:

$$\text{ROE}(t) = \frac{\sum_{Q=1}^{4} \text{AfterTaxStockEarn}(t, Q)}{\text{EquityBase}(t)}. \qquad (12.12.12)$$

12.12.4   Return on Investment

Solving for the ROI of a stream of quarterly distributable earnings will result in a quarterly ROI. The quarterly ROI would then be converted to an annual ROI. For example, an ROI would not be expressed as

3.56% per quarter. Instead, it would be expressed as 15.0% per year. The following conversion formula can be used to obtain an annual ROI:

$$\text{ROI} = (1 + \text{Quarterly ROI})^4 - 1. \qquad (12.12.13)$$

As mentioned above, quarterly distributable earnings can be negative in many quarters. Therefore, the generalized ROI method should be used to obtain meaningful ROIs.

12.12.5 Present Value Profit Measures

A number of profit measures are based on present value calculations, such as embedded value, profit as a percentage of premium, and profit as a percentage of assets. For quarterly calculations, present values are calculated using formulas of the form

$$\text{PV(variable, } n) = \sum_{t=1}^{n} \sum_{Q=1}^{4} \text{variable}(t, Q)\ \text{DiscFactor}(t, Q).$$

$$(12.12.14)$$

Because premiums are paid at the beginning of the quarter, the formula for present value of premiums is slightly different:

$$\text{PVPrem}(n) = \sum_{t=1}^{n} \sum_{Q=1}^{4} \text{Prem}(t, Q)\ \text{DiscFactor}(t, Q - 1).$$

$$(12.12.15)$$

When calculating the present value of income statement items such as premiums, benefits, or expenses, you can use the present value result without adjustment. This is best explained with an example. Example 12.12.1 calculates profit as a percentage of premiums using 12% as the discount rate. The result is $490.93/4,767.79 = 10.30\%$.

Example 12.12.1 Profit as a Percentage of Premiums

t	Profit	PV of Profit	Premiums	PV of Premiums
0.25	100.00	97.21	2,500.00	2,500.00
0.50	200.00	188.98	0.00	0.00
0.75	150.00	137.78	2,400.00	2,267.79
1.00	75.00	66.96	0.00	0.00
Total PV		490.93		4,767.79

PV of profit as a percentage of PV of premiums = 10.30%

When calculating the present value of balance sheet items such as assets, liabilities, or equity, you must adjust the present value result by dividing by four, since the present value counts the balance sheet item four times per year. Again, this is best explained with an example. Example 12.12.2 calculates profit as a percentage of reserves, again using 12% as the discount rate. The proper result is 490.93/18,696.35/4 = 10.50%, not 490.93/18,696.35 = 2.63%.

Example 12.12.2 Profit as a Percentage of Reserves

t	Profit	PV of Profit	Reserves	PV of Reserves
0.25	100.00	97.21	5,000.00	4,860.33
0.50	200.00	188.98	5,010.00	4,734.01
0.75	150.00	137.78	5,020.00	4,610.95
1.00	75.00	66.96	5,030.00	4,491.07
Total PV		490.93		18,696.35

PV of profit as a percentage of PV of reserves = 10.50%

12.13 Pricing Model

We have chosen a slightly modified version of the pricing model for this chapter. Rather than reproduce all the previous tables that were built for the annual model, we produced only enough information to compute pre-tax solvency earnings, by quarter, for the first three policy years.

Table 12.13.1 uses the formulas outlined in Section 12.3 to convert the results of Tables 4.8.1 and 4.8.2 to quarterly values.

To illustrate the effect of modal premiums, we converted from annual premiums to quarterly premiums. Using the information shown at the bottom of Table 12.13.2, you can develop the quarterly premium per unit. Acquisition expenses, commissions, maintenance expenses, death benefits, and claim expense are based on the factors shown in Tables 5.11.1–5.11.3. The pre-reinsurance solvency reserves shown in the table are based on a linear interpolation between beginning- and end-of-the-year terminal reserves.

Table 12.13.1 Survivorship Assumptions and Factors

t, Q	qdQ	qwQ	*SurvFactor*	*Deaths*	*Lapses*
1,0			1.00000		
1,1	0.0002926	0.031453	0.96826	0.00029	0.03144
1,2	0.00	0.00	0.93753	0.00028	0.03045
1,3	0.00	0.00	0.90778	0.00027	0.02948
1,4	0.00	0.00	0.87897	0.00027	0.02854
2,1	0.0004303	0.017979	0.86280	0.00038	0.01580
2,2	0.00	0.00	0.84692	0.00037	0.01551
2,3	0.00	0.00	0.83133	0.00036	0.01522
2,4	0.00	0.00	0.81604	0.00036	0.01494
3,1	0.0005780	0.012741	0.80517	0.00047	0.01039
3,2	0.00	0.00	0.79445	0.00047	0.01025
3,3	0.00	0.00	0.78388	0.00046	0.01012
3,4	0.00	0.00	0.77344	0.00045	0.00998

Table 12.13.2 Premiums, Expenses, Death Benefits, and Pre-Reinsurance Reserves

t, Q	Prem	Comm	MaintExp	DeathBen	ClaimExp	Pre-Reins SolvRes
1,1	1.69700	2.33338	0.14243	0.29279	0.02985	0.42019
1,2	1.64314	2.25932	0.13790	0.28350	0.02890	0.84037
1,3	1.59100	2.18762	0.13353	0.27450	0.02798	1.26056
1,4	1.54050	2.11819	0.12929	0.26579	0.02710	1.68075
2,1	1.49161	0.15662	0.12519	0.37842	0.03858	1.98658
2,2	1.46416	0.15374	0.12288	0.37145	0.03787	2.29242
2,3	1.43722	0.15091	0.12062	0.36462	0.03717	2.59825
2,4	1.41077	0.14813	0.11840	0.35791	0.03649	2.90409
3,1	1.38481	0.14541	0.11622	0.47194	0.00000	3.12481
3,2	1.36638	0.14347	0.11468	0.46565	0.00000	3.34553
3,3	1.34819	0.14156	0.11315	0.45946	0.00000	3.56625
3,4	1.33024	0.13968	0.11164	0.45334	0.00000	3.78696

Assume mode 3 (quarterly)   ROPFactor = 0.0833

ModalFactor = 0.26   AnnlzdPrem_pu = 6.788

ModalPolicyFee = 8.50   ROP_pu = 0.56544

Note: Prem_pu = 1.697, AcqExp(1,1) = 3.625; other values of AcqExp = 0.

Table 12.13.3 Reinsurance Values and Post-Reinsurance Cash Flows and Reserves

t, Q	ReinsPrem	ResCredit	ReinsDeathBen	Post-Reinsurance		
				CashFlowBeg	CashFlowMid	SolvRes
1,1	0.00000	0.52347	0.07302	−4.40380	−0.24962	−0.10329
1,2	0.00000	0.50686	0.07070	−0.75408	−0.24170	0.33351
1,3	0.00000	0.49077	0.06846	−0.73015	−0.23403	0.76979
1,4	0.00000	0.47520	0.06628	−0.70698	−0.22660	1.20555
2,1	0.41051	0.50355	0.09421	0.79930	−0.32278	1.48303
2,2	−0.00553	0.49429	0.09248	1.19308	−0.31684	1.79813
2,3	−0.00362	0.48519	0.09078	1.16931	−0.31101	2.11306
2,4	−0.00178	0.47626	0.08911	1.14602	−0.30528	2.42783
3,1	0.51116	0.50745	0.11734	0.61202	−0.35460	2.61736
3,2	−0.00488	0.50069	0.11578	1.11311	−0.34988	2.84484
3,3	−0.00321	0.49403	0.11424	1.09669	−0.34522	3.07222
3,4	−0.00158	0.48745	0.11272	1.08051	−0.34062	3.29951

Table 12.13.4 Investment Income and Pre-Tax Solvency Earnings

t, Q	InvInt	CashFlowInt	InvIncome	PreTaxSolvEarn
1,1	0.00000	−0.07724	−0.07724	−4.62738
1,2	−0.00176	−0.01492	−0.01668	−1.44926
1,3	0.00569	−0.01444	−0.00875	−1.40921
1,4	0.01313	−0.01398	−0.00085	−1.37020
2,1	0.02056	0.01089	0.03146	0.23050
2,2	0.02530	0.01766	0.04296	0.60410
2,3	0.03067	0.01731	0.04798	0.59135
2,4	0.03605	0.01696	0.05300	0.57897
3,1	0.04142	0.00743	0.04884	0.11674
3,2	0.04465	0.01602	0.06066	0.59643
3,3	0.04853	0.01578	0.06430	0.58839
3,4	0.05241	0.01554	0.06795	0.58054

Note: InvIntRate $= 0.01706$.

Table 12.13.3 develops reinsurance premiums and death benefits based on the reinsurance information provided in Tables 7.6.1 and 7.6.2.

Finally, Table 12.13.4 calculates investment income and pre-tax solvency earnings.

12.14 Exercises

Exercise 12.1

Formulas 12.3.2, 12.3.4, 12.3.6, 12.3.8, 12.3.9, and 12.3.10 can be converted from quarterly to their monthly equivalents merely by replacing Q with M. Develop formulas that are the monthly equivalents to Formulas 12.3.1, 12.3.3, 12.3.5, and 12.3.7.

Exercise 12.2

Assume

- An annual premium rate (Prem_pu(t)) equal to 10.00

- An average size of 100.0

- A modal distribution of 50%, 10%, 15%, and 25% for modes 1 through 4

- The modal factors and modal policy fees shown in Examples 12.4.1 and 12.4.2, and

- A survivorship factor of 1.00

Calculate

1. Modal premiums per unit (Prem_pu(m, t, Q)) for each mode and quarter

2. Annualized premium for each mode, and

3. Premium per unit issued for each quarter (Prem(t, Q)).

Exercise 12.3

Modify Formula 12.4.7 to reflect monthly calculations for dynamic products.

Exercise 12.4

Example 12.4.4 illustrates modal return of premium factors assuming premiums paid beyond the *month* of death are refunded. These factors are applied to annualized premiums to determine the premium refunded at death. Develop or describe a similar table assuming premiums paid beyond the *date* of death are refunded.

Exercise 12.5

Example 12.4.5 illustrates the unearned premium factors as of the end of each quarter. These factors are applied to annualized premiums to determine the premium refunded on lapses. Develop unearned premium factors for lapses that occur at the *middle* of policy months 2 and 5, that is, $\frac{1}{8}$ and $\frac{3}{8}$ of the way through the policy year.

Exercise 12.6

Change the target premium per unit in Example 12.5.1 from 7.50 to 4.50 and describe the resulting values of HighCommPrem and LowCommPrem, keeping all other assumptions the same.

Exercise 12.7

Develop or describe formulas for dynamic products that redistribute monthly premiums, commissions, surrender benefits, and partial withdrawals between beginning-, middle-, and end-of-the-quarter cash flows, as suggested at the end of Section 12.6.1. Use $M1$, $M2$, and $M3$ to represent the three months of quarter Q.

Exercise 12.8

Given the following information, calculate the nonannual interpolated reserves as of the end of the third and ninth policy months for policy year t, assuming premiums are paid (a) semiannually and (b) quarterly:

$$\text{Res\_pu}(t - 1) = 10.00$$
$$\text{NetPrem\_pu}(t) = 6.00$$
$$\text{Exp\_puPrem}(t) = 0.60$$
$$\text{Exp\_puBeg}(t) = 0.40$$
$$\text{Res\_pu}(t) = 14.00.$$

Exercise 12.9

Using the information given for Exercise 12.8, calculate the deferred premium asset as of the end of the third and ninth policy months for policy year t, assuming premiums are paid (a) semiannually and (b) quarterly.

Exercise 12.10

Add together the corresponding answers from Exercises 12.8 and 12.9 and compare the results to the answers from Exercise 6.9. What relationship do you observe? How do you explain this?

Exercise 12.11

Review Formulas 6.4.5 for mean reserves and 6.4.7 for interpolated reserves to observe that the differences between these formulas amount to mean reserves using factors of "$\frac{1}{2}$" and "$\frac{1}{2}$" in place of the interpolation factors "$(1 - \text{Frac})$" and "Frac."

Assume

- 5% of your company's business was issued in each month from January to November and 45% was issued in December (that is, an extra 40% was issued in December)
- Business is issued on average in the middle of the month
- At the end of the year, all business is in policy year t
- On average, initial reserves for year t exceed terminal reserves for year $t - 1$ by 10%
- On average, terminal reserves for year t exceed terminal reserves for year $t - 1$ by 20%
- Total mean reserves at the end of the year equal 1 billion, and
- Exp_puPrem(t) and Exp_puBeg(t) both equal zero.

Calculate interpolated reserves. Is the difference between mean reserves and interpolated reserves significant in this case? Hint: solve the problem separately for the extra 40% issued in December and the other 60% of the business.

12.15 Answers

Answer 12.1

$$i(t, M) = (1 + \text{iAnnual}(t, M))^{1/12} - 1.$$

$$\text{DiscFactor}(n, R) = \left[\prod_{t=1}^{n-1} \prod_{M=1}^{12} \frac{1}{1 + i(t, M)} \right] \prod_{M=1}^{R} \frac{1}{1 + i(n, M)}. \tag{12.3.3}$$

$$qw(t, M) = 1 - (1 - \text{Annual}qw(t, M))^{1/12}. \tag{12.3.5}$$

$$\text{SurvFactor}(n, R) = \left[\prod_{t=1}^{n-1} \prod_{M=1}^{12} (1 - qdM(t))(1 - qw(t, M)) \right]$$

$$\prod_{M=1}^{R} (1 - qdM(n)) (1 - qw(n, M)). \quad (12.3.7)$$

Answer 12.2

Q	m	ModalDist	ModalFactor	ModalPolicy Fee	Prem_pu	Annlzd Prem_ pu	ModalDist × Prem_ pu(m, t, Q)
1	1	0.50	1.0000	50.0000	10.5000	10.5000	5.2500
	2	0.10	0.5100	27.0000	5.3700	10.7400	0.5370
	3	0.15	0.2600	15.0000	2.7500	11.0000	0.4125
	4	0.25	0.2625	18.0000	2.8050	11.2200	0.7013
						Prem(t, Q) =	6.9008
2	1	0.50	0.0000	0.0000	0.0000	0.0000	0.0000
	2	0.10	0.0000	0.0000	0.0000	0.0000	0.0000
	3	0.15	0.2600	15.0000	2.7500	11.0000	0.4125
	4	0.25	0.2625	18.0000	2.8050	11.2200	0.7013
						Prem(t, Q) =	1.1138
3	1	0.50	0.0000	0.0000	0.0000	0.0000	0.0000
	2	0.10	0.5100	27.0000	5.3700	10.7400	0.5370
	3	0.15	0.2600	15.0000	2.7500	11.0000	0.4125
	4	0.25	0.2625	18.0000	2.8050	11.2200	0.7013
						Prem(t, Q) =	1.6508
4	1	0.50	0.0000	0.0000	0.0000	0.0000	0.0000
	2	0.10	0.0000	0.0000	0.0000	0.0000	0.0000
	3	0.15	0.2600	15.0000	2.7500	11.0000	0.4125
	4	0.25	0.2625	18.0000	2.8050	11.2200	0.7013
						Prem(t, Q) =	1.1138

Note: Prem_pu(t) = 10.00, AvgSize = 100.

Answer 12.3

Similar to the adjustment for monthly premiums in (12.4.2), one could assume that some maintenance expenses are not incurred for those policies that die or lapse during the quarter. For those who die or lapse during the quarter, one month of maintenance expenses are saved, on the average. The impact of death and lapses on percentage of premium expenses is already taken into account through Prem(t, Q). Therefore,

$$
\begin{aligned}
\text{MaintExp}(t, Q) = {}& \left(\text{Exp\_pu}(t) + \frac{\text{ExpPerPol}(t)}{\text{AvgSize}} \right) \\
& \times \text{SurvFactor}(t, Q - 1) \\
& \times \left(1 - \frac{qdQ(t)}{3} - \frac{qw(t, Q)}{3} \right) \Big/ 4 \\
& + \text{ExpPrem}(t)\, \text{Prem}(t, Q).
\end{aligned}
$$

Answer 12.4

The difference between refunding beyond the date of death and the month of death is one-half of a month's premium, so add 1/24 (or 0.0417) to all of the factors.

Answer 12.5

Middle of Month	Annual	Semiannual	Quarterly	Monthly
2	0.8750	0.3750	0.1250	0.0417
5	0.6250	0.1250	0.1250	0.0417

Answer 12.6

HighCommPrem is 1.00 through month 4, 0.50 in month 5, and 0.00 thereafter. LowCommPrem is 0.00 through month 4, 0.50 in month 5, and 1.00 thereafter.

Answer 12.7

$$
\begin{aligned}
\text{CashFlowBeg}(t, Q) = {}& \text{Prem}(t, M1) - \text{AcqExp}(t, Q) \\
& - \text{Comm}(t, M1) - \text{MaintExp}(t, Q), \\
\text{CashFlowMid}(t, Q) = {}& \text{Prem}(t, M2) + \text{Prem}(t, M3) - \text{Comm}(t, M2) \\
& - \text{Comm}(t, M3) - \text{SurrBen}(t, M1) \\
& - \text{SurrBen}(t, M2) - \text{PartWithBen}(t, M1) \\
& - \text{PartWithBen}(t, M2) - \text{DeathBen}(t, Q) \\
& - \text{ClaimExp}(t, Q), \\
\text{CashFlowEnd}(t, Q) = {}& -\text{AVComm}(t, Q) - \text{SurrBen}(t, M3) \\
& - \text{PartWithBen}(t, M3).
\end{aligned}
$$

Answer 12.8

a. Assuming semiannual premiums ($m = 2$):
   From Formula 12.7.5,

$$\text{NetPrem\_pu}(2, t) = \text{NetPrem\_pu}(t) = 6.00.$$

From Formula 12.7.7,

$$\text{Exp\_puPrem}(2, t) = \frac{\text{NetPrem\_pu}(2, t)\ \text{Exp\_puPrem}(t)}{\text{NetPrem\_pu}(t)}$$

$$= \frac{6.00 \times 0.60}{6.00} = 0.60$$

From Formula 12.7.8,

$$\begin{aligned}
\text{Res\_puInt}(2, t, \tfrac{1}{4}) = {} & (\text{Res\_pu}(t - 1) \\
& - \text{Exp\_puBeg}(t))(1 - \text{Frac}) \\
& + \text{Res\_pu}(t)\ \text{Frac} \\
& + (\text{NetPrem\_pu}(2, t) \\
& - \text{Exp\_puPrem}(2, t)) \\
& \times (\text{Period}(2) - \text{FracPrem}(2, \text{Frac})) \\
= {} & (10.00 - 0.40)(1 - \tfrac{1}{4}) + 14.00(\tfrac{1}{4}) \\
& + (6.00 - 0.60)(\tfrac{1}{2} - \tfrac{1}{4}) \\
= {} & 12.05,
\end{aligned}$$

$$\begin{aligned}
\text{Res\_puInt}(2, t, \tfrac{3}{4}) = {} & (\text{Res\_pu}(t - 1) - \text{Exp\_puBeg}(t)) \\
& \times (1 - \text{Frac}) + \text{Res\_pu}(t)\ \text{Frac} \\
& + (\text{NetPrem\_pu}(2, t) \\
& - \text{Exp\_puPrem}(2, t)) \\
& \times (\text{Period}(2) - \text{FracPrem}(2, \text{Frac})) \\
= {} & (10.00 - 0.40)(1 - \tfrac{3}{4}) + 14.00(\tfrac{3}{4}) \\
& + (6.00 - 0.60)(\tfrac{1}{2} - \tfrac{1}{4}) \\
= {} & 14.25.
\end{aligned}$$

b. Assuming quarterly premiums ($m = 3$):
   From Formula 12.7.5,

$$\text{NetPrem\_pu}(3, t) = \text{NetPrem\_pu}(t) = 6.00.$$

From Formula 12.7.7,

$$\text{Exp\_puPrem}(3, t) = \frac{\text{NetPrem\_pu}(3, t)\ \text{Exp\_puPrem}(t)}{\text{NetPrem\_pu}(t)}$$

$$= \frac{6.00 \times 0.60}{6.00} = 0.60.$$

From Formula 12.7.8,

$$\begin{aligned}
\text{Res\_puInt}(3, t, \tfrac{1}{4}) &= (\text{Res\_pu}(t - 1) \\
&\quad - \text{Exp\_puBeg}(t))(1 - \text{Frac}) \\
&\quad + \text{Res\_pu}(t)\ \text{Frac} \\
&\quad + (\text{NetPrem\_pu}(3, t) \\
&\quad - \text{Exp\_puPrem}(3, t)) \\
&\quad \times (\text{Period}(3) - \text{FracPrem}(3, \text{Frac})) \\
&= (10.00 - 0.40)(1 - \tfrac{1}{4}) + 14.00(\tfrac{1}{4}) \\
&\quad + (6.00 - 0.60)(\tfrac{1}{4} - \tfrac{1}{4}) \\
&= 10.70,
\end{aligned}$$

$$\begin{aligned}
\text{Res\_puInt}(3, t, \tfrac{3}{4}) &= (\text{Res\_pu}(t - 1) \\
&\quad - \text{Exp\_puBeg}(t))(1 - \text{Frac}) \\
&\quad + \text{Res\_pu}(t)\ \text{Frac} \\
&\quad + (\text{NetPrem\_pu}(3, t) \\
&\quad - \text{Exp\_puPrem}(3, t)) \\
&\quad \times (\text{Period}(3) - \text{FracPrem}(3, \text{Frac})) \\
&= (10.00 - 0.40)(1 - \tfrac{3}{4}) + 14.00(\tfrac{3}{4}) \\
&\quad + (6.00 - 0.60)(\tfrac{1}{4} - \tfrac{1}{4}) \\
&= 12.90.
\end{aligned}$$

Answer 12.9

a. Assuming semiannual premiums ($m = 2$):

From Formula 12.7.9,

$$\begin{aligned}
\text{DefPrem}(t, \tfrac{1}{4}) &= (\text{NetPrem\_pu}(t) - \text{Exp\_puPrem}(t)) \\
&\quad \times \text{FracDef}(2, \tfrac{1}{4}) = (6.00 - 0.60)(\tfrac{1}{2}) = 2.70,
\end{aligned}$$

$$\text{DefPrem}(t, \tfrac{3}{4}) = (\text{NetPrem\_pu}(t) - \text{Exp\_puPrem}(t))$$
$$\times \text{FracDef}(2, \tfrac{3}{4}) = (6.00 - 0.60)(0) = 0.00.$$

b. Assuming quarterly premiums ($m = 3$):

From Formula 12.7.9,

$$\text{DefPrem}(t, \tfrac{1}{4}) = (\text{NetPrem\_pu}(t) - \text{Exp\_puPrem}(t))$$
$$\times \text{FracDef}(3, \tfrac{1}{4}) = (6.00 - 0.60)(\tfrac{3}{4}) = 4.05,$$
$$\text{DefPrem}(t, \tfrac{3}{4}) = (\text{NetPrem\_pu}(t) - \text{Exp\_puPrem}(t))$$
$$\times \text{FracDef}(3, \tfrac{3}{4})$$
$$= (6.00 - 0.60)(\tfrac{1}{4}) = 1.35.$$

Answer 12.10

For semiannual:

$$\text{Res\_puInt}(2, t, \tfrac{1}{4}) + \text{DefPrem}(t, \tfrac{1}{4}) = 12.05 + 2.70 = 14.75,$$
$$\text{Res\_puInt}(2, t, \tfrac{3}{4}) + \text{DefPrem}(t, \tfrac{3}{4}) = 14.25 + 0.00 = 14.25.$$

For quarterly:

$$\text{Res\_puInt}(3, t, \tfrac{1}{4}) + \text{DefPrem}(t, \tfrac{1}{4}) = 10.70 + 4.05 = 14.75,$$
$$\text{Res\_puInt}(3, t, \tfrac{3}{4}) + \text{DefPrem}(t, \tfrac{3}{4}) = 12.90 + 1.35 = 14.25.$$

From Exercise 6.9, $\text{Res\_puInt}(t, 0.25) = 14.75$, and $\text{Res\_puInt}(t, 0.75) = 14.25$.

This shows that a nonannual premium reserve is equal to the annual premium reserve less a deferred premium asset.

Answer 12.11

From the information given, we know that

$$\text{Res\_pu}(t - 1) + \text{NetPrem\_pu}(t) = 1.10 \ \text{Res\_pu}(t), \text{ and}$$
$$\text{Res\_pu}(t) = 1.20 \ \text{Res\_pu}(t - 1).$$

Therefore,

$$\text{Res\_pu}(t - 1) + \text{NetPrem\_pu}(t) = 1.10 \; (1.20) \; \text{Res\_pu}(t - 1)$$
$$= 1.32 \; \text{Res\_pu}(t - 1).$$

So,

$$\text{NetPrem\_pu}(t) = 0.32 \; \text{Res\_pu}(t - 1)$$

From 6.4.5,

$$1 \text{ billion} = \frac{\text{Res\_pu}(t - 1) + \text{Res\_pu}(t)}{2} + \frac{\text{NetPrem\_pu}(t)}{2}.$$
$$= \frac{\text{Res\_pu}(t - 1) + 1.20 \; \text{Res\_pu}(t - 1)}{2}$$
$$+ \frac{0.32 \; \text{Res\_pu}(t - 1)}{2}.$$

So,

$$\text{Res\_pu}(t - 1) = \frac{1 \text{ billion}}{1.26} = 793{,}650{,}794.$$

This leads to:

$$\text{NetPrem\_pu}(t) = 253{,}968{,}254 \text{ and } \text{Res\_pu}(t) = 952{,}380{,}952.$$

Allocating these figures within the following table, we calculate interpolated reserves:

$$\text{Res\_pu}(t - 1) = 793{,}650{,}794$$
$$\text{NetPrem\_pu}(t) = 253{,}968{,}254$$
$$\text{Res\_pu}(t) = 952{,}380{,}952$$

M	Distribution	Frac	Res_puInt
1	0.05	0.958333	47,817,460
2	"	0.875000	48,214,286
3	"	0.791667	48,611,111
4	"	0.708333	49,007,937
5	"	0.625000	49,404,762
6	"	0.541667	49,801,587
7	"	0.458333	50,198,413
8	"	0.375000	50,595,238
9	"	0.291667	50,992,064
10	"	0.208333	51,388,889
11	"	0.125000	51,785,714
12	0.45	0.041667	469,642,857

Total Interpolated Reserves 1,017,460,318

For example, Res_puInt for policies issued in month 7 equals

$$(0.05)[(793{,}650{,}794 + 253{,}968{,}254)(1 - 0.458333)$$
$$+ 952{,}380{,}952(0.458333)].$$

Another approach is to note that, for 60% of the business (5% issued in each month), the mean reserve should match the interpolated reserve, because July 1 is the average issue date. All you need calculate, then, is the difference between interpolated reserves and mean reserves for the extra 40% of the business issued in December.

The difference between mean reserves and interpolated reserves is 17.5 million or 1.75%. This would seem to be a significant difference.

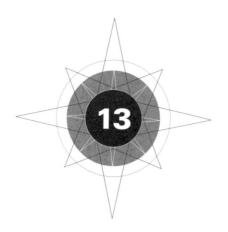

Annuity and Investment Products

13.1 Introduction

Annuity and investment products are close financial cousins to life insurance. They are often sold by the same people and same organizations that offer life insurance. While life insurance products improve financial security in the event of a premature death, annuity and investment products improve financial security primarily for those who do not die prematurely.

This chapter is organized as follows. The first few sections present an overview of annuity and investment products and some of their common features. Differences in the product development process between life and annuity products are discussed, as are differences in assumptions.

The remaining sections present the modifications needed to adapt life insurance pricing to annuity and investment products. In many cases, the formulas presented in Chapters 5 through 12 do not change. Only the differences needed to convert life insurance formulas to properly reflect annuity and investment products are discussed. This approach significantly reduces the size of this chapter.

13.2 Annuity and Investment Products

The products addressed in this chapter are divided into three groups: income annuities, accumulation annuities, and investment products. We will define these three product groups as follows:

- An *income annuity* is a contract that provides a stream of income or annuity payments in return for a single premium.

- An *accumulation annuity* is a contract that accumulates premiums in an account value, with an option to convert the account value to an income annuity. The income annuity feature is a part of the accumulation annuity contract.

- An *investment product* accumulates deposits and provides no option to convert the accumulated funds to an income annuity.

13.2.1 Fixed and Variable Products

Annuities are either fixed or variable products. Fixed products earn credited interest rates or have pre-scheduled income benefits. Variable products typically have account values or income benefits that are tied to investment performance.

13.2.1.1 Fixed Annuities

Fixed annuities are usually backed by high-quality, interest-earning assets, such as bonds and mortgages, in order to protect the principal and earn at least a minimum rate of interest. The assets are usually a part of the company's general portfolio of assets. *Fixed income annuities* are largely driven by the interest rates available on new funds at the time the annuities are sold.

Fixed accumulation annuities credit interest rates to the policyowner based on the interest rates earned by the company on the assets backing the annuities. Interest rates credited by competitors also influence the pricing of the fixed accumulation annuities. Competition may include not only competing annuity products, but also competing investment products, such as certificates of deposit and mutual funds. A minimum interest rate is usually guaranteed.

13.2.1.2   Variable Annuities

A variable annuity typically offers the policyowner a choice of many different investment options, each backed by a separate asset portfolio or fund. Most variable annuity funds are invested in stocks, in contrast to the bonds and mortgages typically associated with fixed annuities. In addition, variable annuities usually offer the policyowner a choice of bond funds and interest-bearing funds. Real estate funds may also be available. The policyowner can allocate premiums or values among multiple funds. Most variable annuities also offer a fixed account option that functions much like a fixed annuity.

Policyowner values or income benefits rise and fall with the market value of the assets backing the variable annuity. Variable annuities typically offer no guarantee with respect to investment performance, such as a minimum interest rate, minimum income benefit, or guarantee of principal. *Variable income annuities* pay income benefits that depend on investment performance.

Variable accumulation annuities work just like variable universal life, but with no COI charges and minimal death benefits, compared to VUL policies. They are something of a cross between fixed annuities and mutual funds, but variable accumulation annuities usually have higher expense charges than comparable mutual funds. However, annuity tax advantages may compensate for the additional expense. In some cases, mutual funds that minimize taxable income may offer better value. In the U.S., mutual funds can minimize taxable income by investing in stocks with low dividend yields and by holding those stocks for many years in order to delay capital gains.

13.2.2   Income Annuities

In most countries, the word *annuity* is used to mean an income annuity. In its simplest form an income annuity pays a periodic (most often monthly) annuity payment to an annuitant for as long as that person lives, in return for a single premium.

Most income annuities in existence today were purchased by employer pension plans to provide monthly retirement benefits to employees. Life insurance policies also generate some income annuities. Beneficiaries who receive life insurance death proceeds are typically offered a number of annuity choices, although most elect to receive the proceeds in cash.

In the decades ahead, income annuities may play an increasing role as baby boomers reach retirement age and look for predictable income streams. In particular, the growing popularity of accumulation annuities in some countries should ultimately result in more income annuities.

Income annuities are used mainly to provide retirement income. However, they are also used in some other situations.

The victim of an accident or other mishap is sometimes awarded a settlement by a court of law to compensate for loss of income, pain and suffering, medical care, and the like. Sometimes part of the settlement is structured as a series of payments so that the victim can be cared for over his or her remaining lifetime. The payments may be provided through an income annuity or a similar product, referred to as a *structured settlement*. Structured settlements sometimes include large, lump-sum payments payable at several dates in the future, in addition to smaller, regular payments. Often, the person receiving the structured settlement payments is impaired in some way and has a reduced life expectancy. This serves to increase the income benefit purchased by a given premium payment.

Big winners of government-sponsored *lotteries* typically receive their winnings in the form of a certain annuity payable over a period such as 20 years.

Homeowners wishing to unlock the equity in their home may execute something called a *reverse mortgage*. This involves selling their home in exchange for an income annuity and the right to live in the home until death. This is sometimes done in countries where real estate is scarce and expensive. It helps a younger couple buy a house by making annuity payments over many years to an older couple who want to unlock their home equity. If the older couple lives longer than expected, the younger couple must wait and continue annuity payments. Sometimes, companies buy houses using the reverse mortgage technique. When a company buys a home in this manner, it can reduce its risk by purchasing an income annuity from an insurance company.

13.2.2.1   Types of Income Annuities

There are many kinds of income annuities: Most annuities pay on a monthly basis, but some annuities pay quarterly or annually. Actually, the word *annuity* implies annual payments.

Immediate annuities begin annuity payments immediately, usually one month after the single premium is paid. Income annuities are sometimes referred to as *single premium immediate annuities* or *SPIAs*.

Deferred annuities begin annuity payments at a later date, usually years after the single premium is paid. Annuity payments are sometimes deferred to a normal retirement age, such as 65.

Certain annuities make annuity payments for a fixed or "certain" number of years, called the certain period, regardless of whether the annuitant is dead or alive. If the annuitant dies, annuity payments are continued to a beneficiary. In some cases the remaining payments at the time of death can be "commuted," especially if there is no surviving beneficiary. This process is referred to as "commutation." It consists of paying the present value of the remaining certain payments in a lump sum to the beneficiary. In essence, this lump-sum payment is a death benefit. Certain periods of 5, 10, and 20 years are the most common.

Life-only annuities make annuity payments for as long as the annuitant lives, no matter how long or how short a period of time that may be. There is no certain period.

Certain and life (C&L) annuities combine the features of certain annuities and life-only annuities. Annuity payments are made for as long as the annuitant lives, but no less than the certain period. "10 year certain and life" is a popular combination. While the certain period results in a higher premium or lower monthly payment, it is often reassuring to the purchaser. It minimizes the loss associated with the annuitant dying a few months after the single premium is paid. As with certain annuities, the remaining certain payments at death can often be commuted, thereby providing a lump-sum death benefit instead of monthly payments to a beneficiary.

Joint and last survivor (JLS) annuities continue annuity payments for as long as either of two people survives. This is popular with married couples who want income to continue as long as either is alive. A variation on this theme is a JLS annuity that pays less after the first person dies. For example, a joint and two-thirds last survivor annuity would pay only two-thirds as much after the first death. A further variation reduces the annuity payment if the primary annuitant dies but not if the secondary annuitant dies.

Indexed annuities provide benefit payments that increase over time, to help the annuitant maintain the same standard of living, despite inflation. Payment amounts would most often be linked to an inflation index. Social security systems often provide inflation-indexed annuity payments. Payments could also increase according to a predefined schedule. Variable income annuities, discussed later, are a form of index annuity.

Combinations of the above kinds of annuities are possible. For example, you could construct an annuity that is deferred for seven years with a ten-year certain period, payable for life to a primary annuitant, with a secondary annuitant receiving 75% of the annuity payment for life if the primary annuitant dies first. Indexing the payments for inflation could further complicate this.

Example 13.2.1

The following chart illustrates the different income benefits and payment periods for various types of annuities that could be purchased by a common single premium. The chart assumes the following:

- The same single premium is paid for each type of annuity.

- For the joint and half survivor annuity, the secondary annuitant receives half of the original annuity benefit after the death of the primary annuitant.

- The primary annuitant lives for 15 years after the annuities are issued.

- The secondary annuitant lives for 25 years after the annuity is issued.

Compared to the life-only annuity, all of the annuities except for the deferred annuity have lower benefit payments. The deferred annuity payment is higher because payments do not begin until five years after the annuity is issued.

Figure 13.2.1 Comparison of Annuity Benefits from a Common Single Premium

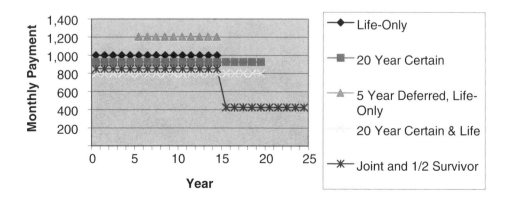

13.2.2.2 Variable Income Annuities

With fixed income annuities, the income benefit is predetermined. The initial and subsequent income benefits for fixed indexed annuities are also predetermined. However, variable income annuities merit a discussion of their own.

With variable income annuities, the initial benefit payment is determined based on guaranteed mortality and an assumed interest rate (AIR). A variable annuity that assumed a given mortality table and 7% interest would have the same initial benefit payment as a fixed annuity that assumed the same mortality table and 7% interest. The variable annuity, however, would have its income benefit periodically adjusted to reflect the investment earnings of the underlying asset portfolio. Subsequent income benefits will increase or decrease, depending on the actual investment performance of the annuity funds compared to the AIR.

The annuity may specify that the income benefit will be adjusted periodically, such as once a year. Each benefit adjustment would reflect investment results since the last adjustment, compared to the assumed interest rate. Assuming income benefits are adjusted annually, the following formula would be used to calculate the monthly income benefit:

Let

$$\text{IncomeBen}(t) = \text{Income benefit for time } t$$
$$\text{NIR}(t) = \text{Net investment return for year } t, \text{ equal to the most recent one-year rate of return on the investments backing the annuity}$$
$$\text{AIR} = \text{Annual assumed interest rate.}$$

Then,

$$\text{IncomeBen}(t) = \text{IncomeBen}(t - 1)\,\frac{1 + \text{NIR}(t - 1)}{1 + \text{AIR}}. \qquad (13.2.1)$$

Example 13.2.2

A variable income annuity has an initial annuity benefit of 1,000 per month. This amount was calculated assuming a 4% AIR. After one year, the investments backing the annuity show an annual return of 1.0%. What will the second year benefit be?

$$\text{IncomeBen}(2) = 1,000 \, \frac{1.01}{1.04} = 971.15.$$

13.2.3 Accumulation Annuities

Accumulation annuities typically function as a tax-advantaged way to save or invest. For example, they may allow buyers to accumulate premiums with interest and not pay tax on the interest until funds are withdrawn. Only a few countries (including the U.S.) allow such tax deferral on interest credited to accumulation annuities. Many restrictions usually apply, such as who is eligible, the maximum amount of premium, and how long the funds must remain within the annuity. In some cases, the entire amount paid into an accumulation annuity may be tax deductible, in addition to interest being tax deferred; all amounts withdrawn are usually fully taxable.

Accumulation annuities usually compete against savings products offered by other financial institutions, such as banks and mutual funds. The success of accumulation annuities is largely driven by the tax advantages they enjoy compared to these other products. Without a tax advantage, buyers often find that other financial products are superior to accumulation annuities. Even where no tax advantages exist, accumulation annuities may still offer features that other savings vehicles do not, such as guaranteed annuitization rates, multiple investment options, and loan provisions.

Accumulation annuities are classified as annuities only by virtue of the right given to policyowners to "annuitize," that is, to use their accumulated funds to purchase income annuities, often at guaranteed single premium rates. Most accumulation annuities are ultimately surrendered for their cash value. Relatively few are annuitized, even though the guaranteed single premium rates may be quite attractive after the passage of many years of mortality improvement, especially if interest rates have dropped.

Where accumulation annuities exist, most people who sell life insurance also sell accumulation annuities. In addition, because accumulation annuities are similar to other financial products, financial institutions such as stockbrokerages and banks often sell them.

Accumulation annuities are most often sold with single premiums. Annuities of this type are generally referred to as *single premium deferred annuities* or SPDAs. In the U.S. market, ongoing, flexible premiums payments are often allowed. Such contracts are referred to as *flexible premium deferred annuities* or FPDAs. However, most policyowners do not take advantage of the flexible premium nature and instead make only one deposit.

Section 13.2.1 included a deferred annuity as a type of income annuity. This kind of deferred annuity has no cash value and has a predetermined income benefit. In contrast, accumulation annuities accumulate premiums with interest. The accumulated cash value or account value can be used to purchase an income benefit.

Example 13.3.1

Figure 13.3.1 illustrates two accumulation annuities with income annuity options. Both annuities build an accumulated value that is used to purchase an income annuity. One annuity is a fixed annuity that earns credited interest of 5% each year. The other annuity is a variable annuity that builds to the same accumulated value at the end of 20 years. However, the pattern of accumulated value is much more volatile for the variable annuity.

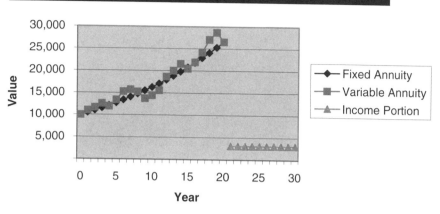

Figure 13.3.1 Accumulation Annuity with Income Annuity Option

Through the late 1990s, variable annuities dominated U.S. sales of new accumulation annuities, for two reasons:

1. The stock market performed exceptionally well in the 1990s. Variable annuities allow the policyowner to invest in stock funds and thereby share in the stock market's performance.

2. Interest rates were relatively low, so credited rates on fixed annuities were low, making them relatively unattractive. Note that there is often a correlation between superior stock market performance and low interest rates.

If stock market performance were poor and interest rates were high, variable annuity sales may still predominate, because many variable annuities offer the policyowner a fixed investment option. Rather than buy a fixed annuity, a policyowner can simply move from stock funds to the fixed option. If market conditions change, the policyowner can move out of the fixed option back into stock funds.

Initial deposits for accumulation annuities often involve substantial amounts. The money used to purchase an accumulation annuity usually comes from personal savings or investments. In some cases, the money comes from a lump-sum retirement benefit received when an employee leaves a company.

FPDAs can be used to create employer-sponsored retirement plans, with premiums usually paid through payroll deduction and based on a percentage of salary. These arrangements are most prevalent in situations where such premiums are tax deductible. FPDAs are also sold without payroll deduction. However, in these cases, the bulk of FPDA premium tends to come from the initial, often single, premium.

Accumulation annuities work much like universal life in terms of how the account value is calculated. The major differences are that accumulation annuities have minimal death benefits, unless they have some of the GMDB features discussed later, and no COI charges.

An accumulation annuity's cash value is usually equal to an account value less a surrender charge. The surrender charge gradually declines and eventually disappears after the contract has been in force for a certain number of years or after a certain number of years has elapsed since the last premium. Account values are calculated by accumulating premiums with interest or investment results and deducting charges for expenses. The accumulation process is usually performed once a month for fixed annuities and daily for variable annuities.

Because ongoing expense charges are relatively minor, accumulation annuities generally persist for as long as the policyowner leaves his or her money with the insurance company. Many accumulation annuities allow for partial withdrawals from the cash value. Some offer policy loans. Most accumulation annuities end in surrender. Fewer end in annuitization or death of the policyowner or annuitant.

Persistency bonuses are not common on accumulation annuities. Two-tier annuities, discussed below, are the normal method used to give policyowners an incentive to keep the funds with the company.

Profit and expense coverage for accumulation annuities generally come from three sources:

1. *Expense charges* usually cover the costs of administration. Expense charges can be periodic, such as an annual or monthly administration

charge, or transaction based, such as a flat charge for exercising a policy loan or transferring funds from one investment account to another. If there are percentage-of-premium expense charges, these often cover all or part of commission expenses.

2. *Surrender charges* encourage persistency and help the company recoup its acquisition costs on premature surrenders.

3. *The spread* between the interest rate earned on invested assets and the interest rate credited to the account value usually provides the most important source of profits. The spread also compensates for decreasing surrender charges. On variable annuities, the spread results from explicit charges against account values and invested assets. The bulk of this charge is typically called a mortality and expense risk charge, or M&E charge. It is deducted from the account value. Explicit investment management expense charges are deducted from the investments themselves to cover the costs of managing the investments.

13.2.3.1   Types of Accumulation Annuities

The *SPDA* is the simplest type of accumulation annuity, with the following typical features:

- Only one premium may be paid, subject to a large minimum.

- For fixed annuities or for the fixed option on a variable annuity, a minimum interest rate, such as 3%, is guaranteed.

- The current interest rate may be guaranteed for one or more years at a time.

- Surrender charges are expressed as a percentage of the account value, with the charges often declining to zero over a period of seven to ten years.

- No expense charges are usually levied, except possibly a monthly or annual fee to cover administrative expenses.

The *FPDA* shares many of the same features as the SPDA, except for the following differences:

- Flexible premiums may be subject to a much smaller minimum payment to encourage regular premium payments.

- The surrender charge schedule may apply separately to each premium payment. In other words, a premium paid in the fifth year may be subject to first-year surrender charges in the fifth year, second-year surrender charges in the sixth year, etc.

- For fixed products, different interest rates may be credited to different premiums, depending on when the premiums were received. This allows the company to reflect the interest rates available when premiums were received. This makes the product responsive to changes in interest rates, making it both more competitive and more equitable. It also makes administration much more difficult.

The *CD annuity* is a type of fixed annuity that competes with certificates of deposit (CDs) offered by banks and some other financial institutions. (CDs commonly offer a guaranteed interest rate for a fixed period of time, with substantial penalties for early withdrawal.) CD annuities are similar to SPDAs but have the following differences:

- The surrender charge period matches the interest rate guarantee period, which is typically three to seven years. Surrender charges may remain high for the entire period.

- At the end of the interest rate guarantee period, the policyowner will have a "window period" to decide whether to surrender with no surrender charge or accept a new guaranteed interest rate (with renewed surrender charges) for another period. The window period is usually fairly short, such as 60 days.

The *two-tiered annuity* is a fixed annuity that accumulates two account values using two different sets of interest rates. One account value applies only to annuitization and is credited with higher interest rates. The other account value applies only to surrender and partial withdrawals and is credited with lower interest rates.

- Two-tiered annuities can be either single premium or flexible premium.

- Higher interest rates are credited to the annuitization account value because the company can expect to earn additional profit after annuitization. The higher interest rates offered for annuitization encourage policyowners to keep their funds with the insurance company. Also, if annuitization occurs, there is no disintermediation. By eliminating this important risk, the company can afford to credit a slightly higher interest rate.

- Lower interest rates are credited to the surrender account value to discourage surrenders and recoup acquisition costs in the event of surrender.

- The difference between the two account values can grow very large over time, depending on the difference in interest rates credited to the two account values. For example, if the surrender account value is credited with 1% lower interest, the difference between the two account values will exceed 20% after 20 years. The result is an implicit surrender charge that may seem onerous and inequitable.

- The two-tiered annuity raises some interesting financial reporting questions, such as which account value to use for reserves and for measurement of profits. The annuitization account value is probably too conservative for reserves, since not all policyowners will annuitize. On the other hand, the surrender account value is probably too liberal, since a significant percentage may annuitize.

The *equity-indexed annuity* (EIA) allows the policyowner to both participate in the stock market and earn at least a minimum interest rate. EIAs are essentially a hybrid between fixed annuities and variable annuities but are classified as fixed annuities. This product is ideal for risk-averse buyers who still want some participation in the equity market.

- Beyond the minimum guaranteed interest rate, the policyowner receives a percentage participation in the appreciation of an equity index, sometimes limited to an overall maximum credited interest rate, or *cap*. The percentage of the equity index credited is known as the *participation rate*. For example, the policyowner may earn 3% interest or 60% of the percentage appreciation in the S&P 500 stock index, whichever is greater, but in no event will more than 15% be credited. In this case, the participation rate is 60% and the cap is 15%.

- To back the liabilities, the company would typically buy the minimum amount of interest-earning assets needed to satisfy the interest rate guarantees by the end of the surrender charge period. The remainder of the funds would be used to purchase hedging securities that track with the upside of the equity index.

- Proper design and pricing depends on the company's ability to purchase appropriate hedging securities. Careful monitoring of experience and periodic adjustments are needed to keep assets well matched with liabilities.

- Many of the required hedging securities are not available in public markets and have to be custom made by banks. Large volumes of sales are necessary in order to purchase the hedging securities at a reasonable rate, because of the significant effort required to create these customized hedges. Also, the availability of hedging instruments will depend on the index being hedged. If a public market does not exist for a particular index, it will be difficult to hedge any liabilities that are determined by that index.

13.2.3.2 Accumulation Annuity Product Features

Accumulation annuities quite often include several of the following product features:

Front-end loads and surrender charges: Accumulation annuities often compete with other financial products such as mutual funds and certificates of deposit. When such competition exists, percentage of premium expense charges or "front-end loads" are not common on accumulation annuities. Instead, most accumulation annuity products have surrender charges or "back-end loads."

Bailout provision: This provision waives the surrender charge if and when the annuity's credited interest rate for a fixed annuity or the fixed account of a variable annuity drops below a specified interest rate called the bailout rate. Bailout provisions, when used, typically apply for a period of a few policy years, called the bailout period. Bailout provisions give the policyowners assurance that the company will credit at least the bailout rate. If not, they can get their money back without penalty. The financial impact on the insurance company is very similar to a guaranteed interest rate equal to the bailout rate for the bailout period.

Medical or nursing home rider: This rider allows the policyowner to surrender the annuity without incurring a surrender charge if the annuitant develops certain medical conditions or is confined to a nursing home or similar facility.

Penalty-free partial withdrawals: Just as with universal life, this feature allows the policyowner to withdraw a portion of the account value without incurring a surrender charge. Some annuities allow any unused penalty-free partial withdrawals to be rolled forward to future years, either completely or partially.

Guaranteed minimum account balance (GMAB): This guarantee assures the policyowner that the total amount available upon surrender will not be less than a certain amount even if this amount is greater than the account value less the surrender charge. Typically, the minimum amount is equal to premiums paid less partial withdrawals. For fixed annuities, this feature essentially guarantees that no surrender charge will be assessed in the early years. For variable annuities, a GMAB feature can be especially valuable, since there is a chance that variable funds will decrease rather than increase.

Simple death benefits: In the simplest case, death benefits are equal to the surrender value or the account value. Because the policyowner is not always the annuitant, it may be possible to pay a different amount upon the death of the policyowner than upon the death of the annuitant. For example, the account value may be payable upon the death of the annuitant while the surrender value is payable upon the death of the policyowner.

Complex death benefits: Some annuities offer a more complicated death benefit, often referred to as a guaranteed minimum death benefit or GMDB. For example, the GMDB could equal the single premium accumulated at 7% interest. There is an ever-expanding universe of GMDB designs.

GMDBs have become an important product-differentiating feature, particularly for variable annuities. GMDB features are rarely found on fixed annuities. The death benefit actually paid is the higher of the GMDB and the account value or, in some cases, the surrender value. The GMDB adds an element of certainty to what may otherwise be viewed as a more uncertain investment.

Because of the uncertainty associated with the performance of variable annuities, the long-term cost of many GMDB designs is very hard to predict. It is often necessary to use stochastic modeling or option pricing to estimate the cost. However, even with the most sophisticated methods and models, the actual cost of GMDBs will likely be much different than expected. This is because, while mortality rates are fairly predictable, investment performance is not.

Some common GMDB designs include the following:

- Return of premium, net of partial withdrawals
- Return of premium, net of partial withdrawals, accumulated at a predefined interest rate
- Ratchet features increase the GMDB every few years to the then-current account value, provided it is higher than the prior GMDB. In other words, the GMDB ratchets up every few years. The ratchet period could be any period, but it is commonly one, three, or five years. Often, ratchet features allow no further increases in the GMDB after a certain attained age, such as 70. In general, ratchet features do not allow the GMDB to decrease. However, reset designs that reset the death benefit when fund performance falls below a certain level can decrease the GMDB amount. Such features allow for greater risk management flexibility.
- Step-up features increase the GMDB by a fixed percentage (such as 3%, 5%, or 7%) each year, regardless of fund performance. The GMDB may be subject to an overall maximum, such as 200% of premiums, net of withdrawals.
- Combination features combine both ratchet and step-up features. For example, the GMDB might be the greater of the death benefit defined by a ratchet feature and one defined by a step-up feature, with the GMDB no longer increasing after a certain age.

Some annuities give the policyowner a choice among several GMDB designs. To compensate for this flexibility, the company may deduct fees from the account value that reflect the expected cost of the GMDB design chosen.

GMDBs can create some interesting situations. Suppose that an annuity developed a 100,000 account value and a 125,000 GMDB. Could the policyowner withdraw 99,000 and be left with 1,000 of account value and 26,000 of GMDB? If so, the long-term cost of the GMDB may be much more than expected. One solution to this situation is to reduce the GMDB by the percentage withdrawn. In other words, a 99,000 withdrawal would reduce the GMDB by 99%.

Guaranteed minimum income benefit (GMIB): This feature guarantees a minimum monthly income from a specified type of income annuity at some date in the future, regardless of investment performance. This guarantee can be thought of as a combination of two guarantees: an investment performance guarantee and a guaranteed price for an income annuity.

The biggest unknown associated with the GMIB feature is the rate at which policyowners will annuitize and utilize the feature. With poor investment performance, mortality improvement and a decline in interest rates, annuitization rates could increase substantially and a GMIB feature could prove quite expensive.

Guaranteed single premium rates for annuitization: This is the feature that distinguishes accumulation annuities from other forms of savings or investment. Most often, a range of income annuity options is provided, such as certain, life-only, and certain and life. What may seem like conservative single premium rates at issue can prove very costly when options are exercised many years later, especially if mortality improves and interest rates decrease. For example, in the U.K. in the late 1990s, the life insurance industry absorbed billions of pounds sterling of losses related to guaranteed single premium rates of annuitization. The guarantees were set when interest rates were much higher than they were in the late 1990s. Such a decline in interest rates was unthinkable only a decade earlier.

Waiver of surrender charge upon annuitization: This is a common feature. It rewards the policyowner for committing funds to the company. If the company offers competitive guaranteed single premium rates for annuitization, this feature may be quite expensive for the older issue ages. For older buyers, significant surrender charges may be waived just a few years after issue, as annuitants approach retirement age, making it difficult for the company to recoup acquisition costs.

Market value adjustment (MVA): Some accumulation annuities feature a market value adjustment that reflects the current market value of the assets backing the cash value. The MVA applies to fixed annuities or to the fixed account under a variable annuity. Amounts allocated to a variable annuity's nonfixed accounts already have a built-in MVA. An MVA protects the company from changes in market value and also rewards the policyowner if market value increases. For example, if the market value of assets drops to 90% of book value, cash values would be multiplied by an MVA of 90% before being paid out. On the other hand, if the market value of assets rises to 120% of book value, cash values would be multiplied by an MVA of 120% before being paid out.

Since market values drop when interest rates rise, an MVA discourages policyowners from surrendering their annuities in order to invest their funds elsewhere and earn higher interest rates. This significantly reduces a company's disintermediation risk, explained in Chapter 10. Market values are impacted by more than just interest rates. Liquidity, credit rating, and market conditions can also impact market values.

Because market values can be difficult to accurately and quickly obtain, the MVA is often based on a formula like the following. Let

s = Number of years remaining for the current interest rate guarantee

i = Interest rate currently guaranteed

j = Interest rate guarantee available for new deposits, with an interest guarantee period of s years

k = A small, additional margin, such as 0.25%, added to provide additional protection for the insurance company. The maximum margin is often limited by statute or regulation.

Then,

$$\text{MVA} = \left(\frac{1 + i}{1 + j + k}\right)^{s}.$$

(13.2.2)

13.2.4 Investment Products

We will define an investment product to be any product (other than life insurance or annuities) offered by financial institutions whose purpose is to increase the buyer's wealth. Financial institutions that offer these products may include banks, investment banks, stockbrokerages, insurance companies, and various types of investment companies, such as mutual funds. Buyers are typically members of the general public, but could also include businesses and even other financial institutions. Investment products may provide buyers the opportunity to invest in just about any type of venture, from stocks, bonds, and real estate to commodities, precious metals, and hedge funds. Local regulations usually govern the permissible types of investment products.

Investment products can be divided into two broad categories:

1. *Variable products* give buyers an interest or percentage ownership in a block of assets. These assets essentially constitute the product. The value of the variable product rises and falls as the value of the assets rise and fall, much like VUL and variable annuities. This is the nature of mutual funds in the U.S. and segregated funds in Canada.

2. *Fixed products* credit the buyers' deposits with interest, either at a fixed interest rate or tied to an interest index, such as LIBOR (the London Inter-Bank Offered Rate). For example, guaranteed interest contracts (GICs) commonly pay a fixed interest rate for a fixed period of time, with no right to receive the funds early.

Investment products use the same three sources of income used by accumulation annuities to cover expenses and provide a profit margin. When commissions are paid, front-end loads or surrender charges are common. Most expenses and profits are provided for by charging an ongoing fee equal to a small percentage of assets under management.

Variable products have an implicit market value adjustment, since the buyer's value is based on the value of assets. Fixed investment products often don't allow premature withdrawals. However, where premature withdrawals are allowed, a market value adjustment is not unusual.

Some variable investment products provide guarantees in excess of the buyer's interest in the underlying block of assets. For example, some U.S. mutual funds now offer guaranteed minimum death benefits and guaranteed minimum income benefits, similar to those provided by accumulation annuities. In general, such features are offered at an extra charge and are backed by an insurance company.

A feature commonly found on segregated fund products in Canada is the guaranteed minimum account value (GMAV). This feature guarantees a return of a minimum value (such as return of premium) upon maturity, regardless of the actual investment performance of the underlying assets. In addition, many such products allow the policyowner to reset the GMAV to the current account value many times during the contract period (as often as once per year, for example) in exchange for extending the maturity date. For example, consider a segregated fund product that guarantees that the maturity value ten years after issue will be no less than the initial account value. The buyer may have an annual option to raise the GMAV to the then-current account value in exchange for resetting the maturity date to be ten years after the current date.

In some markets, insurance companies are permitted to sell investment products. Depending on regulations, these products may be both sold and provided by insurance companies. For example, in Australia and Canada, life insurance companies are allowed to create and sell investment products that resemble mutual funds in the U.S. In some countries, regulations prevent life insurers from providing investment products directly. However, life insurers can often act as intermediaries for other financial institutions, with their agents licensed to sell investment products.

Where possible, many insurance companies offer investment products to provide a more complete spectrum of financial products for their customers and field force. Another motivation may be to sell more business through existing distribution systems. In addition, insurance companies sometimes offer investment products because of tax advantages, regulatory advantages, synergy with their other businesses, or to better balance the company's risk portfolio.

13.3   Product Development

Many of the same considerations that apply to developing life insurance products also apply to developing annuity or investment products. The thinking that goes into product strategies, target markets, pricing strategies, and the organization and process for product development are much the same. Perhaps the biggest difference is in the pricing process, mainly because of the different role that mortality plays.

For most income annuities, premium rates vary only by age and sex. Anti-selection is limited to healthy people deciding to buy annuities because they expect to live too long. As a result, underwriting plays a minor role, although this could change if rates begin to vary by smoker, nonsmoker, and other categories. While the same in-depth type of profit testing used for life insurance should be used to validate the pricing for income annuities, it is still common to use a simple present value formula to calculate single premium rates.

For accumulation annuities and investment products, mortality plays a relatively minor role. Many such products credit the same results and charge the same fees for all ages. Many of these products credit the buyer with the performance of underlying assets. Since investment performance is difficult if not impossible to predict, stochastic modeling is often used to examine and weigh many possible outcomes.

13.4   Pricing Assumptions

Many of the same assumptions are important for both life insurance and annuities. For annuities, we can classify the assumptions as either environmental assumptions (mortality, interest or investment income, and expenses) or policyowner behaviors (lapses, premium payment patterns, and annuitization).

13.4.1 Mortality

The mortality assumption plays varying roles between income annuities and accumulation annuities.

13.4.1.1 Income Annuities

For income annuities, the mortality risk is a longevity risk: the risk of living longer than the insurance company expects. In other words, for income annuities, using lower mortality rates creates a conservative mortality assumption. With the benefit of hindsight, we know that many income annuity products have been priced using mortality assumptions that significantly underestimated mortality improvement. In some cases, this has resulted in significant losses for the insurance companies involved.

When pricing life insurance, many practitioners are cautious of assuming mortality improvement. This same caution can spell disaster when pricing income annuities. It is prudent to assume something *less* than the mortality improvement of the past when pricing life insurance and something *more* than past mortality improvement when pricing income annuities.

Sex-distinct mortality rates are normally used, except where unisex rates are mandated by law, as may be the case for employer-sponsored pension plans. Mortality assumptions for income annuities are highly dependent on the market for the annuities. In general, mortality assumptions vary for individual annuities, group annuities, and structured settlements. These assumptions vary due to the self-selection that takes place at the time of purchasing the income annuity.

Since individual annuities are freely purchased, only healthy lives generally choose to purchase life annuities. Unhealthy individual annuitants will be less inclined to purchase life annuities, since they don't expect to outlive the mortality assumption built into the pricing.

Group annuitants often have little choice but to accept payment in the form of a life annuity. If the annuitant has any choice, it will usually be between various income annuity options, such as life only, certain and life, or JLS. The healthier lives will be tempted to choose the life-only annuity, whereas the unhealthy lives will be more inclined to choose an annuity option with a certain period of guaranteed payments. Little or no choice generally results in higher mortality for group annuities. As a result, group annuity mortality, for both pricing and valuation, is typically higher than that for individual annuities.

Structured settlement annuitants normally have the least amount of selection, since the settlement payments are negotiated in court, and many of the payments to be made are not tied to the annuitant's survival. Population mortality, which can be considered substandard life insurance mortality, may be a fair estimate of mortality.

Standard industry pricing tables exist for individual and group annuitant mortality. These standard tables also include projection factors to project future mortality improvement. As with any industry table, such tables should be adjusted for a company's market and past experience.

13.4.1.2 Accumulation Annuities

For accumulation annuities, mortality assumptions can range from unimportant to moderately important, depending on the extent of the death benefit. While some products may be modeled using mortality based on an average issue age, a greater understanding of profitability by age can be gained by pricing a range of issue ages. Both mortality and persistency vary significantly by age.

For investment products, unless a materially higher benefit is paid in the event of death, mortality rates can be added to lapse rates and otherwise ignored. However, as with accumulation annuities, you may wish to test profitability for a range of ages in order to reflect persistency differences between issue ages.

GMDB features may explicitly charge the policyowner a flat percentage of the account value, such as ten basis points, or 0.10%. In return, the GMDB is paid upon death. Some GMDB features allow the policyowner to choose the type of GMDB feature. Caution should be exercised when determining the mortality assumption for such features, since unhealthy lives may be more inclined to choose the GMDB feature that has the more generous death benefit.

13.4.2 Interest and Investment Income Assumptions

Interest rate or investment income assumptions are crucial to a successful and profitable annuity or investment contract. For accumulation annuity and investment products, the earned interest rate drives the credited rate. The credited rate is the most visible component to the sales agent and the buyer. It makes the difference between a high volume and a low volume of sales. Offering a competitive credited rate while maintaining adequate profitability can become a difficult juggling act.

Accumulation annuity and investment products are usually priced to earn a targeted spread between earned interest rates and credited interest rates. The pricing process is used to determine the targeted spread, which is then used both for setting the credited interest rates for new business and for the resetting of interest rates after issue.

As market interest rates move up and down, the company's earned interest rates should respond similarly, allowing it to move its credited interest rates up and down to remain competitive. In reality, a company's earned interest rates do not track with market interest rates, because a good percentage of its assets have been invested longer term to earn higher interest rates. When interest rates drop, this is a good problem to have. However, when interest rates rise, some difficult choices must be made. It is vital for product development, product management, and investment functions to be in frequent contact to effectively manage credited interest rates in this difficult situation.

For income annuities, the earned interest rate drives the single premiums more than any other assumption. If the company can earn a higher interest rate than its competitors, it likely will be able to offer a more competitive or more profitable product than its competitors.

There are two main interest rate dangers:

1. Guaranteeing current interest rates for a long period of time without investing in assets that will support the guarantees even if interest rates fall. If the company were to back long-term liabilities with short-term assets, a drop in interest rates could cause significant losses for the company.

2. Investing in long-term assets to support a product that has short-term liabilities, such as cash values with no significant surrender charges. If interest rates rise, the company will be stuck with lower-yielding assets that will prevent the company from paying competitive interest rates. If competitive interest rates are not paid, the lack of surrender charges will allow the business to move to a competitor. This could cause significant capital losses if the company has to liquidate lower-yielding assets in a higher interest rate market.

The risk of interest rates deviating significantly from the levels assumed in pricing is so great and so important that at least one of the following two strategies is called for:

1. For single premium products that provide guaranteed benefits, the company must be able to immediately invest in assets that will provide guaranteed returns that closely match the guaranteed benefits. In other words, future asset cash flows must match liability

cash flows. This is especially true for all income annuities and for accumulation annuities with significant interest rate guarantees.

2. For products with cash flows that are highly unpredictable, such as accumulation annuities without MVAs or significant surrender charges, the product must be able to adjust to changing interest rates. This can be accomplished through a combination of conservative interest rate guarantees and an investment strategy that is fairly short term, allowing the company to adjust more quickly to changes in interest rates.

The greatest challenge in designing an annuity product is to achieve both acceptable interest risk and a competitive product. In many cases, the most competitive annuity products are those that take the greatest interest risks. While some interest risk is unavoidable, you don't want to risk the company's solvency, ratings, or reputation to field a more competitive product.

To determine how much risk is involved with a particular product design and investment strategy, it is wise to use stochastic modeling to test many different interest rate scenarios. The modeling would typically adjust credited interest rates to reflect changes in market interest rates and the impact on the company's investment portfolio. Also, lapse rates would vary based on the difference between market interest rates and the product's credited interest rate. This is covered in much greater depth in Chapter 15.

Although disintermediation risk and interest rate risk are very important, you should not overlook default risk and liquidity risk. For example, an economic recession can simultaneously impair the value of real estate, commercial mortgages, junk bonds, and common stocks. Too high a concentration in more volatile assets such as these has resulted in a number of life insurance company insolvencies.

Example 13.4.1 Liquidity Risk

Liquidity risk is often not well understood, but it is dramatized by General American Life Insurance Company's experience in 1999. General American (GA) was a midsize U.S. mutual company, with approximately $22 billion in assets. When $5 billion of short-term investment products were surrendered during a one-week period, the company had to sell $5 billion worth of assets to raise the cash needed. After selling over $2 billion of assets, the U.S. bond market became illiquid, for several reasons:

- GA had flooded the market for certain types of assets, creating a large imbalance between buyers and sellers, which forced prices down.

- Some bond traders became nervous about GA's situation and refused to sell any more bonds for GA.

- Some bond traders became aware of GA's predicament (or, in Wall Street terms, they "smelled blood") and greatly increased the spread they would earn between the price at which they would buy a security from GA and the price at which they would resell it.

- The contracts that were surrendered were large contracts, controlled by 37 corporate clients. The liabilities were too concentrated.

To sell the remaining billions of assets in the short time remaining, General American found they would have had to absorb hundreds of millions of dollars of capital losses, with no guarantee that they could sell all the assets required in such a short time frame. To protect its policyowners' value, GA sought government protection even though the company was financially strong. Within a few weeks, GA was sold to Metropolitan Life Insurance Company, a much larger U.S. mutual insurer. One lesson from this experience is that highly rated, seemingly liquid assets can turn illiquid if you have to sell too much in a hurry.

Unlike fixed annuities, the spread for variable annuities is fixed. As part of the sale of a variable annuity, the company discloses the M&E and investment management charges that will be deducted from gross investment earnings.

The investment management charges vary by the type of fund being managed. In general, money market funds usually charge less than bond funds, which usually charge less than equity funds. The charges may be paid to an outside investment manager or retained by the company, if it manages the funds itself. The charges are usually enough to cover expenses and leave a small margin for profit, either for the outside investment manager or the company.

For fixed products, the company must initially offer and subsequently maintain a competitive credited rate. With variable products, the competitive comparison focuses on the M&E charge.

Once a variable product is purchased, investment performance of the various funds will play a key role in the profitability and persistency of the business. If the funds perform poorly, profitability can be impacted for two reasons: (1) since the M&E charge is a percentage of the fund assets, poor fund performance means a lower absolute amount of M&E charges collected, and (2) poor fund performance will probably mean lower persistency, which again means fewer funds on which the M&E charge is collected.

Since fund performance is such an important item for variable annuities, many insurance companies design their products to include funds managed by established, name-brand mutual fund companies with a long history of successful investment performance.

13.4.3 Expenses

Compared to the other assumptions, expenses pose a relatively small risk for annuity and investment products. Expenses are fairly predictable, unless a company is developing a groundbreaking product or entering a new market. Most often, expenses can be well estimated based on the company's prior experience or based on the experience of other companies. However, there are some important possible variations:

- Sales levels are often quite volatile and dependent on the relative competitiveness of the company's product. This means marketing expenses and other fixed acquisition costs may be spread over a much smaller or much larger base than expected.

- In some cases, a new product can produce a much smaller or much larger average size premium than expected. This means that per policy expenses can have a much larger or much smaller impact than expected.

All annuity and investment products incur some up-front costs to process applications and issue contracts. Income annuity expenses include the costs of making monthly payments and obtaining periodic proof that annuitants are still living. Periodic valuation of income annuities may be relatively labor intensive if there is a small number and a great diversity of products.

Accumulation annuity and investment products can incur significant ongoing costs, such as expenses for the following:

- The tracking and complex commissioning of flexible premiums or deposits.

- Providing periodic customer statements showing activity and accumulation or investment results.

- Handling a significant volume of customer inquiries.

- Processing loan, withdrawal, and surrender requests.

Premium taxes may be assessed on certain types of annuities, although most jurisdictions do not levy such taxes. Front-end loads are sometimes assessed to explicitly cover such taxes. This allows a company to vary its prices to exactly offset the different premium tax rates in various jurisdictions. With this approach, both premium taxes and the matching front-end loads can be omitted from pricing. However, competitive pressures may make it difficult to impossible to levy explicit charges to offset premium taxes. In that case, the cost of premium taxes will be included in pricing along with other expenses.

A similar situation may exist with commissions and matching front-end loads. If they offset one another, it may be possible to omit both from pricing. However, given the importance of each, it is usually best to include both, even when they exactly offset one another. This will result in pricing models that better match reality.

13.4.4 Lapses, Surrenders, and Premium Payment Patterns

We use the terms *lapse* and *surrender* somewhat interchangeably in this book. Policies lapse because of failure to pay premiums, in the case of pre-scheduled products, or because of account values or cash values that are insufficient to cover mortality and expense charges, in the case of dynamic products. Annuities are surrendered, not lapsed. Nonetheless, it is common to refer to annuity termination rates as lapse rates.

Lapse rates rarely apply to income annuities, because they rarely have cash surrender values. To permit surrender would allow those on the verge of death to cash in, thereby defeating the spreading of longevity risk between those who live a short time and those who live a long time.

For accumulation annuities and investment products, lapses are a very important assumption. Lapse rates vary by issue age. Older buyers tend to be more persistent, although they reach retirement age sooner and may surrender their funds at that time. Lapses are sensitive to other factors, such as how credited interest rates compare to interest rates available elsewhere. Larger account values may be more interest sensitive.

Surrender charges can be a major deterrent to surrender. Lapse rates generally increase as surrender charges decrease. As mentioned in Chapter 3, a rough rule of thumb captures this relationship: The surrender charge, as a percentage of the account value, plus the lapse rate is equal to a constant percentage. Such a relationship between surrender charges and lapse rates may be most applicable if agents actively rewrite the business once surrender charges have sufficiently declined.

Also, as mentioned in Chapter 3, there is often a spike in the lapse rate in the first year after the surrender charge vanishes. After the spike, lapse rates usually drop and remain at a lower level. This is especially true if the surrender charge exists for a relatively short period, such as less than ten years. For longer surrender charge periods, there is less of a spike in lapse rates.

Some accumulation annuities and investment products allow flexible premiums or deposits. The pattern of flexible premiums can vary significantly depending on conditions such as how premiums are paid, the purpose of the product, the tax deductibility of premiums, and the resources of the buyer.

Many flexible premium products are sold as single premium products. For example, the agent may look for buyers who have a large lump sum that could be tax sheltered in an accumulation annuity. In these cases, there may be no attempt to sign up the buyer for ongoing premium payments. In other cases, the agent may sell an accumulation annuity with an annual premium, as a means of ongoing savings, with or without a large initial single premium. The experience of the company provides the best means of predicting the average pattern of flexible premium payments. However, it is typical to see a large first-year premium and much smaller renewal premiums.

There is an exception to this: accumulation annuities sold as retirement savings plans through payroll deduction, with tax-deductible premiums. These may experience a fairly level payment pattern. For those who do not surrender their contracts, the premium per unit may decline relatively slowly. The decline in premium per unit in force may be mostly due to employee turnover.

13.4.5   Annuitization

By definition, accumulation annuities offer an option to annuitize—to convert accumulated funds to an income annuity. For some products, such as two-tiered annuities, this can be a critical assumption. On the other hand, some accumulation annuities experience so little annuitization that its impact can be ignored. The rate of annuitization may vary mainly by attained age, with higher annuitization rates expected around retirement ages.

Many products offer a range of annuitization choices, such as certain, life only, certain and life, and JLS, with some offering a range of certain periods. Guaranteed single premium rates for these choices are usually contained in the contract. Many companies override the guaranteed rate with a current single premium rate whenever the current rate produces a larger income benefit. Annuitization rates may be needed for each of the most common annuitization options. To simplify this, you could develop one blended annuitization option, for pricing purposes only, that is a weighted average of the most common options.

There are two main ways to reflect annuitization in pricing:

The simple approach: Include only the present value of all profits and losses resulting from annuitization. In other words, each annuitization would be reflected by showing an immediate gain or loss. This misstates cash flows, reserve changes, capital requirements, the timing of profits and losses, etc., but is a relatively simple and easy solution. This is the approach we will illustrate in this chapter.

The complex approach: Track each annuitization over its lifetime, reflecting factors such as subsequent cash flows, reserve changes, capital requirements, investment income, and taxes. This dramatically complicates the pricing process, especially if many different annuitization choices are modeled. To model one issue age, you must track and summarize all the detailed results of annuitization for each possible annuitization age and option. When annuitization is significant, this is likely to be the preferred approach.

Caution should be exercised when pricing a GMIB feature if the assumption for the cost of the feature is based on historically low annuitization rates. Poor investment performance in the future may make the feature more attractive to policyowners, with annuitization rates well in excess of historical levels. As sensitivity testing is performed on various investment return scenarios, annuitization rates should be adjusted to reflect increased use of GMIB features when investment performance is poor.

13.5   Annuity and Investment Product Cash Flows

In this section, we develop formulas for the annuity and investment product cash flows that differ from life insurance product cash flows. Here is a brief summary of the differences:

Income annuities: Single premiums, low commission rates, and low acquisition costs are the norm. The monthly annuity benefit is unique to income annuities. Death benefits, if any, are associated only with certain periods. There are no surrender benefits, policy loans, partial withdrawals, or dividends. The absence of surrender benefits may change in the future. There is some discussion about allowing annuitants to receive the present value of their future income benefits by providing underwriting information. If such a feature becomes common, modeling the resulting cash flows could prove to be quite challenging.

Accumulation annuities: Single premiums are the most common, but flexible premium contracts also exist. Commissions and acquisition costs are low to moderate. Annuitization options must often be reflected in pricing, although most contracts typically end in surrender. Policy loans and partial withdrawals are common features. Death benefits in excess of account values often exist and can range from minimal to significant. Dividends exist on older annuity products but are uncommon on newer products. Account values accumulate much as for UL or VUL, but without COI deductions. As more choices of features and options are provided to the policyowner, there is a trend to explicitly charge for the features chosen.

Investment products: Single deposits are the most common, but flexible deposit contracts also exist. Commissions and acquisition costs are usually low. Partial withdrawals are often allowed. Contracts end through surrender or maturity of the contract. There are no annuitization options, policy loans, death benefits, or dividends. Account values usually accumulate like the account values of fixed or variable accumulation annuities.

13.5.1 Survivorship

The survivorship formulas for life insurance generally apply to annuity and investment products. However, there are some differences.

13.5.1.1 Income Annuities

For income annuities, mortality is the only decrement needed. We will assume that lapse is not possible. However, if future income annuities allow surrenders as described under income annuity differences, then appropriate adjustments should be made to the formulas.

For annuities with a certain period, we will reflect no death benefits. This assumes that, if the annuitant dies, the certain annuity payments will be continued according to the original schedule and paid to a beneficiary. In reality, the remaining certain payments are sometimes commuted and paid as a lump sum when the annuitant dies. This could be better reflected with a death benefit, which is included as an exercise at the end of the chapter.

For joint and last survivor annuities, the mortality decrements will reflect JLS mortality, that is, the probability of the second of two lives dying. For the more complex JLS designs, the benefits could be broken into two components that could be modeled separately, with their results added together. For example, a joint and two-thirds survivorship annuity could be modeled by adding one-third of a joint-first-to-die annuity to two-thirds of a joint-last-to-die annuity. As another example, consider an annuity that pays two-thirds of the original monthly income to a secondary annuitant if the primary annuitant dies first. This could be modeled as one-third of a single life annuity on the primary annuitant plus two-thirds of a JLS annuity on both annuitants.

13.5.1.2 Accumulation Annuities

Accumulation annuities have three decrements: mortality, lapse, and annuitization. If death benefits are not significant, mortality rates can be combined with lapse rates. If annuitization is not significant, annuitization rates can be combined with lapse rates. Otherwise, the following new decrement must be calculated. The probability of quitting due to annuitization is denoted by qa:

$$qaA(t) = \text{Annual annuitization rate for year } t$$
$$qaQ(t) = \text{Quarterly annuitization rate for year } t$$
$$\text{Annuitizations}(t, Q) = \text{The probability of surviving to and then}$$
$$\text{annuitizing at the end of quarter } Q,$$
$$\text{year } t.$$

We will assume that the quarterly rate $qaQ(t)$ can be calculated from the annual annuitization rate:

$$qaQ(t) = 1 - (1 - qaA(t))^{1/4}. \tag{13.5.1}$$

The formula for survivorship must be expanded to reflect annuitization. We will assume that the quarterly annuitization rate is applied only to those who survive to the end of the quarter:

$$\text{SurvFactor}(t, Q) = \text{SurvFactor}(t, Q - 1)\,(1 - qdQ(t))$$
$$(1 - qw(t, Q))\,(1 - qaQ(t)), \tag{13.5.2}$$
$$\text{Annuitizations}(t, Q) = \text{SurvFactor}(t, Q - 1)\,(1 - qdQ(t))$$
$$(1 - qw(t, Q))\,qaQ(t). \tag{13.5.3}$$

13.5.1.3 Investment Products

For investment products, the only decrement is lapses. This assumes that there are no significant death benefits in excess of cash values, so that mortality rates can be combined with lapse rates.

13.5.2 Units

As with life insurance, annuity pricing results are calculated on a per unit basis. However, the definition of a unit is quite different. For accumulation annuity and investment products, a unit is most often defined as an amount of annuity premium (or investment deposit), such as 1,000 of single premium. For income annuities, units are usually defined in one of two ways: as an amount of premium (for example, 1,000 of single premium) or as an amount of monthly income (for example, ten of monthly income).

Average size follows from the definition of a unit. For example, if a unit is 1,000 of single premium and the average single premium is expected to be 9,876, then the average size is 9.876. If a unit is ten of monthly income and the average monthly income is expected to be 1,234, then the average size is 123.4.

When a unit is defined in terms of premium, the premium per unit is fixed, at least for the first policy year. For example, assume a unit is defined as 1,000 of first-year premium and the expected premium pattern for persisting policies is 5,000 in the first year and 1,500 in renewal years. In this case, the average size will be 5.000, and the premium per unit will be 1,000 in the first year and 300 in renewal years.

When a unit is defined in terms of monthly income, the single premium per unit is often what is being tested or determined by the pricing process. For example, if a unit is defined as ten of monthly income, the premium per unit to be tested might be based on one of the following: an analysis of the competition, an actuarial calculation (such as the present value of future benefits), or a rough estimate that can be refined through successive profit tests.

13.5.3 Premiums and Deposits

Policy fees are the exception for annuity and investment products. Single premiums or single deposits are the norm and result in a very simple premium calculation, equal to the single premium per unit. For flexible premiums or deposits, the premium formula for dynamic life insurance products, Formula 12.5.1, applies.

13.5.4   Expenses

Expenses are reflected in pricing in the same ways that life insurance expenses are reflected. Most annuity and investment product expenses are per policy or percent of premium. Per unit expenses are rare. Acquisition expenses are much lower than for life insurance, because little or no underwriting is necessary.

Commissions and related expenses are handled the same as for life insurance, with most commissions paid as a percentage of premiums. However, many accumulation annuity and investment products compete against investment-oriented products that pay sales representatives a commission that is a small percentage of assets under management. For these products, commissions expressed as a percentage of account value are not unusual.

Maintenance expenses are usually on a per policy basis. Since renewal premiums are rare, maintenance expenses are not normally expressed as a percentage of premiums. All the formulas used for life insurance expenses can be applied to annuity and investment products.

13.5.5   Death Benefits

As explained under survivorship, we assume that income annuities have no death benefits. This ignores the possibility of paying the commuted value of remaining certain payments on death. We also assume that investment products offer no death benefits in excess of cash values.

Only accumulation annuities typically provide death benefits in excess of cash values. The formula for these death benefits is the same as that for dynamic life insurance products with flexible premiums (Formula 12.5.8), with no return of unearned premium on death.

13.5.6   Annuitization Benefits

Annuitization benefits apply only to accumulation annuities. For simplicity, we will calculate the cost of annuitization benefits as the present value of losses resulting from annuitizations. In many cases, annuitizations result in profits, not losses, so this benefit can be a source of additional profit and have a negative net cost.

When calculating annuitization costs, you will want to use an approach that is consistent with your overall approach to pricing. For example, if your pricing results are based primarily on distributable earnings discounted at a certain rate, then annuitization costs should be calculated on the same basis. Annuitization costs should be based on a weighted average of the costs for the most common annuitization options.

Let

$$\text{AnnuitizationCost}(t) = \text{The average present value of losses resulting from one dollar of account value converting to an income annuity during year } t.$$

$$\text{AnnuitizationBen}(t, Q) = \text{The cost of annuitization benefits for year } t, \text{ quarter } Q.$$

The cost of annuitization benefits is equal to the account value times the cost per dollar annuitized times the probability of annuitization:

$$\text{AnnuitizationBen}(t, Q) = \text{AV\_pu}(t, Q) \text{ AnnuitizationCost}(t)$$
$$\text{Annuitizations}(t, Q). \qquad (13.5.4)$$

13.5.7 Income Benefits

To calculate the cost of monthly income benefits, we will need to define the following:

IncomeBen_pu(t, Q) = Monthly income benefit per unit in force that is payable to the annuitant or any beneficiary during quarter Q, year t. This amount would be zero during a deferred period. Otherwise, this amount would usually not vary. However, some annuities have varying benefits, such as those adjusted for inflation.

IncomeBen(t, Q) = The cost of monthly income benefits paid during quarter Q, year t, per unit issued.

We will assume that the same income benefit is paid at the end of each month during the quarter, subject to survivorship. We will assume that mortality decrements for the quarter are spread evenly by month, that is, one-third in each month. This means that the annuity payments at the end of the first, second, and third months of the quarter are decreased by one, two, and three months of mortality decrements, respectively. For simplicity, we will calculate all three payments decreased by an average of two months of mortality decrements.

On average, the monthly annuity payments are made two months into the quarter. For convenience, we will treat all three payments as if they occur at the middle of the quarter. This will understate investment income by half a month's interest on all monthly annuity payments. An easy refinement would be to treat the first two months' payments as middle-of-the-quarter payments and the third month's payment as an end-of-the-quarter payment. This would result in virtually no distortion 'of investment income.

Income annuity benefits for the quarter are calculated as three months of annuity benefits times the probability of surviving, on average, two months into the quarter:

$$
\begin{aligned}
\text{IncomeBen}(t, Q) &= 3\left(\text{SurvFactor}(t, Q - 1) - \frac{2}{3}\,\text{Deaths}(t, Q)\right) \\
&\quad \times \text{IncomeBen\_pu}(t, Q). \\
&= (3\,\text{SurvFactor}(t, Q - 1) - 2\,\text{Deaths}(t, Q)) \\
&\quad \times \text{IncomeBen\_pu}(t, Q). \qquad (13.5.5)
\end{aligned}
$$

The above formula applies to life-only annuities, where payment is contingent on the survival of the annuitant. Some income annuities have a certain period during which payments are made regardless of whether the annuitant has survived. Formula 13.5.5 is replaced with the following formula during the certain period:

$$\text{IncomeBen}(t, Q) = 3 \text{ IncomeBen\_pu}(t, Q). \qquad (13.5.6)$$

13.5.8 Surrender Benefits

Surrender benefits are typically available with accumulation annuities and investment products. The formula for surrender benefits is the same as Formula 12.5.10 for dynamic life insurance products.

13.5.9 Partial Withdrawal Benefits

Partial withdrawal benefits are common features of accumulation annuities and investment products. Most products place restrictions on how much of the account value can be withdrawn without penalty. The formula for partial withdrawal benefits is the same as Formula 12.5.11 for dynamic life insurance products.

13.5.10 Summary of Cash Flows

By Timing: Beginning-of-the-quarter cash flows are the same as for life insurance, equal to premiums less acquisition, commission, and maintenance expenses. Middle-of-the-quarter cash flows consist of monthly income benefits (for income annuities) or death benefits (for accumulation annuities):

$$\text{CashFlowMid}(t, Q) = -\text{IncomeBen}(t, Q) - \text{DeathBen}(t, Q). \qquad (13.5.7)$$

End-of-the-quarter cash flows apply only to accumulation annuities and investment products. These cash flows consist of commissions based on account values, annuitization benefits (for accumulation annuities only), surrender benefits, and partial withdrawal benefits:

$$\text{CashFlowEnd}(t, Q) = -\text{AVComm}(t, Q) - \text{AnnuitizationBen}(t, Q)$$
$$- \text{SurrBen}(t, Q) - \text{PartWithBen}(t, Q).$$
$$(13.5.8)$$

By Type: Premium cash flows are the same as for life insurance. Expense cash flows are the same as for life insurance except that death benefit expenses would normally be omitted, since they are not significant for annuity or investment products. Annuity and investment product benefits do not include dividends or pure endowment benefits:

$$\text{Ben}(t, Q) = \text{IncomeBen}(t, Q) + \text{DeathBen}(t, Q)$$
$$+ \text{AnnuitizationBen}(t, Q) + \text{SurrBen}(t, Q)$$
$$+ \text{PartWithBen}(t, Q).$$
$$(13.5.9)$$

13.6 Reserves

Reserves can have a major impact on annuity pricing. In many countries, solvency reserves can substantially exceed the gross single premium net of acquisition costs. The cost of reserve strain, including acquisition costs, can range from negative, which is unusual, to 10% or more of premium. Using a simplified pricing technique that does not reflect the impact of reserve strain can lead to significant underpricing.

In this section, we will explore solvency, tax, and earnings reserves for income and accumulation annuities.

13.6.1 Solvency and Tax Reserves for Income Annuities

Reserves for income annuities are usually calculated as the present value of remaining annuity benefits. For solvency and tax reserves, the interest rates and mortality rates used to calculate the present values are often prescribed by regulation. The prescribed interest and mortality rates tend to be lower than the general level of interest and mortality rates at the time of issue. This tends to create conservative reserves, at least initially. Over time, actual interest and mortality rates may drop, causing the reserves to become less conservative and perhaps even inadequate.

As with life insurance, the rules for calculating annuity tax reserves tend to produce tax reserves that are equal to or lower than solvency reserves.

13.6.2 Earnings Reserves for Income Annuities

Earnings reserves for income annuities may consist of a benefit reserve and a deferred acquisition cost. The *benefit reserve* would typically use more realistic interest and mortality rates to calculate the present value of remaining annuity benefits, although some margin for conservatism is common. A *deferred acquisition cost* would be established and amortized against future profit margins in the product. Future profit margins would result mainly from differences between actual experience and the assumed interest and mortality rates used to calculate benefit reserves.

Another approach is to calculate a combined earnings reserve without separate benefit reserve and DAC components. With this approach, you would solve for the valuation interest rate that equates the present value of future benefits at issue with the gross single premium net of acquisition costs. The resulting valuation interest rate should be less than the expected earned interest rate. Otherwise, either your valuation mortality rates are too conservative or your product is mispriced. Future earnings should result from the differences between actual interest and mortality rates and those used to calculate earnings reserves.

13.6.3 Solvency and Tax Reserves for Accumulation Annuities

Solvency and tax reserves are rarely allowed to be less than the cash value or more than the account value. When there are no surrender charges and the cash value and account value are one and the same, this means that solvency and tax reserves are usually equal to the cash value. However, when there are surrender charges, the situation can become much more complex.

Accumulation annuities are often designed with declining surrender charges. High early surrender charges protect the company from early lapses and otherwise unrecoverable acquisition costs. Low surrender charges in the later years allow the product to produce a better value for long-term customers. While policies remain in force, the company can earn a spread between the interest rates it earns and the interest rates paid to customers. This spread allows the company to amortize acquisition costs, cover maintenance expenses, and earn a profit.

Such a spread is sometimes used in the calculation of solvency and tax reserves. To the extent that future surrender charge decreases are adequately covered by future interest spreads, the reserve could safely equal the cash value. However, if only a portion of future surrender charge decreases can safely be covered by future interest spreads, then the reserve should equal something more than the cash value. In general, the reserve can be calculated as the current cash value plus future surrender charge decreases net of future interest spreads (but not less than the current cash value). Because future surrender charge decreases and future interest spreads can vary from year to year, this is not a simple determination.

In the U.S., solvency reserves for accumulation annuities are calculated using exactly this kind of approach. The method is called the Commissioners' Annuity Reserve Valuation Method (CARVM, pronounced "carve 'em"). Under CARVM, at each valuation date, the current account value must be projected forward using guaranteed interest rates to calculate projected cash values. The guaranteed interest rates must reflect any interest rates that the company has declared over and above the minimum guarantees in the contract. Next, each projected cash value must be discounted back to the valuation date using the valuation interest rate. The CARVM reserve is the highest discounted value calculated by this process.

Life Insurance Products and Finance

Example 13.6.1 CARVM Reserves

A single premium accumulation annuity has a guaranteed minimum interest rate of 3%, a valuation interest rate of 4.5%, and the following pattern of surrender charges: 10%, 9%, 8%, 7%, 5%, 3%, and 1% for policy years 1–7, respectively, and 0% for policy years 8 and later.

Assuming the company has declared and guaranteed an interest rate of 5% for the fourth policy year, calculate the CARVM reserve at the beginning of policy year 4. The account value at the beginning of policy year 4 is 10,000. It will be projected using an interest rate of 5% for one year and 3% thereafter.

To determine the reserve, it is first necessary to calculate projected account values and cash values as of the beginning of policy years 4, 5, 6, 7, and 8. Cash values beyond policy year 8 are not needed because the valuation interest rate is higher than the guaranteed interest rate and there are no decreases in surrender charges after year 8.

The projected cash values as of the beginning of policy years 4–8 are then discounted back to the beginning of policy year 4. The greatest of these discounted values is the CARVM reserve, shown at the bottom of Table 13.6.1.

Table 13.6.1 Unadjusted CARVM Reserves

t	Guaranteed Credited Rate	Guaranteed Account Value	Surrender Charge	Cash Value	Cash Value Discounted at Valuation Rate
3		10,000.00	8%	9,200.00	9,200.00
4	5%	10,500.00	7	9,765.00	9,344.50
5	3	10,815.00	5	10,274.25	9,408.44
6	3	11,139.45	3	10,805.27	9,468.62
7	3	11,473.63	1	11,358.90	9,525.13
8	3	11,817.84	0	11,817.84	9,483.24

Valuation interest rate = 4.50%   CARVM Reserve = 9,525.13

An adjustment known as the "Continuous CARVM" adjustment is often required. This adjustment recognizes that, if the forward calculation is performed one day beyond the end of the policy year, the surrender charge is reduced, since surrender charges normally apply on a level basis throughout each policy year. Therefore, it is common to make the adjustments shown in Table 13.6.2 to take into account the drop in surrender charge on the policy anniversary.

Table 13.6.2 Adjusted CARVM Reserves

t	*Guaranteed Credited Rate*	*Guaranteed Account Value*	*Surrender Charge Used*	*Cash Value*	*Cash Value Discounted at Valuation Rate*
3		10,000.00	7%	9,300.00	9,300.00
4	5%	10,500.00	5	9,975.00	9,545.45
5	3	10,815.00	3	10,490.55	9,606.51
6	3	11,139.45	1	11.028.06	9,663.85
7	3	11,473.63	0	11,473.63	9,621.35
8	3	11,817.84	0	11,817.84	9,483.24

Valuation interest rate = 4.50%   CARVM Reserve = 9,663.85

13.6.4 Earnings Reserves for Accumulation Annuities

Earnings reserves for accumulation annuities are usually not as complex as solvency reserves. Under U.S. GAAP, the benefit reserve is often set equal to the account value and a deferred acquisition cost is established and amortized against future profit margins. Future profit margins may include revenue from interest spreads, surrender charges applied, and expense charges levied. This is very similar to earnings reserves for dynamic life insurance products.

13.7 Reinsurance

Annuities are less commonly reinsured than is life insurance. There is less perceived need for reinsurance, because a single death cannot produce a large financial loss.

13.7.1 YRT

The YRT reinsurance method, which carves out the mortality risk, is rarely applied to annuities because of the relatively insignificant death benefits offered by most annuity products. One exception to this is reinsurance of GMDB. In its most common form, the reinsurer charges a premium equal to a flat percentage of the account value, such as 10 basis points (0.10%), and in return pays all GMDBs in excess of the account value or cash value.

13.7.2 Reserves Released Reinsurance

A novel form of reinsurance is sometimes used with income annuities. If mortality is much lower than expected, the company will lose money. Such a loss primarily results from the reserves released by death being much lower than expected. The reinsurer could pay the company a reinsurance benefit equal to the reserves expected to be released by death. The company could pay the reinsurer a reinsurance premium equal to the reserves actually released by death. The net effect of this arrangement would be to stabilize the results of the company by passing the fluctuations in reserves released to the reinsurer.

13.7.3 Tail Reinsurance

One form of reinsurance often sought but not often found is reinsurance of the "tail," that is, the income annuity benefits in the later policy years. For example, a company may be comfortable with its matching of assets and liabilities and likely mortality improvement for the first 20 policy years for its income annuities. However, the company would prefer to reinsure all risks beyond the twentieth policy year, which could be called the tail of the annuity benefits. While reinsurers may have the same aversions to the tail, sometimes a reinsurer can be found for this kind of arrangement.

13.7.4 Coinsurance

Coinsurance is the most common form of reinsurance used with annuities. Coinsurance allows the company to share all of the risks associated with a block of annuity business with the reinsurer. This might be done if the company has sold more business than its capital will support. By reinsuring, the company can use the reinsurer's capital to augment its own capital. Alternatively, the company may reinsure because it feels it has too great a concentration of risk in annuity business.

Coinsurance works the same for life insurance and annuities. The company shares an agreed upon percentage of all premiums and benefits with the reinsurer. The reinsurer holds its share of reserves and capital. The company and the reinsurer agree on a formula for reimbursement of the company's expenses related to the business coinsured. Expenses are reimbursed through the payment of expense allowances, which often follow the company's pricing assumptions for expenses.

13.8 Investment Income

Investment income is of critical importance when pricing annuity and investment products. The importance of matching assets and liabilities cannot be overemphasized. For situations where only approximate matching is possible, stochastic modeling, presented in Chapter 15, is an invaluable tool. It will help you better understand the risks related to interest or investment volatility, allowing you to focus on devising strategies to control the most important risks.

The formulas for calculating investment income for annuity and investment products are the same as for life insurance, except that policy loan provisions are rare. Therefore, the formulas for investment income could be simplified to omit policy loans.

13.9 Taxes

Annuity and investment products "enjoy" all of the same types of insurance company taxation that can apply to life insurance products, such as tax on earnings, tax on $I - E$, or tax on capital, as well as many of the same tax adjustments that are applied to assets and liabilities. However, annuity and investment products are sometimes taxed at lower rates or have other tax advantages. This is because some countries encourage investment-oriented products. Seemingly favorable taxation may be necessary to allow annuity and investment products offered by insurance companies to be taxed the same as competing products offered by other financial institutions.

The tax formulas previously provided for life insurance apply to annuity and investment products. However, the tax rates and tax bases that are used for life insurance may differ from those used for annuity or investment products.

13.10 Required Capital

Annuities and life insurance share many of the same risks. Required capital is needed to cover the risks faced by both life insurance and annuity products, namely, asset default risk, insurance risk, interest rate risk, interest spread risk, and other risk. The required capital formulas for life insurance can be used for annuity and investment products by making the modifications described in this section. Annuities rarely have policy loan provisions, so factors related to policy loans can usually be omitted.

Variable accumulation annuities and some forms of investment products pass all or most of the investment risk to the buyer. This is accomplished by basing account values and cash values on the current market value of a segregated portfolio of assets. With such products, required capital is needed only for insurance risk and other risk. If death benefits are not significant, very little required capital might be needed.

Investment and accumulation annuity products that credit interest rates attract buyers who are more focused on current interest rates than are most life insurance buyers. This makes the matching of assets and liabilities even more important than it is for life insurance. In theory, additional required capital is needed when assets and liabilities are not well matched. In practice, most required capital formulas lack this sophistication.

Income annuity products present a different kind of insurance risk: longevity risk, the risk of annuitants living longer than expected. This is the opposite of the risk of premature death associated with life insurance. If significant amounts of both risks exist for a company, these risks may offset one another and, at least in theory, reduce the level of overall required capital. In practice, however, required capital formulas do not allow mortality and longevity risk to be offset against one another.

A required capital component can be calculated for the longevity risk associated with life income annuities. This component is sometimes calculated as a percentage of the reserve, since the reserve measures the present value of future benefits.

Let

> LongevRisk(t) = The longevity risk component of required capital for year t, per unit issued.
>
> LongevFactor = The longevity risk factor, expressed as a percentage of income annuity reserves with life contingencies.

Then,

$$\text{LongevRisk}(t) = \text{LongevFactor Res}(t, Q). \tag{13.10.1}$$

The reserve in this formula should be net of reserves for benefits paid during the certain period, since such benefits are not impacted by the longevity risk.

13.11 Profit Measurement and Analysis

Profit measurement and analysis is much the same as for life insurance. However, there is often a greater focus on ROI and ROE with annuity and investment products. Since these products are simpler to compare than life insurance products, it is possible for products with attractive interest rates or investment results to generate more sales than the company can afford. When a company has limited capital and must choose between different products, ROI or ROE is often used to guide the choice.

13.11.1   Return on Assets

Return on assets (ROA) can be a useful tool in assessing profits on asset-intensive products like annuities. By measuring profits as a percentage of assets, you can compare profit margins to the level of risk associated with the product and the assets. For example, a low ROA such as 0.25% of assets may be barely acceptable for a low-risk product backed by low-risk assets. However, a high ROA such as 2.0% of assets may be needed to compensate for a high-risk product or high-risk assets. The ROA target could be related to the volatility of returns or the probability and extent of a worst-case result.

13.11.2   Capital-Intensive Annuities

Some annuity products can be capital "hogs." For example, the income annuities issued in connection with Chile's privatized social security system often necessitated capital infusions of 20% of single premiums during the late 1990s, with reserve strain, required capital, and acquisition costs all contributing more or less equally to the problem. With so much investment required, it is not surprising that 15% ROIs were elusive. To achieve a 15% ROI on an investment equal to 20% of single premium would require an annual profit equal to 3% of single premium. This would roughly translate to a required interest spread of 3%, with an additional spread of perhaps 0.5% to 1.0% needed to provide for maintenance expenses and amortization of acquisition costs. A total interest spread of 3.5–4% is usually next to impossible to obtain.

13.11.3   Analyzing the Spread

To better understand the economics of an accumulation annuity or investment product, it is often helpful to break its targeted spread into various components. For example, a level portion of all future spreads may be allocated to cover each of the following:

• Expenses, such as acquisition costs and maintenance expenses

- Any losses on surrenders not offset by surrender charges
- Product features, such as bailout features, GMDBs, penalty-free partial withdrawals, and annuitization options
- Risk charges for asset risks such as default, disintermediation, liquidity, and duration mismatch.

After deducting spreads for each of the above from the total spread, the remainder is the spread available for profits. By comparing this to the total investment (consisting of reserve strain, required capital and acquisition costs), you can develop an estimate of ROI. By comparing it to assets, you can develop an estimate of ROA.

Example 13.11.1 Spread Analysis

An accumulation annuity is priced to yield a pre-tax spread of 175 basis points (1.75%) between earned and credited interest rates. The pricing analysis yields the present values shown in Table 13.11.1. The basis points for each component are obtained by dividing by 100 million, the present value of assets.

Table 13.11.1 Spread Analysis

Components	PV in Thousands	Basis Points
Product Features	70	7
Commissions	370	37
Expenses	180	18
Total	620	62

From this, we can determine that 113 bp of the 175 bp pretax spread is available for profit (175 bp − 62 bp = 113 bp).

Example 13.11.2 Income Statement Analysis

Using data consistent with Example 13.11.1, we will display present values and basis points in an income statement format (Table 13.11.2).

Table 13.11.2 Income Statement Analysis

	PV in Thousands	Basis Points
Investment Income	8,000	800
Interest Credited	5,430	543
Other Benefits/Features	70	7
Increase in Reserve	200	20
Commissions	370	37
Expenses	180	18
Total Benefits and Expenses	6,250	625
Income before Tax	1,750	175
Tax at 40%	700	70
Net Income	1,050	105

Basis points equal PV of the income statement item divided by 100 million PV of assets. The net income expressed as basis points is the ROA, which is 105 bp or 1.05%.

13.12   Pricing Example

For this chapter, we will present examples of two products: an income annuity and an accumulation annuity. You will be asked to set up some of the calculations.

13.12.1 Income Annuity Example

The underlying product used here is not a typical income annuity design. The design was established to keep the example within a manageable amount of space. This example should illustrate the pricing mechanics of a typical income annuity product. In addition, we have strayed from the quarterly formulas presented earlier in this chapter. Instead, we have assumed annual payment of income benefits, with payment made in the middle of each policy year to those who are alive at that point in time.

a. Given that IncomeBen_pu = 125.00, verify the values SurvFact, SurvFactMid, and IncomeBen given in Table 13.12.1.

b. Given the following values, verify the calculation of Exp shown in Table 13.12.1.

Prem_pu = 1,000.00	Exp_pu = 0.15 all years
AvgSize = 9.90	ExpPerPol = 25.00 all years
AcqExp_pu = 1.50	CommPct = 5% of premium
AcqExpPrem = 0.02	SalesExpPct = 0.10 (that is, 10%).
AcqExpPerPol = 50.00	

Table 13.12.1 Income Annuity Calculations

t	qd	SurvFactor	SurvFactorMid	IncomeBen	Exp
		1.00000			
1	0.01099	0.98901	0.99451	124.31313	84.22576
2	0.01248	0.97667	0.98284	122.85482	2.64585
3	0.01397	0.96302	0.96985	121.23064	2.61283
4	0.01546	0.94813	0.95558	119.44737	2.57633
5	0.01695	0.93206	0.94010	117.51242	2.53650
6	0.01927	0.91410	0.92308	115.38543	2.49351
7	0.02159	0.89437	0.90424	113.02941	2.44546
8	0.02391	0.87298	0.88368	110.45942	2.39266
9	0.02623	0.85008	0.86153	107.69175	2.33545
10	0.02855	0.00000	0.83795	104.74374	2.27419

c. Given that the reserve interest rate is 5% and given the solvency reserve mortality rates shown in Table 13.12.2, calculate SurvFact,

SurvFactMid, SolvRes_pu, and SolvRes. (Hint: Once you calculate and verify SurvFact and SurvFactMid, work your way up the table to calculate SolvRes_pu. Also, remember that SolvRes is a function of the survivorship factors shown in Table 13.12.1.)

Table 13.12.2 Calculation of Solvency Reserves

t	Solvency Reserve Factors			SolvRes_pu	SolvRes
	q	SurvFactor	SurvFactorMid		
		1.00000			
1	0.00989	0.99011	0.99506	855.88953	846.48330
2	0.01123	0.97899	0.98455	780.07659	761.87518
3	0.01257	0.96669	0.97284	700.60517	674.69897
4	0.01391	0.95324	0.95996	617.02216	585.02017
5	0.01526	0.93869	0.94597	528.83369	492.90679
6	0.01734	0.92242	0.93055	435.85676	398.41798
7	0.01943	0.90449	0.91345	337.36202	301.72564
8	0.02152	0.88503	0.89476	232.52540	202.99077
9	0.02361	0.86413	0.87458	120.41997	102.36719
10	0.02570	0.84192	0.85303	0.00000	0.00000

d. Given that the investment income rate is 7%, verify the values shown in Table 13.12.3 for CashFlowBeg, CashFlowMed, CashFlowInt and InvInt, then calculate PreTaxSolvEarn.

Table 13.12.3 Investment Income and Pre-Tax Solvency Earnings

t	CashFlowBeg	CashFlowMid	CashFlowInt	InvInt	PreTaxSolvEarn
1	915.77424	−124.31313	59.82683	0.00000	4.80464
2	−2.64585	−122.85482	−4.41240	59.25383	13.94887
3	−2.61283	−121.23064	−4.35421	53.33126	12.30980
4	−2.57633	−119.44737	−4.29029	47.22893	10.59373
5	−2.53650	−117.51242	−4.22093	40.95141	8.79495
6	−2.49351	−115.38543	−4.14473	34.50348	6.96861
7	−2.44546	−113.02941	−4.06030	27.88926	5.04643
8	−2.39266	−110.45942	−3.96818	21.12080	3.03541
9	−2.33545	−107.69175	−3.86894	14.20935	0.93678
10	−2.27419	−104.74374	−3.76322	7.16570	−1.24825

13.12.2 Accumulation Annuity Example

With this example, we have again strayed from the quarterly formulas presented earlier in this chapter. We have assumed payment of death benefits in the middle of the year. Surrender benefits and annuitization benefits are assumed to occur at the end of the year.

a. Given that AnnuitizationRate equals 1% for all t, and the values of qd and qw shown in Table 13.12.4, verify Deaths, Lapses, Annuitizations, and SurvFactor for all t.

Table 13.12.4 Accumulation Annuity Calculations

t	qd	qw	SurvFactor	Deaths	Lapses	Annuitizations
0			1.00000			
1	0.01099	0.02	0.95954	0.01099	0.01978	0.00969
2	0.01248	0.03	0.90994	0.01198	0.02843	0.00919
3	0.01397	0.04	0.85273	0.01271	0.03589	0.00861
4	0.01546	0.06	0.78128	0.01318	0.05037	0.00789
5	0.01695	0.08	0.69953	0.01324	0.06144	0.00707
6	0.01927	0.11	0.60448	0.01348	0.07547	0.00611
7	0.02159	0.30	0.40986	0.01305	0.17743	0.00414
8	0.02391	0.05	0.37626	0.00980	0.02000	0.00380
9	0.02623	0.05	0.34459	0.00987	0.01832	0.00348
10	0.02855	1.00	0.00000	0.00984	0.33475	0.00000

b. Given that the premium per unit is the minimum amount paid upon surrender, the account value is paid upon death, and the following values, verify all values in Table 13.12.5.

Investment Income Rate = 7%

Interest Spread = 2%

AnnuitizationCost = 10%

AcqExp_pu = 1.50

AcqExpPrem = 0.02

AcqExpPerPol = 50.00

Prem_pu = 1,000.00

Exp_pu = 0.15 all years

ExpPerPol = 25.00 all years

CommPct = 5% of premium

SalesExpPct = 0.10 (that is, 10%)

AvgSize = 9.90.

Remember that death benefits are paid in the middle of the year, so only half of a year's interest will have been earned at time of death.

Table 13.12.5 Benefits and Expenses

t	Av_pu	SurrChg	CV_pu	DB_pu	DeathBen	SurrBen	AnnuitizationBen	Exp
1	1,050.00	0.10	1,000.00	1,024.70	11.26140	19.78020	1.01769	84.22576
2	1,102.50	0.09	1,003.28	1,075.93	12.88429	28.51997	1.01335	2.56701
3	1,157.63	0.08	1,065.02	1,129.73	14.36099	38.22264	0.99711	2.43433
4	1,215.51	0.06	1,142.58	1,186.21	15.63808	57.55473	0.95925	2.28127
5	1,276.28	0.04	1,225.23	1,245.52	16.49413	75.28199	0.90182	2.09013
6	1,340.10	0.02	1,313.29	1,307.80	17.62906	99.10838	0.81824	1.87142
7	1,407.10	0.00	1,407.10	1,373.19	17.92108	249.65960	0.58254	1.61713
8	1,477.46	0.00	1,477.46	1,441.85	14.12975	29.55353	0.56152	1.09648
9	1,551.33	0.00	1,551.33	1,513.94	14.94140	28.41933	0.53997	1.00658
10	1,628.89	0.00	1,628.89	1,589.64	15.63880	545.27107	0.00000	0.92186

c. Given that solvency reserve per unit in force equals the account value per unit in force, verify SolvRes shown in Table 13.12.6. Then verify the values shown in Table 13.12.6 for CashflowBeg, CashflowMed, CashFlowEnd, CashFlowInt, and InvInt. Finally, calculate PreTaxSolvEarn.

Table 13.12.6 Components of Pre-Tax Solvency Earnings

t	SolvRes	CashFlowBeg	CashFlowMid	CashFlowEnd	CashFlowInt	InvInt	PreTaxSolvEarn
1	1,007.51438	915.77424	−11.26140	−20.79789	63.71671	0.00000	−60.08271
2	1,003.21353	−2.56701	−12.88429	−29.53332	−0.62301	70.52601	29.21923
3	987.14110	−2.43433	−14.36099	−39.21975	−0.66454	70.22495	29.61777
4	949.65301	−2.28127	−15.63808	−58.51397	−0.69776	69.09988	29.45689
5	892.79732	−2.09013	−16.49413	−76.18380	−0.71384	66.47571	27.84951
6	810.05935	−1.87142	−17.62906	−99.92663	−0.73758	62.49581	25.06909
7	576.71368	−1.61713	−17.92108	−250.24214	−0.72983	56.70415	19.53964
8	555.90197	−1.09648	−14.12975	−30.11505	−0.56293	40.36996	15.27745
9	534.56769	−1.00658	−14.94140	−28.95930	−0.58456	38.91314	14.75558
10	0.00000	−0.92186	−15.63880	−545.27107	−0.60263	37.41974	9.55307

13.13 Exercises

Exercise 13.1

A husband age 60 and a wife age 58 purchase a five-year deferred, ten-year certain and life, JLS income annuity, with 50% payable to the survivor upon the first death. The income benefit payable while both are alive is 5,000 per month.

a. Explain the resulting monthly income pattern.

b. Explain how this annuity could be priced as the sum of two single life annuities.

Exercise 13.2

A variable income annuity has an AIR of 3% and experiences the following net investment returns for its first five years: 10%, 15%, 5%, −5%, and 10%. If the initial monthly income is 3,000 and it is recalculated once a year, determine the monthly incomes for years 2 through 6.

Exercise 13.3

An equity indexed annuity product has a participation rate of 75% of the S&P 500 index, a cap of 18%, and a guaranteed minimum interest rate, or floor, of 3%. How much does the S&P 500 index have to rise for the cap or floor to come into play?

Exercise 13.4

An annuity with an MVA guarantees 5.25% interest for the next three years. The three-year interest rate available on new deposits is 7.10%. The company uses an additional margin in its MVA formula equal to 0.35%. Calculate the MVA using Formula 13.2.2.

Exercise 13.5

Rather than ignore death benefits for certain and life annuities, you will develop a formula for income annuity death benefits that reflects the commutation of the remaining certain period payments at the date of death. Use the following notation:

$$\text{CPRemaining}(t, Q) = \text{Average number of certain period monthly payments remaining if death occurs during quarter } Q, \text{ year } t$$

$$\text{CommutRate} = \text{Interest rate at which the remaining certain payments are commuted or discounted to calculate a lump-sum death benefit}$$

$$\text{PctCommute} = \text{The percentage of beneficiaries who opt for a lump-sum death benefit in lieu of continuing monthly payments to the end of the certain period.}$$

Develop a formula for DB_puMid(t, Q), the average death benefit per unit for quarter Q, year t. Assume a unit is defined as a monthly payment of ten. This result can then be used in conjunction with Formula 12.4.10, with no return of premium on death.

Restate Formula 13.5.6 to dovetail with this new approach to death benefits. You will need to reflect different benefits for those who died before the quarter, those who die during the quarter, and those who survive to the end of the quarter.

Exercise 13.6

Calculate AnnuitizationBen(t, Q) and its ratio to earnings, given the following: AV_pu(t, Q) = 10,000, AnnuitizationCost(t) = -0.05 (this means the company makes a 5% profit on annuitization), Annuitizations(t, Q) = 0.01, Assets(t, Q) = 5,000, and ROA(t, Q) = 0.20%. What portion of earnings do annuitization benefits account for?

Exercise 13.7

Modify Formula 13.5.5 to reflect semimonthly income benefits instead of monthly income benefits. Assume that IncomeBen_pu(t, Q) is now defined as the semimonthly income benefit per unit in force. How would IncomeBen(t, Q) be split between middle and end of the quarter cash flows in order to avoid distortion of investment income?

Exercise 13.8

As mentioned in the chapter, it is often necessary to use stochastic modeling to price a GMDB feature. Assume you are pricing a variable annuity that has a GMDB feature that pays upon death the premium accumulated at 5% interest, if that amount is greater than the account value.

Given the mortality rates and investment performance assumptions in Table 13.13.1, calculate the cost of the GMDB design as a percentage of each scenario's account value, assuming all deaths occur at the end of the year and discounting all present values at 5%.

Table 13.13.1 GMDB Scenarios

t	q	Investment Performance Scenario		
		(a)	(b)	(c)
1	0.005	3.0%	5.0%	3.0%
2	0.010	3.0	5.0	5.0
3	0.015	3.0	5.0	7.0
4	0.020	3.0	5.0	3.0
5	0.025	3.0	5.0	−10.0

Exercise 13.9

The following projection of account values shown in Table 13.13.2 assumed that the underlying investments earn a rate of 10% each year and credit interest at a spread of 1.75%. They also assume an annual lapse rate of 10% for all years until the last, when the lapse rate equals 100%.

Table 13.13.2 Account Values

t	AV
0	10,000.00
1	9,742.50
2	9,491.63
3	9,247.22
4	9,009.11
5	8,777.12
6	8,551.11
7	8,330.92
8	8,116.40
9	7,907.40
10	0.00

The initial DAC is equal to 800. Calculate the DAC pattern, assuming the DAC earns 10% less the spread of 1.75%.

13.14 Answers

Answer 13.1

a. For the first five years, no monthly income is paid. For the next ten years, 5,000 per month is paid. After 15 years, the monthly income will be 5,000, 2,500, or 0 depending on whether both, one, or neither are alive, respectively.

b. This JLS annuity is actually the sum of two five-year deferred, ten-year certain and life, single life annuities with income benefits of 2,500 per month. One single life annuity is on the life of the husband and the other is on the life of the wife.

Answer 13.2

$$\text{IncomeBen}(2) = 3{,}000.00 \ (1.10)/1.03 = 3{,}203.88$$

$$\text{IncomeBen}(3) = 3{,}203.88 \ (1.15)/1.03 = 3{,}577.15$$

$$\text{IncomeBen}(4) = 3{,}577.15 \ (1.05)/1.03 = 3{,}646.61$$

$$\text{IncomeBen}(5) = 3{,}646.61 \ (0.95)/1.03 = 3{,}363.38$$

$$\text{IncomeBen}(6) = 3{,}363.38 \ (1.10)/1.03 = 3{,}591.96.$$

Answer 13.3

Let IR equal the index's rate of return. The EIA product credits a floor of 3% or 75% of IR, whichever is greater, but no more than the cap of 18%. If IR is greater than 24%, then the 18% cap comes into play. If IR is less than 4%, then the 3% floor comes into play.

Answer 13.4

$$\text{MVA} = (1.0525/1.0745)^3 = 0.9398 = 93.98\%.$$

Answer 13.5

For convenience, let $n = \text{CPRemaining}(t, Q)$ and $i = (1 + \text{CommutRate})^{1/12} - 1$, which is the monthly interest rate which is equivalent to CommutRate. Let $v = 1/(1 + i)$, which is a monthly discount factor. Assume death occurs at the middle of the quarter, so the first remaining certain payment is half a month after death. The following formula is the present value of n monthly payments of ten each, discounted at a monthly interest rate of i. Let CVRCP = the commuted value of the remaining certain payments. Then, using the algebra of power series we have

$$\text{CVRCP} = 10 \ v^{-1/2} \ \frac{1 - v^n}{i}$$

$$\text{DB\_puMid}(t, Q) = \text{PctCommute CVRCP}.$$

Formula 13.5.6 must be adjusted to reflect certain payments only to those who elect not to receive a lump-sum death benefit after the annuitant has died. This is most easily figured out by breaking the lives at the end of quarter Q, year t, into three groups:

1. Those who survive to the end of quarter Q will receive three monthly payments during the quarter. The probability of this is $\text{SurvFactor}(t, Q)$.

2. The beneficiaries of those who died prior to quarter Q will receive three monthly payments during the quarter, provided they did not

elect to receive lump-sum death benefits. The probability of this is $(1 - \text{SurvFactor}(t, Q - 1)) (1 - \text{PctCommute})$.

3. Those who die during quarter Q will receive one monthly payment before death, and their beneficiaries will receive two monthly payments after death, provided they do not elect to receive lump-sum death benefits. The probabilities of these two events are $\text{Deaths}(t, Q)$ and $\text{Death}(t, Q) (1 - \text{PctCommute})$, respectively.

Combining the three groups into one formula, we have

$$
\begin{aligned}
\text{IncomeBen}(t, Q) &= 3\ \text{SurvFactor}(t, Q) \\
&\quad + 3\ (1 - \text{SurvFactor}(t, Q - 1)) \\
&\quad \times (1 - \text{PctCommute}) + \text{Deaths}(t, Q) \\
&\quad + 2\ \text{Death}(t, Q) (1 - \text{PctCommute}) \\
&= 3 \left[1 - \text{PctCommute} \right. \\
&\quad \times (1 - \text{SurvFactor}(t, Q - 1)) \\
&\quad \left. + \frac{2}{3}\ \text{Deaths}(t, Q)) \right].
\end{aligned}
$$

Answer 13.6

Using Formula 13.5.4,

$$\text{AnnuitizationBen}(t, Q) = (10,000) (0.01) (-0.05) = -5.$$

Earnings can be calculated as

$$\text{Assets times ROA} = (5,000) (0.20\%) = 10.$$

The ratio of $\text{AnnuitizationBen}(t, Q)$ to earnings $= -5/10 = -50\%$. In other words, the profit from annuitization benefits accounts for 50% of earnings.

Answer 13.7

There are now six payments per quarter, one at the end of each half-month during the quarter. If deaths occur, on average, at the middle of the quarter, then 2.5 payments will be made to those who die during the quarter. Therefore,

$$\text{IncomeBen}(t, Q) = (6 \ \text{SurvFactor}(t, Q - 1) - 3.5 \ \text{Deaths}(t, Q))$$
$$\times \ \text{IncomeBen\_pu}(t, Q).$$

To avoid distortion of investment income, $\frac{5}{6}$ of IncomeBen(t, Q) would be allocated to middle of the quarter cash flows and $\frac{1}{6}$ would be allocated to end of the quarter cash flows.

Answer 13.8

Table 13.13.3 Scenario (a)

t	Per Unit In Force			Deaths	Account Value per Unit Issued	NAAR Paid
	Account Value	GMDB	NAAR			
	10,000.00	10,000.00				
1	10,300.00	10,500.00	200.00	0.00500	10,248.5000	1.0000
2	10,609.00	11,025.00	416.00	0.00995	10,450.3955	4.1392
3	10,927.27	11,576.25	648.98	0.01478	10,602.4487	9.5892
4	11,255.09	12,155.06	899.97	0.01941	10,702.1117	17.4644
5	11,592.74	12,762.82	1,170.07	0.02377	10,747.5957	27.8147
				PV at 5%:	45,623.76	49.15
				PV as % of Account Value:		0.1077%

Table 13.13.4 Scenario (b)

t	Per Unit In Force			Deaths	Account Value per Unit Issued	NAAR Paid
	Account Value	GMDB	NAAR			
	10,000.00	10,000.00				
1	10,500.00	10,500.00	0.00	0.00500	10,447.5000	0.0000
2	11,025.00	11,025.00	0.00	0.00995	10,860.1763	0.0000
3	11,576.25	11,576.25	0.00	0.01478	11,232.1373	0.0000
4	12,155.06	12,155.06	0.00	0.01941	11,557.8693	0.0000
5	12,762.82	12,762.82	0.00	0.02377	11,832.3687	0.0000
				PV at 5%:	48,282.90	0.00000
				PV as % of Account Value:		0.0000%

Table 13.13.5 Scenario (c)

| t | Per Unit In Force | | | Deaths | | Account Value per Unit Issued | NAAR Paid |
	Account Value	GMDB	NAAR				
	10,000.00	10,000.00					
1	10,300.00	10,500.00	200.00	0.00500		10,248.5000	1.0000
2	10,815.00	11,025.00	210.00	0.00995		10,653.3158	2.0895
3	11,572.05	11,576.25	4.20	0.01478		11,228.0621	0.0621
4	11,919.21	12,155.06	235.85	0.01941		11,333.6059	4.5768
5	10,727.29	12,762.82	2,035.53	0.02377		9,945.2392	48.3879
				PV at 5%:		46,239.11	44.58
				PV as % of Account Value:			0.0964%

Answer 13.9

Table 13.13.6 calculates each year's profit margin, equal to 1.75% of the beginning of the year account value. The percentage of profit margins needed to amortize acquisition costs, which we will refer to as the "amortization percentage," is calculated as the initial DAC (800.00) divided by the present value of profit margins (1,052.94).

Table 13.13.6 Calculation of DAC

t	AV	Profit Margin	DAC
0	10,000.00		800.00
1	9,742.50	175.00	733.04
2	9,491.63	170.49	663.98
3	9,247.22	166.10	592.56
4	9,009.11	161.83	518.49
5	8,777.12	157.66	441.48
6	8,551.11	153.60	361.20
7	8,330.92	149.64	277.30
8	8,116.40	145.79	189.41
9	7,907.40	142.04	97.12
10	0.00	138.38	0.00
PV at 8.25%:		1,052.94	
Amortization Percentage: 75.98%			

Each successive DAC is calculated starting with the previous year's DAC, adding interest, and then subtracting the amortization percentage multiplied by that year's profit margin. For instance, for year 4,

$$DAC_4 = (592.56)(1.0825) - (0.7598)(161.83) = 518.49.$$

Part III
Modeling and Finance

Part III develops approaches for the modeling of life insurance company financial statements and discusses the management of insurance company finances.

- Chapter 14, "Financial Modeling," explains the modeling of liabilities, introduces a simple asset model, and explores the matching of assets and liabilities.

- Chapter 15, "Stochastic Modeling," introduces the concept of stochastic modeling, applies it to mortality and interest rates, and presents an overview of the most common asset classes.

- Chapter 16, "Financial Management," discusses the tools of financial management and applies them to the management of risk, earnings, and capital.

Financial Modeling

14.1 Introduction

In earlier chapters, we discussed how to calculate life insurance results at the microscopic level. In this chapter, we will explore how to combine many microscopic cells to create a financial model.

This chapter is divided into three main sections:

- Modeling of liabilities
- Asset/liability modeling
- Asset/liability matching or immunization.

14.2 Modeling of Liabilities

In previous chapters, we developed formulas for a single issue age and risk class, on a per-unit-issued basis. The results of such formulas could be used to price one cell at a time. However, such an approach is not often used. More commonly, many cells are combined into a financial model, and the aggregate results of the model are used. To create a financial model, the results of numerous ages and risk classes are combined. This is accomplished by multiplying per-unit-issued results by weights that reflect the distribution of business by age and risk class, and then summing the weighted results. This is the essence of liability modeling. In general, modeling consists of the following steps:

1. Calculate results on a per-unit-issued basis for a number of cells, where each cell is defined by its issue age, risk class, product, issue year, and perhaps other parameters.

2. Multiply each cell's per-unit-issued results by the appropriate number of units (either units in force or units expected to be issued) to create gross results for each cell.

3. Add up the gross results from all cells to calculate total results for the entire model.

Example 14.2.1 Simple Liability Model

As an example, calculate the premium results for a model composed of two cells. The premiums per unit issued are multiplied by the number of units expected to be issued, and the results are added together to obtain total premiums.

Policy Year	Premium Per Unit Issued		Total Premiums
	Issue Age 25	*Issue Age 45*	
1	5.00	20.00	1,100,000
2	4.20	17.00	932,000
3	3.80	16.00	868,000
Number of Units	60,000	40,000	

In Example 14.2.1, the results were summarized by policy year, which is typical for new business models involving a single issue year. For models that involve in-force business or multiple issue years of new business, results are summarized by calendar year.

Example 14.2.1 illustrates only premiums. The same modeling procedure can be applied to obtain total results for all the items you wish to model, such as expenses, benefits, taxes, earnings, assets, liabilities, and capital.

14.2.1 Uses of Liability Models

Liability models are perhaps the most useful and vital tools available to life insurance companies. They are useful for a wide range of difficult decisions. A liability model is the main result of the pricing process. Models are heavily used for product decisions, including the design of product features and the product's price structure. The model's results will influence whether or not a new product is introduced.

By combining the results for a number of products, a company can assess an entire product line. Model results can be used to help decide whether to introduce a new product line or new distribution channel, or whether to discontinue an existing one. Liability models are used to assess the value of a company or block of business to be acquired or sold. They are also essential tools when deciding whether to continue, sell, or close down a line of business or even the entire company.

14.2.2 Types of Liability Models

Liability models can range in complexity from our two-cell example to something that models the entire company. The first step in building a liability model is to understand the kinds of decisions that will be made using that model. The purpose of the model will determine the scope, size, and complexity of the model.

For example, if you are developing cost of insurance factors for female smokers for a Universal Life product, your liability model should include all the pricing cells for female smokers for that product. If you are developing percentage of premium expense charges that will apply to the entire product, then your model should include all pricing cells for the product. If you are deciding the fate of the company, your model should project results for the entire company.

14.2.2.1 Pricing Models

Preliminary pricing models often concentrate on a few representative issue ages for the gender, risk class, and size of policy with the highest expected sales. For example, if 75% of a company's insurance sales are male nonsmokers and issue ages 30 through 55 make up 75% of male nonsmoker sales, then the initial pricing model may concentrate on those cells.

Final pricing models usually include cells for a complete range of representative issue ages, such as every fifth or tenth issue age. Males are usually priced separately from females, so each gender has its own cells. In some markets, female rates are sometimes set equal to male rates with a setback such as four years. In this case females would be charged the same rates as a male four years younger. However, with the growth of advanced pricing software and pricing tools, this method is falling into disuse.

The number of risk classes has been increasing around the world. Not only are smoker and nonsmoker classifications increasingly common, but also one or more preferred classes are sometimes offered. In addition, rates often vary by policy size. As a result, it is possible for a product's pricing model to have hundreds of cells. For example, a product could have cells for every fifth issue age from 20 to 75 (12 representative issue ages), male and female, smoker and nonsmoker, preferred and standard, and four policy sizes, for a total of $12 \times 2 \times 2 \times 2 \times 4 = 384$ cells.

It is highly questionable whether there is value in working with 384 cells for a single product. Often, 20% of the cells will account for 80% of the business. For example, 80% of the business may come from male nonsmokers. It might be best to focus your efforts on this group and develop simplified methods to handle the others.

For example, you may find that smoker rates for the most important smoker pricing cells are two times the nonsmoker rates. If so, you might use two times the nonsmoker rates for all smoker rates. Similarly, you may find that there are simple relationships between the rates for preferred and standard.

Often, the differences between rates for one policy size and the next policy size are fairly constant. You could develop rates for all policy sizes for the most important cells and assume the same differences by policy size apply to all the other cells. The differences between male and female rates usually vary significantly by age and follow no simple pattern. Therefore, it is usually necessary to develop rates for all representative issue ages for both genders, at least for some subset of the cells.

Modeling allows you to cross-subsidize results between pricing cells. For example, to field a product that is competitive across the board, nonsmoker cells may provide extra profits to cover a shortfall in smoker profits. Competitive comparisons are often published for one or two key pricing cells such as male nonsmoker issue age 35 or 45, with a policy size of 100,000 or 250,000. Higher profits from most cells may support lower profits at one or two key cells. Some companies strive to be more competitive for these key cells. In any case, modeling allows you to measure the overall level of profitability.

You can use a model to illustrate a new product being issued over a period of several calendar quarters or years (that is, over the period during which the product is expected to be offered). Such a model would show the cumulative effect of successive quarters or years of sales of the new product, as well as its total effect. This would allow you to compare the cost of developing and implementing the product to the aggregate profits from the product. It would also give you a better sense of the significance and long-term financial effect of the product.

14.2.2.2   New Business Models

For planning and budgeting purposes, it is often necessary to project not only the amount of new business, but also the financial effect of new business. Per-unit-issued pricing results tell you very little about what to expect on an absolute or total basis. What is more useful is a model that reflects the effect of expected new business from all of the company's major products. For example, the total premium, total commission, total expenses, total first-year strain, and total capital contributions associated with new business are important parts of many companies' plans.

If your model will be used to project all new business results, it will often be sufficient to model the results of the company's best selling products and omit the worst selling products. For example, suppose the company's top selling products represent 90% of sales. Suppose all other products are omitted from the model. In this case, the projected results for the top selling products could be divided by 0.9 to gross up to match 100% of expected sales.

A more accurate approach would be to examine each product you wish to omit from the model and match it with the product to be included in the model that is the most similar. The expected sales for each omitted product could be added to the expected sales of its closest cousin.

14.2.2.3 In-Force Models

In-force models have many purposes. They are often used for planning and budgeting purposes. By combining an in-force model with a new business model, it is possible to project total results for an entire company or line of business. An in-force model can be used to calculate the value of a block of business to be sold or acquired. It can be used to determine the adequacy of reserves. A revised dividend scale, revised COI rates, or an interest-crediting strategy can be tested for reasonability or equity by using an in-force model. A model can be used to project future liability cash flows to better match them with asset cash flows.

The gross premium valuation described in Chapter 6 is an in-force model that uses best-estimate assumptions, ignores required capital, and calculates the minimum reserve needed to provide for future cash flows. Gross premium valuation can also be done on a per-unit-in-force basis for one cell or one policy at a time.

Similar products are usually grouped together when modeling a company's in-force business. A company with a long history may have hundreds or even thousands of different products in force. By grouping similar products, the time and effort required to build the model can be significantly reduced.

On the other hand, in order to group products, it is necessary to review each and every product to decide on the product groupings. You would normally start with a summary of all the business in force by product, such as shown in the following example.

Example 14.2.2 Summary of Business in Force by Plan Code

In this example, the plan code identifies the product, gender, and risk class.

Plan Code	Description	Units	Policies	Reserve	Cash Value
17065	Endow to 65—M	987,234	39,489	296,170,200	281,361,690
17075	Endow to 65—F	234,889	10,677	58,722,250	55,786,138
27162	WL to 90—M	12,364	824	3,091,000	2,936,450
27172	WL to 90—F	2,346	196	527,850	501,458
35368	WL to 100—M NS	1,356,257	38,750	162,750,840	146,475,756
35378	WL to 100—F NS	145,678	4,856	14,567,800	13,111,020
36368	WL to 100—M SM	235,879	7,863	35,381,850	31,843,665
36378	WL to 100—F SM	26,447	1,058	3,305,875	2,975,288
75578	10YT—M Pref NS	3,223,639	25,789	35,460,029	0
75678	10YT—M Non-Pref NS	2,263,487	18,862	27,161,844	0
75588	10YT—F Pref NS	890,456	8,095	8,904,560	0
75688	10YT—F Non-Pref NS	794,567	7,357	8,740,237	0
76578	10YT—M Pref SM	1,468,579	12,238	22,028,685	0
76678	10YT—M Non-Pref SM	1,358,549	11,813	19,019,686	0
76588	10YT—F Pref SM	356,957	3,245	4,640,441	0
76688	10YT—F Non-Pref SM	436,807	4,160	6,988,912	0
	Total	13,794,135	195,272	707,462,059	534,991,464

From a summary such as is shown in Example 14.2.2, a company's major products can be determined. Normally, the importance of a product is determined by the size of its premiums, death benefits, or reserves in force.

You should keep the law of diminishing returns in mind when selecting products to be modeled. At some point, the additional accuracy gained by modeling the next product is not worth the time it takes to model that product. In addition, if the prices for all cells were set consistently in the original pricing, then a small number of cells may reasonably project the aggregate results for all cells.

You might vary the number of issues ages modeled by product. The larger products could be modeled using many issue ages. The smaller products may be adequately modeled using only a few issue ages.

14.2.3 Building Data for the Liability Model

Models are usually built to be used repeatedly, with variables changing from one run to the next in order to understand and measure the effect of changes in key variables. Knowing which variables are apt to be changed affects the design and structure of the model. Typically, data input into the model are segregated into two categories: aggregate data and cell data.

Aggregate data are few in number and easily changed. Aggregate data usually include only a few assumptions (such as interest rates) or assumption multipliers (which are applied to mortality, lapse, and expense rates) and perhaps some other parameters. The ability to vary interest rates and multipliers for mortality, lapse, and expense rates allows the modeler to easily test the effect of changes such as a 1% decrease in interest rates, a 5% increase in mortality, a 10% increase in lapse rates, or a 3% decrease in unit expenses.

Cell data are not easily changed because of the vast quantity of data scattered through countless cells. Cell data consist mainly of product parameters and assumptions.

The product parameters included in cell data vary greatly between dynamic and pre-scheduled products. Dynamic products would typically be defined by their cost of insurance rates, expense charges, premium patterns, and interest spreads. Pre-scheduled products would be defined mainly by their per-unit values such as premiums, death benefits, cash values, and dividends.

The assumptions in cell data usually include mortality rates, lapse rates, expense rates, average size, and number of units (either in force or expected to be sold). Many assumptions are derived from pricing assumptions or recent experience studies. The average size and number of units are typically obtained from in-force data.

Rather than reinvent the wheel, many companies purchase modeling software. In this case the division between variable data and static data has already been decided by the software vendor. Modeling software often creates input data from a policy-by-policy electronic extract of the block of business to be modeled. This feature not only speeds the creation of data, but also improves the precision of the model. The extract might contain information for each policy such as

- Product identifier (often called a *plan code*)
- Issue date
- Issue age or date of birth
- Gender
- Risk class
- Number of units
- Solvency reserve
- Tax reserve
- Account value (for dynamic products)
- Amount reinsured.

Each policy is automatically mapped into the most appropriate cell in the model, based on product, issue year, issue age, gender, and so on. The software then projects results forward from the starting point of the model.

The data for each cell might be organized as shown in Example 14.3.2.

Example 14.2.3 Cell Data for a Liability Model

Product parameters:

- Premiums per unit
- Commission rates
- For pre-scheduled products:
    Death benefits per unit
    Cash values per unit
    Dividends per unit
- For dynamic products
    Expected spread between earned and credited interest rates
    Guaranteed interest rates
    Cost of insurance rates
    Surrender charges
    Expense charges
- Reserves per unit or methodology to calculate reserves per unit

Assumptions:

- Number of units (either in force or expected to be sold)
- Average size
- Mortality rates
- Lapse rates
- Expense rates
- Earned interest rates
- For VUL: expected investment performance

Other:

- Information to calculate reinsurance, taxes, and required surplus and interest thereon.

As Example 14.2.3 would indicate, the biggest challenge in building a model is creating the input data. Few companies are able to easily link pricing assumptions, experience study results, in-force data, new business data, product parameters, product calculations, reinsurance data, reserves, and required capital calculations. More often, information must be extracted from many different sources to build the data needed for every cell in the model. At best, this is usually a very difficult and time-consuming process. Over time, many companies automate the extraction of data for their models, but many manual steps often remain.

14.2.4   Liability Model Calculations

For models involving in-force business or several years of new business, you will probably want a model that will reasonably approximate financial statement results. This means you will need the model to realistically project calendar year results. This is usually not the case when pricing a product, where the focus is on all future years combined, not on individual calendar years. There are exceptions to this. For example, if you are developing a new product that is expected to need large amounts of capital, you may want to realistically project the size and timing of the required capital infusions.

Realistic quarterly projections may be needed to help prepare the company's financial plans and budgets. Many companies produce quarterly financial plans for the coming year. Actual results are then compared to plan results each quarter. Investment analysts who track your company's performance develop their own aggregate models of quarterly results. With a realistic quarterly model of your own, you can help them refine their models and develop better quarterly earnings estimates. Realistic quarterly projections can also help you with capital planning.

In this section, we will develop liability model calculations for calendar years, assuming all business is issued on January 1. This allows policy years to match up with calendar years. While no company issues all its business on January 1, business can be grouped so that the average issue date is January 1. For example, all business issued from 1 July 2001 to 30 June 2002 can be grouped together, resulting in an average issue date of 1 January 2002. Exercises at the end of the chapter will explore adjustments needed to develop liability model calculations for calendar quarters.

14.2.4.1 Model Variables

It is common to share the same product parameters and assumptions among multiple issue years of the same product. This cuts down dramatically on the amount of data that must be assembled. However, the amount of business in force or expected to be sold is usually segmented by issue year and sometimes by issue quarter. The rest of this section assumes you will create separate cells for every issue year. This simplifies the presentation. In practice, you will want to share common data among issue years whenever possible. Let

c = Cell identifier. c is a subscript that uniquely identifies a cell, allowing us to keep results separate for each cell. Each cell in the model represents a unique combination of product, issue year, issue age, risk class, gender, and so on.

issyr = Issue year for cell c. Each cell will contain business for only one issue year. The calendar year beginning closest to the issue date will be assigned the business. For example, all business issued from 1 July 2000 to 30 June 2001 will be assigned to calendar year 2001, with an assumed issue date of 1 January 2001. This will allow us to use policy year per-unit-issued results to calculate calendar year results

begyr = iBeginning year for the model, that is, the first calendar year for which model results are desired

calyr = Calendar year; model results will be calculated separately for each calendar year

variable(c, calyr) = Any of the annual per-unit-issued results
calculated in Chapters 5 through 10, such as
Prem, Comm, AcqExp, and so on; for
example, Prem(c, calyr) is the annual
premium per-unit-issued for cell c in calyr.

Calendar year, policy year, and issue year are related through the
following formulas:

$$calyr = issyr + t - 1, \tag{14.2.1}$$
$$issyr = calyr - t + 1, \tag{14.2.2}$$
$$t = calyr - issyr + 1. \tag{14.2.3}$$

Now that we can translate back and forth between calendar year and
policy year, we can calculate all the per-unit-issued values needed for
the model. This will be done using the following simple formula, where
t is determined from issyr and calyr using Formula 14.2.3:

$$variable(c, calyr) = variable(t). \tag{14.2.4}$$

For example, Prem(c, calyr) would be set equal to Prem(t) for cell c.
Prem(c, calyr) would equal the premiums per-unit-issued for cell c that
are projected for calyr. Care should be taken when projecting new
business to be issued after the model starts. For calendar years before
the issue date of the cell, all per-unit-issued variables should be set
equal to zero. In other words, if calyr < issyr, then
variable(c, calyr) = 0.

14.2.4.2 Number of Units

Per-unit-issued results are multiplied by number of units to calculate
aggregate or total results. Number of units also reflects the distribution
of business among the various cells.

Let

NumUnits(*c*) = Number of units for cell *c*. The per-unit-issued results for cell *c* are multiplied by this number of units to calculate gross results for the cell.

NumUnitsIF(*c*) = Number of units in force as of the start of the model for cell *c*. This must be adjusted to determine NumUnits(*c*). This applies only to in-force cells.

For future new business, the number of units represents the expected sales for each cell. If multiple years of new business are to be modeled, it is common to increase the number of units issued each year by the expected growth rate for new business.

If a single product is being modeled, a more sophisticated approach could be taken. The number of units issued over time could reflect a number of factors such as

- A steep ramp-up in sales as the product is introduced

- Seasonal fluctuations in sales from quarter to quarter, based on historical patterns (this would only come into play for quarterly models)

- Annual growth in sales, and

- A gradual drop-off in sales as the product becomes out-of-date or is retired.

For most purposes, such sophistication is unnecessary.

For in-force business, the number of units represents a cell's in-force business at the starting point of the model. This creates a problem because, unlike new business, this number of units cannot be applied to per-unit-issued results without an adjustment. To convert number of units from "per unit in force at the beginning of the model" to "per unit issued," we divide by SurvFactor(*c*, begyr − 1), which is the probability of surviving from issue to the beginning of the model:

$$\text{NumUnits}(c) = \frac{\text{NumUnitsIF}(c)}{\text{SurvFactor}(c, \text{begyr} - 1)}. \tag{14.2.5}$$

Another approach can be taken that makes this adjustment unnecessary:

Calculate per-unit-issued results for in-force cells starting at the beginning of the model rather than starting at the issue date. In other words, if you start with SurvFactor(c, begyr $-$ 1) equal to 1, then Formula 14.2.5 is unnecessary.

14.2.4.3   Total Results

Let

$$NumCells = \text{Number of cells in the model. By summing}$$
cell results from 1 to NumCells, you can combine all the results of the model

$$variable\_tot(calyr) = \text{The total result for a variable. For example,}$$
Prem_(calyr) is the total premium for all cells for calyr.

Total results can be calculated by multiplying per-unit-issued values for each cell by the number of units for each cell and then summing the results:

$$variable\_tot(calyr) = \sum_{c=1}^{NumCells} variable(c, calyr) \, NumUnits(c).$$

$$(14.2.6)$$

For example, the following formula would be used to calculate total premiums:

$$Prem\_tot(calyr) = \sum_{c=1}^{NumCells} Prem(c, calyr) \, NumUnits(c).$$

In practice, most models create one or more levels of subtotals. For example, subtotals by issue year, product, product group, or line of business may be useful.

14.2.4.4   Cell and Total Calculations

If you are building your own modeling software, you will have a choice as to which calculations to perform at the cell level and which to perform at the total level. Product cash flows, reserves, and reinsurance must be calculated at the cell level. However, investment income, taxes, required capital, and profit measures could be calculated at the cell level or the total level. Here are some things to consider when making these choices:

- Calculating more at the cell level is apt to be slower. A minor adjustment in one assumption may require that all cell-level results be recalculated.

- Calculating more at the cell level makes summarization simpler and more flexible. This is good if you want to combine the results in many different ways.

- Calculating more at the total level gives you more control over the final results. It allows you to adjust parameters that affect only the totals and then quickly recalculate results. For example, if total expenses are not credible, you could adjust total expenses and recalculate all the other totals. Using this approach, you could more easily make adjustments to total taxes to reflect tax complexities that do not lend themselves to cell-level calculations.

14.2.5 Validating a Liability Model

Every time you run a model, it is essential that you validate the results before using them. For a new business or pricing model, validation may consist of comparing ratios and patterns over time with those of similar products. For example, comparing the present value of each component of profit to the present value of premiums is often a useful tool. This may help you catch a critical error, such as a mortality assumption that is off by a factor of ten. While such an error may be obvious for a term product, it may not be so obvious for a product with a heavy savings component. With experience, you may be able to quickly tell normal from abnormal results.

For an in-force model, the validation process is more elaborate. First, you must review how closely your model reproduces the starting in-force numbers. Reproducing actual values at a given point in time is known as *static validation*. For example, the model may produce the initial in-force results shown in Example 14.2.4.

Example 14.2.4 Validation of Initial In Force

Model Plan	Description	Units	Policies	Model Reserve	Validation Percentage
1	Endow to 65—M	987,234	39,489	305,009,849	102.98%
2	Endow to 65—F	234,889	10,677	56,854,645	96.82
3	WL to 90 and 100—M NS	1,368,621	39,574	150,000,329	90.45
4	WL to 90 and 100—F NS	148,024	5,052	10,329,809	95.14
5	WL to 100—M SM	235,879	7,863	35,235,664	99.59
6	WL to 100—F SM	26,447	1,058	3,567,890	107.93
7	10YT—M Pref NS	3,223,639	25,789	32,565,445	91.84
8	10YT—M Non-Pref NS	2,263,487	18,862	28,679,043	105.59
9	10YT—F Pref NS	890,456	8,095	9,084,678	102.02
10	10YT—F Non-Pref NS	794,567	7,357	8,657,390	99.05
11	10YT—M Pref SM	1,468,579	12,238	21,957,480	99.68
12	10YT—M Non-Pref SM	1,358,549	11,813	20,984,959	110.33
13	10YT—F Pref SM	356,957	3,245	4,890,375	105.39
14	10YT—F Non-Pref SM	436,807	4,160	7,835,490	112.11
	Total	13,794,135	195,272	695,653,046	98.33

Overall, the model comes close to reproducing the actual reserves shown in Example 14.2.2, with model reserves equal to 98.33% of actual reserves. However, there are certain cells that should be improved. For example, model cell 7, the largest cell by death benefit in force, has model reserves that are off by almost 9%. The model might be improved in a number of ways. For example, you could try changing the representative issue ages or adding more issue ages. If an average issue date is used, you could try adjusting the average issue date or splitting the business into more issue periods.

Example 14.2.4 validates the initial reserves only. Similar validation and adjusting of cells should be done to validate other values, such as cash values, premiums in force, tax reserves, and so on.

Once the initial in force has been validated, you need to check the reasonability of the model going forward. One easy way to accomplish this is to test the model using in-force data from a year earlier. The results of the model can then be compared to the previous year's actual results. If premiums or reserve increases do not match, more adjustments are needed to improve the fit of the model. If death claims, lapses, expenses, investment income, or taxes differ, assumption multipliers or the assumptions themselves can be fine-tuned. Expenses, taxes, and investment income can be variable enough to defy any model. For example, the company's actual capital may significantly exceed its required capital, thereby boosting investment income. Rather than fine-tune certain assumptions, you may want to make some adjustments at the total level. Validating values over a period of time is known as *dynamic validation.*

Some modeling software is capable of modeling both future and past results. This is not difficult, as Formula 14.2.6 can work equally well for past or future periods. With this capability, you can start with current in-force data and produce model results for one or more past years. This gives you another way to validate the results of the model against past experience. Of course, for this approach to work, your model will need to calculate per-unit-issued results for the past.

14.2.6 Liability Model Output

There are many ways to summarize the results of a model. A common structure is to have one row for each important result, with columns for each year or quarter, as shown in Example 14.2.5.

Example 14.2.5 Sample Summary Report for Year 2005

	Quarter			
	1	2	3	4
Premiums	100,000	105,000	110,000	115,000
Solvency Earnings	6,000	5,000	5,000	6,000
Less Incr. in Req. Cap.	(4,000)	(4,000)	(4,000)	(4,000)
Distributable Earnings	2,000	1,000	1,000	2,000
Stockholder Earnings	12,000	11,000	11,000	12,000
Beg. Stockholder Equity	400,000	410,000	420,000	430,000
Annualized ROE	12.00%	10.73%	10.47%	11.16%
Product Cash Flow	50,000	55,000	60,000	65,000
Solvency Assets	2,200,000	2,254,000	2,308,000	2,362,000
Solvency Reserves	2,000,000	2,050,000	2,100,000	2,150,000
Required Capital	200,000	204,000	208,000	212,000

The results of the modeling process can be organized into familiar and useful formats such as income statements and balance sheets. A simple income statement report would show rows for each income and expense item, with columns for each year or quarter, as illustrated in Example 14.2.6.

Example 14.2.6 Sample Stockholder Income Statement

	Calendar Year			
	2001	*2002*	*2003*	. . .
Income				
Premiums	1,000,000	1,100,000	.	.
Investment Income	500,000	550,000	.	.
Total Income	1,500,000	1,650,000	.	.
Benefits				
Death Benefits	100,000	110,000		
Surrender Benefits	100,000	110,000		
Partial Withdrawal Benefits	50,000	55,000		
Dividends	100,000	110,000		
Pure Endowment Benefits	50,000	55,000		
Increase in Benefit Reserve	500,000	550,000		
Total Benefits	900,000	990,000		
Expenses				
Commissions	200,000	220,000		
Acquisition Expenses	100,000	110,000		
Maintenance and Claim Expenses	100,000	110,000		
Amortization of DAC	(100,000)	(120,000)		
Total Expenses	300,000	320,000		
Pre-tax Income	300,000	340,000		
Taxes				
Tax Paid	160,000	180,000		
Provision for Deferred Taxes	(40,000)	(44,000)		
Total Taxes	120,000	136,000		
Net Income	180,000	204,000		

The amortization of DAC includes capitalization of DAC for new business, as well as amortization of DAC for in-force business. In Example 14.2.6, capitalization exceeds amortization of DAC. An income statement similar to Example 14.2.6 could be developed for distributable earnings, with the increase in required capital shown as a deduction from after-tax solvency earnings.

To supplement the information contained in the income statement, an abbreviated stockholder balance sheet could be produced, showing assets (invested assets, policy loans, and DAC) and liabilities (benefit reserve, deferred taxes, and shareholders equity). An even more abbreviated solvency balance sheet could be produced, with invested assets and policy loans as the only assets shown, and solvency reserves and required capital as the only liabilities shown.

While most information of interest is contained in income statements and balance sheets, a few other items are commonly output. Projected product cash flows are useful when planning investment strategies. Many companies measure themselves by the amount of insurance in force and number of policies in force. These totals can be obtained as part of the modeling process by calculating the following per-unit-issued results at the cell level.

Let

$$\text{AmtInsIF}(c, \text{calyr}) = \text{Amount of insurance in force in cell } c \text{ at}$$
$$\text{the end of the year, per unit issued}$$
$$\text{NumPol}(c) = \text{Number of policies issued for cell } c$$
$$\text{NumPolIF}(c, \text{calyr}) = \text{Number of policies in force in cell } c \text{ at the}$$
$$\text{end of the year, per unit issued.}$$

Then,

$$\text{AmtInsIF}(c, \text{calyr}) = \quad \text{DB\_pu}(c, \text{calyr}) \, \text{NumUnits}(c)$$
$$\text{SurvFactor}(c, \text{calyr}). \qquad (14.2.7)$$

Recall that average size is equal to the average number of units per policy issued. We can divide the number of units issued by average size to estimate the number of policies issued:

$$\text{NumPol}(c) = \frac{\text{NumUnits}(c)}{\text{AvgSize}(c)}. \qquad (14.2.8)$$

We can estimate the number of policies in force by adjusting the number of policies issued for survivorship:

$$\text{NumPolIF}(c, \text{calyr}) = \text{NumPol}(c) \ \text{SurvFactor}(c, \text{calyr}). \qquad (14.2.9)$$

The total amount of insurance lapsed can be used to calculate overall lapse rates. This total can be obtained by calculating the following per-unit-issued result at the cell level.

Let

$$\begin{aligned}
\text{AmtInsLapsed}(c, \text{calyr}) &= \text{Amount of insurance lapsed from cell } c \\
&\quad \text{during the year, per unit issued} \\
\text{Annual}qw(\text{calyr}) &= \text{Annualized lapse rate for all business} \\
&\quad \text{during calyr.}
\end{aligned}$$

Then,

$$\text{AmtInsLapsed}(c, \text{calyr}) = \text{DB\_pu}(c, \text{calyr}) \ \text{Lapses}(c, \text{calyr}).$$
$$(14.2.10)$$

An annualized lapse rate can be calculated from the resulting totals as

$$\text{Annual}qw(\text{calyr}) = \frac{\text{AmtInsLapsed\_tot}(\text{calyr})}{\text{AmtInsIF\_tot}(\text{calyr} - 1)}. \qquad (14.2.11)$$

It may be desirable to see reinsurance results by themselves, as well as results before reinsurance. This would require that per-unit-issued results be calculated both before and after reinsurance.

14.2.7 Total Profit Measures

For a new business model, total results can be used to calculate all of the profit measures presented in Chapter 11. However, when in-force business is included in a model, meaningful results can be calculated for only a few profit measures: ROI, ROE, and embedded value.

For a new business model, a meaningful return on investment can be calculated from future distributable earnings, if the projection runs far enough into the future. However, if the model includes in-force business, then future distributable earnings do not tell the entire story. An ROI calculated solely from future distributable earnings would be meaningless, since future earnings are the result of past capital contributions. However, when future earnings are combined with a history of previous capital contributions and distributions, a meaningful return on investment can be calculated.

Return on equity can be calculated for each year. ROE can also be calculated over a multiyear period. In a multiyear calculation, the numerator could be the sum or present value of stockholder earnings. Similarly, the denominator could be the sum or present value of stockholder equity.

Some companies use embedded value. To accurately calculate embedded value, the model must run many years into the future, in order to include all significant future earnings. Embedded value could be calculated separately for in-force business and for each future issue year.

14.2.8   Aggregate Models

When it comes to modeling an entire company or line of business, it is common for a relatively simple aggregate model to outperform an elaborate cell-based model over the short term. Investment analysts create such aggregate models all the time. Their models focus on growth rates and the trends of various ratios. For example, if you track each of the items in your company's income statement as a percentage of premiums over time, you may find some stable relationships and some clear trends, as in the example below.

Some kinds of business may be better predicted as a percentage of assets or a percentage of some other base. There are no standard approaches to aggregate modeling. However, with some experimentation and imagination, you may be able to develop an aggregate model that helps you project short-term aggregate results that are internally consistent and surprisingly accurate.

Example 14.2.7 Sample Aggregate Model

This example uses historical data from 2003 to 2005 to estimate results for 2006. At the bottom of the table, each of the nonpremium items is expressed as a percentage of premiums, except for income tax, which is expressed as a percentage of pre-tax income.

	2003	2004	2005	2006 Estimate	2006 Actual
Revenues					
Premiums	382.6	453.6	578.0	693.6	692.3
Investment Income	63.9	72.1	90.1	107.5	137.7
Total Revenues	446.5	525.7	668.1	801.1	830.0
Benefits and Expenses					
Benefits	372.0	436.8	561.9	672.2	696.9
Expenses	19.6	24.5	31.6	38.8	46.0
Total Benefits and Expenses	391.6	461.3	593.5	711.0	742.9
Pre-tax Income	54.9	64.4	74.6	90.1	87.1
Income Tax	20.2	23.7	27.1	33.0	27.1
Net Income	34.7	40.7	47.5	57.1	60.0
As a Percentage of Premium					
Investment Income	16.7%	15.9%	15.6%	15.5%	19.9%
Benefits	97.2	96.3	97.2	96.9	100.7
Expenses	5.1	5.4	5.5	5.6	6.6
Pre-tax Income	14.3	14.2	12.9	13.0	12.6
Income Tax Rate*	36.8%	36.8%	36.3%	36.6%	31.1%
As a Percentage of Premium					
Net Income	9.1%	9.0%	8.2%	8.2%	8.7%

*As a percentage of Pre-Tax Income.

The estimates for 2006 were developed using the following steps:

- The premium growth from 2003 to 2004 and from 2004 to 2005 was highly inconsistent (18.6% and 27.4%, respectively). Therefore, premium growth was not estimated by trending past results, but by using knowledge of the company. In this way, premium growth for 2006 was projected to be 20%.

- Investment income trended down the last three years as a percentage of premiums. Therefore, a slight decrease in the ratio (to 15.5%) was projected for 2006.

- Benefits jumped around. Therefore, an average of the last three years of benefits as a percentage of premiums (96.9%) was used.

- Expenses trended up as a percentage of premiums. Therefore, the estimate for 2006 (5.6%) continued that trend.

- The income tax rate stayed fairly constant, so a simple average of the past three years of taxes as a percentage of pre-tax income (36.6%) was used for estimated taxes.

Comparing the estimated results for 2006 with the actual results, we find that

- Estimated net income of 57.1 was 95% of actual net income of 60.0. Although this bottom-line estimate is not bad, there were some substantial differences in the individual components.

- The estimated 20% growth in premiums was quite close to actual growth of 19.8%.

- There was a big jump in investment income in 2006, which was not predicted by the model. This was due to a sizable and unexpected increase in the company's savings-oriented business.

- Both benefits and expenses jumped dramatically, as a percentage of premium. The benefit increase was related to the increase in investment income. The expense increase was due to some start-up costs for a new venture.

- The net effect of the previous differences caused pre-tax income to be overestimated.

- The actual tax rate was dramatically below the estimate, due to some one-time tax benefits. This resulted in net income in excess of estimates, even though actual pre-tax income was lower than estimated.

Example 14.2.7 illustrates poor performance of an aggregate model, due to a number of significant changes in the company that the model did not reflect. When a company does not make significant changes from one year to the next, an aggregate model can produce much better estimates of the future.

It is virtually impossible to create a detailed model that contains all of a company's business. There are always products or activities that defy modeling. Making the sum of the pieces add up to equal the total company is a daunting task. Aggregate models can more easily handle such difficulties.

In summary, the best models combine the short-term fit of simple aggregate models with the long-term predictive capability of cell-based models. Once you understand how to adjust the short-term results of your cell-based model to better match aggregate results, you can apply the same techniques to adjust long-term results.

14.3 Asset/Liability Modeling

In this section, we examine why assets and liabilities are increasingly being combined into a single model. We then construct the framework for a simple asset model. Finally, we will bring assets and liabilities together in the same model.

14.3.1 Purpose of Asset/Liability Modeling

Assets are modeled alongside liabilities for reasons such as

- To design an investment strategy that fits the product or liability portfolio
- To more accurately predict investment income
- To determine the potential effect of different interest rate scenarios
- To test strategies used to set credited interest rates.

We will explore each of these purposes below.

It makes little sense to model an insurance company's assets without also modeling the associated liabilities. Asset modeling is driven by the investment strategy. However, an informed investment strategy can only be developed once product cash flows have been estimated.

An asset/liability model can be built for a single product, a product series, an entire line of business, a segregated portfolio, or an entire company. Models may include new business, in-force business, or a combination of both. Regardless of its scope, an asset/liability model can help you identify areas of concern or opportunities for improvement. However, asset/liability modeling is not cheap or simple. It is most cost effective and appropriate for portfolios that are significant to a company.

14.3.1.1   Designing an Investment Strategy

Most products other than term insurance depend heavily on investment returns. It would be unthinkable to design most life insurance products without having some kind of investment strategy in place that guides future investment choices. For example, a five-year endowment product will have a huge cash outflow at the end of the fifth year. If the investment strategy is to invest in ten-year bonds, there could be a problem in meeting the fifth-year cash flow needs. This is the kind of issue addressed by asset/liability management, covered in Section 14.4.

14.3.1.2   Predicting Investment Income More Accurately

In Chapter 7, we calculated investment income as a function of future interest rates. A more accurate approach is to calculate investment income from an asset model that is tied to the liability cash flows. Every company knows a great deal about the assets that it already owns. This knowledge can be used to predict much of the company's future investment income, at least in the short term. You can think of the investment income produced by the asset model as having two parts: (1) investment income expected to be earned on existing assets and (2) investment income expected to be earned on assets to be purchased in the future.

If existing assets are noncallable (for example, loans that cannot be repaid early), investment income on existing assets can be accurately predicted. In this case, only the investment income on future assets is unknown.

However, if assets are callable, a drop in interest rates could result in the prepayment of many assets. This would give the company an abundance of funds to invest while interest rates are low. As a result, the company's average earned interest rate would rapidly drop toward the new money rate. Callable assets result in more variability and uncertainty in investment returns.

14.3.1.3 Testing the Effect of Interest Rate Scenarios

If you can estimate how product cash flows will react to various interest rate scenarios, modeling the assets enables you to test your investment strategy. You will likely find a number of scenarios that produce unsatisfactory investment results.

For example, if a product requires a long-term interest rate of 6% to be fully profitable, you will need an investment strategy that, as much as possible, locks in today's interest rates of, say, 7.5%. You will want to see the results caused by new money rates moving down and staying below 6%. You will want to view the effects of both a sudden and a slow drop in interest rates.

As another example, suppose a product is designed to credit a competitive current interest rate and has minimal surrender charges. If the company decides to invest in long-term assets in order to earn a higher spread between earned and credited rates, you will want to test the effect of both a rapid and a slow rise in interest rates. As you know by now, a rise in interest rates can cause losses for the company:

- If the company subsidizes the credited interest rate to stay competitive, the company will reduce its profits but hold onto the business or

- If the company does not keep the credited interest rate competitive, policyowners will surrender their funds, incur minimal surrender charges, and cause a large cash outflow at a time when the company's long-term assets have depressed market values. The company may be forced to sell assets at a loss and write off deferred acquisition costs.

A model can help management decide which crediting strategy will result in fewer losses. If the company subsidizes interest rates, the company loses money on all policies. If the company does not subsidize interest rates, the company loses money on just the policies surrendered. Depending on the degree of the subsidy and the assumed behavior of the policyowners, one approach or the other may be preferable.

Testing of interest rate scenarios can have several positive effects:

- It should make the company more aware of any significant risks it is taking. This may be the first step toward fixing a significant risk exposure that could threaten the survival of the company. Some people think a significant risk exposure is one that could wipe out the company's capital. However, an event that costs only a fraction of the company's capital could be enough to trigger a run on the bank, which in turn could trigger more losses, leading to the company's ultimate downfall.

- The company may change its investment strategies to reduce its exposure to certain risks. For example, if the company would be hurt by an increase in interest rates, it might purchase options or derivatives to counter the risk.

- The company may change the products it offers to reduce exposure to certain risks. For example, a market value adjustment feature can greatly reduce the disintermediation risk associated with a rise in interest rates.

- The company may limit the total amount of certain kinds of business it will accept, in order to limit the aggregate risk.

- The company may increase certain kinds of business in order to better balance and diversify its risks. For example, annuity longevity risk might be offset by taking more life insurance risk at the older issue ages.

- Some types and levels of risk are acceptable. Every insurance company is in the risk-taking business. By knowing about the risks up front, however, the company can educate its stakeholders and minimize any collateral damage.

14.3.1.4 Developing Interest-Crediting Strategies

Much of the same capability used to test interest rate scenarios is needed to develop and test interest-crediting strategies. In addition, you will need to estimate how competitor's credited rates, your credited rates, and product cash flows will vary with different interest rate scenarios. This topic is covered in Chapter 15.

14.3.2 Introduction to Asset Modeling

An asset model is used to project cash flows, market values, book values, and other items for a portfolio of assets. For our purposes, we will assume that the asset portfolio being modeled is tied to a specific liability portfolio.

The modeling of assets is a subject that deserves a book of its own, as evidenced by the 1,339 pages of *The Handbook of Fixed Income Securities,* edited by Frank J. Fabozzi and T. Dessa Fabozzi (Irwin, 1997). However, by focusing on the simplest asset class—non-callable fixed rate bonds—we can explore some of the basics of asset modeling. By assuming all bonds are held to maturity, we can further simplify the presentation. Market values will be ignored, although market values do play a role in some insurance accounting systems such as U.S. GAAP. Book values will be calculated to produce a constant yield to maturity. An overview of other assets and other items to consider is included in Chapter 15.

We will use the following notation for the parameters that define bonds. Bonds can be purchased at any time. Once purchased, the bond's next coupon could be due anywhere from zero days to six months after the purchase date. However, to keep the formulas a little simpler, we will assume that (1) all bonds are purchased at the end of a quarter, just after any coupon payment for the quarter is made (you will see below that this value could be zero), and (2) all coupon payments and maturity payments occur at the end of a quarter.

Let

$$b = \text{Bond identifier: This uniquely identifies a particular bond}$$

$$\text{Price}(b) = \text{The price of bond } b, \text{ including any commissions, that the company paid to purchase the bond}$$

$$\text{ParValue}(b) = \text{The par value of bond } b, \text{ that is, the amount of principal the company will receive at maturity of the bond}$$

$$\text{CouponRate}(b) = \text{Annual coupon rate paid on bond } b$$

$$\text{Coupon}(b) = \text{The amount of the coupon that is paid to the company every six months as interest on bond } b, \text{ equal to } \tfrac{1}{2} \text{ CouponRate}(b) \text{ ParValue}(b). \text{ Coupon payments are assumed to occur at the end of the quarter.}$$

$$\text{Yield}(b) = \text{The yield to maturity produced by bond } b, \text{ ignoring default and investment expenses. This is an annual effective rate of interest.}$$

$$\text{QtrYield}(b) = \text{The quarterly yield rate that is equivalent to Yield}(b); \text{QtrYield}(b) = (1 + \text{Yield}(b))^{1/4} - 1$$

$$\text{DefaultRate}(b) = \text{The annual cost of default for bond } b, \text{ as a percentage of book value}$$

$$\text{InvExpRate}(b) = \text{The annual investment expense rate for bond } b, \text{ as a percentage of book value}$$

$$\text{cyq} = \text{A single variable that combines calendar year and quarter, equal to 4 calyr} + Q$$

$$\text{Purchase}(b, \text{cyq}) = \text{The purchase price paid for bond } b \text{ during calendar year and quarter cyq. This variable is equal to zero for all quarters except for the quarter in which the bond is purchased.}$$

GrossCashFlow(b, cyq) = The gross cash flow for bond b during cyq. Gross cash flows consist of the receipt of semiannual coupons and the par value at maturity.

CumCashFlow(b, cyq) = The net cash flow for bond b during cyq. Net cash flows consist of the gross cash flows less quarterly deductions for investment expenses and the cost of defaults.

BookValue(b, cyq) = The book value of bond b at the end of calendar year and quarter cyq. The book value is calculated to produce a constant quarterly yield from the purchase date to the maturity date, ignoring default costs and investment expenses.

InvIncome(b, cyq) = The investment income produced by bond b during cyq, consisting of cash flow plus the increase in book value during the quarter.

From the long list of variables needed to model the simplest asset, you can imagine how difficult assets that are more complex may be to model. We will assume we are given all of the above information for each asset except for book values, cash flows, and investment income, which we must calculate.

For the quarter in which bond b is purchased,

$$\text{Purchase}(b, \text{cyq}) = \text{Price}(b). \tag{14.3.1}$$

For all other quarters,

$$\text{Purchase}(b, \text{cyq}) = 0. \tag{14.3.2}$$

For the quarter in which bond b matures, cash flow consists of the final coupon and the maturity value:

$$\text{GrossCashFlow}(b, \text{cyq}) = \text{Coupon}(b) + \text{ParValue}(b). \tag{14.3.3}$$

Coupons are paid every six months up to and including the maturity date. For all the quarters between purchase and maturity, this leads to

$$\text{GrossCashFlow}(b,\ cyq) = 0 \text{ or} \qquad\qquad (14.3.4)$$

$$\text{GrossCashFlow}(b,\ cyq) = \text{Coupon}(b). \qquad\qquad (14.3.5)$$

Book values can be calculated from the gross cash flows and the yield rate. Remember that we have assumed all coupon and maturity cash flows occur at the end of the quarter. The initial book value is equal to the purchase price of the bond. If the bond is purchased in quarter cyq, then

$$\text{BookValue}(b,\ cyq) = \text{Price}(b). \qquad\qquad (14.3.6)$$

The book value at the end of each quarter is the book value at the end of the previous quarter accumulated at the quarterly yield rate, less the gross cash flows that occur on the bond:

$$\text{BookValue}(b,\ cyq) = \text{BookValue}(b,\ cyq - 1)\,(1 + \text{QtrYield}(b))$$
$$- \text{GrossCashFlow}(b,\ cyq). \qquad (14.3.7)$$

Using Formula 14.3.7, you can iteratively calculate all of the book values. Alternatively, the book values can be calculated as the present value of future gross cash flows, discounted using the yield rate. Once the book values have been calculated, you can determine net cash flows. The default costs and investment expenses are deducted from gross cash flows to determine net cash flows:

$$\text{CumCashFlow}(b,\ cyq) = \text{GrossCashFlow}(b,\ cyq) - (\text{DefaultRate}(b)$$
$$+ \text{InvExpRate}(b))\,\frac{\text{BookValue}(b,\ cyq - 1)}{4}.$$
$$(14.3.8)$$

The default rate and the investment expense rate are divided by four to convert them to quarterly rates.

Investment income is calculated as net cash flow plus the increase in book value for the quarter:

$$\text{InvIncome}(b,\ cyq) = \text{CumCashFlow}(b,\ cyq) + \text{BookValue}(b,\ cyq)$$
$$- \text{BookValue}(b,\ cyq - 1). \qquad (14.3.9)$$

Example 14.3.1 Nine-Month Bond

A bond is purchased on 31 December 2001 and matures three quarters later. The coupon rate is 7.00%; the bond is priced to yield 8.00%. Annual default cost and investment expense rates are 0.40% and 0.10%, respectively. Calculate book values, net cash flows, and investment income for the bond from the date of purchase to the date of maturity.

Time	Coupon	Maturity	Book Value	Cumulative Cash Flow	Investment Income
0.00			101.1283		
0.25	3.500		99.5929	3.3736	1.8382
0.50	0.000		101.5277	−0.1245	1.8103
0.75	3.500	100.000	0.0000	103.3731	1.8454

Coupon%:	7.00%
Yield:	8.00%
ParValue:	100.000
DefaultRate:	0.40%
InvExpRate:	0.10%
Qtrly Yield:	1.9427%

The gross cash flows of 3.50, 0.00, and 103.50 are reduced by expected defaults and investment expenses to arrive at the net cash flows of 3.3736, −0.1245, and 103.3731.

Example 14.3.2 30-Month Bond

A bond is purchased that matures ten quarters from the date of purchase. The coupon rate is 6.00%, and the bond is priced to yield 8.50%. Annual default and investment expense assumptions are 0.50% and 0.12%, respectively. Calculate book values, net cash flows, and investment income for the bond from date of purchase to date of maturity.

Time	Coupon	Maturity	Book Value	Cumulative Cash Flow	Investment Income
0.00			94.8447		
0.25	0.000		96.7989	−0.1470	1.8072
0.50	3.000		95.7934	2.8500	1.8444
0.75	0.000		97.7672	−0.1485	1.8253
1.00	3.000		96.7816	2.8485	1.8629
1.25	0.000		98.7758	−0.1500	1.8441
1.50	3.000		97.8110	2.8469	1.8821
1.75	0.000		99.8263	−0.1516	1.8637
2.00	3.000		98.8832	2.8453	1.9021
2.25	0.000		100.9206	−0.1533	1.8842
2.50	3.000	100.000	0.0000	102.8436	1.9230

Coupon%:   6.00%

Yield: 8.50%

ParValue: 100.000

DefaultRate: 0.50%

InvExpRate: 0.12%

Qtrly Yield: 2.0604%

14.3.3   Assembling Data for an Asset Model

Now that we understand all of the components needed to model noncallable fixed rate bonds, we can begin to build the asset/liability model. Assuming we have already developed product (liability) cash flows, the following additional items are needed to model assets:

- A preliminary asset strategy
- An inventory of assets available for purchase
- If modeling an in-force block, an inventory of the assets currently backing the existing liabilities
- Assumptions that describe future interest rate patterns
- A strategy for dealing with negative cash flows.

The rest of this section examines each of the above five items in turn.

14.3.3.1 Preliminary Investment Strategy

A preliminary investment strategy is needed to narrow the universe of assets that will be considered for the model. The investment strategy should specify the attributes of assets that will be considered, such as acceptable asset classes (government bonds, corporate bonds, commercial mortgages, and so on) and acceptable ranges for quality, liquidity, duration, and maturity.

The investment strategy will guide the asset model as to the types and mix of assets that will be purchased from future positive product cash flows. The preliminary investment strategy should be a joint effort between the company's investment managers and those responsible for the liabilities. The characteristics of the assets to be included in the model will depend on factors such as the following:

- The company's general investment philosophy
- Assets and liabilities already on the company's books
- Regulatory restrictions.

Example 14.3.3 Sample Investment Strategy

We will limit our sample investment strategy to noncallable fixed rate bonds, in line with the scope of this chapter. This is not a realistic limitation. The investment strategy is defined by the following quality, liquidity, and maturity constraints:

Quality: Government bonds and AAA bonds have been excluded because of their low current yields compared to bonds of slightly lower quality. Bonds of below investment-grade quality (that is, rated BB or worse) have been excluded because the company is not willing to take that much default risk. As a result, bonds in the quality range of BBB to AA will be considered, with a goal of maintaining an average quality rating of A to A−.

Liquidity: Liquidity is deemed very important due to the nature of the liabilities, which have substantial cash values available on demand. Privately placed bonds will not be considered, since they are fairly illiquid. Only large issues of publicly traded bonds that are widely held and actively traded will be considered.

Maturity: Because the liabilities are unlikely to have any significant cash outflows for at least five years, only maturities of five or more years will be considered. Because the product is expected to generate significant cash outflows starting in ten years and continuing for 20 or more years, no limitation will be placed on the maximum maturity, at least at this point.

14.3.3.2   Assets Available for Purchase

An inventory of assets available for purchase is needed. This inventory should be in line with the preliminary investment strategy. Because thousands of different assets may be currently available, you will want to select a relatively small number of representative assets.

You may want to create "model assets" that reflect a mixture of quality ratings and associated yields, especially if that mixture is part of your investment strategy. You could also combine assets with different liquidity characteristics, such as publicly traded and privately placed bonds. However, you should not mix assets with different maturities, since maturity date greatly affects the pattern of cash flows.

14.3.3.3 Assets Currently Backing Liabilities

If modeling an in-force block, an inventory of the assets currently backing the existing liabilities is needed. This inventory should include all the information needed to project future asset cash flows, book values, and market values. Example 14.3.4 shows some of the information that would be included in such an inventory.

Example 14.3.4 Asset Inventory

Asset ID	Description	Par Value*	Book Value*	Market Value*	Yield Rate	Coupon Rate	Maturity Date
6541987	AA Corporate	1,000	950	960	8.125%	8.000%	5 Aug 2005
6781654	AAA Private	5,600	5,000	5,100	9.500	7.500	12 Sept 2006
9874565	BBB Private	8,000	8,250	8,300	8.250	9.000	31 Aug 2001
8975348	Government	2,000	2,200	2,300	6.500	7.000	30 Apr 2002
5412978	A Corporate	6,000	5,750	5,850	9.250	9.000	31 July 2020
3657128	A Private	8,000	7,750	7,800	9.150	8.000	30 June 2015
9840268	AAA Corporate	7,500	7,000	7,200	9.750	8.000	15 Apr 2012
9824178	AA Corporate	9,600	9,400	9,600	8.250	8.500	30 Sept 2008
1487236	Government	2,400	2,200	2,400	6.750	7.000	31 July 2005
	Total	50,100	48,500	49,510			

*Amounts in thousands.

In addition, a strategy for making future asset purchases is needed. A simplified example of such a strategy is presented in Example 14.3.5.

Example 14.3.5 Strategy for Future Asset Purchases

Description	Book Value Weight	Yield Rate	Coupon Rate	Maturity Date (years)
AA Corporate	40%	7.500%	7.500%	5
AA Corporate	20	8.000	8.000	8
A Private	20	8.250	8.250	7
A Private	10	8.500	8.500	9
Government	10	6.000	6.000	3

The assets available for purchase are a mixture of corporate bonds, privately placed bonds, and government bonds. Although the yield rate on a bond is rarely exactly equal to the coupon rate, for modeling purposes, such an assumption is valid. Actually, the yield rate will be determined by interest rates available at the time of purchase.

14.3.3.4   Future Interest Rate Patterns

Assumptions that describe future interest rate patterns are needed. For purposes of this chapter, we will assume that future interest rates are modeled one set at a time. In Chapter 15, we will use stochastic modeling to develop many random patterns of future interest rates.

For example, the model could have a yield curve structure in place as shown in Example 14.3.6, which shows yield curves at three distinct points in time: at the start of the model, at the end of the fifth year of the model, and at the end of the tenth year of the model.

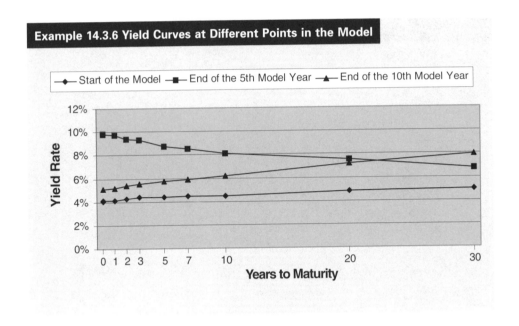

Example 14.3.6 Yield Curves at Different Points in the Model

Legend: ◆ Start of the Model ■ End of the 5th Model Year ▲ End of the 10th Model Year

X-axis: Years to Maturity
Y-axis: Yield Rate

14.3.3.5 Handling Negative Cash Flows

A strategy for dealing with negative cash flows is needed. When product cash flows are negative and exceed asset cash flows, the result is an overall negative cash flow. The shortfall has to be made up in some manner. The two most common approaches to handling negative cash flows are to borrow money or sell assets. The model should reflect the company's intentions for handling negative cash flows. The company's actual practice may vary, depending on the conditions at the company and in the marketplace.

Borrowing: Because of more than sufficient cash flows over the years, the company may have never approached outside parties to help it deal with negative cash flows. However, it is more likely that a product line will incur a cash shortfall. In such a case, the product line can usually borrow cash from other product lines within the same company.

Whether the money is borrowed internally or externally, the model must make an assumption as to the interest rate that will be charged when borrowing is necessary. The interest rate for external borrowing should reflect the company's credit quality. This will be a function of its ratings, capital position, borrowing capacity, and other factors. For internal borrowing, the interest rate could be the same as an external rate, or it could reflect the interest foregone by the product line lending the money.

Funds borrowed will be repaid at the earliest opportunity from future positive cash flows. Therefore, it would make sense to use short-term interest rates in connection with borrowed funds.

Selling Assets: The alternative to borrowing is to make up for cash shortfalls by selling assets. To reflect the sale of assets, the model must calculate the market value of the assets to be sold. The model will need rules to determine which assets to sell first, such as

- Sell assets with the largest capital gains first
- Sell assets with the shortest time to maturity first
- Sell assets that have been held at least one year first.

14.3.4   Asset Adequacy or Free Cash Flows

Asset/liability modeling can be used to test asset adequacy or to calculate the free cash flows generated by a book of business. Free cash flows represent the cash flows that can be withdrawn from the business: the owners of the company are *free* to do what they will with these cash flows. Sometimes free cash flows are negative, in which case the owners must find a way to cover the cash shortfall.

14.3.4.1   Asset Adequacy

Asset adequacy is typically performed on a block of in-force policies to test the adequacy of the assets that are allocated to the block. Most often, assets equal to solvency reserves are allocated to the block. A projection of both assets and liabilities is then performed under various interest rate scenarios. If total assets exceed total liabilities at the end of the projection, then the assets are deemed adequate for that particular interest rate scenario. This process is performed in many countries so that the valuation or appointed actuary can form an opinion as to the

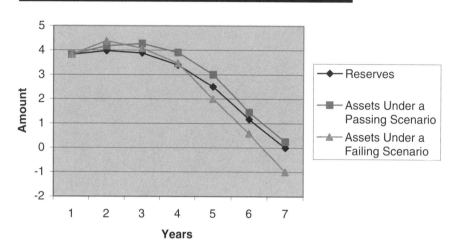

Figure 14.3.1 Sample In-Force Asset Adequacy Scenarios

adequacy of the company's assets. If the allocated assets for a block of business are insufficient under many scenarios, then the actuary may require that the company allocate more assets to the block, to ensure asset adequacy.

Figure 14.3.1 illustrates two interest rate scenarios. In both scenarios, beginning assets equal beginning reserves. In one scenario, assets exceed reserves at the end of the projection period. In the other scenario, assets are less than reserves at the end of the period. If these were the only two scenarios used to form an opinion, the actuary likely would require that additional assets be allocated to the block of business so that the failing scenario would become a passing scenario.

Asset adequacy analysis can be performed with beginning assets less than or greater than the beginning reserves. Regardless of the beginning amount of assets, the purpose is to determine whether the assets allocated are sufficient to satisfy the liabilities over the period tested.

14.3.4.2 Free Cash Flow

Throughout this book, we have emphasized that total assets at the end of each modeling period should equal the sum of solvency reserves and required capital. Asset adequacy analysis ignores this principle; there is no rebalancing performed to keep assets in line with liabilities. Under *free cash flow* testing, however, assets are rebalanced at the end of each period to match solvency reserves plus required capital.

Free cash flow is the amount of cash flow that is either (1) free to be used as the company chooses or (2) required to be contributed to support the business. If free cash flow is positive, then it represents the amount that can be withdrawn from the business. If free cash flow is negative, then it represents the amount that must be contributed to the business.

Free cash flow is useful when projecting new business, particularly if an ROI pricing strategy is being employed. The timing and amount of the free cash flows determine the ROI. Free cash flow is useful with in-force business when determining the capital that will be freed up or required in the future.

14.3.5   Asset Modeling Process under Free Cash Flow Methodology

The following discussion will focus on modeling assets on a policy year basis. This is consistent with the formulas and approach used in Chapters 4 through 11. The annual formulas can be easily adapted to other periods, such as months or quarters.

Rebalancing of the assets backing a portfolio of liabilities can take place every time asset and liability cash flows take place. In an insurance company, cash flows take place every business day. For modeling purposes, we will assume that cash flows occur only at the beginning, middle, and end of the year. We will assume that rebalancing occurs only at the end of the year.

The company's total cash flow for the period must reflect cash received from and paid to all of the parties that the company deals with, including its customers, owners, employees, service providers, tax authorities, lenders, and borrowers. Cash received consists mainly of premiums from customers and investment returns generated by the company's investments, such as coupons, interest payments, dividends, rents, repayments of principal, and proceeds from the sale of assets.

Cash disbursed consists mainly of benefits paid to customers, expenses paid to employees and other service providers, net payments to reinsurers, and taxes paid. The company may also have to make principal and interest payments on any funds it has borrowed. Capital contributions received from stockholders or stockholder dividends paid are part of free cash flow. These amounts will be solved for in the formulas below.

Let

$$
\begin{aligned}
\text{AssetCashFlow}(t) = {} & \text{Asset cash flow for the entire year,} \\
& \text{including coupons, dividends, interest,} \\
& \text{principal repayments, and proceeds from} \\
& \text{the sale of assets. Asset cash flows are} \\
& \text{based on assets invested at the beginning} \\
& \text{of the year.} \\
\text{AssetCashFlowBeg}(t) = {} & \text{Asset cash flow at the beginning of the} \\
& \text{year} \\
\text{AssetCashFlowMid}(t) = {} & \text{Asset cash flow at the middle of the year} \\
\text{AssetCashFlowEnd}(t) = {} & \text{Asset cash flow at the end of the year} \\
\text{LiabCashFlowBeg}(t) = {} & \text{Liability cash flow, consisting of} \\
& \text{premiums less benefits, expenses, and} \\
& \text{taxes, all net of reinsurance, at the} \\
& \text{beginning of the year. Taxes include tax} \\
& \text{on investment income earned on assets} \\
& \text{backing required capital, plus tax on} \\
& \text{interest received less interest paid.} \\
\text{LiabCashFlowMid}(t) = {} & \text{Liability cash flow at the middle of the} \\
& \text{year} \\
\text{LiabCashFlowEnd}(t) = {} & \text{Liability cash flow at the end of the year} \\
\text{IntReceivedRate}(t) = {} & \text{Semiannual interest rate earned on} \\
& \text{positive cumulative cash flows} \\
\text{IntReceivedMid}(t) = {} & \text{Interest received on positive cumulative} \\
& \text{cash flows at the middle of the year}
\end{aligned}
$$

$\text{IntReceivedEnd}(t) =$ Interest received at the end of the year

$\text{IntPaidRate}(t) =$ Semiannual interest paid on funds borrowed to offset negative cumulative cash flows

$\text{IntPaidMid}(t) =$ Interest paid on current year borrowings at the middle of the year

$\text{IntPaidEnd}(t) =$ Interest paid at the end of the year

$\text{CumCashFlowBeg}(t) =$ Cumulative cash flow at the beginning of the year, consisting of asset and liability cash flows at the beginning of the year

$\text{CumCashFlowMid}(t) =$ Cumulative cash flow at the middle of the year, equal to $\text{CumCashFlowBeg}(t)$ plus asset and liability cash flows and interest received or paid at the middle of the year

$\text{CumCashFlowEnd}(t) =$ Cumulative cash flow at the end of the year, equal to $\text{CumCashFlowMid}(t)$ plus asset and liability cash flows and interest received or paid at the end of the year

$\text{AssetsEnd}(t) =$ Book value at the end of the year of beginning-of-the-year assets still in place

$\text{AssetsReq}(t) =$ Assets required at the end of the year, equal to solvency reserves plus required capital

$\text{InvIncome}(t) =$ Investment income earned during the year on beginning-of-the-year assets

$\text{FreeCashFlow}(t) =$ Funds available at the end of the year after bringing invested assets in line with the sum of solvency reserves and required capital.

The following steps are performed at the beginning and middle of the year:

1. Cumulative cash flow is determined.

2. If cumulative cash flow is positive, then interest received at the next cash flow date is calculated as a half-year's interest on this cumulative cash flow.

3. If the cumulative cash flow is negative, then interest paid at the next cash flow date is calculated as a half-year's interest on this cumulative cash flow. This assumes that an amount equal to the cumulative negative cash flow is borrowed, as opposed to selling assets to cover the negative cash flow.

At the end of the year, cumulative cash flow for the year is determined and added to accumulated assets. If accumulated assets are less then the sum of solvency reserves and required capital, then a capital contribution equal to the shortfall is required. If total assets are greater than the sum of solvency reserves and required capital, then the excess can be distributed.

14.3.5.1 Beginning of the Year

The book value of assets at the beginning of the year is the same as the assets required at the end of the previous year, which equals the sum of solvency reserves and required capital at the end of the previous year:

$$\text{AssetsReq}(t - 1) = \text{SolvRes}(t - 1) + \text{ReqCap}(t - 1). \quad (14.3.10)$$

Cumulative cash flow is calculated as the cash flows at the beginning of the year:

$$\text{CumCashFlowBeg}(t) = \text{AssetCashFlowBeg}(t)$$
$$+ \text{LiabCashFlowBeg}(t). \quad (14.3.11)$$

If $\text{CumCashFlowBeg}(t) < 0$, then funds must be borrowed to cover the negative cash flow, so interest paid at the middle of the year is calculated and $\text{IntReceivedMid}(t) = 0$:

$$\text{IntPaidMid}(t) = \text{CumCashFlowBeg}(t)\,\text{IntPaidRate}(t). \quad (14.3.12)$$

If $\text{CumCashFlowBeg}(t) > 0$, then this amount earns interest, so interest received at the middle of the year is calculated and $\text{IntPaidMid}(t) = 0$:

$$\text{IntReceivedMid}(t) = \text{CumCashFlowBeg}(t)\,\text{IntReceivedRate}(t).$$
$$(14.3.13)$$

14.3.5.2 Middle of the Year

Cumulative cash flow is calculated as cumulative cash flow from the beginning of the year plus the cash flows at the middle of the year:

$$\begin{aligned}
\text{CumCashFlowMid}(t) = {} & \text{CumCashFlowBeg}(t) \\
& + \text{AssetCashFlowMid}(t) \\
& + \text{LiabCashFlowMid}(t) \\
& + \text{IntReceivedMid}(t) \\
& - \text{IntPaidMid}(t).
\end{aligned} \qquad (14.3.14)$$

If $\text{CumCashFlowMid}(t) < 0$, then funds must be borrowed to cover the negative cash flow, so interest paid at the end of the year is calculated and $\text{IntReceivedEnd}(t) = 0$:

$$\text{IntPaidEnd}(t) = \text{CumCashFlowMid}(t)\,\text{IntPaidRate}(t). \qquad (14.3.15)$$

If $\text{CumCashFlowMid}(t) > 0$, then this amount earns interest, so interest received at the end of the year is calculated and $\text{IntPaidEnd}(t) = 0$:

$$\text{IntReceivedEnd}(t) = \text{CumCashFlowMid}(t)\,\text{IntReceivedRate}(t). \qquad (14.3.16)$$

14.3.5.3   End of the Year

Cumulative cash flow is calculated as cumulative cash flow from the middle of the year plus the cash flows at the end of the year:

$$\begin{aligned}
\text{CumCashFlowEnd}(t) = {} & \text{CumCashFlowMid}(t) \\
& + \text{AssetCashFlowEnd}(t) \\
& + \text{LiabCashFlowEnd}(t) \\
& + \text{IntReceivedEnd}(t) \\
& - \text{IntPaidEnd}(t).
\end{aligned} \qquad (14.3.17)$$

The book value of the beginning-of-the-year assets still in place at the end of the year can be tracked by making two observations: (1) Investment income includes both asset cash flow and the change in book value and (2) in Formulas 14.3.11, 14.3.14, and 14.3.17, asset cash flow is "diverted" to each period's cumulative cash flow, rather than being allocated to the beginning-of-the-year assets. This means that the book value of these assets can be calculated as beginning assets plus investment income minus asset cash flow:

$$\begin{aligned}
\text{AssetsEnd}(t) = {} & \text{AssetsReq}(t-1) + \text{InvIncome}(t) \\
& - \text{AssetCashFlow}(t).
\end{aligned} \qquad (14.3.18)$$

14.3.5.4 Free Cash Flow

It is given that the book value of assets required at the end of the year is the sum of solvency reserves and required capital at the end of the year:

$$\text{AssetsReq}(t) = \text{SolvRes}(t) + \text{ReqCap}(t). \tag{14.3.19}$$

The actual book value of assets at the end of the year, before any capital contribution or distribution, is AssetsEnd(t) plus the current year cash flow, CumCashFlowEnd(t). Free cash flow is calculated as the amount needed to bring total assets back in balance with required assets at the end of the year:

$$\text{AssetsEnd}(t) + \text{CumCashFlowEnd}(t) - \text{FreeCashFlow}(t)$$
$$= \text{AssetsReq}(t). \tag{14.3.20}$$

Substituting using Formulas 14.3.17, 14.3.18, and 14.3.10, and rearranging terms, we develop the following formula for free cash flow:

$$\begin{aligned}
\text{FreeCashFlow}(t) = {} & \text{SolvRes}(t-1) + \text{ReqCap}(t-1) \\
& - \text{SolvRes}(t) - \text{ReqCap}(t) \\
& + \text{CumCashFlowEnd}(t) + \text{InvIncome}(t) \\
& - \text{AssetCashFlow}(t). \tag{14.3.21}
\end{aligned}$$

Formula 14.3.21 can be restated as

$$\begin{aligned}
\text{FreeCashFlow}(t) = {} & \text{CumCashFlowEnd}(t) + \text{InvIncome}(t) \\
& - \text{AssetCashFlow}(t) - \text{SolvResIncr}(t) \\
& - \text{ReqCapIncr}(t). \tag{14.3.22}
\end{aligned}$$

Example 14.3.7 illustrates free cash flow for two policy years.

Example 14.3.7 Free Cash Flow

The first part of this example illustrates new business, which begins the year with no solvency reserves and no required capital. Therefore, there are no assets at the beginning of the year and no asset cash flows. Liability cash flows consist mainly of premiums less acquisition costs at the beginning of the year, death claims at the middle of the year, and taxes at the end of the year. Assume that positive cumulative cash flows earn interest at a rate of 6% and that debt (negative cumulative cash flows) is charged interest at a rate of 7%.

Policy Year 1	Beg	Mid	End
LiabCashFlow	−5.00000	−1.00000	2.50000
AssetCashFlow	0.00000	0.00000	0.00000
IntReceived	0.00000	0.00000	0.00000
IntPaid	0.00000	0.17204	0.21237
Cash Flow	−5.00000	−1.17204	2.28763
CumCashFlow	−5.00000	−6.17204	−3.88441
InvIncome			0.00000
Incr. in AssetReq			2.00000
Free Cash Flow			−5.88441

The second part of this example illustrates the second policy year, which begins with assets equal to 2.00, earning an interest rate of 6.09%. Asset cash flows consist of the resulting investment income, plus some principal repayment. Liability cash flows consist mainly of premiums at the beginning of the year, death claims at the middle of the year, and taxes at the end of the year. Again, positive cumulative cash flows earn interest at a rate of 6%, and debt (negative cumulative cash flows) is charged interest at a rate of 7%.

Policy Year 2	Beg	Mid	End
LiabCashFlow	3.50000	−1.25000	−1.25000
AssetCashFlow	0.00000	0.06882	0.06882
IntReceived	0.00000	0.10347	0.07161
IntPaid	0.00000	0.00000	0.00000
Cash Flow	3.50000	−1.07771	−1.10957
CumCash Flow	3.50000	2.42229	1.31272
InvIncome			0.12000
Incr.in AssetReq			1.00000
Free Cash Flow			0.29508

14.3.5.5   Free Cash Flow and Distributable Earnings

If we subtract asset cash flows from total cash flows for the year, we are left with liability cash flows and interest received less interest paid. Using this observation, we can alter Formula 14.3.22 to obtain the following:

$$
\begin{aligned}
\text{FreeCashFlow}(t) = {} & \text{LiabCashFlow}(t) + \text{InvIncome}(t) \\
& + \text{IntReceived}(t) - \text{IntPaid}(t) \\
& - \text{SolvResIncr}(t) - \text{ReqCapIncr}(t). \quad (14.3.23)
\end{aligned}
$$

Remembering that liability cash flows consist of product cash flows (premiums less benefits and expenses) and taxes, we find that Formula 14.3.23 is a new formula for distributable earnings. In Chapters 8 and 11, investment income included interest earned on current-year cash flows, so interest received and interest paid were not separate items. Comparing their definitions, it is not surprising that distributable earnings and free cash flow are two names for the same concept.

Several exercises at the end of this chapter will demonstrate that free cash flow and distributable earnings are one and the same. Before performing the exercises, it may be helpful to consider two extreme investment policies:

1. All assets are non-dividend-paying common stocks. Investment income results only from the increasing market value of these assets. As long as these assets are held, no asset cash flows are received.

2. All assets are one-year bonds, with all principal repaid at the end of each year. These assets result in maximum asset cash flow, equal to assets at the beginning of the year plus investment income.

To determine the effect of each of these investment policies on free cash flow, let us examine Formula 14.3.22. Surprisingly, we see that asset cash flows do not affect free cash flow! This gives us an insight into the nature of free cash flow and distributable earnings: While these amounts can be withdrawn (if negative, they need to be contributed), the actual cash needs of the business may be quite different. For example, net cash flow for the year can be negative while distributable earnings are positive. In this case, the company would have to cover the cash shortfall by borrowing money or selling assets. If the company wants to pay out distributable earnings to its owners, additional cash will need to be raised.

14.3.6   Validation of Asset Model

To validate the results of your model, a number of comparisons can be made. You can check the average interest rates for each period by comparing them to the assumed yields earned on new and existing assets. You can compare asset purchases with the resulting asset net cash flows that follow. For example, if the average asset purchased is a ten-year bond, you could compare the assets purchased one year with the resulting asset cash flows ten years later. While these amounts would not be expected to exactly match, they should be in the same range.

If you are modeling a portfolio of existing assets, you will want to match initial values produced by the model with actual starting values such as par value, book value, and average yield. To check the reliability of the asset model, you can model the asset portfolio from a year earlier to see if your model can reproduce the actual investment results of the prior year. If assets were actively traded during the year, the results may be hard to reproduce.

14.3.7 Asset Model Output

The output produced by the asset model may include a number of items for each period, such as

- Liability cash flows (product cash flows net of distributable earnings and taxes)
- Assets purchased
- Asset cash flows
- Loans to fund cash shortfalls and repayment of the resulting principal and interest
- Investment income
- Book value of assets
- Market value of assets
- Average yield on new assets purchased
- Average yield on the entire asset portfolio
- Average duration of new assets purchased, and
- Average duration of the entire asset portfolio.

More sophisticated models may calculate market values and reflect the sale of assets to cover cash shortfalls. In addition, details of each period's asset purchases may be available, such as the asset class, quality, maturity, and yield for each future asset purchased.

14.4 Asset/Liability Matching

By matching assets and liabilities, a company can reduce the financial effect of changes in interest rates. This is the largest risk many companies face. Matching assets and liabilities is also referred to as *immunization,* because it immunizes a company from changes in interest rates. More than a few companies could have been saved from bankruptcy had they employed an asset/liability matching strategy.

This section will develop two basic methods of matching assets and liabilities: (1) exact matching and (2) duration matching. In addition, horizon matching, a hybrid of these two basic methods, will be discussed. If assets and liabilities are well matched, there should be no need to borrow money to cover cash shortfalls.

To simplify the presentation, we will assume that liability cash flows are unaffected by changes in interest rates. For products with a significant savings component, this assumption is not realistic. Chapter 15 will overcome this problem by linking interest rates to liability cash flows.

14.4.1 Exact Matching

Recall that liability cash flows consist of product cash flows (premiums less benefits and expenses, all net of reinsurance) and taxes paid. In a perfect world, future liability cash flows would be exactly known. Assets purchased would result in asset cash flows that exactly matched or offset future liability cash flows. Such a world does not usually exist. However, there are situations in which exact matching of cash flows can be done, although they are rare.

To create an exact matching of assets and liabilities, you begin by matching the final liability cash flows and then work backward to the present time. Often, there are no assets long enough to match the longest or final liability cash flows. (*Long* refers to a long-term asset or liability that lasts many years into the future. *Short* refers to an asset or liability that is relatively short term.) For example, in North America, there are few assets that mature more than 30 years in the future. As a result, exact matching may not be possible for liability cash flows beyond 30 years.

Once the longest liabilities have been matched with noncallable assets, you can then proceed to match the next-longest liabilities. This process continues until all future cash outflows have been matched. There are several practical problems with exact matching:

1. Premium-paying products generate positive cash flows for a number of years, as long as premiums exceed benefits paid. These future positive cash flows will be used to purchase future assets. These future assets cannot be made to match future liabilities until they are

purchased, unless you can devise some other clever solution, as in Example 14.4.5. As a result, the company may have some risk related to future interest rates. More likely, you will need to factor future asset purchases into your matching plans. For example, if there is no disintermediation risk, your strategy might be to purchase assets to match the longest duration liabilities first, to minimize the effect if interest rates were to drop. If there *is* significant disintermediation risk, however, your strategy might be just the opposite: to purchase assets to match the shortest-duration liabilities first.

2. If an asset defaults or repays prematurely, the matching is thrown out of balance. Additional assets must be purchased to rebalance the portfolio.

3. If liability cash flows deviate significantly from expected, the portfolio will need to be rebalanced.

14.4.2 Exact Matching Case Study

The concept of exact matching is best illustrated by working through a case study. Start with the stream-of-liability cash flows shown in Table 14.4.1.

Table 14.4.1 Liability Cash Flows

t	Liability Cash Flow
0.25	−35.00
0.50	−30.00
0.75	−35.00
1.00	−30.00
1.25	−25.00
1.50	−55.00
1.75	−65.00
2.00	−75.00
2.25	−85.00
2.50	−100.00

Further, assume that the assets purchased will be only noncallable bonds that pay semiannual coupons. Bonds that mature at the end of each quarter are available for purchase.

We use the notation defined for bonds in the previous section, but we assume that all of the bond values (price, coupon, par value, and so on) are for one bond unit with a par value of 100. Our goal is to determine how many units of each bond should be purchased at time zero to match future liability cash flows. Let

LiabCashFlow(t) = Liability cash flow at time t

b = Bond identifier; for this example, b will assume values of 0.25, 0.50, . . . , 2.25, and 2.50, which will identify the term or time to maturity of the bond.

BondUnits(b) = Units of bond b that will be purchased at time 0 to match the liability cash flows; for example, Units(2.50) is the number of units of 2.50-year bonds that will be purchased.

By working backwards, we can determine the amount and maturity date of each bond we need to purchase to exactly match the liability cash flows.

First, we will consider the bond that matures at time 2.50. At time 2.50, this bond will generate two cash flows: a coupon payment and a maturity payment. These two cash flows must equal the liability cash flow at time 2.50:

$$\text{BondUnits}(2.50)\ (\text{Coupon}(2.50) + \text{ParValue}(2.50))$$
$$= \text{LiabCashFlow}(2.50). \quad (14.4.1)$$

Rearranging terms, we can determine how many units of 2.50-year bonds we must purchase to match liability cash flows at time 2.50:

$$\text{BondUnits}(2.50) = \frac{\text{LiabCashFlow}(2.50)}{\text{Coupon}(2.50) + \text{ParValue}(2.50)}. \quad (14.4.2)$$

The bond that matures at time 2.25 will generate two cash flows at time 2.25: a coupon payment and a maturity payment. To match the liability cash flow at time 2.25, a similar formula is developed:

$$\text{BondUnits}(2.25) = \frac{\text{LiabCashFlow}(2.25)}{\text{Coupon}(2.25) + \text{ParValue}(2.25)}. \quad (14.4.3)$$

At time 2.00, three cash flows will be generated: a coupon payment and a maturity payment for the 2.00-year bond and a coupon payment for the 2.50-year bond. This results in a slightly different formula to match the liability cash flow at time 2.00:

$$\begin{aligned}
\text{BondUnits}(2.00) \, (\text{Coupon}(2.00) + \text{ParValue}(2.00)) \\
+ \, \text{BondUnits}(2.50) \\
\text{Coupon}(2.50) \\
= \text{LiabCashFlow}(2.00). \quad (14.4.4)
\end{aligned}$$

This results in

$$\begin{aligned}
\text{BondUnits}(2.00) = \\
\frac{\text{LiabCashFlow}(2.00) - \text{BondUnits}(2.50) \, \text{Coupon}(2.50)}{\text{Coupon}(2.00) + \text{ParValue}(2.00)}.
\end{aligned}$$
$$(14.4.5)$$

Extending this logic, you can deduce that there will be three cash flows at time 1.75, four cash flows at times 1.50 and 1.25, five cash flows at times 1.00 and 0.75, and six cash flows at times 0.50 and 0.25. For example, the formula for BondUnits(0.50) is

$$\begin{aligned}
\text{BondUnits}(0.50) = \\
\frac{\text{LiabCashFlow}(0.50) - \sum_{b=1.00,1.50,2.00,\text{and } 2.50} \text{BondUnits}(b) \, \text{Coupon}(b)}{\text{Coupon}(0.50) + \text{ParValue}(0.50)}. \quad (14.4.6)
\end{aligned}$$

Using formulas like 14.4.3, 14.4.4 and 14.4.6, you can calculate bond units for maturity dates starting with 2.50 and working backward to 0.25. The results for this case study are shown in Table 14.4.2. "Coupon Rate" and "Bond Units × Par Value" are associated with the Bond ID. "Asset Cash Flow" is associated with Time (the first column) and consists of cash flows from one to five different Bond IDs.

Table 14.4.2 Exact Matching of Asset and Liability Cash Flows

Time	Liability Cash Flow	b(Bond ID)	Coupon Rate	Bond Units × Par Value	Asset Cash Flow
0.25	−35.00	0.25	4.00%	27.8060	35.0000
0.50	−30.00	0.50	4.50	20.7854	30.0000
0.75	−35.00	0.75	5.00	28.3621	35.0000
1.00	−30.00	1.00	5.50	21.2531	30.0000
1.25	−25.00	1.25	6.00	19.0711	25.0000
1.50	−55.00	1.50	6.50	46.8375	55.0000
1.75	−65.00	1.75	7.00	59.6433	65.0000
2.00	−75.00	2.00	7.50	68.3598	75.0000
2.25	−85.00	2.25	8.00	81.7308	85.0000
2.50	−100.00	2.50	8.50	95.9233	100.0000

14.4.3 Duration Matching

It is not usually practical or even possible to exactly match all future asset and liability cash flows. A more common approach is to match the duration of assets to the duration of liabilities. As we shall see later in this section, duration has another use. It is an excellent predictor of the effect of small interest rate changes on the present value of cash flows.

If asset and liability durations have been matched, then small changes in interest rates will have an equal effect on assets and liabilities. The effect on assets and liabilities will be offsetting, thereby immunizing the company from the risk associated with small changes in interest rates.

The company will have to rebalance its asset portfolio from time to time in order to maintain the matching of assets and liabilities. This periodic rebalancing is needed for a number of reasons, such as changes in interest rates, defaults or sales of assets, and emerging differences between actual and expected liability cash flows.

14.4.3.1 Macaulay Duration

Duration is a measure of the average time of a series of cash flows. *Macaulay duration* is calculated as the weighted average time of a series of cash flows, with the present value of the cash flows used as weights: Let

$$\text{MacDuration}(i) = \text{Macaulay duration of a series of cash flows,}$$
$$\text{with present values based on an interest rate}$$
$$\text{of } i$$

$$\text{CashFlow}(t) = \text{Cash flow at time } t\text{: The series of cash flows is}$$
$$\text{assumed to start at time 0 and end at time } n.$$

Then, using $v = 1/(1 + i)$,

$$\text{MacDuration}(i) = \frac{\sum_{t=0}^{n} t \, v^t \text{CashFlow}(t)}{\sum_{t=0}^{n} v^t \text{CashFlow}(t)} \tag{14.4.7}$$

The Macaulay duration of a single cash flow is the time of that cash flow. For example, the Macaulay duration of a single cash flow at time 10 is ten. The Macaulay duration of multiple cash flows is the weighted average time of the cash flows. For example, the Macaulay duration of three cash flows of one at times 0, 1, and 2 using 11.11% interest is

$$\text{MacDuration}(11.11\%)$$
$$= \frac{0 \, (1.00) + 1 \, (0.90) + 2 \, (0.81)}{1.00 + 0.90 + 0.81} = 0.9299.$$

Liability cash flows are often cash outflows and consist of product cash flows (premiums net of benefits and expenses) less taxes. Asset cash flows are normally cash inflows and consist of coupon payments, maturity payments, mortgage loan payments, principal repayments, sales of assets, and so on.

When matching asset and liability durations, it is crucial that both durations be calculated using the same interest rate. The interest rate used is usually a current interest rate. Rather than use a single interest rate, a series of future interest rates can be used when calculating duration. This approach allows you to reflect the different yields currently available for assets of different maturities. For example, if one-year bonds yield 5% and 30-year bonds yield 7%, you might use a series of interest rates that start with 5% in the first year and rapidly increase over the next few years toward 7%.

14.4.3.2 Modified Duration

The better known and more useful cousin of Macaulay duration is *modified duration,* which is used to estimate the effect of a small change in interest rates on the present value of cash flows. Modified duration is useful in predicting changes in present values due to interest rate changes. Because of this, modified duration is what most professionals mean when they use the term *duration.* Modified duration can be defined as the percentage decrease in the present value of cash flows resulting from a small increase in the interest rate. Let

$$\text{PVCashFlow}(i) = \text{Present value of a series of cash flows}$$
$$\text{discounted at an interest rate of } i$$
$$\text{ModDuration}(i) = \text{Modified duration of a series of cash flows,}$$
$$\text{with present values based on an interest rate}$$
$$\text{of } i.$$

The present value of cash flows is the denominator of Macaulay duration:

$$\text{PVCashFlow}(i) = \sum_{t=0}^{n} v^t \text{CashFlow}(t). \tag{14.4.8}$$

Using calculus, modified duration can be more precisely defined. It is equal to -1 times the derivative, with respect to the interest rate, of the present value of cash flows, all divided by the present value of cash flows. In other words,

$$\text{ModDuration}(i) = -\frac{d(\text{PVCashFlow}(i))/di}{\text{PVCashFlow}(i)} \tag{14.4.9}$$

Because the derivative of v^t with respect to i is equal to $-t\, v^{t+1}$, we have

$$\text{ModDuration}(i) = \frac{\sum_{t=0}^{n} t v^{t+1} \text{CashFlow}(t)}{\sum_{t=0}^{n} v^{t} \text{CashFlow}(t)}. \qquad (14.4.10)$$

Comparing Formulas 14.4.7 and 14.4.10, we can see that the two durations are closely related:

$$\text{ModDuration}(i) = \frac{\text{MacDuration}(i)}{1 + i}. \qquad (14.4.11)$$

Modified duration can be used to calculate the change in PVCashFlow(i) for small changes in interest rates by using the following relationship:

$$\text{Percentage change in PVCashFlow}(i) = - \text{ModDuration}(i) \\ \times (\text{Change in } i). \ (14.4.12)$$

As an example, let us calculate duration for the liability cash flows shown in Table 14.4.1, using an interest rate of 7.00%.

Example 14.4.1 Duration for Liability Cash Flows

t	i = 7.00%		
	Liability Cash Flow	*Present Value*	*t × Present Value*
0.25	−35.00	−34.41	−8.60
0.50	−30.00	−29.00	−14.50
0.75	−35.00	−33.27	−24.95
1.00	−30.00	−28.04	−28.04
1.25	−25.00	−22.97	−28.72
1.50	−55.00	−49.69	−74.54
1.75	−65.00	−57.74	−101.05
2.00	−75.00	−65.51	−131.02
2.25	−85.00	−73.00	−164.24
2.50	−100.00	−84.44	−211.10
Sum:		−478.07	−786.75
Macauley Duration:			1.6457
Modified Duration:			1.5380

The resulting Macaulay duration, the weighted average time for the cash flows, is 1.6457. Modified duration is obtained from Macaulay duration by dividing by 1.07.

As another example, consider a 2.50-year bond with an 8.50% coupon rate. We will calculate durations and PVCashFlow for three different interest rates: 8.50%, 8.51%, and 9.50%.

Example 14.4.2 Duration for a 2.50-Year Bond (Par Value = 100, Coupon = 8.50%)

t	Cash Flow	$i = 8.50\%$		$i = 8.51\%$		$i = 9.50\%$	
		Present Value	$t \times$ Present Value	Present Value	$t \times$ Present Value	Present Value	$t \times$ Present Value
0.25	0.0000	0.0000	0.0000	0.0000	0.0000	0.0000	0.0000
0.50	4.2500	4.0801	2.0401	4.0799	2.0400	4.0615	2.0307
0.75	0.0000	0.0000	0.0000	0.0000	0.0000	0.0000	0.0000
1.00	4.2500	3.9171	3.9171	3.9167	3.9167	3.8813	3.8813
1.25	0.0000	0.0000	0.0000	0.0000	0.0000	0.0000	0.0000
1.50	4.2500	3.7605	5.6407	3.7600	5.6400	3.7091	5.5636
1.75	0.0000	0.0000	0.0000	0.0000	0.0000	0.0000	0.0000
2.00	4.2500	3.6102	7.2204	3.6095	7.2190	3.5445	7.0891
2.25	0.0000	0.0000	0.0000	0.0000	0.0000	0.0000	0.0000
2.50	104.2500	85.0162	212.5405	84.9966	212.4915	83.0885	207.7212
Sum:		100.3841	231.3587	100.3627	231.3072	98.2848	226.2859
Macauley Dur.:			2.3047		2.3047		2.3023
Modified Dur.:			2.1242		2.2106		2.1026

The coupon rate of 8.50% results in an annual effective yield of 8.68%. This explains why PVCashFlow(8.50%) is equal to 100.3841 instead of 100.0000.

We can use Example 14.4.2 to test the accuracy of modified duration in predicting changes in the present value of cash flows. For example, predict the decrease in the present value of cash flows for a 0.01% and a 1.00% increase in interest rates.

Example 14.4.3 Predicted vs. Actual Change in PVCashFlow

Modified Duration	Change in Interest Rate	Predicted PVCashFlow	Actual PVCashFlow	Percentage Error
2.1242	0.01%	100.362737	100.362741	0.000004%
2.1242	1.00	98.251703	98.284846	0.033733

As Example 14.4.3 shows, the percentage error is many times less for the smaller change in interest rate, as a percentage of the present value of cash flows.

Example 14.4.4 Simple Immunization

In this example, we start with the liability cash flows from Table 14.4.1 and design a portfolio of assets that immunizes the company from changes in interest rates. We accomplish this by calculating the duration of the liability cash flows and designing an asset portfolio with matching duration. Convexity is ignored.

Only three bonds are available for purchase: the 0.75-year bond, the 1.50-year bond, and the 2.50-year bond shown in Table 14.4.2. The effective yield to maturity of each bond is equal to its annual coupon rate. Defaults and investment expenses are ignored.

First, the modified duration of the liability cash flows is calculated using an interest rate of 7.00%. The result, shown in Example 14.4.1, is 1.5380. Next, the three bonds are combined into the three different portfolios shown in Table 14.4.3. Each of these portfolios has been designed to produce a modified duration that matches the modified duration of the liabilities. Note that the modified durations for assets have been calculated using the same interest rate used to calculate the modified duration of the liabilities.

Table 14.4.3 Three Asset Portfolios with Matching Durations (*i* = 7.0%)

	Sample Portfolio 1			Sample Portfolio 2			Sample Portfolio 3		
	0.75-year bond weight: 5.00% *1.50-year bond weight: 69.14%* *2.50-year bond weight: 25.86%*			*0.75-year bond weight: 10.00%* *1.50-year bond weight: 60.12%* *2.50-year bond weight: 29.88%*			*0.75-year bond weight: 15.00* *1.50-year bond weight: 51.09* *2.50-year bond weight: 33.91*		
t	*Cash Flow*	*Present Value*	*t × Present Value*	*Cash Flow*	*Present Value*	*t × Present Value*	*Cash Flow*	*Present Value*	*t × Present Value*
0.25	0.59	0.58	0.15	1.18	1.16	0.29	1.77	1.74	0.44
0.50	15.96	15.43	7.72	15.38	14.86	7.43	14.79	14.30	7.15
0.75	24.19	22.99	17.24	48.38	45.99	34.49	72.57	68.98	51.73
1.00	15.96	14.92	14.92	15.38	14.37	14.37	14.79	13.82	13.82
1.25	0.00	0.00	0.00	0.00	0.00	0.00	0.00	0.00	0.00
1.50	346.01	312.62	468.93	302.36	273.18	409.77	258.70	233.74	350.60
1.75	0.00	0.00	0.00	0.00	0.00	0.00	0.00	0.00	0.00
2.00	5.23	4.57	9.14	6.05	5.28	10.57	6.86	5.99	11.99
2.25	0.00	0.00	0.00	0.00	0.00	0.00	0.00	0.00	0.00
2.50	128.40	108.42	271.05	148.37	125.28	313.20	168.34	142.14	355.36
Sum:		479.53	789.15		480.12	790.12		480.71	791.09
Macauley Dur.:			1.6457			1.6457			1.6457
Modified Dur.:			1.5380			1.5380			1.5380

In actual practice, the universe of available investments is much larger than the three investment choices assumed in Table 14.4.3. However, this does illustrate that many different combinations of assets can be used to achieve duration matching.

With duration matching, there is not an exact matching of cash flows. If you compare the asset cash flows in each of the above portfolios to the liability cash flows of Table 14.4.1, you will notice that most of the asset cash flows are less than the liability cash flows at times 0.25, 0.50, 1.00, 1.25, 1.75, 2.00, and 2.25. Asset cash flows mostly exceed liability cash flows in the other periods.

These asset/liability mismatches are important. Duration matching implicitly assumes that the asset/liability mismatches in each period can be offset by investing or borrowing at the interest rate used to calculate the duration. This can be a dangerous assumption. It is possible to match duration and have a terrible mismatch of cash flows.

For example, imagine two liability cash flows at times 0 and 10 that combine to produce a duration of four. If these cash flows were matched with a single asset cash flow at time 4, cash flows would be terribly mismatched while durations matched exactly.

14.4.3.3 Convexity

When we use duration to predict the change in PVCashFlow(i), we are assuming that PVCashFlow(i) varies linearly with i. This is true for only a narrow range of interest rates. Duration is a first-order, linear approximation based on the first derivative of PVCashFlow(i).

To predict changes in PVCashFlow(i) over a wider range of interest rates, we can add a second-order, convex (that is, shaped like x^2) approximation based on the second derivative of PVCashFlow(i). This second-order term is called *convexity* and is calculated as the second derivative of PVCashFlow(i) with respect to i, divided by PVCashFlow(i). Let

> Convexity(i) = The second-order term used in conjunction with modified duration to more accurately calculate the percentage change in PVCashFlow(i) caused by a small change in interest rate.

Because the second derivative of v^t with respect to i is equal to $t(t + 1)v^{t+2}$, we have

$$\text{Convexity}(i) = \frac{\sum_{t=0}^{n} t(t + 1)v^{t+2} \, \text{CashFlow}(t)}{\sum_{t=0}^{n} v^t \, \text{CashFlow}(t)}. \qquad (14.4.13)$$

Modified duration and convexity are combined to more accurately calculate the effect of a change in interest rates on PVCashFlow(i):

Percentage change in PVCashFlow(i)
$$= - \text{ModDuration}(i)(\text{Change in } i)$$
$$+ \tfrac{1}{2} \text{Convexity}(i)(\text{Change in } i)^2. \qquad (14.4.14)$$

While Formula 14.4.14 will produce more accurate results than Formula 14.4.12 over a slightly wider range of interest rates, it also has its limitations. You cannot expect a formula with two terms to reproduce the complexity of the n cash flows contained in PVCashFlow(i).

You could increase the accuracy of Formula 14.4.14 for a wider range of interest rates by adding third and fourth terms based on the third and fourth derivatives. While these additional terms are not difficult to calculate, they do add significantly to the complexity of the matching process.

In practice, few companies go beyond duration and convexity. When matching using convexity, you would first calculate duration and convexity for the liability cash flows. You could then develop different asset portfolios that match the duration of the liability cash flows, as shown in Example 14.4.5. The various asset portfolios with matching durations will likely have different convexities. By blending two of the asset portfolios in the right proportions, you should be able to match the convexity of the liabilities.

For example, suppose the liability cash flows have a convexity of 20.0 and two asset portfolios have convexities of 15.0 and 25.0. The asset portfolios could be blended 50/50 to achieve the desired convexity of 20.0.

14.4.4 Horizon Matching

A third strategy that is often employed is a hybrid between exact matching and duration matching. With horizon matching, assets are purchased to match as closely as possible the liability cash flows for the first several years, such as the first five or ten years. In general, the cash flows in the early durations are more predictable, and therefore easier to match.

The remaining liability cash flows (such as those after the first five or ten years) are then matched using duration matching. As these later cash flows become nearer-term cash flows, the matching process is gradually adjusted to cover these cash flows on an exact matching basis.

14.4.5 Product Cash Flow Matching

The case study in Section 14.4.2 concentrates on using assets available for purchase to match up with the liability cash flows. However, there may be opportunities within a company to use one product's cash flow patterns to help match or offset another product's cash flows. Example 14.4.5 gives a real-life example of product matching.

Example 14.4.5 Matching a Term to 100 Portfolio

An insurance company in Canada insured a large amount of Term to 100 business in the late 1980s. This business had predictable liability cash flows that were positive for the first seven or so years and negative thereafter. Cash surrender values were available, but were much less than reserves held by the company. In other words, an increase in surrenders would generate a windfall for the company.

An important risk in a typical Term to 100 portfolio is that the cash inflows in the early years may have to be invested at rates that are less than those assumed in the original pricing. This would result in investment income earned in the later years not being sufficient to cover cash outflows.

Therefore, at a time when interest rates were relatively high, the company decided to sell short-term immediate annuities with future cash outflows that closely matched the remainder of their Term to 100 cash inflows. The positive Term to 100 cash inflows were then used to pay the annuity cash outflows.

The company was then able to use the annuity premiums to purchase noncallable long-term bonds with cash flows that exactly matched the expected Term to 100 cash outflows for the next 30 or more years. This enabled the company to lock in relatively high interest rates for the next 30 years with virtually no reinvestment risk and no disintermediation risk.

14.4.6   Summary of Asset/Liability Matching

Asset/liability matching is a difficult concept. It is difficult to grasp, even more difficult to communicate, and especially difficult to implement. It requires a degree of collaboration between liability experts (usually actuaries) and investment professionals that is hard to achieve.

Collaboration is needed, not only for the initial matching, but also to ensure that appropriate rebalancing takes place to keep assets matched with liabilities.

We discussed two primary methods of matching assets and liabilities. While exact matching of all cash flows is preferred, it is rarely practical or possible. In most cases, you will be faced with matching duration and possibly convexity too. Matching duration and convexity results in, at best, a rough overall level of matching. Year-by-year cash flows can be significantly mismatched. Because of this, you may want to adopt one of the following strategies, depending on the most significant risk associated with the liabilities:

1. If disintermediation is the most significant risk, your asset duration should be less than your liability duration. This gives you some earlier-than-needed asset cash flows to help offset unexpected liability cash flows that might result from the inaccuracy in duration matching or an increase in interest rates.

2. If reinvestment risk (that is, the risk of not being able to earn at least current interest rates on future positive cash flows) is the most significant risk, your asset duration should match your liability duration.

In this presentation, we have ignored the fact that most liability cash flows are affected by interest rate changes. This is referred to as policyowner *optionality*, since policyowners have the option to demand cash flows such as partial withdrawals, policy loans, and surrenders. If it is advantageous to withdraw funds and invest elsewhere, many policyowners will exercise these options. As a result, when interest rates change, you must reestimate future liability cash flows. In addition, unlike noncallable bonds, many asset cash flows are affected by interest rate changes. The effect of interest rate changes on liability and asset cash flows will be introduced in Chapter 15.

14.5 Exercises

Exercise 14.1

Fill in the missing information below, assuming annual payment of premiums, no policy fees, and DB_pu = 1,000 for all three pricing cells for Year 3.

c	$Prem\_pu(c)$	$NumUnits(c)$	$SurvFactor(c, 2)$	$qd(c, 3)$
Issue Age 25	2.00	45,000.00	0.89	0.00115
Issue Age 45	18.00	?	0.91	0.00450
Issue Age 65	55.00	20,000.00	0.87	?
Total Premium in Year 3:		1,925,000.00		
Total Death Benefits Paid in Year 3:		575,000.00		

Exercise 14.2

Using the definitions below, we develop a method of keeping track of calendar years and quarters assuming that time is measured by the number of calendar quarters since the beginning of calendar year 0. We pretend there was a calendar year A.D. 0 immediately before the year A.D. 1. In fact, the year before A.D. 1 was 1 B.C. This unfortunate choice can be traced to a shortage of trained actuaries when the current system of naming calendar years was established.

Let

iyq = Issue year and quarter for cell c. Each cell will contain business for only one issue year and quarter. The quarter beginning closest to the issue date will be assigned the business. For example, all business issued from 16 November 2000 to 15 February 2001 will be assigned to the first quarter of 2001. This will allow us to use policy quarter per-unit-issued results to calculate calendar quarter results

byq = Beginning year and quarter for the model; the year and end of quarter at which the model begins

cyq = Calendar year and quarter. Model results will be calculated separately for each calendar year and quarter.

variable(c, cyq) = Any of the quarterly per-unit-issued results calculated in Chapter 12, such as Prem, Comm, AcqExp, and so on. For example, Prem(c, cyq) is the quarterly premium per-unit-issued for cell c in quarter cyq.

Combined year and quarter variables are calculated using formulas of the following form:

Combined year and quarter = 4 (Year) + Quarter,

where Year is a number such as 2000 and Quarter ranges from 1 to 4. This results in a time variable that ranges from 7,601 for the first quarter of 1900 to 8,401 for the first quarter of 2100. The four quarters of the year 2000 are numbered 8,001, 8,002, 8,003, and 8,004.

Issue year and issue quarter are combined into a single variable:

iyq = 4 (Issue year) + Issue quarter.

The beginning year and quarter for the model are combined into a single variable:

byq = 4 (Beginning calendar year) + Beginning calendar quarter.

The calendar years and quarters to be projected by the model are combined into a single variable that is used to keep track of time as the model progresses:

cyq = 4 (Calendar year) + Calendar quarter.

Determine values of iyq, byq, and cyq for a model with business issued between 16 February 2000 and 15 May 2000, with the model beginning at the end of the fourth quarter of 2000, and with results calculated through the end of 2001.

Exercise 14.3

Building on the definitions from Exercise 14.2, develop formulas to calculate cyq from policy year t, policy quarter Q, and iyq.

Exercise 14.4

Building on the definitions from Exercise 14.2 and the definition below, develop formulas to calculate policy year t and policy quarter Q from cyq and iyq. Express your answer in terms of duration, to the extent possible, and using INT and MOD:

$$\text{INT}(x) = \text{A function that rounds } x \text{ down to the nearest integer}$$

$$\text{MOD}(x, y) = \text{A function that returns the remainder after integer } x \text{ has been divided by integer } y$$

$$\text{Duration} = \text{The number of whole and fractional policy years that the policy has been in force, equal to (cyq } - \text{ iyq} + 1)/4 \text{ or equal to } t - 1 + Q/4.$$

Exercise 14.5

Using the formulas developed in Exercises 14.2 through 14.4, calculate t and Q as of the following dates for business issued at the beginning of the second quarter of 1985:

1. The end of the third quarter of 2001, and

2. The end of the first quarter of the year 2005.

Exercise 14.6

In this chapter, the emphasis has been on gross yields, which ignore the cost of defaults and investment expenses. In practice, net yields, which are calculated net of the cost of defaults and investment expenses, are often used. In general, the net yield can be calculated as

Net yield for the period

$$= \frac{\text{Investment income for the period}}{\text{Book value at the beginning of period}}.$$

This formula assumes that the asset has cash flows only at the end of the period. Cash flows during the period would require an adjustment to the denominator. Using the notation from Section 14.3.2, the formula for the quarterly net yield would be

$$\text{QtrNetYield}(b, \text{cyq}) = \frac{\text{InvIncome}(b, \text{cyq})}{\text{BookValue}(b, \text{cyq} - 1)}.$$

1. Using only investment income and book values from Example 14.3.1, calculate the quarterly net yield for each period.

2. Using only the annual yield and the annual cost of default and investment expense rates from Example 14.3.1, calculate the annual net yield and convert it to the equivalent quarterly rate.

3. Why do the results from the two previous steps differ? Show algebraically why there is a difference between the two methods of calculating quarterly net yields.

4. What would the result be if the annual default cost and investment expense rates were combined and converted to an equivalent quarterly basis before deducting them from the quarterly yield to determine the quarterly net yield?

5. Which of these methods is most correct?

Exercise 14.7

The values shown in the following table were extracted from policy year 1 of the pricing example that runs from Chapter 4 through Chapter 11. If you attempt to match some of the values shown below from the pricing example in Chapters 4 through 11, remember to include the reinsurance values in Chapter 7.

Fill in the missing values and compute free cash flow. Compare free cash flow to the first policy year's distributable earnings, taken from the pricing example in Chapter 11. Assume that positive cumulative cash flows earn interest at a rate of 7% and debt (negative cumulative cash flows) is charged interest at a rate of 7%.

	Beg	Mid	End
LiabCashFlow	−6.62500	−1.00120	3.43830
AssetCashFlow	0.00000	0.00000	0.00000
IntReceived			
IntPaid			
Cash Flow			
CumCashFlow			
InvIncome			
Incr. in AssetReq			2.19940
Free Cash Flow			

Exercise 14.8

Repeat Exercise 14.7 using the values shown in the following table, from policy year 4 of the pricing example that runs from Chapter 4 through Chapter 11. The value shown for AssetCashFlow is equal to the investment income earned on the assets at the beginning of the year that back solvency reserves and required capital.

	Beg	Mid	End
LiabCashFlow	3.75220	−1.60527	−0.92117
AssetCashFlow	0.00000	0.00000	0.30696
IntReceived			
IntPaid			
Cash Flow			
CumCashFlow			
InvIncome			
Incr. in AssetReq			0.49042
Free Cash Flow			

Exercise 14.9

Recalculate free cash flow in Exercise 14.8, assuming that one-half of investment income generated during the year is from coupon payments and the other half is from an increase in the book value of assets.

Exercise 14.10

Your company's primary objective when selling assets to cover cash shortfalls is to minimize net capital gains and losses. The following three assets are available to cover cash outflows; assets can be partially or wholly sold:

> Asset 1: Book value = 1,000.00, Market value = 1,000.00
> Asset 2: Book value = 1,200.00, Market value = 1,250.00
> Asset 3: Book value =   800.00, Market value =   750.00.

What portion of each of the assets should be sold to raise the following amounts of cash?

1. 1,250.00

2. 2,000.00

3. 2,500.00.

Exercise 14.11

Repeat Exercise 14.10, assuming that, if Asset 3 is sold, then half of it or all of it must be sold. Assume that your company would prefer net capital gains to net capital losses.

Exercise 14.12

Recalculate Example 14.4.1 twice, once with each of the following changes:

1. Replace the first two liability cash flows with 35.00 and 30.00, rather than -35.00 and -30.00.

2. Replace the last two liability cash flows with 85.00 and 100.00, rather than -85.00 and -100.00.

Explain the results.

14.6 Answers

Answer 14.1

We know that

$$\text{Prem\_tot}(3) = \sum_{c=1}^{3} \text{Prem}(c, 3) \, \text{NumUnitsIF}(c)$$

$$= \sum_{c=1}^{3} \text{Prem\_pu}(c, 3) \, \text{NumUnits}(c) \, \text{SurvFactor}(c, 2)$$

$$= 1{,}925{,}000.00.$$

We also know that

$$\text{Deaths\_tot}(3) = \sum_{c=1}^{3} \text{DB\_pu}(c, 3) \, \text{NumUnitsIF}(c) \, \text{Deaths}(c, 3)$$

$$= \sum_{c=1}^{3} \text{DB\_pu}(c, 3) \, \text{NumUnits}(c)$$

$$\times \text{SurvFactor}(c, 2) \, qd(c, 3)$$

$$= 575{,}000.$$

Using these formulas, we can solve for the missing values.

c	$\text{Prem\_pu}(c)$	$\text{NumUnits}(c)$	$\text{SurvFactor}(c, 2)$	$qd(c, 3)$
Issue Age 25	2.00	45,000.00	0.89	0.00115
Issue Age 45	18.00	54,206.35	0.91	0.00450
Issue Age 65	55.00	20,000.00	0.87	0.01764
Total Premium in Year 3:		1,925,000.00		
Total Death Benefits Paid in Year 3:		575,000.00		

Answer 14.2

Business issued between 16 February 2000 and 15 May 2000 is issued on average at the beginning of the second quarter of 2000, which translates to
iyq = 8,002.

The model begins at the end of the fourth quarter of 2000, which translates to byq = 8,004.

The model runs from the beginning of 2001 to the end of 2001, which translates to values of cyq ranging from 8,005 to 8,008.

Answer 14.3

Note that "cyq − iyq + 1" equals the number of calendar quarters since the business was issued. We also know that "$4(t − 1) + Q$" equals the number of calendar quarters since the business was issued. Therefore,

$$cyq − iyq + 1 = 4(t − 1) + Q.$$

This leads to

$$cyq = iyq + 4(t − 1) + Q − 1.$$

This formula gives us a simple way to calculate cyq for a cell from iyq, t, and Q.

Answer 14.4

From the definition of Duration, we know that

$$\text{Duration} = \frac{cyq − iyq + 1}{4} = t − 1 + Q/4.$$

Different formulas for t and Q are needed, depending on whether Duration is a whole number, which it is when MOD(cyq − iyq + 1, 4) = 0.

   If Duration is not a whole number, then $t =$ INT(Duration) + 1 and $Q =$ MOD(cyq − iyq + 1, 4).
   If Duration is a whole number, then $t =$ Duration and $Q = 4$.

Answer 14.5

For both dates, iyq = 4 (1985) + 2 = 7,942.

1. At the end of the third quarter of 2001:
   cyq = 4(2001) + 3 = 8,007.
   Duration = (8,007 − 7,942 + 1)/4 = 16.50, or 16 years and two quarters after the business was issued.

Since Duration is not a whole number,
$$t = \text{INT}(\text{Duration}) + 1 = 17,$$
$$Q = \text{MOD}((byq - iyq + 1)/4) = 2.$$
The third quarter of 2001 is the second quarter of the seventeenth policy year.

2. At the end of the first quarter of 2005,
$$cyq = 4(2005) + 1 = 8,021.$$
$$\text{Duration} = (8,021 - 7,942 + 1)/4 = 20.00, \text{ or exactly}$$
$$\text{20 years after the business was issued.}$$
Since Duration is a whole number,
$$t = \text{Duration} = 20,$$
$$Q = 4.$$
The first quarter of 2005 is the fourth quarter of the twentieth policy year.

Answer 14.6

1. Using investment income divided by beginning book value, the quarterly net yields for the three periods are 1.8177%, 1.8177%, and 1.8176%. The three results are essentially identical and equal to 1.8177%.

2. The annual net yield is 8.00% − 0.400% − 0.100% = 7.50%. The quarterly equivalent net yield is $(1.075)^{0.25} - 1 = 1.8245\%$.

3. The difference in the two results comes from differences in the method of calculating quarterly cost of default and investment expense rates. In the first method, the quarterly yield is reduced by (0.400% + 0.100%)/4, or 0.1250%, for default costs and investment expenses. In the second method, the quarterly yield is reduced by 1.9427% − 1.8245% = 0.1182%. The difference between these two reductions is 0.1250% − 0.1182% = 0.0068%, which fully explains the difference in the two results, since 1.8245% − 1.8177% also equals 0.0068%.

4. If we combine the annual default cost and investment expense rates and convert them to an equivalent quarterly basis, we obtain $(1 + 0.40\% + 0.10\%)^{1/4} - 1 = 0.1248\%$, which is almost no different than simply dividing by four.

5. There is no single correct method. However, the method chosen should be consistent with the method used to develop the cost of default rate and the investment expense rate. For example, if the default and expense rates are developed from quarterly rates multiplied by four, then the consistent method would be the first one, which divides annual default and expense rates by four to obtain quarterly rates.

Answer 14.7

	Beg	Mid	End
LiabCashFlow	−6.62500	−1.00120	3.43830
AssetCashFlow	0.00000	0.00000	0.00000
IntReceived	0.00000	0.00000	0.00000
IntPaid	0.00000	0.22795	0.27025
Cash Flow	−6.62500	−1.22915	3.16805
CumCashFlow	−6.62500	−7.85415	−4.68610
InvIncome			0.00000
Incr. in AssetReq			2.19940
Free Cash Flow			−6.88550

As expected, free cash flow equals distributable earnings for the first policy year, taken from the pricing example in Chapter 11.

Answer 14.8

	Beg	Mid	End
LiabCashFlow	3.75220	−1.60527	−0.92117
AssetCashFlow	0.00000	0.00000	0.30696
IntReceived	0.00000	0.12911	0.07831
IntPaid	0.00000	0.00000	0.00000
Cash Flow	3.75220	−1.47616	−0.53590
CumCashFlow	3.75220	2.27604	1.74014
InvIncome			0.30696
Incr. in AssetReq			0.49042
Free Cash Flow			1.24972

Free cash flow equals distributable earnings for the fourth policy year, taken from the pricing example in Chapter 11.

Answer 14.9

	Beg	Mid	End
LiabCashFlow	3.75220	−1.60527	−0.92117
AssetCashFlow	0.00000	0.00000	0.15348
IntReceived	0.00000	0.12911	0.07831
IntPaid	0.00000	0.00000	0.00000
Cash Flow	3.75220	−1.47616	−0.68938
CumCashFlow	3.75220	2.27604	1.58666
InvIncome			0.30696
Incr. in AssetReq			0.49042
Free Cash Flow			1.24972

The only change compared to Exercise 14.8 is that the AssetCashFlow is half that of Exercise 14.8. However, free cash flow is independent of asset cash flow, other than any effect on interest received or interest paid. Since only the end-of-year asset cash flow changed, there is no effect on interest received or interest paid. Therefore, free cash flow is unchanged.

Answer 14.10

No capital gain or loss is generated by Asset 1. If sold, Asset 2 will generate a capital gain. If sold, Asset 3 will generate a capital loss. Together, Assets 2 and 3 have total book value equal to total market value. Therefore, equal percentages of Assets 2 and 3 can be sold to create no capital gain or loss.

In all three cases, the desired amount of cash can be raised by selling all or part of Asset 1 and equal percentage of Assets 2 and 3. If all of Asset 1 were sold first, then the following percentages of Assets 2 and 3 would be sold to raise the desired amounts of cash:

1. 12.5% to raise 1,250
2. 50.0% to raise 2,000
3. 75.0% to raise 2,500.

Answer 14.11

1. To raise 1,250, sell half of Assets 2 and 3 to generate 1,000 and sell 25% of Asset 1 to generate 250.
2. To raise 2,000, sell all of Assets 2 and 3.
3. To raise 2,500, sell all of Assets 2 and 3 to generate 2,000 and sell half of Asset 1 to generate 500.

Answer 14.12

Part 1 (i = 7.00%)				Part 2 (i = 7.00%)			
t	*Liability Cash Flow*	*Present Value*	*t × Present Value*	*t*	*Liability Cash Flow*	*Present Value*	*t × Present Value*
0.25	35.00	34.41	8.60	0.25	−35.00	−34.41	−8.60
0.50	30.00	29.00	14.50	0.50	−30.00	−29.00	−14.50
0.75	−35.00	−33.27	−24.95	0.75	−35.00	−33.27	−24.95
1.00	−30.00	−28.04	−28.04	1.00	−30.00	−28.04	−28.04
1.25	−25.00	−22.97	−28.72	1.25	−25.00	−22.97	−28.72
1.50	−55.00	−49.69	−74.54	1.50	−55.00	−49.69	−74.54
1.75	−65.00	−57.74	−101.05	1.75	−65.00	−57.74	−101.05
2.00	−75.00	−65.51	−131.02	2.00	−75.00	−65.51	−131.02
2.25	−85.00	−73.00	−164.24	2.25	85.00	73.00	164.24
2.50	−100.00	−84.44	−211.10	2.50	100.00	84.44	211.10
Sum:		−351.24	−740.54	Sum:		−163.20	−36.07
Macauley Duration:			2.1084	Macauley Duration:			0.2210
Modified Duration:			1.9704	Modified Duration:			0.2066

In explaining both results, remember that the duration of your liability cash flows tells you how long or short you need to invest your assets to match the liability cash flows. Therefore, having large upfront positive cash flows, as in Part 1, will allow you to invest your other assets longer. Likewise, having large positive cash flows in the later years, as in Part 2, will force you to invest your existing assets shorter in order to meet the short-term negative cash flows.

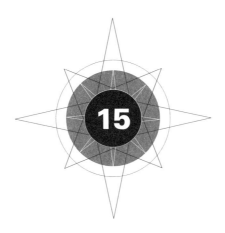

Stochastic Modeling

15.1 Introduction

Stochastic refers to conjecture or guessing. In statistics, it combines random variables and probabilities to guess an outcome, such as a future interest rate. A good stochastic process will produce a collection of outcomes that seems reasonable. For example, if 100 sets of future interest rates are predicted, you would expect to see many interest rate patterns that are consistent with patterns you have observed in the past.

The counterpart to stochastic modeling is often labeled *deterministic,* which means all the assumptions are predetermined. All of the formulas and assumptions presented in previous chapters were deterministic.

This chapter is *not* a highly technical derivation of mathematical formulas. Instead, we focus on practical applications of mathematical and statistical techniques. This chapter will give you an understanding of what is involved in stochastic modeling.

In previous chapters, we established assumptions and then calculated results. For many assumptions, reliable estimates can be established and used with some degree of confidence. However, there is one group of assumptions that is often critical and virtually impossible to predict with confidence: interest rates. To reduce the effect of the unpredictability of interest rates, you can employ several strategies:

- Use a conservative assumption for interest rates
- Offer products that adjust benefits when interest rates change, and
- Match asset and liability cash flows.

All of the above strategies can help reduce interest rate risk but often don't eliminate it. A potentially large, unknown amount of interest rate risk may remain. Using only the tools we have presented so far in this book, you have no way of measuring the significance of the risk to which the company is exposed. While you can develop a worst-case scenario that will severely affect the company, you cannot estimate the likelihood of such an event.

For example, a company may be a big writer of SPDA contracts. Because of fierce competition, the company may invest in long-term assets in order to pick up the extra yield needed to be competitive and still show an acceptable profit. The resulting assets may be much longer than the liabilities, exposing the company to a significant interest rate risk. What tools do we have to measure this risk? Is the risk acceptable in light of the extra sales and profitability being generated by investing in long-term assets? Testing some adverse interest rate scenarios can help you quantify the potential downside, but it does not answer the question of whether the extra risk is worth the extra reward.

In this example, stochastic modeling can be helpful. By randomly generating and testing hundreds of equally likely interest rate scenarios, you can measure the effect of the company's long-term investment strategy over a wide range of likely results. Using a random process, stochastic modeling generates many possible sets of future interest rates. A highly automated process performs asset and liability modeling calculations for all the interest scenarios. These calculations are more sophisticated than those presented in earlier chapters. They can be used to estimate the effect of interest rates on other variables such as credited interest rates, cash values, surrenders, withdrawals, bond calls, and loan prepayments.

You may find that the best interest rate scenarios produce better-than-average results, but not enough to offset the large losses associated with the worst scenarios. As a result, the average returns from all scenarios combined may be significantly less than the returns associated with middle-of-the-road interest rate scenarios.

For example, scenarios with relatively small changes in interest rates over time may produce expected ROIs of 11%, while the average ROI over all scenarios may be only 9%. This may result if the best scenarios produce returns of, say, 17% while the worst scenarios produce returns of, say, −10%. In other words, the potential downside may be much greater than the potential upside. Such insights can be extremely valuable. They can result in a company adjusting product features, altering investment strategy, discontinuing a product, or even exiting a market. On the other hand, by helping a company understand risks and develop strategies to limit those risks, stochastic modeling can also help a company become more aggressive.

Stochastic modeling produces a distribution of likely results. This allows you to answer questions like "What is the probability of ROI being less than 7%?" and "What is the average ROI for the worst 10% of the scenarios?" Answers to questions such as these can help you provide more meaningful insights to those who must make the difficult decisions related to competitive position, risk, and return.

This chapter is not meant to provide the student with the definitive answer for stochastic modeling. The stochastic modeling of interest rates has been researched extensively and is an ongoing topic of research for the actuarial and investment fields. This chapter is intended to give only an introduction to the process of stochastic modeling.

15.2   Overview of Stochastic Modeling

The evolution of computer hardware and specialized life insurance software has made it possible for companies to quickly and efficiently test hundreds or even thousands of randomly generated scenarios. While deterministic models are still the norm, stochastic models are being used in an increasing number of situations.

15.2.1 Uses of Stochastic Modeling

Stochastic modeling can be done for a single product, a portfolio of products, or an entire company. Stochastic modeling is increasingly being used in connection with both pricing and ongoing management of a company's assets and liabilities. The SPDA example in the preceding section could have applied to either new business or in-force business.

Insurance regulators in several countries now require insurance companies to have an actuary annually certify its financial soundness. Regulations or guidelines often require the actuary to perform a sophisticated analysis of assets and liabilities using a number of predetermined sets of interest rates. Stochastic modeling of interest rates would give the actuary a more complete understanding of the company's financial risks and lead to a more informed opinion.

While stochastic modeling can be applied to any variable or assumption, it is most often applied to interest rates and investment returns in the life insurance industry. Other than one section devoted to stochastic mortality, most of this chapter is focused on stochastic interest rates and the resulting effect on liabilities and assets.

Many life insurance products contain options and guarantees. Deterministic pricing is often of little help in figuring an appropriate price or cost for options and guarantees. For example, if a company assumes interest rates will decline from current levels of 7% to an ultimate level of 5% over the next ten years, what is the proper charge for a 3% guaranteed interest rate? Deterministic pricing cannot answer this question. However, by stochastically modeling interest rates, you could estimate how often the 3% guarantee will come into play, as well as the average cost of the guarantee when it does come into play.

Example 15.2.1 Guaranteed Minimum Death Benefits

In Chapter 13, we discussed the increasing variety and significance of guaranteed minimum death benefits (GMDBs) associated with variable annuities. Consider a GMDB that is equal to the single premium accumulated with 7% interest, so that it approximately doubles over a ten-year period. What is the expected cost of this GMDB? Take two scenarios:

1. If the stock market soars soon after the single premium is paid, the account value will likely exceed the GMDB. If the stock market has no significant downturn for a few years, the GMDB may cost the company little or nothing. Because of strong stock market performance during the 1990s, most GMDBs during this period cost much less than expected.

2. If the stock market takes a dive soon after the single premium is paid, the GMDB will likely come into play immediately (that is, it will be "in the money"). If the market languishes for a few years, as it has historically from time to time, the GMDB may increase much faster than the account value. In this case, the GMDB could cost the company much more than expected. This would have been the case in the 1970s, when the stock market made little progress.

While these two scenarios are instructive, they don't begin to answer the question of what to charge for the GMDB. By using stochastic modeling to generate many random but realistic sequences of investment returns, you will find that the GMDB costs very little in most cases; let's call this the "usual cost." However, in a small percentage of scenarios, you will find that the GMDB costs, say, 50 times the usual cost. The relatively few adverse scenarios may result in the average cost being double or triple the usual cost.

Both stochastic modeling and option pricing approaches have been used to develop costs for GMDBs. These two methods have tended to produce consistent results. Interestingly, these theoretical costs have usually been higher than the costs assumed by most companies offering variable annuities with GMDBs.

15.2.2   Steps Involved in Stochastic Modeling

There are four primary steps involved in stochastic modeling:

1. *Select a distribution function.* It is crucial for the distribution function to produce realistic patterns of the variable being stochastically modeled.

2. *Choose a random number generator.* Many software tools can generate random numbers.

3. *Stochastically generate sets of variables.*

4. *Calculate results for each set of interest rates.* This assumes that interest rates are being stochastically modeled. If mortality is being stochastically modeled, the rest of the liability and asset calculations can be done deterministically, based on the mortality rates input. Stochastic mortality will be discussed in its own section. The following would be calculated for each set of interest rates:

    a. *Liability or product-related results.* These results should reflect the relationship between interest rates and other liability-related variables, such as cash values, surrenders, withdrawals, and reserves.

    b. *Asset-related results.* These results should also reflect the relationship between interest rates and other asset-related variables such as calls, prepayments, sales, and purchases of assets.

The next few pages examine each of these steps in more detail.

15.2.2.1 Select a Distribution Function

You need to determine the best distribution function for the variable being stochastically modeled. The distribution function should generate values that best fit the range, frequency, and deviation of possible outcomes for that variable. For example, a mortality distribution function should produce mortality rates that range from zero to one. It should also reproduce the expected mean and variance of mortality.

To stochastically model mortality, it may be intuitively obvious to the most casual observer that the binomial distribution function is a good choice. For interest rates or investment returns, though, the distribution function will likely be based on your own research or the research of others. For example, changes in interest rates may be a function of a variable with a normal or lognormal distribution, though the choice of the proper distribution is the subject of ongoing research. In particular, see "The Sensitivity of Cash-Flow Analysis to the Choice of Statistical Model for Interest Rate Changes," by Gordon E. Klein, published in the Society of Actuaries' *Transactions,* vol. XLV.

The distribution function should be tested to see how well it fits with experience over a number of years. It may take some effort to gather the information needed to compare to past results. Once comparisons have been made, parameters such as mean and standard deviation can be adjusted to improve the fit. For those of you with a working knowledge of statistics, you may want to utilize various statistical tests to measure goodness of fit. The graphs shown in Example 15.6.1 illustrate goodness of fit.

15.2.2.2 Choose a Random Number Generator

A random number generator is used in combination with the distribution function to generate random values of the variable to be stochastically modeled. This process is best illustrated with an example.

Example 15.2.2 Roll of the Die

Suppose you are trying to reproduce the results of rolling a single die with the numbers 1 through 6 on its six sides. The distribution function would have a one-sixth probability of producing each of the numbers 1 through 6. Let the cumulative distribution function $F(x)$ be defined as the probability that the roll of the die will produce a number less than or equal to x. $F(x)$ would have the following values:

x	$F(x)$
1	0.166667
2	0.333333
3	0.500000
4	0.666667
5	0.833333
6	1.000000

Now suppose we have a random number generator that has an equal chance of producing any number between 1 and 1,000,000. Let R be the random number generated by this function. If we let $S = R/1,000,000$, we now have a random number that is evenly distributed between 0.000001 and 1.000000. We can use S in combination with $F(x)$ to generate random values that simulate the roll of a die, as follows:

Result of rolling a die $= x,$ where $F(x - 1) < S \leq F(x).$

For example, if $R = 654,321$, then $S = 0.654321$ and $F(3) < S \leq F(4)$, so a 4 was rolled.

Example 15.2.2 may seem like a lot of trouble to go through to come up with a random number between 1 and 6. It is. However, other distribution functions are not so simple. Steps similar to those outlined above will work for any distribution function and random number generator.

15.2.2.3   Stochastically Generate Sets of Variables

The random number generator is applied to the distribution function to create hundreds or thousands of sets of the variable being stochastically modeled. If mortality were being modeled, one set of mortality rates would consist of separate mortality rates for each cell (product, issue year, issue age, and risk class) in each period (year or quarter) of the model. For example, if the liability model is composed of 1,000 cells and 40 quarters, one set of mortality rates will consist of 40,000 rates. If 1,000 sets of mortality rates are being stochastically generated, you will end up with 40,000,000 randomly generated mortality rates.

If interest rates are being modeled, one set of interest rates could consist of separate yield rates for each type of asset (differentiated by asset class, maturity, and rating) available for purchase in each future time period of the model. In practice, only a few yield rates for key assets for each period would usually be needed, with yields for other assets determined by reference to the yields for the key assets. For example, 90-day London Interbank Offered Rates (LIBOR) and ten-year Eurobonds may be used to generate yield rates for all the other securities in the model. Another common method is to generate yield rates for the local government-sponsored yield rates, such as U.S. Treasury rates. In this case, one set of interest rates for a model with 40 quarters would consist of "only" 80 interest rates.

15.2.2.4   Calculate Results for Each Set of Interest Rates

For each set of interest rates, the liability and asset calculations described in previous chapters are performed. However, a number of variables are directly affected by interest rates. For example, interest rate assumptions will affect

- Credited interest rates and account values for dynamic products
- Dividends for participating products
- Lapse rates, especially when the company does not increase credited interest rates to match increases in market interest rates
- Sales levels

- Premium levels
- Asset market values, and
- Asset calls and prepayments.

A sophisticated stochastic model will automatically adjust these and other variables, to reflect the probable reactions of the company, its customers, and the financial markets to changes in interest rates. Once these adjustments have been made, the normal liability and asset calculations can be performed to determine product cash flows, asset cash flows, distributable earnings, and all the other results of liability and asset models.

15.3 Random Variables

Random variables are developed by combining a distribution function with a random number generator, as illustrated in the roll-of-the-die example in the previous section. In general, the following steps are used to create random variables:

- Develop a cumulative distribution function $F(x)$ that reflects how the random variable should be distributed.
- Calculate a random number S that is evenly distributed between 0.000000 and 1.000000, using your random number generator as input.
- For each random number S, calculate a value x for the random variable:

    For a continuous distribution, determine x from $F(x) = S$

    For a discrete distribution, determine x from

    $$F(x - 1) < S \le F(x).$$

The result is a series of random numbers that are randomly distributed in a pattern that follows the distribution function. Assuming you have a random number generator handy, all you need to generate random variables is a cumulative distribution function. The two most commonly used distribution functions are the binomial distribution and the normal distribution.

15.3.1 Binomial Distribution

The binomial distribution results from the sum of n trials, where each trial results in X equal to 0 or 1. Let p represent the probability that X will equal 1; or, in mathematical terms, let $P(X = 1) = p$. Let X_n be the sum of the results of n trials. Then X_n has a mean of $\mu = np$ and a standard deviation of $\sigma = (np(1 - p))^{1/2}$. If $p = \frac{1}{2}$, then $\mu = \frac{1}{2}n$ and $\sigma = \frac{1}{2}(n)^{1/2}$.

15.3.2 Normal Distribution

In the paper entitled "Interest Rate Scenarios," published in the Society of Actuaries' *Transactions*, Vol. XL, Merlin Jetton uses the binomial distribution to approximate the normal (that is, bell-shaped) distribution. He notes that, for sufficiently large values of n, if we calculate

$$Z_n = \frac{X_n - \frac{1}{2}n}{\frac{1}{2}(n)^{1/2}}, \tag{15.3.1}$$

then Z_n approximates the normal distribution with a mean of zero and a standard deviation of one. Jetton suggests a minimum value of $n = 30$ in order to achieve a satisfactory approximation of the normal distribution. In other words, 30 random numbers can be used to generate each value of X_n, which then determines Z_n. A probability of $p = \frac{1}{2}$ is very easy to simulate using random numbers. All even numbers can be assigned a value of $X = 0$, and all odd numbers can be assigned a value of $X = 1$. By selecting n random numbers, you can quickly and easily generate a value for X_n. Using this technique, Figure 15.3.1 used 60,000 random numbers to generate 2,000 values of X_{30}. As you can see, for 2,000 separate trials, the overall distribution of the occurrences of X_{30} approximates a normal distribution. The resulting distribution of Z_{30} would also be normally distributed, but with a mean of zero and a standard deviation of one.

Given the distribution shown here, we can determine the distribution function $f(x)$, the probability that $X_n = x$, and the

Figure 15.3.1 Occurrences of *X* with *N* = 30 and 2,000 Trials

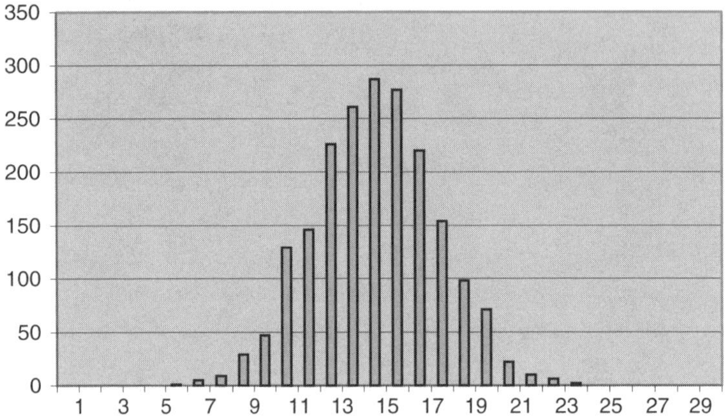

cumulative distribution function $F(x)$, the probability that $X_n \geq x$. These are shown in Table 15.3.1.

Table 15.3.1 Distribution Function Values

x	$f(x)$	$F(x)$	x	$f(x)$	$F(x)$	x	$f(x)$	$F(x)$
1	0.0000	0.0000	11	0.0545	0.1070	21	0.0120	0.9915
2	0.0000	0.0000	12	0.0770	0.1840	22	0.0045	0.9960
3	0.0000	0.0000	13	0.1115	0.2955	23	0.0035	0.9995
4	0.0000	0.0000	14	0.1430	0.4385	24	0.0005	1.0000
5	0.0005	0.0005	15	0.1310	0.5695	25	0.0000	1.0000
6	0.0005	0.0010	16	0.1420	0.7115	26	0.0000	1.0000
7	0.0010	0.0020	17	0.1120	0.8235	27	0.0000	1.0000
8	0.0085	0.0105	18	0.0810	0.9045	28	0.0000	1.0000
9	0.0145	0.0250	19	0.0505	0.9550	29	0.0000	1.0000
10	0.0275	0.0525	20	0.0245	0.9795	30	0.0000	1.0000

Figure 15.3.2 graphs the values shown in Table 15.3.1.

There are other methods that can be used to generate values of Z that are normally distributed with $\mu = 0$ and $\sigma = 1$. For example, Jetton suggests the Box-Muller method, which he describes in his paper.

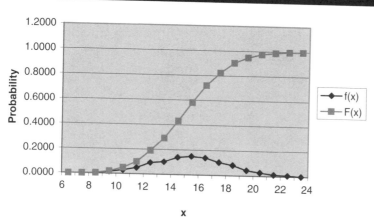

Figure 15.3.2 Distribution Function and Cumulative Distribution Function

15.4   Stochastic Mortality

Larger insurance companies usually insure so many lives that the number of deaths and death benefits are fairly predictable. However, for larger companies with high retention limits and for smaller companies, mortality fluctuations can be quite significant. In addition, mortality variability can be a concern for public companies whose stock price is penalized if earnings per share are even slightly less than expected. In these cases, stochastic models for mortality can be useful. They can help you understand the likely variability of mortality results and design products or programs, such as reinsurance programs, to stabilize those results.

Stochastic models for mortality usually presume that all lives are independent of one another. While this assumption may be good enough for your purposes, it is never quite true, for a couple of reasons:

1. Many insureds have more than one policy in force with the same company. Few, if any, liability models can combine multiple policies on one insured. This is because multiple policies on the same life often fall into different cells, due to different products, issue dates, and issue ages.

2. Disasters such as bombs, fires, and airplane crashes can simultaneously kill many insureds that work or travel together. Such

a catastrophe can severely affect your company's financial results if a number of these insureds are insured by your company.

3. A company may write policies on more than one member of the same family, either as single life coverage on each life or as joint life coverage on perhaps the husband and wife. There is a chance that two or more lives could die simultaneously in a common accident. There is also the *lonely heart syndrome,* which is the increased chance of the second of two spouses dying soon after the first dies.

15.4.1 Seriatim Stochastic Modeling

The simplest approach to stochastic mortality is to model one policy at a time. This approach works best when policies are not grouped into cells. However, it can also be used with a cell-based model if you track how many policies remain in force within each cell. Either way, it is necessary to also use a stochastic approach for lapses and any other decrements, in order to deal with whole policies in force at each point in time.

Seriatim modeling is accomplished by performing the following process for each policy within each period. A period is normally a quarter or a year. Mortality and lapse rates are adjusted to match the length of the period. For each period, the following process is applied.

For each policy in force at the beginning of the period, determine an assumed mortality rate qd and an assumed lapse rate qw for the period. Then,

1. Generate a random number S in the range 0.000000 to 1.000000.

2. If $S \leq qd$, then the policy is terminated by death and qd is set equal to 1; otherwise, qd is set equal to 0.

3. If the policy is not terminated by death, generate another random number S.

4. If $S \leq qw$, then the policy is terminated by lapse and qw is set equal to 1; otherwise, qw is set equal to 0.

Once the policy has terminated, it should be removed from the in force for future periods.

This is a much different approach to modeling. Essentially, every policy is its own cell. Each cell does one of three things: It continues to the end of the model with no deaths and no lapses, it lapses in one period, or it dies in one period. In other words, at any point in time for any cell, SurvFactor is equal to 0 or 1. This, of course, is how actual policies behave.

With today's computing power, a seriatim approach is quite feasible for a model involving tens of thousands of policies. To examine the death claim volatility of the company's largest policies, the seriatim approach is often feasible and is the only way to accurately reflect the death benefit amount of each policy, which should be calculated net of reinsurance.

15.4.2   Alternative to Stochastic Modeling

Before we discuss stochastic modeling for large models involving hundreds of thousands of policies, let us explore a simpler alternative. First, the volatility of the largest policies could be modeled using a seriatim approach, as described above. The volatility of the remaining policies can then be adequately modeled using the following approach:

1. Model the remaining policies deterministically to determine total expected death benefits for each period. Use this to calculate the average expected mortality rate, $q(t)$, for each period.

2. Total variance for each period can then be very roughly estimated as

$$\text{Total variance} = (\text{Number of policies})\, q(t)\, (1 - q(t))$$
$$\times\, (\text{Average death benefit})^2.$$

   This assumes identical policies, which is far from accurate. A better estimate of total variance can be obtained by calculating variance separately for each cell and summing the variances. The best estimate is obtained by calculating variance for each policy and summing the results. Standard deviation is obtained by taking the square root of the total variance.

3. The law of large numbers essentially states that if you have a large number of similar things, they produce results that follow a normal

distribution. Combining the mean and standard deviation of death claims from the first two steps with the normal distribution, you now predict the distribution of death claims and not bother with a stochastic model except for the largest policies.

15.4.3 Binomial Stochastic Modeling

In cases where stochastic modeling is called for and the seriatim approach is not feasible, a binomial approach may be the best answer. This is especially true when dealing with cells that have thousands of policies apiece. If cells have only, say, 10 to 100 policies apiece, it may be more efficient to apply the seriatim approach to each policy than to apply the more complex binomial approach to all policies combined.

The binomial distribution best fits a group of independent lives that share the same mortality rate and death benefit, as is often the case for the policies grouped into a pricing cell. The binomial distribution is applied separately to each pricing or liability cell.

15.4.3.1 Applying the Binomial Distribution

In essence, the binomial approach allows you to use one random number to determine a stochastic outcome for n policies at once, whereas the seriatim approach uses one random number for each policy. With the binomial approach, the following process is repeated once for each period. A period is normally a quarter or a year, and mortality and lapse rates are adjusted to match the length of the period. Here is how the binomial process works for one cell in one period.

At the beginning of the period, determine an assumed mortality rate qd, an assumed lapse rate qw for the period, and the number of policies in force (n). The number of policies in force will decrease from period to period. Then,

1. Using the binomial distribution, create a cumulative distribution function $F(x)$ for the number of deaths x in the period, based on n policies in force at the beginning of the period. The calculation of $F(x)$ will be discussed below.

2. Generate a random number S in the range 0.000000 to 1.000000.

3. If $F(x - 1) < S \leq F(x)$, then x is the number of deaths, and qd is set equal to x/n.

4. Using the binomial distribution, create a cumulative distribution function $F(y)$ for the number of lapses y in the period, assuming $n - x$ policies in force at the beginning of the period, because of the deduction of x deaths.

5. Generate another random number S in the range 0.000000 to 1.000000.

6. If $F(y - 1) < S \leq F(y)$, then y is the number of lapses, and qw is set equal to $y/(n - x)$.

7. The number of policies in force at the beginning of the next period is $n - x - y$.

The result of this process is that whole numbers of policies die or lapse in each period, with a whole number of policies remaining in force for the cell. It is very common for a cell with a small number of policies to have no deaths in the great majority of periods and one death in a few periods.

15.4.3.2   Calculating the Binomial Distribution Function

In this section, we apply the binomial distribution to a cell with n policies with a probability of death equal to q. We assume the reader is already familiar with the binomial distribution. Let

n = Number of policies in the cell at the beginning of the period

q = Probability of any one policy dying during the period

x = Number of deathsout of n policies occurring during the period: x can range from 0 to n

$f(x)$ = The distribution function, equal to the probability that the number of deaths during the period will equal x

$F(x)$ = The cumulative distribution function, equal to the probability that the number of deaths during the period will be less than or equal to x

$$\text{fratio}(x) = \text{The ratio of successive values of } f(x), \text{ equal to}$$
$$f(x)/f(x - 1)$$

$_nC_x$ = Combinatoric factor often described as "n choose x." This is equal to the number of different combinations of x objects that can be chosen from a group of n objects. This factor is the key to the binomial distribution.

$n!$ = n factorial
= Multiplication of all integers from 2 to
n: $= (n) (n - 1) (n - 2) \ldots (2) (1).$

Applying the binomial distribution, we have

$$f(x) = \frac{n!}{(n - x)! \, x!} \, q^x \, (1 - q)^{(n-x)}. \tag{15.4.1}$$

This can be restated in terms of $_nC_x$, as follows:

$$f(x) = {_nC_x} \, q^x \, (1 - q)^{(n-x)}, \text{ where} \tag{15.4.2}$$

$${_nC_x} = \frac{n!}{(n - x)! \, x!}. \tag{15.4.3}$$

Values of $_nC_x$ can be quickly generated using Pascal's triangle, illustrated below, in which values in each row are calculated by adding the one or two values just above them, on the right and left.

n												
0						1						
1					1		1					
2				1		2		1				
3			1		3		3		1			
4		1		4		6		4		1		
5	1		5		10		10		5		1	
6	1	6		15		20		15		6		1

For example, the values of $_2C_x$ for $x = 0, 1,$ and 2 are shown in the third row as "1 2 1." $_2C_0 = 1$ means there is only one way to choose 0 items from a group of 2 items. Similarly, $_2C_1 = 2$ means there are two ways to choose 1 item from a group of 2 items. Finally, $_2C_2 = 1$ means there is only one way to choose 2 items from a group of 2 items. $_nC_x$ is also the coefficient of a^x in the polynomial $(1 + a)^n$.

15.4.3.3 fratio(x)

While $f(x)$ can be calculated directly from the formula above, it is often more efficient to calculate one value of $f(x)$ from the previous value, using fratio(x):

$$f(x) = f(x - 1) \text{ fratio}(x), \quad \text{where} \tag{15.4.4}$$

$$\text{fratio}(x) = \frac{q}{1 - q} \frac{n - x + 1}{x}. \tag{15.4.5}$$

The formula for fratio(x) can be readily derived from the formula for $f(x)$. This is left as an exercise.

Example 15.4.1 Efficiency of fratio(x)

To demonstrate why using fratio(x) might be more efficient, consider the following example. Using $q = 0.01$ and $n = 100$, you could calculate $f(5)$ directly using Formula 15.4.1 or iteratively using Formula 15.4.4:

$$f(5) = \frac{100!}{(100 - 5)! \, 5!} \, 0.01^5 \, (1 - 0.01)^{(100-5)}, \tag{15.4.1}$$

or

$$f(5) = f(4) \frac{0.01}{1 - 0.01} \frac{100 - 5 + 1}{5}. \tag{15.4.4}$$

Which calculation seems simpler and faster?

15.4.3.4 Cumulative Distribution Function F(x)

Once the distribution function $f(x)$ has been calculated, the cumulative distribution function $F(x)$ can be quickly calculated by summing values of $f(x)$:

$$F(s) = \sum_{x=0}^{s} f(x).$$

Life Insurance Products and Finance

Example 15.4.2 Using the Binomial Distribution

In Table 15.4.1, values of $f(x)$ and $F(x)$ have been generated for $n = 10$ and $q = 0.20$. In the next-to-the-last column, ten random numbers distributed between 0.000000 and 1.000000 are shown. These random numbers are *not* related to the first three columns. In other words, do not read across all five columns. The final column shows the value of x that is the result of the random number generated. It is obtained by scanning the $F(x)$ column until a value of x is found such that $F(x - 1) < S \leq F(x)$.

In Table 15.4.1 the probability of death, $q = 0.20$, is a relatively large number. This results in probabilities of multiple deaths that are not infinitesimal. For example, $f(5)$, the probability of five deaths, is 0.026. For smaller, more normal values of q, the probabilities of multiple deaths quickly become infinitesimal. For example, if $q = 0.002$, which is a more typical mortality rate, then the following values of $f(x)$ and $F(x)$ result (see Table 15.4.2).

In Table 15.4.2 you can see that almost all random numbers will result in zero deaths. By specially selecting the last two random numbers, we were able to generate one and two deaths.

As a final example, use the same mortality rate, but increase the number of lives from 10 to 500 (see Table 15.4.3).

Table 15.4.1 Binomial Distribution with $n = 10$ and $q = 0.20$

x	$f(x)$	$F(x)$	S (Random Number)	Resulting Value of x
0	0.1073741824	0.1073741824	0.050000	0
1	0.2684354560	0.3758096384	0.150000	1
2	0.3019898880	0.6777995264	0.250000	1
3	0.2013265920	0.8791261184	0.350000	1
4	0.0880803840	0.9672065024	0.450000	2
5	0.0264241152	0.9936306176	0.550000	2
6	0.0055050240	0.9991356416	0.650000	2
7	0.0007864320	0.9999220736	0.750000	3
8	0.0000737280	0.9999958016	0.850000	3
9	0.0000040960	0.9999998976	0.950000	4
10	0.0000001024	1.0000000000	0.999999	9

Table 15.4.2 Binomial Distribution with $n = 10$ and $q = 0.002$

x	$f(x)$	$F(x)$	S (Random Number)	Resulting Value of x
0	0.9801790434	0.9801790434	0.050000	0
1	0.0196428666	0.9998219100	0.150000	0
2	0.0001771401	0.9999990500	0.250000	0
3	0.0000009466	0.9999999967	0.350000	0
4	0.0000000033	1.0000000000	0.450000	0
5	0.0000000000	1.0000000000	0.550000	0
6	0.0000000000	1.0000000000	0.650000	0
7	0.0000000000	1.0000000000	0.750000	0
8	0.0000000000	1.0000000000	0.850000	0
9	0.0000000000	1.0000000000	0.999000	1
10	0.0000000000	1.0000000000	0.999999	2

Table 15.4.3 Binomial Distribution with *n* = 500 and *q* = 0.002

x	*f(x)*	*F(x)*	*S (Random Number)*	*Resulting Value of x*
0	0.3675112549	0.3675112549	0.050000	0
1	0.3682477504	0.7357590052	0.150000	0
2	0.1841238752	0.9198828804	0.250000	0
3	0.0612516298	0.9811345102	0.350000	0
4	0.0152515331	0.9963860433	0.450000	1
5	0.0030319681	0.9994180114	0.550000	1
6	0.0005012773	0.9999192887	0.650000	1
7	0.0000708935	0.9999901822	0.750000	2
8	0.0000087551	0.9999989373	0.850000	2
9	0.0000009591	0.9999998965	0.950000	3
10	0.0000000944	0.9999999908	0.999999	9

15.5 Stochastic Interest Rates

The stochastic modeling of interest rates involves creating many interest rate scenarios. The more scenarios created, the more credible the results. The number of scenarios is limited by the speed of the software and hardware used for modeling. The time required for additional scenarios should be compared to the value of the additional information that will be gained by adding more scenarios.

Example 14.3.5 in Chapter 14 introduced the concept of interest rate scenarios. Each interest rate scenario consists of a complete set of interest rates for each future period in the model. In practice, a few key interest rates are used to generate all of the others within a period.

Stochastic modeling of interest rates is best performed in the aggregate. Since assets are difficult to purchase in small amounts, modeling a single pricing cell or a small block of business is unrealistic and probably a waste of time. This section will give you a basic understanding of the different methods used to generate interest rate scenarios. To better understand the limitations and biases of the different methods, review Jetton's paper, referred to in Section 15.3.

There are quite a few complexities involved in stochastically modeling future interest rates, such as:

- It is not enough to project one interest rate for each future period. Instead, you must project yield rates for all possible future asset purchases. These same yield rates will allow you to determine the future market values of assets purchased in the past.

- Interest rates are driven by world events such as wars, depressions, and oil shortages. Such events can have unusually significant and long-lasting effects on interest rates. It is questionable whether randomly generated interest rates can adequately reflect such possibilities.

- Interest rates are also driven by the supply and demand for money. Interest rates are essentially the price of money. Some economists argue that studying demographics allows you to predict long-term interest rate trends. Those whose actions will drive the economy for the next 20 years have already been born. For example, in countries where baby boomers are a significant economic force, their aging may boost the savings rate and create an oversupply of money, thereby driving down interest rates. If this is true, should your stochastic model be biased toward declining interest rates?

In the remainder of this section, we will ignore the last two points. However, they deserve careful consideration. To handle the great variety of yields available on different investments, we will consider these yields to be the sum of two pieces: (1) the government yield rate for the same maturity of asset, plus (2) a spread over that yield rate, usually stated in basis points (hundredths of a percent). For example, a ten-year, A-rated corporate bond may have a yield that is 100 basis points (1.00%) over U.S. Treasury bonds of comparable remaining maturity. If the ten-year U.S. Treasury yield is 6.25%, then the A-rated corporate bond will yield 7.25%.

LIBOR yield rates are available for all the major countries. LIBOR rates have become the international standard for short-term interest rate comparisons. However, in certain countries, local government yield rates may still be commonly used. For example, in the U.S., many yields are expressed in terms of basis points over Treasuries, referring to U.S. Treasury notes and bonds.

For simplicity, we will assume that the spread over the government yield rate for a certain type of asset is fixed and unchanging. For example, if a ten-year, A-rated corporate bond currently yields 100 basis points over U.S. Treasuries, we will assume that such bonds will always yield 100 basis points over U.S. Treasuries. In reality, spreads change as supply and demand for different asset classes wax and wane. This complexity could be handled by stochastically modeling spreads, but that is beyond the scope of this chapter. However, the concepts and mechanics of stochastic modeling introduced in this chapter could be applied to spreads.

By assuming that spreads do not change, we have simplified our job of projecting interest rates: All we need to project now are government yield rates for various maturities. This leads us to yield curves.

15.5.1 Yield Curves

A yield curve shows yield rates on one axis and time to maturity on the other axis. This is best illustrated with a graph. The data points on Figures 15.5.1 through 15.5.3 represent yields for investments that mature in 90 and 180 days, and 1, 2, 3, 5, 7, 10, 20, and 30 years.

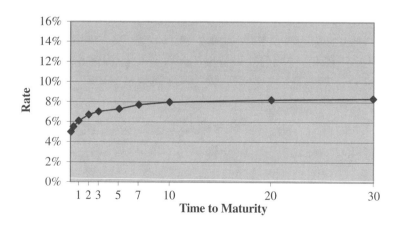

Figure 15.5.1 Normal Yield Curve

Figure 15.5.2 Inverted Yield Curve

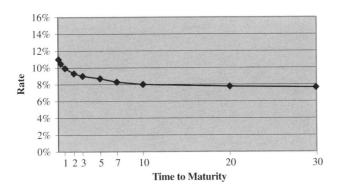

Yield curves normally slope upward with increasing time to maturity, as in Figure 15.5.1. This is called a *normal yield curve*. Yield curves normally slope upward because long-term bonds carry more risk. If interest rates rise, the investor is stuck with lower yielding bonds. The longer the time to maturity, the bigger the gamble the investor is making, so a higher interest rate is demanded.

Occasionally, yield curves slope downward with increasing time to maturity, as in the next graph. This is called an *inverted yield curve*. An inverted yield curve results from a consensus that short-term interest rates are relatively high and are apt to fall. The longer the time to maturity, the more the expectation that interest rates will return to more normal levels.

Figure 15.5.3 Yield Curves of Varying Slopes and Levels

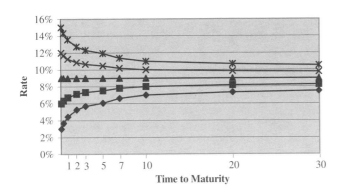

Yield curves can be described by their relative slope and level. The relative slope can range from steeply normal to steeply inverted. Five slopes are shown in the following graph. To spread out the yield curves for easier viewing, we separated the ten-year yields by 1%.

In practice, yield curves are usually defined by one short-term and one long-term rate, such as a 90-day rate and a ten-year rate. The other rates in the curve can usually be determined mathematically from these two rates. This makes our job of generating yield curves much easier: All we need do is generate two rates to define an entire yield curve.

Example 15.5.1 Interpolation of Rates for a Yield Curve

A yield curve might be defined by the rates for 90 and 180 days, and 1, 2, 3, 5, 7, 10, 20, and 30 years. All of these rates can be determined from the 90-day rate and ten-year rate using an interpolation formula such as the following:

$$\text{Interpolated rate} = (1 - \text{Factor}) \times \text{90-day rate}$$
$$+ \text{Factor} \times \text{10-year rate}.$$

The appropriate factors for each maturity can be determined by analyzing actual yield curves. The yield curves in the preceding graphs were generated using the factors shown in Table 15.5.1.

Factors for additional maturities could be developed by interpolating these factors.

Table 15.5.1 Yield Curve Interpolation Factors

Maturity	Factor	Maturity	Factor
90 days	0.0000	5 years	0.7647
180 days	0.1694	7 years	0.9059
1 year	0.3600	10 years	1.0000
2 years	0.5671	20 years	1.0784
3 years	0.6706	30 years	1.1176

15.5.2   Interest Rate Scenarios

An interest rate scenario consists of one yield curve for each future period in the model. Since we need to generate only two rates (a 90-day rate and a ten-year rate) to define a yield curve, all that is left is to generate two random interest rates for each period, right? Unfortunately, it is not that simple.

First, interest rates from one period to the next are highly correlated. The change in interest rates may be random, but the level of interest rates is very much related to the prior period's interest rates. Second, the 90-day rate and the ten-year rate are correlated. They often rise and fall in unison or partial unison. However, at times they move in opposite directions. We will examine three approaches to handling these complexities:

1. The arbitrary method

2. The probabilistic method, and

3. The successive ratios method.

15.5.2.1   Arbitrary Method

The arbitrary method is not a stochastic model. Rather, it involves manually creating a set of interest rate scenarios in an arbitrary fashion. Such scenarios are simple to create. In some jurisdictions, a specific set of rules must be followed to generate specified scenarios. These scenarios are then tested as part of an annual certification of the company's financial condition.

For example, different scenarios may test the effect of gradual or sudden increases or decreases in interest rates. One scenario may have interest rates increasing by 3% over a number of years. Another scenario may have interest rates increase 3% in one year and remain level thereafter.

Creating interest rate scenarios in this way is of limited value. The number of scenarios will rarely be sufficient to perform a thorough test. There is no way to create a conclusion as to the probability of the results of any scenario. In addition, there is no way to combine the result of the various scenarios. Arbitrary input generates arbitrary output.

15.5.2.2 Probabilistic Approach

Let us assume that every yield curve is defined by its level (the ten-year rate) and its slope (the ratio of the 90-day rate to the ten-year rate). Using historical information, we can develop probabilities of each level changing to any other level during the next period. These probabilities could be organized into a grid, such as Table 15.5.2.

Table 15.5.2 Probabilities of Interest Rate Changes

Current 10-Year Interest Rate	*Probability of Ten-Year Interest Rate for Next Period Being*										
	2.00%	*2.25%*	*2.50%*	*...*	*7.00%*	*7.25%*	*7.50%*	*...*	*14.50%*	*14.75%*	*15.00%*
2.00%	0.40	0.30	0.20	...							
2.25	0.10	0.40	0.30	...							
2.50	—	0.10	0.40	...							
...											
7.00	—	—	—	...	0.40	0.20	0.10	...	—	—	—
7.25	—	—	—	...	0.20	0.40	0.20	...	—	—	—
7.50	—	—	—	...	0.10	0.20	0.40	...	—	—	—
...											
14.50								...	0.40	0.10	—
14.75								...	0.30	0.40	0.10
15.00								...	0.20	0.30	0.40

In this table, we have built in several features:

1. The sum of probabilities in each row is 1.000, although not all probabilities are shown.

2. The minimum interest rate is 2% and the maximum interest rate is 15%.

3. In the middle of the table, interest rates are just as likely to go up as go down.

4. At the edges of the table, interest rates are more likely to move in the direction of becoming less extreme.

A similar grid can be developed that shows the probability of each slope changing to any other slope during the next period. Even though we randomly determine both the change in level and slope, we end up generating ten-year rates and 90-day rates that are related.

Using these two grids (for the level and slope of the yield curve), you can develop cumulative probability functions $F(x)$ for each level and slope. You can combine the $F(x)$ for the current level and a random number to stochastically generate the level for the next period's yield curve. Similarly, you can combine the $F(x)$ for the current slope and another random number to generate the slope for the next period's yield curve. This is illustrated in the following example.

Example 15.5.2 Probabilistic Generation of Interest Rate Scenarios

Suppose the current yield curve has a 6% 90-day rate, an 8% ten-year rate, and a slope of 0.75 (6%/8%). The probability of moving from one interest rate level (where the level is defined by the ten-year rate) to another is given by Table 15.5.3, a simplified grid. Notice that the probability of a decrease in interest rates is only 20%, while the probability of an increase is 55%. In other words, the grid is designed to produce interest rates that increase over the long term.

The probability of moving from one slope to another is given by Table 15.5.4.

Twenty random numbers in the range of 0.000 to 1.000 are now selected and used to generate values of level and slope for the next 10 periods (see Table 15.5.5).

The values in Table 15.5.5 can be shown graphically (see Figure 15.5.4). Notice the generally upward trend in the ten-year interest rates. Also, note that the 90-day rates are more volatile than the ten-year rates, since they are the product of two random factors. While the 90-day rates should also trend upwards, the volatility in this short time frame obscures any trend.

Table 15.5.3 Probability Grid for Change in Interest Level

	Probability of Change in Level by				
	−0.50%	−0.25%	0.00%	0.25%	0.50%
$f(x)$	0.05	0.15	0.25	0.35	0.20
$F(x)$	0.05	0.20	0.45	0.80	1.00

Table 15.5.4 Probability Grid for Change in Interest Slope

Current Slope	Probability That Slope for Next Period Is				
	0.60	0.75	0.90	1.05	1.20
0.60	0.40	0.50	0.10	—	—
0.75	0.15	0.55	0.20	0.10	—
0.90	—	0.20	0.60	0.20	—
1.05	—	0.10	0.15	0.50	0.25
1.20	—	—	0.20	0.40	0.40

Table 15.5.5 Randomly Generated Changes in Interest Level and Slope

Period	Random Number	Level (Ten-Year Rate)	Random Number	Slope	90-Day Rate
0	—	8.00%	—	0.75	6.00%
1	0.29419	8.00	0.17107	0.75	6.00
2	0.46285	8.25	0.73454	0.90	7.43
3	0.84673	8.75	0.10351	0.75	6.56
4	0.91231	9.25	0.95458	1.05	9.71
5	0.03333	8.75	0.58342	1.05	9.19
6	0.59102	9.00	0.32648	1.05	9.45
7	0.58078	9.25	0.05276	0.75	6.94
8	0.07409	9.00	0.43711	0.75	6.75
9	0.83582	9.50	0.06886	0.60	5.70
10	0.81573	10.00	0.07167	0.60	6.00

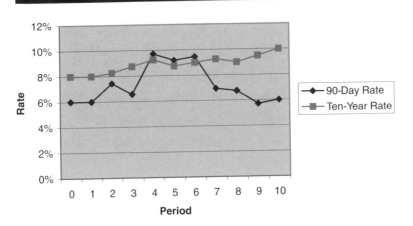

Figure 15.5.4 Randomly Generated Changes in Interest Level and Slope

Jetton's paper (see Section 15.3) describes a slightly different probabilistic approach, where a discrete number of entire yield curves are created. The probabilities of moving from one yield curve to another are used to generate movements in interest rates.

15.5.2.3 Successive Ratios Approach

The successive ratios approach to stochastically generating yield curves uses the assumption that the natural logarithm of the ratio of successive interest rates is normally distributed. In other words, $\ln(i(t + 1)/i(t))$ is normally distributed. By working with successive ratios, you closely tie one interest rate with the next interest rate. The amount of the change in interest rate is random, but not the interest rate itself. By employing the natural logarithm, you can use a random variable with a mean of zero to generate interest rate changes. A natural logarithm of zero results in no change in interest rate, which is what you would like as the mean result.

If the successive ratios approach is applied independently to both the ten-year rate and the 90-day rate, we will end up with two independent interest rates, which would be wrong. To reflect the correlation between the two interest rates, we will do the following:

1. Use one random variable with the successive ratios approach to generate the next ten-year rate.

2. Use a combination of the random variable used for the ten-year rate plus a second random variable to generate the next 90-day rate.

In other words, we will

1. Use random variable 1 to generate the ten-year rate and

2. Use "(random variable 1) × weight 1 + (random variable 2) × weight 2" to generate the 90-day rate.

The weights given to the two random variables will reflect the degree of correlation between the ten-year and 90-day rates. For example, if the rates were 100% correlated, the two weights would be 100% and 0%. The degree of correlation can be determined by performing a statistical study on the ten-year and 90-day rates.

We use the following notation:

$$i90day(t) = \text{90-day interest rate for period } t$$
$$i10year(t) = \text{Ten-year interest rate for period } t$$

VolFactor = Volatility factor, used to control the average volatility of interest rates from one period to the next

Z1, Z2 = Two normally distributed random variables with means of zero and standard deviations of one. Section 15.3 discussed one method that could be employed to generate such variables.

Correlation = The degree of correlation between changes in $i90day(t)$ and $i10year(t)$

Z10year = The random variable used to generate changes in $i10year(t)$, which reflects some correlation with $i90day(t)$.

The following formulas are used to generate the 10-year and 90-day interest rates:

$$i90day(t + 1) = i90day(t)e^{Z1 \text{ VolFactor}}, \tag{15.5.1}$$
$$Z10year = Z1 \text{ Correlation} + Z2 (1 - \text{Correlation}^2)^{0.5}, \tag{15.5.2}$$
$$i10year(t + 1) = i10year(t)e^{Z10year \text{ VolFactor}}. \tag{15.5.3}$$

Examples 15.5.3 through 15.5.5 illustrate interest rates generated using these formulas. Each illustration begins by generating values of X_{30} as was done in Section 15.3, using $p = \frac{1}{2}$. Values of Z_{30} are then calculated using Formula 15.3.1. The three examples use the same random variables and the same pattern of 90-day rates, but with different correlation factors used to produce different ten-year rates.

Example 15.5.3 Successive Ratios Method with Correlation = 1.00

Table 15.5.6 shows ten-year and 90-day rates that are 100% correlated. In Figure 15.5.5, notice how the curves for the two rates follow the same pattern.

Table 15.5.6

t	X_n for Z1	Z1	X_n for Z2	Z2	Z10year	i90day	i10year
0						6.00%	8.00%
1	12	−1.09545	19	1.46059	−1.09545	5.09	6.79
2	14	−0.36515	11	−1.46059	−0.36515	4.82	6.43
3	21	2.19089	20	1.82574	2.19089	6.69	8.93
4	14	−0.36515	16	0.36515	−0.36515	6.34	8.45
5	9	−2.19089	18	1.09545	−2.19089	4.56	6.08
6	16	0.36515	18	1.09545	0.36515	4.82	6.43
7	13	−0.73030	14	−0.36515	−0.73030	4.32	5.76
8	14	−0.36515	18	1.09545	−0.36515	4.09	5.45
9	18	1.09545	15	0.00000	1.09545	4.82	6.43
10	19	1.46059	16	0.36515	1.46059	6.00	8.00

Note: VolFactor = 0.15, Correlation = 1.00.

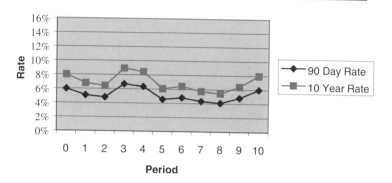

Figure 15.5.5 Successive Ratios Method. Correlation = 1.00

Example 15.5.4 Successive Ratios Method with Correlation = 0.00

Table 15.5.7 shows ten-year and 90-day rates that are completely independent of each other. In Figure 15.5.6, notice how the curves for the two rates move independently of one another.

Table 15.5.7

t	X_n for Z1	Z1	X_n for Z2	Z2	Z10year	i90day	i10year
0						6.00%	8.00%
1	12	−1.09545	17	0.73030	0.73030	5.09	8.93
2	14	−0.36515	13	−0.73030	−0.73030	4.82	8.00
3	21	2.19089	17	0.73030	0.73030	6.69	8.93
4	14	−0.36515	20	1.82574	1.82574	6.34	11.74
5	9	−2.19089	15	0.00000	0.00000	4.56	11.74
6	16	0.36515	16	0.36515	0.36515	4.82	12.40
7	13	−0.73030	11	−1.46059	−1.46059	4.32	9.96
8	14	−0.36515	10	−1.82574	−1.82574	4.09	7.57
9	18	1.09545	18	1.09545	1.09545	4.82	8.93
10	19	1.46059	17	0.73030	0.73030	6.00	9.96

Note: VolFactor = 0.15, Correlation = 0.00.

Life Insurance Products and Finance

Figure 15.5.6 Successive Ratios Method. Correlation = 0.00

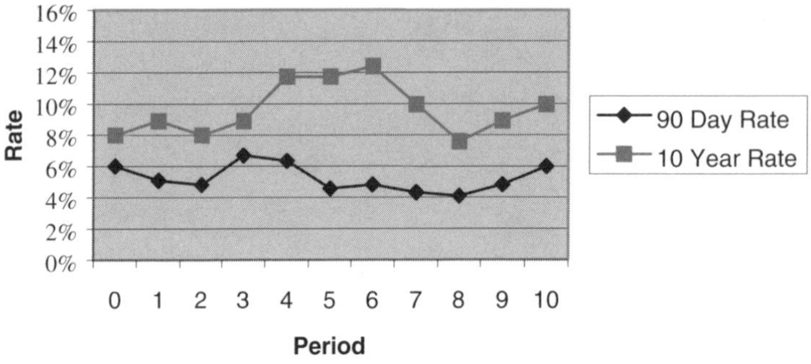

Example 15.5.5 Successive Ratios Method with Correlation = 0.50

Table 15.5.8 shows ten-year and 90-day rates that are somewhat correlated. In Figure 15.5.7, notice how the curves for the two rates follow similar patterns.

Table 15.5.8

t	X_n for Z1	Z1	X_n for Z2	Z2	Z10year	i90day	i10year
0						6.00	8.00
1	12	−1.09545	13	−0.73030	−1.18018	5.09	6.70
2	14	−0.36515	19	1.46059	1.08234	4.82	7.88
3	21	2.19089	16	0.36515	1.41167	6.69	9.74
4	14	−0.36515	12	−1.09545	−1.13126	6.34	8.22
5	9	−2.19089	19	1.46059	0.16947	4.56	8.43
6	16	0.36515	16	0.36515	0.49880	4.82	9.09
7	13	−0.73030	16	0.36515	−0.04892	4.32	9.02
8	14	−0.36515	13	−0.73030	−0.81503	4.09	7.98
9	18	1.09545	15	0.00000	0.54772	4.82	8.67
10	19	1.46059	15	0.00000	0.73030	6.00	9.67

Note: VolFactor = 0.15, Correlation = 0.50.

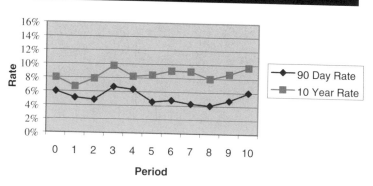

Figure 15.5.7 Successive Ratios Method. Correlation = 0.50

Compared to the probabilistic method, the successive ratios method has two principal advantages:

1. The successive ratios method is not limited to a predetermined number of interest rates or yield curves. The combinations of ten-year and 90-day rates are infinite.

2. It is not necessary to laboriously research and create the large tables of probabilities needed for the probabilistic method. All that is needed is a volatility factor and a correlation factor.

The successive ratios method also has some disadvantages, but these can be corrected by adding adjustments to the method; for example:

1. The successive ratios method can produce some crazy interest rates. Maximum and minimum interest rates are needed.

2. If you think that, over the long run, interest rates will tend to fluctuate mainly within some moderate range such as from 4% to 10%, the successive ratios method will need adjustment. For example, the preliminary result of the successive ratios method could be multiplied by some factor that brings the result a little closer to a targeted interest rate range.

3. The successive ratios method tends to produce more inverted yield curves than would normally be expected. A bias toward normal yield curves could be added to the formulas.

4. The difference between ten-year and 90-day rates can grow to extremes that are not realistic. A modification could be added to

keep the ten-year and 90-day rates within a reasonable range of one another.

15.6 Effect on Liabilities

Each interest rate scenario must then be run through the asset/liability model. The first step for each period of time is to calculate interest rates, including those earned on existing assets, those credited to products, and those available on new investments. The next step is to determine how interest rates affect the product cash flows. The product cash flows then determine the funds available for purchasing new assets or, if there is a cash shortfall, the amount of money that must be borrowed or obtained by selling assets. This sequence of relationships is illustrated in this diagram:

Interest Scenario → Interest Rates → Product Cash Flows → Asset Cash Flows

15.6.1 Determining Interest Rates

At the start of each new period, four interest rates are determined:

- The average interest rate being earned on existing assets
- The interest rates available on new investments
- The interest rates available on competing products, and
- The interest rates credited to the company's products being modeled.

The average interest rate being earned on existing assets can be determined by dividing investment income for the prior period by average assets for the prior period.

The interest rates available on new investments are determined from the interest rate scenario's yield curve for the current period. The yield curve can be filled in for all maturities by interpolating between key rates, such as the 90-day and ten-year rates. The yields for various asset classes and maturities can then be determined by adding spreads to the yield curve rate with the same maturity. These spreads are determined based on current spreads or average historical spreads and are assumed to remain constant.

The interest rates available on competing products will be referred to as *market rates*. They will be discussed in the next section. Then we will discuss the interest rates credited to the company's products.

15.6.2 Modeling Market Interest Rates

The market rate is the interest rate available in financial markets for various financial alternatives, including competing products offered by both life insurers and other financial institutions. Whether policyowners leave their funds with the company or decide to withdraw their funds depends on the alternatives that policyowners face.

If the company is crediting interest rates that are in line with market rates, surrenders and withdrawals should occur at normal rates. If the company credits higher than market rates, persistency should be improved. If the company credits significantly less than market rates, there could be damaging cash outflows. For example, if the company is crediting 8% interest to its SPDA policyowners at a time when short-term money market yields of 15% are available, you can expect a mass exodus of funds.

The market rate is compared to the product's credited rate to determine the effect on product cash flows. The primary effect is on lapse rates, which drives surrender benefits. Also affected are partial withdrawals and policy loans.

If the product being modeled does not have an explicit credited rate, then a proxy could be used. For example, a participating product could compare the dividend interest rate (the interest rate used to calculate dividends) to the market rate. For some products, like term products, the market rate is largely irrelevant. However, if the market rate is high enough, inflation rates may also be high. High, prolonged inflation can significantly reduce the real value of term insurance, leading to premature lapses.

What constitutes a relevant market rate will vary greatly by product and target market. Interviews with ex-customers can be helpful. By asking what interest rates attracted the customer's funds away from your company, you can gain some insight into what kind of products and which companies contribute to the market rate. In any case, you can be sure that the market rate involves more than just the interest rates credited by similar life insurance products. For example, you may want to reflect interest rates on non-insurance products such as the following:

- The interest rates available on money market funds
- The interest rates available on five-year certificates of deposit offered by banks, and
- The interest rates available on ten-year government bonds.

Some insurers use a *new money method* of crediting interest, which tracks assets and credits interest rates according to when funds were received by the company. Other insurers use a *portfolio method* of crediting interest, which credits an average interest rate to a large group of policyowners, regardless of the interest rates available when each contributed funds. When both methods are widely used, this adds another layer of complexity. The relevant market rate could be the greater of that obtained from a new money or portfolio method.

In summary, the market rate should reflect the rates credited by various types of products. These rates can probably be fairly well approximated by subtracting a constant spread from the government yield rate for a given maturity. A portfolio rate might be approximated as an average of rates over the last several years. These different rates might be combined by using the greater or lesser of various combinations of rates. Alternatively, a blend of several different rates might be used as the market rate.

Example 15.6.1 Market Rate Formula

A number of market rate formulas have been developed, based on interest rates credited by various companies on similar products. Below are two formulas derived by Tillinghast–Towers Perrin to approximate the median credited interest rates during the past ten years on the SPDA and UL products in their Wisdom/Flash database for the U.S. market, along with figures showing how well these formulas fit with past results:

SPDA: 55% of three-month average of five-year U.S. Treasury rates, converted to effective yields + 45% of 36-month average of five-year Treasury rates, converted to effective yield − 0.50% (see Figure 15.6.1).

UL: 30% of six-month average of five-year U.S. Treasury rates, converted to effective yields + 70% of 48-month average of five-year Treasury rates, converted to effective yields (see Figure 15.6.2).

Figure 15.6.1 SPDA Competitor Rate Index January 1990–October 1999

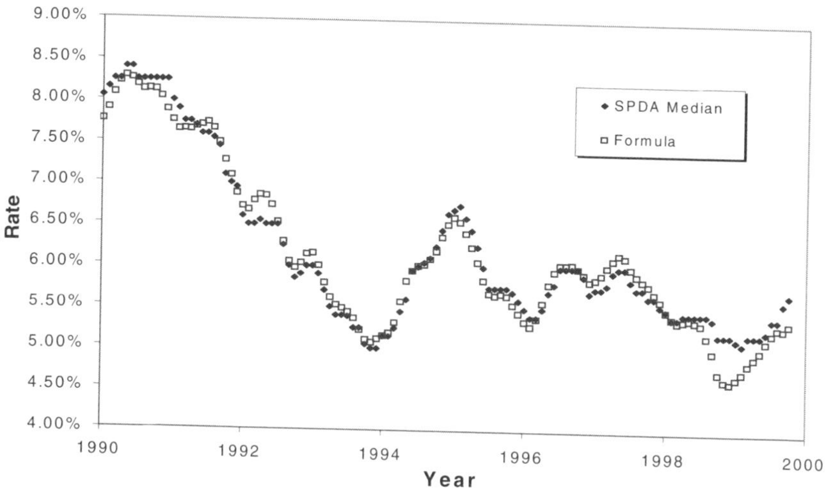

Source: Tillinghast–Towers Perrin.

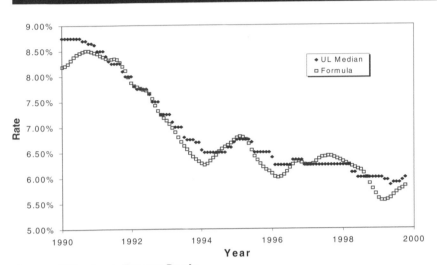

Figure 15.6.2 Universal Life Competitor Rate Index January 1990–October 1999

Source: **Tillinghast–Towers Perrin.**

15.6.3 Modeling Credited Interest Rates

The credited interest rate is a function of four interest rates:

1. The average net interest rate being earned (that is, net of investment expenses and default costs), on existing assets backing the product (the *portfolio rate*)

2. The average net interest rate available on new investments (the *new money rate*)

3. Any interest rate guaranteed by the product, and

4. The market rate.

As you will see below, interest guarantees and market rates act as constraints on what a company can credit, rather than the true driver of the credited rate.

   If a segmentation method is used for crediting interest, then the earned rate for new deposits is equal to the new money rate. The earned rate for existing deposits is the net interest rate earned on the funds backing the segment. If a portfolio method is used for crediting interest, the earned rate is equal to the portfolio rate, with some adjustment for new funds expected to be invested at the new money rate.

If the company segments its assets, the model must be able to track the assets, liabilities, and credited rates for each of the segments and its products. Some products create new segments every time there is a material change in interest rates, thereby generating numerous segments that must be modeled separately. Older segments associated with older products may use a different investment strategy compared to new segments. After a number of years, older segments may be combined, creating a larger pool of assets and liabilities that earn the same credited rates. These variations can add great complexity to your model.

The product could have one or more of the following guarantees:

1. A long-term guaranteed minimum interest rate

2. A short-term current interest rate guarantee, or

3. A bailout rate (if the product has a bailout feature).

The credited interest rate can be no less than any long-term or short-term guarantees. However, the company *can* credit an interest rate less than the bailout rate if it is willing to waive surrender charges. If the surrender charge is small or the end of the surrender charge period is nearing, the company may be willing to credit a rate less than the bailout rate. While the remainder of the discussion will focus on earned rates and market rates, guarantees should not be forgotten.

Most companies will have a targeted spread that they wish to earn. The spread is the difference between the earned rate and the credited rate. In other words, if the market rate is not an issue, most companies will use the following formula to set the credited rate:

Credited Rate = Earned Rate − Targeted Spread.

In practice, market rates often make it difficult to impossible to earn the targeted spread. At other times, the company may be able to earn more than the targeted spread, as is often the case when interest rates have been steadily declining.

Recognizing that spreads may vary according to market conditions, some companies adopt a strategy of earning the largest spread the market will allow, subject to a maximum spread, while maintaining a competitive credited rate, subject to a minimum spread. For example, a company might have a targeted spread of 1.50%, a maximum spread of 2.00%, and a minimum spread of 1.00%.

Most companies want their credited rates to be within a certain range of market rates. For example, a company may want its credited rates to be at least 90% of market rates. Similarly, a company may not want its credited rates to exceed 110% of market rates.

Example 15.6.2 Credited Rate Formula

Given a market rate and an earned rate, the parameters described in the previous two paragraphs can be combined to create the following process for determining credited rate:

1. Calculate maximum possible spread (MPS) = earned rate − 90% of market rate.

2. Set credited rate = 90% of market rate.

3. If MPS is greater than 2.00%, set credited rate = earned rate − 2.00%.

4. If credited rate > 110% of market rate, set credited rate = 110% of market rate

5. If MPS is less than 1.00%, set credited rate = earned rate − 1.00%.

The credited rate formula could also reflect surrender charges. In general, the existence of a surrender charge should help discourage surrenders, allowing the company to credit a slightly lower rate than if there were no surrender charge. The lower the surrender charge, the lower the effect on the credited rate.

15.6.4 Modeling the Effect on Lapses

The next step is to determine how lapses are affected by the crediting rate strategy. Most crediting strategies take some account of market rates. Let us consider the following extreme strategies, one that ignores market rates, and another that reflects only market rates:

Set the credited rate equal to the earned rate less a targeted spread:	Lapses will be highly variable, since no attention is paid to the market rate when setting credited rates. Spreads will always be on target but, with high lapses, recoverability of new business strain may not occur in many scenarios.
Set the credited rate equal to the market rate less a targeted pread:	Lapse rate volatility will be extremely low. However, negative spreads (compared to the earned rate) will be common, causing inadequate profitability in many scenarios.

Life insurance products that are sold as investment vehicles generally have lapses that are quite sensitive to differences between market rates and credited rates. Lapses are especially sensitive if the product has an explicit credited rate. With an explicit credited rate, the policyowner and agent can compare a particular policy to other, competing products. Products without explicit credited rates but with investment features, such as par whole life, have lapses that are less sensitive to differences in interest rates.

To develop formulas that predict changes in lapse rates based on the difference between market rates and credited rates, you can study industry experience and your own company's experience. Generally, the formulas should produce little or no change in lapse rates when the difference between the market rate and the earned rate is small. However, when the difference is large and positive, lapse rates should increase markedly. When the difference is large and negative, lapses should improve, but not disappear.

To give you some ideas on how lapse rates might be related to the difference between the market rate and the credited rate, let us define the following notation:

Difference =	The market rate less the credited rate: If the market rate is 8.00% and the credited rate is 7.00%, then Difference is 1.00% or 0.01
SurrChg% =	Surrender charge, as a percentage of account value

> qwBase = Base lapse rate that applies when there is no difference between market rate and credited rate and no surrender charge.

Here are some examples of formulas for lapse rates:

$$qw(t) = qw\text{Base}(t) \,(1 + \tfrac{1}{2}(100 \text{ Difference})^2) - \text{SurrChg}\%, \text{ with a}$$
minimum of 0.01 and a maximum of 0.50,

$$qw(t) = qw\text{Base}(t) + 1.25 \text{ Difference } 3.25^{|100 \text{ Difference}|} - \text{SurrChg}\%,$$
with a minimum of 0.01 and a maximum of 0.60.

For example, using the first formula with $qw\text{Base} = 0.12$, $\text{SurrChg}\% = 0.05$, and Difference = 0.00%, 1.00%, and 2.00%, we have

$$qw(t) = 0.12 \,(1 + \tfrac{1}{2}\,(0.00)^2) - 0.05 = 0.07,$$
$$qw(t) = 0.12 \,(1 + \tfrac{1}{2}\,(1.00)^2) - 0.05 = 0.13,$$
$$qw(t) = 0.12 \,(1 + \tfrac{1}{2}\,(2.00)^2) - 0.05 = 0.31.$$

Similarly, using the last formula with $qw\text{Base} = 0.12$ and Difference = -1.00%, 0.00%, 1.00%, and 2.00%, we have

$$qw(t) = 0.12 + 1.25 \,(-0.01)\, 3.25^{|(100)(-0.01)|} - 0.05 = 0.029,$$
$$qw(t) = 0.12 + 1.25 \,(0.00)\, 3.25^{|(100)(\,0.00)|} - 0.05 = 0.070,$$
$$qw(t) = 0.12 + 1.25 \,(0.01)\, 3.25^{|(100)(\,0.01)|} - 0.05 = 0.111,$$
$$qw(t) = 0.12 + 1.25 \,(0.02)\, 3.25^{|(100)(\,0.02)|} - 0.05 = 0.334.$$

Keep in mind that these are only examples. In general, a formula should cause lapses to fall below the base lapse rate if the credited rate exceeds the market rate. Only the second of the two lapse rate formulas accomplishes this. Lapses should increase or decrease exponentially, the farther apart the market rate and credited rate. In addition, as shown in the formulas, the existence of a surrender charge should lower the lapse rate.

15.6.5 Modeling Other Product Cash Flows

Credited interest rates directly affect dynamic cash values and reserves. Dividend interest rates affect the amount of dividends paid and the amounts applied to dividend options such as dividend accumulations, paid-up additions, and one-year term additions.

For flexible premium products, partial withdrawals and premium persistency can also be affected by the difference between market interest rates and credited rates. You can develop formulas for partial withdrawals and premium persistency that share similarities with the formulas developed in the previous section for lapse rates.

As market rates increase, you may see an increase in policy loan utilization, especially if policy loan interest rates are fixed. Your own company's experience should allow you to develop a formula to predict policy loan utilization based on interest rates.

High market rates are often associated with high inflation rates, which can cause expenses to increase faster than expected. You could build an inflation rate into your expense calculation. The inflation rate could be calculated as the market rate less a constant.

Finally, as discussed in Chapter 3 under selective lapsation, high lapse rates usually lead to mortality anti-selection. There is a tendency for unhealthy lives to persist, even when the difference between market rates and credited rates is high. If a great majority of the business lapses, the percentage of unhealthy lives may double, triple, or even quadruple, leading to much higher than expected mortality.

Several mortality models can help you estimate the degree of anti-selection resulting from higher-than-normal lapse rates. One model assumes that select and ultimate mortality rates are a blend of mortality rates for healthy and unhealthy lives. This model assumes that a higher proportion of healthy lives lapse. The greater the lapse rate, the greater the proportion of unhealthy lives remaining. The resulting mortality rate can be obtained by blending the mortality rates for healthy and unhealthy lives.

15.7 Effect on Assets

Once the effects of the interest rate scenario on liabilities have been determined, the effects on assets can be determined. The following steps are applied to assets for each period in the model:

1. Asset cash flows are determined, reflecting the effect of the current yield curve.
2. Net cash flow is determined, equal to asset cash flows plus product cash flows less distributable earnings.
3. If net cash flow is positive, new assets are purchased based on the investment strategy.
4. If net cash flow is negative, rules will govern whether to sell assets (and which assets should be sold) or borrow the cash needed.
5. The book value and market value are determined for all assets at the end of the period.
6. Investment income, capital gains, and capital losses are determined for the period.

Steps 1, 3, 4, and 6 will be discussed in more detail in this section. Step 2 is self-explanatory. Step 5 would be more properly discussed in a separate book devoted to the subject of assets.

15.7.1 Major Asset Classes

Setting up a model of asset cash flows begins with a basic understanding of the different types of investments that an insurance company normally makes to back its liabilities. Here are some of questions that need to be answered for each asset:

- What are the typical, regularly scheduled cash flows?
- What are the unusual cash flows, and in what situations can you reasonably assume the unusual cash flows will occur?
  Related to this, what are the rights given to the borrower to alter cash flow payments, by either delaying payments or accelerating payments?
  Does the company have any rights that could affect asset cash flows, such as a put option (that is, the right to force premature repayment)?
- What expenses will the company incur for management and accounting of each particular asset?

- What percentage of your investment will be lost due to asset defaults or asset devaluation?

- How liquid is the asset (that is, how quickly and inexpensively can it be sold)?

Below, we discuss several major asset classes in some detail: government securities, corporate bonds, commercial mortgages, residential mortgages, collaterized mortage obligations, asset-backed securities, real estate, common stock, preferred stock, and policy loans. You should be mindful of each of the above questions as you read the discussion.

15.7.1.1 Government Securities

Most government securities are bonds. Here is a quick review of bonds: Bonds have a stated maturity value, called the *par value,* which is paid at the maturity date. Bonds also have periodic interest payments, called *coupons,* that are typically paid semiannually. The amount of the coupon is equal to the par value times the coupon rate. You can purchase a bond at a discount (a price below par value), at par (a price equal to par value), or at a premium (a price above par value). The difference between the purchase price and the par value is called the *discount* (if price is less than par value) or the *premium* (if price is more than par value). If purchased at a discount, the bond's yield will exceed the coupon rate. If purchased at par, the yield will equal the coupon rate. If purchased at a premium, the yield will be less than the coupon rate. The amount of any discount or premium is amortized to zero over the life of the bond in a fashion that results in a constant yield to maturity, as shown in Chapter 14.

Government bonds are usually not callable. (Refer to the definition of callability in the next section.) Therefore, the asset model can reasonably assume that these securities will be held to maturity, unless the model determines they need to be sold.

Government securities are 100% guaranteed by the government. As a result, these securities are usually the highest rated securities in most countries. The assumed default rate is often zero. In line with their high ratings, these securities are usually the lowest yielding asset class available. Expenses related to government bonds are normally consistent with the expense assumption made for corporate bonds. Finally, these are some of the most liquid assets, with an active market that allows buyers and sellers to efficiently trade.

15.7.1.2 Corporate Bonds

Most corporate bonds are simple in nature, with a stated maturity value and a stated coupon payment. Bonds can have call and put options. A *call option* gives the borrower the option to repay the bond early. A *put option* gives the lender (the insurance company) the option to force the borrower to repay the bond early.

In times of low interest rates, most corporate bonds issued are not callable. However, in times of high interest rates, most corporate bonds issued *are* callable, as borrowers want to be able to refinance if rates fall. Most callable bonds charge a penalty for premature repayment. This penalty is the *call premium* and is equal to the difference between the call price and the maturity value. The call premium usually decreases over time. The call premium helps reimburse the bondholder for lost interest, as bonds will usually be called only when interest rates have dropped below the bond's original yield.

Call premiums commonly take one of two forms:

1. The form most often associated with publicly traded bonds has a call price that gradually decreases as a percentage of the maturity value. For example, the call prices for a five-year bond may be 104%, 103%, 102%, 101%, and 100% of the par value over the five years of the bond.

2. The form most often associated with privately placed bonds is more onerous. The call price is typically equal to the present value of all remaining interest and principal payments, where the present value is calculated using a spread over the yield rate on government securities of the same maturity. The spread is often a low number, like 0.50%, so that future cash flows are discounted at an interest rate lower than the rate at which the borrower could refinance. This results in a substantial penalty for premature repayment. Such a penalty would

provide a windfall to the lender. It would be conservative to ignore the effect of such a call option.

The model must make an assumption as to when the bond will be called. If interest rates move sufficiently below the bond's original yield (such as by 0.50% or 1.00%), then the borrower may be better off calling the bond and refinancing the debt, depending on the call premium. The farther interest rates move below the bond's original yield, the greater the probability of the bond being called. By the time the difference between current interest rates and the bond's original yield reaches some point between 1% and 2%, all bonds are usually called. There are some exceptions to this, such as bonds with onerous call premiums or borrowers with a finance staff that is immersed in other issues.

Put options are uncommon but do exist. They give the bondholder the right to force repayment of the bond. This option would most commonly be exercised when interest rates increased sufficiently beyond the bond's yield. Because the borrower would then have to refinance at higher interest rates, a put option would normally allow the borrower to repay something less than the full maturity value. Many companies avoid bonds with put options because of their lower yields: Put options are not free. Also, companies may have difficultly in tracking put options in order to exercise them at the most opportune time. Finally, companies may be averse to incurring any penalty associated with exercising the put option.

However, put options can be a valuable tool for matching assets and liabilities. Put options give the insurance company the ability to liquidate assets at favorable prices when interest rates are high and market values are depressed. This allows the company to either reinvest at higher interest rates to support higher credited rates or to fund cash outflows caused by not raising credited rates. Either way, put options help the company better match its liabilities.

Most corporate bonds are issued in the public marketplace, with the underwriting and sale of the bond issue managed by one or more investment banking groups. Bonds issued in such a fashion are normally uniform with regard to their provisions. Such bonds are sold to a large audience of investors and can be publicly traded after issue. We will refer to such bonds as *public bonds*. In contrast, *privately placed* corporate bonds, or *privates*, are negotiated and issued directly between a limited number of borrowers and the lender. Many insurance companies have large holdings of privates in their portfolios. The fees paid to investment bankers under public bond issues are saved with private issues. Therefore, all other things being equal, a private bond will normally yield higher than a public bond.

The features and provisions in private bonds vary considerably compared to public bond issues. Therefore, a good understanding of the provisions placed in the private issue is important. For example, privates will often have a sinking fund provision. This requires the borrower to gradually repay a percentage of the bond's principal each year, according to a schedule. The schedule commonly starts out as a small percentage of the bonds and increases over time. Sometimes the borrower is allowed to as much as double the amount repaid each year; this is essentially a "free partial call option." The sinking fund provision allows the borrower to gradually repay the bonds starting some time after issue and continuing to the maturity date, rather than having to repay all of the bonds on the maturity date. The sinking fund is applied across the board, on a pro-rata basis that affects all bondholders equally. A sinking fund provision clearly affects the timing of cash flows. In effect, the bond has no single maturity date. Instead, the bond will be gradually repaid a little each year. This means both the coupons and the remaining par value will drop in a series of steps as bonds are repaid according to the sinking fund schedule.

Call options, put options, and sinking fund provisions can all cause bonds to be repaid prior to maturity. The call option is an option given to the borrower. The put option is an option given to the bondholder. The sinking fund provision is not an option; it is a requirement. There is usually a cost to the borrower associated with a call option. All other factors being equal, a bond with a call option will tend to have a higher interest rate. Conversely, a bond with a put option will tend to have a lower interest rate.

Public bonds are usually more liquid than privates are. Public bonds can usually be sold in a day with low trading costs. Privately placed bonds can often be sold through dealers in a week or less with somewhat higher trading costs. This difference in liquidity causes lenders to demand higher yields from privates.

Some borrowers issue bonds with different levels of seniority. In an insolvency, the most senior bonds are repaid first. The most junior bonds are repaid last and consequently bear the greatest default risk. Each time a borrower issues bonds, the relative seniority of the new issue is clearly stated. When buying lower-rated bonds, it is safer to buy the most senior issues. When buying highly rated bonds, seniority may be of little concern.

Most bonds purchased by insurance companies are investment grade, which means they carry a rating of BBB or better. A bond rated AAA would have almost no chance of default. Such a rating would be given to relatively few, very large, financially secure companies or governments. At the other end of the investment-grade range, a bond rated BBB would have a small but important chance of default, such as 0.10% to 0.20% per year.

Public bonds are typically slightly less expensive to manage than private bonds. This is because good accounting information usually exists for public bonds, whereas private bonds will require more effort to ensure that payments are being made and that the borrower is still a healthy company whose bond deserves to be a part of the company's investment portfolio.

15.7.1.3 High-Yield Bonds

There is an entire spectrum of bonds rated lower than BBB, often referred to as "below investment grade," "high-yield," or "junk" bonds. These are simply corporate bonds with low ratings. A bond rated BB would have a modest chance of default, such as 1.00% to 1.50% per year. A bond rated C or D would have a high probability of default, such as 5.00% to 10.00% per year. To compensate for these relatively high probabilities of default, junk bonds pay high yields—hence the name.

Historically, the extra yield available on below-investment-grade bonds has more than paid for the higher level of defaults. Consequently, investment managers trying to maximize yield and willing to take more risk have been attracted to junk bonds. Because the companies that issue junk bonds are less financially secure, a downturn in the economy can cause the default rate on junk bonds to shoot up. If an insurance company has a large percentage of its assets invested in junk bonds, it could be harmed by such an upshot in defaults.

Companies that issue high-yield bonds can have difficulty refinancing their debt, especially if their financial condition worsens. This means that a call option on a high-yield bond should have a lower chance of being exercised. However, this works much like mortality anti-selection: The healthiest companies are most likely to call their bonds when interest rates fall. The unhealthiest companies are most likely to persist and not call their bonds. This also puts the unhealthiest companies at a competitive disadvantage, as their healthier competitors are able to refinance and reduce their cost of debt. Because of both of these factors, the overall default rate for the bonds that persist may increase.

15.7.1.4 Commercial Mortgages

Commercial mortgages are large loans secured by commercial real estate, most often retail or office buildings. The most common structure requires a monthly payment of principal and interest that would completely amortize the loan over a period of 20 years. However, the loan matures after only ten years, at which time the outstanding principal becomes due. In practice, the borrower usually refinances the mortgage after ten years, with either the same company or a competitor.

The costs of originating the mortgage are usually paid by the borrower. The amount loaned is usually the principal of the loan. In other words, using bond terminology, mortgages are usually purchased at par, so there is no premium or discount to amortize over the life of the mortgage.

Commercial mortgages usually contain a prepayment provision, which is another name for a call option. Prepayment provisions usually charge the borrower a fee for repaying early. Prepayment penalties are usually modest. For example, the prepayment fee could be 5%, 4%, 3%, 2%, and 1% of the principal outstanding for the first five years. After five years, there may be no prepayment fee. Sometimes a more onerous prepayment fee is assessed, similar to that described for privately placed bonds.

As with bonds, commercial mortgages carry a default risk. The default risk for commercial mortgages within a geographical area is highly correlated. When a commercial property has a high level of vacancies, a normal reaction is to lower the rent or offer other financial incentives to attract renters. Such actions can cause problems for other properties in the area, which may have to take similar actions to maintain their occupancy levels. In this way, one default can lead to many defaults.

When the economy turns down, vacancies in retail and office buildings will increase. The average default rate may climb from a fraction of 1% to a multiple of 1%. With time, many of the vacant buildings will once again be occupied. In the meantime, interest payments will be missed, and asset values will be impaired. While commercial mortgages are generally not as risky as junk bonds, the same care should be taken to avoid too high a concentration in assets that are apt to lose value during an economic recession.

Commercial mortgages are fairly illiquid, with no active market. However, a group of commercial mortgages can often be sold in a month or so. The seller must find interested buyers, allow them to do their own due diligence, and offer a competitive price.

Commercial mortgages have high costs of monitoring the asset. Company personnel may need to periodically travel to inspect the property. Outside consultants may be engaged to review and appraise the property on a regular basis.

15.7.1.5 Residential Mortgages

Residential mortgages are loans secured by residential real estate, with most loans usually equal to 50% to 80% of the value of the real estate. In some countries, the borrower makes monthly interest payments and must pay the full principal amount of the loan at maturity. This was the case in the U.K. up until the mid-1990s. Most mortgages in the U.K. today are like those in Canada and the U.S., where the borrower makes monthly payments that are a combination of principal and interest, such that the loan is paid in full when the last monthly payment is made at maturity. This results in a pattern of outstanding principal that decreases slowly at first and more rapidly as the principal is paid down.

Residential mortgages offer either fixed interest rates (most popular in the U.S.) or floating interest rates (common in the U.K. and in Canada, where fixed rates are not available for the entire term of the mortgage). Interest rates are fixed in the U.K. for only a short period, such as two to five years. In contrast, in the U.S., 15- and 30-year fixed rate mortgages predominate. When interest rates float, interest rates and monthly payments are typically adjusted every one to five years, and sometimes even daily in the U.K. The length or term of a new mortgage varies considerably by country. For example, in the U.S., only 15-year and 30-year mortgages are commonly available.

The costs of originating the mortgage are sometimes more than offset by fees charged to the borrower. The lender may initially pay more or less than the ultimate principal to be received. In other words, the mortgage may be purchased at a premium or a discount. Any premium or discount is amortized over the life of the mortgage, altering the yield somewhat from the interest rate paid.

Residential mortgages can always be prepaid. When the borrower sells the real estate, the mortgage is usually repaid. Some mortgages are assumable by the new buyer of the real estate, provided the new buyer qualifies financially. Occasionally, mortgages contain a prepayment penalty to protect the lender, especially if the lender has paid all the costs of originating the mortgage. The prepayment penalty usually lasts for only a few years. Residential mortgages have a substantial risk of prepayment. Few mortgages persist to the maturity date.

The level of prepayment depends on a number of factors. If the economy is strong, more people will move to new houses and mortgages will be prepaid faster. If interest rates fall much below the mortgage interest rate, then prepayments will soar as people refinance their mortgages. However, if interest rates remain higher than the mortgage interest rate, then people will not voluntarily refinance. In this case, prepayments will occur only when people sell their homes. If mortgages are assumable, prepayments will be reduced when interest rates are high.

Residential mortgages carry a default risk, mostly related to the borrower's unemployment, disability, and death. As with high-yield bonds and commercial mortgages, the default rate for residential mortgages is apt to climb during a recession, because of the resulting higher level of unemployment. Again, care should be taken to avoid too high a concentration in assets that are apt to lose value during an economic recession.

Individual residential mortgages are fairly illiquid, with no active market. However, as we will see in the next section, packages or pools of residential mortgages are another story. Because of their smaller size, residential mortgages are more difficult and expensive to sell than commercial mortgages. The cost of due diligence may make it difficult to attract potential buyers, unless the seller is willing to absorb this cost by lowering the price.

15.7.1.6   Collateralized Mortgage Obligations

Through much of the twentieth century, U.S. life insurers were active lenders of residential mortgages. The investment staff of most insurers included specialists in originating and servicing residential mortgages. In the 1980s, that changed. While U.S. life insurers still lend money for residential mortgages, they rarely do so directly.

Instead, mortgage specialists assemble mortgage pools that consist of thousands of individual mortgages. The mortgage specialists then sell slices of these mortgage pools to life insurers and other investors in ever more creative ways. In doing so, they have created a new financial instrument called *collateralized mortgage obligations* (CMOs), which are backed by the cash flows of the underlying pool of mortgages.

The process of creating a new financial instrument or security that is backed by underlying cash flows is known as *securitization.* CMOs were some of the first securitizations done. By purchasing a slice of thousands of mortgages, the buyer can diversify risk, especially if the mortgages are spread out geographically. This is one of the attractions of CMOs. However, this is only the beginning of the slicing that is commonly done to create CMOs.

Under a CMO, different slices, or *tranches,* of the mortgage payments are sold to investors. The payment of interest and principal to each tranche will vary, depending on the cash flow payments of the underlying mortgage payments. Each tranche will receive its share of total interest payments made on the underlying mortgages. The amount of each of the interest payments made to each tranche is set out in the CMO document.

Each interest payment is dependent on the amount of underlying mortgage principal outstanding. As mortgages are prepaid because of the sale of the residences or refinancing of the underlying loan, principal repayments are allocated to each tranche. In general, the shorter tranches receive most, if not all, of the underlying mortgage principal repayments first. The payments to the longer tranches will depend on how quickly the shorter tranches receive their principal. CMOs can be established using a multitude of different structures. Example 15.7.1 sets out a simple sequential tranche structure.

Example 15.7.1 Sequential Tranches

Sequential tranches are set up so that prepayments repay the principal of the first tranche first, then the second tranche, and finally the third tranche, as in the following example:

- Tranche 1: All cash flows associated with the first 30% of the principal to be repaid

- Tranche 2: All cash flows associated with the next 40% of the principal to be repaid

- Tranche 3: All cash flows associated with the last 30% of the principal to be repaid.

Tranche 3 would be called the *senior tranche* and would be the last tranche to be repaid. Variations in interest rates can cause the average duration of all tranches to vary significantly. For example, if interest rates rise dramatically, fewer people will prepay their mortgages, especially if the mortgage is of a fixed rate variety. Conversely, if interest rates fall, prepayments may increase as mortgage holders refinance existing mortgages or move to new homes.

Modeling mortgage cash flows is difficult because of the sensitivity of prepayments to changes in interest rates. Modeling cash flows for the various tranches of CMOs is even more difficult and well beyond the scope of this book. As you model the cash flows, you must separately track principal repayments, interest payments, and any prepayment penalties.

Many investors, particularly insurers, are interested in investments that have stable, predictable cash flows. One type of CMO tranche has been developed to satisfy this desire for predictability of cash flows. It is called a planned amortization class (PAC).

The investor in a PAC tranche is assured of receiving fixed, pre-scheduled payments over a predetermined period of time, under a wide range of prepayment scenarios. In other words, most fluctuations in interest rates will not affect the cash flows of a PAC. In order to create the predictability and certainty for the PAC, more volatile tranches are created to absorb the fluctuations in cash flows. The predictability of the PAC tranche comes with a price tag, in the form of a lower yield. This allows a higher yield to be paid to the other tranches to compensate for their higher volatility and uncertainty of cash flows.

Many CMOs are backed by government guarantees, resulting in no defaults and AAA ratings. Almost all CMOs are investment grade, because of the diversity of risk and the real estate collateral backing the mortgages. Most CMOs are actively traded and quite liquid. However, some of the more volatile tranches may be difficult to sell.

15.7.1.7 Asset-Backed Securities

Having tasted success with the creation of CMOs, investment bankers did not stop there. Instead, they went on a mission to securitize just about every cash flow imaginable. After securitizing residential mortgages, the next targets were just about every other form of consumer and corporate debt, such as credit card balances, automobile loans, home equity loans, bank loans, corporate bonds, and commercial mortgages. In general, the securization of assets such as these is referred to as an *asset-backed security* (ABS). Securitization of corporate bonds is referred to as a *collateralized bond obligation* (CBO).

Securitization spreads risk and increases the availability of funds by tapping the financial markets. It packages a number of similar cash flows into one or more types of tradable securities. In theory, securization should be able to be applied to life insurance cash flows. However, as of this writing, little has been accomplished, mainly because of the unique regulatory and accounting complexities associated with life insurance.

Many of the same considerations that apply to CMOs also apply to ABSs. Prepayment is an important variable that can be somewhat controlled by creating special tranches. However, for every tranche with reduced volatility, there is a buffering tranche with increased volatility. Somehow, buyers of all the tranches must be found.

15.7.1.8 Real Estate

While every real estate transaction is different, most produce cash flows from rental income that are modest and uncertain when compared to bonds and mortgages. Sometimes, cash outflows are required to maintain the property, especially after a tenant has moved out. The largest cash flow comes from the sale of the property.

A sizable portion of the return on real estate often comes from appreciation in the value of the property, although some properties depreciate over time. In most cases, the value of land increases faster than inflation. Buildings are more likely to depreciate. Real estate is perhaps the most illiquid asset. It usually takes months and sometimes years to sell a property for its full value.

Some amount of investment in real estate may be attractive for a company. However, because of its modest and variable cash flow and illiquidity, real estate is a poor match for most insurance liabilities. Real estate may make sense when matched against very long-term liabilities or a portion of the company's capital.

15.7.1.9 Common Stock

The trend in recent years is for common stocks to pay smaller and smaller dividends as a percentage of the stock price. Over the years, the average stock dividend has dropped from over 6% to under 1.5% of the stock price. As a result, stocks are rarely purchased for their ongoing cash flows. Instead, the main attraction is appreciation in the stock price.

Stock prices are highly variable. Declines in stock prices of 50% are not unusual and can occur quickly. Similarly, 100% increases in stock prices over a short period of time are common. On the other hand, common stocks are some of the most liquid investments. The world's stock markets routinely trade tens of billions of dollars worth of stock in a single day. Individual stocks sometimes trade over a billion dollars worth of stock in a single day. A stock's liquidity is related to the number of shares outstanding. Large companies' stocks are generally the most liquid.

Historically, between dividends and price appreciation, U.S. stocks produced total returns in the 9% to 11% range over almost every 20-year period of the twentieth century. Stock returns exceeded the returns produced by bonds and mortgages in every 20-year period.

Because its long-term returns are apt to be superior to just about every other form of investment, common stock is an attractive investment. However, common stocks are a poor match for most insurance liabilities, because of low ongoing cash flows, volatility in price, and accounting treatment. Common stock may make sense when matched against very long-term liabilities or a portion of the company's capital. The liquidity provided by common stocks could be a valuable addition to the portfolio.

15.7.1.10 Preferred Stock

Preferred stock is similar to a bond with no maturity date. Preferred stock dividends are calculated as an interest rate times the par value of the preferred stock, much like coupons. Dividends are usually paid every six months. Preferred stock is junior to all bonds. In the event of insolvency, all bondholders must receive any interest and principal due before any preferred stock dividends are paid. Because of this, preferred stock is of lower quality than the company's lowest rated bonds. Some issues of preferred stock are convertible to common stock at a fixed rate. If the common stock price appreciates sufficiently, this could be a valuable option.

In some jurisdictions, preferred stock dividends affect the borrower's taxes differently than bond coupons, even though both are interest payments. For example, in the U.S., bond coupons are generally tax-deductible for the borrower while preferred stock dividends are not. This causes most U.S. companies to issue bonds rather than preferred stock.

Preferred stocks tend to be fairly liquid, but not as liquid as common stocks or publicly traded bonds. Preferred stock prices vary mainly with interest rates; they behave very much like the prices for 30-year or longer bonds. If the yield and quality are both acceptable, a noncallable preferred stock could make an excellent match for an insurer's longest-term liabilities, especially those longer than the longest bond maturities available.

15.7.1.11   Policy Loans

Policy loans are discussed more fully in Chapter 8. However, it is important to understand how policy loans are affected by changes in interest rates. The effect varies greatly by the method used for policy loan interest.

If the policy loan interest rate is a fixed rate, then policy loan utilization will soar when policyowners can earn an interest rate elsewhere that is sufficiently higher than the policy loan interest rate. A knowledgeable policyowner will take out a maximum policy loan when this is the case. However, many policyowners are unaware of such opportunities and do not take out more policy loans than normal.

To offset the effect of a fixed policy loan interest rate, some products compensate for policy loan activity on a policy-by-policy basis. For example, some dynamic products reduce the credited rate to equal the policy loan interest rate less a spread for the portion of the cash value that is loaned. Some par products have dividends that essentially make the same adjustments for policies with policy loans. Policyowners who understand these adjustments will not be inclined to take out more policy loans than usual. However, some policyowners are apt to not understand this and may mistakenly take out a maximum loan to capitalize on the interest rates available elsewhere.

In summary, when market rates rise above the fixed policy loan interest rate, there will be an increase in the policy loan utilization rate.

The resulting cash outflows will be moderated by policyowners who are unaware of the opportunity and by any adjustments to the credited rate or dividend that are understood by policyowners.

If the policy loan interest rate is a variable rate, policy loan utilization will be more stable. An increase in market rates should not generate significant levels of new policy loans unless many policyowners misunderstand the variable policy loan interest rate—an unlikely event.

If an increase in interest rates causes an increase in surrenders, any policy loans outstanding on surrendered policies will automatically be repaid. This leads to an interesting observation: An increase in interest rates could cause an increase in policy loan repayments, as well as an increase in new policy loans.

15.7.2 Summary of Asset Cash Flows

Now that we have described several different classes of assets, we can discuss asset cash flows in some detail. First, we will summarize all the cash flows related to assets.

Positive asset cash flows result from the following:

- Sales of any type of asset
- For bonds:
  Coupon payments
  Calls (maturity value plus any call premium)
  Puts (maturity value less any put discount)
  Sinking fund payments
  Maturity payments
- For mortgages, CMOs, and ABSs:
  Regular payments of principal and interest
  Prepayments of principal and any prepayment penalties
  Maturity payments (mainly for commercial mortgages)
- Real estate rental income
- Common and preferred stock dividends

- For policy loans:
    Interest payments
    Principal repayments.

Negative asset cash flows result from the following:

- Investment expenses for all types of assets, including real estate maintenance

- Improvements to real estate

- New or additional policy loans

- Asset defaults.

15.7.3   Stochastic Modeling of Asset Cash Flows

The stochastic modeling of asset cash flows is an extremely difficult undertaking. A number of actuarial, investment, and software firms have spent many years building models that have grown increasingly sophisticated and complicated. While the models have become better in many respects, they are about as accurate as the most sophisticated weather prediction models. In other words, the models are not bad, but they cannot and never will be able to predict exactly what will happen—it is an impossible task. Even so, these asset models can be exceedingly beneficial, just like weather forecasts.

Because of the difficulty of the subject, all we can hope to do in these few pages is give you some basic ideas. We will examine cash flows in the following groupings:

- Sales of assets

- Pre-scheduled cash flows (coupons, minimum sinking fund payments, loan payments, rental income, stock dividends, policy loan interest, maturity payments, and investment expenses)

- Premature cash flows (calls, puts, extra sinking fund payments, and loan prepayments)

- Asset defaults.

Once sales of assets, premature cash flows, and asset defaults have been reflected, pre-scheduled cash flows can be easily projected, so they will not be discussed further. We will also not discuss real estate improvements and new policy loans further.

15.7.3.1 Sales of Assets

Many asset/liability models assume that assets are held until they mature or until they are prematurely repaid. This assumption is often at odds with the actual management of the company's investments. Most investment professionals are confident in their abilities and know they can probably beat the market, since the market includes amateurs like the authors, who freely admit their inferiority. However, when you evaluate the performance of the professional investors who manage all of the U.S. mutual funds, you find relatively few who outperform the S&P 500 stock index over a period of several years. While the stocks they picked may have outperformed the S&P 500, the expenses of actively managing the funds, including trading costs, often reduce performance to below that of the S&P 500. The same kind of relative performance applies to insurance company investment managers who actively trade the company's investment portfolio to improve yields. The improved yields net of trading costs may not actually be improved.

This can cause a dilemma for an insurance company. Investment results are critically important to insurers. They need some of the best investment talent available to ensure their investments are expertly managed. However, the best talent is usually loath to follow a buy and hold strategy. They may feel underutilized. They may become bored or feel like they are losing their skills by not trading.

When building your asset model, it is best to reflect reality. If your investment managers intend to actively trade investments, this can work to the company's advantage. A trading strategy that best fits the company's needs should be agreed upon and reflected in your model.

For example, a trading strategy might include targeting capital gains equal to capital losses, if the company is not rewarded for capital gains. A trading strategy could be used to constantly realign assets to better match liabilities. Your asset/liability model could identify assets that would improve the match if sold and reinvested in a different asset. While this is easy to say, it may be quite difficult to model.

15.7.3.2 Premature Cash Flows

Bond calls are driven almost entirely by interest rates. The borrower will call the bond once interest rates fall to the point where refinancing is attractive. Refinancing interest rates must be more than a little below the existing bond's yield, in order to induce the borrower to incur the expenses and effort required to refinance. For example, few borrowers will refinance to save 0.15% of yield. However, almost all borrowers will refinance to save 1.50% of yield. This is mainly true for higher rated bonds. Junk bonds may not be so easily refinanced, because of the borrower's poor credit rating. To model bond calls, you could build a grid of bond call rates that vary by interest differentials and bond quality ratings.

Bond puts are controlled by the insurer. If your company is a buyer of bonds with puts, you should establish some parameters for exercising the puts. For example, you may decide to put the bond anytime the put price (the price the borrower must pay you) is 10% or more above the market value of the bond. Alternatively, you could exercise a put anytime there is a negative net cash flow for the period and the put price exceeds the market value of the bond. Such rules could be built into your model.

Some bonds allow *extra sinking fund payments* to be made, over and above the required sinking fund payments. The amount of extra payments will vary with the ability of the borrower to make the extra payments and the attraction of doing so. As the differential between the bond's yield and current interest rates widen, you can expect extra sinking fund payments to increase. If current interest rates are low enough, a cash-strapped company may be better off borrowing money to make the extra sinking fund payments. Extra sinking fund payments can be modeled using a table of rates that vary with the interest differential.

Similarly, *mortgage prepayments* can be modeled using a table of prepayment rates that vary with the interest differential. Residential mortgages will include a level of prepayments associated with the selling of homes, unrelated to interest differentials.

Prepayments of CMOs and ABSs are much more difficult to model. The brute force approach models all the cash flows of all the tranches in order to predict the behavior of the one tranche in which you are interested. This is the recommended approach, because of the great variety and complexity of securitizations. While it is difficult, there are software packages that make it feasible. A simpler, more dangerous alternative is to resort to a table of prepayment rates that vary with the interest differential. It is dangerous because the pattern of prepayment rates will likely be unique, and you are apt to have no relevant historical data on which to base your guess.

15.7.3.3 Default Assumption

When an asset first defaults, cash inflows are interrupted. In fact, a missed bond coupon or a missed mortgage payment is what usually triggers the default. In many cases, assets in default are rehabilitated, and missed payments are made up. In other cases, the asset ends up being sold at a reduced price, and the insurer experiences a permanent loss. The permanent reduction in price and any missed payments constitute the true cost of default. In some cases it can take years to resolve an asset in default.

When modeling cash flows, how should defaults be reflected? Is it worthwhile to try to model the pattern of missed payments, made-up payments, and a final cash flow when the asset is sold? We will leave that to your judgment, but for our purposes, the answer is a definite "no."

We will take the simple approach of treating a default as a permanent loss of a percentage of the asset. For example, if an asset has a 0.4% annual cost of default, the asset will be carried at 99.6% of book value after one year, 99.2% after two years, and so on. Cash flows resulting from the asset will also be multiplied by the appropriate percentages to reflect defaults.

A default cost of 0.4% does not mean that 0.4% of all securities lose all their value. More likely, it means that 1% of all securities lose an average of 40% of their value. However, for modeling purposes, the result is the same.

Each asset will carry its own default rate, based on the type and quality of the asset. Actual experience shows that default rates tend to increase over time for highly rated securities and tend to decrease over time for poorly rated securities. In practice, such refinements are usually ignored.

An economic downturn will cause an upsurge in default rates for many kinds of assets. If your model can factor in economic cycles, you could vary the default rates with the peaks and valleys of economic activity. For example, a significant rise in interest rates could lead to an economic downturn. Similarly, a significant decrease in interest rates could spur the economy. During an economic downturn, default rates for some assets may double while others may increase by a factor of five or ten. During an economic upturn, default rates may be half of normal levels.

15.7.4 Purchasing New Assets

If the net cash flow for the period is positive, new assets much be purchased. An inventory of possible new assets is part of the input into the model. This inventory is typically based on the assets available shortly before the model is built. The asset model applies the interest rate scenario to determine the interest rates and yields on new assets for each future period. The asset model can apply the company's investment strategy in a number of ways, such as one of the following:

- Input data may specify the percentage of new assets to be invested in various asset classes of various quality and maturity. This distribution of assets may be fine-tuned after each run of the model through all the interest rate scenarios. Such an iterative process could allow the company to develop an investment strategy.

- Input data may specify the distribution of assets by asset class and quality, with the distribution by maturity left for the model to determine, using a goal of matching asset and liability cash flows. The model could dynamically adjust to different interest rate scenarios to better match the changing liability cash flows. By observing the results under various scenarios, the company may gain some insights into how to improve its matching strategies.

Rather than have one overall investment strategy, most companies have a collection of different investment strategies for the assets backing different liability portfolios. For example, a company might have separate investment strategies for universal life, whole life, SPDA, and term insurance portfolios.

15.7.5 Covering Cash Shortfalls

If the net cash flow for the period is negative, the company must borrow money or sell assets to cover the cash shortfall. Borrowing money was discussed in Chapter 14. Here are three examples of strategies for selling assets:

1. A simple strategy would be to sell the assets that are closest to their maturity dates. The market values of these assets would be the least affected by an increase in interest rates, which is the likely cause of the cash shortfall.

2. If the company has avoided taking capital gains in the past because they are largely ignored by investors, it may have built up a large amount of unrealized capital gains. If an increase in interest rates is the cause of the cash shortfall, then the company will likely have many assets with unrealized capital losses. Therefore, a viable strategy may be to sell assets with offsetting capital gains and losses.

3. Another strategy would be to sell assets that help the company better match assets and liabilities. For example, if the company has assets that are longer than its liabilities, it should sell long-term assets. However, the market value of long-term assets could be significantly depressed if the cash shortfall was caused by an increase in interest rates. This strategy could be modified by adding some focus on minimizing net capital gains and losses.

15.7.6 Calculation of Investment Results

Book values, capital gains and losses, and investment income are summarized below.

15.7.6.1 Book Values

For many assets, the book value is simply the price originally paid for the asset. For bonds, mortgages, CMOs, and ABSs, the book value starts out equal to the price paid for the asset and changes over time. The initial difference between the price paid for the asset and either (a) the maturity value, in the case of bonds, or (b) the loan principal, in the case of mortgages, CMOs, and ABSs, is amortized over the lifetime of the asset. At any point in time, the book value is equal to (a) or (b) plus the unamortized difference.

For mortgages, CMOs, and ABSs, regular loan payments gradually reduce the outstanding principal and the book value over the lifetime of the loan. For bonds, sinking fund payments reduce the maturity value and the book value of the bond.

15.7.6.2 Capital Gains and Losses

Sales of assets usually result in a capital gain or loss, which is calculated as the price received at sale less the book value of the asset at time of sale. If this amount is positive, it is a capital gain. If the amount is negative, it is a capital loss. Additionally, when an asset is called, put, or otherwise prepaid, the difference between the cash received and the asset's book value is recorded as a capital gain or loss. Defaults are recorded as capital losses.

15.7.6.3 Investment Income

We will define investment income to include capital gains and losses. This makes the formula for investment income a little simpler:

$$\text{Investment income} = \text{Net asset cash flow} + \text{Increase in book}$$
$$\text{value during the period.}$$

If new asset purchases are included in net asset cash flow as a negative, they will also be included in increase in book value as a positive. If new asset purchases are made only at the end of the period, they will have no effect on investment income for the period. On average, though, new purchases are made at the middle of the period and produce half a period's worth of investment income.

15.8 | Summarizing Stochastic Results

Using the results of stochastic modeling takes some getting used to. For example, instead of solving for the premium rate that produces a 15% ROI, you could take several different approaches with stochastic results. You could solve for the premium that produces

- A weighted average ROI of 15% over all scenarios tested
- An ROI of 15% or higher for half of the scenarios tested
- An ROI of 13% or higher for 75% of the scenarios tested, or
- An ROI of 7% or higher for 95% of the scenarios tested.

Typically, a large number of stochastically generated scenarios will be tested. The number of scenarios will depend on the variability of the results. For example, if every group of 100 scenarios produces materially different results, it may be necessary to test 250, 500, or even 1,000 scenarios before the results stabilize. The number of scenarios tested will also depend on the speed of the modeling software and the complexity of the model being tested. If the model includes thousands of liability cells, for example, it may take much too long to run 1,000 scenarios. It may be necessary to compromise between the desire for stable results and practical limitations.

Once all the scenarios have been tested, the results for the pricing parameter being tested are sequentially ordered. The results are usually summarized by percentile and are sometimes graphed in order to see the range of possible results, as in the following example.

Example 15.8.1 Summarization of Stochastic Results

The present value of pre-tax book profits and distributable earnings are shown in Tables 15.8.1 and 15.8.2 for a sample projection of 100 interest scenarios. The present value of distributable earnings at 10% is shown in Figure 15.8.1.

Figure 15.8.1 gives you a good sense of the variability of results. While the mean and median are both close to 1.1 million, there is less than a 20% chance that results will fall between 600,000 and 1.6 million. There is about a 30% chance that results will be negative. If this block is representative of the entire company's business, the company has a major interest rate risk.

Table 15.8.1 Summary of Present Value of Pre-tax Stockholder Earnings

Percentile	Present Value of Pre-tax Stockholder Earnings, Discounted at			
	6%	10%	15%	Pre-tax Yield
100th	23,099,026	18,527,769	14,567,299	20,188,689
85th	12,921,694	10,563,394	8,523,324	11,901,304
75th	11,332,201	9,373,877	7,632,963	10,611,933
50th	8,300,416	7,020,600	5,825,119	7,926,837
25th	4,953,136	4,571,570	4,159,021	4,824,442
15th	3,408,981	3,154,109	3,386,330	3,511,880
0th	−2,123,567	−1,558,546	−733,039	−1,982,909

Table 15.8.2 Summary of Present Value of Distributable Earnings

Percentile	Present Value of Distributable Earnings, Discounted at			
	6%	10%	15%	Pre-tax Yield
100th	14,294,553	9,216,329	5,102,205	10,939,832
85th	7,280,641	3,638,377	754,151	5,717,390
75th	6,309,503	2,893,450	212,238	4,855,866
50th	4,169,818	1,100,241	−1,117,089	3,152,038
25th	1,617,124	−280,205	−2,215,382	1,040,576
15th	764,837	−1,159,106	−2,615,449	259,719
0th	−2,751,777	−4,590,768	−5,785,222	−3,728,465

Figure 15.8.1 Present Value of Distributable Earnings at 10%

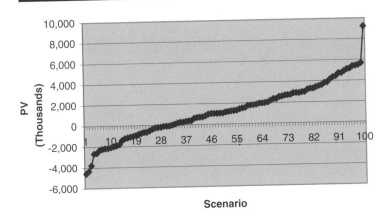

Exercise 15.1

Use the following random values and the table below to estimate how many points the St. Louis Rams will score on any given Sunday.

Random values: 0.25345, 0.32895, 0.45919, and 0.87456.

Points	f(Points)
7	0.04224
14	0.10542
21	0.12434
28	0.08453
35	0.10266
42	0.30894
49	0.15293
56	0.07894

Exercise 15.2

Using Formula 15.3.1, calculate Z_n for X_n = 0, 5, 10, 15, 20, 25, and 30.

Exercise 15.3

Using the distribution function in Table 15.3.1, calculate the following:

$$P(Z_n) = -1.09545$$
$$P(Z_n) = 1.46059$$
$$P(Z_n) = 2.92119.$$

Exercise 15.4

Use Formula 15.4.1 to derive Formula 15.4.5 for fratio(x).

Exercise 15.5

Use Table 15.4.3 to calculate the number of deaths assuming $S = 0.78967$.

Exercise 15.6

Using the binomial distribution, calculate a lapse distribution function and cumulative distribution function, up to and including $y = 20$, where y is the number of lapses. Use $n = 500$ less the number of deaths calculated in Exercise 15.5 and use $qw = 0.01$. Note: $qw = 0.01$ might be viewed as an unusually low lapse rate. It was used to keep the results within a manageable range. When you set up the calculation, try using higher lapse rates and see how long it takes before the cumulative distribution function approaches 1.000.

Calculate the resulting number of lapses and the lapse rate that would be calculated for the following three randomly generated values of S: 0.075, 0.60, and 0.92. Describe the process to calculate the number of deaths and lapses for the next period.

Exercise 15.7

Recalculate the pattern of ten-year rates from Example 15.5.3, using the same random numbers that were generated, but assuming the following distribution function:

	Probability of Change in Level by				
	−0.50%	−0.25%	0.00%	0.25%	0.50%
$f(x)$	0.05	0.20	0.50	0.20	0.05

Exercise 15.8

Using the slope movement probabilities in Example 15.5.3, the slope random numbers in Example 15.5.3, and the 10-year rates in Exercise 15.7, calculate the resulting 90-day rates for

1. Period 4, assuming Period 3's slope was 0.90

2. Period 7, assuming Period 6's slope was 1.05

3. Period 8, using the resulting slope for Period 7.

Exercise 15.9

Using Formulas 15.5.1 through 15.5.3, calculate the 90-day rates and the ten-year rates for the first two periods, using the random numbers below and assuming the beginning 90-day rate is 7.50% and the beginning ten-year rate is 9.25%. Also assume that VolFactor $= 0.25$, Correlation $= 0.35$, and $n = 50$. Use the following values of X_n:

Period	90-day X_n	Ten-year X_n
1	15	29
2	27	22

Exercise 15.10

What problems can be caused by always setting the credited rate equal to the earned rate less the spread needed to achieve the priced-for profit margins?

Exercise 15.11

If you create a lapse rate formula to reflect the differences between credited rates and market rates, what attributes should this formula have?

Exercise 15.12

Of the major asset classes presented in Section 15.7.1, which generally have the following characteristics:

1. The highest liquidity
2. The lowest liquidity
3. The highest quality (or lowest default cost)
4. The lowest quality (or highest default cost)
5. The longest duration or maturity
6. The highest yield, excluding capital gains
7. The highest yield, including capital gains
8. The most predictable cash flows
9. The most volatile cash flows.

Exercise 15.13

Describe the various ways that assets can be repaid prematurely.

Exercise 15.14

Refer to Table 15.8.2. For each discount rate, compare the following pairs of results to the median (50th percentile): 25th and 75th, 15th and 85th, 0th and 100th. For each discount rate, would you say there is more upside potential or downside potential, compared to the median? How would this affect your use of the median result? Discuss the volatility of the results.

15.10 Answers

Answer 15.1

The cumulative distribution function $F(\text{Points})$ results from the distribution function $f(\text{points})$:

Points	f(Points)	F(Points)
7	0.04224	0.04224
14	0.10542	0.14766
21	0.12434	0.27200
28	0.08453	0.35653
35	0.10266	0.45919
42	0.30894	0.76813
49	0.15293	0.92106
56	0.07894	1.00000

Since $0.14766 < 0.25345 \le 0.27200$, Points $= 21$.
Since $0.27200 < 0.32895 \le 0.35653$, Points $= 28$.
Since $0.35653 < 0.45919 \le 0.45919$, Points $= 35$.
Since $0.76813 < 0.87456 \le 0.92106$, Points $= 49$.

Answer 15.2

$$Z_0 = -5.47723 \quad Z_{20} = 1.82574$$
$$Z_5 = -3.65148 \quad Z_{25} = 3.65178$$

$$Z_{10} = -1.82574 \quad Z_{30} = 5.47723$$
$$Z_{15} = \quad 0.00000$$

Answer 15.3

Using Formula 15.3.1 and solving for X_n, we know that the above three values correspond to $X_n = 12$, 19, and 23, respectively. From Table 15.3.1, $f(12) = 0.0770$, $f(19) = 0.0505$, and $f(23) = 0.0035$.

Answer 15.4

Using the definition of fratio(x), we know

$$\text{fratio}(x) = \frac{f(x)}{f(x-1)}.$$

Substituting for $f(x)$ and $f(x-1)$ using Formula 15.4.2, we have

$$\text{fratio}(x) = \frac{{}_nC_x \, q^x \, (1-q)^{(n-x)}}{{}_nC_{x-1} \, q^{x-1} \, (1-q)^{(n-x+1)}}.$$

This reduces to

$$\text{fratio}(x) = \frac{{}_nC_x \, q}{{}_nC_{x-1} \, (1-q)}.$$

Substituting for ${}_nC_x$ and ${}_nC_{x-1}$, we have

$$\text{fratio}(x) = \frac{\dfrac{n!}{(n-x)! \, x!} \, q}{\dfrac{n!}{(n-x+1)! \, (x-1)!} \, (1-q)}.$$

Canceling terms, we have

$$\text{fratio}(x) = \frac{\dfrac{1}{x} \, q}{\dfrac{1}{(n-x+1)} \, (1-q)}.$$

Rearranging terms, we have Formula 15.4.5:

$$\text{fratio}(x) = \frac{q}{1-q} \, \frac{n-x+1}{x}.$$

Answer 15.5

Since $0.7357590052 < 0.78967 \leq 0.9198828804$, the number of deaths equals two.

Answer 15.6

The following table shows the distribution function and cumulative distribution function assuming $n = 498$ (500 less the two deaths from Exercise 15.5) and $qw = 0.01$.

y	$Pr(NumLapse = y)$	$Pr(NumLapse \leq y)$
0	0.0067038905	0.0067038905
1	0.0337226005	0.0404264910
2	0.0846471336	0.1250736246
3	0.1413635632	0.2664371878
4	0.1767044540	0.4431416417
5	0.1763474753	0.6194891170
6	0.1463624669	0.7658515839
7	0.1039110154	0.8697625993
8	0.0644195815	0.9341821809
9	0.0354271548	0.9696093357
10	0.0174988674	0.9871082031
11	0.0078415494	0.9949497525
12	0.0032145072	0.9981642597
13	0.0012138699	0.9993781295
14	0.0004247669	0.9998028964
15	0.0001384425	0.9999413389
16	0.0000422145	0.9999835534
17	0.0000120899	0.9999956433
18	0.0000032633	0.9999989067
19	0.0000008327	0.9999997394
20	0.0000002015	0.9999999409

Since $0.0404264910 < 0.075 \le 0.1250736246$, the number of lapses equals two. The lapse rate equals $2/498 = 0.004016$.

Since $0.4431416417 < 0.600 \le 0.6194891170$, the number of lapses equals five. The lapse rate equals $5/498 = 0.01004$.

Since $0.8697625993 < 0.920 \le 0.9341821809$, the number of lapses equals eight. The lapse rate equals $8/498 = 0.016064$.

To calculate the number of deaths and lapses for the next period:

1. Calculate a new probability table for mortality reflecting the number of lives in force: 500 minus the number of deaths from Exercise 15.5 minus the number of lapses from Exercise 15.6.

2. Generate a random number and use the table calculated in Step 1 to determine the number of deaths.

3. Calculate a new probability table for lapses using the number of lives remaining after subtracting the number of deaths from Step 2.

4. Generate a random number and use the table calculated in Step 3 to determine the number of lapses.

Answer 15.7

Here is the resulting cumulative distribution function:

	Probability of Change in Level by				
	−0.50%	−0.25%	0.00%	0.25%	0.50%
$f(x)$	0.05	0.20	0.50	0.20	0.05
$F(x)$	0.05	0.25	0.75	0.95	1.00

Using the same random values, we now get the following pattern of ten-year rates:

Period	Random Number	Level (Ten-year Rate)
0	—	8.00%
1	0.29419	8.00
2	0.46285	8.00
3	0.84673	8.25
4	0.91231	8.50
5	0.03333	8.00
6	0.59102	8.00
7	0.58078	8.00
8	0.07409	7.75
9	0.83582	8.00
10	0.81573	8.25

Answer 15.8

1. Random number = 0.95458.

   The cumulative distribution function for the current slope of 0.90 is

   Probability that slope for next period is

0.60	0.75	0.90	1.05	1.20
0.00	0.20	0.80	1.00	1.00

   Therefore, Period 4's slope is 1.05.
   90-Day rate = 8.50% from Exercise 15.7 $\times$ 1.05 = 8.925%.

2. Random number = 0.05276.

   The cumulative distribution function for the current slope of 1.05 is

   Probability that slope for next period is

0.60	0.75	0.90	1.05	1.20
0.00	0.10	0.25	0.75	1.00

   Therefore, Period 7's slope is 0.75.
   90-Day rate = 8.00% from Exercise 15.7 $\times$ 0.75 = 6.00%.

3. Random number = 0.43711.

The cumulative distribution function for the current slope of 0.75 is

Probability that slope for next period is

0.60	0.75	0.90	1.05	1.20
0.15	0.70	0.90	1.00	1.00

Therefore, Period 8's slope is still 0.75.

90-Day rate = 7.75% from Exercise 15.7 $\times$ 0.75 = 5.8125%.

Answer 15.9

Period 1:

$$Z1 = (15 - 25)/(\tfrac{1}{2} (50)^{1/2}) = -2.82843.$$

Using Formula 15.5.1:

$$i90day(1) = i90day(0)e^{Z1 \text{ VolFactor}}$$
$$= 7.50\% e^{(-2.82843) (0.25)}$$
$$= 3.6980\%.$$

$$Z2 = (29 - 25)/((\tfrac{1}{2} (50)^{1/2}) = 1.13137.$$

Using Formula 15.5.2:

$$Z10year = Z1 \text{ Correlation} + Z2 (1 - \text{Correlation}^2)^{0.5}$$
$$= (-2.82843) (0.35) + (1.13137)(1 - 0.35^2)^{0.5}$$
$$= 0.06986.$$

Using Formula 15.5.3:

$$i10year(1) = i10year(0)e^{Z10year \text{ VolFactor}}$$
$$= 9.25\% \ e^{ (0.06986) (0.25)}$$
$$= 9.4130\%.$$

Period 2:

$$Z1 = (27 - 25)/(\tfrac{1}{2} (50)^{1/2}) = 0.56569.$$

Using Formula 15.5.1:

$$i90day(2) = i90day(1)e^{Z1 \text{ VolFactor}}$$
$$= 3.6980\%e^{(0.56569)\ (0.25)}$$
$$= 4.2598\%.$$

$$Z2 = (22 - 25)/((\tfrac{1}{2}\ (50)^{1/2}) = -0.84853.$$

Using Formula 15.5.2:

$$Z10year = Z1\ \text{Correlation} + Z2\ (1 - \text{Correlation}^2)^{0.5}$$
$$= (0.56569)\ (0.35) + (-0.84853)(1 - 0.35^2)^{0.5}$$
$$= -0.59687.$$

Using Formula 15.5.3:

$$i10year(2) = i10year(1)e^{Z10year \text{ VolFactor}}$$
$$= 9.413\%\ e^{\ (-0.59687)\ (0.25)}$$
$$= 8.1082\%.$$

Answer 15.10

During a time of rising interest rates, this simple formula could result in a noncompetitive credited rate, leading to an upsurge in surrenders. During a time of falling interest rates, this simple formula could result in too high a credited rate, compared to the rates available on competing products. In summary, the company may be giving away too much profit when interest rates fall and losing too much business when interest rates rise.

Answer 15.11

See the last paragraph of Section 15.6.4. In addition, you may want to impose a minimum and maximum on the results of the formula.

Answer 15.12

1. Government bonds, widely held corporate bonds, widely held stocks

2. Real estate

3. Government bonds, government-guaranteed mortgages (including many CMOs), highly rated corporate bonds

4. Junk bonds

5. Real estate and preferred and common stocks

6. Junk bonds

7. Common stocks

8. Noncallable bonds and some CMO and ABS tranches, designed to generate predictable cash flows

9. Residual CMO and ABS tranches that are designed to absorb cash flow volatility in order to provide cash flow stability to other tranches.

Answer 15.13

Refer to Subsection 15.7.3.2.

Answer 15.14

For the 6% and pre-tax yield discount rates, there seems to be slightly more downside potential, looking at the results for the 15th through the 85th percentile. However, looking only at the 0th and 100th percentiles, there seems to be more upside than downside.

For the 10% and 15% discount rates, there is more upside potential than downside potential, when comparing all pairs of results to the median.

In this case, the magnitude of differences between upside and downside variations is not that significant, so these differences would likely have little impact on the use of the median result. While there is no absolute measure or standard, the volatility of results seems quite significant. Further investigation into the cause of the volatility could lead to improvements in product design, credited rate strategy, or investment strategy.

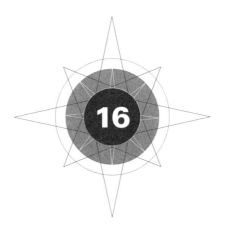

Financial Management

Previous chapters have focused on topics and projects most often handled by actuaries. This chapter covers the fundamentals of financial management, an area that involves accounting, actuarial, and investment professionals. Financial management is commonly headed by a company's chief financial officer (CFO).

As we discussed in Chapter 2, successful companies do a better job than many companies in aligning their vision, mission, strategy, target markets, and products. Their success is often defined by their achievement of financial goals.

In the life insurance industry, financial goals vary widely from company to company. Different companies focus on return on equity, embedded value, consistent growth in earnings and revenue, total return to stockholders, and total return to policyowners. Many factors influence the choice of financial goals: type of company, company tradition, company strengths and weaknesses, past company results, competition, regulation, financial markets, and the personalities and beliefs of the company's senior management and other influential people.

Regardless of the financial goal chosen, there are some basic financial management tools available to life insurance companies that should be understood. Traditions, regulations, and other constraints result in most companies utilizing only a few of these tools. However, the trend is toward developing and using more tools.

No matter what financial goals your company strives to achieve, it must actively monitor and manage its finances in three broad areas:

- Risk management
- Earnings management, and
- Capital management.

Many financial goals are achieved by maximizing earnings, reducing risk and earnings volatility, and optimizing capital. These three components are intimately related. If you change one component, you often affect another component. For example, reinsurance can affect earnings and capital while reducing risk. Buying or selling blocks of business also affects all three components.

To reduce risk, you often have to reduce expected earnings. On the other hand, one way to increase expected earnings is to increase risk. For example, by investing in stocks instead of bonds, you can increase expected earnings, but at a cost of increased risk. In most cases, risk management is motivated by the desire to stabilize earnings. More fundamentally, risk management protects the company's solvency.

Risk management is also linked to capital management. If a company has billions of extra capital, it may be more interested in increasing its returns than avoiding risk. The smaller the capital base (in both absolute terms and as a percentage of assets), the lower the ability to tolerate risk.

16.2 Tools of Financial Management

The tools of financial management can be grouped into informational tools (financial analysis and modeling) and risk transfer options (reinsurance and acquisitions of business). These tools affect all three of the areas of risk, earnings, and capital management. Tools that are specific to each area are discussed in later sections. While selling or acquiring a business is a financial management tool, it is presented as a separate section because of its complexity.

16.2.1   Financial Analysis

Worthwhile financial analysis provides information that leads to decisions. Financial analysis gives a company the ability to analyze and understand its historical results, so it can learn from its own experience. A company must anticipate its future analysis needs, so that it can meticulously collect information over a number of years. This information is often organized in the form of a data warehouse (a central repository of summarized information) with software tools that make the information easy to access and analyze.

Besides income statement and balance sheet results (broken down by line of business, market, product, distribution system, and so on), the company should accumulate other information for financial decisions, such as

- The results of mortality and lapse studies
- Investment results, including net interest rates, default costs, investment expenses, and capital gains and losses, summarized by asset class and asset segment. Net interest rates should be compared to credited interest rates for each asset segment.
- Distribution of sales by product, risk class, gender, and so on
- Relevant unit costs for various levels of decisions (for example, to decide whether to continue a certain product, market, distribution system, line of business, or even the company).

By examining the results of the past, the company can better understand where it is succeeding and where it is failing. A natural reaction to such an understanding would be to put more resources into the areas where the company does the best and shrink the areas where the company does not perform as well. This could change the company's emphasis on different markets, products, and distribution systems.

By better understanding why the company performs well in one area and poorly in another, the company may be able to apply such knowledge to improve its overall performance. For example, by examining why a certain product is successful in one region of the country, the company may learn how to repeat its success in other regions.

16.2.2 Modeling

Modeling is the ability to project future financial results and is discussed in detail in Chapters 14 and 15. Every company needs the ability to model future results, in order to understand the consequences of its decisions.

Often, modeling can produce results at finer levels than financial analysis can. For example, financial analysis may be able to break down results no finer than by line of business or broad product group, because that is all that is tracked by the company's accounting system. Because modeling is the sum of many detailed cells, modeling results can usually be broken down by product, issue year, risk class, and so on. Modeling needs to provide results at least as detailed as the various summaries available from financial analysis.

Modeling can be a useful tool for testing the effect of various decisions on future earnings and other results. For example, a company could ask the following question: If we raise prices by 1%, causing a 25% increase in profit margins and a 20% drop in sales, what is the long-term effect on earnings and return on equity?

Modeling can be used to produce present values of future results. Such present values can be helpful in trying to establish the value contributed by a product, a market, a distribution system, a line of business, or the entire company. For example, the embedded value (based on distributable earnings, in this case) of a block of business can be calculated as shown below. (The formulas presented below are annual formulas. Only minor adjustments are needed to convert to quarterly or monthly values. An exercise at the end of this chapter presents these adjustments.) Let

$$\text{DistrEarn\_tot(calyr)} = \text{Future distributable earnings in calendar year calyr for the business being analyzed}$$

$$i = \text{Hurdle rate at which future distributable earnings will be discounted}$$

$$\text{EmbeddedValue(begyr)} = \text{Embedded value as of begyr, using a hurdle rate of } i.$$

Adapting Formula 11.6.1, we have

$$\text{EmbeddedValue(begyr)}$$

$$= \sum_{calyr=begyr}^{\infty} \text{DistrEarn\_tot(calyr)}(1 + i)^{(begyr - calyr)}. \qquad (16.2.1)$$

Modeling allows you to determine which products, markets, and other factors are contributing the most to the company's financial goals and which are detracting from the goals. In addition, modeling can be used to roughly estimate the costs and potential value of adding new markets, new distribution systems, and new products. Using the results of modeling, the company can make at least a partially informed decision. We say "partially informed" because it is notoriously difficult to make accurate estimates in areas where the company lacks experience.

16.2.3   Combined Financial Analysis and Modeling

The results of financial analysis and modeling can be combined to connect the past and the future, thereby giving the company a more complete view. Combined results are useful for some of the most important decisions a company will need to make. For example, to decide whether to continue a certain distribution system, the company will want to consider past results and future projections to see whether the expenses related to continuing the distribution system will produce acceptable financial results. The company may want to accumulate combined results for other important decisions, such as

- Whether to stop offering certain products
- Whether to exit certain markets
- Whether to sell or close down a certain line of business
- Whether to keep the company independent or seek affiliation with another company, through merger, acquisition, or being acquired.

Oftentimes, the results of the past do not provide enough information to make a certain type of decision. For example, if the company has decided to study the performance of each of its general agencies and close down those that are not adding value, past results do not tell the entire story. For example, a newer general agency may have incurred significant start-up costs, which dwarf the meager profits from the business produced to date. However, when compared to the embedded value of the business produced, the start-up costs may appear to be a good investment. By using financial analysis to determine current expenses for each general agency and by using modeling to calculate the embedded value being created by each general agency, the company can better compare costs and benefits.

By combining historical results with modeled future results, you can calculate long-term performance measures, such as return on investment (ROI) or weighted-average return on equity (ROE). For example, a simple ROI can be calculated as follows. Let

DistrEarn_tot(calyr) = Distributable earnings for the business being analyzed. The same variable is used for past and future results. For example, if a line of business were five years old, the first five values would reflect a large investment (negative distributable earnings) to start up the line of business. The future projected values would show returns on these investments (positive distributable earnings).

ROI = The simple return on investment, to be solved for.

Adapting Formula 11.6.2, we have

$$0 = \sum_{\text{all calyr}} \text{DistrEarn\_tot(calyr)} \ (1 + \text{ROI})^{-\text{calyr}}, \qquad (16.2.2)$$

where calyr starts with the first calendar year in which money was invested in the business and continues until all the business has run out. Keep in mind that simple ROIs can be misleading. When there is more than one sign change in distributable earnings, the proper approach is to calculate a generalized ROI, as described in Chapter 11.

Financial analysis is closely connected to modeling. Modeling is driven by assumptions, which are used to project future values. These assumptions are often based on a financial analysis of past results.

Example 16.2.1

A company has written a five-year term block of business for two years, incurring distributable earnings of -5.8 million and -2.37 million, respectively, for the first two years. A model of the resulting in force business, along with a projection of new sales for the next three years, produces the following pattern of distributable earnings.

Year	DistrEarn (Thousands)
3	$-1,226$
4	-409
5	29
6	$7,677$
7	$4,806$
8	$2,509$
9	875

Combining the two years of historical distributable earnings with the projected distributable earnings shown above allows us to track results from inception until all the business runs off. Table 16.2.1 shows the complete stream of distributable earnings and the resulting ROI.

Table 16.2.1 Calculation of ROI

Year	DistrEarn (*Thousands*)
1	−5,800
2	−2,370
3	−1,226
4	−409
5	29
6	7,677
7	4,806
8	2,509
9	875
	ROI: 9.82%

16.2.4 Reinsurance

Reinsurance is perhaps the most flexible tool a company has for managing its financial position. It is useful for much more than transferring risk. It can also shift earnings, capital, revenue, benefits, expenses, assets, and liabilities from one company to another. The ceding company may have a right to recapture, which allows it to terminate the reinsurance and put the business back on its books.

Many different forms of reinsurance can be used to accomplish different goals. For example, coinsurance can be used to sell all the financial attributes of a block of business to another company. However, the ceding company would typically continue to administer the business in return for an expense allowance from the reinsurer.

Modified coinsurance provides the ceding company with most of the benefits of coinsurance, but with the added benefit that the ceding company gets to retain the reserves for the block and a matching amount of assets. This is very appealing to companies with an aversion to giving up management of assets.

16.2.4.1 Effect on Stability of Earnings

More than any other financial tool, reinsurance can be used to stabilize earnings. Reinsurance can be used to offset virtually every kind of risk. Reinsurance can be used with all kinds of assets and liabilities. In the extreme case, virtually all of a company's risk can be reinsured. In other words, all of the company's assets, liabilities, premiums, investment income, and policy benefits can be reinsured. In this case, the company would be left with only a stream of profits, equal to the difference between expense allowances received from its reinsurers and the company's actual expenses.

More commonly, reinsurance is used to stabilize a company's mortality risk. In many markets there is a trend toward greater use of mortality reinsurance. In some markets, reinsurers end up with more mortality risk than the direct writers retain.

16.2.4.2 Effect on Pattern of Earnings

While yearly renewable term (YRT) focuses on the mortality risk, the pattern of YRT premium rates often does not match the pattern of expected mortality rates. A difference in these patterns, intended or not, can affect the incidence of earnings by policy year.

By varying reinsurance terms and features, it is possible to achieve many different financial objectives. Cash flows between the two parties can be minimized. The ceding company's capital can be enhanced or unaffected. When risk is transferred, required capital is also transferred. The pattern of earnings by policy year can be shifted or left alone. Reinsurance can be designed to have a beneficial effect on taxes, especially when unused tax losses are about to expire.

Reinsurance usually affects the timing of solvency earnings and taxable earnings, including current period earnings. Because of this, reinsurance agreements are sometimes specifically designed to achieve a desired effect on solvency earnings or taxable earnings. In contrast, the effect of reinsurance on expected stockholder earnings is usually spread over the duration of the reinsurance agreement. Different reinsurance designs normally do little to change the pattern of stockholder earnings.

16.2.4.3 Reinsurance as Capital

Compared to debt and equity, reinsurance can be used to obtain financing more quickly, and often at a lower cost. Because risk is transferred, reinsurance of new business has the doubly beneficial effect of financing the strain of new business and lowering the ceding company's capital requirements. In addition, reinsurance of new business provides financing exactly when it is needed, since it reinsures new business as it is produced. By reinsuring a portion of its new business, a company can afford to write much higher levels of new business when sales levels take off. In contrast, debt or equity financing must usually be obtained well in advance of its total deployment.

Companies with too much capital or excess distributable earnings can use reinsurance in the other direction: They can assume reinsurance business to put their excess capital to work. In addition, by assuming reinsurance, it may be possible to generate tax losses. A number of companies have reinsured business over the years just for this reason. To quickly accomplish this without the expense of starting up a reinsurance operation, some companies assume reinsurance from a reinsurer.

Every reinsurance transaction has some effect on the capital of both the ceding company and the reinsurer, either through reserve credits, transfer of cash, or some other effect on assets or liabilities. By using a variety of techniques and a combination of different types of reinsurance agreements, it is possible to construct reinsurance transactions that simultaneously accomplish several targeted objectives, such as

- Transfer of targeted risks
- Transfer of a targeted amount of cash (including no cash transfer)
- Targeted increase or decrease in one or more of the following:
    Solvency earnings
    Solvency capital
    Assets
    Liabilities, and
    Required capital.

Compared to debt and equity, reinsurance not only increases the company's capital, but also decreases the company's need for capital, by reducing its risk and therefore its required capital. The extent to which this can be accomplished is largely determined by a country's reinsurance regulations, which can range from too tough to too loose to just right.

Some countries limit reinsurance so severely that reinsurance is limited to transferring mortality risk using YRT. A number of countries have virtually no reinsurance regulations, which can lead to abusive reinsurance agreements that artificially inflate a company's capital or earnings. A relatively few countries have reinsurance regulations that are "just right," allowing reinsurance the flexibility to play an important and helpful role, without artificially inflating a company's results.

When reinsurance is used primarily to provide capital, the resulting increase in capital can behave more like equity or more like debt. If the reinsurer provided a relatively large amount of capital in relation to future earnings (that is, an amount approaching the present value of future earnings), then the reinsurance would be just as risky as the underlying business. The reinsurer's return would be similar to the ceding company's return; the capital provided through reinsurance would behave much like equity. However, if the reinsurer provided a relatively small amount of capital in relation to future earnings, then the capital provided would almost certainly be repaid by future earnings. In this case, the reinsurance would function more like debt.

16.2.4.4 Reinsurance Leverage

In some cases, reinsurance can be used to leverage a company's returns. For example, if a product produces an ROI of 12.5% and the company can secure a reinsurance agreement that has an ROI of 10.0% for the reinsurer, the company can use this difference to its advantage.

Example 16.2.2 Using Reinsurance to Leverage Returns

Let us assume the product will require a capital contribution of 200 (the "investment") and will produce expected annual earnings of 25 (the "return"). The ROI is $25/200 = 12.5\%$. Let us assume the company reinsures half the business with the following terms: The reinsurer will reimburse the company for half of the capital contribution (100), but will receive only 40% of the expected annual earnings (10).

	Before Reinsurance	Effect of Reinsurance	After Reinsurance
Capital Contribution	200	−100	100
Annual Earnings	25	−10	15
ROI	12.5%	10.0%	15.0%

In this case, the reinsurance agreement helps the company stretch its capital (it can now afford to write twice as much new business) while leveraging its ROI from 12.5% to 15.0%.

16.3 Acquisition or Sale of Business

Selling or acquiring a business is the most complex and difficult way to affect a company's financial results. The results can be dramatic, although not always good.

Companies sometimes sell blocks of business to raise capital. More often, a sale is made to dispose of a business that does not have economies of scale, is no longer a strategic fit, or has a low rate of

return. Companies buy blocks of business to build economies of scale, to add value by cutting expenses, to put idle capital to work, or to grow the company for the benefit of its owners.

For most companies, acquisitions are rare. Many companies would like to grow through acquisition, but relatively few are able to do so. Excess capital among life insurers often leads to fierce price competition for acquisitions. Only a few can afford to pay and have the capability to profit from the resulting high prices. As a result, a relatively small group of buyers often account for a disproportionate number of life insurance acquisitions over time.

16.3.1   Assumption Reinsurance and Indemnity Reinsurance

Acquisition or sale of a block of business (that is, a part of a company) is usually accomplished through a specialized type of reinsurance agreement. The sale of an entire company does not require the use of reinsurance.

Up to this point, discussions of reinsurance in this book have involved only indemnity reinsurance, which indemnifies or reimburses the ceding company for policy benefits paid. Administration and management of the reinsured block of business usually remain with the ceding company. However, the sale of a block of business is usually accomplished by using one of two reinsurance structures: (1) assumption reinsurance or (2) indemnity reinsurance with transfer of administration to the buyer.

Under *assumption reinsurance,* the company that issued the policies is removed from liability after the block of business is sold. Notices are typically sent out to the policyowners notifying them that a new company is now responsible for their insurance policies. In some jurisdictions, regulations require pre-approval from the policyowners before liability can be transferred to the buyer. When faced with these kinds of regulations, which may require the company to contact and gain approval from millions of policyowners, many companies opt to sell blocks of business by using indemnity reinsurance with transfer of administration.

Under *indemnity reinsurance,* the company that issued the policies is *not* removed from the liability stream. Instead, the selling company relies on the reinsurer (the buyer of the block) to reimburse the seller for all benefits paid. Administration is typically transferred to the buyer under these situations. The buyer handles all cash flows related to the business. The selling company, however, must still show the business on its books, although it is 100% offset by indemnity reinsurance.

Indemnity reinsurance accomplishes most of the goals of assumption reinsurance: The seller receives a fair value for the business and no longer has to administer the policies. However, since the seller is still under contractual liability to the policyowners, the seller is ultimately liable for any benefits or other amounts not paid by the reinsurer. For example, if the buyer becomes insolvent and cannot pay policy benefits, the seller must pay them. However, taking this risk is often more attractive than dealing with the onerous requirements that may be imposed in connection with assumption reinsurance.

When business is sold through indemnity reinsurance, the seller has no right to recapture the block, unless the reinsurer does not perform its obligations. When business is sold through assumption reinsurance, the seller has no right to recapture the block under any conditions.

16.3.2 Prerequisites for an Acquisition

An acquisition of a block of business or an entire company requires a number of conditions to be present:

- The buyer must have access to the capital needed to complete the acquisition. A company with excess capital may already have the capital it needs. A company with a good reputation in the financial markets can more easily raise capital for an acquisition, provided the acquisition makes sense to the financial markets.

- The acquisition must be likely to improve the buyer's earnings. The increase in earnings should be commensurate with the risk involved in acquiring the block. The company should be aware of the "buyer's curse." Historically, the results of most acquisitions have been significantly worse than original expectations.

- The buyer must have the resources to complete the acquisition. If the target of the acquisition is to be run as a separate, independent business, this is not an issue. However, if the target is to be fully integrated into the company's existing business, the company must have a team of people who know how to accomplish the integration effectively and who are available to focus solely on the integration until it is completed.

This last point cannot be overemphasized. Combining two operations is an extremely difficult undertaking. Differences in business practice can lead to complex choices. Physically combining operations can lead to logistical nightmares. Adopting common administrative systems is so difficult that it is often not attempted, except for new business.

However, the most difficult aspect is related to people, especially when an acquisition is driven by the expense savings that can be gained by combining two operations. This means firing people. For those with weak stomachs, this means layoffs, early-out programs, downsizing, rightsizing, and even happy-sizing. Whatever you call it, it involves gut-wrenching decisions as to which staff to keep and which to release.

The survivors often wind up feeling guilty and insecure. Many valuable people are lost, both intentionally and unintentionally. Some of them return as consultants, to help the company through the ensuing difficulty caused by losing so many key people. Because of these kinds of problems, it is not surprising that many acquisitions are unsuccessful.

One integration strategy that seems to work better than most is to make very few changes immediately after the acquisition. Let the acquired company show what it can do. Take many months or even a few years to let the organizations get to know each other and learn each other's strengths and weaknesses. Gradually institute changes that build on the strengths and bring the organizations closer together. For example, after a year or two, new product development might be shared. A common software platform might be established for new business.

16.3.3 Prerequisites for a Sale

The sale of a block of business or an entire company requires a number of conditions to be present:

- The seller must have a use for the capital that will be raised by the sale. If the sale simply adds to excess capital and there is no strategy as to how to profitably deploy it, perhaps the time is not right to sell.

- The sale must be likely to improve the seller's earnings. This is usually accomplished by using the proceeds of the sale to earn a higher rate of return than was being earned by the business sold.

- While the "buyer's curse" generally works in favor of the seller, the seller should carefully consider the price currently available for the business. Would the company be better off waiting for a time when the business being sold is more attractive, thereby generating more competition among buyers? Alternatively, is the company better off selling the business before its value drops further? Are insurance properties selling at a relatively high or low price, based on benchmarks such as price to book value or price to earnings ratios?

- If only part of the company is being sold, what effect will the sale have on the remaining staff? Will people wonder which part will be sold next? Will the sale make sense to the staff? Will they understand and accept the wisdom of the sale? Will staff lose confidence in management?

16.3.4 Determining the Purchase Value of an In-Force Block

The sale of a block of business could include both in force and new business. Purchasing the rights to new business is seldom done without first purchasing the future profits of the in-force business. Therefore, the first step in valuing a block of business is to calculate the purchase value of the in-force block of business.

When a block of in-force business is purchased, the parties to the sale have to agree on two primary items:

- What amount of liabilities will the buyer assume? We will assume this amount is the solvency reserves on the block of business being sold.

- What amount of assets will the seller transfer to the buyer in order for the buyer to assume the liabilities?

Most of the time, the amount of assets transferred is less than the amount of liabilities transferred, though this is not always the case. We will define the *purchase value* as the liabilities transferred less the assets transferred.

All of the following variables relate to the block of business being purchased and are as of the purchase date (time zero), unless otherwise noted. Let

$$\text{SolvRes}(0) = \text{Solvency reserves to be transferred}$$
$$\text{Assets}(0) = \text{Assets to be transferred}$$
$$\text{ReqCap}(0) = \text{Required capital for the buyer}$$
$$\text{EV}(0) = \text{Embedded value}$$
$$\text{Tax}(0) = \text{Taxes associated with the acquisition}$$
$$\text{PurchaseValue} = \text{purchase, equal to liabilities less assets transferred}$$
$$\text{TransCosts} = \text{The pre-tax transaction costs associated with the acquisition.}$$

Then,

$$\text{PurchaseValue} = \text{SolvRes}(0) - \text{Assets}(0). \qquad (16.3.1)$$

Typically, the calculation of SolvRes(0) is straightforward, and both parties can agree to it. Often, the buyer will establish the same amount of solvency reserves that the seller was holding. When the buyer restates the amount of solvency reserves, the purchase value is normally based on the seller's solvency reserves. The most difficult part of the negotiations is agreeing on Assets(0).

To calculate Assets(0), the buyer will typically begin with a calculation of the block's embedded value (EV), that is, the present value of future distributable earnings, discounted at the buyer's desired rate of return.

The embedded value calculation assumes initial assets equal to initial solvency reserves plus required capital. Therefore, for an acquisition to be attractive, the buyer must receive initial assets not less than initial solvency reserves plus required capital less embedded value. In other words, the minimum assets received can be calculated as

$$\text{Assets}(0) = \text{SolvRes}(0) + \text{ReqCap}(0) - \text{EV}(0). \qquad (16.3.2)$$

The purchase value is typically tax deductible. However, any difference between initial solvency reserves and initial tax reserves will affect taxes at the purchase date. We can calculate taxes as

$$\text{Tax}(0) = (\text{SolvRes}(0) - \text{TaxRes}(0) - \text{PurchaseValue}$$
$$- \text{TransCosts})\,\text{EarnTaxRate}. \qquad (16.3.3)$$

There may be other tax-related differences that affect Tax(0). These additional items must be taken into account. We can now enhance Formula 16.3.2 to calculate more accurately the minimum assets that must be received, reflecting initial taxes and transaction costs:

$$\text{Assets}(0) = \text{SolvRes}(0) + \text{ReqCap}(0) + \text{Tax}(0) + \text{TransCosts}$$
$$- \text{EV}(0). \qquad (16.3.4)$$

Combining Formulas 16.3.1 and 16.3.4, we can solve for the maximum purchase value:

$$\text{PurchaseValue} = \text{EV}(0) - \text{Tax}(0) - \text{TransCosts} - \text{ReqCap}(0). \qquad (16.3.5)$$

Rearranging terms, we have

$$\text{EV}(0) = \text{PurchaseValue} + \text{Tax}(0) + \text{TransCosts} + \text{ReqCap}(0). \qquad (16.3.6)$$

Formula 16.3.6 can be interpreted as follows: In exchange for incurring an initial purchase value, initial taxes, and transaction costs and setting up initial required capital, the buyer will receive the embedded value of the block of business.

Example 16.3.1 Purchase Value for an In-Force Block of Business

Company ABC has an in-force block of business that it wants to sell with the following balance sheet:

Assets		Liabilities	
Invested Assets	135	Solvency Reserves	120
		Required Capital	15
Total	135	Total	135

Company XYZ has agreed to assume all of the liabilities in exchange for assets equal to 105. Several additional assumptions are needed:

- The buyer establishes the same solvency reserves as the seller (120).

- Pre-tax transaction costs equal 5.

- Tax reserves are less than solvency reserves by an amount of 5, and the buyer is taxed at a rate of 40%.

- The buyer establishes required capital of 12, instead of 15 held by the seller.

From this information, we can impute the buyer's estimate of the embedded value for the block of business, using Formula 16.3.6.

We know the following:

$$\text{PurchaseValue} = 120 - 105 = 15$$
$$\text{Tax}(0) = (5 - 15 - 5)\,40\% = -6$$
$$\text{TransCosts} = 5$$
$$\text{ReqCap} = 12.$$

Using Formula 16.3.6, we have

$$\text{EV}(0) = 15 - 6 + 5 + 12 = 26.$$

This can be calculated a second way: The buyer is going to establish total liabilities of 132, consisting of 120 of solvency reserves and 12 of required capital. After receiving the assets from the seller, paying transaction costs, and incurring taxes, the buyer will end up with assets of 106:

Assets received from seller:	105
Less payment of pre-tax transaction costs:	−5
Less taxes:	− (−6)
	106

The difference between the liabilities established and the net assets received must be funded from the buyer's existing assets.

Therefore, the buyer must believe that the embedded value of the block is 26 (132 − 106).

16.3.5 New Business and Goodwill

If an in-force block of business is sold without ongoing new business, the block is considered a *closed* block of business. Assuming that the purchase value for the buyer is calculated using a discount rate in the embedded value calculation that is acceptable to the buyer, the analysis in Section 16.3.4 is typically the only analysis that has to be performed.

If new business is still being sold and is adding to the in-force block of business, then the sale of the block often is made assuming that new business will continue. However, since the value of new business after the point of the sale is unknowable, it often results in an intangible asset on the buyer's balance sheet. Such an intangible asset is most often reflected only in stockholder accounting. Since solvency accounting is conservative by nature, an intangible asset for the value of future new business is normally not allowed.

The value of future new business is often included as part of *goodwill*. Goodwill is an intangible asset that cannot be directly calculated. It is often described as the value of future new business, intellectual capital, reputation, brand name, and other intangible assets that are impossible to quantify. For stockholder accounting purposes, goodwill is the balancing item that forces assets to equal liabilities at the purchase date.

Example 16.3.2

Company XYZ in Example 16.3.1 has determined a value for future new business associated with the block of business. As a result, it is willing to assume the liabilities of 120 for a reduced amount of assets equal to 85, instead of the original 105, which did not reflect new business. If Company XYZ values the in-force block with an embedded value of 26, then the amount of goodwill would be 20, equal to the 105 of assets they were willing to accept for the in-force business, less 85, the reduced amount they were willing to accept for both the in-force and future new business.

Goodwill is a risky asset. It may be worth much less than initial estimates. For example, suppose much of the value of an acquisition is associated with future new business to be produced through a captive agent distribution system. If the buyer is unsuccessful in retaining most of the agents, much of the goodwill will evaporate.

In most countries, goodwill is amortized and brought into the income statement in a straight line over a number of years, normally between 10 and 40 years. There is often quite a bit of choice as to the proper amortization period. The amortization of goodwill reduces earnings.

In a few countries, goodwill can be expensed (that is, written down to zero) immediately. This practice reduces the company's equity and increases its future returns, because earnings are not reduced by the amortization of goodwill. This has a doubly positive effect on a company's ROE, by increasing "R" and reducing "E."

Goodwill can have a major effect on the attractiveness of an acquisition, depending on how quickly it is amortized and its tax deductibility. For example, suppose half of the purchase value is goodwill. Suppose that goodwill is largely associated with the profits from future new business, which are expected to be earned evenly over the next 20 years. If goodwill must be amortized (deducted from earnings) over the next ten years, then earnings would be depressed for ten years. Few companies would pursue an acquisition that produced depressed earnings for the next ten years. In addition, if goodwill were not tax deductible, the financial effect would be even worse.

There is no simple formula for determining the purchase value for an ongoing business. The value of the intangible assets represented by goodwill is very difficult to determine. Because of the risk and uncertainty associated with future new business, it is common to include the estimated value of no more than three to five years of future new business in the purchase value. A liability model could be used to calculate the embedded value associated with future new business.

16.3.6 Purchase Price and Purchase Value

There is no consistent definition of the *purchase price* of a company or a block of business. What is stated as a purchase price when an acquisition is publicly announced is typically some function of the public accounting standards used by the companies involved. If you ask any two accounting firms for the definition of the purchase price, most likely you will get two different answers.

Because of the lack of a standard definition for purchase price, we defined purchase value earlier in this section. Purchase value is based on solvency accounting: It involves distributable earnings, embedded value, and solvency assets and liabilities.

When formulating a purchase value, there are other considerations to be taken into account beyond distributable earnings and embedded value. For example, a stock company would usually examine the effect of the acquisition on stockholder earnings per share and return on equity. If the acquisition would be dilutive (that is, if it would reduce earnings per share of stock outstanding) for more than a short period, it may not be attractive. If the acquisition produced weighted-average ROEs below the company's targeted ROE, it may not be attractive.

16.3.7   Earnings Management

Acquisitions or sales of business can help the company manage earnings in one of three ways:

- The company can sell a loss-producing business. By taking an earnings hit when the business is sold, the company can avoid future losses, thereby improving future earnings.

- The company can buy a business. This will usually move its earnings up, either a notch or significantly, depending on the size of the acquisition. The added earnings from the acquisition of a closed block will tend to fall off over time. The purchase of an ongoing business may result in added earnings that increase over time.

The company may follow a strategy of growing primarily through acquisitions. In order to continue this strategy, the company must have the confidence and backing of the financial markets, in order to raise more and more capital to finance more and more acquisitions. Alternatively, the company must be able to convince those being acquired to accept the buyer's stock for a major portion of the purchase price.

General Electric (GE), the world's largest corporation by some measures, has profited from an acquisition-related competitive advantage for two main reasons:

1. Life insurance company price to earnings (P/E) ratios are usually, as a group, well below the market average P/E ratio.

2. On the other hand, GE, with its impressive growth and earnings record from 1980 to 2000, enjoyed a relatively high P/E ratio, often more than double that for the average life insurance company.

This means a life insurer owned by GE would be worth more than twice what it would be worth as a stand-alone insurer. This kind of difference has given GE and a few other companies both a strong incentive and a strong ability to acquire life insurers.

16.4　Risk Management

Risk management involves understanding, balancing, and controlling the risks inherent in an insurance company. These risks may come from a number of lines of business, such as life insurance, annuities, health insurance, disability insurance, and so on. Chapter 10 presented risks in a framework that paralleled the components of required capital formulas. In this section, we will organize the risks into the following groupings:

- Market risk
- Credit risk
- Liquidity risk
- Pricing risk.

We will not consider operational risks, property risks, legal liability risks, regulatory compliance risks, and risks related to changes in accounting practices, regulations, legislation, and taxation. As a guide to implementing a thorough risk management program, we recommend the *Standards of Sound Business and Financial Practices*, developed by Canadian regulators and industry groups.

16.4.1　Market Risk

There are a number of risks related to changes in the financial markets. We will examine each of these risks in turn:

- Interest rate risk
- Market fluctuation risk
- Asset valuation risk
- Spread widening risk
- Suboptimal asset allocation
- Currency fluctuation risk.

16.4.1.1 Interest Rate Risk

The effect of changing interest rates on a company's assets and liabilities has been discussed in previous chapters and will not be repeated here. Disintermediation risk is described in Section 10.4. Simple asset/liability management (ALM) techniques are discussed in Chapter 14. In addition, a number of financial derivatives can be purchased as interest rate hedges. For example, a derivative that increases in value with increasing interest rates could help protect a company from increases in interest rates.

Even when assets and liabilities are perfectly matched, there may still be an interest rate risk, because of accounting quirks. This can happen when assets are marked to market value and liabilities are not. A substantial increase in interest rates could cause a financially strong company to appear financially weak or even insolvent. There are several ways to control this risk:

- Encourage sales of products with market value adjustments, including variable products

- Limit sales of products without market value adjustments

- Hold extra capital to be able to withstand interest rate fluctuations

- Work with regulators and accounting bodies to bring the accounting for liabilities in line with the accounting for assets. (This is a long and uncertain process.)

16.4.1.2 Market Fluctuation Risk

Market values of volatile assets, such as common stocks and real estate, are subject to considerable fluctuation over time. A decline in stock or real estate values could cause significant losses for the company. A decline in real estate values could also lead to increased defaults on mortgage loans, as the value of mortgaged properties falls below the outstanding loan principal. There are three main strategies for managing the risk of loss due to a fall in market values:

- Use volatile assets mainly to back products with market value adjustments, including variable products.

- Otherwise, limit volatile assets to a small percentage of overall assets
- Hold extra capital to be able to withstand market fluctuations.

16.4.1.3 Asset Valuation Risk

One risk faced by all companies is that of overly aggressive valuation of assets. If there is not an active market for a particular type of asset, it may be difficult to determine market values. For example, the market values of certain real estate, collateralized mortgage obligations (CMOs), asset-backed securities (ABSs), collateralized bond obligations (CBOs), wholly owned subsidiaries, and thinly traded assets may be uncertain at best. The people who are asked to value these assets are sometimes the same people who made the decision to purchase them in the first place. While this is a clear conflict of interest, it does happen. As a result, a conflicted person may be biased toward overestimating the value, in order to support the original decision to purchase the asset.

When a significant portion of a company's capital is invested in an affiliated company, special care is needed to ensure an unbiased estimate of the value of such an investment.

While asset valuation risk is mainly focused on the overvaluation of assets, undervaluing assets can also be a problem. This is well illustrated by the experience of General American Life Insurance Company and its health maintenance organization (HMO) subsidiary, GenCare. Around 1990, General American had a dispute with the Missouri Department of Insurance (MDI) as to the proper value of GenCare. General American thought it was worth $20 million, and MDI thought it was worth half that. To prove its point, General American sold a portion of GenCare to the public through an initial public offering (IPO), thereby establishing an independent market value for GenCare. It turned out General American was very wrong. GenCare's value increased to about $100 million because of the IPO! When GenCare was sold a few years later, at a time when HMO stocks were particularly hot, it fetched a price of over $500 million.

Several steps can be taken to reduce asset valuation risk:

- Invest the great majority of the company's funds in assets with readily available and verifiable market values, such as publicly traded stocks and bonds.

- Ensure that controls exist so that those who periodically determine the market value of assets do so independently, uninfluenced by senior management or those who purchased the assets. Independent audits should reinforce these controls.

- For a large investment in an affiliate, consider an IPO to sell part of the affiliate to the public and establish an independent market value for it.

16.4.1.4   Spread-Widening Risk

An asset class can fall out of favor, resulting in spreads (that is, the yield rate less a reference rate, like LIBOR) widening. For example, suppose the original spread for a BBB-rated bond with a modified duration of ten years were 1.00% over LIBOR. If the economy turned down, defaults increased, LIBOR remained unchanged, and the spread widened to 2.00%, then the market value of the BBB-rated bond would drop about 10%. This is because a 1.00% increase in the spread has the same effect on market value as a 1.00% increase in interest rates. (This can be calculated using Formula 14.4.11. The change in market value = $-$Modified duration $\times$ Interest change = $-10 \times -1.00\% = 10\%$.)

Spread widening is a function of supply and demand. When demand exceeds supply for a certain kind of asset, its spread drops. When supply exceeds demand, its spread increases. Spread-widening risk is most significant for lower quality, thinly traded, and unusual securities, where supply and demand are most apt to fluctuate.

The experience of Executive Life illustrates the potential effect of spread-widening risk. During the 1980s, Executive Life was a leading buyer of high-yield or "junk" bonds, as they were affectionately called. Although these bonds had relatively high rates of default, the extra spread earned on junk bonds more than compensated for the default cost throughout the 1980s.

By 1990, many large U.S. life insurers were invested in junk bonds, but none more heavily than Executive Life, with some 65% of its investments in junk bonds. When the U.S. economy turned down and default rates increased, there were suddenly many more sellers of junk bonds than there were buyers. This caused junk bond spread to widen, as junk bond market values dropped. This led to much adverse publicity for Executive Life, downgrades by the rating agencies, and a "run on the bank." While Executive Life was able to meet its obligations, the run on the bank led to huge losses that were caused by having to liquidate junk bonds with depressed market values.

By early 1991, the market value of Executive Life's assets was $2.5 billion less than its liabilities. As a result, the California Department of Insurance seized control of Executive Life and quickly sold its junk bond portfolio at a $1–2 billion loss. With the advantage of hindsight, this was unfortunate timing: Junk bond market values appreciated over 50% over the next year. Still, this does point out the danger of having too high a concentration of the company's assets in a volatile asset class such as junk bonds without maintaining substantial extra capital to cover the volatility.

Several strategies can be used to control spread-widening risk:

- Invest mainly in assets with a small risk of spread widening, such as high-quality, heavily traded, widely held securities.

- Use assets with large spread-widening risk mainly in connection with products that have market value adjustments, including variable products.

- Otherwise, limit these assets to a small percentage of total assets.

- Hold extra capital to be able to withstand the effect of spread widening.

16.4.1.5 Suboptimal Asset Allocation

A company's level of asset risk should be tied to its capital position. If a company is overcapitalized, it can afford to take additional asset-related risk in order to earn a higher expected rate of return. For the market risks already discussed, we were concerned that too much risk was being taken in comparison to the company's capital position. For this risk, we are worried about the opposite: Is enough risk being taken to earn the highest expected rate of return, given the company's capital position?

In theory, this risk is easy to manage. If the company's investments are too conservative for its capital position, it can shift a portion of its investments to higher yielding, more volatile assets. Unfortunately, there is no absolute measure to guide when a company's investment risk level optimally matches its capital position. However, a company can compare its investment mix and capital position to similar companies with a similar product mix to get some sense of where it stands.

16.4.1.6   Currency Fluctuation Risk

For a company with the great majority of its business in a single currency, this is not a material risk. However, for an international company with a significant percentage of assets and liabilities in multiple currencies, this risk can be important. There are two primary risks related to currency fluctuations:

- Balance sheet risk: If assets and liabilities are significantly out of balance by currency, a currency change could reduce the company's capital. For example, if the company has 20% of its assets and none of its liabilities in currency X, then a 50% drop in currency X could cost reduce capital by an amount equal to 10% of assets, which could be devastating.

- Income statement risk: If income, benefits, and expenses are significantly out of balance by currency, a currency change could reduce the company's net income. In the insurance business, this risk is usually limited, as income, benefits, and expenses for each international operation all tend to be in the same currency, with income mostly offset by benefits and expenses. However, the net income (income net of benefits, expenses, and taxes) from each international operation is subject to this risk.

Balance sheet risk can be managed simply by balancing assets and liabilities by currency. If liabilities exceed assets for a certain currency, investments in that currency should be increased. If assets exceed liabilities for a certain currency, it may not be possible to reduce the investments in that currency. This is often the case for a foreign subsidiary, which must have assets in excess of liabilities to meet capital requirements. This excess can be offset by borrowing money in that currency at the holding company level.

Income statement risk is trickier. It is possible to buy currency hedges to counter this risk. However, most companies do not attempt to hedge this risk, as the cost of the hedge lowers the level of expected earnings. In addition, normal fluctuations in earnings often exceed the fluctuations due to currency changes. In this case, it may not make sense to stabilize a relatively small currency risk.

16.4.2 Credit Risk

Credit risk is the risk that other parties cannot or will not honor their obligations. Credit risks can be grouped into several categories, the first three of which are related to assets:

- Asset default risk
- Concentration risk
- Risk of inadequate spreads
- Counterparty risk.

16.4.2.1 Asset Default Risk

Asset default risk is discussed in Chapter 10. When managing this risk, we are mainly concerned with excessive asset defaults that may result from prolonged poor economic conditions or poor asset selection. There are several ways to manage this risk:

- Whenever possible, share the risk of asset default with policyowners through market value adjustments and variable products.
- Invest mainly in investment-grade assets.
- Limit investments that are below investment grade to a small percentage of total assets.
- Otherwise, hold extra capital to be able to withstand the effect of excessive asset defaults.

16.4.2.2 Concentration Risk

This is the risk of not being able to pay attention, which is understandable at this point in the chapter. More seriously, concentration risk is the risk associated with having a large portion of a company's investments concentrated in a particular issuer, sector, industry, part of the country, or part of the world. For example, suppose a company invests an amount equal to twice its capital in a concentrated group of assets that proceed to lose 50% of their value. While this sounds far-fetched, it has happened.

During the 1980s, Mutual Benefit Life, a major U.S. life insurer, made significant commitments to develop a large resort area in Florida. When this real estate investment failed to perform as expected, Mutual Benefit invested even more money in an attempt to salvage its original investment. What was originally a large concentration of risk became too large. In 1990, the extent of the loss became clear, and Mutual Benefit was taken over by the New Jersey Department of Insurance. Although Mutual Benefit's policyowners received all of their benefits, Mutual Benefit was never able to work its way out of receivership. It was sold to AIG in 1998.

By the mid-1990s, real estate values in New England were well below their highs of several years earlier. Financial institutions with concentrations of assets in that region experienced significant losses on real estate and mortgage loan investments. New England Mutual, while never close to insolvency, had its ratings lowered because of such a concentration of risk. Because it focused on upper-income customers who were very sensitive to ratings, this was a significant problem for them. The result was a merger with MetLife, a much larger U.S. life insurer, in 1996. By the late 1990s, real estate values in the New England area had soared, which created additional value for the merged companies.

A similar problem contributed to the demise of Confederation Life in Canada in 1994. Depressed real estate values across North America combined with an over-concentration of investments in real estate, along with other factors, led to Confederation's being taken over by OSFI, the Canadian regulator of financial institutions. By the time real estate values recovered a few years later, it was too late for Confederation, which had been dismembered and sold in pieces to other insurers in the meantime.

Concentration risk can be adequately controlled by adopting and following a strict policy of diversification of risk. It requires communication and coordination among all those managing the company's investments, so that accidental concentration of assets is also avoided.

16.4.2.3 Risk of Inadequate Spreads

The credit-related spreads of particular issuers, sectors, countries, or classes of assets may not appropriately compensate the investor for the credit risk assumed. For example, government bonds from country LMNOP may pay an interest rate of LIBOR plus 7.00%. If country LMNOP has only been in existence for a few years or has only issued bonds for a few years, it may be hard to determine whether a spread of 7.00% is appropriate.

The risk of inadequate spreads is smaller where reliable information over a long period is available. This risk can be controlled by limiting the percentage of assets invested in newer and less familiar issuers, sectors, countries, and classes of assets.

16.4.2.4 Counterparty Risk

Counterparty risk is the risk that other parties (such as reinsurers and credit facilities) will not be able to fulfill their obligations to the company. This risk can be controlled by dealing only with high-quality business partners. This requires initial screening, regular monitoring, and a plan for dealing with business partners whose credit quality has deteriorated. Another strategy for controlling this risk is to diversify or spread the risk by dealing with multiple business partners.

Reinsurance is often purchased on a "pay as you go" basis, that is, with annual premiums that approximately cover annual claims. This is the case with most YRT reinsurance and most coinsurance of term products. Counterparty risk is usually insignificant in such cases. When a company reinsures business and transfers a large amount of cash or other assets to the reinsurer, counterparty risk can be reduced by placing the assets in a trust (with the company as beneficiary of the trust) or by securing a letter of credit.

16.4.3   Liquidity Risk

Liquidity risk is the risk of a company not being able to meet its cash flow obligations on time. During a financial crisis, many of a company's sources of cash will be unavailable at precisely the time that cash is needed the most. Because most life insurance products offer cash surrender values available on demand, liquidity risk is often significant. We will examine three types of risk related to liquidity:

- "Run-on-the-bank" risk
- Holding company liquidity risk
- Risk of excessive liquidity.

16.4.3.1   "Run-on-the-Bank" Risk

There is a risk that a ratings downgrade or other adverse publicity could cause many of a company's policyowners to simultaneously demand cash from the company. The experience of General American in 1999, described in Section 13.4.3, dramatizes this risk. Many were surprised that a company with good ratings and strong capital could be brought down by a liquidity problem involving just 37 customers. Not only did it happen, but it happened in a matter of days.

Kentucky Central was a U.S. company that specialized in universal life during the second half of the 1980s. During that time, the company backed a grandiose real estate development with very large commercial loans that turned sour. To hold things together, the company sold some assets and continued crediting high interest rates to its UL policyowners, to encourage persistency. However, rumors of the company's financial problems continued to build and eventually resulted in a run on the bank. While Kentucky Central was still solvent, it could not raise the cash needed to pay all the surrender benefits demanded. As a result, it entered receivership late in 1992 and was sold to Jefferson-Pilot soon thereafter.

The story of Baldwin United (BU) is another example of run-on-the-bank risk. BU was a holding company whose main holdings were in life insurance, property and casualty insurance, and mortgage insurance. In addition, BU owned a few other companies, such as a piano manufacturing company and a trading stamps company.

BU's life insurance companies sold billions of dollars worth of accumulation annuities with high credited interest rates. These high rates were essentially guaranteed by a bailout provision, which waived the surrender charge if the company credited an interest rate lower than a very high bailout rate. BU borrowed a substantial amount of money to purchase a mortgage insurance company and stated publicly that it would repay the debt over a short period. The company was implementing a tax strategy of shifting the gains and losses from its life companies to its property and casualty companies, and for the strategy to work, the mortgage company needed to make money.

When the U.S. economy experienced a downturn in the early 1980s, mortgage default rates increased. Soon the mortgage insurance company was not making enough money for the strategy to work. BU said it would need more time to repay the loan for the mortgage insurance company, and this, in combination with some other negative reporting, caused the "run on the bank." Because the investment in the mortgage insurance company was such a huge part of the portfolio (approximately 20%), the total market value of assets at the time of the run was not enough to support the calls on BU's liabilities. Ironically, this happened in spite of the significant value of the mortgage insurance company: It went public a few years later, with a market value of $1 billion. In the end, policyowners eventually recovered their money with interest, although credited interest rates were substantially less than the bailout rates.

A severe change in economic conditions, such as the worldwide stock market crash of 1929, can lead to a panic among policyowners and a sudden demand for significant cash outflows. A rapid rise in interest rates, such as experienced in North America in 1981, can also lead to significant cash outflows.

There are a few strategies for dealing with the run-on-the-bank risk:

- When designing insurance contracts, give the company an option to delay payments. In the U.S., life and annuity products must reserve the right for the company to delay payments up to six months. This gives the company time to liquidate assets in an orderly fashion and obtain full value. When the company has to rush to sell assets, it often will not receive full value.

- Avoid "hot money" products, which are those sold to buyers who are quick to move their funds when conditions change. For example, products sold to financial institutions and sophisticated investors are more likely to be carefully monitored and quickly cashed out if credit quality or performance deteriorates.

- Maintain some percentage of the company's portfolio in highly liquid assets, such as government securities, short-term investments, and common stocks.

- Establish credit facilities that allow the company to raise cash immediately in a time of need. The cost of such facilities must be balanced with their value to the company.

16.4.3.2 Holding Company Liquidity Risk

This section applies to a life insurance company owned by a holding company. While an insurance company may possess adequate liquidity, there is a risk that its holding company parent may not. Holding companies regularly need cash to pay stockholder dividends, pay interest on debt, cover holding company expenses, and invest in subsidiaries. Cash may also be used to repurchase stock and repay debt principal.

The holding company's only regular source for additional cash is dividends from its subsidiaries. If the subsidiaries are growing and needing additional capital, this could be problematic. In addition, insurance regulations often limit the amount of dividends that can be paid by an insurance company, to protect the company's solvency.

The other source for holding company cash is the capital markets. The holding company can raise cash by issuing additional common stock, preferred stock, bonds, and many variations on those themes. However, if the company is having any financial difficulty, the capital markets may not offer an affordable or attractive option.

Holding company liquidity risk is best managed by planning well ahead. By projecting the holding company's cash needs for the next year or two, a plan can be developed to meet those needs through a combination of subsidiary dividends and capital market activity.

Capital markets blow hot and cold. At times, it is relatively cheap or easy to raise capital. At other times, it can be quite difficult. It is best to raise capital when you sense the timing is right. When in doubt, you should raise capital early, so as not to be caught short during a difficult market.

16.4.3.3 Risk of Excessive Liquidity

To protect itself from the run-on-the-bank risk, a company can go too far and maintain too high a percentage of its assets in more liquid, lower yielding investments, such as government securities and short-term investments. To counter this risk, the company needs to determine the optimal level of liquidity it should maintain. In some cases, a credit facility may provide liquidity protection at a lower cost when compared to the loss of yield rate associated with government securities and short-term investments.

16.4.4 Pricing Risk

Pricing risk can be broken into the following general categories, excluding the risks that have already been addressed in this section:

- Mortality risk
- Morbidity risk

- Longevity risk
- Pricing assumption risk
- Liability option risk.

16.4.4.1 Mortality Risk

Mortality risk has already been addressed in Section 10.3, but some further discussion is in order. Throughout recorded history, epidemics have decimated populations. The last major epidemic to seriously affect the economically advanced countries was the influenza epidemic of 1918–1919, which killed approximately 1% of the population. The current U.S. risk-based capital (RBC) factors for mortality risk are based on this epidemic.

Going forward, advances in medical science may help us contain future epidemics. However, bacteria and viruses can mutate faster than our ability to develop new drugs and treatments to combat them. Combine this with the increasing level of international travel by airplane (which provides a fabulous environment for sharing germs), and we have the potential to quickly spread the latest mutations around the globe.

In addition, natural disasters such as earthquakes and hurricanes (also known as typhoons and cyclones) have the potential of killing many thousands of people in a concentrated area. Manmade disasters, ranging from terrorism to war to a nuclear holocaust, have a frightening potential for killing people.

Mortality can be affected by selective lapsation. For example, widespread use of genetic testing could lead to the best risks canceling their life insurance and the worst risks persisting, thereby raising the mortality of the insured population.

A company should take measures to be able to withstand an epidemic or disaster, within reason. This is primarily accomplished by holding extra capital, but reinsurance is also an important tool. In addition to the common forms of reinsurance described in Chapter 7, most insurance companies also purchase catastrophe reinsurance, to limit their losses from multiple death claims resulting from a single catastrophe.

16.4.4.2 Morbidity Risk

While epidemics and disasters can increase morbidity rates as well as mortality rates, the primary cause of unexpectedly high morbidity costs relates to the ability of the insured to outwit the insurance company. For example, by concealing an existing medical condition, an insured may be able to purchase insurance and make an immediate claim. Alternatively, an insured may successfully claim a disabling condition that is next to impossible to prove or disprove, such as back pain or mental illness.

To illustrate morbidity risk, let us examine the U.S. market for disability income (DI) in the mid- to late 1980s. Two forces combined to sow the seeds of disaster for many companies in the DI business:

- With the U.S. economy booming and the resulting low unemployment level, existing DI policies were producing attractive levels of profit. Competition led to more-liberal underwriting policies and more-liberal definitions of disability, in an attempt to gain more of this lucrative business.

- As the balance of power for setting medical care prices was beginning to shift away from doctors and dentists to HMOs, many doctors and dentists purchased DI policies for large amounts.

By 1990, the tide had turned. The U.S. economy was no longer as robust as it had been just a few years earlier. More importantly, the income levels of many doctors and dentists had fallen to the point where it was more attractive to be disabled than to continue working. Disability rates soared, because of both liberal underwriting and loopholes in the definition of disability that enabled relatively healthy insureds to make legitimate claims against their policies. The major writers of DI lost hundreds of millions of dollars. Many companies exited the DI business. The three leading specialists in the U.S. DI business were eventually merged into a single company in 1999, UNUM/Provident.

Morbidity risk can often be successfully controlled through careful underwriting, clear and verifiable benefit provisions, diligent handling of claims, and designing benefits that encourage beneficial behavior. An example of this last point can be illustrated by the addition of a partial disability benefit: If the insured is able to work part time but will lose all disability benefits by doing so, part time work will be discouraged. If, however, partial disability benefits can be structured so that the insured will be financially better off by working part time, then both the insured and the insurance company will benefit.

16.4.4.3   Longevity Risk

For income annuities, a major risk is annuitants living longer than expected. This happened throughout the twentieth century, with actual mortality improvement almost always exceeding that expected. The results of the human genome project and other areas of medical advancement could lead to even greater mortality improvement, especially at the higher ages, which are the most important ages for income annuities.

Little can be done to control this risk, other than allowing for greater mortality improvement when pricing. Attractively priced reinsurance can be hard to find, as reinsurers generally have similar concerns about this risk.

16.4.4.4   Pricing Assumption Risk

There is always a danger of pricing assumptions being wrong. This risk is heightened when dealing with new markets, new products, new underwriting standards, or a new distribution system, where the company has less experience on which to base its assumptions. Insurance products are very long term. It can take years or even decades for actual experience to unfold sufficiently to assess the original pricing assumptions.

The insurance industry tends to suffer from overcapacity: At any given time, most life insurance companies can afford to and want to issue more new business than they are currently issuing. This can lead to an overly competitive market, where only the most efficient players can make an attractive profit. At times, competitive leapfrogging of prices can lead to inadequate prices for even the most efficient players. This is unlikely to happen when pricing assumptions are based on credible experience, but it can happen when the industry ventures into new products, new underwriting standards, new distribution systems, and so on.

In order to field competitive products, some companies knowingly price using unit costs below their actual unit costs. To compensate, such companies simultaneously pursue an expense reduction campaign, with a goal of bringing actual unit costs down to the level of assumed unit costs, at some time in the not-too-distant future. In some cases, this may be wishful thinking. There is a risk that the cost reduction goals will never be achieved.

On the other hand, some companies base their unit costs on fully allocated expenses, rather than the relevant costs described in Chapter 3. It is possible that such a company may have already achieved the unit costs it uses in pricing, but is unaware of relevant cost pricing.

There are two good ways to reduce pricing risk:

1. Reinsure business that has worrisome levels of pricing risk.
2. Work with pricing experts, such as actuarial consultants and certain reinsurers, to develop assumptions that reflect the latest information and techniques available. This should help your company stay in synch with the market and avoid the risk of being singled out and exploited by sophisticated buyers.

16.4.4.5 Liability Option Risk

Perhaps the greatest shortcoming in life insurance pricing is the lack of ability to properly price the options given to policyowners. What should be charged for a guaranteed minimum interest rate of 3%? What is the right price for the ability to surrender a policy for its cash value at any time with no market value adjustment? While option-pricing models may offer some help in these areas, few insurance companies have tried them. As a result, the cost of most options is never quantified and never explicitly reflected in pricing.

This is unfortunate, as some of the greatest risks faced by life insurers are related to these very options. Ask a U.S. insurer about the cost of premium guarantees, after their experiences with select and ultimate term in the mid-1980s. Ask a Japanese insurance company about the cost of minimum interest rate guarantees, after their experiences of the 1990s. Ask a U.K. life insurer about the cost of annuity purchase rate guarantees, after their experiences of the late 1990s. Ask any company that has experienced a run on the bank about the cost of cash values available on demand.

To manage these risks first requires a greater level of awareness of the existence and cost of such options. Besides the use of reinsurance, one way to control these risks is to consciously avoid too large a concentration of option risk. For example, it would be prudent to limit the company's exposure to "hot money" products (that is, those products with buyers who are quick to move their funds when conditions change) to a small percentage of the company's business. Just as a company manages its concentration risk for assets, it should do likewise for liabilities.

16.5   Earnings Management

Earnings management refers to the many different decisions and actions a company can take to influence future earnings. It is almost always too late to affect current period earnings: They will be what they will be.

When managing earnings, there are usually two common goals: (1) to grow earnings over time, usually at a targeted growth rate, and (2) to minimize unexpected fluctuations in earnings, although some degree of fluctuation is inevitable.

16.5.1   Product Management

Good product management is essential for good earnings management. In the context of this chapter, we will use *product management* to mean a combination of two things: (1) the usual meaning of product management as defined in Chapter 2, related to managing in-force products, and (2) the design and introduction of new products to help the company better meet its financial goals.

The company has some ability to adjust in-force products to achieve its financial goals and manage its earnings. Dividends, nonguaranteed premiums, credited interest rates, and cost of insurance rates can be changed. For example, a company could increase credited interest rates on UL products to improve persistency while simultaneously increasing COI charges to offset the effect of higher credited rates on earnings. Alternatively, the company could simply increase COI charges to increase earnings. When making such adjustments, many considerations must be taken into account, such as delivering on promises, equity among policyowners, the effect on persistency, and regulatory restrictions.

The pricing of new products is perhaps the most important tool the company has to drive future earnings. Profit margins on new products can be increased, but usually at a cost of lower sales and perhaps some loss of loyalty from customers and the distribution system. The company could introduce products with features that reduce risk, increase earnings, improve competitiveness and sales levels, *or* reduce capital needs. It is not possible to do all of the preceding at once! For example, adding a market value adjustment feature will reduce risk but may also reduce sales. Increasing the level of surrender charges in the early policy years may increase earnings and reduce new business strain, but may also reduce sales levels. Last, lower guarantees may reduce risk and new business strain, but may yet again lead to reduced sales.

16.5.2 Asset Management

Assets can be used to help achieve the company's financial goals. Investment strategies can be changed over time. Average yields and earnings can be increased by shifting to riskier or less liquid investments. To the extent that the company can easily handle greater asset risk or fewer liquid assets, it may be wise to improve yields. Alternatively, asset management could focus on reducing the volatility of earnings. It is usually not possible to both increase yield and reduce volatility. Increased yields usually come with increased volatility.

The matching of assets and liabilities is strongly encouraged. However, there will be situations where some degree of mismatching exists:

- When liability cash flows are too unpredictable to match, except over a short horizon.

- When assets and liabilities are purposely mismatched, to improve average yields and expected earnings.

These situations are best handled by a company that is overcapitalized and consciously using its excess capital to support the mismatching.

If the company is not already matching assets and liabilities, then starting to do so may present an opportunity to reduce the volatility of earnings at little to no cost. By better understanding its liabilities, the company may find it needs to invest more in long-term assets. More long-term assets would normally increase yields, unless the yield curve is inverted, while reducing risk at the same time.

Long-term yields can generally be improved by increasing the proportion of assets invested in stocks and real estate. As with mismatching, this requires that the company be strongly capitalized to be able to absorb the ups and downs of the stock and real estate markets.

One disadvantage of investments in both real estate and common stocks is the treatment of capital gains by the stock markets. A large part of the return on common stocks and real estate comes from selling assets for more than their purchase price, thereby generating capital gains. Many times, a company's stock price is largely driven by its *operating earnings,* which is defined as total earnings less capital gains (or losses). The logic is that capital gains are largely under management's control and therefore could be used to manipulate earnings, as in the following example:

Example 16.5.1 Manipulating Earnings Using Capital Gains

Suppose a company has accumulated a large amount of unrealized capital gains over a period of many years. If the company has poor earnings, all it has to do is sell stock or real estate to realize sufficient capital gains to return its earnings to the expected level. Because stock prices are partially driven by P/E ratios, a company could use unrealized capital gains to increase earnings for a number of years, thereby artificially inflating its stock price.

Capital gains are essentially ignored by the stock markets. Therefore, many companies steer away from investments like stocks and real estate that produce low operating income and high capital gains, when compared to bonds and mortgages. Some companies invest in a combination of assets that produce offsetting capital gains and losses over the long term. For example, by investing in a small percentage of junk bonds and stocks, the company may be able to generate capital losses from junk bond defaults that offset capital gains from stocks. While this might be a way to modestly improve long-term yields and operating income, it is definitely riskier and requires more capital.

If the company and the stock markets are focused primarily on operating income, which excludes capital gains and losses, some volatility may be acceptable, as long as it is confined to capital gains and losses. However, the company would not want to increase capital gains at a cost of lower yields, as that would lower its operating income.

16.5.3 Expense Management

Companies with lower expenses generally earn higher profits. Therefore, expense management is often an important part of earnings management. However, lower costs and more efficient processes are not always the best policy. Consider a fine restaurant. It is the pleasure of the dining experience that matters the most, not the efficiency of the kitchen staff. There are parallels in the insurance business, where quality and friendliness of service sometimes matter more than price or efficiency. To cut costs in the wrong places could actually lower earnings.

Therefore, when managing expenses, it is crucial to understand what really matters to your customers and distribution system. When examining an activity, ask not only what it costs, but also what it buys you in terms of customer satisfaction or agent loyalty. In some cases, it may be better to spend more money on an activity, in order to satisfy customers. In other cases, it may be best to cease activities that add no discernible value. Some worthless activities can be ingrained into the organization and therefore very difficult to recognize and eliminate.

16.5.3.1 Major Expense Reductions

Over time, it is normal for companies to develop expense problems. Each year, the tendency is to spend more money on activities that add little or no value to the organization. Eventually, most companies conclude that their expenses have become bloated and need reducing. Common techniques used to achieve a major reduction in expenses include the following:

- An across-the-board cut. For example, every department may be forced to cut its expenses by 10%. While this cuts expenses, it can backfire. Certain areas of the company may need to grow, not shrink. Service, quality, and timeliness may suffer in those areas until money is spent to fix the problems, thereby undoing some of the expense savings.

- "Surgical incisions." By attempting to intelligently reduce expenses in the areas of the company that most need the reductions, the company hopes to reduce expenses without affecting service. If this is done in a rational, nonpolitical manner (a difficult task at best), this can be successful.

- Look at your company from the point of view of a corporate raider: someone who would "slash and burn" areas of the company to shave expenses and boost profits. Ask what a corporate raider would do—then do it yourself.

- Look at your company from the point of view of a new, start-up company. Ask how you would structure such a company to gain competitive advantage over older companies like yours, then re-create your company in that image.

16.5.3.2 Minor Expense Reductions

A number of less radical strategies can be followed to improve expenses:

- Analyze jobs throughout the company and derive the value that each job adds to the company. This process attempts to identify how far removed a particular job is from serving a customer or from satisfying some external requirement. It should lead to identifying which people could be moved closer to the customer. This process also asks what would happen if certain jobs or expenses were cut, or what would happen if a particular person left the company.

    Structural problems can also be identified. For example, if many liaisons are needed to ensure communication, there may be a structural problem, such as too many intermediate levels of management and too few subordinates per manager.

- Pursue outsourcing, which involves paying an outside firm to perform some services that are currently performed within the company. The company should identify which internal services could be outsourced to lower costs and/or improve services. The company should consider giving its business units the authority to outsource certain services rather than use internal or corporate service providers.

    Outsourcing can also be useful in creating competition for internal service providers. If an outside organization can perform a service for a lower price and do it better, it may not make sense to continue to provide the service internally. This strategy may allow your company to focus on what it does best, while outsourcing the rest.

- Reengineer processes, which involves redesigning or automating processes to improve service or reduce costs. Such changes could involve identifying ways to help customers serve themselves.

- Restructure or reorganize all or part of the company, so that its various units work together more effectively.

- Identify ways that the company culture can be shifted to improve collaboration, communication, decision making, initiative, creativity, retention of staff, and so on.

16.5.3.3   Allocation of Corporate Expenses

In Chapter 3, we discussed using relevant expenses in pricing. It is just as important to use the same philosophy when allocating expenses for earnings purposes. Expenses that directly or indirectly relate to a market, product, line of business, distribution system, and so on should be allocated accordingly. However, expenses that are not related to anything but the total company (such as corporate expenses) should not be allocated. Instead, such expenses should be segregated in a corporate "line of business" or segment. One definition of corporate expenses or services is those that would be eliminated or replaced if the company were to be merged into a larger organization.

Allocating corporate expenses to lines of business may disguise the true contribution of each line. Such allocations are always arbitrary, as they are unrelated to the business. The allocation of corporate expenses has led companies to conclude that particular businesses were losers. As a result, companies have closed down businesses that they would have been better off keeping. For example, consider a business that is contributing $5 million of annual profit and an ROE of 15%, before corporate expenses. After $3 million of corporate expenses are allocated, the ROE drops to just 6%, which is deemed a loser. However, if the company closes down this business, they lose $5 million of annual profit and save none of the $3 million of corporate expenses that were allocated to it. Arbitrary allocations are helpful only for making bad decisions.

16.5.3.4   Legacy Systems

Many companies are saddled with *legacy systems,* which is a kindly description for outdated, patched-together computer systems that are used for policy underwriting, issue, billing, accounting, commissioning, policyowner service, lapses, surrenders, death claims, valuation, and so on. These systems form the heart and soul of many life insurance companies. To replace them is an unimaginably difficult task. To continue them becomes increasingly complex and expensive. Older companies with expensive legacy systems run the risk of not being able to compete with younger companies with modern systems. Companies that have acquired a number of companies often have this problem several times over. For some companies, solving the legacy systems problem has the potential to save a significant portion of overall expenses.

One solution is to adopt a modern system for all new business, while building bridges to import data as needed from the old systems. For example, customers and agents will want one set of statements, rather than one statement from the old system and one from the modern system. Modern systems will give the company the ability to implement new products much more quickly. Over the years, the company can gradually move most of the company's older business to the modern system. Years later, when only the most complex, hard-to-move business is left on the legacy system, the company could face some interesting decisions: It may make sense to offer an incentive to the remaining "legacy" policyowners to swap their complex policies for simpler, easy-to-move policies. At some point, it is worth a considerable amount of money to remove the last policies from the legacy system, so it can be laid to rest. Amen.

16.6 Capital Management

Capital management consists of maintaining the proper amounts and types of capital needed to efficiently and safely run the company. On the one hand, the company will want to minimize capital in order to earn a high return on capital. On the other hand, the company will want to maintain extra capital to ensure solvency, customer confidence, and strong ratings. A delicate balance must be achieved in order to meet these conflicting objectives.

In this section, we will examine

- How the "right" amount of capital is determined
- How the "right" capital structure is determined
- What can be done to raise capital
- What can be done to deploy excess capital
- How to internally manage capital.

16.6.1   Determining the Proper Amount of Capital

When determining the proper amount of capital for a company, there are several points of view to consider.

The most important point of view is given by *insurance regulations* that specify the minimum amount of capital required for the company to remain solvent and operate independently. Most economically advanced countries now have such regulations in place, along the lines of the formulas presented in Chapter 10. Companies strive to maintain capital well in excess of the minimum requirement, so that fluctuations in capital do not come close to affecting their solvency.

The next most important point of view is given by independent *rating agencies* that rate the financial strength or *claims-paying ability* of insurance companies. For sophisticated buyers, financial ratings are an important consideration, when both buying and continuing to hold insurance products. Rating agencies use required capital formulas similar to those used by regulators. However, rating agencies are more likely to adjust required capital to reflect their greater familiarity with the business of each particular company.

The company may have its own point of view as to how much capital it thinks is proper. Certainly, the company is in the best position to understand its risks and determine its capital requirements accordingly. However, an outside point of view can often be more objective. In many cases, companies simply strive to have capital in line with their primary competitors. For example, if ratios of actual capital to minimum required capital are published, most companies will want their ratios somewhat near the median ratio for the industry. Too low a ratio could be viewed as financial weakness; too high a rat make it difficult to earn a reasonable return on capital. Of course, if the industry were viewed as over- or undercapitalized, companies may not aim for the median ratio.

Formulas for required capital, whether developed by regulators, rating agencies, or individual companies, are based on an analysis of historical events. They seek to provide enough capital for companies to survive all but the most unusual and extreme events.

16.6.2 Determining the Proper Capital Structure

Corporations in all industries have two primary types of capital available to them: debt and equity. Besides these two, the insurance industry has access to a third type of capital: reinsurance. However, for mutual insurance companies, the options are much more limited. Reinsurance is often the only outside source of capital for mutual insurers. The rest of the discussion of capital structure applies mainly to stock companies.

16.6.2.1 Corporate Structure

Life insurance companies are involved in many different types of corporate structures. These structures may involve multiple insurance companies, holding companies, and other types of companies. The simplest and most common corporate structure is a stand-alone life insurer, with no parent company and no subsidiaries. While such a company can issue stock to raise more equity capital, it usually cannot make effective use of debt. This is because insurance regulations do not normally allow debt to be counted as part of a company's capital for solvency purposes. Instead, debt is treated as a liability, for obvious reasons.

To make effective use of debt, many insurance companies have a parent holding company. (By "holding company," we mean a company that has no business other than the ownership of one or more companies.) The parent company can issue debt and use the proceeds of the debt offering to make a capital contribution to its insurance subsidiary. In other words, debt from the holding company becomes equity to the insurance company. Such a transformation is not possible without a parent company that owns the insurance company.

Having all insurance operations within a single insurance company creates some capital efficiencies: the same capital can be used to support multiple insurance businesses, often with complementary risks. However, some insurance organizations have multiple insurance companies in order to operate in different countries or different markets, or for historical reasons, such as acquisitions.

It is common for a large corporation to have many holding companies and many insurance companies. Additional holding companies are often useful for capital and tax reasons. Figure 16.6.1 illustrates a holding company with two directly owned insurance subsidiaries and two other insurance subsidiaries, owned through insurance company B. A non-insurance company is also owned by company B. Company B could just as easily be a holding company instead of an insurance company. Corporate structures such as these are partly driven by careful planning and partly by historical events, such as past acquisitions.

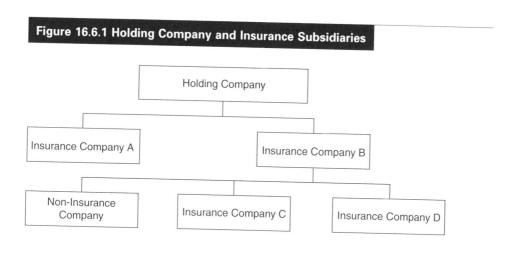

Figure 16.6.1 Holding Company and Insurance Subsidiaries

16.6.2.2 Equity

Equity is usually the largest component of capital. It comes from the owners' capital contributions to the company, plus retained earnings of the company. Equity is the capital with the highest risk. If something adverse happens to the company, equity investors are the investors most likely to lose some or all of their investment. As a result, investors demand the highest rate of return on equity capital, compared to other forms of capital. Equity is most appropriate for supporting high-risk capital needs, such as that portion of its capital that a company feels is truly at risk.

Both common and preferred stock (the two forms of equity) do not have to be repaid; there is no scheduled maturity date and no repayment of principal. However, both normally pay dividends. When the company is under financial pressure, these dividends can be cut or discontinued to give the company more financial breathing room. Common stock dividends must be discontinued before preferred stock dividends are cut. Such actions cannot be taken lightly, as the financial markets view them as a sign of poor performance, weakness, or even financial distress.

16.6.2.3 Debt

Debt is a form of capital that is mainly used by stock companies. As explained earlier in this section, a holding company is needed to make debt useful to an insurance company. Debt is viewed as low-risk capital, at least for companies with good financial ratings. If something adverse happens to the company, equity capital must be wiped out before debt capital can be hit. As long as any equity remains, interest and principal payments must be made as scheduled to holders of debt. In many countries, interest paid on debt is tax deductible to the borrower.

Because of the relative safety of debt, investors settle for a much lower rate of return on debt capital. In most cases, the cost of debt will be only slightly higher than the yield available on new investments of similar quality and maturity. Debt is most appropriate for supporting low-risk capital needs, such as those associated with redundant reserves or excessive capital requirements.

Ideally, the company will structure the maturity of its various debt offerings to match the release of its excess reserves and capital. Debt should be structured in conjunction with asset/liability management, as debt is another form of liability. Bond debt is perhaps the easiest liability to match. To match bond debt, all the company need do is purchase high-quality bonds of matching amounts and maturity dates.

Besides bond debt (debt issued as bonds), the other common form of debt is bank debt (a bank loan). Bank debt is usually short term. The bank usually charges a short-term floating interest rate, such as 30-day LIBOR plus 1.50%. While principal and interest are typically due within a year, the bank loan can usually be extended as long as the company is in good financial condition.

If the company fails to make interest or principal payments on time, the company faces bankruptcy. The more money a company borrows, the greater its risk of failure. As a result, the cost of borrowing increases as a company increases the percentage of its capital in the form of debt. In addition, rating agencies will lower a company's ratings if it adds too much debt. For example, a company with one-third of its capital in the form of debt would have a very hard time earning a rating agency's highest rating. On the other hand, investors will criticize a public company that does not make sufficient use of debt to leverage its returns, as shown in the following example.

Example 16.6.1 Leveraging Returns with Debt

Let us first examine a company with 65 million of after-tax earnings, 500 million of equity capital, and no debt. Its ROE would be 65/500 = 13%. Now suppose that 20% of its capital (100 million) were debt instead of equity and that the after-tax cost of debt were 5%. The company's after-tax earnings would be 65 million less interest on debt of 5 million, for net earnings of 60 million. The company's equity would be 400 million, so its ROE would be 60/400 = 15%. A small percentage of debt can be used to leverage the company's returns from 13% up to 15%, because of the relatively low cost of debt. Equity investors would generally endorse such a move. Rating agencies may be comfortable with a debt ratio of 20%.

The *weighted average cost of capital* (WACC) is a useful concept and is calculated by the following formula:

$$\text{WACC}$$
$$= \text{Percentage of capital in equity} \times \text{Desired return on equity}$$
$$+ \text{Percentage of capital in debt} \times \text{After-tax cost of debt.} \quad (16.6.1)$$

If a company has a long-range target ratio of debt and equity, the WACC can serve as the basis for the hurdle rate to be used in many of the profit objective formulas of Chapter 11. Suppose the equity investors' desired return on equity were 15%. The weighted average cost of capital would then be calculated as follows, for the two alternatives:

No debt: WACC = 100% (15%) + 0% (5%) = 15%,
20% debt: WACC = 80% (15%) + 20% (5%) = 13%.

In other words, increasing debt to 20% of capital lowers the company's WACC from 15% to 13%. However, there is a limit as to how much the WACC can be lowered by using debt.

If a company were to move to 80% debt to lower its WACC, such a move would backfire. The company's equity investors would demand a much higher rate of return, because their capital would be at much greater risk. At the same time, the cost of debt would rise as the use of debt rises. The net result of these forces means that a company cannot significantly lower its WACC by using more than a prudent amount of debt.

Example 16.6.2 Excessive Leverage

To illustrate excessive leverage, suppose the company in the previous example were to shift to a capital structure with 20% equity (100 million) and 80% debt (400 million). It might find that equity investors would demand a 30% return while debt investors would require a 9% after-tax return, with the following result:

80% debt: WACC = 20% (30%) + 80% (9%) = 13.2%.

Looking at the effect of 80% debt on earnings, we would have 65 million of earnings before debt less 36 million of interest on debt, resulting in net earnings of 29 million. ROE would be $29/100 = 29\%$. With net earnings reduced by more than 50%, earnings volatility (as a percentage of net earnings) would more than double. With only 20% equity, if the company were to experience an event that cost it 20% of its capital, the equity investors would be wiped out. For both of these reasons, the demand for a higher ROE is understandable.

16.6.2.4   Combinations of Debt and Equity

Combinations of debt and equity are sometimes referred to as *mezzanine financing,* because they are an in-between level of capital. Convertible bonds and surplus notes are types of mezzanine financing sometimes used by insurance companies.

Convertible bonds have features of both debt and equity. A convertible bond has all the features of a regular bond, except that it pays a much lower rate of interest and is convertible to common stock at a price that is apt to be attractive in a few years. For example, a 1,000 ten-year convertible bond may be convertible to 25 shares of common stock, which implies a conversion price of 40 per share. If the current stock price is 30 and there is a good chance the stock price will climb much higher than 40 per share over the next ten years, then the conversion feature is quite valuable. The lower rate of interest is offset by the value of the conversion option. Both the issuer and investor would view a convertible bond as a bond that will likely never be repaid. Instead, it is most apt to be converted to common stock before the bond matures. As a result, rating agencies might view a particular convertible bond as more equity than debt. This gives the company a tool to lower its short-term WACC without adding significant leverage. However, assuming these bonds are ultimately converted to equity, they would tend to raise the company's long-term WACC.

Surplus notes are a type of debt issued by insurance companies. They function just like bonds, except that coupon and maturity payments are subject to ongoing approval by insurance regulators. This means that, if the insurance regulator prevents the payment of coupon or maturity payments, the company is not in default and the lenders can take no action against the company. This feature allows surplus notes to be treated as equity for solvency purposes. However, rating agencies may view surplus notes as more debt than equity, as they are very likely to be repaid.

16.6.2.5 Reinsurance

Many of the favorable attributes of using reinsurance as a source of capital have been discussed in Section 16.2. These attributes include

- Transfer of risk as well as capital
- Reduction in the need for outside capital
- Access to capital as needed, rather than prematurely raising idle capital in the form of equity or debt.

16.6.3   Methods of Raising Capital

We will present the methods of raising capital separately for mutual and stock companies, with a middle segment that applies to both types of companies.

16.6.3.1   Sources of Capital for Mutual Companies

Mutual companies begin life with some equity. Their equity comes from one of two sources, depending on how the mutual company is formed:

1. If formed by an original group of policyowners, these policyowners would provide the capital needed to start the company.

2. If formed by the mutualization of a stock company, then the capital remaining after the stockholders were bought out would provide the capital needed to start the mutual company.

Once capitalized, mutual companies have no ability to raise additional equity other than by retaining earnings. However, mutual companies have two important levers to keep their actual capital in line with required capital:

1. They can carefully manage their growth so that capital needs do not outstrip growth in capital.

2. They can manage dividends to policyowners so that existing policyowners provide the additional capital needed to finance new policyowners.

16.6.3.2   Sources of Capital for All Companies

There are a few options available to all companies. These can be especially useful for mutual companies:

- In most jurisdictions, reinsurance can be used to provide capital. This can be arranged quickly, often in a matter of one or two months. The amounts and timing of capital provided can be dovetailed to closely match the business needs.

- Where regulations permit it, a company can use surplus notes to increase its capital base. The timing and available amounts of surplus notes are the same as for bonds, described below.

- A company can sell all or part of one of its businesses to raise capital. In particular, moving a successful business into a subsidiary and selling a piece of it to the public can be a particularly effective way for a company to raise capital, as demonstrated in Example 16.6.3.

Example 16.6.3 Raising Capital through a Subsidiary IPO

As 1992 ended, General American (GA) was a fast growing mutual company in need of more capital. The fastest growing segment of GA was its reinsurance business, which had grown to be the second largest in North America. In early 1993, GA moved its reinsurance business and $50 million of capital into a new company called Reinsurance Group of America (RGA). A significant portion (37%) of RGA was then sold to the public through an IPO. After the IPO, RGA's market value was over $400 million. This meant that the 63% of RGA that GA still owned was worth over $250 million. In other words, by establishing a market price for RGA stock, GA was able to add over $200 million to its capital.

When a company sells all or a part of one of its businesses, it may switch from being short of capital to not knowing what to do with all of its excess capital, which is a "high class" problem. Still, careful consideration should be given as to how and when the capital raised by selling a business will be deployed. If too much excess capital will be generated, there may be other ways to structure the sale. For example, by changing terms to reduce the initial excess capital, it may be possible to improve the long-term benefit for the company. The sale of a business ordinarily requires a minimum of several months and could take more than a year.

16.6.3.3 Sources of Capital for Stock Companies

Besides the capital sources described above, stock companies often tap the financial markets to raise debt and equity capital.

Debt is the easier form of capital to raise. The providers of debt, whether investors or banks, are primarily concerned with the security of their loan to the company. If the company has good ratings and can demonstrate its ability to meet its obligations, then securing additional debt is usually not a problem. The greater a company's financial strength, the lower the interest rate on the debt. Large amounts of debt are usually financed by selling bonds to the public. Moderate amounts of bonds are sometimes sold privately. Short-term and smaller amounts are usually provided by bank debt. Bank debt can often be raised in a matter of days. Public bond debt would typically require a couple of months to prepare the required documents, obtain the required approvals, and line up the investors. Private bond debt can be arranged faster.

Raising *equity* can be problematic. Two groups with opposite points of view need to be satisfied: existing stockholders and new investors. While there is often a satisfactory middle ground, this is not always the case.

Existing stockholders may object to additional stock being sold, because it dilutes their ownership of the company. For example, suppose that the majority owner owns 75 shares, equal to 75% of the 100 shares outstanding. Suppose 50 additional shares are to be sold as part of a new equity offering. In this case, the majority owner will end up owning only 50% (75/150) of the company after the new offering. Unless the capital received from selling the additional shares can be immediately deployed to earn the same rate as existing capital, the offering will be dilutive to earnings per share (EPS). That is, the offering will lower EPS, at least for a time. If the offering were permanently dilutive, you would question management's judgment in pursuing the offering.

New investors have many choices as to where to invest their money. To be convinced to purchase your new stock offering, investors must regard your company or the stock price as attractive. A low, bargain stock price may attract investors but will displease existing stockholders. Sometimes it is just not possible to raise the equity capital desired at a price that is fair to existing stockholders. In such a case, the company may have to examine other capital alternatives or reduce its capital needs. Perhaps in six months or a year, the market will react differently to a new stock offering.

Companies can fall into a vicious or virtuous cycle of capital raising: A poorly performing company may find it very difficult to raise additional capital at an acceptable price, causing it to either dilute earnings or forego opportunities that might improve its performance—a vicious cycle. On the other hand, a high performing company may find it easier to raise additional capital at an attractive price, which it can deploy to land more opportunities and further improve its performance—a virtuous cycle.

While an IPO typically requires six months from beginning to end, subsequent stock offerings are much faster because public companies routinely report much of the information needed for stock offerings. Small-scale or private offerings are often completed faster, sometimes in a matter of days or weeks. However, a large-scale subsequent public stock offering would usually require a few months.

16.6.4 Methods of Deploying Excess Capital

Perhaps the most obvious and most often ignored option for deploying excess capital is to distribute it to the owners. The tendency for many companies is to hold onto excess capital for future needs. Given that capital is so hard to come by, many senior executives question why you would want to give it back. The answer may be "Because it is not your money!" On the other hand, extra capital gives the company extra security.

16.6.4.1 Distributing Excess Capital to Owners

There are several ways to distribute excess capital to owners:

- If the company is owned by stockholders, the company could pay a one-time special stockholder dividend to distribute the excess. Alternatively, the company could increase regular stockholder dividends to pay out the excess over a longer period.

- If the company's stock is publicly traded, the company could use excess capital to buy back shares of the company. This would tend to raise the price of the shares, since every remaining share would own a greater portion of the company. In countries where investors are taxed on stockholder dividends, buying back shares is a more tax-efficient method for distributing excess capital.

- If the company is a mutual company, then excess capital could be distributed by enhancing benefits paid to policyowners, such as by increasing policyowner dividends, enhancing credited interest rates, or lowering COI rates.

16.6.4.2 Deploying Excess Capital into Current Operations

When faced with excess capital, perhaps the most natural reaction is to examine your current operations to see where extra capital could do some good, while providing an adequate return on that capital. Some questions you might ask include the following:

- If capital has been the main constraint on pricing, should new, more capital-intensive products be developed? Should existing products be repriced?

- Should distribution capabilities be expanded?

- Should the company undertake significant projects to improve its productivity or service capabilities?

When capital is raised through a debt or equity offering, the company often raises more capital than it can immediately use. It may take a year or two or even longer to deploy all the capital raised. During this time, it may make sense to deploy excess capital through a few large, short-term transactions. Such transactions can be hard to find, but it may be possible to work with a reinsurer to achieve the desired result.

16.6.4.3 Deploying Excess Capital into New Operations

Excess capital may give the company the opportunity to start up a new line of business, enter a new market, build a new distribution system, or pursue an acquisition. Companies must ultimately change or face obsolescence. Starting a new operation can be a great catalyst for changing a company. However, a new operation that has no strategic fit with existing operations is highly questionable. Rather than make such an investment, the company is probably better off giving the excess capital back to its owners, to let them make their own investment decisions.

16.6.5 Internal Capital Management

In order to measure the performance of each of its businesses properly, the company must allocate capital to each business. Assets backing the liabilities and capital of each business must also be allocated, thereby allowing investment income to be calculated for each business. Once relevant expenses have also been allocated to each business, the company can calculate earnings and ROE for each business.

There are two common methods for allocating capital:

The historical method

The required capital method.

16.6.5.1 Historical Method

The historical method tracks the results for a business from inception, accumulating the actual cash flows of the business and ignoring capital requirements. Because most businesses lose money for a number of years, this method results in negative capital in the early years. If the business is a success, the negative capital will eventually turn positive and ultimately exceed the required capital. The one advantage of the historical method is that it tracks the inception-to-date contribution of each business.

However, by ignoring required capital, the historical method ignores reality: Every business must maintain some amount of required capital. As a result, the historical method understates earnings when accumulated earnings are less than required capital and overstates earnings once accumulated earnings exceed required capital. In particular, ROE is grossly misstated, because both earnings and equity are distorted. This can lead to significant misunderstandings and mistakes. A young business with excellent results may be mistakenly closed down, while a mature business with mediocre results may be expanded.

16.6.5.2 Required Capital Method

In contrast, the required capital method allocates the amount of capital required to support a business, ignoring the past results of the business. As a result, actual earnings are determined using logic consistent with distributable earnings. The results for young and old businesses are *not* distorted by their historical results. Past sins are forgiven. Past glories are forgotten. Instead, the focus is on "What have you done lately?" Required capital can also be allocated when calculating results by region, general agency, product, issue year, and so on.

While we strongly believe that the required capital method is the right method for measuring current performance, many experienced professionals, including the authors, have used the historical method. In many ways, it is the more natural approach. If there is no clearly defined standard for required capital, the required capital method may be hard to apply. However, when measuring current performance, the required capital method with any reasonable capital requirement would be preferable to the historical method.

The required capital method requires that the company keep accurate records of capital contributions to and distributions from each business, in order to do historical analyses. Current results can then be viewed in the context of historical capital contributions.

16.6.5.3 Value at Risk

Required capital can be broken into two components:

1. The portion that is truly at risk and

2. The portion that is required to satisfy redundant regulatory reserves or excessive capital requirements.

In recent years, a method of allocating capital has emerged that reflects these two components. This method is known as Value at Risk (VaR).

VaR involves a two-tier approach to calculating required capital *for each business:*

1. The first tier is high-risk required capital, calculated as the amount of capital needed to withstand adverse experience. For example, the amount of capital could be calculated to withstand 99% of one-year fluctuations. This is the "Value at Risk."

2. The second tier is low-risk required capital, equal to the additional capital needed to maintain financial ratings or attain a desired level of financial strength.

In addition, a third tier of capital exists at the company level, equal to the company's overall excess or shortage of capital. The third tier is not allocated to any business. Table 16.6.1 illustrates the three tiers of capital.

Ideally, Tier 1 required capital should be backed by equity, and Tier 2 required capital should be backed by debt. In actual practice, though, it would require a happy coincidence for Tiers 1 and 2 to match up with equity and debt. Often, the amount of debt required to match Tier 2 required capital is not acceptable. For example, Tier 2 may represent 50% of required capital. Few companies would choose a capital structure with 50% debt in order to match Tier 2 needs. A company that finds itself with a significant, ongoing amount of Tier 3 capital should consider the methods of deploying excess capital outlined in Section 16.6.4. If Tier 3 capital is negative, then capital should be raised.

Table 16.6.1 Three Tiers of Capital

Assets	Liabilities and Capital
Total Assets	Total Liabilities
	Tier 1: High-risk required capital, "Value at Risk"
	Tier 2: Low-risk additional required capital, needed to maintain ratings
	Tier 3: Excess or shortage of capital (not allocated by business unit)

16.6.5.4   Using VaR to Allocate Cost of Capital

The VaR method can be used to rationally allocate the cost of capital by business unit, through the following steps:

1. Calculate the company's weighted average cost of capital using Formula 16.6.1, reflecting its mix of debt and equity.

2. Allocate assets backing reserves and Tier 1 required capital to the business units.

3. Retain assets backing Tier 2 required capital in an unallocated corporate segment. Allocate a charge for Tier 2 required capital to the business units.

4. Retain assets backing Tier 3 capital in a separate unallocated corporate segment. Allocate no charge for Tier 3 capital to the business units. Tier 3 capital is true excess corporate capital. Business units should not be penalized if corporate management has been unable to successfully manage and deploy such capital.

5. Calculate ROE using the following formula, where RC = required capital:

$$ROE = \frac{\text{After-tax Business Unit Net Income} - \text{Charge for Tier 2 RC}}{\text{Tier 1 RC}}$$

(16.6.2)

Expect each business unit to earn the company's targeted ROE.

6. Calculate the charge for Tier 2 RC as a percentage of Tier 2 RC. Determine this percentage so that the company will achieve its targeted ROE if all business units achieve the targeted ROE.

Example 16.6.2 Value at Risk Method of Allocating Capital and Calculating ROE

The Value at Risk method is illustrated in this example. The company has a charge for Tier 2 required capital of 2.00% and an ROE requirement for each business unit of 15%, net of charges for Tier 2 required capital. The second and third business units attain the ROE requirement, while the first business unit just misses the mark.

Business Unit	After-tax Net Income	Tier 1 Required Capital	Tier 2 Required Capital	Net Income after Tier 2 Charge	ROE
Individual Life	7,800,000	50,000,000	24,500,000	7,310,000	14.62%
Annuities	2,000,000	12,000,000	10,000,000	1,800,000	15.00
Investment Management	1,100,000	3,000,000	500,000	1,090,000	36.33
Total for Business Units	10,900,000	65,000,000	35,000,000	10,200,000	15.69
Corporate Expenses	0		Tier 1 RC	65,000,000	
Interest on Tier 2 RC	1,750,000		Tier 2 RC	35,000,000	
After-tax Interest on	−1,400,000		Debt	−28,000,000	
Debt					ROE
Total Net Income	11,250,000		Equity	72,000,000	15.63%

Note: Charge for Tier 2 capital = 2.00%, Business unit ROE requirement = 15.00%.

In Example 16.6.2, the charge for Tier 2 RC is given. The development of the theoretically proper charge for Tier 2 RC is left as an exercise.

A company's business units will have different proportions of high-risk and low-risk capital needs. The two-tier, VaR method of allocating capital measures the return on each business unit's high-risk capital while taking into account the cost of additional low-risk capital needed to satisfy solvency and rating agency concerns. While VaR is more commonly used in the banking industry, it applies equally well to the insurance industry.

16.6.5.5   Allocation of Excess or Shortage of Capital

Once required capital has been allocated to all the businesses, what should be done with any remaining excess capital or capital shortfall? We recommend the following approach:

- If the excess or shortfall is viewed as temporary, it should be allocated to a corporate segment.

- If the excess or shortfall is viewed as permanent, the calculation of required capital should be revised to reflect this view. (The company may intend the excess to be permanent, in order to maintain the company's financial strength at a high level; or the company may have no solution to a capital shortfall.)

Another approach is to allocate *all* of a company's capital in proportion to the required capital for each business. Using this approach, there is no excess capital or capital shortfall to deal with. However, this approach can magnify any flaws in the required capital calculations.

Results for a company's businesses can be distorted by reinsurance: If a reinsurance agreement involves a single line of business, that business may receive all the benefits of reinsurance, even if the reinsurance agreement was intended to help the company meet its overall capital needs. Since reinsurance capital is often cheaper than equity capital, the line of business using reinsurance may enjoy a lower cost of capital. In such a case, it may be appropriate to share the costs and benefits of reinsurance among several businesses.

16.6.5.6   Rationing of Capital

The allocation of capital is particularly important when there is a shortage of capital. The company will have to determine which businesses will receive the additional capital they desire and which will not. Those businesses that have achieved the best returns on capital would be the obvious choices to receive additional capital. However, some of the company's up-and-coming businesses that have not yet achieved economies of scale may also warrant additional capital.

The company may face some difficult choices when capital is short. Because of their strategic importance, some businesses may receive additional capital even if they do not earn an adequate return. For example, a mutual company might continue to offer participating whole life business, even if it produces a low rate of return. A company known as a specialist in term insurance would face a difficult choice if the returns available on new term insurance were inadequate. Over the long term, most companies will grow their most profitable businesses and shrink or curtail their least profitable businesses.

16.7 Achieving Financial Goals

This section discusses the achievement of financial goals by first looking at some basic requirements, then offering some simple but helpful techniques, and finally examining the most common financial goals, separately for mutual and stock companies.

16.7.1 Basic Requirements

The achievement of financial goals starts with a simple story. This story explains why your company will succeed. It is told to employees, investors, rating agencies, and perhaps even customers. It explains how the company will apply its competitive advantages to serve markets that provide opportunities for desirable profits and growth. This story is embodied in your company's vision, mission, and strategy.

Many companies lack a plausible story. They may not have competitive advantages. If so, it is time to build some, if they wish to survive. Companies may serve markets with compressed profit margins or little to no growth potential. If so, it is time to find new markets or new approaches to existing markets. A company that is not growing is dying. To survive, a company must periodically make the drastic changes needed to remain competitive and keep growing. Sometimes this means becoming part of a larger organization.

Company size would seem to be a significant factor, for both achieving financial goals in the short run and surviving in the long run. Size breeds economies of scale. Larger companies should have significant cost advantages over smaller rivals. However, smaller companies can often successfully compete with much larger companies by specializing in various market niches or by being affiliated with a larger company. In addition, there are some areas, such as personal service, where small companies often have the competitive advantage.

To achieve a company's financial goals, many areas of the company must work in concert. Products must be developed that generate sufficient sales, limit the company's risk, and provide a sufficient return on capital. Assets must be managed to match the company's products and maximize investment returns while limiting risk. Reinsurance, acquisitions, and divestitures must be coordinated with the management of risk, earnings, and capital. The company has to find just the right balance between growth, profitability, and risk to match the availability of capital.

16.7.2 Financial Management Techniques

There are a number of simple techniques or behaviors that can help a company serve its owners better:

- It is better to underpromise and overdeliver. Do not raise false hopes among investors or policyowners by speculating about good things that could happen. It is much better to stick with what is reasonably certain. Stock prices for companies that overpromise and underdeliver are usually considerably lower than stock prices for otherwise similar companies with the opposite habit. Mutual companies that have overpromised have been sued by their policyowners.

- Make modestly conservative accounting and reserving choices, so that the chances of negative surprises are reduced. This should slightly depress current earnings and current capital, but it should enable the company to build credibility with investors and policyowners over a longer period.

- Increase your vigilance when times are good. Most major financial problems have their seeds sown during good times, when companies tend to get overconfident and more careless. During bad times companies are naturally more vigilant.

- With the capital markets, as in most things, timing is important. You should raise capital when it is cheap, in advance of when you may need it. By looking ahead at your capital needs for the next two or more years, you can take advantage of capital-raising opportunities when they arise, such as relatively low interest rates for debt or a relatively high price for the company's stock.

Have a bias toward opportunities with more upside than downside potential. In particular, options have historically been a major source of added earnings and unexpected losses. Insurance companies routinely face opportunities with options. Life insurance products, assets, reinsurance, and acquisitions usually include some options. Strive to include options that benefit the company and minimize options that could hurt the company.

Build speed into your organization. It is an important competitive advantage. Many opportunities are most attractive to those who react first and less attractive to latecomers.

16.7.3 Achieving Financial Goals for Mutual Policyowners

Mutual policyowners want financial security and maximum value from their policies. Policyowners do not care whether the company grows fast, slowly, or not at all, as long as their value is maximized. In most cases, this is accomplished by continuing to grow the company, so policyowners reap the benefits of increasing economies of scale.

The major question that needs to be answered for a mutual company is "How fast should we grow the company?" This is dictated by the company's capital, acquisition costs, and rates of return on new business. Growth must be controlled so that acquisition costs do not outstrip the ability of the company to build its capital from retained earnings.

However, when acquisition costs are high and rates of return are low, policyowners may actually be better served by closing down new business, running off the in-force business, and returning all the capital to policyowners. This is effectively what is accomplished by the demutualization of a company.

16.7.4   Demutualization

Mutual life insurers seek to provide good value for their policyowners. Because they return much of the value through policyowner dividends, the rate of return (both ROI and ROE) on mutual companies is often far below that for stock companies.

As a result, when a company demutualizes, it starts life as a stock company with a very low ROE. The mutual block of business depresses the company's ROE for years to come. The mutual block slowly runs out and is eventually overshadowed by new business with more normal ROEs. It is not surprising that demutualized insurers are not exactly the darlings of the stock market.

Demutualization is an effective way to unlock the mutual policyowners' value in the company, without dismantling the company in the process. Once policyowners receive stock in the demutualized company, they can keep it or sell it; either way, the company remains capitalized. In fact, most demutualizing companies use the opportunity of the IPO to raise additional capital.

16.7.5   Achieving Stockholder Financial Goals

Stockholders want to maximize the return on their investment, through stock price appreciation and stockholder dividends. The company's stock price is driven by two main factors:

- The outlook for the company and the industry: Does the company have a "story" that sells or sizzles among investors? Are its future growth and earnings prospects dismal, modest, or immense? At what rate will the company be able to grow its future earnings?

- The recent history of the company under the current management team: Has the company produced a track record of stable, predictable earnings, growing at an attractive rate? Is the growth in earnings supported by a comparable growth in revenue? Does historical experience bolster confidence in the ability of the company to keep growing at its current rate? (Note: Stock markets measure growth by comparing results for each quarter with results for the same quarter, one year earlier.)

Stock prices are largely a function of P/E (stock price to earnings per share) ratios. In turn, P/E ratios are largely a function of the expected growth rate for the company, tempered by the current attractiveness of the life insurance industry. For example, a company growing at a 15% rate may have a P/E ratio of 14, while a company growing at a 10% rate may have a P/E ratio of 9. However, if life insurance stocks get "hot," the two companies may see their P/E ratios rise to 18 and 12, respectively. Even when insurance companies are hot prospects, their P/E ratios tend to be significantly below the average for the stock market.

Because of the relationship of P/E ratio and the company's growth rate, a common story is that the company will grow at a rate that is a little below what the company's management feels it can achieve over a number of years. This is in line with the technique of underpromising and overdelivering. While this technique will depress the current stock price, over time it should pay dividends by allowing the company to build its credibility.

If a company is privately held, the owners may depend on the cash they regularly receive from stockholder dividends. For publicly owned companies, stockholder dividends have diminished in importance over time, with stock price appreciation now the main focus.

Surprisingly, investors focus almost all of their attention on stockholder reporting and scant attention on regulatory reporting, unless the company is financially weak. This means the company can show negative solvency earnings and investors will hardly notice. However, rating agencies and regulators will notice. If there is a significant problem, it will be quickly brought to the attention of investors.

A fast-growing company will typically have soaring stockholder earnings and plummeting solvency earnings, because of the extreme conservatism in most solvency reserves. Such a company must actively raise capital to keep up with its growth, tapping most of the sources of capital described in the previous section.

A slow-growing company may experience the opposite: Solvency earnings may exceed stockholder earnings, as conservative solvency reserves are released on old business. The company's capital may grow faster than its ability to deploy capital.

A company should modify its financial goals over time, reacting to changes in the company, the insurance market, and the capital markets. For example, if investors shift their primary focus to ROE, the company should look for ways to improve ROE.

16.7.6   Embedded Value

Embedded value has been gaining acceptance in the capital markets as an important financial measure for insurance companies. Ronald P. McIntosh and Len Savage, of investment banker Fox-Pitt, Kelton, explain the increased interest in embedded value in this section.

Embedded value (EV) is the present value of a company's distributable earnings, including any current excess capital. Value from future new business is not included in EV. Accordingly, embedded value represents a run-off value for the company, discounted at a given rate of return. There are five reasons embedded value may become a key driver of life insurance stock prices:

1. Embedded values are used extensively in Europe. With the growth in international funds and global investing, EV is likely to become the prominent valuation basis for life insurance stocks.

2. EV is an actuarial valuation tool, which is used by buyers to substantiate take-over prices. Buyers typically look at the value of a target in three pieces: (a) the embedded value, (b) goodwill, or the

number of years of future production they will pay for, and (c) a multiple of potential annual cost savings.

3. EV allows investors to see how much of a company's current value is represented by in-force business and how much is based on expected future growth. Obviously, the faster a company is putting profitable business on its books, the more its value should be comprised of future business expectations.

4. EV is a good test of the recoverability of life insurance intangibles. U.S. life insurers, for GAAP accounting purposes, are allowed to initially defer acquisition costs and subsequently amortize them in relation to future years' profits. The embedded value of a company should exceed its DAC. Companies with EV less than DAC plus intangible assets may have been, in retrospect, too aggressive with assumptions or may have overpaid for previous acquisitions.

5. EV should provide a minimum value for life insurance companies. Since most companies are writing profitable new business and have opportunities to improve their profitability, a company's total value should exceed its embedded value.

EV does have some limitations, however. EV can be time- and staff-consuming to implement and maintain; EV can be sensitive and can change significantly with an assumption change; and EV can be difficult to explain to management and outside analysts from one period to the next.

16.8 Conclusion

If you have read the entire book and mastered everything you read, you are now qualified to run any life insurance company. Just walk up to the current head of any insurance organization and explain this to them. Do not stand too close when you explain this. Be ready to run fast!

More seriously, though, we hope you have learned much while reading this book and wish you great success in your future endeavors. If this book helps you do a few things a little better through the course of your career, we will be pleased. Good luck!

James W. Dallas

David B. Atkinson

16.9   Exercises

Exercise 16.1

Using the following variables, develop quarterly formulas equivalent to Formulas 16.2.1 and 16.2.2:

> DistrEarn_tot(cyq) = Future distributable earnings in calendar quarter and year cyq, for the business being analyzed
>
> iQ = Quarterly hurdle rate at which future distributable earnings will be discounted. $iQ = (1 + i)^{.25} - 1$.
>
> EmbeddedValue(byq) = Embedded value as of byq (the year and end of quarter at which the model begins), using a hurdle rate of iQ
>
> ROIQ = The simple, quarterly return on investment, to be solved for. The simple, annual ROI is related to ROIQ as follows: $ROI = (1 + ROIQ)^4 - 1$.

Exercise 16.2

Financial analysis shows that the company's newest line of business seems to be off to a poor start, with the following profits (actually, losses) and new business written in its first three years of operation.

Calendar Year	Profit (Loss) (in Millions)	Amount of Insurance Sold (in Billions)
1	−5	1
2	−10	4
3	−30	16

Because of the accelerating losses, senior management is seriously considering shutting down this new line of business. You have been asked to advise them. Modeling shows the following pattern of profits and losses by policy year, per thousand of insurance sold, excluding expenses that do not vary with the amount of business sold or in force.

Policy Year	Profit (Loss) per Thousand Sold
1	−2
2	1
3	1
4	1
5	1

To simplify this exercise, we will assume that the company is not taxed.

1. Determine how much of the losses are not explained by the model.

2. Assume the excess losses from the previous step are due to the fixed costs of running this line of business. Assuming fixed costs remain constant going forward and the line of business sells 16 billion of new insurance for three more calendar years (years 4–6) and then sells no more business, determine the projected profit for calendar years 4–10.

3. Determine the ROI associated with the results from the previous step.

4. Recalculate the ROI assuming that fixed costs are cut by two-thirds, starting in calendar year 7. (Once sales are stopped, fixed costs should drop significantly.)

5. What is your recommendation? Would you shut down the business immediately or continue the business? If you elect to continue the

business (strong hint), would you reduce sales levels, maintain sales levels, or increase sales levels?

Exercise 16.3

Your company is growing rapidly, selling primarily one product. Sales have increased to a level that will require the company to raise additional capital before the end of the year. A reinsurer has approached you with a proposal to reinsure up to 90% of your company's new business. Your analysis shows that you would be paying the reinsurer an ROI of 11%. Discuss what you would consider in deciding whether to accept the reinsurer's proposal.

Exercise 16.4

Product X earns a meager 10% ROI, before reinsurance. However, you have negotiated a reinsurance agreement that will allow you to reinsure 90% of the business at an ROI of 9%. What ROI would you expect on product X after reinsurance?

Exercise 16.5

DOB, a large insurance organization, has decided to sell its individual life insurance operation, which is respected in the industry as a national leader in the brokerage term market, with the most efficient systems for underwriting and issuing new term policies. Discuss considerations for each of the following potential buyers of DOB:

- Company A is an arch-competitor of DOB in the brokerage term market. They have similar products, prices, agent compensation, and distribution systems. The major difference is that Company A lacks DOB's efficient systems for underwriting and issuing policies. Company A has a publicly traded parent with deep pockets that insists on amortizing goodwill over ten years. Its parent will not settle for anything less than 15% growth and 15% ROE.

- Company B has grown by acquisitions over the years and does a little bit of everything in the market. It is not strong in the brokerage term market. It has many systems in place for underwriting and issue, none of which are very good. It too has a publicly traded parent with deep pockets. However, its parent has so much extra capital that it prefers to expense goodwill immediately. The parent looks for acquisitions that will contribute to its 20% annual growth rate in earnings, revenue, assets, and capital.

- Company C has tried a few acquisitions over the years. While the acquisitions have worked out well financially, the company has not been successful in integrating operations, much like Company B. Company C is a mutual company with just enough excess capital for this acquisition. It specializes in participating whole life products, which produce an ROE of only 8%.

Exercise 16.6

Conduct a risk management review of your company or line of business (or the life insurance company or line of business with which you are the most familiar). Categorize each of the risks as high, moderate, low, or insufficient information. Has your company performed a review of its risks recently? If not, why not? (Perhaps you should volunteer to lead such a review!)

Exercise 16.7

Conduct an earnings management review of your company or line of business (or the life insurance company or line of business with which you are the most familiar). What changes, strategies, or actions would you recommend to

1. Reduce product-related risk without reducing sales levels.

2. Increase investment income without adding too much to earnings volatility.

3. Reduce expenses while improving service. (What major and/or minor expense reduction efforts?)

4. Allocate corporate expenses better.

5. Replace legacy systems. (They cannot last forever, or can they?)

Exercise 16.8

Conduct a capital management review of your company (or the life insurance company with which you are the most familiar).

1. According to insurance regulations, rating agencies, company management, and a comparison to similar companies, is the company over- or undercapitalized? You may get different answers from each. If the company is overcapitalized, how should the excess capital be deployed? If the company is undercapitalized, how should additional capital be raised?

2. What changes to corporate structure would you recommend? Should some companies in the group be merged? Would the addition of a holding company or another insurance company bring tax or regulatory relief?

3. What is the company's capital structure in terms of percentage of capital in debt, equity, and mezzanine financing? Could the company increase its use of debt without endangering its ratings? Should the company decrease its use of debt to improve its ratings?

4. What is the company's use of reinsurance capital? How does it compare in size to debt, equity, and mezzanine financing?

5. How does the company allocate and charge for capital by line of business or other reporting unit? What changes would you recommend?

Exercise 16.9

This exercise expands on Section 16.6.5.4 to develop a theoretical basis for the charge for Tier 2 required capital. Let

$$
\begin{aligned}
\text{Tier1RC} &= \text{Total Tier 1 required capital} \\
\text{Tier2RC} &= \text{Total Tier 2 required capital} \\
\text{ROE} &= \text{The company's desired return on equity} \\
\text{WACC} &= \text{The company's weighted average cost of} \\
&\quad\; \text{capital, reflecting its ROE, after-tax yield on} \\
&\quad\; \text{debt, and capital structure} \\
\text{Tier2IntRate} &= \text{The after-tax interest rate earned on assets} \\
&\quad\; \text{backing Tier 2 required capital}
\end{aligned}
$$

CorpExp = Corporate expenses not allocated to business units. In order to allocate only relevant costs, these expenses could be limited to those related to raising and managing corporate capital.

Tier2ChargePct = The percentage of Tier 2 required capital charged to each business unit for the use of Tier 2 required capital.

Assume the following:

1. Tier1RC earns a return equal to ROE.

2. Tier2RC earns a return equal to Tier2IntRate + Tier2ChargePct.

3. Tier1RC + Tier2RC together earn an overall return equal to WACC, plus an additional amount equal to CorpExp.

The last assumption implies that we will choose a value for Tier2ChargePct that will allow the company to earn its WACC, after first covering corporate expenses.

Use these assumptions to develop a formula for Tier2ChargePct in terms of WACC, Tier2IntRate, CorpExp, ROE, Tier1RC, and Tier2RC.

Exercise 16.10

Assume that ROE = 15%, WACC = 13%, Tier2IntRate = 5%, CorpExp = 0, and Tier2RC = 50% of total required capital. In other words, Tier1RC = Tier2RC = 50% of RC. Calculate Tier2ChargePct using Formula 16.9.2. Explain the result.

Exercise 16.11

Repeat the previous exercise, but assume that Tier2RC = 25% of total required capital. Calculate Tier2ChargePct and explain the result.

Exercise 16.12

Repeat the previous exercise, but assume that Tier2RC = 20% of total required capital. Calculate Tier2ChargePct and explain the result, assuming the cost of debt is 5% and that debt is 20% of capital.

Exercise 16.13

Review how your company (or the life insurance company with which you are the most familiar) achieves its financial goals:

1. What is the company's "story" that explains to investors, rating agencies, employees, and agents how the company will succeed?

2. Which financial management techniques does the company generally use?

3. What are the company's financial goals?

4. What other goals or measures has the company considered? Which have been tried and discarded? Which are currently being considered?

16.10   Answers

Answer 16.1

Adapting Formula 11.6.1, we have

$$\text{EmbeddedValue(byq)}$$
$$= \sum_{\text{cyq}=\text{byq}+1}^{\infty} \text{DistrEarn\_tot(cyq)} \, (1 + iQ)^{(\text{byq}-\text{cyq})/4}.$$

Adapting Formula 11.6.2, we have

$$0 = \sum_{\text{all cyq}} \text{DistrEarn\_tot(cyq)} \, (1+\text{ROIQ})^{-\text{cyq}/4},$$

where cyq starts with the first calendar year and quarter in which money was invested in the business and continues until all the business has run out.

Answer 16.2

1. Three million of loss in each of the first three years is not explained by the model. (Compare the Total Model Profits to Historical Profits in Table 16.9.1.)

2. The projected profits for calendar years 4–10 are −14, 2, 17, 61, 45, 29, and 13, as shown in Table 16.9.1.

Table 16.9.1 Historical and Projected Profits

Cal Yr	Sales	Modeled Profit Resulting from New Sales in Year						Tot Mod. Prof.	Hist. Prof.	Imp. Fixed Costs	Hist. & Proj. Profit	Hist. & Proj. Profit*
		1	*2*	*3*	*4*	*5*	*6*					
1	1	−2						−2	−5	3	−5	−5
2	4	1	−8					−7	−10	3	−10	−10
3	16	1	4	−32				−27	−30	3	−30	−30
4	16	1	4	16	−32			−11		3	−14	−14
5	16	1	4	16	16	−32		5		3	2	2
6	16		4	16	16	16	−32	20		3	17	17
7				16	16	16	16	64		3	61	63
8					16	16	16	48		3	45	47
9						16	16	32		3	29	31
10							16	16		3	13	15
										ROI:	24.4%	25.4%

*With profit increased by 2 in years 7–10.

3. The ROI is 24.4%.

4. Projected profits for calendar years 7–10 are increased by two. The ROI increases to 25.4%.

5. Continue the business. This is likely the company's most profitable business, as ROIs of 24% or more are unusual. Sales should be increased by as much as the company and the market can bear. The company may need to raise additional capital in order to fund the growth of this business. It may be wise to shift resources and capital from other areas of the company to bolster the new line of business.

Answer 16.3

You know you have to do something to raise capital by the end of the year, so you should compare the reinsurance proposal to the other choices, which we will limit to debt and equity. Here are some of the things you might consider:

- How much capital will you need by the end of the year? If only a small amount of additional capital will be needed over the next year or two, then an equity or debt offering is probably not practical. However, bank debt is efficient for smaller capital needs. Alternatively, the company could probably sell a small amount of its stock each day through the stock exchanges without putting too much downward pressure on its stock price. If a large amount of capital is needed, an equity or debt offering is more feasible.

- How much time do you have to raise the capital? If you are pinched for time, the reinsurance solution is probably the fastest. In addition, bank debt can be quickly arranged. A bond or stock offering may take months to complete.

- How leveraged is the company? The company may already have so much debt on its balance sheet that to add any more debt may endanger its ratings. Debt may not be an option for a mutual company.

- What is the company's cost of debt? If the company is highly rated and interest on debt is tax deductible, debt is usually the cheapest form of capital. If the company has poor ratings, the reinsurance proposal may be cheaper than debt.

- How does the cost of reinsurance (11% ROI) compare to the company's weighted average cost of capital (WACC)? Is the cost of reinsurance out of whack with the WACC? If the cost of reinsurance exceeds the WACC, then reinsurance is probably not the best long-term solution. Instead, the company should raise a combination of equity and debt to meet its long-term capital needs.

Answer 16.4

We will assume that the weighted average of (1) the ROI on the 10% of Product X that is retained and (2) the 9% ROI on the 90% of Product

X that is reinsured will equal the 10% ROI on Product X before reinsurance. In other words,

AfterReinROI (10%) + 9% (90%) = 10%.

This leads to

AfterReinROI = (10% − 8.1%)/10% = 19%,
a much more attractive ROI.

Answer 16.5

Company A would love to buy DOB, both to take out a major competitor and to acquire their superior systems. Because DOB is selling an attractive, ongoing operation, a significant portion of the purchase value will be represented by goodwill. Since Company A's parent insists on amortizing goodwill over a ten-year period, without letting ROE fall below 15%, Company A has only two chances of pulling off this acquisition: slim and none. If Company A is earning well in excess of a 15% ROE currently, it may have a slim chance.

Company B is apt to be a serious competitor. While the acquisition of DOB does not have the strategic fit that it would for Company A, Company B's parent is looking for good acquisitions. DOB would seem to be a quality operation that could serve as a model for the rest of the company. The value of DOB would probably be best preserved by running it as a stand-alone operation. There seems to be little opportunity for synergy other than adopting the efficient systems for underwriting and issue throughout the company, although the difficulty and expense of doing so should not be underestimated. Company B may be a serious bidder for DOB.

Company C may think twice before spending its last bit of excess capital on this acquisition. If it chooses to go forward, Company C will be able to make a competitive bid that will likely return much more than its 8% ROE. Goodwill is often not a consideration for a mutual company. Mutual companies tend to focus more on solvency accounting, which typically does not recognize goodwill. If successful, Company C would likely try to preserve the value of DOB by running it on a stand-alone basis, while trying to adapt DOB superior systems to the rest of Company C.

Answer 16.6

Discuss your answers with one or more people who know more about the company's risks, especially the risks you categorized as "insufficient information." If the company has performed a review of its risks recently, compare your answers to the company's analysis. In some companies, this information may be deemed highly sensitive and therefore unavailable.

Answer 16.7

Discuss your answers with one or more people who know more about the company's earnings, products, investments, expenses, and so on. If the company has examined steps it might take to improve earnings, compare your answers to the company's analysis. In some companies, this information may be deemed highly sensitive and therefore unavailable.

Answer 16.8

Discuss your answers with one or more people who know more about the company's corporate and capital structure. If the company has a capital plan or has examined steps it might take to improve its capital position, compare your answers to the company's analysis. In some companies, this information may be deemed highly sensitive and therefore unavailable.

Answer 16.9

The three assumptions can be combined to form the following equation:

$$\text{Tier1RC (ROE)} + \text{Tier2RC (Tier2IntRate} + \text{Tier2ChargePct)} \\ = (\text{Tier1RC} + \text{Tier2RC)} \, \text{WACC} + \text{CorpExp.}$$

$$(16.9.1)$$

Solving Formula 16.9.1 for Tier2ChargePct, we obtain

$$\text{Tier2ChargePct} = \text{WACC} - \text{Tier2IntRate}$$
$$+ \frac{\text{CorpExp} - (\text{ROE} - \text{WACC})\text{Tier1RC}}{\text{Tier2RC}}.$$

$$(16.9.2)$$

Answer 16.10

$$\text{Tier2ChargePct} = 13\% - 5\% + \frac{0 - (15\% - 13\%)(50\% \text{ of RC})}{50\% \text{ of RC}}$$
$$= 6\%.$$

Half of the capital (Tier1RC) earns a rate of 15% and the other half (Tier2RC) earns a rate of 11% (a Tier2IntRate of 5% + a Tier2ChargePct of 6%), for a weighted average rate of return of 13%, which is equal to the WACC. Because only half of the company's capital is earning the ROE, a large Tier2RC charge is needed to raise the average return to match the WACC.

Answer 16.11

$$\text{Tier2ChargePct} = 13\% - 5\% + \frac{0 - (15\% - 13\%)(75\% \text{ of RC})}{25\% \text{ of RC}}$$
$$= 2\%.$$

Seventy-five percent of the capital (Tier1RC) earns a rate of 15%, and the other 25% (Tier2RC) earns a rate of 7% (a Tier2IntRate of 5% + a Tier2ChargePct of 2%), for a weighted average rate of return of 13%, which again is equal to the WACC. Because so much of the company's capital is earning the ROE, only a small Tier2RC charge is needed.

Answer 16.12

$$\text{Tier2ChargePct} = 13\% - 5\% + \frac{0 - (15\% - 13\%)(80\% \text{ of RC})}{20\% \text{ of RC}}$$
$$= 0\%.$$

Eighty percent of the capital (Tier1RC) earns a rate of 15%, and the other 20% (Tier2RC) earns a rate of 5% (a Tier2IntRate of 5% + a Tier2ChargePct of 0%), for a weighted average rate of return of 13%, which once again is equal to the WACC.

From the assumptions, we know that the company's capital structure is 80% equity and 20% debt. In other words, Tier1RC is equal to the company's equity and Tier2RC is equal to the company's debt. Because the company's equity (Tier1RC) is earning the ROE and its debt (Tier2RC) is earning the cost of debt, no Tier2RC charge is needed.

Answer 16.13

Discuss your answers with one or more people familiar with the company's financial management. For a publicly traded company, the answers to these questions are often readily available to investment analysts, rating agency analysts, and, with a little digging, the public.

Glossary

Portions of this glossary are excerpted and adapted from the Life Office Management Association's *Glossary of Insurance Terms* (Atlanta; LOMA, © 1997). Used with permission of the publisher; all rights reserved. For more information about LOMA's glossary and other educational products for insurance and financial services, visit www.loma.org.

AAR   See *net amount at risk*.

accelerated death benefit   A life insurance benefit that allows the policyowner to receive a specified portion of the policy's death benefit before the insured's death if certain conditions are met, such as the insured having a terminal illness and a life expectancy of less than a year. Also known as *living benefit* or *terminal illness benefit*.

accidental death and dismemberment (AD&D)   A life insurance benefit that provides for an amount of money in addition to the basic death benefit of a life insurance policy. This additional amount is payable only if the insured dies as the result of an accident or loses any two limbs or the sight of both eyes as the result of an accident. Some AD&D benefits pay one half of the benefit amount if the insured loses one limb or the sight in one eye.

accidental death benefit (ADB)   A life insurance benefit that provides death benefit only if the insured dies as the result of an accident.

account value   The accumulated fund for an accumulation annuity or universal life policy. The cash value is equal to the account value less any surrender charge. For universal life, premiums and interest are added to the account value while COI and expense charges are deducted from the account value each month.

accrued tax   The amount of tax incurred for the current year, equal to the sum of taxes paid and the provision for deferred taxes.

accumulate To increase a current amount to determine its future value on a given date, reflecting the time value of money.

accumulation An amount that accumulates with interest and perhaps the deposit of additional amounts.

accumulation factor The factor by which a current amount of money is multiplied to determine its future value on a given date.

accumulation annuity An annuity contract under which premiums are accumulated with interest or investment results.

accumulation dividend option A life insurance policy dividend option under which policy dividends are left on deposit with the insurer to accumulate at interest. See *dividend accumulations.*

accumulation reserve method See *retrospective reserve method.*

acquisition costs Costs that are related to the production of new business, such as marketing expenses, distribution expenses, underwriting expenses, policy issue expenses, and first-year commissions.

ADB See *accidental death benefit.*

AD&D See *accidental death and dismemberment.*

adaptive pricing Pricing behavior in which companies review the prices of other companies and then determine where to set their price. Instead of competing mainly on price, companies using adaptive pricing try to compete based on image, quality, and service. See *competitor-oriented pricing strategies.*

additional insured rider A rider that may be added to a life insurance policy to provide term insurance coverage on the life of an individual other than the policy's insured.

adjustable life insurance A type of life insurance that allows the policyholder to change the plan of insurance, raise or lower the face amount of the policy, increase or decrease the premium, and lengthen or shorten the protection period.

adverse deviation Actual conditions that differ from an insurer's assumptions, thus reducing the insurer's revenues, increasing its expenses, or increasing its benefit payments.

age setback   See *setback.*

agency system   A distribution system in which insurance companies use their own commissioned agents to sell and deliver insurance policies. The agency system is the most common system for distributing individual life insurance products and includes the branch office distribution system and the general agency distribution system.

agent   A sales person who represents an insurance company and who sells and services insurance policies.

aggregate model   A simple financial model that attempts to approximate a business or an investment in total or in the aggregate. Aggregate models typically have few, if any, cells. See *model* and *cell.*

aggregate mortality table   A mortality table that aggregates the mortality results of different groups, such as males and females, smokers and nonsmokers, or select and ultimate risks. An aggregate mortality table has mortality rates that vary only by attained age. Compare with *select mortality table* and *ultimate mortality table.*

allowance   See *expense allowance.*

ALM   Usually refers to asset/liability management, but is sometimes used to refer to asset/liability matching.

amortize   **1.** To write off a capitalized expenditure by prorating it over a certain period. See *capitalize.* **2.** To gradually pay off a loan over a certain period.

amount at risk   See *net amount at risk.*

amount of insurance   The amount of benefit provided by an insurance policy. Also known as *face amount, sum assured,* or *volume of insurance.*

annually renewable term (ART) insurance   Term life insurance that automatically renews with the payment of each year's premium, which usually increases. The insurance continues for a specified number of years or until the insured reaches the age specified in the contract. See *increasing premium term.*

annuitant   The person whose lifetime is used as the measuring period to determine how long benefits are payable under a life annuity.

annuity   A policy under which as insurance company promises to make a series of periodic payments to a named individual in exchange for a premium or a series of premiums.

annuity certain   See *certain annuity*.

annuitization   To convert the accumulated funds of an accumulation annuity to an income annuity.

antiselection   The greater tendency of people with a greater-than-average likelihood of loss to apply for or continue insurance, when compared with other people. An increase in antiselection often occurs in connection with increased lapse rates, which lead to increased mortality or morbidity rates.

arbitrary method   A method of estimating future interest rate patterns. This method manually creates a set of interest rate scenarios in an arbitrary fashion. See *probabilistic method* and *successive ratios method*.

ART   See *annually renewable term*.

asset/liability management (ALM)   A program that coordinates the administration of an insurer's investments with the administration of its policy liabilities.

asset/liability matching   A process that attempts to match future liability cash flows with equal and offsetting asset cash flows, to protect the company from changes in interest rates.

asset/liability modeling   A modeling process that projects future liability cash flows, reserve changes, and required capital changes, along with future asset cash flows and changes in book and market value. Contrast with *liability modeling*.

asset share   Insurance cash flows accumulated with interest and net of taxes, calculated on a per unit in force basis, and assuming no capital contributions or distributions. Asset shares are used to determine the share of a company's assets that resulted from a certain group of policies. Asset shares are useful for allocating assets or investment income between different groups of policies,

for setting dividend scales, and for calculating policyowner equity in connection with demutualization.

assets   All things of value owned by an individual or organization. For an insurance company, the principal assets are often bonds, mortgages, real estate, and stocks.

assume   To accept insurance risk from another insurance company, referred to as the ceding company.

assuming company   See *reinsurer*.

assumption reinsurance   A reinsurance agreement in which one company permanently transfers full responsibility for a block of policies to another company. After the transfer, the ceding company is no longer a party to the policy contracts.

assumptions   The mortality, morbidity, interest, expense, and other estimates used for pricing, valuation, and financial modeling.

attained age   A person's current age. Compare to *issue age*.

automatic   A method of ceding reinsurance under which the ceding company and reinsurer agree that all business of a certain description will be ceded to the reinsurer. Neither party has any right to choose particular policies to be ceded—the decision is automatic. Also known as *treaty reinsurance* for non-life business. Contrast with *facultative* and *facultative-obligatory*.

average size   The average amount of insurance purchased, often expressed as a number of units, with 1,000 of benefit being the unit most often used. For example, an average policy size of 120,000 would translate to an average size of 120 units.

avoidable costs   Costs that have not yet been incurred or costs that can be reversed.

bailout provision   A provision that allows an annuity policyowner to surrender the annuity without any surrender charge if the company fails to credit interest at least equal to a certain rate, called the bailout rate, for a number of years called the bailout period. This provision is similar to, though not as strong as, a guaranteed interest rate for the bailout period.

balance sheet   A financial statement that shows a company's assets on the left hand side and its liabilities and equity on the right hand side. It is called a *balance sheet* because assets must balance to liabilities plus equity.

beneficiary   The person or party that the owner of an insurance policy names to receive the policy benefit if the event insured against occurs.

beneficiary insurability option (BIO)   A rider that gives the beneficiary the right to purchase insurance immediately after the insured's death. The new insurance is generally of the same type as the original policy and does not require new evidence of the beneficiary's insurability. A policy with a BIO rider can serve as an alternative to a joint last-to-die policy.

benefit   The amount of money paid when an insurance claim is approved.

benefit reserves   *Stockholder reserves* or *GAAP reserves* excluding *DAC.*

block of business   A group of policies; part of a company's insurance business.

bond   A certificate of debt issued by a government or corporation that guarantees payment of the original investment on a specified date plus periodic, usually semi-annual, payments of interest until that date.

book value   The amount shown on a company's books for a particular asset or liability. A company often maintains separate sets of book values for tax purposes, solvency accounting, and stockholder accounting. Complex rules dictate how book values must be calculated for each type of asset and liability and each set of books.

branch office   A field office that is established and maintained by an insurance company.

breakeven year   The policy year in which accumulated profits first turn positive and remain positive.

broker   A sales person who places business with more than one insurance company. Unlike the agent, who is considered to represent the company, the broker usually is considered to represent the insurance buyer.

brokerage distribution system   A distribution system that relies on commissioned agents, called brokers, who sell the products of more than one insurance company.

brokerage general agency   An agency operated by an independent general agent who is under contract to a number of insurance companies.

buyer-oriented pricing strategies   Pricing strategies that ignore competition. See *penetration pricing, neutral pricing, segmented pricing,* and *skim pricing.* Contrast with *competitor-oriented pricing strategies.*

call option   1. An option to buy a stated amount of stock for a set price at a given time. **2.** An option given to the issuer of a bond to repay the bond before its scheduled maturity date. This option would be exercised most commonly when interest rates fall, allowing the issuer to then refinance at lower rates.

capital   The amount by which an insurance company's assets exceed its liabilities other than debt. Capital generally consists of debt plus equity. See *equity* and *surplus.*

capital contribution   The addition of capital to a company by its owners, usually through a payment of cash.

capital gain   The excess of the market value of an asset over its purchase price. If the asset has not yet been sold, this is referred to as an *unrealized capital gain.* Once the asset is sold, it is a *realized capital gain.*

capital loss   The excess of the purchase price of an asset over its market value. Capital losses can be *realized* or *unrealized.* See *capital gain.*

capitalize   To classify expenditures as assets instead of expenses. Capitalized expenditures are subsequently amortized. See *amortize.*

captive agent   A full-time commissioned salesperson who works out of an insurance company's field office, holds an agent contract with that company, and sends all, or almost all, of his or her business to that company. A career agent may occasionally sell business for other companies. Also known as *career, dedicated, exclusive,* or *tied agent.*

career agent See *captive agent.*

CARVM See *Commissioners' Annuity Reserve Valuation Method.*

cash dividend A dividend option under which dividends are paid to the policyowner in cash.

cash flow When used by an insurance company, this refers to all cash received and paid during a period. Insurance companies receive premiums and investment returns in cash and disburse cash to pay policy benefits, expenses, and taxes and to make new investments. When cash received exceeds cash paid for other than new investments, this is referred to as positive cash flow. Negative cash flow is the opposite, when cash paid for other than new investments exceeds cash received.

cash flow testing An analysis that involves forecasting, under a number of different scenarios, the timing and amount of the cash flows related to some or all of an insurer's business.

cash surrender value See *cash value.*

cash value In a life insurance policy, the amount of money, before adjustment for factors such as policy loans or late premiums, that the policyowner will receive if the policyowner allows the policy to lapse or surrenders the policy to the insurance company.

cede To transfer insurance risk from a ceding company to a reinsurer; the opposite of *assume.*

ceding company An insurance company that cedes insurance risk to a reinsurer.

cell A part of a financial model. See *model.*

certain and life annuity An income annuity that makes payments for as long as the annuitant lives, but for no less than a fixed or *certain* number of years.

certain annuity An income annuity that makes payments for a fixed or *certain* number of years. Also known as *annuity certain.*

chargeback   A charge against an agent's commission account to repay the company for all or part of a commission previously credited to the agent. Commission chargebacks are made on an agent's account, for example, when premiums are returned to the policyowner or when a policy for which an agent received an annualized commission lapses before the end of the first policy year.

children's insurance rider   A rider that may be added to a life insurance policy to provide term insurance coverage on the insured's children.

CI   See *critical illness benefit.*

claim   A demand on an insurer for payment of insurance benefits.

CMO   See *collateralized mortgage obligation.*

closed block   An in-force block of business that is closed to future new business. In other words, no additional new business will be added.

COI   See *cost of insurance charge.*

coinsurance   A form of reinsurance under which the ceding company shares its premiums, death claims, surrender benefits, dividends, and policy loans with the reinsurer and the reinsurer pays expense allowances to reimburse the ceding company for a share of its expenses.

coinsurance with funds withheld (co/funds withheld)   A form of reinsurance under which the basic provisions of coinsurance are modified by having the ceding company withhold funds payable to the reinsurer. The amount of the funds withheld is usually equal to the reserve associated with the business reinsured. Investment income earned on the funds withheld is paid to the reinsurer. This is almost the same as *modified coinsurance (modco)*. The difference between this approach and modco is that the reinsurer holds the reserves as a liability on its books and the funds withheld as an asset on its books, while the ceding company shows a reserve credit for the reserves reinsured and a liability for the funds withheld.

COLA   See *cost-of-living adjustment.*

collateralized mortgage obligation (CMO)   A financial instrument that is backed by the cash flows of an underlying pool of mortgages. Slices of the mortgage cash flows are sold in *tranches.*

compound interest   The payment of interest on principal plus any unpaid interest. Contrast with *simple interest.* Most financial products use the principle of compound interest.

commission   The amount of money paid to an insurance agent or broker for selling or servicing an insurance policy. A commission is usually calculated as a percentage of the premium.

commission override   The portion of the commission received by an agent's general agent in return for providing services such as training, marketing support, and office space to the agent or in return for recruiting the agent for the company.

Commissioners' Annuity Reserve Valuation Method (CARVM)   A retrospective reserve method used in the U.S. for accumulation annuities.

Commissioners' Reserve Valuation Method (CRVM)   A prospective reserve method that produces the same results as the full preliminary term method, except for products with unusually high net premiums. Used primarily in the U.S. See *full preliminary term method.*

common stock   A form of stock that can receive dividends only after preferred stockholders have received all dividends owed them. Most stock is common stock. See *stock.*

competitor-oriented pricing strategies   Pricing strategies that concentrate on the pricing behavior of competitors. See *independent pricing, cooperative pricing, adaptive pricing, opportunistic pricing,* and *predatory pricing.* Contrast with *buyer-oriented pricing strategies.*

conditionally vested commission   A commission that begins as a nonvested commission and becomes vested—guaranteed payable to an agent—after the agent attains a certain age or number of years of service.

contestable period The period of time (usually two years) after a policy is issued during which an insurer may challenge the validity of a life insurance policy due to fraud, misrepresentation, and the like.

continuous-premium whole life insurance Whole life insurance for which premiums are payable throughout the life of the policy.

conversion option The right to change insurance coverage in certain prescribed situations from one type of policy to another without presenting evidence of insurability. Most often, the right to change from a term plan to a permanent plan of insurance.

convertible term insurance Term insurance that can be exchanged, at the option of the policyholder and without evidence of insurability, for another plan of insurance.

cooperative pricing A pricing strategy that anticipates that competitors will follow any price change. Competitors may not charge the same price, but changes in price are often made in parallel. This is common when a few companies dominate a market segment. See *competitor-oriented pricing strategies.*

corridor An amount or percentage that automatically increases the death benefit as the cash value approaches the death benefit. Often, the corridor is a percentage based on the insured's attained age. Some taxing authorities specify minimum corridor percentages to ensure a significant net amount at risk, so the tax-free accumulation of the cash value does not offer too great of a tax advantage when compared to non-insurance products.

cost of capital See *weighted average cost of capital.*

cost of insurance (COI) charge The cost of insurance protection for a universal life policy is reflected by deducting this charge from the account value. The COI charge is calculated as a COI rate times the net amount at risk. The COI rate is similar to a mortality rate and usually varies by age, sex, and risk class.

cost-of-living adjustment (COLA) An automatic increase in a benefit to compensate for an increase in the cost of living.

coupon Bond interest payments, which are usually semi-annual, are called coupons.

covariance   A statistical measure of the correlation of two variables.

crediting rate, credited interest rate   The interest rate that an insurer pays its customers in a given time period for an interest-sensitive product.

critical illness (CI) benefit   A benefit under which the insurer agrees to pay an amount if the insured suffers from one of a number of specified diseases such as cancer, stroke, and heart attack. Also known as *dread disease benefit*.

CRVM   See *Commissioners' Reserve Valuation Method*.

current interest whole life   See *interest-sensitive whole life*.

DAC   See *deferred acquisition costs*.

DD   dread disease. See *critical illness benefit*.

death benefit   The amount paid when a person insured under a life insurance policy dies. This amount does not include adjustments for outstanding policy loans, dividends, paid-up additions, or late premium payments.

debit insurance   See *industrial life insurance*.

debt   A part of the capital structure for many companies, along with equity. Debt usually consists of amounts owed to bondholders and banks.

decreasing term insurance   A type of term life insurance in which the amount of coverage decreases during the term of coverage.

dedicated agent   See *captive agent*.

default   An asset is said to be in default when the borrower fails to make scheduled principal or interest payments on time.

deferred annuity   An accumulation annuity or income annuity whose payouts begin at a future date.

deferred acquisition costs (DAC)   Acquisition costs that are capitalized when policies are issued and then gradually amortized, in order to spread the acquisition costs over the life of the policies. Also known as *expense reserves*, when switched from a positive asset to a negative liability. DAC is used in combination with *earnings reserves*, also known as *GAAP reserves* and *stockholder reserves*.

deferred premiums   Premiums that are due after the close of the financial reporting period but before the next policy anniversary.

deferred tax liability   When reporting liabilities to stockholders, companies must include a deferred tax liability equal to a tax rate times cumulative timing differences. In situations where tax rates have not changed, the deferred tax liability can also be calculated as the cumulative provision for deferred taxes.

demutualization   The process of converting a mutual insurance company to a stock insurance company.

deterministic modeling   A modeling process that uses a fixed set of probabilities to generate a single outcome. Contrast with *stochastic modeling*. See *model*.

direct mail   In insurance, printed solicitations that are addressed directly to prospective purchasers of insurance products.

direct marketing   Any method by which an insurance company sells directly to consumers without the use of agents, such as through direct mail, telemarketing, direct response, and the Internet.

direct response distribution system   In insurance, a distribution system that relies on advertisements, telephone solicitations, and mailings to generate sales. The advertisements and solicitations generally inform the customer how to apply for the insurance or how to contact the insurer.

disability   Inability to work due to an injury or sickness.

disability benefit   A benefit providing for waiver of premium, payment of monthly income, or a lump sum, if the insured becomes disabled.

disability income insurance   A type of health insurance designed to compensate insured people for a portion of the income they lose because of a disabling injury or illness. Generally, benefits for disability income insurance are provided for the disabled person in the form of monthly payments.

discount   To determine the present value of an amount to be paid on a future date, reflecting the time value of money.

discount factor   The factor by which an amount to be paid on a future date is multiplied to determine its present value.

discount rate   The *interest rate* or *yield rate* used to discount future amounts.

disintermediation   Withdrawing money from a financial institution in order to earn a higher yield elsewhere. Disintermediation through policy loans or surrendered policies has been a major problem for life insurers during periods of economic depression and periods of high inflation.

distributable earnings   The earnings that can be distributed to the owners of the company, taking into account not only basic cash flows and solvency reserves, but also required capital. When distributable earnings are negative, they represent an amount that the owners must contribute to the company or allocate to a line of business.

distribution expenses   Expenses involved in making insurance products available to the public. These expenses include agent compensation, sales representatives' salaries, and postal, printing, and telecommunications expenses for those companies that use direct response marketing.

dividend   See *policyowner dividend* or *stockholder dividend.*

dividend accumulations   Amounts that result when a policyowner decides to leave policyowners dividends on deposit with an insurer. See *accumulation dividend option.*

dividend additions   See *paid-up additions.*

dividend interest rate   The interest rate earned on an insurer's investments, used to calculate policyowner dividends.

dividend options   Several alternatives that participating policyowners can choose from to indicate the manner in which they want to receive their dividends.

dread disease (DD) benefit   See *critical illness benefit.*

due and unpaid premiums   Premiums that were due but unpaid as of the end of the financial reporting period.

duration   **1.** For an insurance policy, this is the number of years that the policy has been in force, often used in place of *policy year*. The issue date is duration 0. The first policy anniversary is duration 1. Fractional years are often used. For example, six months after the issue date would be duration 0.5. Compare with *policy year*. **2.** For a series of cash flows, such as from an investment, this is the weighted average time of the series of cash flows.

dynamic product   A life insurance product with cash values that are not predetermined, such as universal life or variable universal life. Cash values depend on premiums paid, cost of insurance and expense charges deducted, and investment results.

dynamic solvency testing (DST)   The use of modeling to project into the future an insurance company's existing and future business and especially its assets, liabilities, and equity.

dynamic validation   Validation of the accuracy of a financial model by comparing its results with actual results over a period of time. Contrast with *static validation*.

earned premium   The portion of a premium that provides insurance coverage for the current financial reporting period is considered earned. Under some forms of insurance accounting, only earned premiums are included in premium revenue. See *unearned premium*.

embedded value (EV)   This is the value of a company or block of business. Embedded value is calculated by discounting future profits using a *hurdle rate*. The hurdle rate is the rate of return demanded by the company's owners or prospective owners. Distributable earnings are often used as the future profits to be discounted.

employer-sponsored distribution   A method of distribution used to sell individual life insurance policies to employees with endorsement from the employer and payroll deductions to pay premiums.

earnings   See *net income*. Also known as *profit*.

earnings reserves   Reserves used for determining stockholder earnings. Also known as *GAAP reserves* and *stockholder reserves*. In some cases, these reserves may be net of *deferred acquisition costs (DAC)*.

endorsement   See *rider*.

endowment benefit   The amount payable when an insured lives to a pre-defined age or policy year.

endowment insurance   A type of life insurance that pays a death benefit to the beneficiary if death occurs during the term of coverage or pays an endowment benefit to the policyowner if, at the end of the term of coverage, the insured is alive.

equity   The amount by which an insurance company's assets exceed its liabilities. The term *equity* is most often used in connection with stockholder reporting. See *capital* and *surplus*.

equity-indexed annuity   An accumulation annuity that allows the policyowner to participate in the stock market while being guaranteed to earn at least a minimum rate of interest.

equivalent single age   An approach used to calculate a single issue age for multiple-life products. It allows a company to use a single life product to insure two lives. For example, two people age 65 might be issued a policy with premiums and cash values that are the same as those for a single insured age 50. Contrast with *joint equal age* and *exact age*.

estate plan   A plan that addresses how best to preserve an individual's assets after the individual dies. Life insurance is often an important part of an estate plan.

EV   See *embedded value*.

exact age   An approach used to calculate issue age and policy values for multiple-life products. It reflects the age, sex, and risk class of each insured. This is most practical for a dynamic product, which can calculate mortality charges for the particular combination of ages, genders, and risk classes for each policy as needed. Contrast with *equivalent single age* and *joint equal age*.

excess of retention   An arrangement that reinsures all of a company's risks in excess of the company's retention limit. The reinsured amount of risk for each policy is calculated by deducting the company's available retention for the insured from the net amount at risk of the policy.

exclusive agent   See *captive agent.*

expenses   Insurance company expenses can be roughly divided between *acquisition costs* and *maintenance expenses.* Policy benefits and taxes are included when *expenses* are used in the broadest possible sense, as when the income statement is said to consist of only *income* and *expenses.*

expense allowance   An amount paid by the reinsurer to the ceding company to help cover the ceding company's acquisition and other costs, especially commissions, and sometimes to provide profit to the ceding company. Expense allowances are usually calculated as large percentages (often 100%) of first-year premiums reinsured and smaller percentages of renewal premiums reinsured.

expense charge   An amount deducted from a dynamic product's account value to offset costs associated with issuing and maintaining the policy.

experience refund   The portion of a reinsurance premium that is returned to the ceding company when claims experience is better than expected.

expire, expiry   When an insured outlives a term policy, the policy expires and the policyowner receives nothing.

extended term insurance (ETI)   A nonforfeiture option in which the net cash value of a policy is used to purchase paid-up term insurance. The amount of term insurance is equal to the death benefit of the policy being surrendered less any outstanding policy loans. The insured maintains the same amount of coverage but usually for a shorter period than the original coverage.

face amount   The amount of insurance benefit shown on the face of the policy. See *amount of insurance.* Also known as *sum assured* (outside North America) or *volume of insurance.* This amount does not include the amount of any paid-up additions, accidental death benefits, or other additional benefits or riders.

fac-ob   See *facultative-obligatory*.

facultative   A method of ceding reinsurance under which the ceding company decides which risks to send to the reinsurer. The reinsurer underwrites each risk sent and decides whether or not to make an offer for the risk and on what terms (such as standard rates, two times standard rates, and so on). The ceding company decides whether to accept each offer. The companies use their *faculties* to decide which risks to send, what to offer, and which offers to accept. Contrast with *automatic* and *facultative-obligatory*.

facultative-obligatory   A method of ceding reinsurance under which the ceding company decides which risks to send to the reinsurer. The reinsurer is obligated to accept any risk sent, unless the risk would cause the reinsurer to exceed its retention limit. Contrast with *automatic* and *facultative*.

family insurance rider   A life insurance policy rider that provides term insurance coverage on the insured's spouse and children, including those born after the rider is issued.

FDQS   First dollar quota share. See *quota share*.

fee-for-service   A distribution system that concentrates on professionals, such as attorneys, accountants, and other financial advisors, who are paid an hourly rate or a consulting fee for a particular assignment. Fee-for-service agents usually do not require a commission on life insurance that is purchased as a result of their advice.

field force   Those insurance agents who work out of an insurer's field offices.

field office   An insurance company's local sales office.

financial institution   An organization that helps channel funds through the economy by accepting the money of savers and supplying that money to borrowers, who pay to use the money. Insurance companies, banks, and mutual funds are examples of financial institutions.

financial reinsurance   Reinsurance designed primarily to serve a financial purpose for one or both of the companies that are party to the agreement. For example, a financial reinsurance transaction can improve the earnings or capital of the ceding company or aid the ceding company's tax planning.

financial services industry   The financial institutions that help consumers and business organizations save, borrow, invest, and otherwise manage money.

first dollar quota share (FDQS)   See *quota share.*

first-to-die life insurance   An insurance policy that covers two or more lives and that provides for payment of the proceeds at the time of the first insured's death.

first year   The first policy year, starting on the issue date and ending just before the first policy anniversary.

fixed annuity   An accumulation annuity that credits an interest rate, or an income annuity with a fixed payout. Contrast with *variable annuity.*

fixed costs   The portion of a company's costs that do not vary with the amount of business sold or serviced.

fixed premium policy   A life insurance or annuity policy under which the premiums are fixed in amount and paid on a regular basis.

fixed premium universal life   See *interest-sensitive whole life.*

flat extra   A substandard premium that is expressed as a flat amount per thousand of insurance. Flat extras are typically charged for people who have dangerous occupations or avocations, such as parachuting.

flexible premium deferred annuity (FPDA)   An accumulation annuity under which a number of flexible premiums can be made.

flexible premium policy   A life insurance or annuity policy under which the policyowner may vary the amount or timing of premium payments.

FPDA   See *flexible premium deferred annuity.*

fractional premiums   Premiums that are paid in installments during a year, such as semiannually, quarterly, or monthly. Fractional premiums are so called because they are fractions of the annual premium.

Frasierization or Frasierized mortality rates   An approach used to calculate joint last-to-die mortality rates, named after Bill Frasier, who first published and popularized this approach in the U.S. in the late 1980s.

free cash flow   The net cash flow that can be withdrawn from the business. The owners of the company are *free* to do what they will with free cash flows. When free cash flows are negative, the owners must cover the cash shortfall. Also known as *distributable earnings*.

front-end load   An expense charge, usually expressed as a percentage of premium, that is deducted from premiums paid for dynamic products or accumulation annuities.

full cost pricing   A method of allocating expenses in which the company allocates *all* of its expenses to the various expense rates used for pricing. When multiplied by the proper units, the resulting expense rates reproduce the company's total expenses. Contrast with *relevant cost pricing*.

full preliminary term (FPT) reserve method   A prospective reserve method that allows for a minimal first-year net premium and slightly higher renewal net premiums, when compared to the net level premium method. This method results in zero first-year terminal reserves, which helps reduce new business strain. The FPT reserve method is used mainly in connection with solvency and tax reserves.

fully allocated expenses   See *full cost pricing*.

function   Many insurance companies are organized by functions such as product development, marketing, distribution, underwriting, policy issue, policyowner service, claims, accounting, valuation, investments, human resources, and so on.

functional cost study   An expense analysis that determines an insurance company's expenses for each of its functions. Unit costs, such as the cost of issuing a policy or paying a claim, are usually determined for each function relevant to product pricing. See *function*.

GAAP   See *generally accepted accounting principles.*

GAAP earnings   Earnings based on generally accepted accounting principles. Contrast with *statutory earnings* and *regulatory earnings.*

GAAP reserves   Reserves that are calculated in accordance with generally accepted accounting principles and used for reporting results to stockholders. Also known as *stockholder reserves* and *earnings reserves.* In some cases, these reserves may be net of *deferred acquisition costs* (DAC).

general account   An undivided investment account in which life insurers maintain funds to support numerous products and lines of business. Contrast with *separate account.*

general agency   An insurance office, headed by a general agent, that provides local sales support. A general agency is often organized to recruit, train, and support agents.

general agent (GA)   The individual in charge of an agency office. The general agent is an independent entrepreneur who is under contract to the insurer.

generally accepted accounting principles (GAAP)   A set of financial accounting principles that U.S. and Canadian companies follow when preparing financial statements for reporting results to stockholders and, in Canada, to regulators.

GIR   See *guaranteed insurability rider.*

GMDB   See *guaranteed minimum death benefit.*

GMIB   See *guaranteed minimum income benefit.*

goodwill   In an acquisition, goodwill is equal to the excess of the purchase price over the tangible value of the business acquired. Goodwill is an intangible asset whose value cannot be directly calculated. It may include the value of future new business, intellectual capital, reputation, brand name, and other intangible assets that are impossible to quantify.

gross premium   The full premium amount that policyowners pay for their insurance.

gross premium method   A prospective reserve method that uses net premiums equal to the full gross premiums. This method calculates the minimum reserve that, together with future premiums and investment income, will be sufficient to cover future policy benefits and expenses. Contrast with *net level premium method* and *modified reserve method.*

gross premium valuation   A valuation that uses realistic assumptions and the gross premium method for calculating reserves. The difference between the assets backing the business and the gross premium reserves is an estimate of the present value of future profits for the business, ignoring taxes.

group life insurance   Life insurance on a group of people, usually issued to an employer for the benefit of the employees. The individual members of the group hold certificates as evidence of their insurance.

group universal life (GUL) insurance   Group life insurance for which the insured can choose the amount of premium to pay, and in which the death benefit is determined by the amount of the premium. The insured can vary the premium and death benefit amounts during the life of the policy. Like individual universal life insurance, GUL is designed to combine insurance protection with a savings element. In addition, GUL is usually "portable," which means that a group member who leaves the group can continue the insurance.

guaranteed insurability rider (GIR)   A supplementary benefit that gives the policyowner the right to purchase additional insurance of the same type as the basic policy without supplying evidence of the insured's insurability. Also known as *guaranteed insurability option (GIO)* and *guaranteed purchase option (GPO).*

guaranteed interest contract (GIC)   An investment product offered by insurance companies that guarantee a rate of return on assets for a fixed period, with payment of principal and accumulated interest at the end of the period.

guaranteed issue underwriting   A streamlined form of underwriting whereby all eligible members of a particular group of proposed insureds who apply for insurance and who meet minimal conditions—such as having actively worked a minimum number of hours per week for a certain number of months with no significant medical absences—automatically qualify for insurance. Compare with *medical* and *simplified issue underwriting.*

guaranteed minimum death benefit (GMDB)   A death benefit offered in connection with an accumulation annuity that may exceed the annuity's account value.

guaranteed minimum income benefit (GMIB)   A benefit offered in connection with an accumulation annuity that guarantees a minimum monthly income, regardless of future investment performance.

guaranteed purchase option (GPO)   See *guaranteed insurability rider.*

guaranteed upgrade   A provision that guarantees that a policy will receive any upgrades or improvements in terms available on similar, newly issued policies.

heaped commission schedule   A commission schedule that pays relatively high first-year and low renewal commission percentages, such as 70% first-year and 10% renewal. Also known as a traditional commission schedule.

holding company   A company that has no business other than owning one or more other companies.

home service agents   Exclusive or captive agents who collect premiums and provide service at the policyowner's residence. Home service agents market products primarily to lower-income individuals and families.

home service distribution system   A distribution system used to sell small amounts of individual insurance using home service agents.

hospital indemnity insurance   A type of health insurance that provides a predetermined flat benefit amount for each day an insured is hospitalized. The benefit amount does not vary according to the amount of medical expenses the insured incurs, although some policies provide higher benefit amounts if the insured is in an intensive or cardiac care unit.

hurdle rate   This is the discount rate used to discount future profits in the calculation of embedded value. It is the rate of return demanded by the company's owners or prospective owners. See *embedded value.*

immediate annuity   An income annuity with payouts that begin immediately or within one year.

immunization   The matching of asset and liability cash flows so that they cancel one another and thereby protect or *immunize* the company from changes in interest rates. See *asset/liability matching.*

income   For a life insurance company, income consists primarily of premiums and investment income.

income annuity   An annuity with scheduled income payments.

income statement   A financial statement that shows a company's income (premiums, investment income, and miscellaneous income), outgo (policy benefits, expenses, and taxes), and net income (income less outgo), also known as *earnings* or *profit.*

increasing premium term insurance   A form of term insurance with annually increasing premiums and level death benefits. It is better known as *annually renewable term.*

incremental costs   Changes in costs associated with changes in pricing and sales levels.

indemnity reinsurance   A form of reinsurance in which the risk is passed to a reinsurer that reimburses the ceding company for covered losses. The ceding company retains its liability to and contractual relationship with its policyowners.

independent agent   An agent who represents more than one insurance company; the opposite of a captive agent. Compare with *broker.*

independent marketing organization (IMO)   A non-company-affiliated organization that contracts with an insurance company to perform distribution and other marketing functions for one or more of the company's products or product lines. Also known as a *producer group.*

independent pricing   Pricing that is done by a company that has no real competitors in its target market. The company sets a price that is independent of prices charged by any other companies. See *competitor-oriented pricing strategies.*

indeterminate premium life insurance   A type of nonparticipating life insurance that specifies both a maximum potential premium rate and a lower current premium rate. The lower rate is paid by the policyowner for a specified period. Later, the premium rate may fluctuate according to the mortality, expense, and investment experience of the insurance company, but the premium rate will never be larger than the maximum premium rate.

indexed annuity   An income annuity that makes payments whose amounts are linked to an index, such as an inflation index.

industrial life insurance   Life insurance issued in small amounts, with premiums payable weekly or monthly. Premiums are generally collected at the insured's home by an agent. Also called *debit insurance*. See *home service distribution system.*

in force   When an insurance policy is in effect.

in-force business   Insurance business that is currently in effect or in force.

in-force model   A model that consists of cells that represent in-force business. An in-force model projects cash flows and profits for an existing book of business.

initial public offering (IPO)   A corporation's initial offering of common stock to the public. This is generally a six-month-long process that culminates in a large amount of the corporation's stock being purchased by many investors on a single day.

initial reserve   The reserve for a policy at the beginning of the policy year. The initial reserve is generally equal to the terminal year at the end of the prior policy year plus the net annual premium due on the anniversary.

insolvency, insolvent   The inability of an insurer to meet its financial obligation on time.

insurability   Acceptability to an insurance company of an applicant for insurance.

insurable interest   A condition in which the person applying for an insurance policy and the person who is to receive the policy benefit will suffer a genuine loss or detriment if the event insured against occurs. In most jurisdictions, without the presence of insurable interest, an insurance contract is invalid.

insured   A person whose life is insured by a life insurance policy.

interest rate   The amount charged for a loan or the amount earned on a deposit, usually expressed as an annual percentage of the loan or deposit.

interest-sensitive whole life insurance   A type of whole life insurance in which premium rates and cash values vary according to the insurer's assumptions regarding mortality, investment, and expense factors. Each policyowner can decide whether he or she wants favorable changes in assumptions to result in a lower premium or a higher cash value for the policy. If changes in assumptions result in a higher premium than that paid when the policy was purchased, the policyowner may choose to lower the policy's death benefit and maintain the previous premium or pay the higher premium and maintain the original death benefit. As with indeterminate premium life insurance, interest-sensitive whole life insurance guarantees that the premium will not increase above the rate guaranteed when the policy was purchased. Also called *current interest whole life* and *fixed premium universal life.*

interest spread   The assumed spread or margin between the net interest rate earned on assets backing the product and the interest rate credited (either explicitly or implicitly) to policyowners. The profitability of interest-sensitive products is often highly dependent on achieving the priced-for spread.

internal rate of return (IRR)   See *return on investment.*

investment   An asset acquired for future financial return or benefit.

investment income   The returns earned on an investment, often consisting of interest income or capital gains.

investment product   A product that accumulates deposits and provides no option to convert the accumulated funds to an income annuity.

IPO   See *initial public offering.*

issue   A policy is issued when it is put together for delivery to the policyowner, after the underwriter approves the applicant for insurance.

issue age   The age of the insured as of the issue date. This age is usually shown on the face page of the policy.

issue date   The date the policy is said to be issued, usually shown on the face page of the policy. This date determines the policy anniversary. Policies are sometimes issued before or after their issue dates.

IRR   *Internal rate of return.* See *return on investment.*

JLS   See *joint last survivor.*

joint equal age   An approach used to calculate issue age for multiple-life products. It allows a company to develop a joint life product that assumes that every joint policy is issued to two people of the same age and same risk class. The joint equal age is adjusted to reflect the actual ages, genders, and risk classes of the two insureds, based on company rules. Contrast with *equivalent single age* and *exact age.*

joint first-to-die   A form of insurance that insures two or more people and that pays a death benefit when the first of the people insured dies.

joint last survivor (JLS)   A form of insurance that insures two or more people and that pays a death benefit when the last of the people insured dies. A JLS policy most commonly insures a husband and wife. Also known as *joint last-to-die* and *joint and last survivor.*

joint last-to-die   See *joint last survivor.*

joint last survivor annuity   An income annuity that makes payments for as long as one of two annuitants remains alive. Also called a *joint last-to-die annuity* and a *joint and last survivor annuity.*

lapse   The termination of an insurance policy because a renewal premium is not paid by the time required.

lapse rate   For a block of policies, the percentage of in force policies that terminate as a result of nonpayment of renewal premiums or surrender during a given policy year. The lapse rate is determined by dividing the number of policies that lapse during a given policy year by the number of policies in force at the beginning of that policy year.

lapsed policy   An insurance policy terminated because of nonpayment of premiums. See *nonforfeiture options.*

lapse-supported products   Products that depend on most buyers lapsing for the product to achieve adequate profitability. If lapses are lower than originally expected, profitability will be eroded.

law of large numbers   The theory of probability that specifies that the greater the number of observations made of a particular event, the more likely it will be that the observed results will approximate the results anticipated by the mathematics of probability.

legacy systems   Outdated, patched-together computer systems that are used by life insurance companies for policy underwriting, issue, billing, accounting, commissioning, policyowner service, lapses, surrenders, death claims, valuation, and so on.

level commission schedule   A commission schedule that provides the same commission rate for the first year and renewal years.

level premiums   Premiums that remain the same each year that the life insurance policy is in force.

level term insurance   A type of term insurance that provides a death benefit that remains the same during the term of coverage.

levelized commission schedule   A commission schedule that pays slightly different percentages for first-year and renewal commissions. The differences between first-year and renewal commission percentages are smaller than those under traditional or *heaped* commission schedules.

leverage   The use of borrowed funds to increase the rate of return for a business or an investment. Also known as financial leverage.

Leverage is possible only if the cost of borrowed funds is less than the expected rate of return for the business or investment.

liabilities   A company's debts and future obligations. For an insurance company, liabilities include amounts owed to creditors and the actual unpaid and future expected claims of its policyowners and their beneficiaries.

liability cash flows   Cash flows consisting of premiums less benefits, expenses, and taxes, all net of reinsurance.

liability modeling   A modeling process that projects future liability cash flows, reserve changes, and required capital changes. Asset cash flows are not explicitly modeled. Instead, investment income is calculated by applying interest rates to the required amount of assets. Contrast with *asset/liability modeling*.

life or life-only annuity   An income annuity that makes payments for only as long as the annuitant lives.

life expectancy   The average number of years of life remaining for persons of a given age, according to a mortality table. Most often, life expectancy is calculated from birth and is equal to the average age at death in this case.

limited-payment whole life insurance   An insurance policy for which premiums are payable for some stated period that is less than the insured's lifetime. Some limited-payment policies specify the number of years during which premiums are payable, while other policies specify an age after which premiums are no longer payable. Single-premium whole life insurance, in which only one premium payment is made, is an extreme type of limited-payment insurance.

liquid, liquidity   The ability to sell an asset quickly for a fair price.

living benefit   See *accelerated death benefit*.

long-term care (LTC) insurance   A form of insurance that typically pays a monthly benefit while the insured is unable to perform certain activities of daily living.

lonely heart syndrome   The increased chance of the second of two spouses dying soon after the first dies.

loss **1.** Negative profit, negative earnings, or negative net income. See *net income.* **2.** Claims paid or incurred on a policy.

M&E risk charge See *mortality and expense risk charge.*

maintenance expenses The expenses of maintaining an in force policy, such as the expenses associated with billing and collection of renewal premiums, calculation and payment of renewal commissions, policyowner service, annual or quarterly policy statements, and financial reporting.

marginal expense pricing See *relevant cost pricing.*

market rate The interest rate(s) available on competing financial products.

market value The amount for which an asset or liability could be currently sold.

market value adjustment (MVA) A feature that adjusts a policy's cash value for increases or decreases in the market value of assets backing the policy. In most cases, the adjustment approximates the market value of the assets, using a formula based on interest rates.

mature When an insured outlives a permanent policy, the policy is said to mature or endow, and an endowment benefit is paid to the policyowner.

maturity The scheduled final date for an insurance policy or asset, such as a bond or mortgage.

MCCSR See *Minimum Continuing Capital and Surplus Requirement.*

mean reserve The average of a policy's initial reserve and terminal reserve for a given policy year.

medical expense rider A supplementary benefit sometimes attached to a life insurance policy that reimburses medical expenses up to a certain amount per day while the insured is hospitalized.

medical underwriting A form of underwriting that includes a review of complete medical information, including a medical or paramedical exam for the prospective insured in order to determine insurability. Contrast with *guaranteed issue* and *simplified issue underwriting.*

minimum capital, minimum surplus   See *required capital.*

Minimum Continuing Capital and Surplus Requirement (MCCSR)   A system used by Canadian regulators for evaluating the adequacy of an insurer's capital based on the insurer's size and the riskiness of its assets and liabilities. See *required capital.*

mixed costs   Expenses that are fixed for a range of growth and variable when certain thresholds are exceeded. Many expenses within a company fall into this *mixed category* of "fixed to some extent but variable with sufficient growth."

modal   Having to do with the *mode of premium payment.*

modco   See *modified coinsurance.*

mode of premium payment   The frequency of premium payments, such as annual, semiannual, quarterly, and monthly.

model, modeling   A financial model attempts to reproduce past results and predict future results through calculations that approximate the financial workings of a business or an investment opportunity. Models are sometimes composed of many cells, each of which approximates a part of the business or investment portfolio being modeled.

modified coinsurance (modco)   A form of reinsurance under which the basic provisions of coinsurance are modified by having the ceding company maintain the entire solvency reserve. Periodically, the reinsurer transfers back to the ceding company an amount equal to (1) the increase in the solvency reserve for the reinsured portion of the policy less (2) the interest earned by the ceding company on the solvency reserve for the reinsured portion of the policy. In the event of a claim, the reinsurer is responsible for the death benefit net of the solvency reserve for the reinsured portion of the policy. Similarly, for surrenders, the reinsurer pays the cash value net of the solvency reserve for the reinsured portion of the policy.

modified net premiums   Net premiums that are lower for the first year than for subsequent years, as a percentage of gross premiums. See *modified reserve method.*

modified reserve method   A prospective reserve method that allows for a much-reduced first-year net premium and slightly higher renewal net premiums, when compared to the *net level premium method.* This method creates smaller first-year reserves than those calculated using the net level premium method. Modified reserve methods reduce new business strain. The most common modified reserve method is the *full preliminary term* method. Modified reserve methods are used mainly in connection with solvency and tax reserves.

money market fund   A low-risk mutual fund that achieves great liquidity by investing primarily in short-term securities.

morbidity rate   The rate at which sickness, injury, and failure of health occur among a defined group of people. The premium that a person pays for health insurance is based in part on the morbidity rate for that person's age, sex, and risk class.

mortality   Having to do with the chance of dying.

mortality and expense (M&E) risk charge   For variable annuities and variable life insurance, the monthly charge deducted from the account value to cover expenses and mortality costs. This charge is usually a small percentage of the account value.

mortality charge   For universal life policies, the monthly charge deducted from the account value for the cost of insurance protection. See *cost of insurance charge.*

mortality rate   The probability of death. Mortality rates vary by gender, age, policy year, risk class, and other factors.

mortality table   A chart that displays mortality rates by age and other characteristics. See *aggregate mortality table, select mortality table,* and *ultimate mortality table.*

mortgage loan   A loan backed by a pledge of property as security for repayment of the loan.

mortgage protection   Life insurance designed to repay the outstanding balance of a mortgage or other loan in the event of death. This protects both the lender and the beneficiaries who no longer have to worry about paying off the loan if the insured dies.

mutual fund   An investment fund with shares sold to the public. A mutual fund usually has a clearly defined investment policy, such as a high-growth stock fund, a long-term bond fund, or a money market fund. A mutual fund allows an individual investor to own a small percentage of many investments.

mutual life insurance company   A life insurance company without stockholders whose management is directed by a board elected by the policyowners. Mutual companies generally issue participating insurance policies and are owned by their participating policyowners. Contrast with *stock life insurance company.*

MVA   See *market value adjustment.*

net amount at risk (NAAR, NAR, AAR)   The difference between the death benefit of a life insurance policy and the amount of the policy's reserve or cash value.

net income   The earnings or profit for a period, usually shown in an income statement. Net income is equal to income (premiums, investment income, and miscellaneous income) less outgo (policy benefits, expenses, and taxes). Policy benefits include both benefits paid in cash and the increase in reserves for future benefits.

net interest rate   See *net yield.*

net level premium method   A prospective reserve method that assumes that a policy's net premiums are a constant percentage of gross premiums over the life of the policy. This method often creates significant first-year reserves that can lead to significant new business strain. Contrast with *modified reserve method.*

net premium   The premium used to calculate reserves.

net single premium   The present value of the expected benefits of an insurance policy. The net single premium is the amount of money that would have to be collected at the time a policy is issued to assure that there will be enough money to pay the death benefit of the policy, assuming that interest is earned at the expected rate and that claims occur at the expected rate.

net yield   An asset's yield is calculated as its gross yield less deductions for investment expenses and the cost of defaults.

neutral pricing   Setting prices at a level that most buyers would consider reasonable. See *buyer-oriented pricing strategies.*

new business   Business that first became in force during the current reporting period.

new business model   A model consisting of cells that estimate future new business. A new business model projects cash flows and profits for future policies that have not yet been sold.

new business strain   Because of the conservatism of solvency accounting, it is quite common for life insurance companies to suffer initial losses when writing profitable new business. These losses "strain" the company's capital or surplus, at least temporarily. New business strain results because the sum of acquisition costs, first-year solvency reserves, and first year benefits often greatly exceeds the first-year premium. Also known as *surplus strain.*

new money method   A method of crediting interest that reflects the interest rates earned on funds according to when the funds were received.

nonforfeiture options   The various ways in which a policyowner may apply the net cash value of a life insurance policy if the policy lapses, such as *automatic premium loan (APL), cash surrender, extended term insurance (ETI),* and *reduced paid-up insurance (RPU).*

nonguaranteed elements   Product design elements that may be subject to periodic updates to reflect actual experience. These features could include premium rates, cost of insurance rates, interest rates, and expense charges. Nonguaranteed elements are primarily associated with dynamic products, but pre-scheduled products can also have nonguaranteed elements, such as dividends and indeterminate premiums. Account values, cash values, and even death benefits may be determined by formulas that reflect changes in nonguaranteed elements.

nonmedical limit   The maximum death benefit that a given company will issue without the applicant taking a medical examination.

nonparticipating policy   A life insurance policy for which the policyowner does not receive dividends. Contrast with *participating policy*.

nonsmoker risk class   An underwriting risk class that includes people who are standard risks and who have not smoked cigarettes or used tobacco for a specified period before applying for insurance. People in the nonsmoker risk class pay lower than standard premiums.

nontraditional products   Products with premiums, cash values, or death benefits that are not pre-scheduled. Also known as *dynamic products*.

one-year term (OYT) dividend option   A dividend option under which dividends are used as a single premium to purchase one-year term insurance.

operating income   The earnings resulting from the regular operations of the company, equal to *net income* excluding capital gains and losses.

opportunistic pricing   Pricing behavior used by the most efficient companies to drive down prices to a level where only the most efficient can survive. See *competitor-oriented pricing strategies*.

option A, option B   These are the two death benefit options offered in connection with most universal life products. Under option A, the death benefit is level, except that it is reduced by any partial withdrawals. Under option B, the death benefit is equal to a specified amount plus the account value, which results in a level net amount at risk. *NAR = DBEN - AV*

ordinary income   See *operating income*.

overhead expenses   General corporate expenses, commonly including the expenses of executives, the board of directors, public relations, investor relations, accounting, financial reporting, auditing, and other functions not connected with providing products and services to customers.

PAD   See *provision for adverse deviation*.

paid-up additional insurance dividend option   The dividend option under which the insurer uses each policy dividend to purchase paid-up additional insurance on the insured's life.

paid-up additions (PUAs)   Additional life insurance purchased with policyowner dividends. Paid-up additions increase the policy's death benefit and cash value and require no additional premiums. Also known as *dividend additions.*

paid-up insurance   Insurance that requires no further premium payments.

paramedical exam   An abbreviated physical examination given to a prospective insured for insurance underwriting purposes, often including physical measurements, medical questions, and the collection of blood and urine specimens, and usually administered by a nurse.

partial withdrawal provision   A policy provision that permits the policyowner to withdraw money from the policy's cash value or accumulated value. This provision is often included in universal life policies and accumulation annuity contracts.

participating policy   An insurance policy under which the policyowner shares or *participates* in the insurance company's results by receiving policy dividends.

payor   The person who pays the policy's premiums.

P/E ratio   See *price-to-earnings ratio.*

penalty-free partial withdrawal   Universal life and accumulation annuities often allow the policyowner to withdraw up to a certain percentage of the account or cash value each year without incurring a surrender charge on the amount withdrawn. Amounts withdrawn in excess of the penalty-free amount are charged a pro-rated surrender charge.

penetration pricing   Setting prices low enough to generate a much higher level of sales. See *buyer-oriented pricing strategies.*

permanent difference   A difference between pre-tax earnings and taxable earnings that is permanent in nature and that will not reverse over time. For example, when a company receives a special tax credit or is denied a tax deduction, this often creates a permanent difference. Permanent differences do *not* create a distortion between the taxes currently paid and the taxes that will ultimately be paid.

permanent life insurance Any form of life insurance other than term insurance; generally, life insurance with cash values, such as whole life or universal life.

persist A policy is said to persist when it remains in force. This requires that any required premiums be paid.

persistency The tendency of policies to persist or remain in force.

persistency bonus **1.** A bonus paid to agents and agency managers to reward favorable persistency. **2.** A bonus paid to a policyowner after a policy remains in force for a specified number of years.

persistency rate For a group of policies, the share of business that remains in force. The persistency rate is calculated as either (1) the business in force at the end of the period divided by the business in force at the beginning of the period or (2) one minus the lapse rate. There is a difference between these two definitions because policies can terminate for reasons other than lapse, such as death.

personal producing general agent (PPGA) An agent who generally works alone and engages primarily in prospecting and sales. PPGA contracts are often identical to those for general agents, so they receive the commission rates payable to general agents, which are higher than those for regular sales agents. PPGAs often contract with several insurance companies and must meet minimum production requirements in order to maintain their general agent contract with each insurer.

per unit in force Per unit of insurance currently in force, used mainly for traditional or pre-scheduled products. Premiums, cash values, death benefits, and reserves are calculated for each policy as a value per unit in force times the number of units in force for that policy.

per unit issued Per unit of insurance originally issued, used mainly in insurance pricing and modeling calculations. Amounts that are *per unit in force* can be multiplied by *survival factors* to produce amounts that *per unit issued.*

plan of insurance   A specific type of insurance product. See *product.*

policy   A written document that contains the terms of the contractual agreement between an insurance company and a policyowner.

policy benefits   All amounts paid to policyowners and beneficiaries, consisting mainly of death benefits, surrender benefits, policyowner dividends, maturity payments, and disability benefits. In the income statement, policy benefits would include both benefits paid in cash and the increase in reserves for future benefits.

policy fee   A flat amount that is charged for each policy to cover the costs of administration. Sometimes, the policy fee is higher in the first year.

policy loan   A loan that is made to the policyowner and secured by the policy's cash value. The policy loan cannot exceed the cash value. When death benefits or surrender benefits are paid, the amount of any outstanding policy loan is deducted from the benefits.

policy premium method (PPM)   The prospective reserve method used by Canadian life insurers. PPM reserves are calculated as the present value of future benefits less the present value of future gross premiums. While the formula is essentially the same as that used for gross premium reserves, the assumptions used for PPM tend to be more conservative than realistic. As a result, new business strain is quite common.

policy size   The amount of coverage provided on a policy. Policy size is usually expressed as the amount of death benefit in force or the number of units.

policy value   A generic term sometimes used to mean account value, accumulation value, cash value, or cash surrender value.

policy year   The 12-month period between a policy's anniversaries. The first policy year begins on the issue date. The second policy year begins on the policy's first anniversary.

policyholder   See *policyowner*.

policyowner   The person or party who owns an individual insurance policy. The policyowner is not necessarily the person whose life is insured. The terms policyowner and policyholder are frequently used interchangeably.

policyowner dividend   An amount of money returned to the owner of a *participating policy*. The dividend is a partial refund of the premium paid. It results from actual mortality, interest, and expenses that are more favorable than those that were expected when premiums were set.

portfolio   **1.** A group of investments managed or owned by an individual or organization. **2.** All of the products offered by an insurance company.

portfolio method   A method of crediting interest in which each policyowner receives a rate of interest equal to the average rate of interest earned on the entire portfolio of assets in the insurer's general account. Contrast with *new money method*.

PPGA   See *personal producing general agent*.

PPM   See *policy premium method*.

predatory pricing   Charging a price that is below the cost of the product, for the purpose of driving competitors out of the business, often at a financial loss to the predator. See *competitor-oriented pricing strategies*.

preferred risk class   A risk category composed of proposed insureds who present a significantly less-than-average likelihood of loss.

preferred stock   A form of stock that pays the stockholder a fixed dividend interest rate. Preferred stockholders must receive all dividends owed them before common stockholders can receive any dividends. See *stock*.

premium   The payment(s) required to establish and keep an insurance policy in force.

premium tax   A tax on insurance premiums similar to sales tax or value-added tax, except that it is paid by insurance companies instead of policyowners. It is levied as a percentage of premium, such as 2%.

premium reduction dividend option   A life insurance policy dividend option under which the insurer applies policy dividends toward the payment of renewal premiums.

pre-scheduled products   Life insurance products with premiums, death benefits, and cash values that are fixed or known well in advance, such as whole life, endowment, and term insurance. Also known as *traditional products.*

present value   The amount of money that must be invested to accumulate to a specified amount on a given date is called the present value of that specified amount. See *accumulate* and *discount.*

preservation of total deaths theory   A theory that assumes that the total number of deaths between those who lapse and those who persist remains the same, regardless of the lapse rate. It is used to estimate the mortality rate of the remaining group when excess (selective) lapses occur.

principal   A sum of money that is loaned or invested.

price-to-earnings ratio   The ratio of a company's stock price to its earnings per share.

producer group   See *independent marketing organization.*

plan of insurance   A specific type of insurance product. See *product.*

probabilistic method   A method of estimating future interest rate patterns. This method uses historical information to develop probabilities of interest rates changing from one level to other levels. See *arbitrary method* and *successive ratios method.*

product   In insurance, a specific type or plan of insurance. Most life insurance companies offer many different insurance products. Whole life, universal life, and 10-year term are examples of different products. Products are defined by the benefits they provide and the premiums that are charged. Also known as *plan of insurance.*

premium margin   The change in the present value of profits caused by a 1% change in the premium level divided by the present value of a 1% change in the premium level. Premium margin tells you the percentage of an increase or decrease in premium that will add to or subtract from profits.

profit   See *net income*. Also known as *earnings*. Profit is the opposite of *loss*.

profit margin   The present value of profits divided by the present value of premiums. Profit margin tells you the percentage of added premiums from selling more policies that will add to profits.

prospective reserve method   A method of calculating reserves that looks ahead to a policy's future premiums and benefits to calculate the current reserve. The current reserve equals the present value of future benefits and expenses less the present value of future net premiums. Contrast with *retrospective reserve method.*

provision for adverse deviation (PAD)   Adjustments to assumptions that serve as a safety margin to allow for unfavorable variations from expected values.

provision for deferred taxes   When reporting earnings to stockholders, companies must set aside a provision for deferred taxes equal to accrued taxes less taxes paid. Accrued taxes are usually determined by applying a tax rate to pre-tax stockholder earnings, adjusted for permanent differences. Pre-tax stockholder earnings are reduced by taxes paid and the provision for deferred taxes to calculate after-tax stockholder earnings.

pure broker   An insurance salesperson who is not under an agency contract with any insurance company, and who is usually considered to be an agent of the client rather than of the insurer.

pure endowment   An amount payable only to those people who survive to a certain date; those who do not survive to that date receive nothing. Unless combined with some form of life insurance such as whole life or endowment insurance, pure endowments are generally illegal.

put option   An option to sell a stated amount of stock or bonds for a set price at a given date. For a bond, this option would be exercised most commonly when interest rates rise, allowing the seller of the bond to then purchase a new investment with a higher yield.

quota share   A reinsurance arrangement in which the reinsurer receives a certain percentage of each risk reinsured. Also known as *first dollar quota share (FDQS)*.

rate of return   An after-tax interest rate or *return on investment*.

rating   **1.** A measure of financial strength assigned to a company by a rating agency. **2.** An estimate of additional mortality risk assigned to a prospective insured by an insurance company underwriter. See *substandard risk class*.

rating agencies   Independent firms that objectively rate the financial status of companies. Insurance companies are most often rated on their ability to repay debt and their ability to pay future claims.

RBC   See *risk-based capital*.

real estate   Land, including all the permanent buildings and natural resources associated with it.

recapture   In reinsurance, the process by which the ceding company takes back from the reinsurer a portion of its reinsured business. The right of recapture is normally subject to a number of limits and conditions. Normally, only the ceding company can initiate recapture; the reinsurer cannot force it.

reduced paid-up (RPU) insurance   A nonforfeiture option under which the net cash value of a life insurance policy is used as a net single premium to purchase a smaller amount of fully paid insurance of the same kind as the policy being lapsed.

reentry   Also known as requalification, this involves re-underwriting the insured and allowing the insured to pay the same premium rates that a new applicant for insurance would pay. In addition, the agent usually receives a new commission. For policies with steeply increasing premiums, reentry will significantly reduce the premium. This privilege can be very valuable for the insured and agent and very costly for the insurance company.

regulatory accounting principles See *solvency accounting principles.* Also known as *statutory accounting principles.*

regulatory earnings See *solvency earnings.* Also known as *statutory earnings.*

regulatory reserves See *solvency reserves.* Also known as *statutory reserves.*

reinstatement Restoration of a lapsed policy to premium-paying status.

reinsurance Insurance of insurance. A type of insurance that one insurance company, known as the *ceding company,* purchases from another insurance company, known as the *reinsurer,* in order to transfer risks that the ceding company insures.

reinsure To transfer insurance risk from one insurer to another insurer.

reinsurer The insurance company that accepts the risk transferred from another insurance company, the *ceding company,* in a reinsurance transaction.

relevant cost pricing A method of allocating expenses in which the company allocates only those expenses that are relevant to pricing decisions. Relevant (or marginal) expenses are those expenses that are affected by changes in sales levels. Contrast with *full cost pricing.*

renewable term Term insurance that gives the policyowner the right to renew the insurance coverage at the end of the specified term without submitting evidence of insurability. Premiums generally increase at each renewal.

renewal Any time after the first policy year.

renewal year Any policy year after the first policy year.

renewal commissions Commissions paid to the agent for a specified number of years after the first policy year. See *heaped commission schedule, level commission schedule,* and *levelized commission schedule.*

renewal premiums Premiums payable after the first year's premium.

required capital   The capital that regulators, rating agencies, or the company itself deem necessary for the company to be able to withstand reasonable fluctuations in financial results. Also known as *minimum capital, minimum surplus, required surplus, capital adequacy reserve,* and *solvency margin.*

required surplus   See *required capital.*

reserve   The amount of funds that an insurer must set aside as a liability, to meet future policy obligations. This amount, together with future premiums and interest, must be adequate to pay future insurance benefits and related expenses.

residual risks   The "non-preferred" risks that remain when preferred risks are split out of a group of insureds or potential insureds.

retained amount   The amount of insurance risk that a company keeps on a policy and does not reinsure.

retention limit   The maximum amount of insurance that an insurance company will carry on any individual without ceding part of the risk to a reinsurer. Retention limits are often reduced for the highest issue ages and highest substandard ratings.

retrospective reserve method   A method of calculating reserves that looks back at a policy's past premiums and benefits to determine the current reserve. The current reserve equals the accumulated value of past net premiums less the accumulated cost of insurance. This method is used mainly for dynamic products and accumulation annuities, with reserves based on account values or cash values. Contrast with *prospective reserve method.*

return of premium on death   Most insurance policies return premiums paid for coverage beyond the month or date of death. For example, if the insured dies one month after paying an annual premium, 11 months of premium will usually be refunded when the death claim is settled.

return on assets (ROA)   A measure of a company's financial performance, calculated as its earnings divided by its assets.

return on equity (ROE)   A measure of a company's financial performance, most often calculated as its stockholder earnings divided by its average stockholder equity.

return on investment (ROI)   A solved-for after-tax discount rate that results in the present value of a series of cash flows (or profit flows) equal to zero. When applied to the cash flows of an investment, the IRR is the yield rate or interest rate. Also known as *internal rate of return (IRR)*.

rider   An amendment to an insurance policy that becomes a part of the insurance contract and expands or limits the benefits payable. Also called an *endorsement*. See *ADB, GIR,* and *WP.* Term insurance is sometimes issued as a rider.

risk-based capital (RBC) requirements   A system used by U.S. regulators for evaluating the adequacy of an insurer's capital based on the insurer's size and the riskiness of its assets and liabilities. See *required capital*.

risk class   A group of insureds who present a substantially similar risk to the insurance company. Among the most common risk classes used by life insurance companies are standard, preferred, nonsmoker, smoker, substandard, and uninsurable.

ROE   See *return on equity*.

run on the bank   A sustained outflow of funds when many customers withdraw their funds from a financial institution within a short period.

salaried sales representatives   Insurance sales representatives who are employees of the insurer and who are usually paid on a salary plus incentive compensation basis. Salaried sales personnel may work with agents or independently, may make sales directly to customers or promote the sale of an insurer's products through other intermediaries, and are often used to distribute group insurance and pension products.

sales level   Sales levels are most often measured by amount of insurance sold or amount of premium sold. Some companies use number of policies sold or amount of first-year commission as important sales measures.

scenario   A plausible set of consistent assumptions about the future, most often used in connection with insurance pricing and financial models.

second-to-die life insurance   Life insurance that covers two persons and provides for payment of the proceeds when both insureds have died. It is generally designed to pay estate taxes.

securities   Stocks and bonds.

segmentation   A process by which an insurer divides its general account investments into distinct parts, or segments, that correspond with particular products or lines of business. Also called *segregation*.

segmented pricing   The practice of setting different price levels for different kinds of buyers with different behaviors. See *buyer-oriented pricing strategies*.

segregated account   See *separate account*.

segregation   See *segmentation*.

select and ultimate mortality table   A mortality table that shows select mortality rates as well as the ultimate mortality rates that follow the select period.

select mortality table   A mortality table that shows only the mortality rates of people who have recently been accepted for life insurance, which is a *select* group. See *select rates*.

select period   The period of years immediately following underwriting during which there is a significant difference in mortality rates between persons whose good health was proved at the beginning of the period (the select group) and other persons of the same age. The underwriting process allows an insurance company to *select* the better risks.

select rates   The premium or mortality rates that apply during the select period. Select rates vary by issue age and policy year. They are lower and increase much faster than ultimate rates.

selection of risks   See *underwriting*.

selective lapses   The lapses associated with healthy lives, which lead to *antiselection*. Healthy lives are more likely to *select* to lapse and purchase new insurance. Unhealthy lives are more likely to continue their current insurance.

sensitivity testing   Profit testing by varying key assumptions (such as mortality, lapse, interest, expense, sales levels, or tax rates) and observing the effect on profit margins and other measures.

separate account   An investment account maintained separately from an insurer's general investment account to manage the funds placed in variable policies. Also called a *segregated account.*

seriatim valuation process   A valuation process that calculates reserves *serially*, that is, for one policy at a time. The alternative is to calculate reserves for groups of similar policies.

service fee   A form of agent compensation that constitutes a small percentage of the premium and that is usually payable only after renewal commissions on a policy have ceased.

setback   A number of years subtracted from a person's actual age in order to use the mortality, premium, cash value, or reserve rates for another issue age. A setback is most commonly used to equate a female with a male a few years younger, in recognition of the longer life span of females.

settlement options   The several ways, other than immediate payment in cash, that a policyowner or beneficiary may choose to have policy benefits paid. See *supplementary contract.*

shareholder   See *stockholder.*

shareholders fund   The share of a company's assets that are held solely for the benefit of shareholders. This concept is used in English-speaking countries outside of North America. Contrast with *statutory fund.*

simple average   A simple average of *n* numbers is calculated by summing the numbers and dividing by *n*. Contrast with *weighted average.*

simple interest   The payment of interest on principal only, ignoring any unpaid interest. Contrast with *compound interest.* Simple interest is most often used to calculate interest over short periods, such as days, weeks, or months. It is rarely used for periods of more than one year.

simplified issue underwriting   A form of underwriting similar to guaranteed issue underwriting, but with the addition of one or more questions about the insured's medical history. If the questions turn up any significant medical concerns, then medical underwriting may be an option. Compare with *medical* and *guaranteed issue underwriting.*

single premium deferred annuity (SPDA)   An accumulation annuity for which only one premium payment is made.

single premium policy   A policy purchased with a single, lump-sum premium.

size band   A range of policy face amounts (sizes) that share the same premium rates.

skim pricing   The practice of setting a high price to maximizes a company's profit margin. See *buyer-oriented pricing strategies.*

soliciting agent   Typically, an insurance agent who works under a general agent or a branch manager. The soliciting agent is the person who contacts prospective customers, sells insurance, delivers policies, and collects initial premiums.

solvency   An insurer's ability to pay its debts and to pay policy benefits when they come due.

solvency accounting principles   Accounting principles used when reporting financial results to insurance regulators, who are focused on maintaining insurer solvency. Also known as *regulatory accounting principles* and *statutory accounting principles.* Contrast with *stockholder accounting principles* and *tax accounting principles.*

solvency earnings   Earnings based on solvency accounting principles. Also known as *statutory earnings* and *regulatory earnings.*

solvency margin   Systems used by E.U., Australian, and other regulators for evaluating the adequacy of an insurer's capital based on the insurer's size and the riskiness of its assets and liabilities. See *required capital.*

solvency reserves   Reserves calculated in accordance with standards established by insurance regulators, who are focused on maintaining insurer solvency. Also known as *regulatory reserves* and *statutory reserves.*

SP   Abbreviation for *single premium.*

SPDA   See *single premium deferred annuity.*

split dollar insurance plan   An insurance plan under which an employee is covered by individual life insurance that is paid for jointly by the employee and the employer. The employee names the beneficiary. Each year, the employer pays a portion of the premium equal to the increase in the policy's cash value for the year; the employee pays the balance of the premium. If the employee dies, the employer receives death proceeds equal to the cash value of the policy and the beneficiary receives the remainder of the death benefit.

split rider   A rider added to a joint last survivor insurance policy which allows the policy to be split into two single-life insurance policies under certain conditions, such as divorce or a change in tax law, with no new evidence of insurability required.

standard risk class   A risk class made up of individuals whose anticipated likelihood of loss is not significantly higher or lower than average. Unless there is a preferred risk class, most insureds are included in the standard risk class.

static validation   Comparing the initial results of a financial model with the company's actual values at the starting point of the model. Contrast with *dynamic validation.*

statutory accounting principles   See *solvency accounting principles.* Also known as *regulatory accounting principles.*

statutory earnings   Earnings based on statutory accounting principles. Also known as *solvency earnings* and *regulatory earnings.*

statutory fund   The share of a company's assets that are set aside to back certain policyowner liabilities. This concept is used in English-speaking countries outside of North America. In those countries, insurance companies have one shareholders fund and one or more statutory funds. See *shareholders fund.* There is no parallel for North American companies, whose assets are held in one *general account* and sometimes one or more *separate accounts.*

statutory reserves   See *solvency reserves.* Also known as *regulatory reserves.*

stochastic modeling   A modeling process that uses random variables and probabilities to generate a series of possible outcomes. A mathematical process is used to create one possible outcome after another. A good stochastic model generates a distribution of outcomes that seems reasonable in light of past experience. Contrast with *deterministic modeling.* See *model.*

stock   The capital that a corporation raises by selling shares that entitle the stockholder to dividends and other rights of ownership. Some companies have both voting stock and non-voting stock. See also *common stock* and *preferred stock.*

stock life insurance company   A life insurance company that is owned by stockholders. Contrast with *mutual life insurance company.*

stockholder   One of the owners of a corporation. Also known as *shareholder.* See *stock.*

stockholder accounting principles   Accounting principles, such as GAAP, that are used when reporting financial results to stockholders and stock markets. Contrast with *solvency accounting principles* and *tax accounting principles.*

stockholder dividend   An amount paid by a corporation to its stockholders, most often on a quarterly basis. Stockholder dividends are part of the stockholders' return on their investment in the corporation.

stockholder earnings   Earnings based on stockholder accounting principles, such as GAAP. Also known as *GAAP earnings.*

stockholder equity   The amount by which an insurance company's assets exceed its liabilities under stockholder accounting principles, such as GAAP.

stockholder reserves   Reserves used for reporting results to stockholders. Also known as *GAAP reserves* and *earnings reserves.* In some cases, these reserves may be net of *deferred acquisition costs* (DAC).

stock market   A financial market in which shares of stock in many corporations are bought and sold.

strain   See *new business strain.*

structured settlement   A series of payments awarded by a court of law to provide for a victim's care over the victim's lifetime. The person or company that must make these payments often transfers the liability for the payments to an insurance company in exchange for a lump-sum premium payment.

substandard risk class   A risk class made up of people with medical or nonmedical impairments that give them a greater than average likelihood of loss. Substandard risks pay higher-than-standard premiums, based on *ratings* assigned by underwriters.

successive ratios method   A method of estimating future interest rate patterns. This method stochastically generates yield curves using the assumption that the natural logarithm of the ratio of successive interest rates is normally distributed. In other words, $\ln(i(t+1)/i(t))$ is normally distributed. See *arbitrary method* and *probabilistic method*.

suicide exclusion   A provision contained in most life insurance policies that requires the insurance company to return premiums in lieu of paying a death benefit if death occurs due to suicide within a certain period of time after policy issue, such as two years. This is considered to be in the public's best interests. Without such a provision, some disturbed people may purchase insurance and then kill themselves to benefit their loved ones.

sum assured   The term most commonly used in English-speaking countries outside of North America for *amount of insurance, face amount,* or *volume of insurance.*

sunk costs   Costs that a company is irreversibly committed to bear.

supplementary benefit   A rider that is added to an insurance policy to provide additional benefits. Some typical supplementary benefit riders are accidental death coverage, waiver of premium, and the guaranteed insurance rider. See also *rider.*

surplus   The amount by which an insurance company's assets exceed its liabilities, also known as its capital. The term *surplus* is most often used when referring to a company's capital for solvency purposes. See *capital* and *equity.*

surplus strain   See *new business strain*.

surrender   When a policyowner terminates an insurance policy to receive its cash value. See also *lapse*.

surrender charge   Expense charges sometimes imposed when a policyowner surrenders an accumulation annuity or dynamic product. Surrender charges usually decline to zero over a period of five to twenty years.

survival, survivorship   The act of keeping a policy in force. The opposite of termination.

survival factor   The probability of a policy remaining in force from the issue date to a given point in time.

target market   A group of policyowners or potential policyowners that a company has chosen to serve. A company's target markets help define which products the company should offer. The company's strategy should guide how it will evolve to better serve its target markets.

target premium   For flexible premium products, premiums up to the amount of the target premium receive a high commission rate, while premiums in excess of the target premium receive a low commission rate.

tax   Insurance companies pay many different kinds of taxes such as income tax, premium tax, excise tax, payroll tax, sales tax, and surplus tax (tax on capital).

tax accounting principles   Accounting principles that are used when calculating and reporting taxable income. Contrast with *solvency accounting principles* and *stockholder accounting principles*.

tax loss carryforward or carryback   If a company has tax losses (that is, negative taxable income), it can use the losses to offset past or future positive taxable income. Most governments will not pay companies to lose money. Tax regulations specify limits as to how many years tax losses can be carried back or carried forward. For example, tax losses might be allowed to offset taxable income in the three previous years or the next fifteen years. When carrying losses back, the company would receive a refund of prior years' tax payments. When carrying losses forward, the company would reduce taxes it otherwise would have to pay.

tax reserves Reserves that are used in the calculation of taxable income. In most countries, tax reserves are equal to *solvency reserves*.

temporary differences See *timing differences*.

terminal dividend An extra dividend or pro-rated dividend covering the period between the last policy anniversary date and the termination date of the policy.

terminal illness (TI) benefit See *accelerated death benefit*.

terminal reserve The reserve on a policy at the end of the policy year.

term life insurance Life insurance under which the benefit is payable only if the insured dies during a specified period, or *term*.

tied agent See *captive agent*.

timing difference A difference between pre-tax earnings and taxable earnings that is temporary in nature and that will reverse over time. For example, when a different method is used to calculate an asset or liability for tax purposes, a timing difference results. It is a temporary difference because all assets and liabilities are eventually extinguished. A timing difference means that taxes currently paid are not representative of the taxes that will ultimately be paid.

total and permanent disability (TPD) A form of insurance that pays the insured a lump sum benefit when the insured is certified as totally and permanently disabled.

traditional products Products with pre-scheduled premiums, cash values, and death benefits, such as whole life, endowment, and term insurance. See *pre-scheduled products*.

tranche A particular slice of cash flows sold to investors under a collateralized financial instrument. The payment of interest and principal to each tranche depends on the cash flows of the underlying assets. For example, under a CMO, each tranche receives its share of cash flows received from the underlying pool of mortgages. The procedure for allocating cash flows to the various tranches is set out in the CMO document.

treaty   A reinsurance agreement between a reinsurer and a ceding company. The three most common methods of accepting reinsurance are *automatic, facultative,* and *facultative-obligatory.* The three most common types of reinsurance treaties are *YRT, coinsurance,* and *modified coinsurance.*

treaty reinsurance   See *automatic.*

ultimate mortality table   A mortality table that shows mortality rates for people who have not recently been underwritten. See *ultimate rates.*

ultimate period   The period after the select period, when the effect of underwriting (selection) has worn off.

ultimate rates   Premium or mortality rates that apply during the ultimate period. They vary by attained age rather than by issue age and policy year. Ultimate rates increase more slowly than select rates.

underwriter   An individual employed by an insurance company who decides whether or not the company will accept a risk and how it should be classified. A century ago, acceptance of a risk was indicated by signing at the bottom of a document (that is, "underwriting"). Companies that accept risks are sometimes referred to as underwriters.

underwriting   The process of screening applicants for insurance and classifying them so that appropriate premiums may be charged. Also called *selection of risks.*

underwriting class   See *risk class.*

underwriting requirements   Printed instructions that indicate what evidence of insurability is required for a given situation and which of several optional information sources will be needed to provide underwriters with necessary information. Sources of information may include medical records and the results of physical examinations. Underwriting requirements are graduated based on the proposed insured's age and the amount of coverage requested.

unearned premium   The portion of a premium that provides insurance coverage beyond the current date. Under some forms of insurance accounting, unearned premiums are excluded from revenue. See *earned premium*.

uninsurable risk class   The group of people with a risk of loss so great that an insurance company will not offer them insurance.

unit   **1.** a small amount of insurance, such as 1,000 of initial death benefit. For convenience, insurance companies calculate premiums, cash values, dividends, and reserves on a per unit basis for *pre-scheduled products*. **2.** For *variable products*, a unit represents a share of an investment fund. Premiums purchase additional units; withdrawals and surrenders reduce the number of units.

unit cost   The cost of handling one unit, such as the cost to issue a policy or pay a claim. Insurance expenses are often expressed in terms of unit costs. See *functional cost study*.

unit-linked life insurance   A variety of variable universal life offered in the U.K. and some other countries. Older unit-linked products often have front-end loads and a bid/offer spread, which is similar to a small front-end load on premiums combined with a small surrender charge on withdrawals and surrenders.

unitised-with-profits life insurance   A product that is a hybrid between unit-linked and with-profits products, offered mainly in the U.K. The product looks and behaves much like a unit-linked product, but the product's unit values do not track the market value of an underlying investment fund. This allows the insurance company to smooth the investment results.

universal life insurance   A form of permanent life insurance that is characterized by its flexible premiums, flexible face amounts, and unbundled approach that resembles a savings account combined with term insurance.

validation   See *dynamic validation* and *static validation*.

valuation   The process of establishing a value for all of an insurer's reserves, usually at the end of a month or quarter.

value at risk (VaR) An approach for measuring returns and allocating capital that requires increased returns and more capital for greater risks.

vanishing premium The use of accumulated values, policyowner dividends, or excess interest credits to discontinue payment of premiums while continuing the insurance in force.

VaR See *value at risk.*

variable annuity An annuity under which the policy's accumulated value, and sometimes the amount of monthly annuity benefit payments, fluctuate with the performance of one or more investment funds. See *variable products.*

variable costs The portion of a company's costs that vary with the amount of business sold or serviced.

variable products Insurance products in which the policy benefits vary according to the performance of one or more investment funds. With variable products, policyowners share in the investment risk. Death benefits and cash values cannot be predetermined. Variable products include variable annuities, variable life insurance, and variable universal life insurance. Also known as *dynamic products.* Contrast with *pre-scheduled* and *traditional products.*

variable life insurance A form of whole life insurance under which the death benefit and the cash value of the policy fluctuate according to the performance of an investment fund. Most variable life insurance policies guarantee that the death benefit will not fall below a specified minimum. See *variable products.*

variable universal life insurance A form of life insurance that combines the premium and death benefit flexibility of universal life insurance with the investment flexibility and risk of variable life insurance. See *variable products* and *variable life.*

vested commissions Commissions that the agent will receive regardless of whether or not the agent continues to represent the insurance company. The agent's contract determines the conditions under which commissions will be vested.

volume (of insurance) See *amount of insurance* and *face amount.* Also known as *sum assured* outside North America.

WACC See *weighted average cost of capital.*

waiver of premium (WP) A supplementary benefit under which the insurer waives renewal premiums that become due while the insured is totally disabled.

waiver of premium for payor (WPP) A supplementary benefit often included in juvenile policies which provides that the insurer will waive the policy's renewal premiums if the payor, not the insured child, dies or becomes disabled.

weighted average An average calculated by multiplying each number to be averaged by its weight and then dividing the sum of the results by the sum of the weights. The weight applied to a number usually reflects the present value, the probability of occurrence, or the relative importance of the number. Contrast with *simple average.*

weighted average cost of capital (WACC) A company's weighted average cost of capital is calculated as a weighted average of its cost of equity (its ROE) and cost of debt (after-tax interest on debt), with weights that represent its desired proportions of equity and debt.

whole life insurance Life insurance that remains in force during the insured's entire lifetime, provided premiums are paid as specified in the policy. Whole life insurance also builds a savings element called the cash value.

with-profits life insurance A form of participating life insurance offered mainly in English-speaking countries outside of North America. Compared to North American participating products, with-profits products tend to have higher premiums and lower guaranteed cash values and tend to be backed by higher-yielding, more risky investments.

yearly renewable term (YRT) A type of reinsurance in which the ceding company purchases yearly renewable term insurance from the reinsurer for the net amount of risk of each policy reinsured.

Premium rates typically vary by gender, issue age, policy year, and risk class. Zero first-year YRT rates are sometimes used to help offset the ceding company's new business strain.

yield curve A graph that shows the yield rates available for investments of various maturities. A *normal yield curve* has higher yield rates for longer maturities. An *inverted yield curve* has some instances of lower yield rates for longer maturities.

yield rate The profit obtained from an investment, expressed as a percentage of the investment, or the interest rate earned on an investment. See *interest rate*.

Zillmer reserve method A prospective reserve method that reflects a first-year expense charge equal to 3.5% of the death benefit. This method results in reserves that are generally lower than full preliminary term reserves, thereby reducing or eliminating new business strain. The Zillmer reserve method is used mainly in connection with solvency and tax reserves.

Index of Variable Definitions

Index